HANDBOOK OF READING INTERVENTIONS

HANDBOOK OF
READING
INTERVENTIONS

edited by
Rollanda E. O'Connor
Patricia F. Vadasy

THE GUILFORD PRESS
New York   London

© 2011 The Guilford Press
A Division of Guilford Publications, Inc.
72 Spring Street, New York, NY 10012
www.guilford.com

Printed in the United States of America

This book is printed on acid-free paper.

Last digit is print number: 9   8   7   6   5   4   3   2   1

Library of Congress Cataloging-in-Publication Data

Handbook of reading interventions / [edited by] Rollanda E. O'Connor, Patricia F. Vadasy.
    p. cm.
  Includes bibliographical references and index.
  ISBN 978-1-60918-151-2 (hardback)
  1. Reading—Remedial teaching—Handbooks, manuals, etc.   I. O'Connor, Rollanda E.
II. Vadasy, Patricia F.
  LB1050.5.H267 2011
  372.43—dc22

2010052974

*To the funding agencies that have supported the research
reported by the authors of these chapters—*

*in particular, the U.S. Department of Education
Office of Special Education Programs and Institute of Education Sciences,
along with the National Institute of Child Health and Human Development*

About the Editors

Rollanda E. O'Connor, PhD, is Professor of Education at the University of California, Riverside. She taught reading in special and general education classrooms for many years and has conducted numerous intervention studies in special and general education settings, explored procedures to predict in kindergarten and first grade which children are likely to develop reading difficulties, and followed the reading progress of children who received early intervention. Her longitudinal studies of intervention and assessment led to the development (with Patricia F. Vadasy) of *Ladders to Literacy,* a collection of phonological and print awareness activities and scaffolding suggestions for children at risk for reading problems, and the book *Teaching Word Recognition: Effective Strategies for Students with Learning Difficulties.* Dr. O'Connor's current research includes evaluating the effects of early, continuous intervention across the first 4 years of schooling and developing research-based interventions for students with reading difficulties in the intermediate grades.

Patricia F. Vadasy, PhD, is Senior Researcher at the Washington Research Institute in Seattle, Washington. Her background is in early reading acquisition and instruction, instructional design, and intervention research. Dr. Vadasy oversees a research team engaged in research on effective school-based literacy interventions for at-risk and struggling students. She has published findings on her grant-funded intervention research widely in peer-reviewed journals. She is the lead author (with Rollanda E. O'Connor) of the *Sound Partners* code-oriented supplemental tutoring program and coauthor (with Rollanda E. O'Connor) of the *Ladders to Literacy* preschool and kindergarten programs.

Contributors

Mary Abbott, PhD, Juniper Gardens Children's Project, University of Kansas, Kansas City, Kansas

Isabel L. Beck, PhD, Learning Research and Development Center, University of Pittsburgh, Pittsburgh, Pennsylvania

Peter Bryant, PhD, Department of Education, University of Oxford, Oxford, United Kingdom

Jay Buzhardt, PhD, Juniper Gardens Children's Project, University of Kansas, Kansas City, Kansas

Susan De La Paz, PhD, Department of Special Education, University of Maryland, College Park, Maryland

Amy Eppolito, MEd, School of Education, University of Colorado at Boulder, Boulder, Colorado

Ralph P. Ferretti, PhD, School of Education, University of Delaware, Newark, Delaware

Meenakshi Gajria, PhD, Division of Teacher Education, St. Thomas Aquinas College, Sparkill, New York

Michael M. Gerber, PhD, Graduate School of Education, University of California, Santa Barbara, Santa Barbara, California

Vanessa Goodwin, PhD, Graduate School of Education, University of California, Riverside, Riverside, California

Charles R. Greenwood, PhD, Juniper Gardens Children's Project, University of Kansas, Kansas City, Kansas

Roxanne Hudson, PhD, Area of Special Education, University of Washington, Seattle, Washington

Asha K. Jitendra, PhD, Department of Education Psychology, University of Minnesota, Minneapolis, Minnesota

ix

Janette K. Klingner, PhD, School of Education, University of Colorado at Boulder, Boulder, Colorado

Margaret G. McKeown, PhD, Learning Research and Development Center, University of Pittsburgh, Pittsburgh, Pennsylvania

Ann Morrison, PhD, Department of Teacher Education, Metropolitan State College, Denver, Colorado

Terezinha Nunes, PhD, Department of Education, University of Oxford, Oxford, United Kingdom

Rollanda E. O'Connor, PhD, Graduate School of Education, University of California, Riverside, Riverside, California

Michael J. Orosco, PhD, Graduate School of Education, University of California, Riverside, Riverside, California

Lisa S. Pao, MA, Department of Human Development, Teachers College, Columbia University, New York, New York

Catherine Richards-Tutor, PhD, College of Education, California State University, Long Beach, Long Beach, California

Theresa A. Roberts, PhD, Department of Child Development, California State University, Sacramento, Sacramento, California

Louise Spear-Swerling, PhD, Department of Special Education and Reading, Southern Connecticut State University, New Haven, Connecticut

Barbara Terry, PhD, Juniper Gardens Children's Project, University of Kansas, Kansas City, Kansas

Patricia F. Vadasy, PhD, Washington Research Institute, Seattle, Washington

Joanna P. Williams, PhD, Department of Human Development, Teachers College, Columbia University, New York, New York

Howard P. Wills, PhD, Juniper Gardens Children's Project, University of Kansas, Kansas City, Kansas

Contents

1

Introduction

Patricia F. Vadasy
Rollanda E. O'Connor

The chapters in this book provide windows into the research on effective interventions to help students learn to read and write. The importance of preparing all students to be skilled readers is a widely embraced value. Teachers across the grade levels immediately appreciate this objective, because, as one first grader informed us, "Reading affects everything you do." Proficient literacy skills are critical to negotiate life in the complex 21st-century world. Many students face special challenges in acquiring these skills. Students who do not acquire a strong foundation in reading skills may experience continued and broadening poor school outcomes in reading and in content area learning, and diminished motivation to succeed in school.

Effective reading instruction today is richly informed by research extending from cognition and neuroscience to school-based intervention studies on components of the reading process. One of the early research summaries on reading instruction was conducted by Jeanne Chall (1967) in her review of beginning reading approaches. In her final book, Chall (2000) lamented that teaching practices in reading often follow "a direction opposite from the existing research evidence" (p. 180). She wrote of the need for teachers to have access to research, and a consensus on which practices have adequate research evidence to support their use. Chall noted the beginning of this evidence in the research on first-grade reading instruction by Bond and Dykstra (1967), followed by more recent reports supporting benefits of systematic instruction in phonics (Adams, 1990; National Reading Panel, 2000; Snow, Burns, & Griffin, 1998). This evidence continues to be summarized in published research syntheses, although these reports are rarely written specifically for practitioner audiences. In this volume, chapter authors summarize evidence on specific reading interventions and approaches designed for preschool, younger, and older students.

Certain facts make it clear that instruction across the grade levels must be informed by this evidence. In 2005, 69% of all fourth graders performed at basic or below basic levels of performance. This proportion is considerably larger for minority students. The challenges teachers face in preparing students to achieve at high levels in literacy skills are daunting. Because reading skills are taught and learned across content areas, all teachers must utilize evidence-based practices that benefit low-skilled students.

The chapters in this book describe the areas of reading instruction in which this evidence has been translated into effective instructional practices. This translation process has been supported in large-scale efficacy studies. Researchers have tested research-based approaches in real-world settings. Furthermore, the research tools available in recent studies allow researchers to frame their findings and recommendations for specific subgroups of students more carefully and take into account student characteristics. Not surprisingly given the complexity of the act of skilled reading, an intervention is often not equally effective for all students.

Chapters address the major components of reading and reflect the developmental course of reading skills. Several chapters address the development and support of early reading skills, including preschool literacy instruction. A growing body of research describes the emergent literacy skills that support later reading achievement and effective classroom activities to develop these foundation skills. Other chapters review the research on early stages of word reading and tutoring approaches for primary-grade students in beginning reading skills. The complexity of reading comprehension warrants several chapters that focus on specific types of comprehension instruction, including vocabulary skills prerequisite for understanding texts, skills in negotiating text structures and themes, cooperative learning approaches, skills in constructing the meaning of texts, and applying effective strategies for comprehension. Chapters on spelling and writing reflect the reciprocal relationship of reading and spelling, and the shared influence of language skills on reading and writing. Many of the chapters include information from meta-analyses on reading topics that synthesize these research studies.

The studies described in these chapters directly reflect the role of federal support for research on reading development and instruction. Most of the research summarized by chapter authors has been supported by the National Institute of Child Health and Development and the U.S. Department of Education. This research has helped us understand how children learn to read, how to identify students at risk for reading disability, and effective interventions for children with reading difficulties.

Finally, as the table of contents reflects, the chapters do not fall easily into clear themes based on developmental stages or reading subprocesses. In fact, the chapters may appear to present a sampler, which in a sense is accurate. We confess that we chose topics and chapters based on a match between the practical needs of teachers and the reading topics in which a strong body of research has developed to inform instruction. We invited authors whose work in these areas builds upon strong research foundations and offers valuable models and guiding principles for practitioners. As noted earlier, readers will note a concentration of chapters on comprehension themes. The nonunitary nature of comprehension calls for taking it apart and considering the multiple processes and subskills involved in understanding text. Different types of text, for example, present different comprehension challenges. Comprehension is also influenced by readers' purposes for reading. Chapters 9 through 11 examine various aspects of comprehension and intervention targets.

In each of the chapters of this book authors summarize research and theory in broad areas of reading that have influenced and provided a foundation for their work. Contributors summarize the research and its relevance for the audience of practitioners with whom they have also worked in their own intervention studies. These studies allow researchers to draw increasingly clear lines from research to applications for effective instruction. Wherever it is appropriate, authors outline features of instruction and teaching principles identified in intervention studies that reflect a research-to-practice framework.

Chapter 2 begins with an overview of the development of phonemic and alphabetic skills from preschool into kindergarten, and a history of research on these precursor skills. Research on the important role of phonemic awareness in early reading development has strongly influenced how educators identify children at risk for reading disabilities. Research on the role of phonemic awareness in predicting reading achievement led to the development of effective interventions to teach these skills to kindergarten and preschool children. In this chapter, O'Connor reviews the developmental course of phonemic awareness skills and their transfer to phoneme segmenting, blending, and, finally, skilled word reading. Chapter 2 highlights features of these interventions that are of particular interest to practitioners, including their average intensity and duration, and ways in which this instruction has been effectively delivered. Phonemic skills are most effectively taught in combination with alphabetic skills, and O'Connor provides examples of what this may look like in practice. The chapter concludes with a sample instructional routine and sequence to teach phoneme segmenting skills and spelling.

It is well appreciated that literacy skills begin to develop long before children enter kindergarten, and in Chapter 3, Roberts describes the preschool foundations for literacy success. She summarizes research on the foundation skills for literacy development: phonological awareness, oral language, and alphabetic knowledge, including basic learning mechanisms that support preschool instruction and learning. Research firmly establishes the important role of these skills in literacy development, and Roberts notes seminal studies in each area and evidence from preschool intervention studies that support recommendations for instruction. Roberts acknowledges special features of preschool instruction and corresponding principles of effective interventions implemented at the preschool level. Finally, the chapter includes a summary of "important details" that characterize each area of literacy instruction and are essential aspects of instruction teachers can easily incorporate as they plan instruction for their preschool students.

Chapter 4, by Spear-Swerling, describes the development of word reading skills, word reading problems, and features of effective interventions. This chapter provides a summary of information on phases of word recognition development that is essential for differentiating beginning reading instruction. Spear-Swerling reviews features of core phonics instruction, as well as phonics interventions for children who struggle to acquire accurate and efficient word reading skills, including strategies for reading more complex and multisyllabic words. Based firmly on the robust research on word reading instruction, Spear-Swerling's chapter offers teachers practical advice for assessment and instruction that supports word reading development. Sample teaching scripts include a word building activity used with poor decoders, and scripts for teaching syllable types and phonetically irregular words, and providing feedback and support during oral reading practice.

In Chapter 5, Nunes and Bryant summarize research on the role of morphemic knowledge in word reading. This chapter includes a summary of their work on how to assess children's knowledge of morphemes and interventions to teach children about morphology. Students are often unaware of the morphological information encoded in words. As Nunes and Bryant share in this chapter, instruction in morphology has both reading and spelling benefits for both lower and higher skilled students. Furthermore, these morphological interventions have benefits for students beginning in the primary grades. This chapter includes examples of specific teaching activities from the authors' training program to develop aspects of morphological awareness.

In Chapter 6, Gerber and Richards-Tutor summarize the history of encoding language with print and how language mergers contribute to the spellings of words today. Using research findings from the past 40 years, they show the instructional principles that generate the strongest gains for poor spellers. They also capture how excellent spellers study the morphology and language origins of words, and draw implications for how teachers can structure spelling lessons more effectively in schools. Drawing on stage theories of learning to spell, Gerber and Richards-Tutor demonstrate how correct letter sequences in children's spelling attempts can be used to monitor progress of emerging spellers and show their improvement over time.

In Chapter 7, McKeown and Beck describe the deep divide between our understanding of vocabulary acquisition and how vocabulary has been taught in the classroom. They review the research on how word meanings are acquired and stored as connections with other word meanings and contexts. Effective vocabulary instruction builds upon this knowledge base of the role of context in learning words and the incremental nature of vocabulary learning. McKeown and Beck summarize research on effective vocabulary instruction and promising new approaches for young students. The authors address the categories of words that leading researchers judge to be most worthwhile to teach. The chapter concludes with a summary of features of effective instruction, the use of dictionary definitions, and a sample weeklong instructional sequence illustrating vocabulary instruction that builds upon storybook reading with kindergarten students.

In Chapter 8, Hudson summarizes the research informing a multicomponent view of reading fluency. This expanded and developmental conceptualization of fluency encompasses automaticity, efficiency, and fluency at the sublexical, lexical, and text levels. This view reinforces the value of fluency as an instructional objective across the reading acquisition continuum. The evidence-based fluency approaches Hudson describes are clearly linked to specific aspects of fluency that hinder coordinated and fluent text reading. These interventions include methods to develop underlying word level accuracy, reading rate, and multilevel approaches. Hudson addresses the challenge that this expanded view of fluency creates for student assessment and emphasizes the importance of correctly identifying the type or level of fluency impediment prior to matching the student to an intervention.

Jitendra and Gajria, in Chapter 9, summarize research on teaching main idea and summarization skills to students with learning disabilities. They describe their work on instructional programs for teaching main idea and summarization skills to middle school students with learning difficulties. Features of their effective interventions, which characterize the interventions summarized across many chapters in this volume, include explicit instruction in strategies with extensive practice opportunities and ongoing assessment in student use of the strategies. Jitendra and Gajria provide extended teaching scripts and sample passages that clearly illustrate how teachers can implement this instruction.

In Chapter 10, Klingner, Morrison, and Eppolito consider the role of metacognition in comprehension instruction. Students who struggle with reading often have less knowledge about the cognitive processes that support comprehension and difficulty managing the comprehension process. This chapter presents a summary of metacognitive strategies that help students become aware of and regulate their thinking processes surrounding comprehension. Three types of metacognitive strategies are reviewed: planning, monitoring, and evaluating. The authors review the research and outline procedures for evidence-based single strategies, including purpose setting, activating prior knowledge, and prediction. They describe strategies that can be implemented before, during, and after reading, including summarization and main idea instruction. Finally, they describe more time-intensive multicomponent strategies that include cooperative group learning activities.

Reading comprehension is further "unpacked" in Chapter 11, on text structures and theme. Williams and Pao lay out distinguishing features of narrative and expository text structures that enable the reader to organize text content, and to construct a mental representation necessary for comprehension. The authors describe research on two programs designed for use with either narrative or expository text. The Theme Identification program provides instruction to help students identify plot elements that underlie story theme in narrative texts. The Close Analysis of Texts with Structure program targets strategies for use with cause–effect expository text structure. The chapter includes examples of each type of lesson that illustrate teaching activities and features of instructional design that characterize each program. Writing activities in each program provide scaffolded practice with text structure and help students learn how to organize and edit their writing about narrative and expository texts.

In Chapter 12, on peer-mediated approaches, Abbott, Greenwood, Buzhardt, Wills, and Terry summarize the contributions of these approaches to Tier 1 instruction in classrooms where fewer than 80% of students are meeting literacy benchmarks. Abbott and her colleagues focus on two widely used and studied peer-mediated approaches: Classwide Peer Tutoring (CWPT) and Peer-Assisted Learning Strategies (PALS). Both approaches provide dedicated time for reading aloud, with clearly sequenced peer interactions to develop comprehension. The authors summarize research supporting the benefits of these approaches for both literacy outcomes and academic engagement across diverse student populations. The chapter includes a detailed description of the CWPT basic protocol. Abbott and her colleagues draw upon their research on CWPT implementation to discuss training and fidelity procedures associated with improvements in student outcomes.

Chapter 13, on supplemental interventions, summarizes research on effective instruction by paraeducator tutors in early word reading and in fluency skills. As Vadasy summarizes, a growing research base on tutoring by paraeducators or teaching assistants supports their training for roles in supplementing instruction in specific foundation reading skills. The research summarized in this chapter supports the use of these support staff particularly for instruction in specific skills that present common obstacles to reading development: early decoding, word identification, and fluency, areas in which lower performing students often need more explicit instruction and more frequent and scaffolded practice opportunities. High-quality instructional design and training are consistent features of effective supplemental interventions. The chapter highlights design and implementation features that characterize effective supplemental tutoring interventions.

As Ferretti and De La Paz address in Chapter 14, more specialized skills are required to read and write effectively as content area texts and topics become increasingly challenging. Students must learn to coordinate specialized vocabulary, domain-specific knowledge, and complex text structures. Strategies and skills in interpreting information assume a larger role in text comprehension. The authors describe reading and writing activities that teachers can use to teach students collaborative reasoning and writing strategies with social studies and history content-area texts. The strategic reading and writing behaviors they outline offer a means for teachers to organize cooperative group inquiry on content topics that require skills in evaluating and interpreting texts, and debating and defending different points of view.

Teachers today work with classrooms of increasingly diverse students from many language and cultural backgrounds. Many students from low socioeconomic backgrounds, as well as language-minority students, are not attaining proficient levels of reading. In Chapter 15 Orosco and O'Connor summarize the work of several groups of researchers who have studied the benefits of early reading interventions for primarily Spanish-speaking English language learners (ELLs), the largest language-minority student population in the United States. Not surprisingly, this research reveals that features of instruction found effective in many interventions for English-only students also help ELL students make progress in language and reading skills. Researchers have identified and continue to investigate promising approaches to instruction in reading and vocabulary skills for ELL students in more rigorous studies. Orosco and O'Connor conclude, as Goldenberg, Rueda, and August (2006) concluded in their review, that research is needed to understand better how sociocultural characteristics of teachers and students influence literacy outcomes of language-minority students.

The sobering findings from the 2005 National Assessment of Educational Progress (NAEP) on the large numbers of fourth graders who are not reading at proficient levels remind us of challenges that face us in teaching older students. These challenges expand as older students encounter a broader range of texts, more difficult text features, and more demanding writing assignments that hinge upon text comprehension. Early instruction in decoding skills is often supported by reading specialists. Middle school classroom teachers become responsible for teaching literacy skills in comprehension strategies, vocabulary, and writing in the context of challenging content-area instruction. In Chapter 16, on older readers, O'Connor and Goodwin address the specific reading needs of students in grades 5–12. Breakdowns in reading skills for older students may occur at word or text levels. The authors summarize interventions that address problems students encounter in reading multisyllabic and affixed words that require knowledge of morphological structures and multiletter spelling patterns. As the proportion of more difficult and lower-frequency vocabulary words increases in their school texts, many older students begin to struggle due to their limited vocabulary knowledge. O'Connor and Goodwin review findings on keyword and interactive strategies that may help students learn, remember, and productively use new vocabulary. Confronted with word- and text-level obstacles, many students develop decreased motivation for reading. Research on computer-assisted and individualized approaches to reading instruction suggests ways to maintain students' engagement and interest in reading. Finally, the chapter includes an overview of research on fluency and comprehension interventions found to benefit older students, including repeated reading and comprehension instruction in story content, text structures, and strategy application.

This book is written for teachers, teacher trainers, and graduate students, with chapters chosen to help readers access the broad research bases on these topics and gain a more in-depth understanding of the interventions and research by the chapter authors. In Michael Pressley's (1998) excellent book on the state of the art of research on reading instruction, he concluded that much more research and implementation are needed. We hope that the chapters in this book engage readers and aid them in continuing to build background knowledge in reading research and refine their implementation of research-based literacy instruction. The evidence-based literacy interventions described in these chapters can be integrated in whole-class, small-group, or individual instruction. Much more remains to be learned about the widespread scale-up of these interventions in response-to-intervention applications.

References

Adams, M. J. (1990). *Beginning to read: Thinking and learning about print*. Cambridge, MA: MIT Press.

Bond, G. L., & Dykstra, R. (1967). *Coordinating center for first grade reading instruction programs*. (Final Report of Project No. x-001, Contract No. OE-5-10-264). Minneapolis: University of Minnesota.

Chall, J. S. (1967). *Learning to read: The great debate*. New York: McGraw-Hill.

Chall, J. S. (2000). *The academic achievement challenge: What really works in the classroom?* New York: Guilford Press.

Goldenberg, C., Rueda, R. S., & August, D. (2006). Synthesis: Sociocultural contexts and literacy development. In D. August & T. Shanahan (Eds.), *Developing literacy in second-language learners: Report of the National Literacy Panel on Language Minority Children and Youth* (pp. 249–267). Mahwah, NJ: Erlbaum.

National Reading Panel. (2000). *Teaching children to read: An evidence-based assessment of the scientific research literature on reading and its implications for reading instruction*. Washington, DC: National Institute of Child Health and Human Development.

Pressley, M. (1998). *Reading instruction that works: The case for balanced teaching*. New York: Guilford Press.

Snow, C. E., Burns, S., & Griffin, P. (Eds.). (1998). *Preventing reading difficulties in young children*. Washington, DC: National Academy Press.

2

Phoneme Awareness and the Alphabetic Principle

ROLLANDA E. O'CONNOR

A mother sits with her son and a book in her lap. "Rattle rattle, clink clink. Here comes the *milkman*." She points to the *m* in milkman. "You know that letter."

"*M*!" he proudly exclaims. "*M* for *Miles*! That's me!"

"Yes, *Mmmiles* starts with *m*. And *mmm*ilk starts with m. And *mmmilkman* starts with *m*." She stretches the first sound of each word to demonstrate the sound for the letter *m* and to assist her son with hearing the sound.

"*Mmm*." Miles looks around the bedroom and spots a different book on the floor. "Me and My Dad!" He points to Mercer Mayer's *Just Me and My Dad* on the floor. "*Mmme*." He exaggerates the sound for *m*, as his mother did earlier.

"*Mmme* starts with *m*," she agrees. Do you see another word with *m*?"

This mother and her son are playing the kind of word games that countless parents enjoy with their young, prereading children. She is also teaching her son that letters have sounds, that those sounds are often similar across words in which those letters appear, and that the sound that begins her son's name is found in many words he knows from his favorite stories. Although she may be unfamiliar with the terms, she is teaching phoneme awareness and the alphabetic principle.

These days kindergarten teachers know that "phoneme awareness"—a conscious attentiveness to the individual speech sounds that comprise spoken words—is an important step toward reading and spelling. Although alphabet

9

books have been available since colonial times, and attention to letter names and sounds has figured into first-grade phonics instruction for over 50 years, the focus on phoneme awareness in preschool and kindergarten was rare until about 15 years ago.

There are good reasons for this shift toward prereading skills prior to first grade. Adams (1990) pointed out the enormous gap in experience with books and parental reading to children between low- and high-income families on average. Hart and Risley (1995) demonstrated how differences in story reading and substantive conversations between parents and their children play out in differences in vocabulary development prior to school entry. The early literacy studies in preschool (see Roberts, Chapter 3, this volume) have shown that while this gap is pronounced, children with minimal literacy experience and children learning English as a second language can make good gains in vocabulary and phonological skills with instruction that focuses on these areas. Teachers and researchers have learned that waiting until a child demonstrates readiness to learn certain prereading skills can increase the achievement gap. Rather, instruction that assists low-skilled children to catch up to their peers can have immediate and long-term effects on their reading trajectory. Although many kinds of early interventions can improve academic outcomes for children at risk, this chapter outlines studies and intervention activities that highlight the role that phoneme awareness and the alphabetic principle play in learning to read and spell.

The Trail toward Phoneme Awareness

The passage of Public Law 94-142, the Education for All Handicapped Children Act of 1975, established guidelines for identifying children with disabilities, including reading disability (RD), which is a type of learning disability. Under those guidelines, children became eligible for special education services for RD when their reading achievement fell significantly below what might be expected by their cognitive ability. Although defined somewhat differently across states, for most children, eligibility for special services meant falling about 2 years or more behind their peers in reading achievement. Such low achievement is difficult to identify until late in second grade or later, because children are not expected to read well in kindergarten or first grade. Several research teams in the United States and elsewhere were concerned about delaying services for children due to the difficulty of identifying RD in the first few years of school.

Several research teams in the 1980s and early 1990s (Felton, 1992; Lundberg, Frost, & Petersen, 1988; Share, Jorm, MacLean, & Matthews, 1984) took a similar approach to the problem:

1. Because most children enter the public school system in kindergarten, kindergarten is the first opportunity to try to identify potential early markers of RD.

2. Kindergarten readiness tests in the 1980s used to permit and to deny entrance to kindergarten gave few indicators of what the problems might be or how readiness might be improved, so they sought skills that might be malleable through intervention.

3. Theories of potential indicators ranged widely across reading and developmental milestones, so it made sense to measure broadly and determine which indicators were most tightly linked with real reading in the future.

In their view, early identification of children likely to develop reading problems constituted the first step toward solving the problem of RD. Researchers measured many characteristics of these 5- and 6-year-old children and their families, including gross and fine motor skills, knowledge of letters, shape copying, book handling, rhyming, picking off the first or last sounds in words, vocabulary, TV watching, and parental income and education, among other things. These studies converged on the finding that among the many skills that can be measured in kindergarten, phoneme awareness was a consistently strong predictor of later reading achievement.

By the late 1980s, the link between "phoneme segmenting" (i.e., the ability to break apart a spoken word into individual speech sounds) and reading achievement a year later had been well established (Juel, 1988; Perfetti, Beck, Bell, & Hughes, 1987; Share et al., 1984). The studies were correlational, meaning that researchers measured children's phoneme awareness and other prereading skills in kindergarten or first grade, and measured their reading ability one or more years later to determine which relationships were strongest. Researchers were just beginning to think about how they might intervene and teach phoneme awareness to children who did not acquire it naturally, and whether intervention could improve reading and spelling development.

Bradley and Bryant (1983) were among the first to tackle the instructional implications of teaching phoneme awareness to children who lacked that understanding. They began their study by measuring 4- and 5-year-old nonreading children's ability to match first sounds in words, and following their reading and spelling progress over the first 4 years of schooling. In the second year, as students entered school, they measured children's sound matching again and selected students who lagged behind their peers. They assigned some students to an intervention that included 40 lessons targeting phoneme awareness over a 2-year period. They taught some children the same phoneme awareness activities but also included plastic letters to represent sounds. A third group practiced categorizing the words by meaning and features (e.g., items of clothing or farm animals), and a fourth group received no training from the research staff. At the end of the training period, children who had received the combination of phoneme awareness plus letter manipulation outscored other groups in spelling, and both phoneme awareness groups scored better in reading than the categorization or control group.

Bradley and Bryant's (1983) study is widely cited as one that proposed a causal connection between phoneme awareness and reading development. Additional correlation and prediction studies fueled intense interest in phonological awareness instruction (Juel, 1988; Liberman & Shankweiler, 1985; Tunmer, Herriman & Nesdale, 1988) and reported high correlations among quite a few different phoneme awareness tasks and reading achievement. For example, Bradley and Bryant used an "Odd Man Out" task to measure phoneme awareness ("Bit, bone, flat. Which word doesn't belong?") and sound categorization to teach students to identify words that shared the same first sound, middle sound, or last sound in pairs and trios of words. Studies were needed to explore ways to measure phoneme awareness effectively and to determine the component skills that comprise the construct (Calfee, Lindamood, & Lindamood, 1973; Stanovich, Cunningham, & Cramer, 1984; Tunmer et al., 1988; Wagner, Torgesen, Laughon, Simmons, & Rashotte, 1993; Yopp, 1988).

Logically, blending and segmenting may relate to reading and spelling differently. Reading an unfamiliar printed word would seem to require two interrelated skills: (1) Children must identify the letters and produce sounds the letters are likely to make, and (2) children must blend those phonemes together to produce a likely pronunciation for the word. While blending phonemes seems necessary for reading, segmenting spoken words would appear to be more related to spelling: (1) First, children must segment the word into speech sounds, and (2) then associate an alphabet letter with each sound produced to spell the word. In a test of this progression, Fox and Routh (1976) measured 4-year-old children's ability to blend and segment speech sounds, then provided half of the children with auditory blending training. All of the children were taught to identify some letter-like shapes and sounds to be used later in a reading analogue task. Half of the children in the blending group could segment before the training began; the other half could not. What Fox and Routh found was surprising: Blending instruction did not improve word reading unless children were already able to segment words into speech sounds prior to treatment.

Later, studies with normally achieving kindergarten children found that "segmenting interventions" (e.g., teaching children to say the first sound in spoken words, or to separate all of the sounds in short words) and *combinations* of blending (e.g., /c/–/a/–/t/ = *cat*) and segmenting interventions produced improvements in reading (Ball & Blachman, 1991; Cunningham, 1990; Torgesen, Morgan, & Davis, 1992). Torgesen et al. proposed that teaching *both* blending and segmenting may produce a more complete, decontextualized understanding of the phonemic structure of words than training in blending or segmenting alone.

The Components of Phoneme Awareness

Studies have helped to shape the nuances around the kind of intervention that may be useful in preschool and kindergarten. One important question is which skill to start with given the range of possibilities. Slocum, O'Connor, and Jenkins (1993) designed a study to determine whether blending or segmenting was easier to teach. Using only spoken words (no print), they taught children in a Head Start preschool (average age 5 years, 2 months) to blend word parts ("What word is this? *M–ix*?") or segment words into parts ("Tell me two sounds in *fat*"). The researchers kept track of how many instructional sessions it took to learn each task. After children learned their first skill (either blending or segmenting), the researchers taught the other skill (either blending or segmenting) to determine whether blending was easier to learn after learning to segment, or vice versa. They found no evidence that learning to blend or segment transferred to the other phonological task for children at this age, which suggested that if both are important in learning to read and spell, both should be taught to students who do not acquire these skills independently.

In a further exploration of intervention content, O'Connor, Jenkins, and Slocum (1995) compared effects of teaching kindergartners who lacked phoneme awareness either to blend *and* segment, or to blend, segment, rhyme, *and* delete phonemes. They found it very difficult to teach phoneme deletion to prereading children; however, children who learned to blend and segment ended the study able to rhyme as well as those who had been taught to rhyme, and both treatments outperformed the control group on phonological and reading measures. Their results suggested that an intervention content of blending and segmenting, along with a few letters and sounds to demonstrate the alphabetic principle, might be sufficient for 5- and 6-year-old children with poor literacy skills.

Most of these studies were conducted one on one or in small groups of three to five children. Two studies in the 1990s also investigated whole-class instruction in phoneme awareness and letter knowledge. The focus of instruction was on the children most at risk for reading difficulties; however, the researchers were also interested in the effects of whole-group activities for students who did not appear to need additional phoneme awareness intervention. O'Connor, Notari-Syverson, and Vadasy (1996) assigned classes of students in high-risk urban schools to implement whole-class and center-based activities to teach phoneme blending and segmenting, and letter knowledge. The classes included children at risk, children with special education needs, and children with average literacy scores. Children across abilities made strong gains in phonological and reading skills, which is an important finding, because teachers would not want to hold back their high-performing children while attending to low-skilled children in particular. Blachman, Tangel, Ball, Black, and McGraw (1999) produced similar findings with whole-class instruction in an urban, low-income community.

More recently, Yeh and Connell (2008) taught 4- and 5-year-olds in Head Start preschools either to (1) blend and segment with a few letter sounds, as in O'Connor et al. (1995); (2) recognize and produce rhymes; or (3) learn the meanings of new words, which can help students with comprehension of language. Although each group of children learned the skills in their assigned groups, only children in the blend and segment intervention learned those particular skills. As in the O'Connor et al. study, children who learned to blend and segment could also produce rhymes as well as the children who were taught to rhyme specifically.

These studies had two features in common. First, the children learned to blend and segment in about 6–10 hours of instructional time. Second, interventions were delivered in small doses of 10–20 minutes per session, which is a reasonable amount of time to devote to literacy improvement in most preschool or kindergarten settings.

In summary, intervention research with children at risk for RD reports positive effects for children in kindergarten (Blachman, Ball, Black, & Tangel, 1994; O'Connor et al., 1995, 1996) and first grade (Blachman et al., 1999; Foorman, Francis, Fletcher, Schatschneider, & Mehta, 1998; Vellutino et al., 1996). Converging evidence suggests that a combination of segmenting and blending for average learners may provide a basis for transfer to learning to read words (Berninger, 1986; Torgesen et al., 1992).

Who Can Teach Phoneme Awareness?

For teachers who might find individual or small-group interventions like those in the previously described studies difficult to manage, researchers have also studied interventions delivered by adults who were not trained teachers or graduate students. Allor and McCathren (2004) found positive effects for first-grade students tutored by college undergraduates. Children at risk of reading failure were taught phoneme awareness and decoding with 10–14 hours of tutoring, which resulted in significant gains in those areas. Vadasy, Sanders, and Peyton (2006) used paraeducators (teaching assistants) in kindergartens to tutor students who were at risk due to low literacy skills. In 18 weeks of tutoring, the paraeducators achieved strong and lasting effects in phoneme awareness, reading accuracy, and developmental spelling.

In a similar study in England that used instructional assistants, Hatcher et al. (2005) considered the amount of intervention that might be necessary for kindergartners with low literacy skills. They assigned some at-risk kindergartners to 20 weeks of intervention and others to a wait-listed group that began 10 weeks of intervention nearer the end of the school year, overlapping with the second 10 weeks of the 20-week group. Instruction was delivered by trained teaching assistants in daily 20-minute sessions. Children who began intervention earlier performed better at the midway point, but those who started in the second 10 weeks appeared to catch up to those who started earlier, suggesting that a full 20 weeks of intervention might be unnecessary for many children. Hatcher et al. also cautioned, however, that about one-fourth of the children in each treatment made very little gain in reading skills, and that more intensive intervention (perhaps by a trained teacher) might improve responsiveness.

These studies converge on the finding that many children who begin kindergarten with poorly developed preliteracy skills can learn phoneme awareness skills in just 10–14 weeks in short, well-planned lessons delivered frequently during the week, whether taught by certified teachers, graduate students, undergraduate students, or teaching assistants.

A second commonality across these studies is that not all children respond well to small-group instruction. Keeping in mind that the students selected were already delayed in literacy skills relative to their peers, about 20–25% did not make the hoped-for gains during these interventions.

These notions led researchers to suggest that early intervention efforts should encourage children to learn about sounds in words and features of print. To close the achievement gap, it would be useful for children to learn these skills within the window of time during which these understandings develop for typically achieving children. In this view, if by the end of kindergarten all children could blend and segment spoken words (phoneme awareness) and link these speech sounds to letter sounds (the alphabetic principle), they would be prepared to learn to decode and recognize words in first grade.

The Alphabetic Principle

The ability of children to blend, segment, and in other ways manipulate the sounds in spoken words produces phoneme awareness, but an additional step in which children realize that sounds in words can be represented by letters—the alphabetic principle—makes learning to read a reasonable and motivating activity. Even for young children, phoneme awareness instruction that includes alphabet letters is more effective than instruction without them (for discussions of this issue, see Ball & Blachman, 1991; Hatcher, Hulme, & Ellis, 1994). We often think of the alphabetic principle as knowledge we need to impart to children, but Mattingly (1992) places the alphabetic principle in a larger context by suggesting that phoneme awareness is the critical insight that made an alphabetic writing system possible; the alphabetic principle is the method by which the alphabetic writing system works. Letters represent phonemes.

An advantage is usually reported for phoneme awareness interventions that include a phoneme–grapheme correspondence component (i.e., teaching letters and their sounds), suggesting that the *minimal content* of instruction should include blending and segmenting, along with at least a limited number of letter–sound correspondences. Byrne and Fielding-Barnsley (1991) found strong effects for their training in phoneme identity, in which children learned to isolate the first or last sound in words and also learned some letter–sound correspondences; however, they concluded that this training was insufficient for some children to learn the alphabetic principle.

Phoneme awareness and letter–sound correspondences can each be learned in isolation from the other; nevertheless, children with reading difficulties may need specific instruction to learn to link these two understandings. As an example, O'Connor and Jenkins (1995) selected kindergartners from a special education kindergarten class who were learning to read with a code-emphasis reading curriculum. Pretests showed that these children were good segmenters, with over half of the children at ceiling on a segmenting task. They were also reasonably strong on letter–sound correspondences (knowing over half of the letter sounds in the alphabet in kindergarten). The researchers paired students by ability and randomly assigned one student in each pair to 10-minute sessions in which he or she segmented, then spelled, the words from the reading curriculum. The matched-pair students read the same words as many times as the spellers spelled the words. At the end of the study, children in each group had attained the same lesson level in their reading curriculum; however, the children in the spelling condition read more words accurately from that curriculum, and also read and spelled words they had not practiced that contained similar patterns. The researchers attributed these differences in outcomes to the fact that students in the spelling treatment had more opportunity to learn and practice the alphabetic principle, and thereby to gain more functional use of their understandings.

A critical notion here is that teaching the alphabetic principle is not the same as teaching phonics. Children can (and, unfortunately, many do) learn letters and sounds, and still not understand how to apply this knowledge to reading and spelling words. Direct demonstrations of the alphabetic principle may be necessary. For children beyond first grade who read very poorly, a few days of instruction in the alphabetic principle can help to make their spelling less capricious and word analysis activities more interesting (O'Connor et al., 2002).

Despite the utility that intervention in phoneme awareness and the alphabetic principle might have for struggling learners, research suggests that for average readers, the role that phoneme awareness plays in reading and spelling may be developmentally limited; that is, once children read words fairly well, perhaps by second grade, phoneme awareness ceases to have a direct effect on reading, because it has been superseded by higher level skills, such as word recognition, reading rate, and comprehension of language.

Whether phoneme awareness continues to have a role in interventions for older poor readers is less well understood. Working with second- through fourth-grade poor readers, McCandliss, Beck, Sendak, and Perfetti (2003) found that these students did not use knowledge of segmenting and letter sounds to spell the interior of words correctly, which suggests a lack of understanding of the alphabetic principle. Using Beck's instructional procedure Word Building, students learned to identify one-letter differences among words, first with one-syllable words, then graduating to longer words as they mastered easier sets. Students in this intervention improved their reading and spelling, and most remarkably in the difficult-to-hear middle sections of words.

In a study of second- through sixth-grade children, Lovett and Steinbach (1997) developed a reading intervention that included the alphabetic principle, blending, and spelling. Like McCandliss et al. (2003), their intervention program began with easy examples and proceeded with more difficult words as students' skills improved. Students made strong gains in phoneme awareness and in real and nonsense word reading, and were able to use the alphabetic principle to generalize to reading words they had not been taught.

In a study with contrary findings, Bhat, Griffin, and Sindelar (2003) developed an intervention for middle school poor readers that focused on phoneme awareness. Following 4 weeks of one-to-one instruction, students improved in phoneme awareness but did not improve in reading or spelling. O'Connor and Goodwin (Chapter 16, this volume) speculated that for phoneme awareness interventions to be useful for older poor readers, they should include opportunities to apply phoneme awareness and the alphabetic principle to words with multiple syllables that are closer to what these students see in textbooks and are required to read in their classes. The interventions used in the studies with positive effects mentioned earlier moved students quickly from one-syllable words to longer, more grade-appropriate word forms.

Do Effects Last?

These studies all reported immediate gains in phoneme awareness and, in some cases, other aspects of reading, but what long-term effects can be expected from interventions in phoneme awareness and the alphabetic principle? O'Connor, Notari-Syverson, and Vadasy (1998) followed the students who received the phoneme awareness instruction from their kindergarten teachers into their first-grade classes. By the end of the year, the early boost shown by the average readers who jumped ahead at the end of kindergarten had disappeared; however, lasting positive effects were found for the low-skilled children, who maintained their advantage over students who had not received phoneme awareness instruction in kindergarten. Other studies that have followed the reading progress of students who received phoneme awareness instruction as preschoolers (Byrne & Fielding-Barnsley, 1991, 1993; Lundberg, Frost, & Petersen, 1988) or kindergartners (Blachman et al., 1999; Bradley & Bryant, 1983; Elbro & Petersen, 2004) have also found effects lasting into first or second grade or beyond, although the students do not necessarily catch up to their typically developing peers.

Moreover, findings across long-term follow-up studies differ. Some studies reveal that students maintain gains in some skills but that gains do not necessarily transfer to more advanced reading skills. As an example, Coyne, Kame'enui, Simmons, and Harn (2004) intervened with kindergartners in phoneme awareness and found short-term (kindergarten) and long-term (first grade) effects on phoneme awareness and decoding; however, children who had received the kindergarten intervention still had a seriously delayed reading rate in first grade.

Others find good transfer effects for phoneme awareness interventions. In a study that contextualized phoneme awareness interventions in whole-language classrooms, Ryder, Tunmer, and Greaney (2008) delivered 24 weeks of small-group instruction to struggling readers in kindergarten, using teaching assistants as instructors. Not only did treated students outperform controls at the end of the year but they also maintained their gains into second grade, which required generalization of phoneme awareness and decoding to reading words and reading connected text.

Together these findings suggest that teachers should assess students' understanding of phoneme awareness early in schooling and deliver short, focused lessons on blending and segmenting spoken words, along with representing sounds in letters, to children who lack this understanding. Findings from studies suggest also that it doesn't hurt to include students with higher skills levels, probably because these activities tend to be engaging and fun. In fact, these higher-skilled students may find that the phoneme awareness activities help them to cement their understanding and to link it with printed words in ways that stimulate self-teaching of decoding skills (Share, 1995).

The relationship between phoneme awareness and the alphabetic principle is intuitive for some children, but others need to be shown this relationship through extensive practice. To keep the early gains strong, teachers may need to structure opportunities for students who have had phoneme awareness interventions to apply phoneme awareness to more advanced reading and spelling activities. For students who begin schooling with low literacy skills, it is unlikely that intervention in phoneme awareness *only* will close the gap with their more advantaged classmates.

And What about English Language Learners?

In California, as in many areas of the country, including students who are learning English in effective interventions maintains a high priority. Several studies in the last 10 years have shown transfer of phoneme awareness from a student's primary language to English (Lesaux & Siegel, 2003; Linan-Thompson, Vaughn, Prater, & Cirino, 2006). More importantly, studies that include English language learners (ELLs) with serious delays in reading have shown that instruction in phoneme awareness improves ELLs' reading skills in English (Healy, Vanderwood, & Edelston, 2005; Justice & Pullen, 2003; O'Connor, Bocian, Beebe-Frankenberger, & Linklater, 2010; Quiroga, Lemos-Britton, Mostafapour, Abbott, & Berninger, 2002). A recent study of first- and second-grade ELLs who were making poor progress in whole-class instruction (Kamps et al., 2007) showed that ELLs included in small-group interventions that focused first on phoneme awareness and letter sounds, and then progressed to more advanced reading skills in first and second grades, made stronger reading gains than those in control schools without these interventions.

Moreover, growth in phoneme awareness across kindergarten (Linklater, O'Connor, & Palardy, 2009) and first grade (Lesaux & Siegel, 2003; O'Connor et al., 2010) is similar for ELLs and students whose first language is English. These studies suggest that ELLs can and should be included in effective phoneme awareness interventions, and that doing so may improve their reading acquisition over time. Although it has received little specific research attention, small-group activities designed to teach phoneme awareness often include pictures of objects and actions, which may improve ELLs' English vocabulary, as well as their phoneme awareness.

How Much Phoneme Awareness Is Enough?

One useful way of thinking about phoneme awareness is the way in which it facilitates reading. Hearing phonemes within words enables children to make sense of letter-sound instruction and to apply the link between phonemes and letters to develop a strong sense of the alphabetic principle. Once children have that understanding, word reading ability can develop rapidly for most. Certainly children can be taught to identify sounds in words with more than three or four phonemes, just as children can be taught through extensive practice to get increasingly faster at naming letters. But how good is "good enough" at these skills?

Research has established that in the early stages, growth in phoneme awareness and letter-sound knowledge is linked to improvement in decoding in a nearly linear manner. Scatterplots of growth, which plot how well children segment words against how well they read, presents an important caveat. After children can segment one-syllable words into constituent phonemes, getting even better at segmenting has no identifiable effect on getting better at reading. What this relationship suggests is that interventions aimed at helping children to hear three or four sounds in a short word probably produce sufficient skill at segmenting. Once children get this good at phoneme awareness, their teachers should move on to instruction focused on reading words and running text.

Likewise, scatterplots of letter naming and identifying letter sounds against decoding shows a linear relationship up to about 50 letters or sounds per minute. Thereafter, getting faster at naming letters or sounds may take time away from the more important tasks of reading and spelling words.

And speaking of taking time away from reading instruction, teachers need not wait or withhold instruction in decoding, vocabulary, and high-frequency words until students reach these "good enough" levels (about 30 segments identified in 10 words, or 50 letters or sounds per minute), particularly if students are in first grade or older. Phoneme awareness can be learned alongside reading instruction, as well as prior to it.

In measurement studies, we sometimes call this "good enough" phenomenon *gating*. Specifically, prior to first grade, it can be useful to measure lower-level skills like phoneme awareness and letter knowledge up to the point where children exceed the ability of these readiness tasks to enable further reading development (e.g., they are good enough on these skills). For phoneme awareness and the alphabetic principle, once children can segment 30 or so sounds in 10words and name all the alphabet letters or sounds, it is time to shift away from measuring, as well as teaching, these skills. Instead, teachers can teach students to decode words, recognize words that are irregularly spelled, read sentences and running text, and develop vocabulary and comprehension, all of which can be taught in integrated reading interventions that combine these crucial features of reading development. At that point, measurement, too, should shift to measures of reading words and comprehending text.

Closing Thoughts

So, must phoneme segmenting and blending be taught to young children? It might be useful here to consider individual differences among children and their life circumstances. The mother and child in our opening exchange were reading and talking about storybooks. The mother took the time to point out the sameness among words that began with the same letter; in essence, she was teaching the child that the letters on the page represent speech sounds, and that spoken words can be broken into collections of speech sounds—the phonemes in a language. Perhaps the only teaching this child will need to grasp phoneme awareness and the alphabetic principle is this kind of interplay—time and again—with an adult who reads aloud and invites the child to explore the words and letters on the page and the sounds they make.

A child in a similar life circumstance may have just as much read-aloud time with his or her mother, but without the conversation about letters, sounds of letters, and sounds in words. Despite similar amounts of exposure to books and literacy, one child may "pick up on" the alphabetic principle, while another may not. The combination of studies discussed in this chapter suggests that many children need some instruction in phoneme awareness, because it does not develop spontaneously necessarily. The difference may not be *whether* to teach it but how intensively and to whom.

Keep in mind that many students learn to blend and segment spoken words without specific instruction in kindergarten or first grade, because they have been made aware of how the reading and writing system works in home or play settings. The focus of this chapter is on students who have failed to acquire these skills prior to school entry. Informal and formal assessments can help to identify the students who need instructional support. Many schools already have such systems in place, particularly if they have participated in the Reading First initiative or response-to-intervention models. Keep in mind, also, that phoneme awareness instruction is not the same as phonics instruction. "Phoneme awareness" concerns how well children hear and can play with sounds in spoken words; "phonics" refers to linking letters of the alphabet to sounds in logical and lawful ways. The combination of these important endeavors generates an understanding of the alphabetic principle.

Last, it is crucial to understand that although problems with phoneme awareness and the alphabetic principle interfere with reading and spelling development, solving these problems does not ensure that students will read well. Phoneme awareness is best conceived as a bridge to decoding and spelling. Once children get the words off the page accurately, they still must understand what they mean, combine the words into meaningful phrases and sentences, and relate sentences to other sentences that come before and after. As students progress through school, excellent reading also requires cross-linkage of one piece or type of text to others, to background knowledge, and to many other aspects of prior learning. Nevertheless, these sophisticated acts of comprehension start with reading the words, and for that, phoneme awareness is foundational.

Activities to Teach Phoneme Awareness

Children may have difficulty identifying the first, or last, or all sounds in spoken words. A main problem with hearing individual phonemes is the rapidity of the speech stream as phonemes are coarticulated in a word. One of the easiest ways for children to slow down the pronunciation of a word so that they can hear the phonemes is just that—to slow down the pronunciation. This activity called "stretched segmenting" was designed to help students slow down their pronunciation and attend to each change in speech sound.

Stretched Segmenting

TEACHER	STUDENT
I can say a word really slowly. Listen and watch me. I'll say *fin*. See the *fin* on the fish in the water? I'll say *fin* slowly. *Fffiiinnn*. Say it with me: *Fffiiinnn*. [Guides the slow pronunciation by raising his left arm toward students and slowly moving his left hand out from his body as he says the phonemes: *Fffiiinnn*.]	*Fffiiinnn*.
That was really slow! Let's say *fin* slowly again. *Fffiiinnn* [Again, provides a visual cue by guiding the slow pronunciation of each sound with his left hand as he and the students say the word slowly together.]	*Fffiiinnn*.
Now you do it. [Silently guides the slow pronunciation with his left hand as the group of students stretches each sound in the word.]	*Fffiiinnn*.
[If the students have difficulty, say an incorrect sound, or fail to articulate the /f/ and /i/ long enough to hear the sound, the teacher coarticulates the sound with the students, provides another model ("Listen: *Fffiiinnn*. Do it with me: *Fffiiinnn*."), and reinforces students' attempts ("That was really slow! Great!").]	

Once children can stretch the sounds in a word, teachers can help them to identify each phoneme individually in a one-syllable word. Children often benefit from visual guidance and prompts. Three-square forms like the one below (also called Elkonin boxes; Elkonin, 1973) can be used to show children how many phonemes they are seeking and to provide a tactile surface to touch as they identify the speech sounds.

Segmenting into Three Phonemes

TEACHER	STUDENT
Let's say all the sounds in *pat*. We'll *pat* cookie dough! Watch me. [Touches the first box.] /p/. [Touches the middle box.] /a/. [Touches the last box.] /t/.	
Watch me again. [Touches each box as the phoneme is pronounced.] /p/–/a/–/t/.	
Do it with me. [Touches each box in sequence as she and the students say the three sounds together.] /p/–/a/–/t/.	/p/–/a/–/t/.
Now you say the sounds in *pat*. [Silently touches each box as students say the three sounds.] Just right!	/p/–/a/–/t/.
Zoom! Watch the airplane *zoom* across the sky. Let's say all the sounds in *zoom*. Watch me. [Touches the first box.] /z/. [Touches the middle box.] /oo/. [Touches the last box.] /m/.	
Watch me again. [Touches each box as the phoneme is pronounced.] /z/–/oo/–/m/.	
Do it with me. [Touches each box in sequence as she and the students say the two sounds in *zoom* together.] /z/–/oo/–/m/.	/z/–/oo/–/m/.
Now you say the sounds in *zoom*. [Silently touches the first box, then the next one as students say the sounds.]	/z/–/oo/–/m/.
[Continues with *man* and *like*.]	

Activities to Teach the Alphabetic Principle

The difference between these phoneme awareness activities and those that teach the alphabetic principle is the addition of alphabet letters. A simple way to begin is with first-sound activities. You can use the same three-square box used earlier for segmenting.

First Sound with Letter Representation

TEACHER	STUDENT
The *rain* got me all wet. Say *rain*.	Rain.
What's the first sound in *rain*?	/r/.
Do you know a letter that makes that sound?	R.
Yes! Put [or write] *r* in the first box.	[Writes *r* or moves letter tile *r* into the box.]

Once children can segment into three phonemes and link the first sound to an appropriate letter in the alphabet reliably, they can begin Segment to Spell, in which children first verbally segment a spoken word, then represent each phoneme they identify with an alphabet letter and read the spelled word aloud. In most classrooms we have observed, children can do this type of activity near the end of kindergarten or at the beginning of first grade.

Segment to Spell

TEACHER	STUDENT
The *bat flew* ran through the forest. Say *bat*.	Bat.
What's the first sound in *bat*?	/b/.
Do you know a letter that makes that sound?	B.
Yes! Put [or write] *b* in the first box.	[Writes *b* or moves letter tile *b* into the box.]
Say all the sounds in *bat*.	/b/–/a/–/t/.
Touch the boxes and say the sounds in fox.	[Touches the boxes.] /b/–/a/–/t/.
What do you have so far?	/b/.
What comes next?	/a/.
Do you know a letter that makes that sound?	A.
Put *a* in the middle box.	[Writes *a* or moves letter tile *a* into the box.]
What do you have so far?	/b/–/a/.
What comes next?	/t/.
Do you know a letter that makes that sound?	T.
Put *t* in the last box.	[Writes *t* or moves letter tile *t* into the box.]
What word did you spell?	*Bat.*
Sound it out.	*Baaat. Bat.*

References

Adams, M. (1990). *Beginning to read: Thinking and learning about print.* Cambridge, MA: MIT Press.

Allor, J., & McCathren, R. (2004). The efficacy of an early literacy tutoring program implemented by college students. *Learning Disabilities Research and Practice, 19,* 116–129.

Ball, E., & Blachman, B. (1991). Does phoneme awareness training in kindergarten make a difference in early word recognition and developmental spelling? *Reading Research Quarterly, 26,* 49–66.

Berninger, V. (1986). Normal variation in reading acquisition. *Perceptual and Motor Skills, 62,* 691–716.

Bhat, P., Griffin, C. C., & Sindelar, P. T. (2003). Phonological awareness instruction for middle school students with learning disabilities. *Learning Disability Quarterly, 26,* 73–87.

Blachman, B. A., Ball, E., Black, R. S., & Tangel, D. M. (1994). Kindergarten teachers develop phoneme awareness in low-income, inner-city classrooms. *Reading and Writing: An Interdisciplinary Journal, 6,* 1–18.

Blachman, B. A., Tangel, D. M., Ball, E. W., Black, R. S., & McGraw, C. K. (1999). Developing phonological awareness and word recognition skills: A two-year intervention with low-income, inner-city children. *Reading and Writing: An Interdisciplinary Journal, 11,* 239–273.

Bradley, L., & Bryant, P. E. (1983). Categorizing sounds and learning to read: A causal connection. *Nature, 303,* 419–421.

Byrne, B., & Fielding-Barnsley, R. (1991). Evaluation of a program to teach phoneme awareness to young children. *Journal of Educational Psychology, 83,* 451–455.

Byrne, B., & Fielding-Barnsley, R. (1993). Evaluation of a program to teach phonemic awareness to young children: A 1-year follow-up. *Journal of Educational Psychology, 85,* 104–111.

Calfee, R., Lindamood, P., & Lindamood, C. (1973). Acoustic-phonetic skills and reading: Kindergarten through twelfth grade. *Journal of Educational Psychology, 64,* 293–298.

Coyne, M., Kame'enui, E., Simmons, D., & Harn, B. (2004). Beginning reading intervention as inoculation or insulin: First grade reading performance of strong responders to kindergarten intervention. *Journal of Learning Disabilities, 37,* 90–106.

Cunningham, A. (1990). Explicit vs. implicit instruction in phonemic awareness. *Journal of Experimental Child Psychology, 50,* 429–444.

Elbro, C., & Petersen, D. K. (2004). Long-term effects of phoneme awareness and letter sound training: An intervention study with children at risk for dyslexia. *Journal of Educational Psychology, 96,* 660–670.

Elkonin, D. (1973). U.S.S.R. In J. Downing (Ed.), *Comparative reading* (pp. 551–579). New York: Macmillan.

Felton, R. H. (1992). Early identification of children at risk for reading disabilities. *Topics in Early Childhood Special Education, 12,* 212–229.

Foorman, B. R., Francis, D. J., Fletcher, J. M., Schatschneider, C., & Mehta, P. (1998). The role of instruction in learning to read: Preventing reading failure in at-risk children. *Journal of Educational Psychology, 90,* 37–55.

Fox, B., & Routh, D. K. (1976). Phonemic analysis and synthesis as word-attack skills. *Journal of Educational Psychology, 68,* 70–74.

Hart, B., & Risley, T. R. (1995). *Meaningful differences in the everyday experience of young American children.* Baltimore: Brookes.

Hatcher, P., Hulme, C., & Ellis, A. (1994). Ameliorating early reading failure by integrating the teaching of reading and phonological skills: The phonological linkage by hypothesis. *Child Development, 65,* 41–57.

Hatcher, P. J., Hulme, C., Miles, J. N. V., Carroll, J. M., Hatcher, J., Gibbs, S., et al. (2005). Efficacy of a small group reading intervention for beginning readers with reading-delay: A randomized controlled trial. *Journal of Child Psychology and Psychiatry, 47,* 820–827.

Healy, K., Vanderwood, M., & Edelston, D. (2005). Early literacy interventions for English language learners: Support for an RTI model. *The California School Psychologist, 10,* 55–64.

Juel, C. (1988). Learning to read and write: A longitudinal study of 54 children from first through fourth grades. *Journal of Educational Psychology, 80,* 437–447.

Justice, L. M., & Pullen, P. C. (2003). Promising interventions for promoting emergent literacy skills: Three evidence-based approaches. *Topics in Early Childhood Special Education, 23,* 99–114.

Kamps, D., Abbott, M., Greenwood, D., Arreaga-Mayer, C., Wills, H., Longstaff, J., et al. (2007). Use of evidence-based, small-group reading instruction for English language learners in elementary grades: Secondary-tier intervention. *Learning Disability Quarterly, 30,* 153–168.

Lesaux, N. K., & Siegel, L. S. (2003). The development of reading in children who speak English as a second language. *Developmental Psychology, 39,* 1005–1019.

Liberman, I., & Shankweiler, D. (1985). Phonology and the problems of learning to read and write. *Remedial and Special Education, 6,* 8–17.

Linan-Thompson, S., Vaughn, S., Prater, K., & Cirino, P. T. (2006). The response to intervention of English language learners: At-risk for reading. *Journal of Learning Disabilities, 39,* 390–398.

Linklater, D., O'Connor, R. E., & Palardy, G. (2009). Kindergarten literacy assessment of English only and English language learner students: An examination of the predictive validity of three phonemic awareness measures. *Journal of School Psychology, 47,* 369–394.

Lovett, M. W., & Steinbach, K. A. (1997). The effectiveness of remedial programs for reading disabled children of different ages: Is there decreased benefit for older children? *Learning Disability Quarterly, 20,* 189–210.

Lundberg, I., Frost, J., & Petersen, O. (1988). Effects of an extensive program for stimulating phonological awareness in preschool children. *Reading Research Quarterly, 23,* 263–284.

Mattingly, I. G. (1992). Linguistic awareness and orthographic form. In R. Frost & L. Katz (Eds.), *Advances in psychology: Vol. 94. Orthography, phonology, morphology, and meaning* (pp. 11–26). Amsterdam: Elsevier Science.

McCandliss, B., Beck, I., Sendak, R., & Perfetti, C. (2003). Focusing attention on decoding for children with poor reading skills: Design and preliminary tests of the Word Building intervention. *Scientific Studies of Reading, 7,* 75–104.

O'Connor, R. E., Bell, K. M., Harty, K. R., Larkin, L. K., Sackor, S. M., & Zigmond, N. (2002). Teaching reading to poor readers in the intermediate grades: A comparison of text difficulty. *Journal of Educational Psychology, 94*(3), 474–485.

O'Connor, R. E., Bocian, K., Beebe-Frankenberger, M., & Linklater, D. (2010). Responsiveness of students with language difficulties to early intervention in reading. *Journal of Special Education, 43,* 220–235.

O'Connor, R. E., & Jenkins, J. R. (1995). Improving the generalization of sound/symbol knowledge: Teaching spelling to kindergarten children with disabilities. *Journal of Special Education, 29,* 255–275.

O'Connor, R. E., Jenkins, J. R., & Slocum, T. A. (1995). Transfer among phonological tasks in kindergarten: Essential instructional content. *Journal of Educational Psychology, 2,* 202–217.

O'Connor, R. E., Notari-Syverson, A., & Vadasy, P. F. (1996). Ladders to literacy: The effects of teacher-led phonological activities for kindergarten children with and without disabilities. *Exceptional Children, 63*, 117–130.

O'Connor, R. E., Notari-Syverson, A., & Vadasy, P. (1998). First grade effects of teacher-led phonological activities in kindergarten for children with mild disabilities: A follow-up study. *Learning Disabilities Research and Practice, 13*, 43–52.

Perfetti, C. A., Beck, I., Bell, L., & Hughes, C. (1987). Phonemic knowledge and learning to read are reciprocal: A longitudinal study of first grade children. *Merill–Palmer Quarterly, 33*, 283–319.

Quiroga, T., Lemos-Britton, Z., Mostafapour, E., Abbott, R. D., & Berninger, V. W. (2002). Phonological awareness and beginning reading in Spanish-speaking ESL first graders: Research into practice. *Journal of School Psychology, 40*, 85–111.

Ryder, J. F., Tunmer, W. E., & Greaney, K. T. (2008). Explicit instruction in phoneme awareness and phonemically based decoding skills as an intervention strategy for struggling readers in whole language classrooms. *Reading and Writing, 21*, 349–369.

Share, D. (1995). Phonological recoding and self-teaching: Sine quo non of reading acquisition. *Cognition, 55*, 151–218.

Share, D., Jorm, A., MacLean, R., & Matthews, R. (1984). Sources of individual differences in reading acquisition. *Journal of Educational Psychology, 76*, 1309–1324.

Slocum, T. A., O'Connor, R. E., & Jenkins, J. R. (1993). Transfer among phonological manipulation skills. *Journal of Educational Psychology, 85*(4), 618–630.

Stanovich, K., Cunningham, A., & Cramer, B. (1984). Assessing phonological awareness in kindergarten children: Issues of task comparability. *Journal of Experimental Child Psychology, 38*, 175–190.

Torgesen, J. K., Morgan, S. T., & Davis, C. (1992). Effects of two types of phonological awareness training on word learning in kindergarten children. *Journal of Educational Psychology, 84*, 364–370.

Tunmer, W., Herriman, M., & Nesdale, A. (1988). Metalinguistic abilities and beginning reading. *Reading Research Quarterly, 23*, 134–158.

Vadasy, P. F., Sanders, E. A., & Peyton, J. A. (2006). Code-oriented instruction for kindergarten students at risk for reading difficulties: A randomized field trial with paraeducator implementers. *Journal of Educational Psychology, 98*, 508–528.

Vellutino, F. R., Scanlon, D. M., Sipay, E. R., Small, S. G., Pratt, A., Chen, R., et al. (1996). Cognitive profiles of difficult-to-remediate and readily remediated poor readers: Early identification as vehicle for distinguishing between cognitive and experiential deficits as basic causes of specific reading disability. *Journal of Educational Psychology, 88*, 601–638

Wagner, R. K., Torgesen, J. K., Laughon, P., Simmons, K., & Rashotte, C. A. (1993). Development of young readers' phonological processing abilities. *Journal of Educational Psychology, 85*, 83–103.

Yeh, S. S., & Connell, D. B. (2008). Effects of rhyming, vocabulary, and phoneme awareness instruction on phoneme awareness. *Journal of Research on Reading, 31*, 243–256.

Yopp, H. (1988). The validity and reliability of phonemic awareness tests. *Reading Research Quarterly, 23*, 159–177.

3

Preschool Foundations
for Reading and Writing Success

THERESA A. ROBERTS

Ample evidence demonstrates that the foundations for strong reading and writing are formed in preschool (Duncan et al., 2007; Snow, Burns, & Griffin, 1998). Preschool children who *enter* kindergarten with higher levels of literacy skills and language competencies are likely to be better readers (e.g., Duncan et al., 2007; Hammer, Lawrence, & Miccio, 2007; National Institute of Child Health and Human Development (NICHD) Early Child Care Network, 2005; Storch & Whitehurst, 2002). Alphabetic knowledge, phonological awareness, and oral language are three of these important foundations (Biemiller, 2006; Bradley & Bryant, 1983; Ehri & Roberts, 2006; Scarborough, 2001; Tunmer, Herriman, & Nesdale, 1988; Whitehurst & Lonigan, 1998).

There are striking differences in the alphabetic knowledge, phonological awareness, and oral language competence of preschool-age children, and evidence that there is stability in these competencies across the preschool through elementary developmental periods (Lonigan, Burgess, & Anthony, 2000; Storch & Whitehurst, 2002). In other words, preschool children who have high or low literacy foundations are likely to remain so as they progress into the early grades and formal reading instruction. Children who are from low-socioeconomic-status families and learning English as a second language are less likely to have the necessary foundations in these core areas at preschool entry or exit (Bowey, 1995; Chaney, 1994), although preschool experience can help to close the gap between these children and their more advantaged counterparts (Administration on Children, Youth, and Families [ACYF], 2003). Yet preschool settings differ markedly in the degree to which they stimulate literacy foundations (e.g., Dickinson, McCabe, & Clark-Chiarelli, 2004; Mashburn et al., 2008; Whitehurst & Massetti, 2004). In addition, children who are more at risk for reading difficulties are less likely to have the benefit of high-quality preschool experiences (e.g., LoCasale-Crouch et al., 2007; McGill-Franzen, Lanford, & Adams, 2002). Both the promise and the necessity of developing and bringing to scale high-quality preschool intervention are underscored in the presence of this knowledge.

An important component of high-quality preschool is the availability of carefully designed and sequenced instruction that draws on the basic learning mechanisms that underlie literacy acquisition. This high-quality instruction is characterized by "important details" that can be drawn from preschool intervention research. For example, the details of alphabet instruction that result in robust learning are different from those that lead to vocabulary learning (Aram, 2006; Roberts & Neal, 2004). This chapter reviews these basic mechanisms and summarizes "important details" of alphabet, phonological awareness, and oral language interventions that lead to significant learning.

The chapter begins with a brief introduction that explains why alphabetic knowledge, phonological awareness, and oral language are important literacy foundations. This introduction is followed by review of the evidence related to intervention to enhance preschool-age children's skills in these areas. Experimental studies with a comparison group and random assignment of children to intervention groups provide the clearest evidence of an intervention's effectiveness, because they reduce the possibility that intervention effects are due to children's growth or differences in the groups of children being compared. Evidence from smaller scale, researcher-designed interventions, as well as findings from larger scale and/or teacher-implemented interventions, are discussed. The available evidence specific to English learners is interwoven into this discussion. Each chapter section concludes with a summary of instructional principles that can be drawn from research. Sample lessons illustrate how these principles may be incorporated. In the final section of the chapter I discuss issues associated with the implementation of effective preschool interventions.

Knowledge of the alphabet is one of the two best predictors of beginning reading, and the number of letters that children know at kindergarten entry is associated with eventual levels of reading competence (Adams, 1990). Deep familiarity with letter shapes, names, and sounds is the foundation for word reading skill. Accuracy and automaticity (speed) are two components of children's performance that demonstrate this deep familiarity with the alphabet. Children must be able to identify accurately the names and sounds of letter shapes. They also must do so quickly, because rapid conversion from printed words to their oral language pronunciation allows children to access word meanings at a rate that enables good reading comprehension (Roberts, Christo, & Shefelbine, 2010). As preschool children begin to develop this deep familiarity with the alphabet, they use their growing knowledge to make sense of the print they are exposed to, and to create meaningful print. Specific instructional practices help children form basic connections between letter names and sounds, and appreciate how print works in real life. These practices are elaborated in the section "Interventions to Increase Children's Alphabetic Knowledge."

Phonological awareness is the ability to attend to and perform tasks on the phonemic structure of words rather than their meanings. Phonemes are the smallest units into which speech can be divided, and that make a difference to the meaning of a word. The word *mist* has four phonemes, while the word *miss* has only three. Phonological awareness is an oral language skill and is the anchor for connecting the speech that children already know with print. Phonemic awareness reflects a more precise and advanced level of phonological awareness, and refers to the ability to attend to and perform tasks on the individual phonemes in words. Phonemic awareness and alphabetic knowledge at kindergarten entry are the two best predictors of beginning reading (Adams, 1990). There is a strong relationship between preschool children's performance on a variety of phonological/phonemic awareness tasks and later reading (e.g., Burgess, 2002). Learning the connections between phonemes in speech and the alphabetic elements of print is the backbone of beginning reading. Furthermore, competence with the smallest units of word structure—phonemes—revealed in tasks such as substituting one phoneme in a word for another, or segmenting each phoneme in a word, has the most telling influence on later literacy (NICHD, 2000). Instructional practices that help children gain a hold of the individual phonemes of words within instructional sequences that progress from easier to more challenging phonological awareness tasks are elaborated in the section "Interventions to Increase Children's Phonological Awareness."

Oral language competence before children reach kindergarten has a strong relationship to literacy achievement for children learning to read in their first language (NICHD Early Child Care Research Network, 2005; Snow et al., 1998). Differences in oral language competence are clearly observable in preschool-age children (Hart & Risley, 1995; Scarborough, 2001). These initial differences in oral language have far-reaching implications for later literacy (Scarborough, 2001; Stanovich, 1986). Oral language contributes to learning phonological awareness skills and is a foundation for reading comprehension. Research specific to English language learners (ELLs) indicates that oral language competence in both first and second language supports literacy in either language, as English learners draw upon experiences and knowledge coded in their first language to meet the demands of second-language literacy (Ordonez, Carlo, Snow, & McLaughlin, 2002).

The recent report of the National Early Literacy Panel (NELP; 2008) concluded that preschool oral language, broadly conceptualized, is strongly related to later literacy, but vocabulary knowledge has only a weak or moderate relationship with both decoding and comprehension skills. However, the panel tracked the influence of vocabulary only to the end of kindergarten and first grade, and the influence of vocabulary on literacy begins to be expressed most clearly after grade

2 (Biemiller, 2006). The panel also did not consider the influence of vocabulary size on kindergarten or first-grade literacy for ELLs whose English vocabularies are typically of a size similar to those of English-only preschool children. As vocabulary grows, children's representations of words they know include more detail about the individual phonemes that comprise them (Metsala & Walley, 1998). Therefore, children's vocabulary size may influence the development of phonological awareness and early word reading, particularly for children who are more likely to have smaller vocabularies, such as ELLs (Roberts, 2005). For these reasons, in this chapter vocabulary is treated as an important component of preschool oral language that influences later literacy achievement. Instructional practices and adult–child interaction patterns that enhance oral language in both more and less structured contexts are elaborated in the section "Interventions to Increase Children's Oral Language and Vocabulary."

Thinking about Intervention in Preschool

Several factors warrant consideration when thinking about preschool literacy intervention. The first is that preschool children have not yet expressed evidence of reading and writing difficulty, because they are prereaders. Yet, as already noted, there is a fair amount of stability in literacy foundations from preschool to the elementary years, and early competence is associated with higher rates of later growth (Stanovich, 1986). In addition, many children from low-socioeconomic-status families and families in which the primary language is not English enter and exit preschool substantially behind other children (Snow et al., 1998). This stability, growth, and demographic-related pattern provides an impetus for viewing comprehensive preschool programs that target academic literacy foundations as early intervention to prevent later reading difficulty (Snow et al., 1998). An important component of intervention is identification and more intensive follow-up for children who experience difficulty in mastering literacy foundations taught in the classroom instructional program. Response-to-intervention (RTI) models are a promising approach in which participation in core literacy instruction is followed with tiered levels of more intensive support in smaller instructional settings, with participation determined by frequently measured progress (Fuchs & Fuchs, 2006; Gettinger & Stoiber, 2009; VanDerHeyden, Snyder, Broussard, & Ramsdell, 2007). In this chapter, "preschool intervention" is defined broadly and includes both classroom programs that provide instruction in one or more of the core literacy foundations to all children and small-group differentiated instruction.

A second important feature of the early childhood education field is the long-standing commitment to fostering social-emotional development (Bredecamp & Copple, 1997; National Association for the Education of Young Children, 2009; National Research Council, Institute of Medicine, 2000). Many have commented on the tendency to view social-emotional and cognitive/academic emphases as competing (e.g., Dickinson, McCabe, & Essex, 2006). Recent studies, however, have portrayed the reciprocal relationships among preschool literacy competencies and the motivational and self-regulatory orientations that can either support or impede learning to read (Chang & Burns, 2005; Chapman, Tunmer, & Prochnow, 2000; Lepola, Poskiparta, Laakkonen, & Niemi, 2005; Turner & Johnson, 2003). Other evidence has documented the important role that adult responsiveness, shared attention, and positive emotions play in learning, although most of this evidence does not clearly show that these features of adult–child relationships actually *cause* learning (Baumeister & Vohs, 2004; Bus, Belsky, van IJzendoorn, & Crnic, 1997; Pianta, 2006; Pianta, Hamre, & Stuhlman, 2003). A potential legacy of the early childhood field for literacy intervention may be to increase the prominence of the complementary benefits to be realized from instructional practices that promote cognitive learning and social-emotional well-being. These important social-emotional influences on learning are included as specific features of high-quality alphabet, phonemic awareness, and oral language intervention detailed within subsequent sections of the chapter.

Another noteworthy feature of preschool education is the relatively recent emphasis on academic preparation and use of intentional pedagogies (e.g., Lee & Ginsburg, 2007). Consequently, teacher knowledge of the three core literacy areas, skill in intentional teaching practices, and positive valuing of these practices are issues. Preschool teachers tend to endorse literacy practices in which children choose their own activities within a print-rich environment (Lee & Ginsburg, 2007). In another study, fewer than 50% of Head Start teachers reported daily phonological awareness, writing, or alphabet letter activities (Hawken, Johnston, & McDonnell, 2005). Explicit instruction was not a strategy these teachers reported using frequently.

A final feature that characterizes preschool literacy intervention is that many programs are only half-day or about 3½ hours in duration. Thus, time constraints to implement preschool literacy intervention are significant and have implications for instructional design.

General Principles of Effective Preschool Instruction and Intervention

Research on interventions to promote preschool children's competence in core literacy foundations of alphabetic knowledge, phonological awareness, and oral language is burgeoning. This research indicates that intentionality underlies effective intervention, whether that intentionality is expressed through structured and explicit group instruction, in a conversation between an adult and individual child, or in a dramatic play center. A critical aspect of intentionality is selecting instructional strategies and child activities on the basis of their effectiveness for achieving specific instructional goals. Preschool children learn literacy foundations in diverse ways and benefit from teacher-guided, child-guided, explicit, and less structured experiences (e.g., Connor, Morrison, & Slominski, 2006; Ehri & Roberts, 2006; Graue, Clements, Reynolds, & Niles, 2004). Effective interventions for promoting alphabetic and phonological skills can be characterized by teacher-guided explicit instruction in small groups, clearly defined instructional goals, careful sequencing of instructional elements, and significant teacher modeling and child practice (Ehri, Nunes, Willows, Yaghoub-Zadeh, & Shanahan, 2001; Phillips, Clancy-Menchetti, & Lonigan, 2008). In comparison, effective intervention for oral language is characterized by similar kinds of structured lessons and greater reliance on less structured interactions between children and adults.

Another general principle of effective instruction and intervention is that small differences in instruction influence what is learned (Byrne, 1992; Byrne & Fielding-Barnsley, 1991; Connor et al., 2006; Nelson, Sanders, & Gonzalez, 2010; Roberts & Meiring, 2006). Effective interventions embed important details about how children learn alphabet, phonological, and oral language skills into learning experiences. Large differences in student performance can be accounted for by these details. For example, Byrne (1992) discussed experiments using different approaches to improve children's phonemic awareness. He found that children needed to read printed words containing target phonemes, to learn the letters that represent phonemes, and to hear the target phoneme in different parts of the word in order to gain deep knowledge of *phoneme identity*. Instruction that did not include all these key features was not nearly as effective (32% performance vs. 95% performance). Variation on these instructional principles accounts for a portion of the growing evidence documenting that some preschool teaching programs and practices are more effective than others (e.g., Debarysche & Gorecki, 2007; Fischel et al., 2007; Han, Roskos, Christie, Mandzuk, & Vukelich, 2005; Preschool Curriculum Evaluation Research [PCER] Consortium, 2008; U.S. Department of Education, Institute of Education Sciences [IES], What Works Clearinghouse, 2004). English-only children are the dominant group in most studies, with children from low socioeconomic backgrounds well represented. Emerging evidence supports that ELLs can also learn literacy foundations in English at the preschool level (Ehri & Roberts, 2006; Roberts, 2009).

Studies of preschool intervention can be classified into two major categories. One group of studies includes researcher-designed comparisons between different instructional approaches that differ in small ways. These studies are designed to compare interventions based on theory and existing evidence. They frequently include carefully scripted instructional protocols, with a significant level of detail specified in the teaching routines. The instruction within these studies is often delivered in small groups or one-on-one by trained researchers. They provide the clearest available evidence of the potential of a particular intervention. The studies have in aggregate demonstrated that it is possible to increase preschool children's performance on alphabet, phonological awareness, and oral language (including vocabulary) measures, with impressive educational advances often demonstrated. However, an important qualification is that they do not reveal what may be accomplished by teachers implementing a particular type of instruction in a regular classroom setting.

The second group of intervention studies examines literacy outcomes associated with instruction delivered by regular classroom teachers. These interventions often target several literacy goals and are typically implemented on a larger scale, often in many classrooms and schools. A subset of these studies compares particular literacy curricula, many of which are commercially available. The most comprehensive report reviewed 15 literacy curricula that had been tested with rigorous research designs (PCER Consortium, 2008). Only two programs led to significant gains in alphabetic, phonological, or oral language skills. Participating children were mostly from low-income families. Factors that may have contributed to these disappointing results include details of instruction and breadth of implementation of the curricula. I turn now to a discussion of research that details characteristics of effective intervention specifically for alphabetic knowledge, phonological awareness, and oral language learning.

Interventions to Increase Children's Alphabetic Knowledge

Small-scale experimental studies designed and implemented by researchers offer robust evidence that children's alphabetic knowledge can be enhanced in preschool. "Small scale" refers to studies with about 50 or fewer children, distributed among two to four different instructional groups. These studies have identified specific instructional practices, strategies, and materials that promote children's learning of the names and sounds of letter shapes. Importantly there is evidence that instruction in alphabet knowledge has a causal influence on preschool children's ability to learn and remember simple written words (Roberts, 2003; Share, 2004). Some studies have demonstrated positive effects from intervention on alphabet knowledge for children who are English learners at the very initial stages of English acquisition (Nelson et al., 2010; Roberts & Neal, 2004). Carefully designed instruction to teach alphabet knowledge benefits later literacy achievement in elementary school (NICHD, 2000). There is also evidence that larger-scale interventions implemented by regular teachers can increase children's alphabetic knowledge, although the number of letters known at the end of preschool in these studies has varied between 10 and 23 (Diamond, Gerde, & Powell, 2008; Nelson et al., 2010; U.S. Department of Education, IES, National Center of Educational Evaluation and Assistance, 2007; U.S. Department of Health and Human Services, 2005).

Important Details for Letter–Name and Letter–Sound Intervention

Interventions that lead to the necessary accuracy and speed in identifying letter names and sounds should be grounded in the basic learning mechanisms that enable children to acquire names and sounds of letters. Memory of specific pairings between what is initially an arbitrary shape and its name or sound—or *paired associate learning*—is the fundamental mechanism involved in learning each pair. Letter shapes are formed from the same small set of lines (horizontal, curved, vertical, and slanted) and curves (whole and part circles). Since each letter shape and letter-name or letter-sound pair is part of a complex system, the alphabet, discriminating the shape and verbal label (letter name or letter sound) of each pair from the others is a second basic learning mechanism. Memory for each pair is strengthened by focusing children's attention on the letter shape and its name or sound, and by having children pronounce it. It is like sewing on a button; the more times the button and fabric are stitched together, the more strongly attached together they become. Exercises in discriminating one letter from the others help to stitch together letter shapes, names, and sounds. Ample practice and repetition of each pair contribute to both accuracy and automaticity of learning. In addition to forming strong memories that can be quickly accessed, children should be helped to understand the purposes of the alphabet and to appreciate how it works in meaningful print. While learning individual shapes, names, and sounds leads some children to insight about how speech and print connect, many children need to have this relationship explained to them. Opportunities for children to explore and examine how the alphabet works in meaningful print can hone this insight, while simultaneously "sewing" the print and speech pairings tightly together.

Working with and Selecting Alphabet Books

During storybook reading, most children focus on language meaning, and neither adults nor children show much attention to print (Yaden, Smolkin, & Conlon, 1989). Yet during alphabet book reading, both teachers and parents direct significant attention to print, and the amount of attention to print is associated with children's ability to name letters (Bus & van IJzendoorn, 1988; van Kleeck, 1998; Yaden, Smolkin, & MacGillivray, 1993). Including alphabet books in alphabet letter instruction can give children additional practice in linking letter shapes with their names and sounds. Alphabet books can also help children see how letters function in print when books include printed words, and when pronunciations of pictured words provide clear examples of alphabet letter names or sounds. For example, an alphabet book that shows only pictures of words that begin with the letter *A* and a printed letter "A" provides less material for learning about the relationship between print and phonemes in words than do alphabet books with words written under each picture. An alphabet book page for the letter *A* that includes a picture of an acorn, ape, apple, and alligator (with each word printed under the picture) contributes to learning the letter name and short vowel sound for *A* more than does a page that includes a picture of an artichoke and an arm, because *artichoke* and *arm* do not include the letter name or sound for *A* in their pronunciation.

Using Personal Names

Knowledge of letters in personal names emerges earlier than knowledge of other letters, and children are particularly aware of the first letter in their own names (Bloodgood, 1999; Treiman, Cohen, Mulqueeny, Kessler, & Schechtman, 2007). Knowledge of written personal names appears to pave the way for alphabetic learning. While the mechanisms for this connection between personal names and alphabetic letter knowledge are not understood, motivation, personal meaningfulness, and letter exposure have been suggested. Others have noted that young children draw on the letters in their personal names in early writing and alphabet learning (Levin, Both-De Vries, Aram, & Bus, 2004; Treiman & Kessler, 2004). Recommendations to use children's personal names to teach alphabet letters are frequently made, although there have been few experimental studies of the effectiveness of this practice. In a small-scale experiment, Justice, Chow, Capellini, Flanigan, and Colton (2003) included personal names as part of a multifaceted curriculum that also relied on the alphabet song and alphabet games. In this study with children from low-income families, gains in alphabet letter naming were obtained.

Teaching Letter Writing

Preschool children's ability to write letters is also associated with their alphabetic knowledge and phonemic awareness (Diamond et al., 2008). One experimental study demonstrated that teaching 4-year-old preschool children how to write letters led to better letter recognition than typing letters on the computer (Longcamp, Zerbato-Poudou, & Velay, 2005). Experimental training studies with primary-grade children have shown that letter-writing instruction can increase both the accuracy and speed of children's handwriting, and that such improvement leads to more fluent and higher quality writing (Berninger et al., 1997). These researchers found that instructing children to study letter shapes, with numbers embedded in the shapes indicating the sequence and direction of writing strokes, followed by limited practice writing each letter (three to five times), was the most beneficial strategy. The benefits of teaching children the correct sequence of strokes to write letters appears to be twofold. It both improves recognition of alphabet letters and sets the foundation for the handwriting accuracy and fluency that lead to more and better quality writing (Graham, Harris, & Fink, 2000).

A number of unanswered questions about how best to teach the alphabet remain. We do not yet know whether teaching letter names or letter sounds is more advantageous, although arguments have been made that letter names may be more efficient (Ehri & Roberts, 2006). This argument hinges on the fact that most letter names contain clues to the letter sounds, and children figure this out as they learn letter names (Roberts, 2003; Treiman, Weatherston, & Berch, 1994). It is also not known whether teaching uppercase, lowercase, or both together is

TABLE 3.1. The Details That Matter: Alphabet Intervention

- Explain the purpose of the lesson and reason for learning the alphabet.
- Clearly and repeatedly pair the letter shape and its letter name or letter sound.
- Compare and contrast (discriminate) new letters with known ones.
- Model/demonstrate all instructional tasks.
- Elicit oral participation in naming letters from all children.
- Help children to say the letter names/sounds correctly.
- Provide sufficient practice and repetition.
- Connect letter names/sounds to children's personal names.
- Use alphabet books with written words that clearly include target letter names and letter sounds.
- Teach how to write letters efficiently and practice writing letters three to five times.
- Respond to all children's participation and show positive emotions during instruction.
- Promote self-regulation by allowing children control and choice in some activities.
- Implement consistent routines and have activities well-prepared and well-organized.
- Provide many opportunities for children to observe, explore, and generate meaningful use of alphabet knowledge.
- Monitor progress in speed and accuracy of alphabet knowledge.
- Provide differentiated/individualized small-group intervention.

optimal. However, introducing uppercase and lowercase letters together significantly increases the amount of paired-associate learning and letter discrimination that children must accomplish. Another question for the design of alphabet interventions is the best sequence in which to teach the letters. These are very important applied questions for future research.

Table 3.1 summarizes the important details for the design of alphabet intervention. These elements can be woven explicitly into alphabet lesson planning forms, used to evaluate the quality of alphabet instruction within a program, or used to coach teachers for improving alphabet instruction.

The following plan outlines 3 days of instruction using many of the details in Table 3.1. The activities are for small-group intervention for children needing more intensive support.

Each Day

Teacher explains that the goal of the lesson is to learn alphabet letter names, and that the purpose of this learning is to use letters to help in learning to read in kindergarten. Children sing the alphabet song. They feed letters to "Ms. Letter Muncher" puppet. Children name the letter as they feed the puppet. Children play the game with the puppet in pairs on their own to promote self-regulation.

Day 1: Letter B

   1. Children are shown a large letter card with an uppercase *B*. The teacher names the letter. Children repeat the name several times in a back-and-forth, playful manner, accompanied by positive teacher emotion.

   2. The teacher models how to write the letter on a whiteboard. Children practice writing letter *B* three to five times on their own whiteboard, saying, "Down, around, around, makes letter *B*."

   3. Children read a "big book" alphabet book turned to page "B," where they name pictures and then use a small picture frame to "frame" the letter *B* in the words on the "B" page (choose pictures with letter name, such as *bee, beet, bean,* if possible).

Day 2: Letter M

   1. Children are shown a large letter card with an uppercase *M*. The teacher names the letter. Children repeat the name several times in a back-and-forth, playful manner, accompanied by positive teacher emotion.

   2. The teacher models how to write the letter on a whiteboard. Children practice writing letter *M* three to five times on their own whiteboard, saying, "Up, down, up, down makes letter *M*."

   3. Letters *B* and *M* are placed in a pocket chart. The teacher guides children in comparing the two letters. Children use their own letter cards and show the *B* or *M* several times when asked by the teacher.

   4. Children read a "big book" alphabet book, naming pictures then using a small picture frame to "frame" the letter *M* in the words on the "M" page.

   5. Children look for letters *B* and *M* in children's names that begin with each letter that have been written on a large card. They use the small frame again to frame the beginning letters *B* or *M*.

   6. Each child is provided a small frame and a sheet with children's names or an alphabet book and looks for and frames letters *B* and *M*.

Day 3: Letter R

   1. Children are shown a large letter card with an uppercase *R*. The teacher names the letter. Children repeat the name several times in a back-and-forth, playful manner, accompanied by positive teacher emotion.

   2. The teacher models how to write the letter on a whiteboard. Children practice writing letter *R* three to five times on their own whiteboard, saying "Down, around, slant makes letter *R*."

   3. Letters *B*, *M*, and *R* are placed in a pocket chart. The teacher guides children in comparing the three letters: "Letters *B* and *R* both have a down and around.

Letter *B* has another 'around.' But look, letter *R* has a 'slant'"! Children use their own letter cards and show the *B*, *M*, or *R* several times when asked by the teacher. Then, using small letter cards of their own, children place them in a line, rearrange them, and so forth, while naming them.

4. Children read a "big book" alphabet book for page "R," naming pictures, using a small picture frame to "frame" the letter *R* in the book.

5. Children look for letters *B*, *M*, and *R* in children's names that begin with each letter that have been written on a large card. They self-regulate and use the small frame again to frame the beginning letters *B*, *M*, or *R*.

6. Each child is provided a small frame and a sheet with children's names or an alphabet book, and looks for and frames letters *B*, *M*, and *R*.

Interventions to Increase Children's Phonological Awareness

Phonological awareness refers to the ability to be conscious of, attend to, and manipulate phonemes, the speech sounds that make words. It is typically less well-developed than alphabetic knowledge in preschool children. Preschool phonological and phonemic awareness instruction is effective and leads to better performance in conventional reading in the elementary years (Fox & Routh, 1976; Lundberg, Frost, & Petersen, 1988; NICHD, 2000). These findings lead to the defensible conclusion that phonological awareness, like alphabetic knowledge, plays a causal role in learning to read (Ehri et al., 2001). Children's phonological awareness in one language can also be shared with another language, although this sharing is influenced by how similar languages are in phonological structure and how effectively instruction promotes the use of phonological awareness knowledge across languages (Bialystok, Majumder, & Martin, 2003; Durgunoğlu, Nagy, & Hancin-Bhatt, 1993; López & Greenfield, 2004).

Small-scale, researcher-designed and implemented interventions to teach phonological skills to preschool children can be very effective. Almost all of the experimental studies include small groups (two to five children) or individual instruction. The benefit of phonological awareness instruction for a preschooler is almost twice that for an older child (NICHD, 2000). In addition, instruction targeting fewer rather than more phonological skills is most effective, highlighting the importance of planning focused instruction (NICHD, 2000). The NICHD report also noted that these successful interventions targeted individual phonemes in skills such as identifying beginning and ending phonemes in words, recognizing the same phoneme in different words, and blending and segmenting phonemes into simple words.

Larger-scale studies implemented with regular teachers and/or specific curricula have produced notably poorer results (Byrne & Fielding-Barnsley, 1995; Preschool Curriculum Evaluation Research Consortium [PCER], 2008; Whitehurst et al., 1999). The first report on Early Reading First outcomes reported no evidence of improvement on phonological awareness (U.S. Department of Education, IES, 2007). Early Reading First programs entail large-scale interventions implemented by regular classroom teachers who receive professional development in phonological or phonemic awareness instruction. The PCER Consortium (2008) review of 15 different preschool curricula similarly reported that only two of them produced significant phonological awareness gains.

An exception to this pattern of low phonological awareness performance was a randomized controlled trial by Nelson et al. (2010). In this experiment, trained paraeducators implemented a phonological awareness intervention with children attending Head Start, and obtained an approximate 45% advantage over the control group (1.31 effect size). In this study, 82% of participating children came from families whose primary language was not English. The intervention featured 25 lessons that were approximately 20 minutes long. Instruction began with rhymes and syllables, followed quite soon by phoneme-level activities, and alphabetic skills were also taught throughout the lessons. At the end of the program children switched middle phonemes in words and segmented phonemes in simple words. This program targeted phoneme-level skills within consistent and specified instructional routines.

Results such as these in combination with conclusions from the National Reading Panel (NICHD, 2000) support the value of instruction in phoneme-level skills. Yet many comprehensive PreK commercial programs, including those reviewed in the PCER report, devote many initial lessons to phonological sensitivity exercises to draw children's attention to environmental sounds; to have children clap as they say each syllable in their names and other words; and to recognize, generate, or discriminate rhyming words before phoneme skills are taught. Some programs do not include any phoneme-level activities, because they are believed to be too challenging for young children. Syllable-level activities focus on only a beginning level of phonological awareness. A recent review by Castles and Coltheart (2004) concluded there is no strong evidence that syllable-level activities lead to phonemic awareness, although some critics have suggested that the criteria for acceptable evidence applied in the review were too stringent (Phillips & Torgesen, 2006). Another review by MacMillan (2002) was similarly skeptical about the link between rhyming exercises and later literacy (Martin & Byrne, 2002; Muter, Hulme, Snowling, & Stevenson, 2004; Walton, 1995). Efforts to teach rhyming to preschool ELLs have also not been very successful (Barnett, Yarosz, Thomas, Jung, & Blanco, 2007; Roberts & Neal, 2004). The data are sufficient to suggest limiting the amount of rhyming activity in phonological intervention. The discussion of details for phonological awareness instruction that follows focuses on phoneme-level intervention.

Important Details for Phonological Awareness Intervention

Several learning mechanisms are called upon during phonological awareness instruction. In order to successfully attend to the structure of a word rather than its meaning and thereby set the stage for phonological awareness learning, children must exercise a fair amount of attention control, because their more automatic response is to pay attention to word meaning rather than word structure. Children must also be able to perceive differences between the individual phonemes in speech. Most typically developing preschool children, including English learners can be expected to have this ability, although children with language impairments may have trouble (Fowler, 1991). In addition children must be able to form accurate mental representations of the individual phonemes that comprise words. This ability is needed, for example, to identify a beginning or ending phoneme in a word, to determine that an individual phoneme and the beginning or ending phoneme in a word match, or to strip off a phoneme in a word and say what remains (Elbro, 1996; Roberts, 2005). Therefore, a critical starting point for teachers to teach phonological skills successfully is to ensure that individual phonemes stand tall and still in children's minds. Children need to hear phonemes pronounced accurately both within and outside the context of whole words. Many children also need help to correctly pronounce, or articulate these phonemes to make each phoneme clear. The challenges inherent in teaching phonological skills to ELL children are apparent, because they must perceive, remember, and focus on the phonemes of a language they are just beginning to learn. These challenges, together with evidence that once the skill of attending to phonemes is learned in any language, that skill can be used in another language, suggest that children will benefit from learning phonological awareness in their primary language (Durgunoğlu et al., 1993; López & Greenfield, 2004). Instructional conditions that help children to stay focused on word structure, to develop accurate knowledge of individual phonemes, to make the phonemes in words concrete and prominent, and to understand the conceptual requirements embedded in the language of phonological awareness instruction are key elements for phonological awareness success. Interventions that systematically foster these multiple competencies are needed.

Focusing Attention on Word Structure

Teachers help children focus on word structure by giving frequent reminders to listen to little bits of words. It is helpful to use a consistent cue to signal this listening, such as pairing the word *listen* and cupping an ear with one's hand. Again, because preschool children are oriented to language meaning, helping them to stay focused on word structure is an important instructional detail. For example, in the lesson that follows, the word *bug* is used in teaching the phoneme /b/. Avoiding meaning-based digressions during the lesson such as "I like bugs" or "I found a tick on my dog last night" will help children to stay focused on word structure. One likely reason that phonological awareness instruction targeting fewer tasks is more effective than phonological awareness instruction targeting several tasks (NICHD, 2000) is that having one or two tasks helps children focus their attention and avoid potential confusion about what is expected.

Modeling Individual Phonemes

Clear and accurate pronunciation of individual phonemes, with many repetitions by both teacher and child during each lesson, helps each phoneme to stand tall in children's minds. This decontextualized presentation of individual phonemes helps to etch their individual identities in children's minds. Progressive stretching of word pronunciations can help children to hear the individual phonemes in whole words. Children initially repeat the whole word, followed by several progressions, each modeled by the teacher, in which they speak the word more and more slowly until each phoneme is spoken individually. Teachers help children learn phoneme identity by explaining that certain words are alike because they begin with the same phoneme, then having children find pictures or objects that begin with the same phoneme (Byrne & Fielding-Barnsley, 1991). The ability of teachers to pronounce the individual phonemes correctly in a consistent manner helps children in this effort (NICHD, 2000). Some commercial programs include CDs to help teachers and even families learn how to pronounce English phonemes correctly. Helping teachers to develop accurate pronunciations of English phonemes should be addressed sensitively in professional development.

Using Articulatory Cues

Recent studies have shown that training children to focus on how phonemes are produced is effective in enhancing phonemic awareness. Ehri and Sweet (1991), Castiglioni-Spalten and Ehri (2003), and Boyer and Ehri (in press) reported that segmentation training, using articulatory pictures of mouth movements adapted from Lindamood and Lindamood (1998), improved phonemic awareness in 4- and 5-year-old children. Drawing children's attention to this useful information provides learning opportunities in the motoric modality and helps to make phonemes concrete. Teachers can help children by using a chart to depict the speech apparatus and how different phonemes are made, and by teaching the meaning of the words that describe speech production such as *tongue*, *throat*, and *lips*. This may be particularly useful to ELL children. Children can also examine how phonemes are made by using small mirrors and watching the teacher's mouth. Of course, to obtain the full benefit of articulatory feedback, all children need to pronounce the phonemes and words used in phonological awareness intervention many times. Dialect differences and second language status can influence how phonemes are represented in children's minds and influence later spelling development (Kamp, 2009; Treiman & Kessler, 2004). Therefore, ensuring that children can pronounce phonemes accurately is important.

Making Phonemes Concrete

Individual phonemes are ephemeral and short-lived compared to whole spoken words. They literally take only milliseconds to pronounce. In addition, in actual speech, phonemes are tied together, and their contours depend on the surrounding phonemes. I liken this to a watercolor painting in which individual colors blend. Instructional routines to help make these slippery phonemes stand still and be concrete will help children attend to and ultimately manipulate them. A variety of techniques have been used in instructional research to accomplish this: hand clapping and other hand movements, stick tapping, and moving small tiles. I have used little individual "Make It Concrete" kits that include inexpensive materials to help make phonemes stand tall and still (Roberts, 2009). The kits include a phone made of 1½-inch polyvinyl chloride (PVC) pipe, a small mirror, 1-inch tiles, and a large rubber band. The mirrors, for example, allow children to see and explore how their speech apparatus produces different phonemes. The kits are used regularly with established routines to ensure that they efficiently support rather than detract from phonological awareness learning.

Connecting Print and Speech

As children acquire alphabetic knowledge, it is helpful to show them written forms of words having the same initial phoneme, and point out words that contain these letters and phonemes (Byrne & Fielding-Barnsley, 1991; NICHD, 2000). Pointing out the letter sound that is embedded within most letter names is another way to tie together print and phonemes that benefit phonemic awareness (Treiman & Kessler, 2003). For example, when the letter name s is pronounced, the letter sound is heard at the end of the letter name. Phonological awareness interventions often include the use of small (1 × 1 inch) tiles to count phonemes. Alphabet letters can be added to the tiles as children's alphabetic knowledge increases. This practice draws on the potential of written letters to strengthen phonemic learning (NICHD, 2000). Children develop phonemic skills when they attempt to write words on their own (Ehri & Roberts, 2006; Martins & Silva, 2006), because writing involves decomposing words into phonemes, then deciding which letters to use to represent those phonemes. To achieve the most effective pairing of alphabetic knowledge and phonological awareness learning, teachers should coordinate the order of introduction of alphabet letters and the phonemes targeted in phonological awareness instruction.

Using Simple, Familiar Words

Children are likely to manage more of the phonemes of words that (1) are learned earlier, (2) occur more frequently in spoken language, (3) are familiar, (4) comprise phonemes most 3- and 4-year-olds can pronounce and (5) have fewer phonemes closely tied to neighboring ones. The use of these types of words during phonological awareness activities makes it easier for preschool children and particularly ELLs to remember and accurately pronounce phonemes (e.g., Storkel & Rogers, 2000). Instruction should target words of two to four phonemes (pig, boat, hi, dog, jump) in which the phonemes are not closely tied to each other (e.g., the /f/

and /r/ in the word *frog*). The words should also have regular grapheme–phoneme correspondences that help children understand the alphabetic system (therefore, the word *car* would not support teaching phoneme correspondences for the letters *a* and *r*). The words and phonemes used in phonological awareness instruction should be carefully selected. There are websites, phonological awareness teaching resources, and some curricula that provide lists of good words for teaching phonological awareness. Try Googling "CVC words."

Teaching Words of Instruction

Children need to understand a number of words used in phonological awareness instruction if they are to be clear about what they are expected to do. Words such as *first*, *last*, *same*, *different*, *sound*, and *word* are used frequently in phonological awareness instruction. Teachers should not assume that these words are understood by all preschool-age children, particularly ELLs. Some children also may not know other, more concrete words, such as *lips*, *tongue*, and *throat*, that are important in helping to make phonemes concrete. An important detail of phonological awareness instruction is to explicitly teach and review these words of instruction. I have used a large chart of the speech apparatus, with written labels for the various parts to teach this learning vocabulary.

Table 3.2 summarizes the important details for designing phonological aware-

---

TABLE 3.2. The Details That Matter: Phonological Awareness Intervention

- Explain the purpose of the lesson and the reason for learning phonological awareness.
- Teach only one to two phonological awareness skills in each lesson.
- Maintain a focus on the individual phonemes in words (rather than meaning).
- Model/demonstrate all instructional tasks with correct pronunciation.
- Elicit oral participation in pronouncing target phonemes from all children.
- Help children to say the target phonemes correctly.
- Include instructional practices to make phonemes concrete.
- Provide sufficient practice and repetition.
- Select familiar and simple words (CVC, CV) to use in lessons.
- Teach and review language-of-instruction words (e.g., *sound*, *first*, *last*, *lips*, *tongue*).
- Include alphabet letters in phonological awareness instruction after children have acquired alphabetic knowledge.
- Include writing activities that incorporate words with target phonemes.
- Respond to all children's participation and show positive emotions during instruction.
- Promote self-regulation by allowing children to control and to choose in some activities.
- Implement consistent routines and have activities well prepared.
- Monitor progress in phonological awareness learning regularly.
- Provide differentiated/individualized small-group intervention.

ness instruction. These elements can be explicitly woven into phonological awareness lesson plans, used to evaluate the quality of phonological awareness instruction within a program, or used to coach teachers for instructional growth.

A sample lesson that includes many of the details in Table 3.2 follows.

Main Lesson

The teacher begins:

> "Our lesson today is to hear the little bits of sound in words. You will have
> to listen very hard when I say these little bits and try to feel them in your
> own mouth. Remember to listen [Cups ear.] to the little bits of sound in the
> words.
>
> "What is the first sound in *bug*? /b/ is the first sound in *bug*. You say /b/,
> /b/. What is the first sound in bug? Everybody say it. Push one of your tiles
> forward each time you say /b/ like this. [Models. The children practice saying
> /b/.]
>
> "Look at your mouth with your mirror while you say /b/ like this. Look at
> your lips. Feel your throat while you say /b/. Do it lots of times! [Models. The
> children practice saying /b/.]
>
> "Now I am going to show you some objects that start with /b/. What
> sound? Say it three times." [Holds up three fingers and holds up one finger
> each time the children all together say '/b/, /b/, /b/'.]

Next, the teacher brings out a small plastic tub that has five to six miniature
objects whose spoken names begin with the sound /b/. Objects with short and
familiar names are selected from the tub: bug, bat, bike, book, boy. The objects are
shown one at a time and named with correct pronunciation by the teacher.

> The teacher says the letter sound, the name of the object, and the letter sound
>   again: /b/, *bug*, /b/.
> The children participate with the teacher two to three times for each object.
> The teacher checks that each child is saying the "sound, word, sound"
>   sequence and engages all children in pronunciation.

> "Now take out three [Holds up three fingers.] tiles and place them beside each
> other on your whiteboard. *Bug* has three sounds, so I need three tiles. [Mod-
> els by placing the three tiles in a row one by one, saying "/b/ /u/ /g/" as she
> adds each tile.] You do it. Do it three more times. [Models each time, saying
> *bug* and running her hand under the three tiles as she says the word. Repeats
> this activity for the other words.]"

The following activity is done after children have learned a number of letter
names or sounds.

"Watch how I write some words that begin with /b/. Says "bug" and writes the letter *b* as she says the first sound. Repeats for *big* and *bat*, and other short words in which each sound maps onto one letter.] You are learning about these sounds in words to help you read in kindergarten!"

Follow-Up Activities

The teacher informs the children that the tub will be available at a center, where they can play with the /b/ sound. Other materials include alphabet books with the "B" page held open; letter models of *b*, pictures of children from the class who have the phoneme /b/ in their names, with their name written on the photograph; a large tub in which children place items they bring from home or find in the classroom that begin with /b/; and art media, so that children can draw pictures of objects that begin with the phoneme /b/.

Individualizing Instruction

After whole-class instruction, the teaching assistant works with a smaller group of children who did not participate or were having difficulty. The children play with the items in the tub, so that each child has many turns naming an item. The children can sort items into piles (big or little; three favorites, etc.); ask for objects from the tub the teacher has hidden; and put the object in their pile, saying the initial phoneme /b/ and the full name of the object many times. The children use individual small mirrors and practice saying the phoneme /b/ many times, watching their own mouths as they say it.

Interventions to Increase Children's Oral Language and Vocabulary

Effective interventions for oral language development, like those for the alphabet and phonological awareness, include structured intervention. Experimental studies have demonstrated that children's overall oral language and vocabulary knowledge can be enhanced with a variety of interventions, including storybook reading, explicit vocabulary instruction, language-rich and responsive interactions, and complex dramatic play (Biemiller, 2006; Bodrova & Leong, 2007; Dickinson & Tabors, 2001; Girolametto, Weitzman, & Greenberg, 2003; Morrow & Schickedanz, 2006). The largest gains in oral language development (effect sizes ranging in size from 0.7 to over 2.00) have been found for learning vocabulary words, typically with storybook reading as the instructional context within small-scale, researcher-developed, structured interventions. More modest effects are typically reported for overall language development or standardized vocabulary scores, measured by tests such as the Peabody Picture Vocabulary Test. These interventions have been effective with both English-only and ELL children

(Roberts, 2008; Roberts & Neal, 2004). Teachers who promote significant oral language growth in children find ways to respond meaningfully to the comments and queries of individual children during book reading and other structured oral language instruction (Huttenlocher, Vasilyeva, Cymerman, & Levine, 2002). Similar to what has been found for phonological awareness, the large-scale Early Reading First program evaluation and the IES evaluation of experiments comparing different preschool curricula found no evidence of oral language gains from these well-supported programs implemented by regular classroom teachers (U.S. Department of Education, IES, 2007; PCER, 2008).

Adult–child interactions associated with oral language growth are characterized by adult responsiveness and extension of language interactions that occur "in the moment." Thus, oral language interventions often appear more unstructured and spontaneous than interventions for alphabetic knowledge or phonological awareness. However, skilled teachers are intentional and principled in how they use language in these interactions. Many studies have found relationships between the quality of these more unstructured interactions and child language growth. Yet research showing that implementation of these practices produces language growth in preschool settings is very limited. More research is needed to test the idea that purposeful implementation of these features of language interaction can result in oral language growth in group settings such as preschool.

The complexity of language learning requires that classroom interventions to foster language growth be extensive, sophisticated, and multifaceted (Hart & Risley, 1995; Pinker, 1994). Advancing oral language competence has proven to be more challenging than advancing other components of preschool literacy foundations—a pattern found in both the smaller-scale experimental and larger-scale studies (PCER Consortium, 2008). Research suggests that socioemotional variables such as emotional warmth, shared attention, and responsiveness are necessary for effective oral language intervention (Pianta, 2006).

Important Details for Oral Language and Vocabulary Intervention

The following simple model highlights the complex learning mechanisms involved in language acquisition:

> Language *input* + Language *intake* + Language *production* = Language learning

Language *input* refers to the ambient language environment provided by teachers, other adults, and materials that support language learning. Language *intake* refers to the process of the child engaging with this language and internalizing the words, linguistic structures, and discourse that form the architecture of strong language. Language *production* refers to the child's active use of language. Language *production* promotes both language learning and children's personal ownership of language. This basic representation of language learning applies to both first- and second-language acquisition. The elements in this simplified model capture the fundamental role that interactions between the language model and language learner play in language development. Adult guidance that provides high-quality *input* and ensures child *intake* and *production* often occurs informally during one-on-one and small-group interactions. This multicomponent language acquisition model suggests several details that are important for the design of effective oral language interventions.

Exposure to a great deal of language with an extensive variety of common and rare words, modeling of simple and increasingly complex language structures, and explanations of words provide important language *input* (Hart & Risley, 1995; Dickinson & Tabors, 2001). A very important type of input is "decontextualized language," in which children are exposed to experiences and ideas, developed through language, that are not occurring in the child's immediate environment (Hindman, Connor, Jewkes, & Morrison, 2008; Olson, 1977). Examples of decontextualized language include imagining, talking about past and future events, and talking about unfamiliar animals shown in a picture book. It is important language input because it sharpens children's ability to use language by itself as a tool for learning. Exposure to these important types of language can be provided through structured group lessons and through more informal but nevertheless intentional interactions. Language *intake* is sensitive to social and emotional conditions that promote children's willingness and interest in appropriating the language input provided to them. Foremost among the socioemotional yet intentional strategies to foster language *intake* are adult responsiveness, expression of positive emotion, and sharing in a back-and-forth interaction where communication is emphasized (Pianta, 2006). Adults can activate cognitive mechanisms promoting language intake through expanding on the child's language; adding new, related information to the interaction; and answering children's questions (Wells, 1985). *Intake* is further promoted by language related to topics, concepts, and experiences that are meaningful to children (Bernhard et al., 2006; Bernhard, Winsler, Bleiker, Ginieniewicz, & Madigan, 2008).

Intake is also sensitive to the intentional activation of specific cognitive learning mechanisms that children use to learn words and to build their sophistication with language structures (Bloom, 2000). Children use fast mapping (Carey, 1978), theory of mind (Bloom, 2000), and object principles and labeling (Blewitt, Rump, Shealy, & Cook, 2009; Spelke, 1994) to learn words. Knowledge of these mechanisms can inform explicit and informal instructional strategies for teaching words, although the research base documenting use of these strategies leading to oral language growth is limited. "Fast mapping" means that children quickly link a spoken word and the meaning to which it refers. The fast mapping mechanism allows preschool children to rapidly acquire new word meanings, although meanings may be incomplete. Establishing high expectations for the number of words to target in preschool interventions follows from this fast mapping capability. Children also use social cues from others, such as gaze and gestures, to puzzle out the meaning of individual words (Bloom, 2000). These strategies reflect children's theory of mind. The value of gestures, gaze, and interaction are suggested by this mechanism. An additional word-learning mechanism is children's orientation first to label new words, assumed most often to refer to objects, followed by later learning of deeper meaning (Blewitt et al., 2009). This mechanism suggests that vocabulary instruction begin with simply associating the word pronunciation with what it refers to, followed by activities to develop deeper word meaning.

Language *production* consolidates language learning. When children learn words, they must store the words' pronunciation and meaning in memory. Saying the words helps children learn its pronunciation. When children produce oral language, they refine their understanding of the individual phonemes of the language they are speaking, because the phonemes of a language reside in speech movements that produce them (Liberman, 1999). Language is also used to build social relationships. Thus, language production confers vocabulary, phoneme representation, and social relationship benefits. Teachers encourage language production by creating a desire to speak; opportunities for emotionally safe production, such as choral responding; and a warm emotional climate. Teachers who structure production requests to align with children's current first- or second-language proficiency encourage language production. For example, "yes" or "no" questions may be appropriate for children with very limited English, whereas others with more developed English skill may add missing words to a sentence, and more proficient children may create a complete utterance.

Reading Books

Children love to have books read over and over and three to five repeated readings foster oral language. Explanations of word meanings, either embedded within reading or taught explicitly prior to reading, produce vocabulary and oral language gains for both English-only and young ELL children (Penno, Wilkinson, & Moore, 2002; Robbins & Ehri, 1994; Roberts & Neal, 2004; Roberts, 2008; Sénéchal & Cornell, 1997; Sénéchal, Thomas, & Monker, 1995; Whitehurst et al., 1988). Explaining word meanings can produce additional gains of 14–30% when compared with learning words from repeated readings alone. Teachers can use a range of strategies to promote language development during book reading. These effective strategies include teacher–child interaction around the story and talk that requires thinking and analyzing. Teacher questioning, including both simple "What is _____?" and more complex questions (e.g., "What might Willie do next?"), and teacher expansion of children's language is beneficial (Biemiller, 2006; Dickinson & Smith, 1994; Pemberton & Watkins, 1987; Sénéchal & Cornell, 1993; Wasik, Bond, & Hindman, 2006). One effective intervention had children create stories based on their personal experiences (Bernhard et al., 2008). These books were read both in classrooms and at home. The authors reported oral language gains for Hispanic children from low-socioeconomic-status families, but not on all measures.

Engaging in Extended Language Interaction

Extended adult–child interactions and conversation provide language modeling and build children's motivation to engage in language interactions. A number of characteristics of extended adult–child language interactions and conversations are strongly associated with child language competence. These characteristics include adult responsiveness, emotional warmth, following the child's lead in conversational development, meaningful exchanges of information, and exposure to rich language (Landry, Smith, & Swank, 2006; Pianta, 2006). They are remarkably similar to the characteristics identified in the experimental research on book reading.

The research on these characteristics comes primarily from studies of mother–child interactions and child language competence in home settings, with some nonexperimental research documenting a strong relationship between quality of teacher–child conversation and children's language ability (Dickinson & Tabors, 2001). Research has also found low levels of conversation and extended adult–child interaction in many preschool classrooms (Dickinson et al., 2004). Small-scale experimental interventions have shown that the quality of mother–child interactions can be increased in dyads from a variety of ethnic groups, and this change subsequently leads to significant language gains (Landry et al., 2006). Girolametto et al. (2003) conducted one of the few experimental studies documenting that extensive training of teachers, accompanied by classroom coaching and self-analysis, led to changes in teacher behavior that then resulted in more talkativeness and more complex oral language in children.

Correlational evidence shows that both cognitive and socioemotional features of conversations and dyadic interaction are associated with strong language outcomes. Experimental studies are needed to determine whether and how adult–child conversations and extended interactions in preschool settings can cause oral language growth. Whether and how extended interactions can occur frequently enough in preschool settings (with the typical high child-to-adult ratio) to provide sufficient intervention to make a difference in oral language growth is an important question.

Teaching Vocabulary

A variety of interventions have been successful in teaching children new words. Teachers provide definitions and use other explicit strategies to teach children word meanings and to prompt frequent word use in effective interventions (Biemiller, 2006). Repeated oral production of instructed words in multiple contexts helps children remember the pronunciation of words and their meanings (Blewitt et al., 2009). The importance of children remembering the pronunciation of a word is often overlooked in vocabulary instruction. Monolingual and ELL children can learn about 40–60% of tested storybook words they don't know when they are provided word definitions, prop boxes, or vocabulary cards with pictures and words written on them. Vocabulary instruction with brief word explanations can be effective whether it occurs before or during reading. A combination of primary language and English storybook reading can produce English vocabulary gains for ELLs at the same rate as English-only storybook reading (Roberts, 2008). Exposure to rare and content-rich words is another valuable strategy for increasing children's vocabulary (Dickinson & Tabors, 2001; Hart & Risley, 1995).

Deciding which words to teach and the number of words to target is an important issue in vocabulary instruction. Vocabulary words to be used for instruction are beginning to be identified within commercial PreK literacy programs. These words are typically selected from storybooks or themes and units within programs. Biemiller (2006) suggests selecting words on the basis of empirical data that specify when various words are acquired, targeting 25–30 words per week that are well above children's current vocabulary levels. Words that build basic communication competence and words used frequently in instruction are also important criteria to be considered for selecting words, perhaps particularly for ELLs.

Creating Language–Rich Sociodramatic Play

Complex sociodramatic play can be an effective preschool intervention for language development (Bodrova & Leong, 2007). These play experiences can be structured to promote children's rich language production and to extend their exploration of themes, plots, and story lines. Interestingly, children's ability to construct connected chains of language to build story narratives has been increased in small-scale experiments (Mages, 2008; Morrow & Schickedanz, 2006). The relationship of this competence to reading comprehension is straightforward. Teachers who help children initiate and elaborate stories and plots, and who provide challenging language without "taking charge" of the sociodramatic play can also contribute to language development.

Extensive implementation of the details in Table 3.3 ensures that the simple *input + intake + production = language learning* model guides language development intervention.

Issues in Preschool Literacy Intervention

A complex system of cognitive, motivational, emotional, and institutional factors influences the ultimate effectiveness of preschool literacy interventions. In the following section I briefly outline factors to be accounted for formally in planning and implementing these interventions. These factors include frequency and intensity of instruction, fidelity of implementation, levels of needed performance, and differentiation of instruction.

TABLE 3.3. The Details That Matter: Oral Language and Vocabulary Intervention

- Provide exposure to a large number of words.
- Provide exposure to rare and content-rich words.
- Provide exposure to decontextualized language.
- Read the same book three to five times over several days.
- Give short explanations of selected words before or during book reading.
- Use a variety of simple and more challenging questions that require thinking and analysis.
- Teach vocabulary words explicitly, with instruction that incorporates the mechanisms children use to learn words (fast mapping, watching adults, labeling objects).
- Teach 25–30 words weekly.
- Carefully select words to teach that facilitate story understanding, content knowledge, communication, and understanding of instruction.
- Provide multiple opportunities for meaningful language exchanges of several turns with adults.
- Talk often about topics, ideas, and experiences of interest to children.
- Elicit oral language production from all children.
- Provide complex dramatic play where language use is structured into the play to expand themes and story lines.
- Respond to, expand, and elaborate on children's language initiations.
- Demonstrate positive emotions during oral language interactions.
- Promote self-regulation by allowing children to initiate and guide oral language interactions and plan sociodramatic play.
- Implement consistent routines and have activities well prepared.
- Monitor progress in oral language and vocabulary growth regularly.
- Provide differentiated and individualized small group intervention.

Sufficient Frequency and Intensity of Instruction

We are far from knowing the optimal number of intervention sessions (frequency) and duration of these sessions (intensity) needed in each of the core literacy areas. There is great variability in the intensity of instruction provided within commercial programs. Instructional time may vary from 2 to 3 minutes to 30 minutes. For example, Connor et al. (2006) found in their video analysis of preschool classrooms that teachers spent only about 2 minutes per hour on vocabulary activities. About 10–12 minutes of well-designed alphabet instruction or 10–20 minutes a day of phonological awareness instruction resulted in significant learning in a number of studies (Byrne & Fielding-Barnsley, 1989; Nelson et al., 2010; Roberts, 2003; Roberts & Neal, 2004). Preschool intervention studies focusing on vocabulary suggest that daily instruction of 15–20 minutes can lead to mastery of 40–60% of instructed words (Biemiller, 2006). It is more difficult to calculate how much rich language time is needed to result in oral language growth. Both more- and less-structured efforts to build oral language must permeate the day, be ever present in teacher's minds, and be predicated on firm understanding of the intentional and principled ways of using language that provide rich input, ensure intake, and inspire production.

Fidelity of Implementation

The challenge of ensuring that a particular intervention or curriculum is carefully implemented is widely acknowledged in educational research. The PCER Consortium (2008) reported that preschool curricula are not typically implemented with full fidelity. In a more fine-grained analysis of one of these studies, Pence, Justice, and Wiggins (2008) found that even after a year of program implementation with a modest professional development component, instructional processes embedded in the curriculum were implemented only moderately. Both Byrne and Fielding-Barnsley (1995) and Whitehurst et al. (1999) attributed attenuated effects for the Sound Foundations intervention to the low levels of implementation by regular teachers. Whitehurst et al. noted that some teachers implemented the Sound Foundations program 1–2 days per week (rather than the prescribed 5 days). Wasik et al. (2006) found the level of child outcomes correlated .69 with the level of program implementation in their vocabulary instruction study. In the context of these findings, increased attention to conditions that promote strong implementation of intervention programs is clearly warranted.

Levels of Needed Performance

Benchmarks and standards for preschool children in the core literacy foundations are rapidly being specified by states and local educational agencies. These efforts reflect increasing awareness that preschool literacy foundations are important. However, scientific evidence that unambiguously documents the level of skill needed in preschool in these core literacy areas is not yet clear. McGee (2005) performed a detailed and careful review of the evidence available at that time to derive target levels of performance in alphabet knowledge and phonemic awareness. She concluded that children should possess the following skills at the end of preschool:

1. Knowledge of 50–75% of the uppercase and lowercase letters, and knowledge of six to nine letter–sound relationships.

2. The ability to identify six to nine different phonemes at the beginning and end of words, and to recognize how these phonemes operate in written words.

3. The ability to use some letter name–sound relationships in invented spelling.

The most recent studies suggest that when instruction draws on basic learning mechanisms and important details of effective instruction, and is of sufficient intensity and duration, realistic literacy targets for 4-year-olds at the end of pre-school are knowledge of most of the uppercase and lowercase letters, more than half the letter sounds, and ability to isolate initial phonemes and to blend and segment two- to three-phoneme common words (NICHD, 2000; Nelson et al., 2010).

Benchmarks and learning expectations for vocabulary can be drawn from Biemiller (2006). Children learned about 35–40% of unknown words embed-ded in storybook reading accompanied by brief teacher explanations of 25–30 challenging words per week. This would aggregate to between 400 and 500 new words a year, a rate that could lead to gains of up to 6 months on standardized vocabulary measures. This level of vocabulary instruction far exceeds the vision and practice in current preschool classrooms, where as little as 1% of the interac-tion between children and teachers during choice time involves discussion about words (Dickinson et al., 2004). Consensus and recognition of attainable literacy targets for high-quality interventions are needed.

Assessment and Grouping

Preschool teachers need skill in both assessment and grouping in order to plan and modify their basic literacy program, and to implement differentiated instruc-tion for individual children, perhaps using an RTI model. Assessment instru-ments that are sensitive to children's differing levels and rates of learning are an important tool for planning both individual and small-group interventions. Yet only very recently have assessment and screening tools specific to literacy founda-tions become available for young children. *Get Ready to Read!* (Phillips, Lonigan, & Wyatt, 2009), *Get It, Got It, Go!* (McConnell, Priest, Davis, & McEvoy, 2002) and the *Test of Preschool Early Literacy* (Lonigan, Wagner, & Torgesen, 2007) are examples of these instruments. Therefore, many experienced preschool teachers have had little exposure to these instruments and how to use them. In addition, many teachers have been taught that these instruments are not appropriate for preschool children, because they focus on academic skills, are isolated from real reading and writing activities, and do not adequately take into account important individual differences indexed by informal teacher observations (e.g., Bredecamp & Copple, 1997). Utilizing data on individual and group performance to plan supplemental instruction for children that vary in level and rates of learning is not commonplace in preschool instruction. Small groups are used infrequently to explicitly teach specific skills (e.g., Connor et al., 2006; National Center for Early Development and Learning [NCEDL], 2005). Practices designed to develop knowledge and positive teacher orientations to assessment and grouping are needed to maximize the effectiveness of intervention.

Final Words

It is necessary to look beyond the simple presence or absence of practices that target alphabetic knowledge, phonological awareness, and oral language to determine that preschool children are receiving the high-quality interventions that build strong foundations in these skills. Effective interventions are based on the "important details" that underlie high-quality instruction and maximize children's learning. Regular and sustained implementation of high-quality instructional practices is critical. These high-quality instructional practices activate basic learning mechanisms, include specific practices shown by research to promote learning, and establish responsive and positive adult–child relationships that foster engagement and self-regulation. Finally, monitoring child progress and differentiating learning experiences, particularly for children in need of additional learning support, have emerged as important features of effective preschool literacy intervention. The research suggests that careful orchestration of all these elements into preschool interventions can enhance literacy foundations for reading and writing for both English-only and ELL children. Although many important questions remain, there is a sufficient knowledge base to guide the design and implementation of effective preschool interventions.

References

Adams, M. (1990). *Beginning to read: Thinking and learning about print.* Cambridge, MA: MIT Press.

Administration on Children, Youth, and Families (ACYF). (2003). *Head Start FACES 2000: A whole-child perspective on program performance: Fourth progress report.* Washington, DC: U.S. Department of Health and Human Services.

Aram, D. (2006). Early literacy intervention: The relative roles of storybook reading, alphabetic activities, and their combination. *Reading and Writing, 19,* 489–515.

Barnett, S. W., Yarosz, D. J., Thomas, J., Jung, K., & Blanco, D. (2007). Two-way and monolingual immersion in preschool education: An experimental comparison. *Early Childhood Research Quarterly, 22,* 277–293.

Baumeister, R. F., & Vohs, K. D. (Eds.). (2004). *Handbook of self-regulation.* New York: Guilford Press.

Bernhard, J. K., Cummins, J., Campoy, F. I., Ada, A. F., Winsler, A., & Bleiker, C. (2006). Identity texts and literacy development among preschool English language learners: Enhancing opportunities for children at risk of learning disabilities. *Teachers College Record, 108,* 2380–2405.

Bernhard, J. K., Winsler, A., Bleiker, C., Ginieniewicz, J., & Madigan, A. L. (2008). "Read My Story!": Using the Early Authors Program to promote early literacy among diverse, urban preschool children in poverty. *Journal of Education for Students Placed at Risk, 13,* 76–105

Berninger, V., Vaughan, K., Abbott, R., Abbott, S., Brooks, A., Rogan, L., et al. (1997). Treatment of handwriting fluency problems in beginning writing: Transfer from handwriting to composition. *Journal of Educational Psychology, 89,* 652–666.

Bialystok, E., Majumder, S., & Martin, M. M. (2003). Developing phonological awareness: Is there a bilingual advantage? *Applied Psycholinguistics, 24*, 27–44.

Biemiller, A. (2006). Vocabulary development and instruction: A prerequisite for school learning. In D. Dickinson & S. Newman (Eds.), *Handbook of early literacy research, Vol. II* (pp. 41–51). New York: Guilford Press.

Blewitt, P., Rump, K. M., Shealy, S. E., & Cook, S. A. (2009). Shared book reading: When and how questions affect young children's word learning. *Journal of Educational Psychology, 101*, 294–304.

Bloodgood, J. (1999). What's in a name?: Children's name writing and name acquisition. *Reading Research Quarterly, 34*, 342–367.

Bloom, P. (2000). *How children learn the meanings of words.* Cambridge, MA: MIT Press.

Bodrova, E., & Leong, D. J. (2007). *Tools of the mind.* Upper Saddle River, NJ: Pearson Education.

Boyer, N., & Ehri, L. C. (in press). Contribution of phonemic segmentation instruction with letters and articulation pictures to word reading and spelling in beginners. *Scientific Studies of Reading.*

Bowey, J. A. (1995). Socioeconomic differences is preschool phonological sensitivity and first-grade reading achievement. *Journal of Educational Psychology, 87*, 476–487.

Bradley, L., & Bryant, P. E. (1983). Categorizing sounds and learning to read—a causal connection. *Nature, 301*, 419–421.

Bredecamp, S., & Copple, C. (Eds.). (1997). *Developmentally appropriate practice in early childhood education* (Rev. ed.). Washington, DC: National Association for the Education of Young Children.

Burgess, S. R. (2002). The influence of speech perception, oral language ability, the home literacy environment, and pre-reading knowledge on the growth of phonological sensitivity: A one-year longitudinal investigation. *Reading and Writing: An Interdisciplinary Journal, 15*, 709–737.

Bus, A. G., Belsky, J., van IJzendoorn, M. H., & Crnic, K. (1997). Attachment and book reading patterns: A study of mothers, fathers and toddlers. *Early Childhood Research Quarterly, 12*, 81–98.

Bus, A., & van IJzendoorn, M. (1988). Mother–child interactions, attachment, and emergent literacy: A cross-sectional study. *Child Development, 59*, 1262–1272.

Byrne, B. (1992). Studies in the acquisition procedure for reading: Rationale, hypotheses and data. In P. Gough, L. Ehri, & R. Treiman (Eds.), *Reading acquisition* (pp. 1–34). Hillsdale, NJ: Erlbaum.

Byrne, B., & Fielding-Barnsley, R. (1989). Phonemic awareness and letter knowledge in children's acquisition of the alphabetic principle. *Journal of Educational Psychology, 81*, 313–321.

Byrne, B., & Fielding-Barnsley, R. (1991). Evaluation of a program to teach phonemic awareness to young children. *Journal of Educational Psychology, 83*, 451–455.

Byrne, B., & Fielding-Barnsley, R. (1995). Evaluation of a program to teach phonemic awareness to young children: A 2- and 3-year follow-up and a new preschool trial. *Journal of Educational Psychology, 87*, 488–503.

Carey, S. (1978). The child as word-learner. In M. Hale, J. Bresnan, & G. A. Miller (Eds.), *Linguistic theory and psychological reality* (pp. 264–293). Cambridge, MA: MIT Press.

Castiglioni-Spalten, M. L., & Ehri, L. C. (2003). Phonemic awareness instruction: Contribution of articulatory segmentation to novice beginners' reading and spelling. *Scientific Studies of Reading, 7*, 25–52.

Castles, A., & Coltheart, M. (2004). Is there a causal link from phonological awareness to success in learning to read? *Cognition, 91,* 77–111.

Chaney, C. (1994). Language development, metalinguistic awareness, and emergent literacy skills of 3-year-old children in relation to social class. *Applied Psycholinguistics, 13,* 371–394.

Chang, F., & Burns, B. M. (2005). Attention in preschoolers: Association with effortful control and motivation. *Child Development, 76,* 247–263.

Chapman, J. W., Tunmer, W. E., & Prochnow, J. E. (2000). Early reading-related skills and performance, reading self-concept, and the development of academic self-concept: A longitudinal study. *Journal of Educational Psychology, 92,* 703–708.

Connor, C. M., Morrison, F. J., & Slominski, L. (2006). Preschool instruction and children's emergent literacy growth. *Journal of Educational Psychology, 98*(4), 665–689.

Debaryshe, B. D., & Gorecki, D. M. (2007). An experimental validation of a preschool emergent literacy curriculum. *Early Education and Development, 18,* 93–110.

Diamond, K., Gerde, H., & Powell, D. (2008). Development in early literacy skills during the pre-kindergarten year in Head Start: Relations between growth in children's writing and understanding of letters. *Early Childhood Research Quarterly, 23,* 467–478.

Dickinson, D. K., McCabe, A., & Clark-Chiarelli, N. (2004). Preschool-based prevention of reading disability: Realities vs. possibilities. In C. A. Stone, E. R. Silliman, B. J. Ehren, & K. Apel (Eds.), *Handbook of language and literacy: Development and disorders* (pp. 209–227). Hillsdale, NJ: Erlbaum.

Dickinson, D. K., McCabe, A., & Essex, M. J. (2006). A window of opportunity we must open to all: The case for preschool with high quality support for language and literacy. In D. Dickinson & S. Newman (Eds.), *Handbook of early literacy research, Vol. 2* (pp. 11–28). New York: Guilford Press.

Dickinson, D. K., & Smith, M. W. (1994). Long-term effects of preschool teachers' book readings on low-income children's vocabulary and story comprehension. *Reading Research Quarterly, 29,* 105–122.

Dickinson, D., & Tabors, P. O. (2001). *Beginning literacy with language: Young children learning at home and school.* Baltimore: Brookes.

Duncan, G. J., Claessens, A., Huston, A. C., Pagani, L. S., Engel, M., Sexton, H., et al. (2007). School readiness and later achievement. *Developmental Psychology, 43,* 1428–1446.

Durgunoğlu, A. Y., Nagy, W., & Hancin-Bhatt, B. J. (1993). Cross-language transfer of phonological awareness. *Journal of Educational Psychology, 85,* 453–465.

Ehri, L. C., Nunes, S. R., Willows, D. M., Yaghoub-Zadeh, Z., & Shanahan, T. (2001). Phonemic awareness instruction helps children learn to read: Evidence from the National Reading Panel's meta-analysis. *Reading Research Quarterly, 36,* 250–287.

Ehri, L. C., & Roberts, T. A. (2006). The roots of learning to read and write: Acquisition of letter and phonemic awareness. In D. Dickinson & S. Neuman (Eds.), *Handbook of early literacy research, Vol. 2* (pp. 113–131). New York: Guilford Press.

Ehri, L. C., & Sweet, J. (1991). Fingerpoint-reading of memorized text: What enables beginners to process the print? *Reading Research Quarterly, 26,* 442–462.

Elbro, C. (1996). Early linguistic abilities and reading development: A review and a hypothesis. *Reading and Writing: An Interdisciplinary Journal, 8,* 453–485.

Fischel, J. E., Bracken, S. S., Fuchs-Eisenberg, A., Spira, E. G., Katz, S., & Shaller, G. (2007). Evaluation of curricular approaches to enhance preschool literacy growth. *Journal of Literacy Research, 39,* 471–501.

Fowler, A. E. (1991). How early phonological development might set the stage for phonological awareness. In S. Brady & D. Shankweiler (Eds.), *Phonological processes in literacy: A tribute to Isabelle Y. Liberman* (pp. 97–117). Hillsdale, NJ: Erlbaum.

Fox, B., & Routh, D. (1976). Phonemic analysis and synthesis as word-attack skills. *Journal of Educational Psychology, 68,* 70–74.

Fuchs, D., & Fuchs, L. S. (2006). A framework for building capacity for responsiveness to intervention. *School Psychology Review, 35,* 621–626.

Gettinger, M., & Stoiber, K. (2009). Applying a response-to-intervention model for early literacy development in low-income children. *Topics in Early Childhood Special Education, 27,* 198–213.

Girolametto, L., Weitzman, E., & Greenberg, J. (2003). Training day care staff to facilitate children's language. *American Journal of Speech–Language Pathology, 12,* 299–311.

Graham, S., Harris, K., & Fink, B. (2000). Is handwriting causally related to learning to write?: Treatment of handwriting problems in beginning writers. *Journal of Educational Psychology, 92,* 620–633.

Graue, E., Clements, M. A., Reynolds, A. J., & Niles, M. D. (2004, December). More than teacher directed or child initiated: Preschool curriculum type, parent involvement, and children's outcomes in the child–parent centers. *Education Policy Analysis Archives, 12*(72). Retrieved May 14, 2008, from *epaa.asu.edu/epaa/v12n72.*

Hammer, C. S., Lawrence, F. R., & Miccio, A. W. (2007). Bilingual children's language abilities and early reading outcomes in Head Start and kindergarten. *Language, Speech, and Hearing Services in Schools, 38,* 237–248.

Han, M., Roskos, K., Christie, J., Mandzuk, S., & Vukelich, C. (2005). Learning words: Large group time as a vocabulary development opportunity. *Journal of Research in Childhood Education, 19,* 333–346.

Hart, B., & Risley, T. R. (1995). *Meaningful differences in the everyday experience of young American children.* Baltimore: Brookes.

Hawken, L. S., Johnston, S. S., & McDonnell, A. P. (2005). Emerging literacy views and practices: Results from a national survey of Head Start preschool teachers. *Topics in Early Childhood Special Education, 25*(4), 232–242.

Hindman, A. H., Connor, C. D., Jewkes, A. M., & Morrison, F. J. (2008). Untangling the effects of shared book reading: Multiple factors and their associations with preschool literacy outcomes. *Early Childhood Research Quarterly, 23,* 330–350.

Huttenlocher, J., Vasilyeva, M., Cymerman, E., & Levine, S. (2002). Language input and child syntax. *Cognitive Psychology, 45,* 337–374.

Justice, L. M., Chow, S., Capellini, C., Flanigan, K., & Colton, S. (2003). Emergent literacy intervention for vulnerable preschoolers: Relative effects of two approaches. *American Journal of Speech–Language Pathology, 11,* 17–29.

Kamp, N. (2009). The spelling of vowels is influenced by Australian and British English dialect differences. *Scientific Studies of Reading, 13,* 1–25.

Landry, S. L., Smith, K. E., & Swank, P. R. (2006). Responsive parenting: Establishing early foundations for social, communication, and independent problem-solving skills. *Developmental Psychology, 42,* 627–642.

Lee, J. S., & Ginsburg, H. P. (2007). Preschool teachers' beliefs about appropriate early literacy and mathematics education of low- and middle-socioeconomic status children. *Early Education and Development, 18,* 111–143.

Lepola, J., Poskiparta, E., Laakkonen, E., & Niemi, P. (2005). Development of and relationship between phonological and motivational processes and naming speed in predicating word recognition in grade 1. *Scientific Studies of Reading, 9,* 367–399.

Levin, I., Both-De Vries, A., Aram, D., & Bus, A. (2004). Writing starts with own name writing: From scribbling to conventional spelling in Israeli and Dutch children. *Applied Psy-cholinguistics, 26,* 463–477.

Liberman, A. M. (1999). The reading researcher and the reading teacher need the right theory of speech. *Scientific Studies of Reading, 3,* 95–111.

Lindamood, P., & Lindamood, P. (1998). *The Lindamood Phoneme Sequencing Program for Reading, Spelling and Speech: The LIPS Program.* Austin, TX: Pro-Ed.

LoCasale-Crouch, J., Konold, T., Pianta, R., Howes, C., Burchinal C., Bryant, D., et al. (2007). Observed classroom quality profiles in state-funded pre-kindergarten programs and asso-ciations with teacher, program and classroom characteristics, *Early Childhood Research Quarterly, 22,* 3–17.

Longcamp, M., Zerbato-Poudou, M., & Velay, J. (2005). The influence of writing practice on letter recognition in preschool children: A comparison between handwriting and typing. *Acta Psychologica, 20,* 67–79.

Lonigan, C. J., Burgess, S. R., & Anthony, J. L. (2000). Development of emergent literacy and early reading skills in preschool children: Evidence from a latent variable longitudinal study. *Developmental Psychology, 36,* 596–613.

Lonigan, C. J., Wagner, R. K., & Torgesen, J. K. (2007). TOPEL: *Test of Preschool Early Literacy.* Austin: TX: Pro-Ed.

López, L. M., & Greenfield, D. B. (2004). The cross-language transfer of phonological skills of Hispanic Head Start children. *Bilingual Research Journal, 28,* 1–18.

Lundberg, I., Frost, J., & Petersen, O. P. (1988). Effects of an extensive program for stimulating phonological awareness in preschool children. *Reading Research Quarterly, 23,* 263–284.

MacMillan, B. (2002). Rhyme and reading: A critical review of the research methodology. *Journal of Research in Reading, 2,* 4–42.

Mages, W. K. (2008). Does creative drama promote language development in early childhood?: A review of the methods and measures employed in the empirical literature. *Review of Educational Research, 78,* 124–152.

Martin, M., & Byrne, B. (2002). Teaching children to recognize rhyme does not directly pro-mote phonemic awareness. *British Journal of Educational Psychology, 72,* 561–572.

Martins, M. A., & Silva, C. (2006). The impact of spelling on phonemic awareness. *Learning and Instruction, 16,* 41–56.

Mashburn, A. J., Pianta, R. C., Hamre, B. K., Downer, J. T., Barbarin, O. A., Bryant, D., et al. (2008). Measures of classroom quality in prekindergarten and children's development of academic, language and social skills. *Child Development, 79,* 732–749.

McConnell, S. R., Priest, J. S., Davis, S. D., & McEvoy, M. (2002). Best practices in measuring growth and development for preschool children. In A. Thomas & J. Grimes (Eds.), *Best practices in school psychology IV* (Vol. 2, pp. 1231–1246). Betheseda, MD: National Asso-ciation of School Psychologists.

McGee, L. (2005). The role of wisdom in evidence-based preschool literacy curricula. In B. Maloch, J. Hoffman, D. Schallert, C. Fairbanks, & J. Worthy (Eds.), *54th yearbook of the National Reading Conference* (pp. 1–21). Oak Creek, WI: National Reading Confer-ence.

McGill-Franzen, A., Lanford, C., & Adams, E. (2002). Learning to be literate: A compar-ison of five urban early childhood programs. *Journal of Educational Psychology, 94,* 443–464.

Metsala, J. L., & Walley, A. C. (1998). Spoken vocabulary growth and the segmental restruc-turing of lexical representations: Precursors to phonemic awareness and early reading ability. In J. L. Metsala & L. C. Ehri (Eds.), *Word recognition in beginning literacy* (pp. 89–120). Hillsdale, NJ: Erlbaum.

Morrow, L. M., & Schickedanz, J. A. (2006). The relationships between sociodramatic play and literacy development. In D. Dickinson & S. Neuman, (Eds.), *Handbook of early literacy research, Vol. 2* (pp. 269–280). New York: Guilford Press.

Muter, V., Hulme, C., Snowling, M. J., & Stevenson, J. (2004). Phonemes, rimes, vocabulary, and grammatical skills as foundations of early reading development: Evidence from a longitudinal study. *Developmental Psychology, 40*, 665–681.

National Association for the Education of Young Children. (2009). Developmentally appropriate practice in early childhood programs serving children from birth through age 8. Washington, DC: Author.

National Center for Early Development and Learning (NCEDL). (2005). *NCEDL Pre-Kindergarten Study.* Retrieved April 22, 2009, from *www.fpg.unc.edu/~ncedl/pdfs/ed9_1. pdf.*

National Early Literacy Panel. (2008). Developing early literacy: Report of the National Early Literacy Panel. Washington, DC: National Institute for Literacy. Available at *www.nifl. gov/earlychildhood/NELP/NELPreport.html.*

National Institute of Child Health and Human Development (NICHD). (2000). Report of the National Reading Panel. *Teaching children to read: An evidence-based assessment of the scientific research on reading and its implications for reading instruction.* (NIH Publication No. 00-4769). Washington, DC: U.S. Government Printing Office.

National Institute of Child Health and Human Development (NICHD) Early Child Care Network. (2005). Pathways to reading: The role of oral language in the transition to reading. *Developmental Psychology, 25*, 428–442.

National Research Council and Institute of Medicine. (2000). *From neurons to neighborhoods: The science of early childhood development.* Committee on Integrating the Science of Early Childhood Development. (J. Shonkoff & D. Philips, Eds.). Washington, DC: National Academies Press.

Nelson, J. R., Sanders, E. A., & Gonzalez, J. (2010). The efficacy of supplemental early literacy instruction by community-based tutors for preschools enrolled in Head Start. *Journal of Research on Educational Effectiveness, 3*(1), 1–21.

Olson, D. R. (1977). From utterance to text: The bias of language in speech and writing. *Harvard Educational Review, 47*, 257–281.

Ordonez, C. L., Carlo, M. S., Snow, C. E., & McLaughlin, B. (2002). Depth and breadth of vocabulary in two languages: Which vocabulary skills transfer? *Journal of Educational Psychology, 94*, 719–728.

Pemberton, E. F., & Watkins, R. V. (1987). Language facilitation through stories: Recasting and modeling. *First Language, 7*, 79–89.

Pence, K. L., Justice, L. M., & Wiggins, A. K. (2008). Preschool teachers' fidelity in implementing a comprehensive language-rich curriculum. *Language, Speech, and Hearing Services in Schools, 39*, 329–341.

Penno, J. F., Wilkinson, I. A. G., & Moore, D. W. (2002). Vocabulary acquisition from teacher explanation and repeated listening to stories: Do they overcome the Matthew effect? *Journal of Educational Psychology, 94*, 23–33.

Phillips, B. M., Clancy-Menchetti, J., & Lonigan, C. J. (2008). Successful phonological awareness instruction with preschool children. *Topics in Early Childhood Special Education, 28*, 3–17.

Phillips, B. M., Lonigan, C., & Wyatt, M. (2009). Predictive validity of the Get Ready to Read! screener: Concurrent and long-term relations with reading-related skills. *Journal of Learning Disabilities, 42*, 133–147.

Phillips, B. M., & Torgesen, J. K. (2006). Phonemic awareness and reading: Beyond the growth of initial reading accuracy. In S. Neuman, & D. Dickinson (Eds.), *Handbook of early literacy research* (Vol. 2, pp. 101–112). New York: Guilford Press.

Pianta, R. C. (2006). Teacher–child relationships and early literacy. In S. Neuman & D. Dickinson (Eds.), *Handbook of early literacy research* (Vol. 2, pp. 149–162). New York: Guilford Press.

Pianta, R. C., Hamre, B., & Stuhlman, M. (2003). Relationships between teacher and children. In W. Reynolds & G. Miller (Eds.), *Comprehensive handbook of psychology: Vol. 7. Educational psychology* (pp. 199–234). Hoboken, NJ: Wiley.

Pinker, S. (1994). *The language instinct.* New York: Morrow.

Preschool Curriculum Evaluation Research (PCER) Consortium. (2008). *Effects of preschool curriculum programs on school readiness* (NCER 2008–2009). Washington, DC: U.S. Government Printing Office.

Robbins, C., & Ehri, L. C. (1994). Reading stories to kindergartners helps them learn new vocabulary words. *Journal of Educational Psychology, 86,* 54–64.

Roberts, T. A. (2003). Effects of alphabet letter instruction on young children's word recognition. *Journal of Educational Psychology, 95,* 41–51.

Roberts, T. A. (2005). Articulation accuracy and vocabulary size contributions to phonemic awareness and word reading in English language learners. *Journal of Educational Psychology, 97,* 601–616.

Roberts, T. A. (2008). Home storybook reading in primary or second language with preschool children: Evidence of equal effectiveness for second-language vocabulary acquisition. *Reading Research Quarterly, 43,* 103–130.

Roberts, T. A. (2009). *No limits to literacy for preschool English learners.* Thousand Oaks, CA: Corwin Press.

Roberts, T. A., Christo, C., & Shefelbine, J. A. (2010). Word recognition. In M. Kamil, P. D. Pearson, E. Moje, & P. Afflerbach (Eds.), *Handbook of reading research* (Vol. IV, pp. 229–258). London: Routledge.

Roberts, T. A., & Meiring, A. (2006). Teaching phonics in the context of children's literature or spelling: Influences on first grade reading, writing and spelling and fifth grade comprehension. *Journal of Educational Psychology, 98,* 690–713.

Roberts, T., & Neal, H. (2004). Relationships among preschool English language learner's oral proficiency in English, instructional experience and literacy development. *Contemporary Educational Psychology, 29,* 283–311.

Scarborough, H. S. (2001). Connecting early language and literacy to later reading (dis)abilities: Evidence, theory, and practice. In S. B. Neuman & D. K. Dickinson (Eds.), *Handbook of early literacy research* (Vol. 1, pp. 97–110). New York: Guilford Press.

Sénéchal, M. (1997). The differential effect of storybook reading on preschoolers' acquisition of expressive and receptive vocabulary. *Journal of Child Language, 24,* 123–138.

Sénéchal, M., & Cornell, E. H. (1993). Vocabulary acquisition through shared reading experience. *Reading Research Quarterly, 28,* 360–375.

Sénéchal, M., Thomas, E. H., & Monker, J. A. (1995). Individual differences in 4-year-old children's acquisition of vocabulary during storybook reading. *Journal of Educational Psychology, 87,* 218–229.

Share, D. (2004). Knowing letter names and learning letter sounds: A causal connection. *Journal of Experimental Child Psychology, 88,* 213–233.

Snow, C. E., Burns, S., & Griffin, P. (Eds.). (1998). *Preventing reading difficulties in young children.* Washington, DC: National Academy Press.

Spelke, E. S. (1994). Initial knowledge: Six suggestions. *Cognition, 50,* 443–447.

Stanovich, K. (1986). Matthew effects in reading: Some consequences of individual differences in reading. *Reading Research Quarterly, 21,* 360–407.

Storch, S. A., & Whitehurst, G. J. (2002). Oral language and code-related precursors of reading: Evidence from a longitudinal structural model. *Developmental Psychology, 38,* 934–945.

Storkel, H. L., & Rogers, M. A. (2000). The effect of probabilistic phonotactics on lexical acquisition. *Clinical Linguistics and Phonetics, 14,* 407–425.

Treiman, R., Cohen, J., Mulqueeny, K., Kessler, B., & Schechtman, S. (2007). Young children's knowledge about printed names. *Child Development, 78,* 1458–1471.

Treiman, R., & Kessler, B. (2004). The case of case: Children's knowledge and use of upper and lowercase letters. *Applied Psycholinguistics, 25,* 413–428.

Treiman, R., Weatherston, S., & Berch, D. (1994). The role of letter names in children's learning of phoneme–grapheme relations. *Applied Psycholinguistics, 15,* 97–122.

Tunmer, W. E., Herriman, M. L., & Nesdale, A. R. (1988). Metalinguistic abilities and beginning reading. *Reading Research Quarterly, 23,* 134–158.

Turner, L. A., & Johnson, B. (2003). A model of mastery motivation for at-risk preschoolers. *Journal of Educational Psychology, 95,* 495–505.

U.S. Department of Education, Institute of Education Sciences (IES), National Center of Education Evaluation and Regional Assistance (2007). *National Evaluation of Early Reading First: Final Report to Congress.* Retrieved April 22, 2009, from *ies.ed.gov/ncee/pdf/20074007.pdf.*

U.S. Department of Education, Institute of Education Sciences, What Works Clearinghouse. (2004, December). *Topic report: Early childhood education.* Retrieved March 15, 2009, from *ies.ed.gov/ncee/wwc/reports/topic.aspx?tid=13.*

U.S. Department of Health and Human Services. (2005). *Head Start impact study: First year findings.* Washington, DC: Author.

VanDerHeyden, A. M., Snyder, P. A., Broussard, C., & Ramsdell, K. (2007). Measuring response to early literacy intervention with preschoolers at risk. *Topics in Early Childhood Special Education, 27,* 232–249.

van Kleeck, A. (1998). Preliteracy domains and stages: Laying the foundations for beginning reading. *Journal of Children's Communication Development, 20,* 33–51.

Walton, P. D. (1995). Rhyming ability, phoneme identity, letter–sound knowledge, and the use of orthographic analogy by prereaders. *Journal of Educational Psychology, 87,* 587–597.

Wasik, B. A., Bond, M. A., & Hindman, A. (2006). The effects of a language and literacy intervention on Head Start children and teachers. *Journal of Educational Psychology, 98,* 63–74.

Wells, G. (1985). Preschool literacy-related events and success in school. In D. Olson, N. Torrance, & A. Hilliard (Eds.), *Literacy, language, and learning: The nature and consequences of reading and writing* (pp. 229–255). Cambridge, UK: Cambridge University Press.

Whitehurst, G. J., Falco, F. L., Lonigan, C. J., Fischel, J. E., De-Baryshe, B. D., Valdez-Menchaca, M. C., et al. (1988). Accelerating language development through picture book reading. *Developmental Psychology, 24,* 552–559.

Whitehurst, G. J., & Lonigan, C. J. (1998). Child development and emergent literacy. *Child Development, 69,* 848–872.

Whitehurst, G. J., & Massetti, M. (2004). How well does Head Start prepare children to learn to read? In E. Zigler & S. J. Styfco (Eds.), *The Head Start debates (friendly and otherwise)* (pp. 251–262). New Haven, CT: Brookes.

Whitehurst, G. J., Zevenbergen, A. A., Corne, D. A., Schultz, M. D., Velting, O. N., & Fischel, J. E. (1999). Outcomes of an emergent literacy intervention from Head Start through second grade. *Journal of Educational Psychology, 91,* 261–272.

Yaden, D., Smolkin, L., & Conlon, A. (1989). Preschoolers' questions about pictures, print conventions, and story text during reading aloud at home. *Reading Research Quarterly, 24*, 188–214.

Yaden, D. B., Smolkin, L. B., & MacGillivray, L. (1993). A psychogenetic perspective on children's understanding about letter associations during alphabet book readings. *Journal of Reading Behavior, 25*, 43–68.

4

Phases in Reading Words and Phonics Interventions

LOUISE SPEAR–SWERLING

Recently, I spent some time observing reading instruction in a first-grade classroom where the teacher heavily emphasized contextual strategies for reading unfamiliar words. These strategies involved using context cues, such as pictures, and the initial letter to guess the word, or skipping the word entirely, reading to the end of the sentence, then guessing the word based on sentence context. One particular first grader, whom I'll call Jennie, was an excellent reader, among the best in the class.

"Jennie knows what to do when she comes to a hard word," the teacher commented to the class one day. "She knows all her strategies."

"Yep," Jennie piped up matter-of-factly, "but I don't use 'em. If I don't know a word, I just sound it out!"

Contrary to the teacher's assumption, what likely made Jennie such a strong reader was not her ability to use contextual strategies to read words, but her knowledge about common letter–sound relationships and her skill in decoding. Here I use the term "decoding" to mean reading an unfamiliar word by applying knowledge about letter sounds and common letter patterns in words, that is, phonics knowledge. Application of phonics knowledge can involve a variety of tactics, including "sounding out" unknown words (e.g., sounding out and blending the individual sounds represented by the letters *sh*, *a*, *ck*, to read the word *shack*), or reading them by analogy to known words (e.g., reading the unknown word *shack* by analogy to the known word *back*). Unskilled beginners do frequently rely on contextual cues, such as pictures and sentence context, to help them read unfamiliar words. However, progress in reading is strongly associated with the development of phonics knowledge and decoding skills, not with reliance on context to aid decoding (Adams, 1998; Stanovich, 2000). Decoding skills constitute a subset of broader word recognition skills, which also include the ability to read familiar words quickly ("by sight") and to use morphemic knowledge, such as knowledge about common roots and affixes, to read words.

In the early grades, a high proportion of struggling readers have problems in word recognition, either alone or in combination with core comprehension weaknesses, such as limitations in vocabulary knowledge (Catts, Hogan, & Adlof, 2005; Leach, Scarborough, & Rescorla, 2003). Reading difficulties based solely in poor comprehension, despite adequate word reading, become much more frequent from about grade 4 onward; however, even among older children, the incidence of word recognition problems is not trivial. For example, Leach et al. found that over 90% of struggling readers identified in the primary grades, and over 60% of those identified after grade 3, had problems that included accuracy or speed of word recognition. Furthermore, phonics knowledge and decoding skills are a key weakness for most readers who struggle with word recognition (Fletcher, Lyon, Fuchs, & Barnes, 2007; Stanovich, 2000), making effective phonics interventions essential tools for educators who work with at-risk and struggling readers. Fortunately, there is an extensive research base about how to help struggling readers in the area of phonics and decoding skills. This research base and its practical implications for teachers are the topics of this chapter.

The chapter begins with a review of research findings on the development of word recognition skills in typical children. These findings offer important insights about how to identify at-risk readers early. In the second section of the chapter I discuss characteristics of core general education instruction in the primary grades that can prevent or ameliorate word recognition problems in many children, and that provide a crucial foundation for school-based approaches to intervention. The next sections summarize basic features of interventions that are successful with poor decoders, followed by examples of specific interventions with strong research support. These sections of the chapter also include sample teaching scripts for developing decoding and word recognition skills in struggling readers. The chapter concludes with some practical tips for educators and a list of references.

Typical Development in Reading Words

Nearly all children learning to read in English and other alphabetic languages appear to pass through a series of similar phases in their word recognition development. Here I summarize the phases, which I have described elsewhere (Spear-Swerling, 2004) in more detail and in relation to a variety of reading problems. Borrowing from the seminal work of Ehri (1991), I use the terms "visual cue word recognition," "phonetic cue word recognition," "controlled word recognition," and "automatic word recognition" for the four phases. The descriptions below are based heavily on the work of Ehri and her colleagues (e.g., Ehri, 1991, 2004, 2005; Ehri & McCormick, 1998), as well as on that of numerous additional investigators (e.g., Adams, 1990; Carver & David, 2001; Stanovich, 2000). Word recognition development also involves other essential skills such as phonemic awareness, discussed elsewhere in this volume.

Children in the phase of visual cue word recognition do not yet understand the alphabetic code and rely primarily on visual cues, such as a distinctive logo or word shape to read words, rather than letter sounds. This phase characterizes a young child who can recognize the word *stop* on the red octagonal stop sign or the word *Pepsi* based on the flowing shape of the Pepsi logo, but is unable to read the same words printed in conventional type on paper. Due to children's lack of understanding of the alphabetic code, this phase is sometimes termed "prealphabetic" (Ehri, 2005). Visual cue word reading is typical of most preschoolers and of some kindergarten children, especially early in kindergarten.

In the phonetic cue word recognition phase, also called "partial alphabetic" (Ehri, 2005), children understand that written English is a code in which letters map onto sounds in spoken words. However, their knowledge of letter–sound relationships is incomplete, and they usually rely only on some letters in a word, especially the first and last letters, rather than looking carefully at all the letters. Decoding the vowel part of the word is especially problematic, because vowel sounds are highly variable in English, and because the vowel is frequently contained in the less salient, medial part of a word. For example, a child in the phonetic cue phase might confuse words such as *sack* versus *sock* or *lake* versus *like*. Because of these limitations in decoding, children in the phonetic cue phase remain heavily dependent on pictures and sentence context when they encounter unfamiliar words. Phonetic cue word recognition is characteristic of many kindergartners and first graders, especially those in the first half of first grade.

Children in the phase of controlled word recognition, also termed "full alphabetic" (Ehri, 2005), have more complete knowledge of letter–sound relationships than do children in the previous phase. Thus, they have better ability to decode unfamiliar words and become less reliant on context cues for reading words. However, their word recognition skills continue to involve primarily controlled rather than automatic processes; that is, children must put effort into reading unknown words instead of recognizing most words quickly and automatically. Controlled word recognition is typical of children later in first grade, as well as in second grade.

Finally, in the phase of automatic word recognition, children recognize most common words automatically, that is, without effort and "by sight." When they encounter an occasional unknown word, they can apply their extensive knowledge of letter–sound relationships to decode it quickly. Therefore, they do not often need to use context cues as an aid to decoding words, and their increasingly rapid word recognition skills facilitate fluency in reading grade-appropriate text. Automatic word recognition and fluent text reading enable children to focus more of their mental resources on the meaning of the text than on decoding individual words, providing an important underpinning for the more sophisticated comprehension demands of texts used in the middle and upper grades. Because automatic word recognition appears to involve consolidating knowledge of common letter patterns in words, including common affixes, such as *tion*, and common rimes, such as *ight* or *ake*, this also has been termed the "consolidated alphabetic" phase (Ehri, 2005). Knowledge of letter patterns greatly facilitates children's ability to read multisyllabic words such as *invention* or *misunderstanding*, as well as shorter words. Typical readers achieve this phase in about late second to third grade.

Transitions between phases are generally gradual, not abrupt. For instance, children in the phase of phonetic cue or controlled word recognition may recognize some very common words automatically; children in the phase of automatic word recognition may occasionally need to use controlled decoding processes to read long or unusual words. In addition, the meaning of the term "sight word" as used in research on children's word recognition development must be differentiated from the use of the same term in education. Educators often use the term "sight word" to refer to phonetically irregular or common words that are taught as whole words (e.g., using flash cards) to facilitate rapid recognition or because they are exceptions to common phonics rules. However, in research on typical reading development, "sight word" means any word read automatically, that is, quickly and without effort. As outlined earlier in the description of phases, phonics knowledge and decoding skills enable children to achieve sight word recognition of most words. After seeing a word several times and using knowledge of common letter–sound relationships to read it, children usually begin to recognize the word automatically on subsequent exposures (Ehri, 2005).

Research on children's word recognition development has some important implications for early identification of difficulties in reading words:

• Beginning and struggling readers tend to rely on contextual cues to compensate for limitations in word recognition. To assess children's word recognition skills accurately, teachers must use a measure that presents words out of context (e.g., in a list).

• The development of phonics knowledge and decoding skill is particularly central to children's progress in word recognition. Pseudowords such as *sneck* or *grike* tap this kind of knowledge more reliably than real words, which children sometimes may be able to read from memory. Thus, it is helpful to use an out-of-context word recognition measure that includes pseudowords. Assessment of decoding difficulties also should include a measure of phonemic awareness, because poor phonemic awareness often contributes to decoding problems.

• Typical readers develop extensive phonics knowledge and decoding skill in the earliest grades. Most children progress from being nonreaders at kindergarten entrance to being able to decode a wide variety of one-syllable words by the end of first grade, to having extensive knowledge for decoding multisyllabic words and automatic recognition of most common words by the end of third grade. To enable struggling readers to keep up with grade expectations, teachers must identify children with word recognition problems early, set ambitious goals, and employ interventions that facilitate rapid progress in decoding.

Core General Education Instruction in Phonics

Many authorities (e.g., Fletcher et al., 2007; Torgesen, 2004) have emphasized the importance of effective core general education instruction as a base for intervention efforts in reading. Ineffective core instruction in reading can undermine intervention efforts by creating a steady stream of children who require intervention because of inadequate instruction, not because of genuine learning problems. Conversely, simply enhancing classroom instruction can provide substantial benefits to many, though not all, at-risk readers (Mathes et al., 2005).

Studies of classroom reading instruction have usually compared overall instructional approaches or specific features of instruction rather than different commercial programs. These studies (e.g., Christensen & Bowey, 2005; Connor, Morrison, & Underwood, 2007; Mathes et al., 2005; National Reading Panel, 2000) suggest that although a variety of general approaches to teaching phonics can be effective, certain characteristics of instruction are associated with greater effectiveness. In particular, effective phonics instruction is both explicit and systematic. "Explicit" means that teachers directly teach and model key letter–sound relationships and decoding skills; children are not expected to acquire these skills simply from exposure to words or incidental learning opportunities. "Systematic" means that teachers carefully plan and organize instruction so that children learn prerequisite skills before they learn more complex skills. The sequence of instruction also takes into account research on children's early reading development. For example, beginning readers tend to find short vowel sounds highly confusable, so a well-sequenced phonics program should avoid introducing many different short vowel sounds at once (Carnine, Silbert, Kame'enui, & Tarver, 2004).

Phonics approaches can vary in numerous ways. Analogy and analytic phonics are whole-to-parts approaches: They teach children to decode new words based on their similarities to known words, as in the *shack–back* example discussed earlier. Synthetic phonics approaches are parts to whole: They teach children to sound out letters or letter patterns and blend them. Synthetic phonics approaches also vary in the size of the initial unit of instruction. Onset–rime approaches teach children to blend "onsets" (the initial consonant or consonant cluster) and "rimes" (the vowel and any subsequent letters) in words, whereas grapheme–phoneme approaches focus on blending smaller units, individual sounds or phonemes, right from the start. In an onset–rime approach, words such as *feet* or *snap* would be decoded by blending two parts (*f-eet* and *sn-ap*), whereas in a grapheme–phoneme approach, children would need to blend additional parts, *f-ee-t* or *s-n-a-p*. The use of synthetic phonics approaches at the grapheme–phoneme level, integrated with blend-and-segment phonemic awareness instruction (i.e., instruction that explicitly teaches children how to blend and segment individual phonemes orally), appears to be especially effective for beginning readers, with benefits for reading comprehension and spelling, as well as word decoding (Christensen & Bowey, 2005; Ehri, 2004; National Reading Panel, 2000). In addition, although most authorities have emphasized the importance of teaching phonics in kindergarten and first grade, continuing phonics instruction into second grade may be critical, especially for weak first-grade readers (Connor et al., 2007).

Different types of texts are used to teach reading in the earliest grades, including predictable books, which use repetition and pictures to help beginners predict words, and decodable books, which use words controlled to specific phonics patterns that children have been taught. Research on the relative effectiveness of different text types is decidedly mixed. Some intervention studies (Jenkins, Peyton, Sanders, & Vadasy, 2004; Mathes et al., 2005) have found no additional benefit to using decodable texts in phonics instruction. However, Menon and Hiebert (2005) did find benefits to using "little books" leveled according to a variety of criteria that included both decodability and predictability, as compared to a literature-based basal, for all types of first-grade readers (low-, middle-, and high-achieving).

Although research does not support rigid prescriptions about the types of texts beginners must read, beginners do need opportunities to apply their developing decoding skills in reading books and other texts (Ehri, 2004). For instruction they also should read texts at an appropriate level of difficulty, those they can read with 90–95% word accuracy and about which they can respond successfully to at least 75% of comprehension questions. Many popular leveling systems for beginners' texts fail to increase consistently in word-level demands and do not provide good support for decoding instruction (Cunningham et al., 2005). If children are placed for instruction in books with numerous words that are too difficult for them to decode, then they may resort to frequent guessing at unknown words based on context and partial letter cues, unpromising strategies for long-term progress in reading. Teachers also must provide appropriate feedback when children are reading orally. For example, rather than encouraging a child to guess based on pictures or to skip over unknown words, teachers can point to letters or word parts that a child has read incorrectly, give feedback about the correct sounds of letters, and encourage the child to blend sounds to form words.

Overview of Successful Phonics Intervention Approaches

Even with the best core general education instruction, some children still will have reading difficulties. Many contemporary authorities recommend addressing these difficulties through "layering" of interventions over evidence-based core reading instruction, as in response-to-intervention (RTI) models (e.g., Fletcher et al., 2007; Mathes et al., 2005; O'Connor, Fulmer, Harty, & Bell, 2005; Vadasy, Sanders, & Abbott, 2008). Research suggests that a variety of specific intervention activities and methods for teaching decoding can be effective if instruction is explicit and systematic, and if the decoding intervention is well integrated with other important components of reading (Denton, Vaughn, & Fletcher, 2003; Mathes et al., 2005; Torgesen et al., 2001). For example, transfer of decoding gains to fluency and comprehension may be facilitated by having children read texts that contain a high proportion of words or word patterns that they can decode successfully, as well as by teacher feedback during oral reading that encourages application of decoding skills (McCandliss, Beck, Sandak, & Perfetti, 2003). Placing poor decoders in appropriate texts for instruction usually requires employing different texts, or at least different levels of texts than those used in the general education classroom, because grade-appropriate texts are often too difficult for poor readers to decode successfully.

Synthetic phonics approaches at the grapheme–phoneme level may be more difficult initially for struggling readers than larger-unit approaches, such as those involving onsets and rimes, because they make relatively heavy demands on phoneme blending abilities, often a weakness in poor decoders. However, grapheme–phoneme level approaches emphasize attention to all letters in a word right from the start, which, in the long run, may facilitate faster learning of the alphabetic code (Christensen & Bowey, 2005). Numerous phonics interventions for struggling readers have combined activities involving grapheme–phoneme decoding with activities involving analysis of larger units in words. Examples of these latter types of interventions include multisensory structured language programs (e.g., Birsh, 2005; Henry, 2003), which combine teaching of grapheme–phoneme decoding with instruction in common syllable patterns, and the Phonological and Strategy Training (PHAST) program of Lovett, Barron, and Benson (2003), which combines grapheme–phoneme decoding instruction with teaching of strategies such as word recognition by analogy and "peeling off" prefixes and suffixes from a longer word.

For children who are unresponsive to core general education reading instruction or initial interventions, increases in explicitness and intensity of instruction, as opposed to changes in overall instructional method, appear to be most important (Torgesen, 2004). Ways to increase intensity include devoting more time to intervention and decreasing the size of the intervention group (e.g., one teacher to three students vs. one teacher to five students). Intervention delivered in small homogeneous groups generally appears to be as effective as one-to-one tutoring (Elbaum, Vaughn, Hughes, & Moody, 1999; National Reading Panel, 2000; Torgesen, 2004). Phonics interventions implemented by well-trained volunteers and paraprofessionals can benefit many struggling readers (Invernizzi, Rosemary, Juel, & Richards, 1997; Vadasy, Sanders, Peyton, & Jenkins, 2002), as can interventions implemented in the context of a supervised field work program for teacher candidates (Spear-Swerling, 2009; Spear-Swerling & Brucker, 2004).

However, children who are not responsive to initial levels of intervention may require more highly trained and experienced teachers (Vadasy et al., 2008).

To group children effectively, place them in appropriate texts for instruction and decide where to begin instruction, formative assessment of children's decoding skills is very important. Assessment should determine which letter sounds, word patterns, and syllable types children can decode and which still need work. Children at beginning levels of decoding may only be able to read simple consonant–vowel–consonant words such as *sat* and *lip*; slightly more advanced readers may be able to decode short vowel words but may have difficulty with vowel–r patterns (e.g., *star*, *first*) or vowel diphthongs (e.g., *boil*, *frown*); and older struggling readers may be able to decode a wide variety of one-syllable words but have difficulty primarily with words of more than one syllable (e.g., *targeted*, *explanation*). Including some pseudowords along with real words in assessment is helpful to determine whether children can decode unfamiliar words as opposed to recognizing specific words from memory. Several commercially available tests can be used to assess decoding skills, such as the CORE Phonics Survey (Consortium on Reading Excellence, 2008). Teachers can also develop informal assessments of decoding skills.

Examples of Research-Based Interventions for Decoding

In this section, I discuss examples of specific interventions for decoding and word recognition that have strong research support. Citations are provided for further information about each intervention, along with Web-based information in some cases. The interventions involve a continuum from whole-class groupings to more individualized, tutorial interventions. Many of these interventions have elements that extend beyond decoding to other components of reading, such as comprehension; I discuss only the decoding interventions and their application to text reading. My colleagues and I (Spear-Swerling, 2009; Spear-Swerling & Brucker, 2003, 2004) have employed activities adapted from many of these interventions in a teacher preparation program for special educators and dually credentialed elementary/special education teachers. The descriptions below include sample teaching scripts based on these adaptations. Numerous variations of each script are possible, including not only those suggested at the end of the script but also, for example, alterations in the teacher's language to make the wording more appropriate for older struggling readers.

Direct Instruction

Direct Instruction (Carnine et al., 2004), a specific approach to teaching reading based heavily on the work of Engelmann and his colleagues (e.g., Engelmann & Bruner, 1974, 1988; Engelmann & Carnine, 1991), has been published as several different commercial programs. The decoding component of these programs involves synthetic phonics instruction at the grapheme–phoneme level. Direct Instruction can be used in a general education setting but has most often been employed with at-risk populations, such as children from low socioeconomic status backgrounds. Lessons can be taught in both small- and large-group formats. There is a high degree of teacher–student interaction through frequent teacher questioning and unison oral responding by students. Teachers use signaling techniques, such as a hand signal or a finger snap, to cue students when to respond, with teachers providing clear, unambiguous feedback to children's errors. Lessons are briskly paced and scripted.

Direct Instruction emphasizes a carefully planned sequence of skills, with very explicit teaching of important prerequisite skills before children move on to more complex skills, and with particular attention to avoiding potential confusions. For example, because the sounds for *sh* and *ch* are similar, beginning readers often confound them; therefore, teachers would separate the two patterns in instruction and ensure that children have mastered the first pattern prior to introducing the second one. Direct Instruction also highlights careful selection of examples in teaching. For instance, if children are learning the vowel–consonant–*e* phonics pattern, where the final *e* makes the first vowel long (*shine, ate, hope*, etc.), teachers must be mindful of exception or irregular words, such as *come*. Furthermore, careful selection of examples can facilitate efficient learning of phonics generalizations. In the case of the vowel–consonant–*e* pattern, the number of consonants that precede the pattern is irrelevant: *Shine, ate, hope*, and *throne* all have a final *e* that is silent and a first vowel that is long. Teachers can facilitate children's understanding of this point by selecting examples that vary the number of initial consonants.

Some aspects of Direct Instruction programs have been widely criticized, especially their highly scripted nature and their reliance on signaling and unison responding techniques. Nevertheless, a substantial research base supports the effectiveness of the programs (Adams & Carnine, 2003; Adams & Engelmann, 1996; Carlson & Francis, 2002). The emphasis of Direct Instruction on effective instructional design and delivery principles, such as well-sequenced instruction, clear teacher feedback, avoidance of inadvertently confusing instruction, and careful selection of examples, is especially valuable.

Peer-Assisted Learning Strategies

Peer-Assisted Learning Strategies (PALS) developed in part from work on collaborative learning (e.g., Jenkins & O'Connor, 2003). Lynn and Douglas Fuchs (Fuchs & Fuchs, 2005) and their colleagues at Vanderbilt University have designed PALS programs for both reading and mathematics. All of the PALS programs involve pairing academically stronger students with weaker ones to provide additional practice in important academic skills, as well as to foster social learning and cooperation. Pairs are rotated periodically. Prior to instituting the program, teachers train students carefully to implement the PALS procedures. These procedures include basic rules for behavior (e.g., talk quietly and talk only about PALS tasks) and simple tutoring routines (e.g., the use of modeling and immediate corrective feedback to errors). Abbott, Greenwood, Buzhardt, Wills, and Terry (Chapter 12, this volume) describe PALS and other peer-mediated approaches.

Word–Building Interventions

Word-building interventions (Beck, 2005; Beck & Juel, 1992; Cunningham & Cunningham, 1992) encompass a range of activities to develop children's decoding skills using chains of words. The chains are sets of words that comprise letter sounds children have been taught, where the progression from one word to the next involves a change in a single phoneme. For instance, children who have learned single consonant and short vowel sounds might be working with the following series of words: *mat, hat, sat, sad, sag, sap, slap, slip, snip,* and so forth. Note that the phoneme change can occur in a variety of places, not just in the initial phoneme; this feature of word building is important to develop children's understanding of the alphabetic code, as well as their attention to all letters in a word. Word-building activities can involve letter cards or tiles, with words constructed on a pocket chart by the teacher or children, on a magnetic board, or on children's desks. Activities can also involve writing in lieu of letter cards, with words written in a grid or set of boxes, and with each box devoted to a single phoneme. For example, the word *thick* would use three boxes, with *th* in the first box, *i* in the second, and *ck* in the third. If letter cards are used, they should be arranged in alphabetical order to facilitate finding specific letters. A detailed description of the word-building intervention developed by Beck and her colleagues is at *www. education.pitt.edu/leaders/decoding/wordbuilding.aspx.*

Research on word-building interventions (e.g., Blachman et al., 2004; McCandliss et al., 2003; Spear-Swerling & Brucker, 2004; Spear-Swerling, 2009; Stahl, Duffy-Hester, & Stahl, 1998) suggests that these interventions can be very effective in developing the decoding skills of beginning and struggling readers. Furthermore, word building is an especially engaging way to give children practice in decoding. Teachers can easily incorporate word-building activities designed for groups into general education reading instruction. Intensive word-building activities involving smaller groups or tutorial instruction are useful interventions for poor decoders. Appendix 4.1 provides a sample script for a word-building activity my colleagues and I have used in a tutorial intervention that is part of a field work program for teacher candidates in elementary and special education.

PHAST Track Reading Program

PHAST (Phonological and Strategy Training) is a research-based intervention for word recognition and decoding developed by Lovett and her colleagues (2003; Lovett, Lacerenza, et al., 2000; Lovett, Warren-Chaplin, Ransby, & Borden, 1990). PHAST combines instruction in two programs, PHAB/DI and WIST. PHAB/DI

(Phonological Analysis and Blending/Direct Instruction) is an adaptation of Reading Mastery (Engelmann & Bruner, 1988), a DI program with an emphasis on grapheme–phoneme blending. WIST (Word Identification Strategy Training) involves an adaptation of the Benchmark School program developed by Gaskins, Downer, and Gaskins (1986) that uses keyword spelling patterns organized by vowel and rime units, and that teaches decoding by analogy. For example, the three key words for the three common sounds of the vowel *y* are *cry*, *baby*, and *gym*. A child might decode words such as *try* and *fly* by analogy with *cry*; *lady* by analogy with *baby*; and *myth* by analogy with *gym*. WIST also teaches three additional word recognition strategies: vowel variation (trying different sounds for the vowel in a given word in order of the frequency of the vowel sounds), spy (looking for parts of a word the child already knows), and peeling off prefixes and suffixes in a multisyllablic word.

PHAST lessons include a metacognitive Game Plan that gives children practice in applying various decoding strategies in a coordinated way and in monitoring that their efforts produce a recognizable word. The steps of the Game Plan involve choosing a decoding strategy or strategies (e.g., for a multisyllablic word, peeling off affixes and decoding the base word by grapheme–phoneme blending); applying the strategies (e.g., reading the base word, then the entire word with affixes); checking whether the word makes sense as a real word; and "scoring" the application (e.g., if the child's attempt did not produce a recognizable word, then he or she would repeat the process by choosing a different decoding strategy).

Studies have consistently shown the PHAST combination of PHAB/DI and WIST to have stronger benefits for word recognition and decoding than either program alone (Lovett et al., 2003; Lovett, Steinbach, & Frijters, 2000). The combined program has yielded positive effects even with upper elementary and middle school students, including some with severe, long-standing reading difficulties. It would be an especially appropriate choice for a small-group or tutorial intervention with struggling decoders, in Tier II or III for schools utilizing tiered intervention models.

Multisensory Structured Language Programs

Multisensory structured language (MSL) programs include a variety of contemporary programs developed from the foundational work of Samuel Orton, Anna Gillingham, and Betsy Stillman (e.g., Gillingham & Stillman, 1970). As outlined in Birsh (2005) and Henry (2003), these programs emphasize explicit, systematic teaching of language structure, in combination with multisensory methods that involve making visual, auditory, and/or tactile–kinesthetic associations among sounds, letters, and words. For example, as children learn the sound for the letter *s*, they would be simultaneously looking at the letter, tracing it, and saying the sound /s/. Unlike some multisensory approaches that focus on whole-word learning (e.g., Fernald, 1943), MSL programs emphasize learning of the alphabetic code, not memorization of sight words. MSL programs typically begin decoding instruction by teaching grapheme–phoneme correspondences and synthetic blending strategies, but they also teach language structure well beyond the grapheme–phoneme level, including aspects of morphology, grammar, and syntax.

One useful aspect of many of these programs involves instruction in syllable types. Vowel sounds in English are highly variable; for example, the letter *a* can represent the different vowel sounds heard in *back, cake,* and *car,* as well as several other sounds. Syllable types provide a way to predict the likely vowel sound of a word. Syllable types commonly taught in MSL programs include the following:

- Closed: A syllable that has a single vowel and ends in a consonant; the vowel sound is short (e.g., *math, crunch, spend, on, flip*).

- Silent *e* (or magic *e*): A syllable that ends in a vowel–consonant–*e* pattern; the vowel sound is long (e.g., *ice, flame, use, strode, theme*).

- Open: A syllable with a single vowel that is the last letter of the syllable; the vowel sound is long (e.g., *flu, go, me, try*).

- Vowel–*r*—closed (or *r*-controlled or "bossy *r*"): A syllable that contains a single vowel followed immediately by an *r*; the vowel sound of the specific vowel–*r* pattern (*ar, er, or, ur, ir*) must be memorized (e.g., *car, dirt, spurn, herd, born*).

- Vowel team (or vowel combination or vowel digraph/diphthong): A syllable that contains one of many specific vowel patterns (e.g., *ai, ay, all, igh, oy, oo*) whose sounds must be memorized (e.g., *plain, stray, stall, sight, toy, bloom*).

- Consonant–*le*: A syllable comprised of a consonant–*le* pattern (e.g., *-dle, -ble, -gle*) that is always part of a longer word; the vowel sound is a schwa (e.g., *dazzle, bugle, marble, needle*).

Appendix 4.2 shows a sample script for teaching the syllable type that is usually taught first, the closed syllable.

The highly explicit, systematic teaching of phoneme–grapheme decoding and higher levels of language structure characteristic of MSL programs is well supported empirically (e.g., Foorman, Francis, Fletcher, Schatschneider, & Mehta, 1998; Joshi, Dahlgren, & Boulware-Gooden, 2002; Torgesen et al., 2001). However, the specific contribution of multisensory techniques to successful outcomes remains controversial (Birsch, 2005). Most intervention studies have not isolated the influence of multisensory methods specifically. Occasional studies comparing similar forms of systematic phonics teaching with and without the multisensory component have not found multisensory techniques to improve outcomes beyond the advantages conferred by systematic phonics alone (Clark & Uhry, 1995; Fletcher et al., 2007).

However, multisensory techniques do provide a useful way to focus children's attention on letters and print. For instance, in traditional activities for teaching letter sounds such as those involving flash cards, children may repeat responses after the teacher without actually looking carefully at the letter on the card; the use of a multisensory tracing technique ensures that they are looking at the letter at the same time that they say its sound. Multisensory methods can also be especially useful for teaching phonetically irregular words (see the sample teaching script in Appendix 4.3). The International Dyslexia Association (2009), a professional organization devoted to dyslexia and related reading difficulties, has endorsed multisensory methods used in combination with structured language teaching (see *www.interdys.org/factsheets.htm*). MSL programs are especially appropriate as small group or tutorial Tier II or III interventions.

All of the interventions just described emphasize the importance of encouraging children to apply their developing decoding skills in reading text that is at an appropriate level of difficulty. Skillful teacher guidance and feedback on errors during children's oral reading are essential. Appendix 4.4 displays a sample script for teacher guidance and feedback during a child's oral reading in context.

Some Practical Advice

To conclude, here are some practical tips for teachers and teacher educators on how to intervene successfully with struggling decoders:

• Use appropriate assessments to target instruction and monitor progress. Children's word recognition development involves a progression of phases and learning of increasingly complex skills. Efficient, effective intervention hinges on determining where a given child or group of children functions along this continuum of development. For planning intervention and monitoring progress in decoding, criterion-referenced or informal tests of children's decoding skills, using both real words and nonsense words presented out of context, are especially useful.

• Teach decoding skills explicitly and systematically out of context, but be careful to provide many opportunities for children to apply skills in reading of text, both at an instructional level, with teacher guidance and feedback, and at an easier, independent level for practice and enjoyment. Some out-of-context instruction usually is indispensable for children to acquire decoding skills in an efficient manner. However, without sufficient opportunities to read passages and books, decoding gains may not transfer to fluency or comprehension, and children's motivation to read may suffer.

• Find ways to accelerate progress in decoding. For example, build on known decoding skills as determined by criterion-referenced testing and observation rather than focusing on low-level skills a child already knows. Emphasize the most useful letter patterns and phonics generalizations (e.g., the sounds of *igh* and *tion*) and skip the less useful ones (e.g., the six different sounds of *ough*). Set ambitious decoding goals that enable struggling readers to catch up to grade expectations. In order for a struggling first-grader to remain on track with regard to grade-level expectations in decoding, he or she needs to be able to decode one-syllable words involving numerous syllable types (e.g., closed, silent *e*, open, vowel–*r*, vowel team) by the end of the school year. With well-planned, explicit teaching and timely intervention, these kinds of goals are attainable for most struggling decoders.

• Use some low-frequency words (or nonsense words) in phonics instruction. If teachers use primarily high-frequency words (e.g., *cat, man, sit, fast, stop*), children may know these words from memory but not practice use of a decoding process. In addition, they may falsely appear to be progressing in decoding and may fail to grasp the entire point of phonics instruction: that knowledge of the alphabetic code gives them the power to figure out unknown words. The use of low-frequency words (e.g., *wit, vast, crop*) can help to avoid these problems.

• Emphasize recognition of common letter patterns and application of phonics knowledge in actual reading of words—not verbalization of phonics rules. Although it is important for teachers to verbalize rules clearly, many children become confused when trying to state phonics rules. Application, not recitation of rules, is the point. If a child can consistently recognize a particular pattern (e.g., that the vowel–consonant–*e* pattern at the end of a syllable makes the first vowel long and the *e* silent) and use that pattern to decode unfamiliar words, then he or she is demonstrating adequate knowledge of the rule.

• Emphasize oral reading and interactive activities with teacher guidance and feedback rather than silent reading and independent worksheet activities. Some silent reading (e.g., silent reading in easy texts to promote fluency) and independent worksheets (e.g., to provide additional practice of learned skills) are certainly appropriate. However, oral reading at their instructional level is vital for children with decoding problems; without oral reading, teachers cannot adequately monitor children's progress in decoding and application of decoding skills in reading text. Furthermore, oral reading and interactive activities are generally much better ways than worksheets to engage children's interest and motivation.

Phonics knowledge and decoding skills are not sufficient for good reading comprehension; children who are able to decode unfamiliar words can have poor comprehension for other reasons, such as limitations in vocabulary or background knowledge. However, without accurate word recognition skills, children lack an essential foundation for reading comprehension. They also are likely to lose motivation for reading, because early success in acquiring basic reading skills is a key predictor of avid reading later on (Cunningham & Stanovich, 1997). Although reliance on contextual strategies may provide a limited, short-term fix for the problems of some struggling decoders, an instructional emphasis on contextual strategies actually encourages children to stay "stuck" in a beginning phase of reading development, a bit like encouraging a baby to keep crawling when he or she is ready to walk. Teachers can best ensure children's reading progress by developing their knowledge about the alphabetic code and their abilities to apply that knowledge in reading unfamiliar words and text, using research-based instruction and interventions.

References

Adams, M. J. (1990). *Beginning to read: Thinking and learning about print*. Cambridge, MA: MIT Press.

Adams, M. J. (1998). The three-cueing system. In F. Lehr & J. Osborn (Eds.), *Literacy for all: Issues in teaching and learning* (pp. 73–99). New York: Guilford Press.

Adams, G. L., & Carnine, D. W. (2003). Direct Instruction. In H. L. Swanson, K. R. Harris, & S. Graham (Eds.), *Handbook of learning disabilities* (pp. 403–416). New York: Guilford Press.

Adams, G. L., & Engelmann, S. (1996). *Research on Direct Instruction: 25 years beyond DISTAR*. Portland, OR: Educational Achievement Systems.

Beck, I. L. (2005). *Making sense of phonics: The hows and whys*. New York: Guilford Press.

Beck, I. L., & Juel, C. (1992). The role of decoding in learning to read. In S. J. Samuels & A. E. Farstrup (Eds.), *What research has to say about reading instruction* (pp. 101–123). Newark, DE: International Reading Association.

Birsh, J. R. (2005). *Multisensory teaching of basic language skills* (2nd ed.). Baltimore: Brookes.

Blachman, B. A., Schatschneider, C., Fletcher, J. M., Francis, D. J., Clonan, S., Shaywitz, B., et al. (2004). Effects of intensive reading remediation for second and third graders. *Journal of Educational Psychology, 96*, 444–461.

Carlson, C. D., & Francis, D. J. (2002). Increasing the reading achievement of at-risk children through Direct Instruction: Evaluation of the Rodeo Institute for Teacher Excellence (RITE). *Journal of Education for Students Placed at Risk, 7*, 141–166.

Carnine, D. W., Silbert, J., Kame'enui, E., & Tarver, S. (2004). *Direct Instruction reading* (4th ed.). Upper Saddle River, NJ: Merrill.

Carver, R. P., & David, A. H. (2001). Investigating reading achievement using a causal model. *Scientific Studies of Reading, 5*, 107–140.

Catts, H. W., Hogan, T. P., & Adlof, S. M. (2005). Developmental changes in reading and reading disabilities. In H. W. Catts & A. Kamhi (Eds.), *The connections between language and reading disabilities* (pp. 25–40). Mahwah, NJ: Erlbaum.

Christensen, C. A., & Bowey, J. A. (2005). The efficacy of orthographic rime, grapheme–phoneme correspondence, and implicit phonics approaches to teaching decoding skills. *Scientific Studies of Reading, 9*, 327–349.

Clark, D. B., & Uhry, J. K. (1995). *Dyslexia: Theory and practice of remedial instruction*. Baltimore: York Press.

Connor, C. M., Morrison, F. J., & Underwood, P. S. (2007). A second chance in second grade: The independent and cumulative impact of first- and second-grade reading instruction and students' letter-word reading skill growth. *Scientific Studies of Reading, 11*, 199–233.

Consortium on Reading Excellence. (2008). *CORE assessing reading: Multiple measures for kindergarten through twelfth grade* (2nd ed.). Novato, CA: Arena Press.

Cunningham, A. E., & Stanovich, K. E. (1997). Early reading acquisition and its relation to reading experience and ability ten years later. *Developmental Psychology, 33*, 934–945.

Cunningham, J. W., Spadorcia, S. A., Erickson, K. A., Koppenhaver, D. A., Sturm, J. M., & Yoder, D. E. (2005). Investigating the instructional supportiveness of leveled texts. *Reading Research Quarterly, 40*, 410–417.

Cunningham, P. M., & Cunningham, J. W. (1992). Making words: Enhancing the invented spelling–decoding connection. *Reading Teacher, 46*, 106–115.

Denton, C. A., Vaughn, S., & Fletcher, J. M. (2003). Bringing research-based practice in reading intervention to scale. *Learning Disabilities Research and Practice, 18*, 201–211.

Ehri, L. C. (1991). Learning to read and spell words. In L. Rieben & C. A. Perfetti (Eds.), *Learning to read: Basic research and its implications* (pp. 57–73). Mahwah, NJ: Erlbaum.

Ehri, L. C. (2004). Teaching phonemic awareness and phonics: An explanation of the National Reading Panel meta-analyses. In P. McCardle & V. Chhabra (Eds.), *The voice of evidence in reading research* (pp. 153–186). Baltimore: Brookes.

Ehri, L. C. (2005). Learning to read words: Theory, findings, and issues. *Scientific Studies of Reading, 9*, 167–188.

Ehri, L. C., & McCormick, S. (1998). Phases of word learning: Implications for instruction with delayed and disabled readers. *Reading and Writing Quarterly, 14*, 135–163.

Elbaum, B., Vaughn, S., Hughes, M. T., & Moody, S. W. (1999). Grouping practices and reading outcomes for students with disabilities. *Exceptional Children, 65*, 399–415.

Engelmann, S., & Bruner, E. (1974). *DISTAR Reading I*. Chicago: Science Research Associates.

Engelmann, S., & Bruner, E. (1988). *Reading Mastery I*. Columbus, OH: Science Research Associates.

Engelmann, S., & Carnine, D. (1991). *Theory of instruction: Principles and applications* (rev. ed.). Eugene, OR: ADI Press.

Fernald, G. (1943). *Remedial techniques in basic school subjects*. New York: McGraw-Hill.

Fletcher, J. M., Lyon, G. R., Fuchs, L. S., & Barnes, M. A. (2007). *Learning disabilities: From identification to intervention*. New York: Guilford Press.

Foorman, B. R., Francis, D. J., Fletcher, J. M., Schatschneider, C., & Mehta, P. (1998). The role of instruction in learning to read. *Journal of Educational Psychology, 90*, 37–55.

Fuchs, D., & Fuchs, L. S. (2005). Peer-Assisted Learning Strategies: Promoting word recognition, fluency, and reading comprehension in young children. *Journal of Special Education, 39*, 34–44.

Gaskins, I. W., Downer, M. A., & Gaskins, R. W. (1986). *Introduction to the Benchmark School Word Identification/Vocabulary Development program*. Media, PA: Benchmark School.

Gillingham, A., & Stillman, B. (1970). *Remedial training for children with specific language disability*. Cambridge, MA: Educators' Publishing Service.

Henry, M. K. (2003). *Unlocking literacy: Effective decoding and spelling instruction*. Baltimore: Brookes.

International Dyslexia Association. (2009). *Multisensory structured language teaching fact sheet*. Retrieved August 11, 2009, from *www.interdys.org/factsheets.htm*.

Invernizzi, M., Rosemary, C., Juel, C., & Richards, H. C. (1997). At-risk readers and community volunteers: A 3-year perspective. *Scientific Studies of Reading, 1*, 227–300.

Jenkins, J. R., & O'Connor, R. (2003). Cooperative learning for students with learning disabilities: Evidence from experiments, observations, and interviews. In H. L. Swanson, K. R. Harris, & S. Graham (Eds.), *Handbook of learning disabilities* (pp. 417–430). New York: Guilford Press.

Jenkins, J. R., Peyton, J. A., Sanders, E. A., & Vadasy, P. F. (2004). Effects of reading decodable texts in supplemental first-grade tutoring. *Scientific Studies of Reading, 8*, 53–85.

Joshi, R. M., Dahlgren, M., & Boulware-Gooden, R. (2002). Teaching reading in an inner city school using a multisensory teaching approach. *Annals of Dyslexia, 52*, 229–242.

Leach, J. M., Scarborough, H. S., & Rescorla, L. (2003). Late-emerging reading disabilities. *Journal of Educational Psychology, 95*, 211–224.

Lovett, M. W., Barron, R. W., & Benson, N. J. (2003). Effective remediation of word identification and decoding difficulties in school-age children with reading disabilities. In H. L. Swanson, K. R. Harris, & S. Graham (Eds.), *Handbook of learning disabilities* (pp. 273–292). New York: Guilford Press.

Lovett, M. W., Lacerenza, L., Borden, S., Frijters, J., Steinbach, K., & DePalma, M. (2000). Components of effective remediation for developmental reading disabilities: Combining phonological and strategy-based instruction to improve outcomes. *Journal of Educational Psychology, 92*, 263–283.

Lovett, M. W., Steinbach, K. A., & Frijters, J. C. (2000). Remediating the core deficits of developmental reading disability: A double-deficit perspective. *Journal of Learning Disabilities, 33*, 334–358.

Lovett, M. W., Warren-Chaplin, P., Ransby, M., & Borden, S. L. (1990). Training the word recognition skills of reading disabled children: Treatment and transfer effects. *Journal of Educational Psychology, 82*, 769–780.

Mathes, P. G., Denton, C. A., Fletcher, J. M., Anthony, J. L., Francis, D. J., & Schatschneider, C. (2005). The effects of theoretically different instruction and student characteristics on the skills of struggling readers. *Reading Research Quarterly, 40*, 148–182.

McCandliss, B., Beck, I. L., Sandak, R., & Perfetti, C. (2003). Focusing attention on decoding for children with poor reading skills: Design and preliminary tests of the word building intervention. *Scientific Studies of Reading, 7*, 75–104.

Menon, S., & Hiebert, E. (2005). A comparison of first graders' reading with little books or literature-based basal anthologies. *Reading Research Quarterly, 40*, 12–38.

National Reading Panel. (2000). *Teaching children to read: An evidence-based assessment of the scientific research literature on reading and its implications for reading instruction.* Washington, DC: National Institutes of Health.

O'Connor, R. E., Fulmer, D., Harty, K., & Bell, K. (2005). Layers of reading intervention in kindergarten through third grade. *Journal of Learning Disabilities, 38*, 440–455.

Slingerland, E. (1971). *A multisensory approach to language arts.* Cambridge, MA: Educators' Publishing Service.

Spear-Swerling, L. (2004). A road map for understanding reading disability and other reading problems: Origins, intervention, and prevention. In R. Ruddell & N. Unrau (Eds.), *Theoretical models and processes of reading* (Vol. 5, pp. 517–573.) Newark, DE: International Reading Association.

Spear-Swerling, L. (2009). A literacy tutoring experience for prospective special educators and struggling second graders. *Journal of Learning Disabilities, 42*(5), 431–443.

Spear-Swerling, L., & Brucker, P. (2003). Teachers' acquisition of knowledge about English word structure. *Annals of Dyslexia, 53*, 72–103.

Spear-Swerling, L., & Brucker, P. (2004). Preparing novice teachers to develop basic reading and spelling skills in children. *Annals of Dyslexia, 54*, 332–364.

Stahl, S. A., Duffy-Hester, A. M., & Stahl, K. A. L. (1998). Everything you wanted to know about phonics (but were afraid to ask). *Reading Research Quarterly, 33*, 338–355.

Stanovich, K. E. (2000). *Progress in understanding reading: Scientific foundations and new frontiers.* New York: Guilford Press.

Torgesen, J. K. (2004). Lessons learned from research on interventions for students who have difficulty learning to read. In P. McCardle & V. Chhabra (Eds.), *The voice of evidence in reading research* (pp. 355–381). Baltimore: Brookes.

Torgesen, J. K., Alexander, A. W., Wagner, R. K., Rashotte, C. A., Voeller, K. K. S., & Conway, T. (2001). Intensive remedial instruction for children with severe reading disabilities: Immediate and long-term outcomes from two instructional approaches. *Journal of Learning Disabilities, 34,* 33–58.

Vadasy, P. F., Sanders, E. A., & Abbott, R. D. (2008). Effects of supplemental early reading intervention at 2-year follow up: Reading skill growth patterns and predictors. *Scientific Studies of Reading, 12,* 51–89.

Vadasy, P. F., Sanders, E. A., Peyton, J. A., & Jenkins, J. R. (2002). Timing and intensity of tutoring: A closer look at the conditions for effective early literacy tutoring. *Learning Disabilities Research and Practice, 17,* 227–241.

APPENDIX 4.1. Sample Teaching Script for Word-Building Activity

Skill Addressed: Decoding of phonetically regular words.

Prerequisites: The child must know sounds for all letters used in the activity, including the correct vowel sounds for the words used. The example shown here involves a child who knows all single consonant sounds; the short vowels *a*, *i*, and *u*; and the digraph *sh*.

Materials: Magnetic letter board and lowercase letter tiles; letter tiles should accurately represent phonemes (e.g., digraphs such as *sh* on a single tile, but blends such as *sl* represented by two tiles, *s* and *l*).

Preparation: The teacher arranges in alphabetical order the letter tiles to be used around the perimeter of the magnetic board. Consonant letters, vowel letters, and digraphs may be grouped separately. Organization of materials prior to the lesson is essential to avoid wasting time hunting for letters. Letter tiles not in use should be put away to limit potential distraction. The teacher also should prepare a preliminary list of words to be used in the lesson, with an emphasis on words the child is unlikely to know by sight and will therefore have to decode.

Procedure: The teacher introduces the task by saying, "Now we are going to work on reading new words. I am going to use some words you probably have not seen before, but you can sound them out if you look carefully at all the letters."

- In the middle of the magnetic board, the teacher puts together the three letter tiles *s*, *a*, *p*, to spell *sap*. "What's this word?" [If the child has difficulty, the teacher encourages the child to sound out individual phonemes, then to blend sounds by saying, "Good—now say it fast."]
- Next, the teacher says, "I am going to change just one sound in the word. What's this new word?" The teacher returns *s* to the correct spot on the perimeter of the board and replaces it with *m*. "Right, *map*." The teacher uses a few additional examples involving substitution of the initial sound, such as *map* to *rap* to *lap*.
- The teacher says, "Now I am going to try to trick you. Watch carefully. What's this word?" The teacher makes a change in a final phoneme, for example, *lap* to *lag*. [If the child makes a mistake, the teacher gives corrective feedback, such as pointing to the letter the child read incorrectly. If the child is successful, the teacher says, "I couldn't trick you—good for you! You knew you had to look at all the letters, not just the first letter."] The teacher tries some additional examples involving substitution of the final sound, such as *lag* to *lam* to *lash*.
- Next, still encouraging careful attention to all the letters in the word, the teacher tries more difficult substitutions of letters involving known vowel sounds and blends,

for example, *lush, flush, flash, flat, flit, slit, spit, spat.* [If the child has difficulty, encourage phonemic blending strategies; if the words remain too difficult, drop back to simpler words by eliminating blends or using fewer vowel sounds. If the child does well, try more difficult blends, for instance, *split* or *splint.*]

• Try to achieve a brisk pace in the activity, so that the child has the opportunity to decode many words. The teacher may also wish briefly to discuss meanings of the unfamiliar words, but this is not the primary focus of the activity.

Variations: Helpful variations include individual letter cards and pocket charts to facilitate the use of the activity in groups, as well as variations involving writing of words. Writing activities can also be helpful for children unduly distracted by the tiles and magnetic board.

APPENDIX 4.2. Sample Teaching Script
for Teaching Syllable Types

Skill Addressed: Learning syllable types to determine the vowel sound of individual syllables; the example shown here addresses the first syllable type commonly taught, closed syllables.

Prerequisites: The child must be able to classify individual letters as vowels or consonants; the letter *y*, which can be both a vowel and a consonant, is used only as a consonant in the activity below. The child also should be familiar with the term "short vowel" and know at least a few short vowel sounds; however, he or she does not necessarily have to know all short vowel sounds.

Materials: Dry-erase board, markers, introductory word list with appropriate examples of closed syllables, 10–15 index cards with some words that are closed syllables and some that are not.

Preparation: The main preparation for this activity involves selection of the words for the introductory word list and for the index cards. The teacher should be careful to use a variety of closed syllables with all vowels, including long words such as *splash* and *brick*, as well as consonant–vowel–consonant (CVC) patterns like *hip* and *lot*, because in this activity the child only has to classify the words, not decode them. For beginning readers, only one-syllable words should be used. The teacher must include low-frequency words the child is unlikely to know by sight. Phonetically irregular words (e.g., *what*, *of*), vowel–*r* closed words (e.g., *barn*, *first*), and vowel teams with a single vowel (e.g., *small*, *flight*) must be filtered out of the word lists for closed syllables. (The other syllable types will be taught later.)

Procedure: The teacher introduces the task by saying, "Today you are going to begin learning about syllable types. Syllable types can give you a way to figure out the vowel sound of a word. Today we are going to learn the first syllable type, closed syllables."

- The teacher writes a set of closed syllables on the dry-erase board that has the characteristics discussed earlier under *Preparation*, such as *splash, inch, lot, blend, up.* Pointing to the first word, the teacher says: "How many vowels does this word have?" [The child should say, "One."] "Does it end in a consonant?" [The child should say, "Yes."] "So it is a closed syllable, and it will have a short vowel sound."
- The teacher proceeds through each of the sample words on the list using the procedure discussed earlier, gradually eliciting more information from the child, for example, "So it is what kind of syllable? And what will the vowel sound be?"
- Next, the teacher gives the child the index cards with closed and not-closed syllables mixed together, for example, *hog, sprint, yeast, swell, lime, flu, chump, task, ape, cloud.*

The teacher says, "Some of these words are closed syllables and others are not. Separate them into two piles, one for the closed syllables and another for the not-closed syllables." The teacher monitors the child's performance and provides coaching for errors.

• When the task is completed, the teacher has the child go back and give the vowel sound for each closed syllable. If the child only knows a few short vowel sounds, pick the words with the vowels he or she knows.

• As the child learns additional syllable types, add more piles to the sorting task (e.g., closed syllables, silent-*e* syllables, and neither).

Variations: For groups of children, instead of a sorting task, the teacher can use a paper-and-pencil task in which children circle the closed syllables, cross off the not-closed syllables, and take turns giving vowel sounds. For more advanced decoders who are learning syllable types mainly to assist in decoding long words, present words in divided form (e.g., *mag–net, splen–did*) or teach strategies for dividing words prior to introducing syllable types.

APPENDIX 4.3. Sample Teaching Script for Teaching Phonetically Irregular Words

Skill Addressed: Reading of phonetically irregular words.

Prerequisites: The child must be able to identify the names of all letters.

Materials: Index cards, pen, and pencil.

Preparation: The teacher prints in pen each of the new irregular words to be taught on an index card. The card should be sufficiently thick, so that the teacher's writing does not show through the back of the card. The new word to be taught in this sample lesson is *come*.

Procedure: The teacher introduces the task by saying, "Today you are going to learn a new word that is a 'rule breaker' (or 'exception word'). Because these words don't follow the rules you have learned, you can't sound them out in the usual way, so you will learn them another way. You still need to look carefully at all the letters in the word, because this will help you to remember it."

- The teacher places the index card for *come* in front of the child and says, "This word is *come*—as in the sentence, 'Come here.' Trace the letters and say them with me." [The teacher has the child trace each letter with a pencil as teacher and child together say the letter names—*c, o, m, e*—and then say the whole word, *come*.]
- The teacher says, "Good—now try it yourself." [The teacher has the child repeatedly trace the word, saying the letter names while tracing them, then saying the whole word.]
- When the teacher thinks the child has had sufficient practice, he or she says, "Now turn the card over and see if you can remember how to write the word. Remember to say the letter names and then the whole word as you are writing." [If the child makes an error, have the child turn to the front of the card and help him or her find the error. Repeat the tracing process several additional times and try the writing-from-memory task again. After the child writes the word from memory successfully, keep the card for review in future lessons.]

Variations: Instead of using pencil and paper, some children enjoy using a chalkboard or small slate board; as they trace the word with their fingers, the word gradually becomes fainter and eventually disappears, at which point they write it from memory. A variation of this activity for groups (see, e.g., Slingerland, 1971) uses a piece of paper folded in thirds. The teacher writes the new word on the far-left third of the paper; the children copy the word in the middle space; then they fold the paper over (to cover the teacher-written and copied versions) to write the word from memory. At each step, children repeatedly trace and quietly say the word, while the teacher circulates among them to monitor their work and let them know when they are ready to move on to the next step.

APPENDIX 4.4. Sample Teaching Script
for Feedback during Oral Reading in Context

Skill Addressed: Application of decoding skills to reading text.

Prerequisites: The child must be placed in a book written at an appropriate instructional level, where he or she can read with 90–95% word accuracy and answer at least 75% of comprehension questions correctly. The book should also contain a reasonable number of words from the phonics categories the child has learned to decode.

Materials: The only necessary material is an appropriate book.

Preparation: The teacher previews the book for words the child will find difficult to decode, such as names and irregular words. (Although application of decoding skills is the focus of this sample teaching script, of course, the teacher also will want to preview the book for content, for example, for unfamiliar vocabulary and to develop appropriate comprehension questions.)

Procedure: The teacher introduces the book by discussing the title and cover, activates relevant background knowledge by asking questions, and reviews about three to six words that the child is likely to find difficult. The teacher then says, "Now let's find out what happens in the story. Read aloud for me, using your best reading. If you make a mistake on a word, I will help you by pointing to the mistake." When the child reads a word incorrectly or has difficulty decoding, the teacher responds with the following sequence of steps:

- Allow a few seconds of wait time to see whether the child recognizes that he or she has made an error in word recognition, especially if the incorrect word does not make sense in the sentence. Recognition of errors and attempts to correct them show that the child is actively engaging with the text and monitoring comprehension. Because this kind of monitoring is critical to good reading, it should be acknowledged and encouraged by the teacher, for instance, by saying, "You knew that what you read did not make sense and you tried to fix it—good for you."
- If the child does not attempt to self-correct quickly, point to the word or the part of the word with which the child is having difficulty. For example, if the child skips a word, the teacher would point to the entire word; if the child reads *ship* for *sheep*, the teacher would point to the *ee* pattern.
- If the child does not succeed in decoding the word with the pointing cues, follow up with verbal cues, such as "Remember, *ee* says /e/."
- The teacher should tell the child the word only as a last resort, unless the word is an unfamiliar irregular word or an unusually complex word that the child is unlikely to be able to decode. If the child is placed in an appropriate book, few words

should fall into this category. After the teacher supplies the word, the child should repeat it.

   • Once the child has successfully decoded the word or has repeated the word after the teacher, the teacher says, "Good, now read the whole sentence one more time." The repetition of the sentence helps to establish fluency and comprehension.

Variations: If a child has slow, labored reading despite meeting the criteria for word accuracy and comprehension mentioned earlier, teacher and child can take turns reading, which helps to reduce the reading load for the child. When the teacher reads, he or she models good fluency and expression.

5

Morphemic Approaches for Reading Words

TEREZINHA NUNES
PETER BRYANT

In this chapter we briefly explain what morphemes are and review research on the importance of morphemes for the development of children's literacy. We then describe some assessments we have designed to help teachers and researchers assess whether children are using their knowledge of morphemes in word reading and spelling. Finally, we describe ways in which we have taught children to use their knowledge of morphemes in spelling, and the impact of this learning on the children's progress in literacy.

Morphemes and Their Importance in Word Reading

In English orthography, as in many other written languages, words represent two aspects of oral language: the sounds of the language and also meanings that go beyond the sounds. Most people easily recognize that letters represent sounds, even if there isn't a one-to-one correspondence between all the sounds in a language and the letters we use to represent the sounds. We do not dwell here on this aspect of learning to read, though it is an important one. We focus instead on a related but distinct aspect of what words represent: the meanings that are conveyed by some letters or group of letters that represent "morphemes" (i.e., units of meaning that form words).

Suppose you read sentences (1) and (2) below in a book about a new planet on which some new things were found. The astronauts had to create names for these things in order to write their diaries, and they also wrote a glossary of the new words, but reading the glossary seemed boring (who wants to read a dictionary?), so you went straight to the diary, which you found fascinating. These two sentences were taken from their diary.

1. Before we entered the spaceship, we placed the glocks in a basin.
2. Just before we closed the door, we noticed the trox on the window.

You don't know yet what was put into the basin and what was on the window because you didn't read the glossary. But can you tell whether the astronauts were talking about one or more than one of each of these items?

Written words in English, as in many other languages, use letters or sequences of letters to represent meaning beyond the representation of sounds. The two words that the astronauts invented sound the same at the end, but the way they spelled these words should give you a clue to how many of these things they were talking about. In English, plural nouns end with the letter s (even though we sometimes pronounce the s with a /z/ sound, like in the words *bees*, *birds*, and *toys*). On the whole, if an English noun is spelled with an x at the end, it is a singular form; the plural should end in *xes* (as in *fox* and *foxes*). So the clue that you have on the number of things that the astronauts were writing about is that one word ends in s and the other in x.

The smallest units of meaning in a language are called "morphemes." The word *bird* has one morpheme and the word *birds* has two, *bird* + *s*. The first part, *bird* is called "root," and the *s* is called an "affix." When an affix is placed before a root (e.g., *un-happy*), it is called a "prefix": if it is placed after the root (e.g., *happiness*), it is called a "suffix."

Morphemes tend to have fixed spellings in English even when their pronunciation changes across words. This is true both of roots and suffixes. For example, we pronounce the root in the words *magic* and *magician*, *heal* and *health*, and *know* and *knowledge* quite differently, but we spell them in the same way. Think also of how you pronounce the words *kissed* and *opened*: *Kissed* sounds like it has a /t/ at the end and "opened" sounds like the sequence /nd/, as if there were no *e* there. But *ed* is a suffix that marks the past tense of regular verbs, so we write it at the end of regular verbs even though we do not pronounce the words in this way.

Suffixes tell us something about the meaning of words; this information is related to the word's grammatical class. In English, the morpheme s at the end of nouns marks the plural; at the end of verbs, the s marks the third-person singular. Suffixes are of two types:

- Inflectional suffixes, like the s at the end of nouns or verbs, do not change the grammatical class of the word.
- Derivational suffixes, like *ion* at the end of *confession*, *ness* at the end of *happiness*, and *ian* at the end of *magician*, change the meaning of the word and

place it in a particular category of words (e.g., *ian* words are agentives, such as *magician*, *mathematician*, *politician*, and *ion* words are abstract nouns, such as *confession*, *destination*, and *combination*).

The distinction between these two types of affix morphemes is important, because derivational suffixes affect the meaning of words more radically than inflectional suffixes. But the similarity between these two types of morphemes is just as important: When they are added to a word, they change meaning in predictable ways (for a more detailed definition of morphemes and a discussion of their importance in literacy, see Nunes & Bryant, 2006, 2009).

How Morphemes Participate in Word Reading

Think of how you read the words *dishwasher* and *disheartened*. Both words contain the letters *sh*, which very often in English form a "digraph" (i.e., two letters that represent a single sound). Most times when you come across *sh*, you read it as you would in *dishwasher*. But in words such as *dishearten*, *dishonest*, and *dishonor*, you automatically separate out the prefix *dis* from the rest of the word, and you do not treat *sh* as a unit in reading. This may seem like an isolated instance, but it is not. For example, whenever the prefix *un* is followed by a vowel, you read the consonant *n* as belonging to a different syllable than the vowel: Think of *unaccompanied*, *uneven*, and *unidentified*. But words can also start with the prefix *uni*, and in this case the *n* and the *i* are part of the same syllable, as in *uniform* and *unilateral*.

Researchers have for some time suggested that people don't read long words in a letter-by-letter fashion: They parse these words into units that are larger than a letter but smaller than the word. Leong (1989) made use in his research of this process of parsing, which takes place very rapidly and without the reader's conscious engagement. He designed a series of studies in which he tried to find out what units readers use in parsing words. He reasoned that if he mixed lower- and uppercase letters in a word, this mixture would disrupt reading more if the mixture crossed the boundaries of the readers' way of parsing the word than if the mixture coincided with these boundaries. He expected that if the uppercase and lowercase letters matched the reader's parsing of the words, this would facilitate reading, thus speeding up word recognition.

Leong showed Canadian students in fourth, fifth, and sixth grades (ages 10–12 years) words that contained different mixtures of upper- and lowercase letters. When this mixture is random within the word, it usually makes word reading more difficult: For example, reading "mAcHInE" is much more difficult than reading either "machine" or "MACHINE." However, Leong expected the mixture to have a facilitating effect if it were not random, but rather coincided with the way readers parse the words during word recognition. Leong showed students two types of upper- and lowercase letter mixes: for example, "tractOR" and "tracTOR." In the first type of presentation, "tractOR," the word is analyzed into morphemes;

in the second type of presentation, "tracTOR," the word is analyzed in sequences of sounds that can be pronounced together, "trac" and "tor," but do not coincide with the morpheme boundaries. Because this process of parsing takes place so quickly, instead of asking the students to pronounce the words, Leong asked them to indicate whether letter sequences they saw on a screen were words or not by pressing a key in a computer keyboard. The time between the appearance of the letter sequence on the screen and the student pressing the key is called "reaction time." Students' reaction times were indeed faster when the boundaries of the upper- and lowercase letter groups coincided with the morphemes. This facilitating effect was larger for older students and also for those with higher reading ability within their grade level. Thus, Leong found that students use morphemes as units during word recognition, and that the better they are at word recognition, the more they rely on morphemes.

In his subsequent work, Leong (1991, 1992) went on to suggest that morphological skills affect word reading, alongside phonological skills, and sentence comprehension, in more advanced readers (10- to 12-year-olds). He measured the students' morphological skills, using tasks originally designed by Carlisle (1988). In one task, students are asked to judge whether two words that share a phonological element are related to each other (e.g., *doll* and *dollar*); in another task, students are asked to complete a sentence by using a word cue provided by the researcher (e.g., *farm*; *My uncle is a _____?*). Leong found that the students' morphological skills were an important factor in predicting how they would perform in a test of reading fluency later on.

Morphemes affect fluent word reading directly, through this parsing process, but also indirectly, through an increase in children's reading vocabulary. Nagy and Anderson (1984) analyzed the vocabulary used in primary school books and found that most long words in English comprise more than one morpheme. When children come across a multimorphemic word for the first time in a book, they need to use their morphological knowledge to infer the word's meanings and, in some cases, its pronunciation, too. To refer back to our earlier example: If we encounter the word *disheartened* for the first time in print and are able to analyze it into morphemes, we can make connections between its parts (*dis*, *heart*, *en*, and *ed*) and the way this word should be pronounced and interpreted. The prefix *dis* is kept as a separate pronunciation unit from *heart*. The suffix *en* is added to a noun to form a verb: *hearten* means "to make cheerful" (Collins English Dictionary, 1991; or to give heart in the sense of giving courage). And we might also know that the *ed* at the end is a mark of the past or past participle. So we could pronounce *disheartened* correctly and have a good stab at its meaning even if we had never heard the word before coming across it in a book.

Nagy, Berninger and Abbott (2006) suggest that if we use only letter–sound correspondences to read, we cannot be certain how to read words like *disheartened*. However, by using our morphological skills, we can add this word to our reading vocabulary, because we know something about its pronunciation and meaning. So our morphological knowledge should contribute to our word-reading skill, at least when we need to read multimorpheme words with a pronunciation not entirely predictable from letter–sound correspondences.

Nagy and his colleagues (2006) assessed morphological skills of a large number of students (about 600) selected from four different grade levels—from fourth grade (approximate average age 10 years) to ninth grade. They also gave the children a variety of literacy outcome measures, including reading comprehension, reading vocabulary, and decoding of inflected words. Similarly to Leong, they found that the children's morphological skills were strongly related to their performance in reading comprehension, reading vocabulary, and decoding of inflected words, alongside and distinct from the children's knowledge of letter–sound correspondences (for further readings, see Mahony, 1994; Mahony, Singson, & Mann, 2000; Singson, Mahony, & Mann, 2000).

In summary, there are two ways in which knowledge of morphemes contributes to children's success in reading. One is by parsing long words into morphemes, thus speeding word recognition. The other is that when we come across a multimorphemic word for the first time in print, our morphological knowledge gives us clues regarding the word's pronunciation and meaning, thus promoting our reading comprehension, too (for further discussion, see Nunes & Bryant, 2009).

How Can We Know Whether Our Students Are Using Their Morphological Knowledge in Reading?

We designed a relatively short reading task that teachers can use to find out whether their children are using different units in word reading (Nunes, Bryant, & Olsson, 2003). Standardized reading tests are useful as a measure of how far children have progressed, but they do not give teachers information about the types of skills that the children use (or fail to use) in word reading. The children themselves often cannot explain this process to the teachers: Word recognition processes take place too quickly for us to become aware of them.

Our reading test contains real words and also invented words called "pseudowords" in the research literature. Pseudowords are used in assessments of decoding, because they eliminate the possibility that the child partially guesses the word from some letters or groups of letters: They require the child to rely entirely on decoding skills, because it is not possible to support decoding with semantic knowledge (i.e., previous knowledge of words). Suppose you come across the word *grape* in a reading test but do not yet know how to read words with this final *e*. You might try to pronounce it as /grap/ or /grapee/, but you would know that these are not words. You might know that the letter *a* represents different vowel sounds in different words, then try varying its sound, until you come up with *grape*, which you know to be a word, so your knowledge of decoding would be complemented by your semantic knowledge. This process does not work with pseudowords: If you have been told that you are reading invented words, which you cannot recognize, you have to do your best with just your decoding skills.

In our assessment, we presented children with a list of words and a separate list of pseudowords: So the children always knew whether they should recognize the word they pronounced or pronounce what they decoded, without expecting this to sound like a real word.

We used words and pseudowords that depended on different types of processes, as indicated below, but the different types of words and pseudowords were mixed in each list. When the words had a final *e*, we chose words that would still sound like another word if the reader did not use the information about the final *e* in decoding (e.g., *hope* could be read as *hop* if the child did not know about the final *e*).

The words and pseudowords were chosen to assess three distinct but related processes that influence word reading. The examples listed here are separated by the type of unit that children used in reading: We refer to these as different subtests.

- Subtest 1 contained words and pseudowords that can be pronounced on the basis of *single letter–sound correspondences* (e.g., words: *hop, tap, sit, cut, hug, fat*; pseudowords: *tok, dut, sof, smap*).

- Subtest 2 contained words and pseudowords that require the use of *phonological units larger than single letter–sound correspondences*, such as digraphs and double letters (e.g., words: *site, fated, hope, wives, dive, hive, cute, cuter, huge, hopper, hugger, fate, taped, sitter, fatter, tapped, dishwasher, dashing*; pseudowords: *smape, sofe, duter, dape, lishing*).

- Subtest 3 contained words and pseudowords in which pronunciation depended on the use of morphological units (e.g., words: *universe, uninterested, unity, unusual, union, unimportant, uninvolved, unilateral, uniform, dishonest, mishap, mishandle*; pseudowords: *uninverted, misheaded, unisided, unimatched, mishammer, uninset, uningest, unishaped*).

The children's performance in each of these subtests was highly related to performance in the other two subtests, but the subtests had very different levels of difficulty.

Table 5.1 shows the proportion of correct responses by children in different grade levels. The children's mean ages went from 7 years, 6 months, in grade 3 to 10 years, 7 months, in grade 6. Table 5.1 shows quite clearly that it was much easier for children in the four grade levels to read words and pseudowords that could be pronounced using simple letter–sound correspondences (subtest 1) than to read those that required the use of more than one letter to represent a particular sound (subtest 2). It was even more difficult to use morphological units (subtest 3).

When we looked at individual children's performance, we found that 90% of

TABLE 5.1. Percentage of Correct Responses by Type of Word and Pseudoword for Each Grade Level

Type of unit needed to read the words and pseudowords	Grade 3 (N = 239)	Grade 4 (N = 222)	Grade 5 (N = 229)	Grade 6 (N = 236)
Subtest 1: Simple letter–sound correspondences	80	86	90	91
Subtest 2: Phonological units larger than one letter	52	65	74	76
Subtest 3: Morphological units	32	46	60	64

the children scored higher in subtest 1 than in subtest 2; 97% scored higher in subtest 1 than in subtest 3; and 88% of the children had a better performance in subtest 2 than in subtest 3. Because the subtests have different levels of difficulty, we should expect all children to show a difference in the percentage of correct responses across the subtests. On average, the children scored 20% higher in subtest 1 than in subtest 2 and 36% higher in subtest 1 than in subtest 3. This means that we can expect all children to differ in the proportion of correct responses across the subtests due to the differences in their level of difficulty. But about 4% of the children read more than twice as many words in subtest 1 as in subtest 2, and about 10% read twice as many words in subtest 1 as in subtest 3. Table 5.2 presents the proportion of correct responses for the children in each of these groups for each subtest.

Table 5.2 shows clearly that the children in the different groups performed quite similarly when reading words and pseudowords that can be decoded on the basis of simple letter–sound correspondences. All four groups read almost 90% of these words and pseudowords correctly: They made only occasional errors. In contrast, when the words and pseudowords could only be decoded by using larger units, the groups' performances are quite different. This pattern of scores suggests that the children in our study, who were in grade 3 or above, were competent in using letter–sound correspondences in word reading, but some children found it quite difficult to use the other types of units. Identifying children who have difficulty with one of the more advanced processes in word reading is of particular importance in the design of personalized educational programs. Thus, a very large discrepancy across subtests can be used as an indication that a child needs explicit teaching about the reading units that are important for the subtests in which he or she did not do well.

One could argue that the types of words and pseudowords in our subtests 2 and 3 are not typical of what children need to know to be good decoders. It is possible to test whether this is true by seeing how well the children's performances in each of these three subtests predict their performance in a standardized reading test, which is taken as a good general measure of decoding. In order to find out the relative importance of each of these subtests for predicting children's achievement

TABLE 5.2. Percentage Correct by Group and by Subtest

Group	Percentage correct in subtest 1	Percentage correct in subtest 2	Percentage correct in subtest 3
Not more than twice as many correct in subtest 1 than in 2	86	52	67
More than twice as many correct in subtest 1 than in 2	88	11	17
Not more than twice as many correct in subtest 1 than in 3	86	55	70
More than twice as many correct in subtest 1 than in 2	89	13	38

in a standardized word-reading test, we saw a sample of the children ($N = 197$) again about 5 months later in the academic year. On this second occasion, we gave them an intelligence test (Wechsler Intelligence Test for Children [WISC] and the Schonell Word Reading Test (a standardized reading test to obtain a measure of the children's reading age). This allowed us to use a statistical technique called regression analysis to see whether the subtests made independent contributions to the prediction of word reading later, and also the importance of each subtest in this prediction. We gave the children the intelligence test to separate out the effect of general verbal intelligence on decoding: It is possible that success in each of the three subtests and in the word reading could just be a matter of how intelligent the children were.

The regression analysis showed that each subtest made an independent contribution to predicting the children's word reading scores 5 months later. This is an important result, because it indicates that mastery of simple letter–sound correspondences and knowledge of digraphs are not sufficient on their own to explain children's achievement in word reading tests: Performance in subtest 3, which assesses whether the children use morphemes in reading words, makes an independent contribution to the prediction of children's word reading scores. The analysis also showed that for children in these grade levels, the importance of subtest 3 for predicting achievement in word reading was roughly equivalent to that for the other two subtests together. Figure 5.1 shows this result schematically.

The values indicated by the arrows can vary between –1 and 1. A positive value indicates that the higher the child's score in the measures on the left side of the picture, the better the child's performance in the Schonell Word Reading Test. In this case, all values are positive. The closer the value is to 1, the more important it is in predicting the child's word reading result. Thus, for these grade levels, performance in subtest 3, which assesses whether the children are using morphological units in word reading, is the best predictor of their overall word reading performance.

Our general conclusions so far were the following:

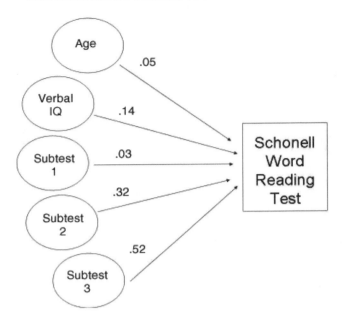

FIGURE 5.1. Predicting achievement in word reading.

- Children use at least three types of units in reading: simple letter–sound correspondences, digraphs, and morphemes.
- The more proficient children become, the more likely they are to use morphemes.
- The use of each of these three types of units makes an independent contribution to children's word reading achievement.
- From about grade 3, the importance of morphemes for word reading is relatively higher than that of the other units, which represent sounds; this may be due to the fact that by then, most children have a better grasp of phonological units (letters, digraphs) than of morphological units.
- Most children show a discrepancy between the use of simple letter–sound correspondences and the other two types of units, but in some children this discrepancy is considerable, and they may require explicit teaching.

Designing Teaching Programs to Help Students Use Their Morphological Knowledge in Reading

The design of a teaching program involves making decisions about what to teach, with what aim, how to teach, how to assess the benefits of teaching, and who might reap these benefits. If we look at different studies rather than try to find all the answers in a single study, we can base each of these decisions on research already available in the literature. Although some of the answers may be tentative, and further corroborating evidence is required for firmer conclusions, we believe that there is much evidence of methods that can be used to teach children how to make the best of their morphological knowledge in reading.

What Aims Can We Achieve through Morphological Instruction?

The research reviewed in the previous sections suggests that teaching children about morphology should help them to become better at word reading and reading comprehension (see also Carlisle & Stone, 2005), and that it should also have a positive effect on their development of vocabulary (see also Baumann, Edwards, Boland, Olejnik, & Kame'enui, 2003; Nunes & Bryant, 2006). There is also evidence that instruction on morphology has a positive effect on children's spelling (e.g., Arnbak & Elbro, 2000; Nunes & Bryant, 2006; Nunes, Bryant, & Bindman, 1996), particularly when the spelling of the words cannot be based on the way the words sound. Some of the examples presented earlier illustrate this well: If we try to spell words like *magician* and *confession* based on the way they sound, we most certainly are doomed to fail. Finally, there is also evidence to support the idea that teaching children about morphology should help them learn a second language: Children's awareness of morphemes in their own language predicts their second language learning (e.g., Deacon, Wade-Woolley, & Kirby, 2007), and those who have English as an additional language could also benefit from morphological instruction (e.g., Carlo, August, Snow, Lively, & White, 2004).

The studies reviewed here were not teaching studies; therefore, they provide a rationale for the idea that teaching children about morphology *should* help them in all these domains, but they do not demonstrate the benefits of morphological instruction. Later in this chapter we look at some teaching studies and the benefits of morphological instruction for children.

What Do We Teach When We Teach Children about Morphology?

Teaching studies in the literature have aimed at different forms of knowledge of morphemes in the context of literacy. Some studies have highly specific aims: For example, Wysocki and Jenkins (1987) aimed at teaching children specific base forms and affixes, so that they could use this specific knowledge to infer the meanings of new words in which the same stems and affixes appeared. They found that children can indeed infer the meanings of new words by using their knowledge of stems and affixes.

Fayol, Thenevin, Jarousse, and Totereau (1999) carried out a specific study of discrimination of plural marks in French, a language in which plurals often are not marked in spoken language but are marked in writing. French plural nouns are marked by s at the end and verbs in the third person plural are marked by *nt*, but these endings are not pronounced in speech. Fayol and colleagues found that children can learn from instruction in how to use the appropriate spellings for the plural and also improve their reading comprehension of sentences that require interpreting the plural marks.

Bryant et al. (2006) investigated different ways of teaching children about the distinction between the suffixes *ion* and *ian*. They found that children can learn how to spell words not specifically included in the training, and correctly spell them with *ion* or *ian* by using their knowledge of morphology.

These basic studies demonstrate that it is possible to teach children to use their knowledge of morphology for other purposes—to infer the meaning of words, to understand written sentences, and to spell.

Other studies have the aim of helping children become aware of morphemes in a more general way and use this knowledge to read and spell words, and to infer the meanings of new words (e.g., Lyster, 2002; Nunes & Bryant, 2006; Nunes et al., 2003). This much broader aim is in line with the view that children can learn about a morphological principle and use it in reading and spelling, in the same way that they learn an alphabetic principle. This type of intervention is the focus of the next section.

Previous research shows that at the time children start to learn to read, most (if not all) have some knowledge of morphology. Thus, any teaching they receive should take into account what they already know and what further learning teachers want to promote.

Young children's knowledge of morphology has been investigated for more than 50 years. Jean Berko (1958), a pioneer in this domain of investigation, suggested that as children learn their first language, they encounter words that are related morphologically, and they make connections between the forms and meanings of these words. For example, they hear *dog* and *dogs*, and know that *dogs* has as /z/ sound at the end, and that this ending indicates more than one dog. She hypothesized that they infer rules about how differences between the forms of the words are related to their meanings, even if these rules are known only implicitly. She used an ingenious method to test this idea. She showed children drawings of bird-like creatures that were not actual birds and said to them: "Here is a wug." *Wug* is a pseudoword, so the children were experiencing an entirely new verbal form. If they could make the plural of this verbal form correctly, then the achievement could not be explained by a specific memory: The verbal form was a pseudoword that they would not have encountered. So she showed the children a picture with two "wugs" and said to the children: "Here comes another wug. Now there are two of them; there are two ... " She encouraged the children to complete the sentence. If the children were able to complete the sentence with the form "wugs," then they would have demonstrated that they knew something about what happens to the meaning of a noun when you add an *s* at the end.

The children she assessed were either in kindergarten, ages 4–5 years, or in first grade, ages about 6–7 years. Both groups of children were competent in forming the plural of some words but not others. If all they needed to do was add an /s/ or a /z/ sound to the pseudoword, they were right most of the time: Kindergarten children were correct about 80% of the time, and first graders about 90%.

However, when the stem itself ended in an /s/ or a /z/ sound, the children had much more difficulty: The plural of *nizz*, which should be *nizzes*, turned out to be very difficult: Only 14% of answers by kindergarteners and 33% of the answers by first graders were correct. So children do not learn about morphology in an all-or-nothing fashion. The fact that they could correctly make the plural of *wug*, but not of *nizz*, suggests that they learn the basic rules first and gradually refine their knowledge of plural forms over time. Incidentally, this is in a way similar to the use of different units in reading: Children seem to learn simple letter–sound correspondences first and refine this knowledge by learning to use other units over time.

The sort of the knowledge that was demanded in this type of task is called "implicit knowledge": The children are using knowledge of morphemes to speak or to understand language. But children can be asked to use their knowledge of morphemes to do something other than speak; they can be asked to identify morphemes explicitly; count the morphemes in a word; subtract a morpheme to see what is left; or explain how they know, for example, that the plural of "wug" is "wugs." These tasks demand awareness of morphemes. Tasks that require children to be aware of morphemes are more difficult than those that can be solved without awareness, using only implicit knowledge.

Berko's work provides an example of this difference. She presented the children with 14 compound words, such as *fireplace*, *football*, *newspaper*, and *birthday*, and asked them to define each word. The words are quite common and were probably known to the children. Her aim was to see whether the children could use their knowledge of morphemes to explain what these compound words mean— for example, by saying that football is a ballgame that you play with your feet or newspaper is paper on which news stories are written. She classified the children's answers into different categories: The category of interest here is the one that she called "etymological explanations," which consisted of using morphemes in the compound words to explain their meanings. This was not an easy task, and only 13% of all the responses were classified as etymological. *Birthday* was only defined as "a day" by 2% of the children, and none appeared to have said anything about a connection to one's birth; children's answers relied on associations with getting presents and eating cake. *Fireplace* was the word that elicited the largest number of responses using the elements of the compound in the definition: 72% of the answers indicated that people put fire in a fireplace, but Berko remarks that this may have been due more to the fact that fire is a salient feature in a fireplace than to an etymological analysis of the word.

There are many differences between the two tasks employed by Berko that we described here, but one of these is salient: In the task where the children had to inflect words to make plurals or other verb tenses, they could use implicit knowledge, whereas in the definition task, they had to make their knowledge explicit enough to explain it verbally. Even though the implicit knowledge task involved pseudowords with which the children were not familiar, it resulted in a higher level of success than the explicit knowledge task, which used only words that were very familiar to the children.

Several subsequent studies carried out in English and also in French have confirmed that when children first start on the road to literacy, their awareness of morphemes is limited, and many do not make a link between their implicit knowledge of morphemes and the way words are written (e.g., Kemp & Bryant, 2003; Notenboom & Reitsma, 2007; Walker & Hauerwas, 2006). Their awareness of morphemes is a stronger predictor of their use of morphemes in spelling than their implicit knowledge of morphemes (Nunes, Bryant, & Bindmand, 1997). These findings have a clear implication for teaching: When we teach children about morphemes, we should try to improve their awareness or explicit knowledge of morphemes.

In summary, children's implicit knowledge of morphemes develops from an early age, but their awareness of morphemes is still limited when they start learning to read. In the same way that they need to become aware of the sounds of their language to understand the alphabetic principle, children need to become aware of morphemes to understand the morphemic principle. So teaching programs should aim at promoting children's awareness or explicit knowledge of morphemes, which can then be used in word reading and spelling.

How Can We Teach Children about Morphemes So That They Can Use This Knowledge in Word Reading?

Different researchers (e.g., Arnbak & Elbro, 2000; Berninger et al., 2003; Lyster, 2002; Nagy et al., 2002; Nunes et al., 2003; Nunes & Bryant, 2006; Nunes, Bryant, Pretzlik, & Hurry, 2011) have designed morphological interventions, with the aim of promoting children's awareness and use of morphemes in word reading and spelling. Several common features in these interventions provide the basis for describing how we can help children to improve their awareness and use of morphemes in word reading and spelling. These features are included in the interventions because research, sometimes in other domains of learning, shows that such principles work well. We summarize these below and refer to research that suggests that the form of teaching adopted in these studies is more effective than others (for further discussion, see Nunes & Bryant, 2006).

• Children should have experiences with both inflectional and derivational morphemes. Many programs give the children experiences with inflectional morphemes first, because past research has shown that children succeed more in tasks about inflectional morphemes than in those about derivational morphemes (e.g., Berko, 1958; Nunes et al., 1996).

• Children should be actively making decisions during the process of instruction rather than simply repeating the same answers. For example, instead of being asked to add *ian* to words to make agents, they should be deciding how to spell words such as *magician* and *confession*, which end in the same sound but are spelled differently for morphological reasons. Our research that supports this principle was not carried out with morphemes but with the orthographic units *k* and *ck* at the end of words (Nunes & Bryant, 2009). The distinction between words that end in *k* or *ck* is based on neither phonology nor morphology: those that end in *ck* just have one vowel in the coda before the /k/ sound (e.g., *brick*, *lock*, *back*), and those than end in *k* have more than one letter in the coda between the vowel and the /k/ ending (e.g., *risk*, *book*, *task*, *pink*). We taught two groups of children to distinguish these spellings. One group practiced the spelling of each type of word separately; they did not have to make decisions about the spelling, because during each block of trials they always used the same spelling. The second group practiced exactly the same words, but the words were mixed within the blocks of trials, so they always needed to make a decision about which spelling to use. Our two groups had the same amount of practice with the same words and pseudowords. Both taught groups made more progress than an untaught control group from pre- to posttests and differed from the control group at an immediate posttest, given right after they finished the training. However, only the second group, which had to decide which spelling to use during the training, still differed from the control group 8 weeks later. So the children in this group were able to retain what they had learned better than the group that just used the same spelling in each block of trials and did not have to make any decisions. We noticed that during the training, children who used the same spelling over and over, without having to make any decisions, felt that they had already learned what we were teaching them and would rather stop practicing before they reached the end. In contrast, the group that had to make decisions made more mistakes during training and continued to try to learn throughout the practice trials. We extended the use of this principle about children having to be actively making decisions from the study of orthographic patterns to our training program about morphemes.

• Instruction should contain an element of explicitness about morphemes. In our study about learning the distinction between *ian* and *ion* (Nunes & Bryant, 2006), we compared the learning progress and retention of three groups of children that had the same amount of practice on the same tasks, using the same words. One group was asked to answer the questions and given feedback; group members were asked at the end of the tasks whether they could explain how they decided to use *ian* or *ion* at the end of words. The second group started out pretty much like the first one, but halfway through the task they were asked whether they could explain how to choose *ian* or *ion* to complete the word. They were then told explicitly that *ian* is a suffix that forms person words and *ion* forms other types of words (e.g., words about events, feelings). Finally, the third group was told the difference between *ian* and *ion* words from the start. When these groups were compared to a control group, it became quite clear that the two groups that received some explicit instruction learned more and retained their learning until 8 weeks later, after the teaching had ended; the group that only received implicit instruction did better than the control group in an immediate posttest, just after the training finished, but not 8 weeks after the training had ended. Other studies (e.g., Fantino, Jaworski, Case, & Stolarz-Fantino, 2003) have also found that explicit instruction on rules facilitates later learning in problem-solving situations when other rules have to be used to solve problems.

• There should be variation in the procedures and cognitive demands of the activities that children carry out during the training. For example, they might be asked to subtract affixes (e.g., "What word is left if you take the *less* out of *fearless*?"), add affixes (e.g., "How can you change the word *lucky* to make it mean the opposite?"), count morphemes in multimorphemic words (e.g., "How many parts are there in the word *unimaginable*?"), generate different words with the same stem, or say whether two words that share a phonological segment are related (see the word relatedness task designed by Carlisle [1988], referred to earlier on). Studies about children's problem solving (e.g., Chen, 1999) have shown that primary school children are better at forming a scheme for solving a problem if they are engaged with more different procedures than just one during learning trials.

• Activities should help the children make connections between morphemes and meaning, and between morphemes and the way words are spelled. When activities such as counting morphemes are used, children should be aware that the units that they are looking for have a meaning function in the structure of the word. This should help the children differentiate a search for morphemes from a search for phonological units, such as syllables or rimes. Our own work shows that in order to use morphemes in spelling, children (Nunes et al., 2003; Nunes et al., 2011) as well as teachers (Hurry et al., 2005) must make a connection between the letter strings that represent the morphemes and the meaning function that they have. If this connection with meaning is not made, the letter strings are perceived as patterns that appear in spelling but are not predictable.

• Many researchers have attempted to make the activities in which the children engage similar to games. This game format is likely to help maintain children's interest and motivation. There is evidence from previous research (e.g., Parker & Lepper, 1992) that children have stronger intrinsic motivation and learn better in the context of games than when they are presented with the same materials in an abstract teaching context.

These principles were common across many training studies, even though not all researchers listed them explicitly. The principles seem sensible and are supported by research, but it must be acknowledged that only some of them have been tested specifically in the context of research on how to teach children about morphology; others have been tested in different contexts. Together, the principles make for a sound design of how to teach children about morphemes to improve their literacy skills.

We used all these principles in designing our own program for teaching children about morphology (Nunes & Bryant, 2006), which can be downloaded from *www.education.ox.ac.uk/research/child-learningresources*. The program is not limited to games that focus on morphology: we found it necessary to start the program by providing for the children some explicit knowledge of grammar, because many of the activities and the discussions in which we expected children to engage would require at least a basic understanding of word classes. For example, when we ask children to change nouns into verbs, they need to have a basic understanding of nouns and verbs. English language presents challenges to a teacher who wants to explain verbs and nouns to children for two reasons. First, the same word (i.e., the same sequence of sounds) can often be a noun and a verb: for example, in the sentences *I bought a book* and *I will book the seats for the theater*, *book* changes grammatical categories. Second, some definitions that are used for nouns and verbs in primary school seem to confuse children: in our pilot studies of the intervention, we found that children could not agree on the classification of the word *fight* in the sentence *My friend and my brother had a fight*. The children had been taught that verbs are action words, and some argued that "a fight" is full of action, so it must be a verb.

We decided to capitalize on children's intuitions about grammar, which appear in judgments of grammaticality, and develop their grammatical awareness by asking them to discuss and explain whether some sentences were right or wrong. There is some doubt regarding preschool children's ability to discriminate grammatically correct sentences from verbal strings that are grammatically incorrect and not proper sentences in the language (Bialystock, 1986; Gombert, 1992), but there is clear evidence that primary school children are able to make judgments of grammaticality (Papandropoulou & Sinclair, 1974), and that their performance in such tasks is related to their ability to use sentence context in word reading (e.g., Bowey, 1986; Rego & Bryant, 1993; Stanovich & West, 1983; Tunmer, Nesdale, & Wright, 1987).

The ability to make grammaticality judgments can be based on implicit knowledge: The child might compare the sentence heard in the task with one that he or she would say without explicit knowledge of why the sentences in the task are right or wrong. This is not the same as the ability to explain the basis of the judgment. Hakes (1980), for example, presented children with grammatically correct and incorrect sentences, such as "The string chased the kitten," in which the object and the subject are in the wrong positions. Nearly all the participants between ages 5 and 6 years were able to distinguish grammatically correct and incorrect sentences, but only a minority of children between 7 and 9 years of age could use grammatical justifications to explain why the sentences were incorrect.

In our training, we set out to use children's implicit knowledge to develop their awareness of grammar. We proposed to draw on the children's intuitions by asking them to make grammaticality judgments, and to promote their awareness of grammar by having them justify and discuss their arguments. Their intuitions about grammar were made more explicit during their discussions about morphology.

Table 5.3 presents the aims of the program and illustrates how they were pursued with some of the activities designed for each of the aims.

How Do We Assess the Benefits of Teaching?

We have suggested that children can benefit in many ways from morphological instruction, so different assessments should be used depending on the aims of the program. In the case of word reading, which is the focus of this chapter, we have opted for two approaches: use of traditional standardized tests that provide a reading age and also a factor score obtained from an analysis of the three subtests described earlier, plus a standardized reading test.

The measurement of children's word reading has developed over a long period of time, and standardized tests in common use today were not inspired by contemporary views of how children's word reading develops. The Schonell Word Reading Test (Schonell & Schonell, 1950), which we have found to be a useful and reliable instrument, starts with words that occur frequently and are short (e.g., *tree, little, milk, red, book*), and those that appear later in the test are longer and less common (e.g., *island, soloist, somnambulist, procrastination*). The testing is interrupted when the children make 10 consecutive errors. Thus, many younger children do not reach the longer and less frequently used words. This test design is based on the idea that both word frequency and word length affect word reading, an assumption that is supported by research. We use a standardized reading test to evaluate our interventions, because this gives us an assessment designed quite independently of our theories and methods.

However, we know that this measure can be improved. Our own three subtests provide information on other aspects of children's word reading ability, namely the extent to which they use different types of units in reading. In order to combine the scores of different tests, it is not possible just to add their scores: A simple addition would bias the measure by giving more importance to the test that has a larger number of items. Thus, it is necessary to use a statistical procedure called factor analysis, which produces a score for each child based on the four tests and weights the tests by their relative importance in measuring word reading. We ran a factor analysis with the Schonell Word Reading Test and our three subtests together, which showed that there is a single ability underlying these four different tests; all four tests had a factor loading greater than .9. Because the highest value that factor loadings can have is 1, this means that all four tests were very well connected to the children's word reading ability. This combination of different approaches to measuring word reading gives us a more powerful measure of children's word reading ability.

We realize that this procedure cannot be easily applied outside the academic community, and that teachers may decide simply to use a standardized word reading test. Yet the procedure is quite simple, with the support of the right computer software (we use SPSS, Statistical Package for the Social Sciences), and is recom-

TABLE 5.3. Aims of the Teaching Program and Examples of Activities Used to Pursue Each Aim

Aims	Examples of activities
To develop awareness of sentence structure and word order	*Grammaticality judgments.* Sentence frames were presented with a missing word; the children made grammaticality judgments if the gaps were to be filled with given words. [*We saw a* _____ *in the town center.* Words to be used to fill the gap: *car, computer, sing.*] The children were also asked to provide words that fit into the sentence. They presented justifications for their answers orally and discussed the alternatives. Some grammatically correct answers that were provided led the children to discuss the difference between grammar and semantics (e.g., *I saw a cow in the town center* provoked comments that the sentence was correct but unlikely to be true).
To promote awareness of inflections	*Grammaticality judgments.* Sentence frames were presented with a missing word; among the choices for the children were words that did not match the sentence in number agreement. [*There are many* _____ *in London.* Words to be used to fill the gap: *doctors, bus, new.*]
To promote awareness of grammatical word class	The children were shown pictures with corresponding words and asked to find other words of the same type. They then discussed the words each child had produced. *Using different suffixes to form words of a specific class.* The children were asked to choose suffixes to form words of the same class and later asked what sort of words these are.
To promote awareness of word structure with free morphemes	The children were presented with two words (e.g., *pea–nut*) and asked what word they form together. They were asked to explain whether they could see how the two words related to the meaning of the compound. Sometimes this was actually not possible (e.g., *butterfly*) but most of the time the connection could be found.
To promote awareness of grammatical and semantic word class using the same stem in base and derived form; also to promote awareness of suffixes and prefixes	*Name the person.* The children were presented with two suffixes (*er* and *ist*) and asked to name the person. [*A person who cleans is a* _____.] Games with abstract words involved deciding whether the suffix to be added is *-ion* or *-ness*. *Make a verb.* The children made verbs by adding *en* at the end (*strength + en*) or at the beginning (*en + large*) of words. *Distinguishing* ian *and* ion *spellings.* The children were shown how to choose the spelling for the right type of word.
To promote awareness of prefixes	*Choose the beginning of the word.* The children had base forms to which they should add *dis, un, in,* or *im* (we provided both variations here). At the end of the activity, they were asked how the addition of these prefixes changed the meaning of the words.
To learn to distinguish stems and affix boundaries	*Words that have an /s/ sound at the end compared with words where the /s/ sound (or es) marks the plural.* The children were taught the strategy of taking out the end of the words to see whether a proper word still remains (e.g., *carrots–bus*). These examples were followed by making person-words and then identifying stems in pseudowords that are about persons. *Counting morphemes in words.* The children were shown multimorphemic words and asked to count the morphemes.

(*continued*)

TABLE 5.3. (*continued*)

Aims	Examples of activities
To develop awareness of how knowledge of prefixes and suffixes helps infer the meaning of words	*Change the words by adding* ful *or* less. At the end, the children discussed how these suffixes change the meaning of words.
	Do it again or undo it. The children were asked to fill in the prefix depending on the meaning (e.g., *redo* vs. *undo*).
	Prefixes that tell us about number. The children looked for number cues in the words and pseudowords (e.g., compare *bicycle* and *tricycle*; "What does a *biheaded* monster look like?").
	Making words with the same stem and different affixes. The children were given a stem and several affixes and looked for combinations that were real words. They explained the meaning of words that others doubted were real words and checked the dictionary.
To look for patterns that relate to the choice of suffix	*Making person words from nouns and verbs.* At the end of the session, the children discussed whether there was a pattern in the choice of suffixes.

mended for the assessment of intervention programs. The risk of deciding that an intervention is not successful when it actually is successful can be reduced by putting in place good measures.

Who Can Benefit from Instruction about Morphology?

We consider here some studies that help to answer this question. We treat each successful study as an effective demonstration that benefits can be accrued by the children, without attempting to present a full overview of results available in the literature.

1. *Can young children benefit from teaching about morphology?* Lyster (2002) implemented a teaching program with a large number of kindergarten children ($N = 273$). Its aim was to develop children's phonological awareness (Group 1) and morphological awareness (Group 2) to see whether they would subsequently develop better literacy skills when they were taught how to read. The teaching lasted about 30 minutes per week for 17 weeks. These intervention groups were compared to a control group that only received extra exposure to print. The two intervention groups performed better than the control group when they were compared in a Word Reading and a Text Reading test on school entry and at the end of first grade. They also outperformed the control group in two other tasks, Word Identification (marking word boundaries in a text printed without word boundaries) and Orthographic Coding (a test that requires the children to identify real words in a list of homophones in which some spellings were not appropriate for real words; e.g., "droar" for *drawer*). This study was carried out in Norway, with children learning to read Norwegian, a phonologically regular language. For this

reason, it provides support for the idea that children can learn to use morphemes in word reading, even if they do not have to do so because they rely on effective phonological strategies.

We conclude that young children can benefit from morphological instruction even when this instruction is provided before they start to learn to read in school.

2. *Can children learn to use morphemes in reading at a later stage, after instruction about phonology?* Nunes et al. (2003) carried out a large-scale study ($N = 468$) in which they taught four groups and had one unseen control group. Two taught groups received teaching on phonology (with or without emphasis on spelling) and two received teaching on morphology (with or without emphasis on spelling). The children received about 40 minutes of teaching a week over 12 weeks, during the time when the children were expected to have literacy lessons; there was no extra teaching time. The children were in grades 3 and 4, and had received instruction with a predominant focus on phonology.

All the taught groups outperformed the control group in a standardized reading test. There were no overall differences between the groups in a standardized spelling test that did not use multimorphemic words. However, the difference approached statistical significance when the control group was compared to those groups for which there had been emphasis on spelling, irrespective of whether the teaching was about phonology or morphology. Only the groups that were taught about morphology outperformed the control group in a spelling test, in which they had to spell correctly suffixes such as *ion, ian, ed,* and *ness* at the end of words. Finally, whereas the taught groups did not differ from the control group in reading words that involve the use of morphemes (e.g., those in subtest 3, presented earlier) both morphology groups and the phonology group that worked with emphasis on spelling outperformed the control group in reading pseudo-words that involve the use of morphemes.

In conclusion, morphological instruction can benefit children's word reading if introduced in their third or fourth year of literacy instruction. It also provides them with effective word analysis strategies for reading entirely new words, as demonstrated in their ability to read pseudowords that required recognizing morphological boundaries.

3. *Can high and low achievers benefit from morphological instruction?* Birgis-dottir et al. (2006) and Nunes, Bryant, Pretzlik, et al. (2006) assessed the effects of morphological training on children's spelling and vocabulary. Their measures did not include word reading. They were able to separate out the analysis for children whose results at pretest were up to the median from the analysis for children who at pretest performed above the median. They compared the children's result with two programs: morphological teaching with or without emphasis on spelling.

On the spelling assessment, the children who had been in the lower group at pretest performed statistically better than the controls, irrespective of whether there had been an emphasis on spelling or not, but the higher performing group members differed significantly from the control only if they had participated in a program with an emphasis on spelling.

In one of the measures of vocabulary, there was a statistically significant difference between the children in the lower performing group who received morphological instruction and the control group, but the difference was not significant for those in the higher performing group. In the measure of pseudoword definition, both the lower and higher performing groups showed a statistically significant difference compared to the control group.

In conclusion, it is possible that high-performing children develop their awareness of morphology to a large extent without the need for instruction but still show some benefits from teaching, particularly when the teaching focuses on spelling and morphemes at the same time. In contrast, children in lower attainment groups seem to be less likely to learn about morphemes on their own and benefit significantly from instruction.

4. *Can poor readers improve their word reading through morphological teaching?* Nunes et al. (2011) carried out an intervention study with a sample of children selected for a discrepancy between their chronological age and their reading and spelling age. The children (N = 59) were in grades 4 or 5; their mean chronological age at pretest was about 121 months; their mean reading age was approximately 93 months, and their mean spelling age was 91 months; thus, they were more than 2 years behind in their reading and spelling. All the children's verbal and general IQ scores were in the normal range.

The children were randomly assigned to a control, a phonological intervention, or a morphological intervention group. They received approximately 20 sessions of individual tuition (five children did not complete the 20 sessions) of about 45 minutes each, during a time that was timetabled for literacy instruction in their classroom. So they had no extra time on literacy instruction. The children had not received a diagnosis of dyslexia and were not receiving additional remedial instruction during this period.

The instruction followed the same general pattern as the one described earlier. However, we conducted this study before our computer-based resources were developed, and teaching did not involve computer presentations: We used paper and pencil, as well as pictures, during the teaching sessions.

The interval between the pre- and the posttest was about 7 months. The mean increase in reading age (assessed by the Wechsler Objective Reading Dimensions [WORD] Reading Test) in the control group was 6.86 months, which is roughly equivalent to the time elapsed between pre- and posttest. The mean increase in reading age in the phonological intervention group was 13.09 months, and in the morphological treatment group was 11.70 months. We used a statistical analysis to test for the significance of these differences, controlling for the children's verbal intelligence and their performance on the WORD Reading Test at pretest. This analysis showed that the children in the phonological intervention performed significantly better at posttest than those in the control group; the results for the children in the morphological intervention group were not statistically significant, but they did show a trend ($p = .058$). Similar results were observed when we used the measure of word reading that combined our three subtests with the standardized word reading test: The phonological intervention group's gains were significantly greater than the gains obtained by the control group, but the morphological intervention group did not differ from the control group statistically.

Arnbak and Elbro (2000) have also studied the effects of morphological interventions for poor readers in grades 4 and 5. The participants in their study were older (mean age 11 years). They had been diagnosed as dyslexic, had received remedial instruction, and were still receiving it during the study. The teaching program included 36 individual lessons of about 15 minutes three times a week. The taught group showed statistically significantly better performance than the control group in measures of awareness of morphology but not in a measure of reading morphologically complex words. However, the taught group showed significantly better performance than the control group in the posttests of reading comprehension and spelling morphologically complex words.

In summary, the results of studies with poor readers seem to vary. In our study, the poor readers' gains approached statistical significance in comparison to controls in a standardized word reading test, but not in a more comprehensive measure of word reading. In the Arnbak and Elbro (2000) study, there were statistically significant gains in reading comprehension and spelling. In neither study were there marked gains in reading morphologically complex words in comparison to the control group. Our study also included a group taught to use larger phonological units than letter–sound correspondences, and this group outperformed the control group in both measures of word reading; thus, the study shows that poor readers at these age levels can benefit from special tutoring delivered within the same time constraints and using similar delivery format. Our tentative conclusion is that it is possible that morphological intervention for poor readers should be associated with phonological intervention. This was the case in the Arnbak and Elbro study, in which morphological teaching was effective in promoting reading comprehension, even though the control group was also receiving remedial instruction.

General Conclusions

There is overwhelming evidence now that morphemes are units used in word reading by children. They are used more consistently as children improve their reading skills. There is also clear evidence that children benefit from instruction that raises their awareness of morphemes in their language, and from teaching about how to use morphemes in reading and spelling. Younger children in kindergarten and older children up to fifth grade have participated in studies that show that they make clear progress in reading, spelling, and vocabulary when they are taught about morphemes. Students who start out weak, as well as those who are at the top half of the class, benefit from such instruction.

There is, however, one group of children for whom the benefits are not as clearly documented: children who have fallen considerably behind in reading and spelling by the time they reach grade 4 or 5. The reasons for the lower levels of success with poor readers are not clear. It is possible that they require both phonological and morphological teaching to make progress, because they have already fallen behind in their use of phonological units in reading. It is also possible that earlier interventions would be more successful, but one must not forget that in our study a phonological intervention did succeed with the poor readers. Finally, it is also possible that poor readers form a diverse group in which some make progress and others do not. This possibility can only be evaluated in studies using larger samples, and these so far are not available in the literature.

References

Arnbak, E., & Elbro, C. (2000). The effects of morphological awareness training on the reading and spelling skills of young dyslexics. *Scandinavian Journal of Educational Research*, *44*, 229–251.

Baumann, J. F., Edwards, E. C., Boland, E. M., Olejnik, S., & Kame'enui, E. J. (2003). Vocabulary tricks: Effects of instruction in morphology and context on fifth-grade students' ability to derive and infer word meanings. *American Educational Research Journal*, *40*, 447–494.

Berko, J. (1958). The child's learning of English morphology. *Word*, *14*, 150–177.

Berninger, V. W., Vermeulen, K., Abbott, R. D., McCutchen, D., Cotton, S., Cude, J., et al. (2003). Comparison of three approaches to supplementary reading instruction for low-achieving second-grade readers. *Language, Speech, and Hearing Services in Schools*, *34* 101–116.

Bialystock, E. (1986). Factors in the growth of linguistic awareness. *Child Development*, *57*, 498–510.

Birgisdottir, F., Nunes, T., Pretzlik, U., Burman, D., Gardner, S., & Bell, D. (2006). An intervention programme for teaching children about morphemes in the classroom. In T. Nunes & P. Bryant (Eds.), *Improving literacy by teaching morphemes* (pp. 104–120). London: Routledge.

Bowey, J. (1986). Syntactic awareness in relation to reading skill and ongoing comprehension monitoring. *Journal of Experimental Child Psychology*, *41*, 282–299.

Bryant, P., Nunes, T., Pretzlik, U., Bell, D., Evans, D., & Olsson, J. (2006). From the laboratory to the classroom. In T. Nunes & P. Bryant (Eds.), *Improving literacy by teaching morphemes* (pp. 65–103). London: Routledge.

Carlisle, J. (1988). Knowledge of derivational morphology and spelling ability in fourth, sixth and eighth graders. *Applied Psycholinguistics*, *9*, 247–266.

Carlisle, J. F., & Stone, C. A. (2005). Exploring the role of morphemes in word reading. *Reading Research Quarterly*, *40*, 428–449.

Carlo, M. S., August, D., Snow, C. E., Lively, T. J., & White, C. E. (2004). Closing the gap: Addressing the vocabulary needs of English-language learners in bilingual and mainstream classrooms. *Reading Research Quarterly*, *39*, 188–215.

Chen, Z. (1999). Schema induction in children's analogical problem solving. *Journal of Educational Psychology, 91*(4), 703–715.

Collins English Dictionary. (1991). (3rd ed.). Glasgow: HarperCollins.

Deacon, S. H., Wade-Woolley, L., & Kirby, J. (2007). Crossover: The role of morphological awareness in French immersion children's reading. *Developmental Psychology, 43,* 732–746.

Fantino, E., Jaworski, B. A., Case, D. A., & Stolarz-Fantino, S. (2003). Rules and problem solving: Another look. *American Journal of Psychology, 116*(4), 613–632.

Fayol, M., Thenevin, M.-G., Jarousse, J.-P., & Totereau, C. (1999). From learning to teaching to learn French written morphology. In T. Nunes (Ed.), *Learning to read: An integrated view from research and practice* (pp. 43–64). Dordrecht, The Netherlands: Kluwer.

Gombert, J. E. (1992). *Metalinguistic development.* Hemel Hempstead: Harvester Wheatsheaf.

Hakes, D. T. (1980). *The development of metalinguistic abilities in children.* Berlin: Springer-Verlag.

Hurry, J., Nunes, T., Bryant, P., Pretzlik, U., Parker, M., Curno, T., et al. (2005). Transforming research on morphology into teacher practice. *Research Papers in Education, 20*(2), 187–206.

Kemp, N., & Bryant, P. (2003). Do beez buzz?: Rule-based and frequency-based knowledge in learning to spell plural -*s. Child Development, 74,* 63–74.

Leong, C. K. (1989). The effects of morphological structure on reading proficiency—a developmental study. *Reading and Writing: An Interdisciplinary Journal, 1,* 357—379.

Leong, C. K. (1991). Modelling reading as a cognitive and linguistic skill. In R. F. Mulcahy, R. H. Short, & J. Andrews (Eds.), *Enhancing learning and thinking* (pp. 161–173). New York: Praeger.

Leong, C. K. (1992). Cognitive componential modelling of reading in ten- to twelve-year-old readers. *Reading and Writing: An Interdisciplinary Journal, 4,* 327—364.

Lyster, S. H. (2002). The effects of morphological versus phonological awareness training in kindergarten on reading development. *Reading and Writing, 15,* 261–294.

Mahony, D. L. (1994). Using sensitivity to word structure to explain variance in high school and college level reading ability. *Reading and Writing: An Interdisciplinary Journal, 6,* 19–44.

Mahony, D., Singson, M., & Mann, V. (2000). Reading ability and sensitivity to morphological relations. *Reading and Writing, 12,* 191–218.

Nagy, W. E., & Anderson, R. C. (1984). How many words are there in printed school English? *Reading Research Quarterly, 19,* 304–330.

Nagy, W. E., Berninger, V. W., & Abbott, R. D. (2006). Contribution of morphology beyond phonology to literacy outcomes of upper elementary and middle-school students. *Journal of Educational Psychology, 98,* 134–147.

Nagy, W. E., Kuo-Kealoha, A., Wu, X., Li, W., Anderson, R. C., & Chen, X. (2002). The role of morphological awareness in learning to read Chinese. In W. Li, J. S. Gaffney, & J. L. Packard (Eds.), *Chinese language acquisition: Theoretical and pedagogical issues* (pp. 59–86). Norwell, MA: Kluwer Academic.

Notenboom, A., & Reitsma, P. (2007). Spelling Dutch doublets: Children's learning of a phonological and morphological spelling rule. *Scientific Studies of Reading, 11,* 133–150.

Nunes, T., & Bryant, P. (Eds.). (2006). *Improving literacy by teaching morphemes.* London: Routledge.

Nunes, T., & Bryant, P. (2009). *Children's reading and spelling. Beyond the first steps.* Oxford, UK: Wiley/Blackwell.

Nunes, T., Bryant, P., & Bindman, M. (1996). Morphological spelling strategies: Developmental stages and processes. *Developmental Psychology, 33,* 637–649.

Nunes, T., Bryant, P., & Bindman, M. (2006). The effects of learning to spell on children's awareness of morphology. *Reading and Writing, 19,* 767–787.

Nunes, T., Bryant, P., & Olsson, J. (2003). Learning morphological and phonological spelling rules: An intervention study. *Scientific Studies of Reading, 7,* 289–307.

Nunes, T., Bryant, P., Pretzlik, U., Burman, D., Bell, D., & Gardner, S. (2006). An intervention programme for classroom teaching about morphemes. In T. Nunes & P. Bryant (Eds.), *Improving literacy by teaching morphemes* (pp. 121–133). London: Routledge.

Nunes, T., Bryant, P., Pretzlik, U., & Hurry, J. (2011). *The effect of phonological and morphological interventions on poor readers' word reading and spelling.* Manuscript under review.

Papandropoulou, I., & Sinclair, H. (1974). What is a word?: Experimental study of children's ideas on grammar. *Human Development, 17,* 250–256.

Parker, L. E., & Lepper, M. R. (1992). The effects of fantasy contexts on children's learning and motivation: Making learning more fun. *Journal of Personality and Social Psychology, 62,* 625–633.

Rego, L. L. B., & Bryant, P. E. (1993). The connection between phonological, syntactic and semantic skills and children's reading and spelling. *European Journal of Psychology of Education, 8,* 235–246.

Schonell, F. J., & Schonell, F. E. (1950). *Diagnostic and attainment testing: Including a manual of tests, their nature, use, recording, and interpretation.* Edinburgh: Oliver & Boyd.

Singson, M., Mahony, D., & Mann, V. (2000). The relation between reading ability and morphological skills: Evidence from derivational suffixes. *Reading and Writing: An Interdisciplinary Journal, 12,* 219–252.

Stanovich, K., & West, R. (1983). On priming by a sentence context. *Journal of Experimental Psychology: General, 112,* 1–36.

Tunmer, W. E., Nesdale, A. R., & Wright, A. D. (1987). Syntactic awareness and reading acquisition. *British Journal of Developmental Psychology, 5,* 25–34.

Walker, J., & Hauerwas, L. B. (2006). Development of phonological, morphological, and orthographic knowledge in young spellers: The case of inflected verbs. *Reading and Writing: An Interdisciplinary Journal, 19,* 819–843.

Wechsler Objective Reading Dimensions (WORD) Reading Test. (1993). London: The Psychological Corporation.

Wysocki, K., & Jenkins, J. R. (1987). Deriving word meanings through morphological generalization. *Reading Research Quarterly, 22,* 66–81.

6

Teaching Spelling to Students with Learning Difficulties

Michael M. Gerber
Catherine Richards-Tutor

Students with learning disabilities often struggle not only in learning to read but also in learning to spell, and in many cases spelling is more difficult for them. Like reading, spelling is a *cultural* artifact and, unlike oral language, neither is a direct product of evolution. We used our evolved oral language abilities to create a system for representing spoken language in graphic form. Most children develop whatever oral language is used in their respective cultures naturally, but they must be taught to read and, if their culture uses an alphabet, to spell. When writing systems, like English, are inconsistent in how the alphabet is used to represent the spoken language, spelling can be difficult even for children without reading problems.

It is not surprising that observation and comment on "good" spelling instruction are as old as public education itself (e.g., see Almack & Staffelbach, 1934; Horn, 1919; Lull, 1917; Tidyman, 1919; Sudweeks, 1927). Many of these early recommendations seem reasonable and have been deeply ingrained in practice. Unfortunately, the perceived value of spelling in the school curriculum has receded over the years, and there has been far less research on spelling instruction than on teaching reading or other aspects of writing, especially for students with learning difficulties.

We cannot correct this deficiency in this short chapter, but our aim is to provide teachers and other practitioners with some background about spelling, why

113

it is so difficult for students, and what kinds of progress monitoring and interventions might be adapted to classroom use. We highlight particularly those that conform with contemporary ideas about a multi-tiered, response-to-intervention (RTI) strategy for addressing learning problems.

A Quick History of English Spelling

There are complex reasons why letters and speech sounds lack reliable correspondence in American English spelling, and why alternative and implausible spellings have been historically preserved. The general reasons for spelling variations of sounds in English are rooted in historical events lost in the mist of time. Written English in Britain, the parent language of American English, used the Roman alphabet to represent Anglo-Saxon words. The problem with this approach was use of an alphabet representing the spoken sounds of one language (Latin) to represent the sounds of an entirely different language. So already there was a problem that scribes had to solve: How could these additional sounds be represented? Choices were made writer by writer, not dissimilar to the choices that children puzzle over until they learn (remember) conventional spellings. To make the problem worse, there are also spoken language variations in cultures—dialects—that influence spelling choices.

Every spoken language evolves over time, sometimes abruptly and dramatically, and at other times creating pronunciation shifts while spelling is left unchanged. For example, the Norman Conquest brought domination of French in official writing, but rulers eventually yielded to the language of their subjects: English. Gradually, with the advent of political and cultural reconciliation, translation of government and church documents (1200s), the influence of universities (1300s), and the growth of printing (1400s), the cumulative effects of choices about spelling became more stable in everyday writing.

But even in the late 16th century, English orthography showed much of the seeming arbitrariness and compromise that had already occurred historically. The following is a short excerpt from a letter sent by Elizabeth I, Queen of England, in her own handwriting to James VI, King of Scotland, around 1585. This is a political letter and not really about playing musical instruments. Rather, Elizabeth is playing on the dual meanings of the word *instrument* to make a point.

> "Tochinge an 'instrument,' as your secretarye terme it, that you desiar to haue me signe, I assure you, thogh I can play of some, and haue bine broght up to know musike. Yet this disscord wold be so grose as wer not fit for so wel-tuned musicke" (Bruce, 1849, p. 30).

When read by a modern, literate, English-speaking person, Elizabeth's unexpected spellings (e.g., tochinge/touching, secretarye/secretary, terme/term, desiar/desire, haue/have, signe/sign, thogh/though, bine/been, musike and musicke/

music, disscord/discord, wold/would, grose/gross, wer/were) are immediately noticeable. These are not spelling "errors," because a common agreement about spelling these particular words and spelling in general was just then emerging. Rule-governed spelling evolved as a consensus in how writers wrote and how adults taught children. Some decisions appealed to rules (conventions) that had been handed down, but other decisions merely created rules on the fly, based on the importance or influence of the writer.

In America, perhaps no single person had as much influence on contemporary American English spelling as Noah Webster. He published his first speller in 1783 (Micklethwait, 2000), revising it several times over the years, and these various versions were the most prevalent texts for teaching American children for over a century. As a scholar of language, Webster, of course, was guided by his knowledge of spellings proposed by many other authors from preceding dictionaries, particularly the *Dictionary of the English Language*, published by Samuel Johnson in England in 1755. But Webster had his own opinions about not only how individual words ought to be spelled (e.g., to make them more phonetic or more consistent with common usage) but also who should control language—scholars or the people who use it. Webster had strong patriotic, as well as scholarly, motives to make American English distinct, and millions of American schoolchildren were eventually taught spellings determined by Webster alone. Today, we have mostly forgotten why these various orthographic decisions were made.

Spelling Is a Solvable Puzzle

This apparent arbitrariness in spelling "rules" is the source of great frustration for many children (and some adults) of otherwise normal intelligence and motivation. One of this chapter's authors (Gerber & Hall, 1989) once conducted research with intermediate-grade students who had learning disabilities and were poor spellers. He asked them during an interview if they knew that some words sound the same but are spelled differently, such as *through* and *threw*. Most of the students had encountered this puzzle. He also asked if they knew that some words that sound different but are spelled the same, such as *read* and *read*. The students knew this to be true as well. Then he asked, "Why do you think this is so?" One student, with unwavering conviction, replied, "The teacher is trying to trick us." In the end, most children merely accept, without more than a puzzled protest, that teachers or dictionaries are the final authorities on how words should be spelled. Perhaps with somewhat greater protest, normally achieving students submit themselves to the arduous task of studying words and memorizing spellings that appear to make no sense because they are not spelled as they are pronounced.

Spelling difficulties across languages vary because of differences in the cognitive *transparency* of different alphabetic writing systems; that is, different cognitive effort is required by children to learn which speech sounds are intended by which letters, and what special conventions must be followed to spell words so that others will read them correctly. Spanish and Italian, for example, are considered to have highly *transparent* orthographies, because the relationship between alphabet letters and speech sounds is reliably the same from word to word. English and French, on the other hand, are *opaque* orthographies, because the relationship between speech sounds and alphabet is variable. American English, for example, has about 44 discrete phonemes, or spoken sounds, but only 26 letters available to represent those sounds. Obviously, some letters have to do double duty: There are over 500 ways to spell those 44 phonemes. As a result, many children experience difficulty learning to spell.

However, children generally vary in how much formal instruction they require to learn to spell. Just as there may be precocious readers, those who seem to figure out the code for representing letters of the alphabet with sounds, there are also children who early on figure out the conventions for spelling words in their language. Fortunately for teachers, most normally achieving students do most of the work themselves; that is, they take the instructional experiences that teachers provide and construct for themselves strategies to remember or reconstruct particular spellings. Also, although segmented phonemes do not entirely correspond reliably to spellings, English spelling is not as hopelessly irregular as often thought. Spelling rules often fail to capture the regularity in English spelling patterns.

For example, in 1966, Stanford University researchers programmed a computer with 200 rules for translating speech sounds to spellings (Hanna, Hanna, Hodges, & Rudorf, 1966). The program could spell 80% of phonemes correctly, but only about half of the 17,000 words on the Lorge–Thorndike list of the most common words in English (Simon & Simon, 1973). This result may seem somewhat discouraging, because it is unlikely that students learn or are taught 200 discrete rules, and we expect them to spell with very low error rates by the time they finish high school.

Simon and Simon (1973) pointed out that students have available a large amount of information about words other than the "rules" that tie letter choices to speech sounds. For example, reading practice builds memory for patterns of letter sequences of words that help children become better readers and spellers (Nathan & Stanovich, 1991). Until students build this knowledge of orthographic patterns through experience that allows them to recall difficult spellings of words reliably, initial instruction should help students to segment the intended word into its phonemes, then select appropriate letters to represent each phoneme in turn. Students, then, can regard their spelling attempt and apply other information they possess about the target or related words (e.g., pronunciation, sentence context).

Simon and Simon (1973) refer to this strategy as "generate and test"; that is, students first produce simple and direct representations of the phonemes they perceive—and perhaps alternate simple spellings, depending on how many "rules" they know. But then the word has become an object for reading, and another set of skills can be employed. They may, for example, recognize one of the spellings or feel more confident that one "looks right." This supplemental *testing* procedure may not guarantee a correct spelling, but it may improve on their first attempt and lead to further revisions. In fact, Read (1975) demonstrated that as early as preschool, before any formal instruction, children try to puzzle out how this system works. They want to write down the words they know, and with limited knowledge they make bold attempts to do so. These attempts are not so much "errors" as they are revealing demonstrations of active, creative problem-solving with limited tools (Steffler, Varnhagen, Friesen, & Treiman, 1998; Treiman & Bourassa, 2000). Older students, including older students with learning disabilities (Boder, 1973; Cassar, Treiman, Moats, Pollo, & Kessler, 2005; Gerber, 1984, 1985; Gerber & Hall, 1987; Siegel, Share, & Geva, 1995), continue to show this same inventiveness as they slowly trade simple assumptions for educated guesses.

For example, consider the following words: *closed*, *peeked*, and *united*. These words are pronounced, respectively, /klozd/, /pEkt/, and /UnItid/. Young students and students with learning disabilities using a simple strategy of selecting letters to represent each phoneme will almost certainly misspell one or more of these words, because the past-tense marker *-ed* is spelled the same but pronounced differently for each. In fact, to spell these words correctly, students have to ignore the final phonemes and recognize instead that each word is a past tense form of the root verb. If they do, they can apply a different kind of rule, one that specifies that past-tense for most verbs is spelled *-ed*.

We used these exact words in a study of fifth-grade students with learning disabilities (Gerber & Hall, 1989). One student demonstrated the benefit of the generate-and-test strategy when spelling the word *closed* in a clearly observable sequence of writing, inspecting, and self-correcting. The four examples below are all part of the same spelling attempt. Each line, however, shows what the attempt looked like after each reflective pause. The ^ indicates that the student sometimes squeezed letters between those he had already written (e.g., the *l* added to *kosd*). In his next-to-last attempt to repair the spelling, he crossed out *k* and wrote *c*.

```
k o s d
k l o s d
   ^
k̶ c l o s d
c l o s e d
         ^
```

If we had not been watching this process as it unfolded, we would have seen only the ultimately correct spelling, albeit with some obvious self-corrections. However, it was clear from observing this student that quite a bit of active problem solving was going on. There were clear pauses before each attempted self-correction. He could be seen looking intently at his spelling during these intervals, and each interval ended with a self-correction attempt. We thought it was noteworthy, too, that the final correction was to write the *e* before the *d*, an apparent recognition that the spelling convention for "past tense" was required, regardless of how the word sounded when pronounced.

From this one observation, we cannot predict that the student eventually will be a fluent speller. Good spellers are fluent when they write words rapidly and accurately. There seems to be no uncertainty, no delay, between thinking of the word they wish to write and producing it with a pencil or keyboard. Such fluency in performance is typical of successful learners in all areas of the curriculum, especially performance of basic or foundational skills such as word reading or simple arithmetic, and it represents an important qualitative change in thinking that students must undergo to retrieve or formulate correct responses; that is, students are not only accurate (as was our student with learning disabilities), but they also are fast and automatic (unlike our student). However, students with learning disabilities show a prolonged tendency to make errors, including different errors for the same word, and they appear not to possess sufficient knowledge or strategies to resolve their chronic uncertainty about how to spell intended words. As a consequence, they write slowly rather than fluently, which distracts them from their attempts to communicate ideas because of the inordinate amount of attention required in trying to spell correctly. Moreover, they display a persistent and high error rate in the writing they do produce (Graham, 1999).

Although we now have good evidence from brain imaging studies that students with learning disabilities across languages have similar difficulty processing word-level information efficiently, *regardless* of how transparent their orthography may be (e.g., see Paulesu et al., 2001). Opaque orthographies like English present those with learning disabilities with additional challenges and the cognitive demands in learning to spell are even greater. Different kinds of information have to be rapidly and effortlessly retrieved, evaluated, and coordinated.

Consider, for example, *expert* spellers. Tim Ruiter, the 12-year-old runner-up in the 2009 Scripps National Spelling Bee, was quoted as saying about the word he ultimately missed, "I had absolutely no clue about that word. I was just racking my brain for *anything possible that could help me*" (emphasis added). The winner, Kavya Shivashankar, 13, "wrote out every word on her palm and always ended with a smile" (White, 2009).

She went on to beat Tim and 291 other very skilled competitors. When asked how she prepared and what strategies she used while spelling, Kavya very succinctly explained:

> I used two sources to start off, Spell It and the Consolidated Word List. My dad is my *coach*, so we both worked a lot on *root words* and expanded the *study lists* from there. I also studied many *etymology patterns*. *I didn't just memorize the words*, and instead I used *clues* like the *language of origin, roots and the definition* to put the words together. With the nerves, I just took the spelling bee one word at a time, which helped me calm down. I was enjoying myself out there, so I had fun and I wasn't too nervous. (Gopalakrishnan, 2009, emphases added)

Interestingly, she never asked for words to be used in a sentence, which is how teachers usually teach and test spelling. When asked why, Ms. Shivashankar explained, "I don't know. I just never found that useful. *I don't get any information from it*" (transcript of CNN interview, May 29, 2009, emphasis added).

Clearly, she had some natural abilities to perform at this level, but it is striking how she learned to use a rich variety of information and strategies. She used word lists, but also she *studied* words with a coach (read, "teacher" instead of "coach") who provided guidance about how to use different kinds of information. Most importantly, she did not simply *memorize* words. Therefore, her statement is informative for teachers.

For over a century, teachers have used word lists to teach spelling. These lists have varied according to what theory of spelling skill acquisition has guided compilation of the lists. Today, lists are usually provided as part of commercial curriculum materials, so that the theory of teaching or learning spelling is strongly influenced by the decision to use a particular spelling resource. Some lists are compiled to represent words most frequently used in writing. Other lists are created to illustrate useful spelling patterns. Still other lists are meant to facilitate vocabulary development and may contain words that are used less frequently.

Like all Scripps competitors, Kavya studied word lists, too. Her mention of Spell It is in reference to a website (*myspellit.com*) established by Merriam-Webster as a study resource for the Scripps National Spelling Bee. It contains 1,150 words selected to illustrate spelling variations associated with language of origin. The site also offers direct access to dictionary entries for words and their oral pronunciation. In addition, the Spell It site provides a second list, "Words You Need to Know," based on words commonly used in students' academic writing. These are 140 words that are frequently misspelled (e.g., *occurrence*), homonyms (e.g., *cereal–serial*), and commonly confused words (e.g., *desert–dessert*). The Consolidated Word List, also provided by Scripps, contains about 23,413 unique words, along with illustrations of definitions, sentences, parts of speech, language origins, pronunciation tips, and relative frequency of use.

Both of these word lists are primarily intended to direct students' attention to the nonphonetic information (e.g., language of origin) that historically has determined contemporary American English spellings. There is nothing inherently wrong about using word lists. But there is nothing inherently better about one list or another, as long as it is relevant to actual usage in reading and writing. Clearly, students should not—cannot—simply memorize the more than 472,000 words in *Webster's Third New International Dictionary* (2002; the official Scripps Spelling Bee dictionary). Therefore, the explicit studying that they do in preparation must focus on learning how nonphonetic information, rules, and strategies can help them resolve uncertainty when spelling in competition.

Modern spellings represent the result of a sequence of barely remembered but once logical decisions about how origin words are represented in written English. In general, similar features in the language of origin result in similar derivations for English spellings. These are hard to express as a "rule," but with sufficient exposure to writing and written language they become discernable to students as *probabilities*. Recall Simon and Simon's (1973) generate-and-test notion. It is the probability of a spelling that helps students manage options and generate good choices. But it is the amount of deliberate instructional attention that spelling receives (as well as the amount of reading practice that helps students develop spelling representations) that determine outcomes, particularly for students who need that instruction.

For primary-grade children and those with learning disabilities, learning even common words can be a challenge. If there is indeed a useful "trick" for learning to spell common words in American English, it is that children can learn to use a variety of associations (the "probabilities" mentioned earlier), *only one of which relies on direct matching of speech sounds to alphabet letters*. Children can, for example, remember a salient visual feature, such as the double consonants in *rubber* or recurring consonants in *baby*. Children may use an analogy to a known word (e.g., *ate*, *crate*), or associate a particularly salient word meaning with its spelling (e.g., *stop*). Children can even remember a spelling because they have had past difficulty remembering it. For example, after repeatedly dictating a list of words over a series of days to a student with learning disabilities, the student suddenly volunteered, "Oh, yeah! This is the one I always miss," then spelled it correctly. The point is that students use a variety of linguistically sophisticated, logical, and sometimes idiosyncratic strategies to spell specific words.

For unusually expert spellers such as spelling bee champions, it is clear that they *study* words and information about the spelling of these words—patterns, etymologies, roots, language origins. That is, they *learn* actively to construct the spelling from many different categories of knowledge, along with rules and probabilities for using this knowledge in any particular spelling attempt (Berninger et al., 2000). Less gifted and less competitive students, particularly those with learning disabilities, still have to consult various sources and make decisions about many different kinds of word knowledge to arrive at a correct spelling in English. Examples include spelling options for different speech sounds, rules or conventions that might apply, and other strategies that might be used to obtain useful clues when letter–sound or sound–letter correspondence is insufficient. Nevertheless, students with learning difficulties are susceptible to direct instruction, guided practice, and appropriate use of explicit strategies (Gerber, 1984, 1985; Swanson, 1999).

How to Teach Spelling on Purpose

It is somewhat discouraging to see in recent national surveys of spelling practice (Fresch, 2003, 2007; Graham, 1999; Spear-Swerling & Brucker, 2004) that teachers' knowledge and instructional methods have changed little, if at all, in decades. Why, despite better language arts curricula and more research, have things remained much the same? One reason may be that teachers—as well as teacher training programs and curriculum publishers—still regard spelling as a relatively minor skill and/or one that will develop naturally as students learn and read more words. Another reason may be that teachers tend to implement published curriculum materials and the instructional activities they dictate. Although these recommended instructional activities may have value, teachers may use them without extracting any general instructional principles, particularly for students who spell poorly. Finally, it may simply be that teachers don't understand spelling development very well and are unsure how to make use of information from students' erroneous, but natural, attempts to spell (see Kwong & Varnhagen, 2005; Read, 1975; Varnhagen, McCallum, & Burstow, 1997). Conversely, some teachers may think that students have to be encouraged to "invent" spellings, or that because such errors are in some sense "developmental," they should not be corrected.

Actually, students do *not* need to be encouraged to "invent" solutions to spelling problems they encounter. They apply what understanding they possess naturally, but they might need some systematic guidance, including correction, to be motivated to attempt to spell at all. Spelling skills develop, following a well-described general sequence in which students first learn which letters conventionally represent which phonemes. Phonemic awareness is also a fundamental precursor to word-level reading, but the cognitive task in spelling—to generate letters from phonemes—is the inverse of the cognitive task in early decoding—to generate spoken phonemes from letters (Ehri, 2000). For most students with reading difficulties, spelling is also considerably more difficult to master. Performance on both reading and spelling eventually becomes fluent for most students, although in early grades, performance on one task is not necessarily a reliable indication that students can perform the inverse operation. For example, young students may readily produce a spelling for a word but, when asked to read it back, are unable to read what they've written. For students with learning disabilities in particular, teachers have to instruct students in both tasks and cannot expect that teaching word-decoding skills simultaneously includes spelling skills.

Most characterizations of spelling development posit a skill level or stage at which students can reliably produce a legal spelling of all phonemes heard in a word and even recognize that alternative legal spellings exist. Some authors have referred to this stage as "transitional." At this stage, students with learning disabilities often can accurately represent phonemes but cannot determine on the basis of phonological information alone which alternative spelling is correct. Therefore, in solving a spelling problem, students at this transitional stage have to know or seek other information, if they are to reduce response uncertainty to zero and produce a correct spelling. Students who struggle to learn to apply phonological information to spelling, as well as to word reading, are frustrated at the transitional stage of spelling skill acquisition when more and different kinds of information about the word are needed. Normally achieving students pass through this stage, because they have read many more words, have larger reading and writing vocabularies, have seen and used many more variations of spelling patterns, and have learned to associate more fluidly the kinds of relevant information that particular spelling decisions require.

One useful way to think about students' responsiveness to intervention is to imagine every request to spell a word is a problem to be solved. Problems exist when we are uncertain about what response is required in a situation. It is no different for students. Normally intelligent, knowledgeable, and skilled students seek to reduce uncertainty about the needed response. They do this by remembering past learning and how they solved particular kinds of problems with specific kinds of information. For example, when asked to spell a word (the problem), a student may know how to determine a correct response (the solution) by thinking about the sequence of speech sounds (i.e., phonemes) heard when saying the word, and which letters can be used to represent each of these sounds. If students have previously learned how to map phonemes and alphabet letters as part of learning to decode words, they might apply this knowledge to their current spelling problem. When instruction is explicit, practice is guided, and appropriate motivation is stimulated, we may monitor progress by watching students' attempts to spell and examining the trajectory of their performance compared to peers.

It is important to understand, however, that students must be taught to use new strategies as they acquire new knowledge. In general, when faced with a spelling problem, good spellers know to seek certain kinds of information, based on previous learning, that will help them reduce response uncertainty as close to zero as possible. Remember our spelling bee champion. Such students are reliably correct. Students with learning disabilities, however, have a great deal of difficulty reducing their uncertainty about how to spell words, even after they have been exposed to some basic strategies, such as matching alphabet letters to sounds. Teachers have to plan the time to explain such a strategy and provide guided practice in its use, so that students learn not only to recognize that they can employ it successfully, but also when it is insufficient and new information is required (Valmont, 1972).

Students with learning disabilities require *purposeful* instructional interventions—a kind of "coaching"—not only to learn useful patterns of spelling but also how and when to apply what they have learned. Swanson's (1999) meta-analysis of intervention research with students who have learning disabilities demonstrated that two frequent components of successful interventions are direct, explicit instruction and strategy training. In terms of spelling interventions, the former implies direct instruction in spelling knowledge (e.g., phonemic analysis, spelling of affixes) and ample guided practice in its application. At transitional stages of spelling acquisition when distinctive vowel sounds are absent, especially in unstressed syllables, strategies must be taught that focus on knowledge of morphology, etymology, and less common linguistic features of particular words. Much of this knowledge for normally achieving students comes from reading. Each new word encountered is associated with the spelling and meaning of already known words. The greater the number of associations available, the easier it will be to reconstruct the spelling. Students with learning disabilities suffer from not only inefficiencies in their current problem solving but also the cumulatively smaller network of associated information that they can access when they need to recall the spelling of a less frequently encountered word.

Response to Spelling Instruction

With regard to RTI, spelling also may be a particularly informative domain, because it helps us understand the ways in which instruction, rather than curriculum, is critical to supporting students who do not meet achievement benchmarks with their peers. Most extant examples of RTI focus on an increased *amount* of instructional time rather than the specific techniques or methods of instruction; that is, secondary, or Tier 2, interventions often consist of *additional* time (e.g., 30 minutes) several days a week for a period of 9–10 weeks. Clearly, teachers need to be concerned about the *efficiency* as well as the content, of their intervention time with students. Efficient teaching uses direct instruction to increase the number of response opportunities (e.g., spelling attempts, or attempts to retrieve relevant associated information) in the time allocated, so that students either receive confirmatory reinforcement when they are correct or corrective feedback (i.e., evaluation plus appropriately modified new instruction) when they are incorrect. In primary-grades, the content of such intervention should be spelling patterns or "families." In this way, students consolidate knowledge about a number of words and syllables.

Supplementary interventions for primary-grade students who have not yet reached a transitional stage of spelling might be constructed somewhat differently than those for intermediate and secondary students. First, for primary-grade students, the content of intervention is likely to focus on phoneme selection for regular spellings. By third grade, these interventions might include morphological awareness (i.e., knowledge of the spelling of common affixes such as -*s*, -*ing*, -*ed*). For intermediate students, or students at the transitional stage of spelling acquisition, interventions might focus on word roots and derivations. Filippini (2007) demonstrated that morphological awareness and semantic analysis skills can be taught to first graders along with phonemic awareness to improve and expand oral vocabulary. She used a combination of direct instruction and simple strategy training. Although she did not attempt to teach spelling, her instructional intervention is a promising model for teaching even primary-grade students nonphonological information that is useful for making decisions about spelling.

Most teachers prefer to teach spelling from word lists. The source and purpose of word lists in published curriculum materials varies. They may represent high-frequency words from reading or writing, and therefore contribute to students' reading and writing ability. They may represent "word families" or common linguistic patterns. Learning high-frequency patterns helps students spell by analogy when they need to spell a related word. Word lists might be formulated as vocabulary lists tied to a particular reading content. These lists are intended to have utility through their relationship to content about which students will read and write.

Effective spelling instruction requires that teachers know their students' level of spelling development, so that they can craft instruction and other supportive learning activities accordingly. Any given published curriculum can be helpful, but for students who are struggling, some amount of individually tailored instruction is necessary. Teachers are able to design and deliver necessary interventions more effectively if they can generate appropriate exemplar words to teach specific knowledge and skills. The best place to search for such exemplar words is students' current curriculum, because such words are relevant to students' age and the curriculum standards of their grade level. Beyond spelling instruction, these words also are likely to be encountered again by students in other learning activities and contexts, where reading and writing them reinforces knowledge of their spelling.

Spelling instruction should be a part of the general language arts curriculum for many of the reasons we have discussed thus far (Berninger et al., 2000). For example, vocabulary instruction that includes exposure to word spellings, in addition to oral exposures to the words and meanings, results in better memory for the pronunciations and meanings of the taught vocabulary (Rosenthal & Ehri, 2008). Most often, core curriculum materials include spelling words each week that coincide with the reading text, demonstrate a particular focus in learning phonics (e.g., word families), or illustrate linguistic features (e.g., learning affixes and inflected forms). However, spelling instruction tends to be the poorer relative of reading instruction, and not always effectively integrated with word reading, writing, and vocabulary instruction. Research surveying teachers about spelling instruction shows that although teachers devote specific time each week to spelling instruction, many feel that having enough time and adequate materials is a concern (Fresch, 2003, 2007). Often spelling gets pushed aside as other academic areas take precedence.

Fresch's (2003) research indicates that many of the surveyed teachers (72%) used one list of spelling words with all students in a class, and only 20% of teachers organized spelling instruction in small groups. Students' spelling skills may vary greatly and individual differences may determine the rate at which students learn words, how many words they learn at a time, and how well they generalize the spelling of individual words to their writing. To provide individualized instruction, it is necessary for teachers to collect data on student progress to guide intervention. Several methods have been used to assess spelling. In this next section we discuss methods for assessing students' spelling skills prior to planning instruction.

Using Assessment Information to Design Instruction

Using data-based decision-making processes to inform spelling instruction requires a cyclical process of assessment, analysis and reflection, then teaching. Traditional assessment instruments may be useful for estimating achievement but are less useful for monitoring progress in an RTI model (Gerber & Cohen, 1985).

Spelling is a developmental process, and observation and evaluation of the errors students make when asked to attempt difficult spellings can provide valuable insight into how students solve spelling problems, what knowledge they use, and what knowledge they lack. This insight can inform the construction of appropriate interventions. In this closing section, we discuss various measures and scoring procedures to inform spelling instruction in this way: curriculum-based measurement using correct letter sequences, and qualitative developmental analysis.

Curriculum–Based Measurement

Curriculum-based assessment (CBA), meaning assessment derived from the curriculum, is probably the most commonly used assessment of spelling. Generally, language arts programs provide a weekly list of spelling words featured in the reading or phonics study for the week, or both. These words are generally introduced to students on Monday, taught during the week, and tested on Friday. These tests usually take about 10 minutes and are scored as words correct or incorrect. However, these common measures are not necessarily reliable or valid measures of general spelling achievement. Rather, they measure short-term learning over the course of a week.

Another common assessment is curriculum-based measurement (CBM), which is a type of CBA. Curriculum based measures of spelling can assess students' progress over time on grade level curriculum. These measures are reliable and valid and easy for teachers to administer and interpret (Deno, 1985). The spelling lists comprise words from across the grade level, so that some words are easier and others are more difficult. Because CBM is used frequently, Wright (1992) recommends that the assessment probe take only about 2 minutes to administer. For younger students 12 words are usually presented, one every 10 seconds; for older students, 17 words are administered every 7 seconds, for a total of 2 minutes for the assessment.

Spelling CBM is generally scored as correct two-letter letter sequences, and Table 6.1 shows several examples. This method is preferable to scoring words as correct or incorrect, because students receive credit for partially correct spellings. Scoring correct letter sequences is also preferable to counting the number of correct letters written, because it takes into account the placement of letters (including the leading and trailing blank spaces around a word) relative to each other. For example, if John wrote *arec* for *race*, counting up the letters would generate a score of 4, because all of the individual letters are represented, although the sequence is incorrect. John would receive a higher score than Mary, who spelled *race* as *rac*, which would generate a score of 3, although Mary's spelling represents the correct letter sequences. When a word is scored correctly, one point is added to the correct letter sequences.

Using correct letter sequences also provides an accuracy score, another important piece of information for designing instruction. Using the total number of letter sequences possible and the students' scores on correct letter sequences,

TABLE 6.1. Scoring Using Correct Letter Sequences

Word	Total possible score: Correct letter sequences	Student spelling	Scored: Correct letter sequences
cake	5	Cak	3
storm	6	Strm	4
spotted	8	spooted	6
artist	7	Artest	5
communicate	12	cumunecate	7

divide the number of correct letter sequences by the total letter sequences possible. For example, using the words in Table 6.1, which have 38 total possible letter sequences, a student who scores 25 would have an accuracy score of 66%.

Using CBM, correct letter sequences can be tracked over time using graphs.
Teachers can also track the accuracy score and total words spelled correctly to
have more data to guide instruction. Figure 6.1 shows ongoing data from Ricky, a
third-grade student, over the course of 10 weeks of intervention.

Developmental Spelling Analysis

Another way to use spelling data is to analyze spelling according to developmental
stages, which can help teachers understand the spelling strategies that students
use and need to be taught. For example, to rate spellings, Tangel and Blachman
(1992) created a 7-point scale (0 = *random string of letters*, 2 = *correct initial phoneme*, 6 = *correct spelling*). A teacher can review the score pattern and see that one
student may still use phonetically related letters rather than conventional letters
(perhaps needing more alphabetic instruction), whereas another may consistently
fail to represent both letters in a consonant blend (perhaps needing more phonemic segmenting and two-letter spelling pattern practice). Stage models of spelling
development often describe four or five stages, including a preliterate/preread-
ing stage (spelling that uses jumbles of letters and numbers), a prephonetic or
letter-naming stage (spelling that uses letter names), phonetic/word pattern stage
(spelling that uses phonics and words pattern "chunks"), and transitional stages
that include errors but are closer approximations of the correct spelling (Gerber,
1985). Several methods for scoring use developmental analysis. Screening measures exist to pinpoint a student's spelling stage (i.e., Ganske, 1999; Developmental Spelling Analysis [DSA]). Then, based on the score and the developmental
stage, students are given a more detailed assessment for that stage that examines
various features of spelling. Although using DSA can provide detailed information
on errors students make, it is likely that development of spelling is a continuous
process, with changing understandings that tend to be word-specific rather than
a pure sequence of stages (Varnhagen et al., 1997). Therefore, struggling spellers

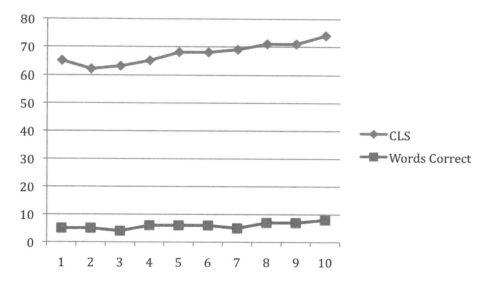

FIGURE 6.1. Ricky's growth on correct letter sequences (CLS) and words correct over 10 weeks of intervention.

may spend more time in between what we think of as distinct stages and show a mixture of understandings in their attempts rather than always produce only one kind of error that fits neatly into one stage or another.

Moreover, the words that students are given to spell may require features of one stage over another; that is, to spell grade-level words, students sometimes need to fall back on phonological information that would put them in a lower stage for some words but a higher stage for words they are able to spell accurately from memory. Additionally, DSA is not useful for ongoing progress monitoring, because it does not consider small amounts of growth students might make, even within or between stages. Therefore, it may be useful to consider a scoring system that takes into account development on a continuum rather than in stages.

Key Features of Spelling Interventions Based on Progress Monitoring

Research investigating spelling interventions has demonstrated a common set of both *methods* for delivering intervention and *content* of the intervention. In this section we first describe the key features for delivering effective intervention, then the content of spelling interventions.

Swanson's (1999) synthesis, mentioned earlier, provides the key features of many interventions, including spelling interventions, that have proved effective for students with learning disabilities and other at-risk students. Two common features of effective intervention are direct instruction and strategy instruction. "Direct instruction" includes breaking down a task; modeling; and providing corrective feedback, small-group instruction, and independent practice. "Strategy instruction" includes systematic explanations, use of advanced organizers, modeling of the strategy by the teacher, verbal questioning, demonstrating use of the strategy, step-by-step prompts, dialogue between students and teachers about the strategy, and metacognitive questioning of the spelling process by the teacher. Successful spelling interventions over the last decade have incorporated many of these elements of instruction.

Effective instruction for at-risk primary-grade students should include explicit instruction in the alphabetic principle, beginning with phoneme–grapheme correspondences for single letters (see Edwards, 2003). Following this basic instruction, alternative spellings should be introduced, providing explicit instruction in alternative ways to spell the /k/sound (e.g., with *c*, *k*, *ck*), or the long-*e* phoneme (as in *equal*, *eagle*, *creek*, and *baby*) (Berninger et al., 2002).

Interventions for students in kindergarten through second grade are conducted typically in small groups for about 20–30 minutes each day (Edwards, 2003; Graham et al., 2008; Santoro, Coyne, & Simmons, 2006). There is ample modeling and scaffolding to help students get to the correct spelling. For example, Santoro and colleagues explicitly taught kindergarten students letter sounds and how to write letters by modeling and having students trace and copy letters. Teachers demonstrated phoneme segmenting multiple times before having students independently apply spelling and writing skills. Teachers used segmenting blocks to scaffold isolating sounds and letters. This process improved both word reading and spelling.

Additionally, these interventions systematically control for task difficulty by restricting words to those including taught letter–sound correspondences (Santoro et al., 2006), and keeping word lists short enough for students to master within an instructional week, often in sets of 5–10 words (Berninger et al., 2002; Graham, Harris, & Chorzempa, 2002; Roberts & Meiring, 2006). Error correction, another common feature of effective spelling interventions and correcting errors as they are made (wordwise), is more effective than waiting until the end of a long spelling dictation list (listwise) (Bryant, Drabin, & Gettinger, 1981). For older students modeling and error correction continue to be important; however, interventions may need to last longer and be more individualized to meet student needs (Wanzek et al., 2006). These interventions often include strategy instruction as part of the intervention.

For many students, direct teaching of strategies is necessary. Strategy instruction includes providing students with problem-solving skills; the problem in this case is spelling an unknown word. Students can then use these "backup" strategies when they cannot directly retrieve the word from memory. These strategies include using letter names (pen = pn (*n* name to make the -*en* sound), phonological information (sounding it out, *c-a-n*), analogy ("I know how to spell *bake*, because I can spell *cake* and take the *c* off and put a *b*"), orthographic rules (-*e* at the end makes the *a* say its name), and morphological information (*thanked* is past tense, so add *-ed*) (Kwong & Varnhagen, 2005; Varnhagen et al., 1997). Strategies vary in sophistication and students who have more developed spelling skills generally use more sophisticated strategies. Students who struggle with spelling tend to use less sophisticated strategies and may not develop them without direct instruction. Therefore, spelling interventions should include these strategies to teach students how to approach spelling words they do not know. For young students, phonological and analogy strategies are appropriate, but as students get older, a focus on orthographic rules and morphological strategies may be more useful for the types of words they spell. Strategy instruction for older students may integrate spelling with composition, with students learning independently to check their writing at word, sentence, and text levels (see Berninger et al., 2002).

One simple and flexible intervention that has proved effective is imitation–modeling (Gerber, 1986; Kauffman, Hallahan, Haas, Brame, & Boren, 1978; Nulman & Gerber, 1984). Students respond to dictated words with illustrative sentences, as in many typical spelling tests. When they produce an error, however, the teacher responds as follows, incorporating a wordwise correcting procedure:

> "That is not correct."
> "This is what you wrote." [The teacher reproduces the student's error exactly beneath the error. This is the *imitation* step, which helps the student to change focus from spelling production to reading. The teacher's imitation is now a word to be regarded and evaluated in a reading, rather than writing, process.]
> "The correct spelling is _____" [The teacher writes the correctly spelled word beneath her imitation. This is the *model* step. It induces the student to make a visual comparison of the two—the imitated error and the correctly spelled word—and to see which features discriminate between them.]

Imitation–modeling is efficient. Immediate corrective feedback is provided, another feature of effective spelling interventions (Wanzek et al., 2006). Teacher talk is kept to a minimum, and student attention is directed to the specific features—the specific spelling of phonemes in a particular word—that differentiate correct from incorrect spelling. It is, in essence, a dynamic assessment in which teachers note errors and respond specifically to them. Specific strategy or general concept teaching can follow. In clinical experiments, when repeated dictations of short lists (e.g., 10 words) were presented with contingent imitation–modeling, until all words are correctly spelled, students were able to spell successive lists of words with the same features in fewer and fewer trials (Gerber, 1986; Gettinger, Bryant, & Fayne, 1982; Kauffman et al., 1978; Nulman & Gerber, 1984).

Content of Instruction

One of the most common questions teachers ask is "What words do I teach?" This question is not easily answered. To back up and reiterate, beginning in kindergarten, instruction in letter knowledge and phonemic segmenting facilitates early spelling and reading. Early invented spelling attempts reflect the student's level of linguistic knowledge and help the teacher choose words for appropriate instruction. For example, a kindergartner who spells the word *tag* as *t* is able to represent the initial sound correctly, and instruction might offer practice in segmenting consonant–vowel–consonant (CVC) words into phonemes and using alphabet tiles to match the correct symbol to each sound. Research strongly supports teaching of alphabetic and phonological skills to provide the early foundation for spelling (Treiman, 2006).

Spelling instruction in the primary grades is typically organized around word lists. Graham and his colleagues have developed lists of words used most frequently in students' writing and divided by grade level (for the lists, see Graham, Harris, & Loynach, 1993, 1994). Teachers can also develop words lists. Most language arts curricula have spelling programs, including word lists and lessons. Lists of word families with similar orthographic patterns (i.e., *-op*, *-ight*) are useful for spelling intervention and often correspond with the language arts curriculum. Content-area reading and language arts stories or novels provide opportunities to teach spelling of key vocabulary words (i.e., *molecule*, *ancestor*). Often, more than one spelling list is useful. Individualized spelling lists can be created for struggling students.

Research clearly supports the idea that instruction in spelling transfers to word recognition, and effective instruction coordinates reading and spelling words, and matches the increasing complexity of words that students encounter. Spelling instruction must therefore include related skills that contribute to spelling development, including phonological awareness, alphabetic principle, phonics, letter writing, orthographic rules, and morphology. These skills relate to both reading and spelling therefore direct instruction in these skills, and their interrelations improve spelling outcomes (Wanzek et al., 2006). For young children beginning to learn to read and write in preschool and kindergarten the phonological awareness skill of segmenting is critical to spelling and is a precursor skill that can be taught to young students before they can formally read or write (Ritchey, 2008; Santoro et al., 2006). Focusing on letter names and sound–letter relationships is also critical for kindergarten and first-grade students, because these skills are strongly related to later spelling and writing (Roberts & Meiring, 2006; Schneider, Roth, & Ennemoser, 2000). For students in second grade or older who have developed these precursor skills, spelling intervention content should focus on spelling patterns and rules (Graham et al., 2002), along with phonics. For older, struggling spellers, besides phonics instruction, spelling intervention should include morphemic analysis (Wanzek et al., 2006), so that students learn to recognize and combine meaningful parts of words (see Nunes & Bryant, Chapter 5, in this volume).

Case Studies

To conclude, we provide illustrations of RTI-type decision making and spelling intervention based on progress data from case studies for students K–5. Each case study illustrates the kind of student performance that data revealed, the teacher's decision-making process, and a sketch of an appropriate intervention.

Kindergarten Student: Miwa

Miwa is in the middle of the kindergarten year, and Dynamic Indicators of Basic Early Literacy Skills (DIBELS) testing has identified her as at-risk on phoneme segmenting, nonsense words, and letter-naming fluency. The intervention team has recommended explicit spelling instruction in daily, individual, 15-minute sessions for 10 weeks. Instruction will target phoneme segmenting, alphabetics, and spelling CVC words (see Figure 6.2).

This explicit instruction in alphabetic and phonemic skills, with spelling practice in regular CVC words containing taught letters, includes practices found effective in improving spelling, phonemic segmentation, and nonsense word read-

---

Objective: Students match letter sounds to words, segment CVC words, and spell CVC words.

Materials: Cards for a small set of letter sounds (6 consonants, 3 vowels), letter tiles, segmenting boxes, paper and pencil.

Activity 1: Letter–sound naming cards

Teacher shows card, and students tells name and sound of the letter.

Activity 2: Segmenting sounds in CVC words

Teacher dictates CVC word, and student uses segmenting box to point and say each sound in the word.

□   □   □

Activity 3: Spelling and reading with letter tiles

Teacher dictates a CVC word, student repeats it, and student uses letter tiles to spell the word. Student pronounces the sound as she moves each tile, then blends the sound and reads the word.

Activity 4: Spelling, writing, and reading CVC words

Teacher dictates a CVC word for student to spell on paper. Student repeats and segments word, and says each sound as she writes it in on paper, then reads the word.

FIGURE 6.2. Lesson plan for kindergarten student at risk.

ing skills (Ehri & Wilce, 1987; O'Connor & Jenkins, 1995; Vandervelden & Siegel, 1997).

First-Grade Student: Jesse

Jesse is in the middle of his first-grade year. District assessments show that Jesse is behind in both his reading and spelling skills. Ms. Valdez collects data and finds that Jesse is at risk on three key skills: letter–sound naming, phoneme segmenting, and spelling CVC words. She decides to focus on these skills to boost Jesse's reading and spelling. See Figure 6.3 for a lesson plan for a small group of students who are performing like Jesse.

Note how this activity extends segment-to-spell, introduced by O'Connor (Chapter 2, this volume) by requiring students to write letters to represent sounds. The activity integrates spelling and reading phonetically regular words, which have a positive influence on both reading and spelling outcomes (O'Connor & Jenkins, 1995; Roberts & Meiring, 2006; Santoro et al., 2006)

Third-Grade Student: Herman

Herman, a third grader, continues to have difficulty reading and spelling multisyllabic words. Scores from a DSA show that Herman can chunk words and spell two to three letter patterns correctly, including vowel teams and consonant blends. However, his spelling reflects limited morphological awareness—under-

Objective: Students will spell and read CVC words.	**Materials:** Letter cards, placeholders (blank tiles or foam shapes), picture cards with words, white boards, small Post-its
Activity 1: Letter–sound naming flashcards	Show flash card and students tell name and sound of the letter.
Activity 2: Segmenting–tapping sounds on placeholder	Students get three placeholders and tap sounds of CVC words: *s-a-d.* ☐ ☐ ☐
Activity 3: Letter–sound relationship	Show picture card with word. Say "This is a *cap*." What letter makes the *c* sound in *cap*? Write the letter on your white board."
Activity 4: Spelling and reading CVC words	Give students a word to spell: *sat*. Have students put out a Post-it for each sound they hear, spell the word, then blend the sounds and read the word. ☐ ☐ ☐

FIGURE 6.3. Lesson plan for a first-grade student at risk.

standing of word stems and affixes, and how many longer words are formed. His teacher, Ms. Conway, reviews the DSA to plan a lesson to teach a small group of students who are ready to learn about multisyllablic words formed with two common suffixes: *-tion* and *-ness*.

This lesson (see Figure 6.4) includes explicit instruction in spelling derived word forms, practice in checking on whether students have used the correct form (noun or verb), practice in using taught words in a scaffolded writing task—practices found to be effective for students at risk and that benefit spelling and writing (Berninger et al., 2002; see Nunes & Bryant, Chapter 5, this volume).

Fifth-Grade Student: Maribel

Maribel, a Spanish-speaking English language learner, has recently been redesignated as fluent English proficient. She is a good decoder and can read fluently at 120 words per minute at the middle of the year, which is above the threshold usually considered to be at risk for reading problems. She also is able to comprehend text at grade level. However, writing is a problem, particularly spelling. Her teacher, Mr. Harding, decides to collect baseline data on her spelling using CBM spelling assessment. The results indicate that she is a slow speller and makes errors spelling even single-syllable words with vowel combinations. Mr. Harding is going to conduct an intervention for Maribel in a small group with other students who also have difficulty with spelling words. He begins the intervention using CVVC words, using word families, and systematic error correction (see Figure 6.5).

Objective: Students spell words with target derivational suffixes (e.g., combination, fitness).	**Materials**: Word cards for target root words, derived words, and isolated suffixes (e.g., *rich*, *ill*, *elect*, *inspect*, *richness*, *illness*, *election*, *inspection*, *-ness*, *-tion*)
Activity 1: Review words and suffixes.	Introduce suffixes, root words, derived words. Model how to produce correct spellings of affixed words.
Activity 2: Spell words with and without suffixes.	Have students complete cloze sentences by choosing and inserting correct word forms [e.g., "Dad took his car in for an _____ (*inspect, inspection*)"].
Activity 3: Teach grammatical categories of derived words.	Discuss with students which form of the word (i.e., *inspect, inspection*) is correct in the sentence above, and how *-tion* makes the word a noun.
Activity 4: Use taught words in writing.	Provide writing frame with topic and words to include in a four-sentence paragraph (e.g., "Going camping" using the derived words *vacation*, *destination*, *fitness*). Guide students in checking their writing at the word and sentence levels.

FIGURE 6.4. Lesson plan for third-grade student at risk.

Objective: Students spell CVVC words and begin to develop spelling fluency.	**Materials**: Flash cards with words, whiteboards, small Post-its, index cards with word family endings *-eat -oat, -aid*.
Activity 1: Vowel team review.	Teacher models vowel team and letter combinations and students review sounds they make: *ea, oa, ai*.
Activity 2: Spelling words with short and long vowels, including vowel combinations.	Teacher dictates words with both short and long vowels (e.g., spell *ran*, make *ran* into *rain*; spell *cot*, make *cot* into *coat*; spell *bet*, make *bet* into *beat*). Students write words on whiteboards.
Activity 3: Using words in writing.	Teacher provides a writing frame to scaffold student practice incorporating CVVC words in sentences or paragraphs to increase generalization. Teacher reviews student writing, and students discuss word choices and spelling.

FIGURE 6.5. Lesson plan for fifth-grade student at risk.

Conclusion

Research indicates very clearly that effective spelling instruction helps student develop spelling *and* reading skills. Although English spelling has many irregularities resulting from its historical influences, it has regularities at letter and morpheme levels that skilled spellers recognize, and that good instruction can help at-risk students to learn. Because there is often little dedicated time for spelling in the school day, spelling instruction warrants a focused and effective approach. Effective practices we have discussed in this chapter include the following:

- Assessment that inform and pinpoint the focus for spelling instruction through DSA, CBA, or CBM.
- Explicit instruction in the alphabetic principle, including single letters, alternate spellings, and multiletter spelling patterns, provides the foundation for spelling simple words for beginners.
- Explicit instruction for beginners combines alphabetic and phonemic skills.
- For older students, explicit instruction includes morphemes (e.g., root words, inflections, and affixes).
- Effective instruction integrates practice in reading and spelling words, because transfer goes both ways.
- Instruction aims for transfer to authentic tasks, with scaffolded practice applying spelling in writing tasks to induce generalization of skills.
- Instruction for older students includes a metacognitive focus to help stu-

dents learn to check their spelling and their word choices independently to match the sentence context (i.e., word form, number, tense).

References

Almack, J. C., & Staffelbach, E. H. (1934). Spelling diagnosis and remedial teaching. *Elementary School Journal, 34,* 341–350.

Berninger, V. W., Vaughn, K., Abbott, R. D., Begay, K., Coleman, K. B., Curtin, G., et al. (2002). Teaching spelling and composition alone and together: Implications for the simple view of writing. *Journal of Educational Psychology, 94,* 291–304.

Berninger, V. W., Vaughn, K., Abbott, R. D., Brooks, A., Begay, K., Curtin, G., et al. (2000). Language-based spelling instruction: Teaching children to make multiple connections between spoken and written words. *Learning Disability Quarterly, 23,* 117–135.

Boder, E. (1973). Developmental dyslexia: A diagnostic approach based on three atypical reading–spelling patterns. *Developmental Medicine and Child Neurology, 15,* 663–687.

Bruce, J. (Ed.). (1849). *Letters of Queen Elizabeth and King James VI of Scotland.* London: J. H. Nichols & Son, Printers.

Bryant, N. D., Drabin, I. R., & Gettinger, M. (1981). Effects of varying unit size on spelling achievement in learning disabled children. *Journal of Learning Disabilities, 14,* 200–203.

Cassar, M., Treiman, R., Moats, L. C., Pollo, T. C., & Kessler, B. (2005). How do the spellings of children with dyslexia compare with those of nondyslexic children? *Reading and Writing: An Interdisciplinary Journal, 18,* 27–49.

Deno, S. L. (1985). Curriculum-based measurement: The emerging alternative. *Exceptional Children, 52,* 219–232.

Edwards, L. (2003). Writing instruction in kindergarten: Examining an emerging area of research for children with writing and reading disabilities. *Journal of Learning Disabilities, 36,* 136–148.

Ehri, L. C. (2000). Learning to read and learning to spell: Two sides of a coin. *Topics in Learning Disorders, 20,* 19–49.

Ehri, L. C., & Wilce, L. S. (1987). Does learning to spell help beginners learn to read words? *Reading Research Quarterly, 22,* 37–65.

Filippini, A. (2007). *Project WORD: Effects of adding vocabulary to early reading instruction for English learners at-risk of reading disabilities.* Unpublished dissertation, University of California, Santa Barbara.

Fresch, M. J. (2003). A national survey of spelling instruction: Investigating teachers' beliefs and practice. *Journal of Literacy Research, 35,* 819–848.

Fresch, M. J. (2007). Teachers' concerns about spelling instruction: A national survey. *Reading Psychology, 28,* 301–330.

Ganske, K. (1999). The Developmental Spelling Analysis: A measure of orthographic knowledge. *Educational Assessment, 6,* 41–70.

Gerber, M. (1984). Orthographic problem-solving ability of learning disabled and normally achieving students. *Learning Disability Quarterly, 7,* 157–162.

Gerber, M. M. (1985). Spelling as concept driven problem solving. In B. Hutson (Ed.), *Advances in reading/language research* (Vol. 3, pp. 39–75). Greenwich, CT: JAI Press.

Gerber, M. M. (1986). Generalization of spelling strategies by LD students as a result of contingent imitation/modeling and mastery criteria. *Journal of Learning Disabilities, 19,* 530–537.

Gerber, M. M., & Cohen, S. (1985). Assessment of spelling skills. In A. F. Rotatori & R.

Fox (Eds.), *Assessment for regular and special education teachers: A case study format* (pp. 249–278). Austin, TX: Pro-Ed.

Gerber, M., & Hall, R. (1987). Information processing approaches to studying spelling deficiencies. *Journal of Learning Disabilities, 20,* 34–42.

Gerber, M. M., & Hall, R. J. (1989). Cognitive-behavioral training in spelling for learning handicapped students. *Learning Disability Quarterly, 12,* 159–171.

Gettinger, M., Bryant, N. D., & Fayne, H. R. (1982). Designing spelling instruction for learning disabled children: An emphasis on unit size, distributed practice, and training for transfer. *Journal of Special Education, 16,* 339–448.

Gopalakrishnan, M. (June 11, 2009). Stellar speller: Kavya Shivashankar's road to victory. Retrieved from *Espnrise.com*. Retrieved September 7, 2010, *http://rise.espn.go/com/s/conversations/show/story/4250637*

Graham, S. (1999). Handwriting and spelling instruction for students with learning disabilities: A review. *Learning Disability Quarterly, 22,* 78–98.

Graham, S., Harris, K., & Chorzempa, B. (2002). Contribution of spelling instruction to the spelling, writing, and reading of poor spellers. *Journal of Educational Psychology, 94,* 669–686.

Graham, S., Harris, K., & Loynanch, C. (1993). The basic spelling vocabulary list. *Journal of Educational Research, 86,* 363–368.

Graham, S., Harris, K., & Loynanch, C. (1994). The spelling for writing list. *Journal of Learning Disabilities, 27,* 210–214.

Graham, S., Morphy, P., Harris, K., Chorzempa, B., Saddler, B., Moran, S., et al. (2008). Teaching spelling in the primary grades: A national survey of instructional practices and adaptations. *American Educational Research Journal, 45,* 796–825.

Hanna, P. R., Hanna, J. S., Hodges, R. E., & Rudorf, E. H., Jr. (1966). *Phoneme–grapheme correspondences as cues to spelling improvement.* Washington, DC: U.S. Government Printing Office.

Horn, E. (1919). Principles of method in teaching spelling. In *Eighteenth Yearbook of National Society for Study of Education* (Part 2, pp. 52–95). Bloomington, IL: Public School Publishing.

Kauffman, J. M., Hallahan, D. P., Haas, K., Brame, T., & Boren, R. (1978). Imitating children's errors can improve their ability to spell. *Journal of Learning Disabilities, 11,* 217–222.

Kwong, T., & Varnhagen, C. (2005). Strategy development and learning to spell new words: Generalization of a process. *Developmental Psychology, 41,* 148–159.

Lull, H. G. (1917). A plan for developing a spelling consciousness. *Elementary School Journal, 17,* 355–361.

Micklethwait, D. (2000). *Noah Webster and the American dictionary.* Jefferson, NC: McFarland & Co.

Nathan, R. G., & Stanovich, K. E. (1991). The causes and consequences of differences in reading fluency. *Theory Into Practice, 30,* 176–184.

Nulman, J. H., & Gerber, M. M. (1984). Improving spelling performance by imitating a child's errors. *Journal of Learning Disabilities, 17,* 328–333.

O'Connor, R. E., & Jenkins, J. R. (1995). Improving the generalization of sound/symbol knowledge: Teaching spelling to kindergarten children with disabilities. *Journal of Special Education, 29,* 255–275.

Paulesu, E., Démonet, J.-F., Fazio, F., McCrory, E., Chanoine, V., Brunswick, N., et al. (2001). Dyslexia: Cultural diversity and biological unity. *Science, 291,* 2165–2167.

Read, C. (1975). *Children's categorization of speech sounds in English.* Urbana, IL: National Council of Teachers of English.

Ritchey, K. (2008). The building blocks of writing: Learning to write letters and spell words. *Reading and Writing, 21*, 27–47.

Roberts, T. A., & Meiring, A. (2006). Teaching phonics in the context of children's literature or spelling: Influences on first-grade reading, spelling, and writing and fifth-grade comprehension. *Journal of Educational Psychology, 98*, 690–713.

Rosenthal, J., & Ehri, L. C. (2008). The mnemonic value of orthography for vocabulary learning. *Journal of Educational Psychology, 100*, 175–191.

Santoro, L., Coyne, M., & Simmons, D. (2006). The reading–spelling connection: Developing and evaluating a beginning spelling intervention for children at risk of reading disability. *Learning Disabilities Research and Practice, 21*, 122–133.

Schneider, W., Roth, E., & Ennemoser, M. (2000). Training phonological skills and letter knowledge in children at risk for dyslexia: A comparison of three kindergarten intervention programs. *Journal of Educational Psychology, 92*, 284–295.

Siegel, L. S., Share, D., & Geva, E. (1995). Evidence for superior orthographic skills in dyslexics. *Psychological Science, 6*, 250–254.

Simon, D. P., & Simon, H. A. (1973). Alternative uses of phonemic information in spelling. *Review of Educational Research, 43*, 115–137.

Spear-Swerling, L., & Brucker, P. O. (2004). Preparing novice teachers to develop basic reading and spelling skills in children. *Annals of Dyslexia, 54*, 332–364.

Steffler, D., Varnhagen, C., Friesen, C., & Treiman, R. (1998). There's more to children's spelling than the errors they make: Strategic and automatic processes for one-syllable words. *Journal of Educational Psychology, 90*, 492–505.

Sudweeks, J. (1927). Practical helps in teaching spelling: Summary of helpful principles and methods. *Journal of Educational Research, 16*, 106–118.

Swanson, H. L., with Hoskyn M., & Lee, C. (1999). *Interventions for students with learning disabilities: A meta analysis of treatment outcomes.* New York: Guilford Press.

Tangel, D. M., & Blachman, B. A. (1992). Effect of phoneme awareness instruction on kindergarten children's invented spelling. *Journal of Reading Behavior, 24*, 233–261.

Tidyman, W. F. (1919). *The teaching of spelling.* Yonkers-on-Hudson, NY: World Book Co.

Treiman, R. (2006). Knowledge about letters as a foundation for reading and spelling. In R. M. Joshi & P. G. Aaron (Eds.), *Handbook of orthography and literacy* (pp. 581–599). Mahwah, NJ: Erlbaum.

Treiman, R., & Bourassa, D. (2000). The development of spelling skill. *Topics in Language Disorders, 20*, 1–18.

Valmont, W. J. (1972). Spelling consciousness: A long neglected area. *Elementary English, 49*, 1219–1221.

Vandervelden, M. C., & Siegel, L. S. (1997). Teaching phonological processing skills in early literacy: A developmental approach. *Learning Disability Quarterly, 20*, 63–81.

Varnhagen, C., McCallum, M., & Burstow, M. (1997). Is children's spelling naturally stage-like? *Reading and Writing, 9*, 451–481.

Wanzek, J., Vaughn, S., Wexler, J., Swanson, E., Edmonds, M., & Kim, A. (2006). A synthesis of spelling and reading interventions and their effects on the spelling outcomes of students with LD. *Journal of Learning Disabilities, 39*, 528–543.

Webster's Third New International Dictionary of the English Language. (2002). Springfield, MA: G. and C. Merriam.

White, J. (2009, May 28). Kavya Shivashankar, 13, Kansas girl, wins National Spelling Bee. Associated Press.

Wright, J. (1992). *Curriculum-based measurement: A manual for teachers.* Syracuse, NY: Syracuse City Schools.

7

Making Vocabulary Interventions
Engaging and Effective

MARGARET G. MCKEOWN
ISABEL L. BECK

Vocabulary is currently a hot topic in the reading field. But for a very long time it was not hot, getting little attention in materials, research funding, or publications. Those of us who do research on vocabulary have always thought vocabulary should be a hot topic. And in fact, the International Reading Association reflected the status of vocabulary as "not hot but should be" over a number of years prior to 2000, in its annual survey of reading topics that appears in its *Reading Today* publication.

The reason that vocabulary development should be hot is that vocabulary is strongly tied to reading comprehension. This is a long-standing finding (Davis, 1944; Singer, 1965; Snow, Tabors, Nicholson, & Kurland, 1995; Spearrit, 1972; Thurstone, 1946). But despite that solid relationship, vocabulary was cool (in the cold sense, not in the "way cool" sense) for a long time.

Vocabulary Knowledge, Literacy,
and Traditional Vocabulary Instruction

The reason that vocabulary has become a hot topic seems to be a growing awareness of the stark consequences of the vocabulary–comprehension relationship. From a number of studies over the past decade, it has become clear that an individual's vocabulary knowledge has a limiting effect on his or her literacy future. The dawning of vocabulary's role might be traced to Hart and Risley's study (1995) showing that the vocabulary children know at age 3 strongly predicts their reading comprehension status in third or fourth grade. The researchers demonstrated this by following children in their homes from the time they spoke their first words until they were age 3. Talk in the children's homes was recorded one full day per month over that time. Hart and Risley found that the number of words spoken in the home determined the number of words in a child's vocabulary, and that this number differed for children at different socioeconomic status (SES) levels, such that children of university professors knew about three times as many words as children of welfare families. Hart and Risley showed that this gap does not narrow, with children who start behind becoming low-ability readers by the time they reach the intermediate grades.

Hart and Risley's (1995) findings are consistent with earlier work that pointed out vast differences in vocabulary knowledge among learners from different SES groups, from toddlerhood through high school. For example, several studies showed that first graders from higher-SES backgrounds knew at least twice as many words as children from lower-SES background (Graves, Brunetti, & Slater, 1982; Moats, 2001; White, Graves, & Slater, 1990). But more recent studies, including that of Hart and Risley (1995), have added the revelation of stark consequences on students' later literacy growth (Biemiller & Slonim, 2001; Cunningham & Stanovich, 1997; Wagner et al., 1997). These studies indicate that school experiences have little effect on students' vocabulary development, so however ill- or well-equipped children are in vocabulary when they start school, is how they will be when they finish their schooling. This may seem counterintuitive, in that school provides an enormous input of words. Students are presented in a variety of subject areas with words that are highlighted, defined, and hung on the wall. However, the way that words traditionally are dealt with in classrooms is not particularly effective.

In early grades, the "vocabulary" that gets attention comprises words that students know from oral language but need to learn to recognize in print, and this is, of course, a vital aspect of children's literacy education. Very few words that are unfamiliar in meaning are contained in the material that children themselves read in the first and second grades, and even in third grade to a great extent. Children may meet new words (i.e., whose meanings are unknown) in read-alouds. And when such words occur, the most that is done usually is to provide a brief meaning, such as a teacher reading about an enormous turnip, saying, "*Enormous* means very, very big." But the word *enormous* is rarely followed up in any systematic way.

In intermediate grades, vocabulary is dealt with usually as part of the reading lesson, with a set of words introduced before reading. The introduction is most often a brief definition or a sentence containing the word, constructed so that the meaning can be gleaned from context. But, again, little, if any, follow-up is provided. This has been the pattern until very recently. A change has begun in basal reading materials in the past couple of years. Some publishers are giving attention to more deliberate word selection, carefully explained word meanings, and provision of follow-up attention, so that students have opportunities to think about and use the words. Those materials have just begun to make their way into the schools, so it will be some time before we are able to assess their effects.

When students get to middle and high school, the true scourge of vocabulary instruction is thrust upon them; that is, students typically are given a list of words and required to look each one up in the dictionary, record its definition, and use it in a sentence. This work is not only tedious but also ineffective—except in causing students to hate vocabulary.

Principles of Vocabulary Learning

The typical patterns of school vocabulary instruction produce a deep divide between what is done in classrooms and what is understood about vocabulary learning. Instruction is not effective if it is not consistent with what is known about how vocabulary is acquired. What is known about vocabulary acquisition might be summarized in three principles. First, vocabulary knowledge is a network of connected concepts; second, vocabulary is learned from context, but context is an inefficient learning medium; and third, learning is incremental.

Networks of Vocabulary Knowledge

When a learner acquires information about a word's meaning, connections form in his or her brain to other words and to experiences related to what has been learned previously (Perfetti, 2007; Reichle & Perfetti, 2003; Wolf, 2007). So if you were to think about the word *party*, what would come to mind? Probably not "an event held to celebrate an occasion or entertain friends." More likely you would think about parties you have been to or given, perhaps a favorite party food, and so forth. All the contexts in which you have encountered the word *party* or experienced such an event lead to building an abstract representation of the word's meaning. The abstract nature of the representation means that when you read the word in a new context, you are not dependent on specific information from an individual context that you have encountered before, which could limit your understanding of that new context. Rather, the representation you have created is rich and nuanced, meaning that it has many associated concepts and can bring the most relevant ones to the surface to help make the new context meaningful. Representations of word meaning, if they are of high quality, are flexible and allow rapid retrieval of meaning when we meet the word in context (Perfetti, 2007).

Perfetti (2007) finds that skilled comprehenders make better uses of experiences with words: They more quickly come to recognize a word's meaning. This is a finding along the way to Perfetti's development of the lexical quality hypothesis (LQH) (Perfetti & Hart, 2002), which holds that a learner's ability to use experiences to advantage is, in turn, constructed from the accumulation of the learner's experiences with words encountered in informative contexts. The notion that the greater the accumulation of experiences with a word, the greater likelihood that a precise, nuanced understanding of a word's meaning will be acquired is also an aspect of Nagy and Scott's (2000) view of how word meaning develops. LQH also posits that what may seem to be a deficit in ability for less able comprehenders is more likely the result of knowledge differences—knowledge that has not been acquired or practiced to a high enough level. When we consider what this means for instruction, this is good news, because it implies that we can help students to become good comprehenders by providing high-quality practice with words and meanings. We can provide the experiences to build the knowledge they are lacking and support their practice of it.

Learning Vocabulary from Context

Context is the major resource for learning new vocabulary. For young children beginning to learn their language, this means everyday oral, conversational contexts. Children acquire words from oral contexts quite readily, because these contexts provide a great deal of support. The first line of support is our use of a limited set of words in oral language. Hayes and Ahrens (1988), in a study of samples of college-educated adults, found that nearly 95% of conversational language is made up of the most frequent 5,000 words in English vocabulary. Thus, the same words are repeated in conversations with great frequency, so their meanings are more accessible and are reinforced frequently. Moreover, oral contexts are redundant in that gesture, voice intonation, and surrounding physical context reinforce word meanings. For example, a mother may say to her child, "Here is your cup of milk," as she hands it to him, thus signaling the meanings of *cup* and *milk*.

However, everyday oral contexts cease to be a rich source for vocabulary growth as children reach school age. Oral language—even between college-educated adults—contains an average of 17 "rare" words per 1,000 running words (Hayes & Ahrens, 1988). "Rare" words are those whose frequency in the language is less than that of the 10,000 most frequent words. Examples include *alias*, *nation*, *cautious*, and *participate*. The lack of such words in oral language means that children informally begin to encounter fewer and fewer words that they do not yet know. Written language, on the other hand, contains many more rare words, about 30 per 1,000 in books written for children—nearly twice as many as in adult conversation. In comparison, books for adults contain about 52 per 1,000. Consequently, for children to continue to experience effective vocabulary growth, they will have to learn new words from written sources. But turning to written language for vocabulary growth presents new challenges. Because written language lacks the immediacy and redundancy of oral language, reading requires us to develop ideas from words alone. This makes figuring out the meanings of unfamiliar words much more difficult.

Although the bulk of a person's vocabulary is learned from printed context, written language is not a reliable source for word meaning information (Beck, McKeown, & McCaslin, 1983; Nagy & Herman, 1987; Sternberg, 1987). Authors do not write in order to teach the meanings of words—they write to express ideas. So the extent to which a word's meaning is apparent is rather random. For example, compare the following sentences and consider the quality of information you would have about each word if you were encountering it for the first time:

> Lisa got to the party late, and as she pushed through the crowd, she couldn't help thinking that everyone there looked *distinguished*.
>
> We weren't looking forward to the scolding Mama would give us when we got home, so we *dawdled* along the way for as long as we could.

Upon reading the first sentence, many possibilities might come to mind for the meaning of *distinguished*: Were the partygoers looking placid? Gloomy? Bored? Dressed to the nines? In the second sentence, however, it would likely be clear to the reader that *dawdled* signals going as slowly as possible.

Consider Nagy, Herman, and Anderson's (1985) calculation that of every 100 unfamiliar words encountered in reading, about five of them are learned. Although other researchers have estimated word learning as high as 15 per 100 words, they measured learning immediately after reading, while Nagy et al. measured learning 7 days later (Swanborn & de Glopper, 1999). It is also the case that lower-ability readers have a very difficult time making use of clues to word meaning in written language (McKeown, 1985). Thus, the students most in need of vocabulary enhancement are further disadvantaged.

Learning the vocabulary of written language, although challenging, is critical to achieving literacy. The task's importance is captured by Corson's concept of the lexical bar (1985, 1995). According to Corson, a barrier—a lexical bar—exists between everyday meaning systems and the meaning system created by academic, literate culture. In talking about a barrier between everyday language and text language, Corson reflects the findings of Hayes and Ahrens (1988), who noted the sharp distinctions between the word stock of informal oral language and that of written language. For individuals to achieve any measure of literacy, they need to cross the lexical bar (Corson, 1995).

Learning Is Incremental

The third principle of vocabulary acquisition is that learning is incremental. Understanding of a word's meaning accumulates as a learner encounters the word in different contexts. These different contexts are necessary to provide the nuances of meaning that lead to a decontextualized representation of meaning—a representation that the reader can use to make sense of subsequent contexts containing the word. Multiple contexts are needed even if an initial encounter provides strong clues to the word's meaning. Consider, for example, the following sentence as a reader's first encounter with the word *accumulate*: "Each day at the beach we collected more shells, until by the end of the week we had accumulated more than we could fit in our pail." It seems likely that the reader would readily infer that *accumulate* means that a bunch of things had been collected. But even with that clear a context, the reader wouldn't yet know, for example, whether the word was used only for something deliberately gathered, only for something being sought for a collection, or whether it always indicated getting too much of something. Further experiences with the word would be needed to clarify those aspects.

Recent and very intriguing perspectives on learning word meanings suggest that knowledge of a word can be enhanced not only by encountering the word in context but also in contexts that do not even contain the word being learned. Several recently developed models of word learning allow for this possibility, including Landauer's latent semantic analysis (Landauer & Dumais, 1997), the REAP model (Heilman, Zhao, Pino, & Eskenazi, 2008), and Reichle and Perfetti's word-experience model (2003; as described in Bolger, Balass, Landen, & Perfetti, 2008).

Opportunities to enhance word knowledge with contexts that do not contain the word arise because of the way readers process text. In the process of reading, the reader activates words related to the context. This activation creates a connection between the activated word and the context in the reader's semantic network. Thus, words in a context that may be associated with a newly learned word can add to a reader's knowledge of that word. Imagine, for example, a student who has just learned that the word *drowsy* means "feeling like you are going to fall asleep." Further imagine that the student then encountered a sentence such as "I was fighting to stay awake, but I finally stretched out on the couch." As he reads the sentence, the reader might activate a scenario of not being able to stay awake, feeling sleepy, then giving in to sleep. Within that scenario, the word *drowsy* could be activated, adding to the student's mental representation of the word, also called his "semantic network" for the word.

Additional encounters, either with a word being learned or with words that can be associated with the word, allow a learner to add to or refine aspects of what is understood about a word's meaning, and to figure out which aspects apply generally across the uses of a word and which are context-specific.

What We Have Learned
about Vocabulary Instruction from Research

Instruction can play a role in literacy development if it has features that conform to the principles of how vocabulary is acquired, by helping students form connections to new words through experiences with many different contexts. This conclusion was reached over decades of research.

Early vocabulary research tended to focus on the ability to associate a word with a definition or synonym and, as measured by typical multiple-choice tests, was successful. This early research is discussed in several reviews of the field (e.g.,

Baumann, Kame'enui, & Ash, 2003; Beck & McKeown, 1991; Graves, 1986). The basic message they convey is that all instructional methods produce better word learning than no instruction, no particular method seems consistently superior, and advantages accrue from repeated exposures to the instructed words. Given the strong correlational relationship between vocabulary and comprehension, improvement in comprehension might also have been expected from gains in vocabulary. But prior to the 1980s, evidence of comprehension improvement from vocabulary instruction was elusive, with most studies finding no effects (e.g., Baumann et al., 2003; Stahl & Fairbanks, 1986).

As researchers sought to understand why vocabulary instruction generally did not improve comprehension, evidence began to indicate that the semantic network connections built over time and across multiple experiences when learners spontaneously acquire vocabulary play a key role in vocabulary's effect on comprehension. Because comprehension is a complex process, a reader must actively work on information encountered in text in order to build understanding. This requires readers to call on their semantic networks to bring meaning to the words that are read. Thus, it became apparent that to affect comprehension, instruction needed to provide learners with more than simple associations between words and definitions. Key research that brought the field to the conclusion that vocabulary instruction needs to aim for more than mastering definitions included Mezynski's review of instruction (1983), Stahl and Fairbanks's meta-anlaysis (1986), and research studies by Beck and McKeown and their colleagues (Beck, Perfetti, & McKeown, 1982; McKeown, Beck, Omanson, & Perfetti, 1983; McKeown, Beck, Omanson, & Pople, 1985), and others (Kame'enui, Carnine, & Freschi, 1982; Margosein, Pascarella, & Pflaum, 1982).

The instruction in Beck and McKeown's work included frequent encounters with each word and used an assortment of activities to engage student processing. For example, after being introduced to word meanings and contextual examples, students were asked to discuss whether they would *berate* someone who had *inspired* them, or whether a *tyrant* could be a *miser*. Following the Beck et al. (1982) and McKeown et al. (1983) studies, two reviews analyzed features of instruction in studies that succeeded or failed to affect comprehension. Mezynski (1983), in a review of eight studies, and Stahl and Fairbanks (1986), in a meta-analysis of about 30 studies, concluded that instruction that succeeded in affecting comprehension includes three features: more than one or two exposures to each word; both definitional and contextual information; and engagement of students in active, or deep, processing.

A subsequent study by McKeown et al. (1985) directly compared instruction designed to engage active processing with instruction that focused on practice of definitions. High (12) and low (4) frequencies of encounters with the words were also investigated for both types of instruction. For accuracy of knowledge, as measured by a multiple-choice test, high frequency of instruction led to better results, but whether instruction emphasized active processing or practice of definitions did not make a difference. However, on measures of comprehension, type of instruction *did* make a difference, with only instruction that encouraged active processing of words and featured 12 encounters showing comprehension effects.

Our understanding of the relationship between vocabulary instruction and comprehension still has some gaps, especially in terms of general gains and long-term consequences. Typically, gains on standardized tests of comprehension are rare. But this result needs to be considered in the context of the state of the field's ability to assess vocabulary learning in a general way. As Pearson, Hiebert, and Kamil (2007) note, "Measures of vocabulary are inadequate to the challenge of documenting the relationship between word learning and global measures of comprehension. ... Measures are so insensitive that they prevent us from documenting that relationship" (p. 283).

A recent meta-analysis by Elleman, Lindo, Morphy, and Compton (2009) speaks to the challenges of understanding the vocabulary–comprehension relationship. The authors report finding good news—that vocabulary instruction improves comprehension when assessed by experimenter-designed measures. Better yet, they found that students with reading difficulties received even greater benefit from vocabulary instruction. Elleman et al.'s analysis could not identify qualities that made vocabulary instruction more effective, because not enough studies systematically compared the different components, such as levels of processing, and number and types of encounters. However, they did find that more effective instruction included high levels of discussion.

When the researchers examined the results from standardized measures, in contrast to experimenter-designed measures, no effects of instruction were found. Elleman et al. (2009) echo the conclusion of Pearson et al. (2007) that until we have more sensitive measures, "we will not be able to determine to what extent vocabulary knowledge contributes to comprehension" (p. 36).

The field is very much in need of assessments that show what students do gain from vocabulary instruction. For example, when does instruction lead students to learn words beyond the words taught? And what mechanism causes that to occur? It seems that knowing some words makes learning other words easier—but is that because with more known words, new contexts have proportionally more known material to assist with learning words in contexts that remain unfamiliar? Latent semantic analysis (Landauer & Dumais, 1997) would imply a "yes" to that question, suggesting that every word learned reduces the number of sentences a reader will encounter with unknown words, and that learning one word, even partially, helps the reader learn other words (Landauer, 2009).

Or is the mechanism that leads to independent learning the richer semantic network created from learning more words? The greater amount of connections in a richer semantic network could allow a learner to make meaningful associations to new words more easily as they are encountered. Perfetti's (2007) LQH would seem to support the idea that the key to comprehending a text is the reader's ability to retrieve the meanings needed in a given context. The speed and quality of retrieval are driven by the connections in one's semantic network.

Instruction for Younger Learners

In the past decade or so, research has shown us that instruction can, and needs to, start early. Traditionally, vocabulary instruction started around third grade. Now we understand that if we wait to help children acquire the words they need to comprehend the academic language in their textbooks and at the same time expect them to be learning content from those texts, we will be too late. We need to give students a head start, so that when faced with more difficult content, they already have some of that vocabulary as a foundation. Thus, students will be well-equipped to learn both content and words that are new to them. Researchers have examined the results of teaching new word meanings to children in kindergarten, and now even to preschoolers (Justice, Kaderavek, Fan, Sofka, & Hunt, 2009; Leung, 2008; Roskos et al., 2008).

The most common context for studies of vocabulary learning for younger learners is a story read aloud. Reading to children has been characterized as "a cornerstone of literacy development" (Brabham & Lynch-Brown, 2002, p. 465), and positive correlations between being read to and eventual reading achievement have been published in journals for over 50 years (Teale, 2003). Thus, reading aloud seems to be a natural vehicle for developing ways to enhance vocabulary.

The read-aloud vocabulary research began with investigation of the extent of incidental word learning from a single reading of a story (Biemiller & Boote, 2006; Elley, 1989; Nicholson & Whyte, 1992; Penno, Wilkinson, & Moore, 2002; Robbins & Ehri, 1994; Sénéchal, Thomas, & Monker, 1995). Researchers generally found a learning effect, but a disappointingly small one. Some researchers then augmented the read-alouds with direct explanation of word meanings as the story was read (e.g., Biemiller & Boote, 2006; Elley, 1989; Penno et al., 2002) or repeated readings of the stories (Elley, 1989; Penno et al., 2002). Adding these strategies brought greater effects for acquiring vocabulary. However, what we know about effective vocabulary instruction might call into question the approach of repeated readings, even when bolstered by explanations. The studies based on reading aloud provide both contextual and definitional information, but only the single context from the read-aloud. They provide multiple encounters, but only with that single context and an explanation of its meaning. They do not provide the variety of encounters or the depth of processing identified by Stahl and Fairbanks (1986) and Mezynski (1983) as needed for instruction that affects complex language situations.

A few studies based on reading aloud do include instructional activities that might address the deep processing feature (e.g., Beck & McKeown, 2007; Coyne, McCoach, Loftus, Zipoli, & Kapp, 2010; Coyne, Simmons, Kame'enui, & Stoolmiller, 2004; Silverman, 2007; Wasik & Bond, 2001). The approaches used in these studies prompt students to interact with target words through activities that pose questions about the words, or ask students to create uses for the words. In Beck and McKeown's work, the interactions were based on the instruction that they developed to engage student processing in their initial vocabulary research with fourth graders (Beck et al., 1983; McKeown et al., 1985). Coyne et al. (2004) used an approach with a number of components, including explanation of word meanings during reading and follow-up activities that promote interaction, for example, "Is a *rumpus* more like sitting quietly or wild play?" Silverman (2007) used similar approaches, providing contexts for children to reflect on and discuss. Wasik and Bond's approach (2001) included introducing words before reading; interactive discussion during book reading, prompted by questions such as "What can I do with this [pointing to object pictured in story]?"; and follow-up activities related to the words.

Both Coyne and his colleagues and Silverman have compared types of instruction. Coyne, McCoach, and Kapp (2007) and Coyne et al. (2010) compared repeated readings of stories (1) with embedded instruction, which presented explanations of word meaning during the readings, and (2) with extended instruction, which provided activities asking children to respond to a variety of contexts. They found the extended instruction significantly better on all measures, which included expressive and receptive definitions, and recognition of uses in context. Silverman (2007) compared approaches, again implemented after story read-alouds. The analytic approach, which asked children to think and talk about various contexts for the words, was compared to a contextual approach, in which activities were limited to asking children to supply associations to words based on their own experiences. She found that the analytic approach, which offered a variety of contexts for children to consider, was significantly more effective. Coyne et al. (2007, 2010) and Silverman (2007), by directly comparing types of instruction, help us to zero in on the features of instruction that most effectively produce learning.

Based on theory and prior research with older students, we might expect comprehension to be impacted by the instruction in these studies as well. However, studies with younger students have not examined the effect of these strategies on comprehension. One recent exception is a study by Coyne, McCoach, Loftus, Zipoli, Ruby, et al. (2010) in which kindergartners who learned vocabulary through interactive, robust instruction showed enhanced comprehension relative to control students on a listening comprehension measure.

Which Words to Teach?

The first decision to make in the development of instruction in vocabulary is which words to teach. That is an issue that has received surprisingly little attention, a point that Coyne et al. (2004) also make. In both commercial instructional materials and instructional research on vocabulary, we see a range and variety of words, even within the same lessons. Consider, for example, the following list of words whose meanings were to be introduced in conjunction with a reading selection in a third-grade basal: *gym, recite, prefer, perform, enjoying,* and *billions* (Farr et al., 2000). Consider the difference in the utility and familiarity of the words.

For example, not only is *gym* most likely known by third graders, but it also has a much more limited role in a literate repertoire relative to *prefer* and *perform*.

Similarly, consider words included in several research studies: *corridor*, *elderly*, *gazing*, and *satchel* (Sénéchal & Cornell, 1993); *anguish*, *parasol*, *calamity*, and *tilted* (Elley, 1989). Consider the utility of words such as *parasol* and *satchel* compared to *gazing*, *anguish*, and *calamity*.

Historically, most researchers spent very little time providing a rationale for the words they selected to be taught. Often they dealt with that issue by simply saying that words believed to be unfamiliar to students were selected as targets of the instruction. The earliest attention to the kinds of words to be taught was Beck and McKeown's concept of word tiers, initially discussed in Beck, McKeown, and Omanson (1987). The concept of word tiers became more prominent when it was discussed and expanded in Beck, McKeown and Kucan's books, *Bringing Words to Life* (2002) and *Creating Robust Vocabulary* (2008). We conceptualized a three-tier heuristic as a means of identifying a potentially manageable set of words for reading and language arts instruction by considering that different words have different utility and roles in the language (Beck et al., 1987).

We designated Tier 1 as words typically found in oral language, including those likely found in conversations with young children (e.g., *bed*, *boy*, *run*, *busy*). Children entering school typically know the meanings of such words, and there is little need for direct instruction of the meanings of these words in school.

Tier 3 consists of words with quite low frequency of use that usually apply to specific domains. Many Tier 3 words represent new concepts and, as such, are part of the content being learned in a particular subject area, such as *peninsula* in association with geography. Other examples include words such as *isotope*, *colonists*, and *legislate*. These words are taught to build students' content knowledge rather than to expand their general language repertoire. Knowledge of Tier 3 words as independent items would not be of high utility for most learners.

But a word in Tier 3 is not necessarily conceptually difficult. Because tiers are determined by the roles words play in the language, Tier 3 words are those with particular and narrow roles in the language. So Tier 3 includes words of science, engineering, and economics—words that would be unfamiliar to many literate adults and, indeed, conceptually challenging. But Tier 3 also includes words that may be familiar, such as *piano*, the use of which is restricted to the domain of music.

Even young children add Tier 3 words to their vocabularies as they build knowledge of the world. *Butterflies*, *earthworms*, and *chipmunks* are all Tier 3 words. Such words are appropriate for young students to know, and they can be taught through simple explanation or illustration. Thus, they are not good candidates for rich vocabulary instruction.

We turn now to Tier 2, which contains words of high utility for literate language users. These words characterize text and are not so common in conversation (Hayes & Ahrens, 1988). They are also words of general utility, not limited to a specific domain. Some examples might be *versatile*, *cherish*, *awe*, and *emerge*.

Because of the role they play in a language user's verbal repertoire, rich knowledge of words in Tier 2 can have a significant impact on verbal functioning.

Although we believe that Tier 2 words should be the major focus of vocabulary instruction, even for young students, we acknowledge that not all children know the meanings of all Tier 1 words when they enter school. Thus, some attention to Tier 1 words may be called for in school. Because Tier 1 words are used in everyday conversation, it seems that lots of conversational talk is the best way to help children become familiar with and able to use these words. As Stahl and Nagy (2006) noted, directly explaining the meanings of common words is not a useful instructional task.

Several other scholars of vocabulary have provided input on the kinds of words best targeted for instruction. The approaches can be roughly divided by researchers who, like Beck and McKeown, describe criteria for choosing words (Nation, 2001; Stahl & Nagy, 2006) and those who have developed procedures for identifying specific words (Biemiller, 2001, 2005; Hiebert, 2005).

Biemiller (2001, 2005) and Hiebert (2005) have developed well-specified approaches to selecting words to teach primary-grade children. Biemiller has been working on a system for selecting words based on testing words from several levels of the Living Word Vocabulary (LWV; Dale & O'Rourke, 1979), developed from a study of the vocabulary knowledge of students in grades 4, 6, 8, 10, 12, and early college. The LWV is dated in some respects, and its methodology has been called into question (Hiebert, 2005). But it is the only available source about vocabulary based on students' knowledge of words. Other sources that provide grade-level vocabulary are based on frequency counts—analysis of the frequency of words in printed school materials.

Biemiller began testing words from LWV's fourth-grade level and initially found that most of the words known by 80% of fourth graders were actually already known by children at the end of second grade (Biemiller & Slonim, 2001). Biemiller and Slonim's results also suggested that words are learned in a roughly sequential order. From these results, Biemiller reasoned that since words seem to be acquired in a roughly sequential order, teaching them in that order would be beneficial. He identified as optimal candidates for instruction those words that 30–70% of children knew when tested, and that seemed likely to be learned *next*.

Hiebert's (2005) approach to selecting words for vocabulary instruction aims to identify words that are unknown to students in first through fourth grades, but that account for a significant portion of texts in grades 5 and above. To define her vocabulary curriculum, Hiebert has selected a database of words from the texts used in the fourth-grade versions of prominent standards-based tests (three state tests and the National Assessment of Educational Progress [NAEP]), and categorized the words according to zones that correspond to bands of frequency. Zones 1 through 4 contain 5,586 words that Hiebert has designated for teaching in grades 1 through 4. With instruction directed to Zones 1 through 4, students would have been taught about 92% of the words on the prominent tests.

Other scholars have taken an approach more similar to that of Beck and

McKeown, categorizing words based on their role and utility in the language, and laying out guidelines for selecting words to teach. Stahl and Nagy (2006) approached the issue of which words to select and what kind of attention to devote to different words using characteristics such as frequency, utility, and requirements for learning to create descriptive categories of word types. Two key categories that to Stahl and Nagy merit significant attention are "high-frequency words" and "high-utility general vocabulary." They characterize high-frequency words as those that make up the bulk of words in any genre, spoken or written. This category is similar to our Tier 1 words. Stahl and Nagy suggest that many, if not most, students are familiar with these words early in their school careers. However, given the importance of these words, Stahl and Nagy suggest providing many opportunities for students to deal with these words in context.

Stahl and Nagy's high-utility general vocabulary words, similar to our Tier 2 words, are described as those that "may be uncommon in conversation but are part of the core of written language that students encounter in their texts . . . words you'd expect to be part of a literate person's vocabulary" (2006, p. 61). They offer examples for the first nine letters of the alphabet: *abolish, banish, chamber, deliberate, exceed, frequent, genuine, hospitable, initiative.*

Nation (2001) provides similar consideration of which words merit instruction, and although the discussion is targeted to learning English as a second language (ESL), the constructs he presents are relevant for first language (L1) learning as well. Nation identifies four kinds of vocabulary to consider when designing instruction: high-frequency, academic, technical, and low-frequency. Nation points out that almost 80% of the running words in any text are high frequency. Such words would generally be included in our Tier 1 category. Nation asserts that the high-frequency words are important enough to merit significant attention—but recall that this is aimed at second language (L2) learners.

Nation's category of academic words comprises common words across domains of academic texts, and they typically make up about 9% of running words in a text. Here Nation cites Coxhead's Academic Word List (1998) as a good database. Coxhead's list of 570 word families is drawn from a corpus of 3,500,000 running words from academic journals and university textbooks in four broad academic areas: arts, commerce, law, and natural science. Both range and frequency were considered in selecting the words, such that all word families on the list occur in all four academic areas and are used at least 100 times in the corpus. Nation views academic words as essential to teach, because of their range of coverage over various types of text and the meaning they bring to a text. These words would overlap our Tier 2 category.

The two remaining categories in Nation's scheme, technical words and low-frequency words, cover the remaining 10% of running words, with each approximated at 5%. Technical words are those closely related to a specific topic or subject area but not so common beyond it. Nation's technical words are similar to our Tier 3 words, and he asserts that teaching such words makes sense only when learning the specialized subject matter. Low-frequency words in Nation's view require little instructional time, because they make up a very small percentage of any single text. Yet they are the largest group of words in the language, and Nation acknowledges that the boundary between high and low frequency is an arbitrary one in which the low-frequency category includes both words that almost got into the high-frequency category and words that are truly rare.

Despite the different criteria and procedures discussed, each approach finally comes to rely on subjective judgment for selecting words to teach. Biemiller and Boote (2005) acknowledge this aspect in two ways. First they discuss the lack of clear criteria for distinguishing *teachable* and *too hard* words, saying that they are "left with testing and some uses of intuition for identifying word meanings for instruction" (p. 4). Second, they mention their research group's need to evaluate "word importance" to distinguish words that are most useful to learn. Hiebert (2005) acknowledges the judgment component in discussing implications for teachers, for example, pointing out the relative utility of words *checkpoint* and *cautiously* that appear in the same text (pp. 260–261). The approaches espoused by Stahl and Nagy, Nation, and Beck and McKeown all inherently view judgment as a key component, in that these approaches describe criteria for choosing words rather than procedures for identifying specific words.

All of the approaches to selecting words for instruction have a common purpose: to identify words that are most productive for students' literacy outcomes, primarily the ability to comprehend text by teaching words that will be encountered often enough to be useful, while avoiding words that are already familiar or so rare as to be of little future use. But these parameters of usefulness are specified very differently for the various approaches and result in targeting different parts of the English lexicon for instruction.

Instructional Features and Activities

What is the starting point for vocabulary instruction? Most commonly it is a text, either a text read aloud to students or one that students are reading together or on their own as part of classroom work. Typically, a set of words is drawn from the text as target words for the lesson. When we began our study of vocabulary with fourth graders (Beck et al., 1982), however, we did not organize words around texts. Rather, we organized each week's word set around a (loose) theme; for example, the set for "Speaking" included *wail, chorus, proclaim, mention, commend, berate,* and *urge.* We began each week's instruction by announcing the theme to students.

Our more recent vocabulary work, however, begins with a read-aloud, and we think this works very well, because after the story is read, there is a ready context in which to introduce the words. For example, we can begin instruction by saying, "In the story, Jessica and her friend were inseparable. That means they never wanted to be apart from each other." Note that the context from the story is restated, then paraphrased using familiar words rather than the target word. Thus, the meaning of the context is fully explained.

Our work using read-alouds has been with kindergarten and first-grade children, but the read-aloud can be an effective choice even with older students. Many students, even at intermediate and middle school grades, can understand more sophisticated text than they can read themselves. And if students are reading below grade level—and students most in need of vocabulary development often are—the texts they read may have few Tier 2 words. Choosing words from more sophisticated texts that can be read aloud provides a richer word choice.

In our vocabulary instruction, the text is read once, then the lesson moves to work with the words. Other researchers have the text read several times. The multiple readings seem to have grown from early efforts to influence vocabulary by simply reading aloud and increasing exposure to the text in an effort to produce more learning. But, as discussed earlier, researchers have moved beyond reading alone as a way to develop vocabulary, and have added explanations of the words and other activities. There may indeed be reasons to read texts twice—because children want to hear it, because parts of the text can be discussed more closely, or for purposes such as attending to the descriptions an author uses, and so forth. But it is unclear what multiple readings add to vocabulary learning, especially if there is a good amount of language interaction in the instruction itself.

The Role of Definitions

Providing a definition can be a strong starting point for understanding a word. Several caveats operate here, however. The definition has to be explanatory; it has to describe the meaning in terms that are readily understood by the student, and that provide a sense of what the particular word means. Definitions should not come one right after the other; rather, some work should be done with each individual word before going on to the next. Note that this means that having students look up a list of words in the dictionary is not recommended. In fact, it should be prohibited!

The benefit of a definition is that it provides an explicit, general meaning, not tied to a specific context. If a context alone is presented as a starting point, elements from the context that are not part of the word's meaning might be understood as part of the meaning. For example, in *Charlotte's Web*, Templeton the rat announces, "I am a glutton but not a merry-maker," and goes off to eat the breakfast that Wilbur left untouched. If students were introduced to the word *glutton* using only this context, they might get the idea that being a glutton means eating someone else's food.

A major drawback of definitions from traditional dictionaries is that students do not understand them. Several research studies have shown that students have difficulty making sense of dictionary definitions (McKeown, 1993; Miller & Gildea, 1985). There are, however, some better choices in dictionaries. They include the *Collins COBUILD English Dictionary* (1987) and the *Longman*

Advanced American Dictionary (Delacroix et al., 2007), both of which were developed as learner dictionaries—learners for whom English is not their L1. These dictionaries are, however, extremely useful for native English speakers of all ages. COBUILD is "designed to read like ordinary English" (1987, p. xvi) and its definitions (actually, they call them *explanations*) appear as full sentences and show how the words are used in the language. *Longman* constructs all of its definitions using the 2,000 most common words in the language. Table 7.1 shows definitions of the words *devious* and *exotic* from a traditional dictionary, COBUILD, and *Longman*. It's easy to see why a student using the traditional dictionary might interpret *devious* as not going straight, and end up with the sentence "The boy was devious on his bike."

When we began our vocabulary research, neither COBUILD nor *Longman* dictionaries were available, so we reformulated the definitions we found into what we call "friendly explanations." But even definitions from COBUILD or *Longman* may need tweaking, depending on the age of the students. So let's take a look at what goes into a friendly explanation.

A "friendly explanation" defines a word's meaning in everyday, connected language. Like the COBUILD definitions, it exemplifies use of the word. Friendly explanations strive to present a clear, distinct meaning for a word. For example, a glossary or dictionary might define *conspicuous* as "easy to see." But that could fit *visible* as well. So a friendly explanation also makes clear the distinct character of the word: "If something is conspicuous, you see it right away, because it stands out." Or consider this friendly explanation for *illusion*: "something that looks like one thing, but is really something else or is not there at all." Contrast this to a traditional dictionary definition: "appearance or feeling that misleads because it is not real," which could apply to anything from fake flowers to a toupee!

Interactive Practice

After introducing a word by talking about its context within a text and providing an explanation of its meaning, the teacher should then actively engage students with the meaning. Even good contexts and explanations are static information, and learners need to act on information if they are to truly come to own it. The

TABLE 7.1. Comparing Definitions from Different Dictionaries

Word	Traditional	COBUILD	Longman
devious	Straying from the right course; not straightforward	Someone who is devious is dishonest and secretive, often in a complicated way	Using tricks or lies to get what you want
exotic	Foreign; strange; not native	Something that is exotic is strange, unusual, and interesting because it comes from a distant country	Unusual and exciting because of a connection with a foreign country

most effective and efficient activity elicits quick responses and multiple associations. The activity we have used most often goes something like this:

> "I'm going to say some things, and if you think they would be *conspicuous*, say '*conspicuous*'; if not, say 'no.' Ready?
>> 'Someone wearing rainboots on a sunny day.'
>> 'A tree in the forest.'
>> 'A gorilla in a first-grade classroom.'"

The activity also includes asking why or why not after students respond, first, to be sure students are making the correct association, and, second, to strengthen the connection between the word and its meaning. For example, a student might say, "Wearing rainboots would be *conspicuous* because most people wouldn't have boots on if it was sunny, so you'd look pretty funny if you did." This would reinforce being *conspicuous* as looking unusual compared to others around you.

For a vocabulary lesson following reading of a text, each word in the set to be targeted is introduced in this way; that is, the context for the story is reviewed, a friendly explanation is offered, and an interaction follows. Visual and phonological representations are also provided. A card with the word on it is held up as each word is introduced. The teacher says the word, then asks students to repeat it. Several studies have shown that providing visual and phonological representations makes the instruction more effective (Rosenthal & Ehri, 2008; Silverman, 2007).

Over the subsequent 3 or 4 days, activities including the taught words are presented. The following illustrates a follow-up activity for the word *conspicuous* and describes what the activity is asking of students.

TEACHER	STUDENTS
Which would be *conspicuous*, a man walking down the street carrying a briefcase, or a man carrying a live alligator?	*Students choose the example of something conspicuous from the pair of descriptions that are similar (man walking down the street carrying something) but distinguished by something related to the target word.*
What would be *conspicuous* on the playground? What would be *conspicuous* in your bookbag?	*Students respond to questions that ask them to place the word within their own experiences, thus forming a connection between the word and their own lives.*
If a friend was trying to find you in a crowd of people, how would you make yourself look *conspicuous*?	*Again students are asked to place the word within their own lives. But here they generate a way to be conspicuous.*

The car looked *conspicuous* because
_____.

Students complete a context to create a scenario for a conspicuous car. We find that asking for sentence completion prompts much better uses of words than asking students to produce a sentence (often resulting in, for example, "He was conspicuous").

Notice that the word *activity* here doesn't mean asking students to go do something, but rather asks them to be mentally active in thinking about and using the word. Also notice that these activities are very simple: They ask for oral responses and do not require materials or organization. The intent is to spend the maximum amount of time and attention thinking about the words. So, for example, drawing in response to a word can be a good activity, but to provide maximum effect children should not spend too much time on an illustration for one word. An effective format might be to allow children a few minutes to draw something about a word they choose, then have a discussion in which children can share their words, drawings, and ideas. Thus, children get input from more than just their own drawing, and they also explore language related to their ideas.

Assessing Students' Vocabulary Learning

A sequence of lessons most typically concludes with an assessment. Why is that? Presumably, it is to understand what students have learned. Assessments for vocabulary can take many forms depending on the teacher's purpose. For example, an easy assessment might be designed around recognizing definitions of the words. This lets a teacher know whether students have some minimal familiarity with the words, and it might give students a feeling of accomplishment.

More challenging assessments can be created that, for example, require students to complete sentence stems for each word. Alternatively, cloze sentences can be created that require students to fill in the correct target word. For students who cannot yet respond in writing, developing a useful and feasible assessment is more difficult. So sentence completions are possible, but they require each student to give an individual oral response. A format we have used with young learners is "Yes–No"—essentially a true–false test. The content can be definition-like, with items such as "Does *avoid* mean stay away from? … Does *avoid* mean having a good time?" Or contexts can be queried: "If I am afraid of dogs, would I *avoid* them? … If I love ice cream, would I *avoid* it?" The fullest test of this form would have a "yes" and a "no" item for each definition, and a "yes" and a "no" item built around contexts for each word.

The design of an assessment should depend on what you want to know about what students have learned. The purpose of effective vocabulary instruction is for students to learn more than a definition for a word. Students should also be able to use the word in speaking or writing, and to make sense of contexts in which the word appears. This would suggest that the best assessments require students to create or identify contexts. However, when instruction is interactive and requires students to respond to and develop contexts, and discuss the words and their uses, assessments may not be necessary; that is, during the lesson interactions a teacher may be able to take stock of what students are able to do with the words.

A Sample Instructional Sequence

This section presents a sample of a week's sequence of instruction for a set of words. The lesson is based on words from the story *A Pocket for Corduroy* (Freeman, 1978), about a stuffed bear who gets lost in a laundromat, then is found the next day by a very relieved little girl. The instruction is adapted from lessons developed for a recently completed study in kindergarten classrooms. Optimal vocabulary instruction for kindergartners is from six to eight words per week. This sample shows the material for four words. Often with younger students we introduce half of the words right after story reading and wait until later in the day, or even the next day, to introduce the others.

Because the excerpts are taken from a script for a study, notes to the teacher are also included, such as indications of expected responses. We have retained these notes in the material that follows to provide a fuller idea of how the instruction is carried out. Annotations have been added for initial items in some of the activities to explain their purpose, point out their features, or relate them to the features discussed earlier.

Day 1: Introduction

(*Show each word card as you are introducing the word.*)

1. **Reluctant:** In the story, Lisa was *reluctant* to leave the laundromat without Corduroy. That means Lisa did not want to leave the laundromat because Corduroy was lost.

   Story context and paraphrase of context

   When you are *reluctant*, you are worried about doing something and you don't want to do it.

   Friendly explanation

   Let's say that word again. (*reluctant*)

   Phonological representation

   - Let's think about being *reluctant*. I will say some things and if you think you would be *reluctant* to do it, say, "Reluctant." If not, say, "No!"

   Interactive practice

(For each item, call on a student to explain his or her response. For example, for the first item, ask, "Why would you be reluctant *to hold a spider?")*	*Explanation is prompted.*
○ Holding a tarantula spider. (*reluctant*) ○ Petting a kitten. (**no**) ○ Jumping out of a tall tree. (*reluctant*)	*Both positive and negative examples are included.*

2. **Insist:** In the story, Lisa's mother *insisted* that she leave the laundromat when it was closing. That means Lisa's mother said she must leave the laundro-mat—Lisa did not have a choice.

   If someone *insists* that you do something, they say that you have to do it.

   Let's say that word again. (*insist*)

   • Let's think about someone *insisting*. I will say some things and if you think the person would be insisting, say, "Insist." If not, say, "No!"

   (For each item, call on a student to explain his or her response.)

   ○ A teacher tells you to finish your work before lunch. (*insist*)

   ○ A babysitter tells a child to jump on the bed. (**no**)

   ○ A policeman tells a driver to slow down. (*insist*)

3. **Rummage:** In the story, Corduroy *rummaged* through the laundry bag, hop-ing to find something he could use to make a pocket. That means he looked for something by moving things around.

   If you *rummage*, you look for something by moving things around kind of carelessly.

   Let's say the word again. (*rummage*)

   • Let's think about *rummaging*. I'm going to say some things and if you think you would *rummage*, say, "Rummage." If not, say, "No!"

   (For each item, call on a student to explain his or her response.)

   ○ Looking in your desk for a pencil right before a test is about to begin. (*rummage*)

   ○ Reading the pages of a magazine. (**no**)

   ○ Going through the cupboards for a missing box of sugar. (*rummage*)

4. **Eager:** In the story, Corduroy was *eager* to find something he could use to make a pocket. That means he really wanted to make the pocket.

   If you are *eager* to do something, you really want to do it.

   Let's say the word again. (*eager*)

   • Let's think about being *eager*. I am going to say some things and if you think you would be *eager* to do them say, "Eager." If not, say, "No!"

(For each item, call on a student to explain his or her response.)

○ Eat a piece of your favorite cake. (*eager*)

○ Go into a dark, scary alley. (**no**)

○ Read your favorite story. (*eager*)

Day 2: Review and Practice

Review with Questions

Notice in the activity below that for each word there is a question about the meaning and one that asks students to choose which of two contexts goes with the word.

We learned some new words yesterday. These words were *reluctant, insist, rummage,* and *eager.* I'm going to ask you some questions to review these words. (**Show the card as you review each word.**)

> *(If a student gives a wrong answer, call on another student, then remind students of the definition.)*

1. Does *reluctant* mean you don't want to do something or that you are very excited?

   Students are asked to choose the correct meaning rather than recall it, so that the task is more game-like and removed from the realm of memorization.

2. What would you be *reluctant* to do: eat something that smelled funny, or eat your favorite cookie?

   When a student responds, ask why. If a student says "favorite cookie," and can give a good reason, such as "It might be the last one and I'd want to save it," accept the response. But then call on another student to respond, so that a more typical connection can be made.

3. Does *insist* mean that you laugh so hard you get the hiccups or that someone tells you to do something and you don't have a choice?

4. What would your dad *insist* that you do: hold his hand when crossing the street, or cross the street without looking both ways?

5. Does *rummage* mean to look for something and move things around carelessly, or to climb up a tree?

6. Who is *rummaging*, a man going through trash looking for his credit card, or a man pinning a receipt to a bulletin board?

7. Does *eager* mean that you can't wait to do something, or that you are feeling cold?

8. What would you be *eager* to do, turn off your favorite video game, or go to your best friend's birthday party?

Situations and Examples

In this activity students are asked to explain contexts that contain the target words.

(Show card for each word.)

1. Think about the word *insist*.

   If you were talking loudly when your brother was taking a nap, your mom might *insist* that you be quiet.

   • Can you think of something else that your mom might *insist* that you do? (*As children provide examples, respond by stating the connection between the word and its meaning. For example, "Yes, your mom might* insist *that you clean your room because she wants it to look nice."*)

2. Let's think about the word *reluctant*.

   • Why would you be *reluctant* to take out the kitchen trash? (*For example, it smells bad; it's hard work; maybe it's cold outside.*)

3. Think about the word *rummage*.

   • When might you *rummage* through your backpack? (*For example, if you have a lot of stuff in it and you are looking for your homework.*)

4. Think about the word *eager*.

   • Why would you feel *eager* to go swimming on a hot day? (*For example, because swimming is a fun way to get cool.*)

Day 3: Practice with Words

Actions with Words

In this activity students respond physically to the words. Students seem to have a lot of fun with this, and to remember the motions associated with the words very well.

1. Let's think about the word *rummage*.
   - Pretend that you have a big bag full of stuff in front of you, and you want to pull out a pencil. What would you look like if you were *rummaging* through a bag? **(Students should be moving their hands in a way that looks like they are searching through a bag.)**

     (If students are unable to demonstrate, you should demonstrate, and explain your actions for the word.)
   - *(Call on a student to describe what he or she is doing and why that goes with* **rummage**.*)*

     The teacher asks for an explanation to make sure that the students understand appropriate actions and can relate them to the meaning elements of the word.

     (If students are unable to answer, describe what the student is doing and explain how this goes with **rummage**.*)*

2. Now I want you to think about the word *eager*.
   - If I asked you a question and you knew the answer and were *eager* to say it, what would you do? Act like I just asked you a question and you are *eager* to answer. **(Students may quickly raise a hand in air and start shaking it wildly, as is commonplace when students really wants to answer a question.)**

     (If students are unable to demonstrate, you should demonstrate, and explain your actions for the word.)
   - *(Call on a student to describe what he or she is doing and why that goes with* eager.*)*

     (If students are unable to answer, describe what the student is doing and explain how this goes with eager.*)*

3. Think about the word *reluctant*.
   - If I told you that it is time for gym class but you are *reluctant* to go, what would you look like? Act like you are feeling *reluctant* to go to gym (**arms crossed, frowning**).

     (If students are unable to demonstrate, you should demonstrate, and explain your actions for the word.)
   - *(Call on a student to describe what he or she is doing and why that goes with* **reluctant**.*)*

     (If students are unable to answer, describe what the student is doing and explain how this goes with **reluctant**.*)*

4. Think about the word *insist*.

  - If you *insisted* that your sister clean up the mess she made in your bedroom, what would you look like? Act like you are *insisting* (**hands on hips, moving finger, curled brow**).

    (If students are unable to demonstrate, you should demonstrate, and explain your actions for the word.)

  - *(Call on a student to describe what he or she is doing and why that goes with* insist.*)*

    (If students are unable to answer, describe what the student is doing and explain how this goes with insisted.*)*

Yes–No

I have some sentences that make sense and some that don't make sense. You decide. If you think it makes sense, everybody say, "Yes." If it doesn't make sense, say, "No."

Listen carefully!

(Show card for each word.)

(For several of the sentences, ask a child to explain why it does or does not make sense. For example, "The sentence 'Jan was reluctant *to go outside when it was stormy' makes sense, because you don't want to go outside and get all wet.")*

1. Jan was *reluctant* to go outside when it was stormy. (**yes**)

2. Mom *insisted* that Chris eat some green beans. (**yes**)

3. Linda *rummaged* through the empty drawer. (**no**)

4. Lauren felt very sick after riding on the merry-go-round and so she was *eager* to ride it again. (**no**)

Day 4: Practice with Words

Idea Substitution

I am going to read a sentence that has something to do with one of your vocabulary words. Then I want you to tell me which new word the sentence has to do with.

(Show cards for each set of words.)

1. The first two words we're using are *reluctant* and *insisted*. (**As needed, repeat the two words.**)

  - Carol didn't want to put on her coat. What word goes with that sentence, *reluctant* or *insisted*? *(reluctant)*

Now let's say the sentence but use *reluctant* in it.

Carol was (*pause for students to say* **reluctant***)* to put on her coat.

Good. Carol was *reluctant* to put on her coat.

As written, the activity directs the teacher to lead students to place the target word within the sentence. Older or more able students could be called on to restate the sentence however they like, as long as it includes the target word.

- Mike's mom said that he had to wash his hands before dinner. What word goes with that sentence, *reluctant* or *insisted*? (*insisted*)

  Now let's say the sentence but use *insisted*.

  Mike's mom (*pause for students to say* **insisted***)* that he wash his hands before dinner.

  Good. Mike's mom *insisted* that he wash his hands before dinner.

2. The two words that I want you to think about are *rummage* and *eager*.
   - Brian dug through his toy box searching for his baseball glove. What word goes with that sentence, *rummage* or *eager*? (**rummage**)

     Now let's say the sentence but use *rummage*.

     Brian (*pause for students to say* **rummaged***)* through his toy box, searching for his baseball glove.

     Good. Brian *rummaged* through his toy box, searching for his baseball glove.
   - Lou couldn't wait to go on vacation because he loved the beach. What word goes with that sentence: *rummage* or *eager*? (**eager**)

     Let's say the sentence but use *eager*.

     Lou was (*pause for students to say* **eager***)* to go on vacation because he loved the beach.

     Good. Lou was *eager* to go on vacation because he loved the beach.

Day 5: Review

I am going to ask you some questions to review the words we've learned this week.

(*Show word card as you review each word.*)

1. Does *reluctant* mean not sure you want to do something, or does it mean to be sad?

2. Does *insist* mean to tell someone to do something, or does it mean to whine?

3. Does *rummage* mean to curl up and go to sleep, or does it mean search for something by throwing things around?

4. Does *eager* mean feeling like you want to do something, or does it mean to feel happy?

Good job, class. Let's give a cheer for our new words!

A Few Further Comments

Because the kinds of activities we have presented are done in an oral mode, they are accessible to all students. Oral responses are easier for students to produce than written responses, and they allow students a window on the thinking of their peers. The intensity of the activities—the multiple encounters and the extended talk around examples produced by asking "why"—helps to ensure students' success, even those students who often struggle with language activities, especially activities that focus on reading.

There are some general ways to get even more from the activities. One is to call attention to good responses by asking other students what they think or asking them to comment on peers' responses. For example, if Tyrone says, "I'm *eager* to eat dinner after I play soccer," you might say, "Tyrone says he is *eager* to have dinner after he plays a soccer game. What do you think? Are you *eager* to eat after you play hard?" Or you could say, "Why do you think Tyrone is so *eager* to eat then?" Questions that prompt a brief response from all students are another way to ensure that more students are actively processing. For example, "Tell me one thing you sometimes have to *rummage* around to find" and call on each student for a one-word response.

Effective vocabulary instruction is motivating. What makes instruction for vocabulary effective is actively processing and manipulating words and contexts, which is exactly what makes the activities engaging and fun. What this means is that we really don't need to create special activities in vocabulary just to motivate students. Good instruction will do that! This point is important, because often teachers think they need to do something out of the ordinary to motivate students, such as create or play a game with words, or have students put on skits. These activities can be reasonable choices *if* most of the time and attention are on connecting words to meanings and contexts. Too often, however, attention to word meanings is only a small side effect of such activities, yet teachers believe they are valuable because they prompt students to enjoy something related to words. It is easy to have fun with words!

In a nutshell, effective vocabulary instruction begins with carefully choosing the words to teach, most often Tier 2 words that represent general concepts but are not commonly used in conversation. Initial instruction for each word is explicit and includes providing student-friendly explanations of words in a clear and familiar context. Depth of word knowledge can then be developed through oral language activities that present the selected words in multiple contexts. These oral activities initially provide students with opportunities to respond to and recognize the correct use of the words. Later practice offers opportunities for students to use and talk about the words in their own ways. These vocabulary interactions allow teachers to monitor individual student learning and to correct word misunderstandings or usage. The repeated practice and peer learning opportunities lead to engaging and intensive investigations into the meanings of new words.

References

Baumann, J. F., Kame'enui, E. J., & Ash, G. E. (2003). Research on vocabulary instruction: Voltaire redux. In J. Flood, D. Lapp, J. R. Squire, & J. M. Jensen (Eds.), *Handbook of research on teaching the English language arts* (pp. 752–785). Mahwah, NJ: Erlbaum.

Beck, I. L., & McKeown, M. G. (1991). Conditions of vocabulary acquisition. In R. Barr, M. L. Kamil, P. Mosenthal, & P. D. Pearson (Eds.), *Handbook of reading research* (Vol. 2, pp. 789–814). New York: Longman.

Beck, I. L., & McKeown, M. G. (2007). Increasing young low-income children's oral vocabulary repertoires through rich and focused instruction. *Elementary School Journal, 107*(3), 251–271.

Beck, I. L., McKeown, M. G., & Kucan, L. (2002). *Bringing words to life: Robust vocabulary instruction.* New York: Guilford Press.

Beck, I. L., McKeown, M. G., & Kucan, L. (2008). *Creating robust vocabulary: Frequently asked questions and extended examples.* New York: Guilford Press.

Beck, I. L., McKeown, M. G., & McCaslin, E. S. (1983). Vocabulary contexts development: All contexts are not created equal. *Elementary School Journal, 83*(3), 177–181.

Beck, I. L., McKeown, M. G., & Omanson, R. C. (1987). The effects and uses of diverse vocabulary instructional techniques. In M. G. McKeown & M. E. Curtis (Eds.), *The nature of vocabulary acquisition* (pp. 147–163). Hillsdale, NJ: Erlbaum.

Beck, I. L., Perfetti, C. A., & McKeown, M. G. (1982). Effects of long-term vocabulary instruction on lexical access and reading comprehension. *Journal of Educational Psychology, 74*(4), 506–521.

Biemiller, A. (2001). Teaching vocabulary: Early, direct, and sequential. *American Educator, 25*(1), 24–28.

Biemiller, A. (2005). Size and sequence in vocabulary development: Implications for choosing words for primary grade vocabulary instruction. In A. Hiebert & M. Kamil (Eds.), *Teaching and learning vocabulary: Bringing research to practice* (pp. 223–242). Mahwah, NJ: Erlbaum.

Biemiller, A., & Boote, C. (2005, April). *Selecting useful word meanings for instruction in the primary grades.* Paper presented at AERA annual meeting, Montreal.

Biemiller, A., & Boote, C. (2006). An effective method for building meaning vocabulary in primary grades. *Journal of Educational Psychology, 98*(1), 44–62.

Biemiller, A., & Slonim, N. (2001). Estimating root word vocabulary growth in normative and advantaged populations: Evidence for a common sequence of vocabulary acquisition. *Journal of Educational Psychology, 93*(3), 498–520.

Bolger, D. J., Balass, M., Landen, E., & Perfetti, C. A. (2008). Contextual variation and definitions in learning the meaning of words. *Discourse Processes, 45*(2), 122–159.

Brabham, E. G., & Lynch-Brown, C. (2002). Effects of teachers' reading-aloud styles on vocabulary acquisition and comprehension of students in the early elementary grades. *Journal of Educational Psychology, 94*(3), 465–473.

Collins COBUILD English language dictionary. (1987). London: William Collins Sons.

Corson, D. J. (1985). *The Lexical Bar.* Oxford, UK: Pergamon Press.

Corson, D. J. (1995). *Using English words.* Dordrecht: Kluwer Academic.

Coxhead, A. (1998). *An Academic Word List* (Occasional Publication Number 18, LALS). Wellington, New Zealand: Victoria University of Wellington.

Coyne, M. D., McCoach, D. B., & Kapp, S. (2007). Vocabulary intervention for kindergarten students: Comparing extended instruction with embedded instruction and incidental exposure. *Learning Disabilities Quarterly, 30*(2), 74–78.

Coyne, M. D., McCoach, D. B., Loftus, S., Zipoli, R., & Kapp, S. (2010). Direct vocabulary instruction in kindergarten: Teaching for breadth vs. depth. *Elementary School Journal, 110*(4), 1–18.

Coyne, M. D., McCoach, D. B., Loftus, S., Zipoli, R., Ruby, M., Crevecoeur, Y., et al. (2010). Direct and extended vocabulary instruction in kindergarten: Investigating transfer effects. *Journal of Research on Educational Effectiveness, 3*(2), 93–120.

Coyne, M. D., Simmons, D. C., Kame'enui, E. J., & Stoolmiller, M. (2004). Teaching vocabulary during shared storybook readings: An examination of differential effects. *Exceptionality, 12*(3), 145–162.

Cunningham, A. E., & Stanovich, K. E. (1997). Early reading acquisition and its relation to reading experience and ability 10 years later. *Developmental Psychology, 33*(6), 934–945.

Dale, E., & O'Rourke, J. (1979). *Living word vocabulary.* Boston: Houghton Mifflin Company.

Davis, F. B. (1944). Fundamental factors in reading comprehension. *Psychometrika, 9*(3), 185–197.

Delacroix, L., et al. (Eds.). (2007). *Longman advanced American dictionary* (2nd ed.). Edinburgh: Pearson Education Limited.

Elleman, A. M., Lindo, E. J., Morphy, P., & Compton, D. L. (2009). The impact of vocabulary instruction on passage-level comprehension of school-age children: A meta-analysis. *Journal of Research on Educational Effectiveness, 2*(1), 1–44.

Elley, W. B. (1989). Vocabulary acquisition from listening to stories. *Reading Research Quarterly, 24,* 174–186.

Farr, R. C., Strickland, D. S., Beck, I. L., Abrahamson, R. F., Ada, A. F., Cullinan, B. E., et al. (2000). *Trophies.* Orlando, FL: Harcourt.

Freeman, D. (1978). *A pocket for Corduroy.* New York: Puffin Books.

Graves, M. F. (1986). Vocabulary learning and instruction. *Review of Research in Education, 13*(1), 91–128.

Graves, M. F., Brunetti, G. J., & Slater, W. H. (1982). The reading vocabularies of primary-grade children of varying geographic and social backgrounds. In J. A. Harris & L. A. Harris (Eds.), *New inquiries in reading research and instruction* (pp. 99–104). Rochester, NY: National Reading Conference.

Hart, B., & Risley, T. (1995). *Meaningful differences.* Baltimore: Brookes.

Hayes, D. P., & Ahrens, M. G. (1988). Vocabulary simplification for children: A special case of "motherese"? *Journal of Child Language, 15*(2), 395–410.

Heilman, M., Zhao, L., Pino, J., & Eskenazi, M. (2008, June). *Retrieval of reading materials for vocabulary and reading practice.* Presented at the 3rd Workshop on Innovative Use of NLP for Building Educational Applications, Association for Computational Linguistics, Columbus, OH.

Hiebert, E. H. (2005). In pursuit of an effective, efficient vocabulary curriculum for elementary students. In E. H. Hiebert & M. L. Kamil (Eds.), *Teaching and learning vocabulary* (pp. 243–263). Mahwah, NJ: Erlbaum.

Justice, L., Kaderavek, J., Fan, X., Sofka, A., & Hunt, A. (2009). Accelerating preschoolers' early literacy development through classroom-based teacher–child storybook reading and explicit print referencing. *Language, Speech, and Hearing Services in Schools, 40*(1), 67–85.

Kame'enui, E. J., Carnine, D. W., & Freschi, R. (1982). Effects of text construction and instructional procedures for teaching word meanings on comprehension and recall. *Reading Research Quarterly, 17*(3), 367–388.

Landauer, T. K. (2009, February). *Towards teaching the right words in the right way for the right student at the right time.* Invited seminar, Learning Research and Development Center, University of Pittsburgh, Pittsburgh, PA.

Landauer, T. K., & Dumais, S. T. (1997). A solution to Plato's problem: The latent semantic analysis theory of acquisition, induction, and representation of knowledge. *Psychological Review, 104*(2), 211–240.

Leung, C. (2008). Preschoolers' acquisition of scientific vocabulary through repeated read-aloud events, retellings, and hands-on science activities. *Reading Psychology, 29*(2), 165–193.

Margosein, C. M., Pascarella, E. T., & Pflaum, S. W. (1982, March). *The effects of instruction using semantic mapping on vocabulary and comprehension.* Paper presented at the meeting of the American Educational Research Association, New York.

McKeown, M. G. (1985). The acquisition of word meaning from context by children of high and low ability. *Reading Research Quarterly, 20*(4), 482–496.

McKeown, M. G. (1993). Creating effective definitions for young word learners. *Reading Research Quarterly, 28*(1), 16–31.

McKeown, M. G., Beck, I. L., Omanson, R. C., & Perfetti, C. A. (1983). The effects of long-term vocabulary instruction on reading comprehension: A replication. *Journal of Reading Behavior, 15*(1), 3–18.

McKeown, M. G., Beck, I. L., Omanson, R. C., & Pople, M. T. (1985). Some effects of the nature and frequency of vocabulary instruction on the knowledge and use of words. *Reading Research Quarterly, 20*(5), 522–535.

Mezynski, K. (1983). Issues concerning the acquisition of knowledge: Effects of vocabulary training on reading comprehension. *Review of Educational Research, 53*(2), 253–279.

Miller, G. A., & Gildea, P. M. (1985). How to misread a dictionary. *AILA Bulletin,* 13–26.

Moats, L. C. (2001). When older students can't read. *Educational Leadership, 58*(6), 36–39.

Nagy, W. E., & Herman, P. A. (1987). Breadth and depth of vocabulary knowledge: Implications for acquisition and instruction. In M. G. McKeown & M. E. Curtis (Eds.), *The nature of vocabulary acquisition* (pp. 19–36). Hillsdale, NJ: Erlbaum.

Nagy, W. E., Herman, P. A., & Anderson, R. (1985). Learning words from context. *Reading Research Quarterly, 20*(2), 233–253.

Nagy, W. E., & Scott, J. A. (2000). Vocabulary processes. In M. L. Kamil, P. B. Mosenthal, P. D. Pearson, & R. Barr (Eds.), *Handbook of reading research* (Vol. 3, pp. 69–284). Mahwah, NJ: Erlbaum.

Nation, I. S. P. (2001). *Learning vocabulary in another language.* Cambridge, UK: Cambridge University Press.

Nicholson, T., & Whyte, B. (1992). Matthew effects in learning new words while listening to stories. In C. K. Kinzer & D. Leu (Eds.), *Literacy research, theory, and practice: Views from many perspectives* (pp. 499–503). Chicago: National Reading Conference.

Pearson, P. D., Hiebert, E. H., & Kamil, M. L. (2007). Vocabulary assessment: What we know and what we need to learn. *Reading Research Quarterly, 42*(2), 282–296.

Penno, J. F., Wilkinson, I. A. G., & Moore, D. W. (2002). Vocabulary acquisition from teacher explanation and repeated listening to stories: Do they overcome the Matthew effect? *Journal of Educational Psychology, 94*(1), 23–33.

Perfetti, C. (2007). Reading ability: Lexical quality to comprehension. *Scientific Studies of Reading, 11*(4), 357–383.

Perfetti, C. A., & Hart, L. (2002). The lexical quality hypothesis. In L. Verhoeven, C. Elbro, & P. Reitsma (Eds.), *Precursors of functional literacy* [Published as Vol. 11 of the series Studies in Written Language and Literacy]. Philadelphia: Benjamins.

Reichle, E. D., & Perfetti, C. A. (2003). Morphology in word identification: A word-experience model that accounts for morpheme frequency effects. *Scientific Studies of Reading, 7*(1), 219–238.

Robbins, C., & Ehri, L. C. (1994). Reading storybooks to kindergartners helps them learn new vocabulary words. *Journal of Educational Psychology, 86*(1), 54–64.

Rosenthal, J., & Ehri, L. C. (2008). The mnemonic value of orthography for vocabulary learning. *Journal of Educational Psychology, 100*(1), 175–191.

Roskos, K., Ergul, C., Bryan, B., Burstein, K., Christie, J., & Han, M. (2008). Who's learning what words and how fast: Preschoolers' vocabulary growth in an early literacy program. *Journal of Research in Childhood Education, 22*(3), 275–290.

Sénéchal, M., & Cornell, E. H. (1993). Vocabulary acquisition through shared reading experiences. *Reading Research Quarterly, 28*(4), 360–374.

Sénéchal, M., Thomas, E., & Monker, J. A. (1995). Individual differences in four-year-olds' ability to learn new vocabulary. *Journal of Educational Psychology, 87*(2), 218–229.

Silverman, R. (2007). A comparison of three methods of vocabulary instruction during read-alouds in kindergarten. *Elementary School Journal, 108*(2), 97–113.

Singer, H. (1965). A developmental model of speed of reading in grade 3 through 6. *Reading Research Quarterly, 1*(1), 29–49.

Snow, C. E., Tabors, P. O., Nicholson, P. A., & Kurland, B. F. (1995). SHELL: Oral language and early literacy skills in kindergarten and first-grade children. *Journal of Research in Childhood Education, 10*, 37–47.

Spearrit, D. (1972). Identification of subskills of reading comprehension by maximum likelihood factor analysis. *Reading Research Quarterly, 8*(1), 92–111.

Stahl, S. A., & Fairbanks, M. M. (1986). The effects of vocabulary instruction: A model-based meta-analysis. *Review of Educational Research, 56*(1), 72–110.

Stahl, S. A., & Nagy, W. E. (2006). *Teaching word meanings.* Mahwah, NJ: Erlbaum.

Sternberg, R. J. (1987). Most vocabulary is learned from context. In M. G. McKeown & M. E. Curtis (Eds.), *The nature of vocabulary acquisition* (pp. 89–105). Hillsdale, NJ: Erlbaum.

Swanborn, M. S. L., & de Glopper, K. (1999). Incidental word learning while reading: A meta-analysis. *Review of Educational Research, 69*(3), 261–285.

Teale, W. H. (2003). Reading aloud to young children as a classroom instructional activity: Insights from research and practice. In A. van Kleeck, S. A. Stahl, & E. B. Bauer (Eds.), *On reading books to children* (pp. 114–139). Mahwah, NJ: Erlbaum.

Thurstone, L. L. (1946). A note on a re-analysis of Davis' reading tests. *Psychometrika, 11*(4), 185–188.

Wagner, R. K., Torgeson, J. K., Rashotte, C. A., Hecht, S. A., Barker, T. A., Burgess, S. R., et al. (1997). Changing relations between phonological processing abilities and word-level reading as children develop from beginning to skilled readers: A 5-year longitudinal study. *Developmental Psychology, 33*(3), 468–479.

Wasik, B. A., & Bond, M. A. (2001). Beyond the pages of a book: Interactive book reading and language development in preschool classrooms. *Journal of Educational Psychology, 93*(2), 243–250.

White, T. G., Graves, M. F., & Slater, W. H. (1990). Growth of reading vocabulary in diverse elementary schools. *Journal of Educational Psychology, 82*(2), 281–290.

Wolf, M. (2007). *Proust and the squid.* New York: HarperCollins.

8

Fluency Problems

When, Why, and How to Intervene

ROXANNE HUDSON

Teachers who work with struggling readers often encounter students who exhibit problems with reading fluently. These students read slowly and with great effort, stop to decode unknown words either silently or aloud, may skip difficult words altogether, and read in short phrases that frequently sound disjointed. Nonfluent readers often focus on decoding at the word level, which makes comprehension of the text difficult, if not impossible. While many students in the primary grades have difficulty with developing phonemic awareness or reading accurately, students in the intermediate or upper grades often have trouble with reading fluently (Biancarosa & Snow, 2006).

The Multidimensional Nature of Reading Fluency

What is meant by reading fluency has received considerable attention and discussion since the National Reading Panel (NRP) published its report in 2000, reigniting interest in this aspect of reading proficiency. "Reading fluently" is often defined by researchers as accurate reading of connected text at a conversational rate, with appropriate prosody or expression (e.g., Armbruster, Lehr, & Osborn, 2001; Hudson, Lane, & Pullen, 2005; NRP, 2000), and often measured as a combination of rate and accuracy—the number of correct words read aloud in 1 minute (e.g., Fuchs, Fuchs, & Maxwell, 1988; Shinn, Good, Knutson, Tilly,

& Collins, 1992; Torgesen, Rashotte, & Alexander, 2001). Other researchers omit rate from their conception and define fluency "in terms of phrasing, adherence to the author's syntax, and expressiveness" (Daane, Campbell, Grigg, Goodman, & Oranje, 2005, p. v), and measure it using a scale of prosodic reading (Daane et al., 2005; Zutell & Rasinski, 1991). While some researchers include comprehension in their definition of reading fluency (Samuels, 2006), in this chapter, I focus primarily on quick and accurate reading of words, in and out of context, with appropriate prosody. In addition I provide an explanation of the multidimensional nature of reading fluency, explain why it is important to overall reading proficiency, and describe the evidence and instructional methods for interventions that address reading fluency at different levels (sublexical, lexical, and textual).

Word reading accuracy and reading fluency are important aspects of reading proficiency; each aspect has a clear connection to text comprehension, the purpose of reading. Without accurate word reading, the reader will have trouble accessing the author's meaning. Slow, laborious reading taxes the reader's capacity to construct an ongoing interpretation of the text, while poor prosody can lead to confusion through inappropriate or meaningless groupings of words.

Reading fluency is a complex and multidimensional construct that incorporates many aspects of proficient reading (Berninger, Abbott, Billingsley, & Nagy, 2001; Kame'enui & Simmons, 2001; Torgesen & Hudson, 2006; Wolf & Katzir-Cohen, 2001) and develops slowly over time (Kame'enui & Simmons, 2001). The multifaceted aspect makes it both intriguing and difficult to research and remediate in students with reading problems. Wolf and Katzir-Cohen (2001) conclude that "reading fluency involves every process and subskill involved in reading. ... Fluency is influenced by the development of rapid rates of processing in all the components of reading" (p. 220). It is the development of automaticity, efficiency, and fluency at different levels of written language—sublexical, lexical, and textual—that allows a fluent reader to read effortlessly, flexibly, and with comprehension. In this chapter, I use the terms "automaticity," "efficiency," and "fluency" to refer to different levels and types of quick processing of written text.

Automaticity, Efficiency, and Fluency

Automatic processes involve direct memory retrieval (Logan, 1988). For a process to be automatic, it must be fast, effortless, autonomous, and able to be completed without conscious control or attention (LaBerge & Samuels, 1974; Logan, 1988, 1997; Posner & Snyder, 1975). When applied to reading, these elements are easily identified. Speed can be seen in the instantaneous reading of "sight words," words that are read as a whole from memory—a process much quicker than any analytic process, such as using analogy or phonemic decoding (Ehri, 1998). Effortlessness is obvious when observing a fluent reader read for hours without a break or fatigue. Effortlessness is also linked to lack of demand on attentional resources, meaning that when word recognition is automatic, attention can be devoted to understanding what is read (Laberge & Samuels, 1974). Autonomy is most easily seen by the lack of control a reader has over word recognition; the process is encapsulated and occurs whether a reader wishes to read the words or not (Ehri, 1987). Finally, automatic processes happen so quickly that they are beyond conscious control or analysis by the reader. It is impossible for a good reader to explain how he or she automatically reads a word by sight.

Automaticity in reading is a race between memory (e.g., sight word reading) and use of an algorithm involving analysis (e.g., use of analogy, context, or phonemic decoding) (Logan, 1988). When a reader recognizes a word automatically, the memory trace always produces faster identification of the word than a process that requires analysis and application of an algorithm. Automaticity is not an all-or-nothing proposition; rather, it follows a predictable curvilinear pattern of increasing speed to an asymptote. The main mechanism for improvement in automaticity is practice with consistent input (letters) and consistent output (sound and meaning) pairings (Rayner, Foorman, Perfetti, Pesetsky, & Seidenberg, 2001). Automaticity is also item-specific. Because it is based on memory traces (Logan, 1988, 1997), each letter, each rime, each word becomes automatic, with little transfer to other letters, rimes, or words; however, there is transfer between words that share the same letter patterns (Berends & Reitsma, 2007; Ehri, 2002).

"Efficiency" refers to how quickly various processes can activate and be completed. Unlike "automaticity," which is a direct link to memory, efficiency is involved in processes with multiple steps, such as decoding unknown words (Berninger et al., 2001). When readers are very efficient, they may engage in strategic processing very quickly (Perfetti, 1985). This can be seen and heard when an accomplished reader decodes unknown words so quickly that there is no break in his or her pace or prosody.

"Fluency" is the flexible coordination of multiple processes to accomplish a reader's particular goals. A fluent reader can change pace to meet the demands of a text or particular purpose for reading, and develops "control over surface-level text processing so he or she can focus on understanding the deeper levels of meaning" (Rasinski, 2004, p. 46). When a reader is fluent, multiple serial items and processes are coordinated in time "so that they are synchronized to support all aspects of oral or silent reading of text in real time" (Berninger et al., 2010, p. 5).

The Importance of Automaticity, Efficiency, and Fluency to Reading Comprehension

According to Perfetti's (1985) verbal efficiency model, reading processes share limited-capacity processing resources, often termed "working memory." These resources limit the amount of processing and storage that may occur simultaneously in memory. As processes become more efficient or automatic, they use fewer of the resources of working memory, allowing other processes to proceed more completely. The higher-order processes of comprehension are, by their very nature, resource-intensive. In contrast, processes such as letter recognition, word recognition, and access to the word's contextual meaning may become extremely efficient or automatic. When these processes are sufficiently automatized, according to verbal efficiency theory, working memory space is freed for additional, more complex comprehension processes. Conversely, when word recognition processes are not efficient, they cause a bottleneck that constrains the operation of comprehension processes in working memory.

Multiple Levels of Reading Fluency

Reading fluency is a complex orchestration of multiple subprocesses working at different levels, from letters to connected text (Berninger et al., 2001; Breznitz, 2006; Fuchs, Fuchs, Hosp, & Jenkins, 2001; Kame'enui & Simmons, 2001; Torgesen & Hudson, 2006; Torgesen, Rashotte, et al., 2001; Wolf & Katzir-Cohen, 2001), a whole that is greater than its parts (Katzir et al., 2006). When this whole functions well, reading is effortless and facilitates reading comprehension.

Sublexical Level of Reading Fluency

Phonemic Awareness and Letters

Research over 20 years has established the importance of phonemic awareness in learning to read (e.g., NRP, 2000; Rayner et al., 2001; Wagner & Torgesen, 1987). Automaticity with phonemic blending is essential for efficient and effective decoding, and learning grapheme–phoneme (letter–sound) relationships is at the heart of the alphabetic principle. Without the knowledge of how sounds are systematically represented by letters, children cannot be successful readers in an alphabetic language (e.g., Adams, 1990; Ehri, 1998; NRP, 2000; Speece & Ritchey, 2005). According to Adams (1990), speed and accuracy in letter recognition are critical to the entire word recognition endeavor. If letter recognition is too slow, the activation of the first letter is gone before the last is activated, and the spelling pattern is not perceived.

Rapid Automatized Naming

A part of this rapid retrieval of letters is influenced by how quickly readers can name familiar stimuli, or "rapid automatized naming" (RAN). The relation between RAN and reading achievement has repeatedly been demonstrated across various samples of typical and atypical readers, even after IQ, processing speed, and phonological skill have been partialed out (Denckla & Rudel, 1976; Kail & Hall, 1994; Manis, Doi, & Bhada, 2000; Schatschneider, Fletcher, Francis, Carlson, & Foorman, 2004; Wolf, 1997; Wolf & Bowers, 1999; Wolf, Bowers, & Biddle, 2000). This relationship varies according to the stimuli used. Naming letters or digits is more related to reading achievement than naming of pictures or colors (Schatschneider et al., 2004) and RAN-digits is more related to reading speed than to reading accuracy (Savage & Frederickson, 2005). While it is clear RAN is related to reading, its exact relationship is unclear. Some researchers suggest that RAN is a measure of lexical access (Wagner, Torgesen, Laughon, Simmons, & Rashotte, 1993), while others suggest it is a measure of the speed of general information processing (Catts, Gillispie, Leonard, Kail, & Miller, 2002; Kail & Hall, 1994), a marker of orthographic processing (Manis et al., 1999), or an index of a precise timing mechanism in reading (Berninger et al., 2001; Wolf, Bowers, et al., 2000).

A timing deficit in RAN has been found in poor readers in comparison to good readers (Catts et al., 2002; Wolf, Bowers, et al., 2000), and Thomson et al. (2005) found a direct relationship between rapid naming and reading rate in connected text in children and adolescents with dyslexia. Wolf, Bowers, et al. (2000; Wolf & Bowers, 1999) found that readers with a double deficit in both phonological processing and RAN have more severe reading disabilities than those with a deficit in just one.

Larger Letter Patterns

Automaticity in recognition of larger letter groups that share a pattern across words such as digraphs, trigraphs, rimes, and suffixes is also critical in the development of reading fluency. Without knowledge of these widely occurring letter patterns, students are not able to move to more advanced, efficient decoding of longer and more complex words (Ehri, 2002). Rapid word identification is facilitated by the reader's ability to use multiletter patterns rather than decoding letter by letter. This consolidation of letters into larger patterns is at the heart of the development of word reading automaticity (Ehri, 1997): "Repeated experience reading a letter sequence that symbolizes the same phoneme blend across different words yields a consolidated unit in which several graphemes become bonded to a blend of phonemes. Consolidation allows readers to operate with multiletter units that may be parts of morphemes, syllables, or parts of syllables" (p. 178).

Lexical Level of Reading Fluency

I define "lexical reading fluency" as reading words out of context, either automatically by sight or by slower processes such as decoding or analogy.

Word Reading Automaticity

Automatic recognition of words plays a large role in reading fluency (Berninger et al., 2010) and reading comprehension (Schwanenflugel et al., 2006), and distinguishes skilled from less skilled readers (Jenkins, Fuchs, van den Broek, Espin, & Deno, 2003). The size of a reader's "sight word vocabulary," or the proportion of words in any given passage that can be recognized by sight, plays a pivotal role in how quick and accurate a reader is (Torgesen, Rashotte, et al., 2001), particularly for students who are below average in reading rate. Development of word reading automaticity is influenced by how well word-specific orthographic knowledge is represented in a reader's lexicon (Ehri, 1992). Knowledge of the specific, unique visual spelling patterns in words plays a role separate from that of sound–symbol relationships (Vellutino, Scanlon, & Tanzman, 1994). There is a direct relationship between orthographic knowledge and (1) reading accuracy, (2) reading rate in connected text, (3) reading comprehension, (4) spelling, and (5) written composition in children and adolescents with dyslexia (Thomson et al., 2005).

Word reading automaticity follows a predictable pattern of development from the use of simple visual cues for words through use of the alphabetic principle to identify unfamiliar words, and finally to reading words "at a single glance" using fully amalgamated representations in memory (Ehri, 1992). As Ehri (2005) comments: "How do children learn to read words by sight? The process at the heart of sight word learning is a *connection-forming* process. ... Readers learn sight words by forming connections between letters in spellings and sounds in pronunciations of the words" (p. 170).

For a more detailed discussion of development of automaticity in reading words, interested readers are directed to Ehri (1998, 2002, 2005) and to Spear-Swerling (Chapter 4, this volume).

Decoding Efficiency

No matter how efficient a reader becomes at decoding or reading by analogy, automatic recognition of a word is always faster and a critical component of reading fluency. However, for readers who encounter a large number of unfamiliar words, as many do in the elementary and middle school grades, efficient decoding processes are essential. "Phonological decoding appears to be a bridge to real-word reading, which as it improves, increasingly becomes a bridge to reading comprehension" (Berninger, Abbott, Vermuelen, & Fulton, 2006, p. 340). Slow or inaccurate operation of any of the analytic or knowledge retrieval processes required for decoding unknown words will have a noticeable impact on reading fluency (Fien et al., 2008; Good, Baker, & Peyton, 2009; Good, Simmons, & Kame'enui, 2001; Katzir et al., 2006). When children are not efficient in the use of analytic decoding processes to read unknown words, they often fail to use those processes when reading text, and their accuracy suffers. Students who need to expend considerable effort to decipher one word may expend that same level of effort for the next one but are unlikely to do so for a third or fourth. It is exhausting for students to read text with unfamiliar words when their decoding processes are not efficient.

Text Level of Reading Fluency

Passage reading fluency in connected text is even more complex than fluency at the sublexical or lexical levels because of the increased role meaning plays.

While meaning is activated to a limited extent when one reads words in isolation (Adams, 1990), it is activated to a much greater degree in reading a passage of connected text. When describing passage reading fluency, Fuchs et al. (2001) recognize the role of meaning:

> Oral reading fluency represents a complicated, multifaceted performance that entails, for example, a reader's perceptual skill at automatically translating letters into coherent sound representations, unitizing those sound components into recognizable wholes, and automatically accessing lexical representations, processing meaningful connections within and between sentences, relating text meaning to prior information, and making inferences to supply missing information. (pp. 239–240)

Comprehension

There is considerable evidence to suggest that the relationship between reading fluency and comprehension is reciprocal. Reading rate and accuracy have been identified as important facilitators of reading comprehension in average and disabled readers (Adams, 1990; Berninger et al., 2006; Breznitz, 1987; Chard, Vaughn, & Tyler, 2002; Dowhower, 1987; Fuchs et al., 2001), and it appears that comprehension also facilitates quick and accurate reading of text (Biemiller, 1977–1978). This bidirectional relation is supported by Berninger et al. (2010), who found that automatic word reading, efficient decoding, and reading comprehension predicted oral passage reading fluency in second and fourth grades, while reading comprehension was also predicted by oral passage reading fluency in both grades. This relation is also supported by Jenkins et al. (2003), who found that reading words in context explained more variance in reading comprehension among fourth graders than did reading the same words in a list (70 vs. 9%). They also found that a student's reading comprehension score explained more variance in oral reading rate and accuracy in connected text than did reading the same words in a list (70% vs. 54%). Jenkins et al. hypothesized that certain "automatic" comprehension processes develop when students read large amounts of text while attending to meaning, and because of the reciprocal nature of reading fluency and comprehension, these relatively "automatic" comprehension processes are instrumental in the development of reading fluency.

Prosody

While the aspects of reading fluency related to rate and accuracy are evident at all levels of text (sublexical, lexical, and textual), prosody is uniquely associated with reading connected text, because syntax and meaning determine the appropriate intonation, rhythm, and pitch of what is being read (Breznitz, 2006); isolated words do not provide the necessary context. As in spoken language, written text incorporates phonological, morphological, syntactic, and semantic information.

"Prosody" is a linguistic term that describes the rhythmic and tonal aspects of speech: the "music" of oral language. Prosodic features are variations in pitch (intonation), stress patterns (syllable prominence), and duration (length of time) that contribute to expressive reading of a text (Allington, 1983; Dowhower, 1991; Schreiber, 1980, 1991). Prosody develops over time from grade 1 to grade 2 as readers improve, with fewer pausal intrusions and shorter pause durations (Miller & Schwanenflugel, 2008), and more-skilled readers read more prosodically than less-skilled readers (Schwanenflugel, Hamilton, Kuhn, Wisenbaker, & Stahl, 2004). Longitudinally, as readers develop from grades 1–3, pausal intrusions and word reading automaticity are highly related; as intrusions decrease, word reading automaticity increases (Miller & Swanenflugel, 2008). In contrast to other research that did not measure development over time, Miller and Schwanenflugel found that a decrease in pausal intrusions in grades 1 and 2 was related to higher reading comprehension in grade 3, even after they accounted for word reading automaticity.

The exact role that prosody plays in passage reading fluency and comprehension is unclear. Some research indicates that prosodic reading is a sign that a reader can quickly and accurately read words (Miller & Schwanenflugel, 2006; Schwanenflugel et al., 2004). Other research suggest that prosody indicates the reader can comprehend what is being read (Kuhn & Stahl, 2003), while still other research suggests that prosodic reading of text is necessary for comprehension (Breznitz, 2006; Cohen, Douaire, & Elsabbagh, 2001). Better, more appropriate prosody is associated with better comprehension (Breznitz, 1990; cited in Breznitz, 2006). Prosody may help listeners and readers better understand this language by creating a prosodic representation similar to phonological and orthographic representations in working memory (Cohen et al., 2001). A prosodic representation organizes language using semantic and syntactic information, which helps memory. The key aspect appears to be that a prosodic representation is auditory— a translation of written text to auditory language (Breznitz, 2006). While clearly critical, more research is needed to understand prosody's role in reading fluency and comprehension.

Vocabulary

It seems likely that automatic or efficient access to word meanings also affects passage reading fluency. Because Perfetti (1985) suggests that both lexical access (word name) and semantic encoding (contextual word meaning) processes must be efficient, it is reasonable to think that reading fluency would be limited if semantic activation is not automatic. Evidence of this possible relationship can be found in studies by Perfetti and Hogaboam (1975). In addition to finding that good comprehenders read low-frequency and nonsense words more quickly than do poor comprehenders, Perfetti and Hogaboam also found that when reading words they do not know, poor comprehenders are both slower and less accurate than when reading words whose meaning they know, while good readers were equally fast and accurate with both types of words. As long as readers are under obligation to actively think about the meaning of what they are reading, speed of identification of word meanings may play a role in passage reading fluency.

Metacognition

While generally considered part of reading comprehension, metacognitive differences are also likely to influence passage reading fluency. Difficulty with executive management of processes when reading is common in students with reading disabilities (Berninger et al., 2001). This difficulty often leads to problems with self-monitoring or self-correction while reading. Although beginning readers often see reading as word recognition, better readers likely view reading as a problem-solving activity (Walczyk et al., 2007). Because metacognition refers to being aware of and regulating one's own thinking, its application to this problem solving is clear. Readers make many conscious and unconscious decisions, based on a wide range of factors, about how to approach a reading task, and these decisions are likely to affect how accurately, quickly, and expressively they read the text. For example, the value readers place on accuracy versus speed affects how quickly they read (Colón & Kranzler, 2006).

Summary

Quick, accurate prosodic reading is the result of accomplishing multiple subprocesses efficiently and automatically, at multiple levels of text that interact with each other (Breznitz, 2006). Without automatic access to letter names and letter–sound relationships, efficient operation of phonemic analysis and blending processes, automatic access to knowledge of larger letter patterns, large numbers of words recognized by sight, and quick access to word meaning, reading fluency in connected text suffers. I now discuss the implications of this framework for instruction.

Research–Based Methods to Improve Reading Fluency

Many struggling readers fail to gain reading fluency incidentally. In contrast to skilled readers, they often need direct instruction in how to read fluently and sufficient opportunities for intense, fluency-focused practice incorporated into their reading program (Allinder, Dunse, Brunken, & Obermiller-Krolikowski, 2001). A vicious cycle can develop, in which reading is so difficult and time-consuming that poor readers avoid practice and do not improve. Without reading practice, fluency does not increase, which makes reading laborious, and the cycle continues.

Wolf and Katzir-Cohen (2001) emphasize the importance of early instruction that ensures the growth of accuracy before problems in fluency can develop. They support approaches such as that of Ehri (1998), which begins with emphasis on the development of word reading accuracy and shifts to a focus on increasing the rate of processing. Ehri recommends that a primary goal of first-grade reading instruction should be to help children reach the full alphabetic phase of word reading. Practice at this level develops decoding accuracy and readies students to read letter chunks and, eventually, whole words automatically. In addition, Berninger et al. (2006) recommend a set of sequential instructional steps that begin with accuracy in the use of the alphabetic principle and phonological decoding, which leads to the quick and accurate decoding of unknown words. This is necessary for readers to develop a large number of words they can read automatically, which in turn is necessary for fluent passage reading. See in this volume O'Connor (Chapter 2), Roberts (Chapter 3), and Spear-Swerling (Chapter 4) for evidence-based practices designed to develop the necessary foundation in accuracy.

For many of the reading fluency interventions I review, research results are presented in terms of "effect sizes" (ESs), which are estimates of the power of an intervention. ESs are calculated by comparing the outcome for the intervention group with a comparison group, while taking into account the variability within the groups. ESs differ from statistical significance, because two groups can be statistically significantly different, but not by very much, making the difference meaningless in terms of educational impact. Because they are standardized, ESs can be used to evaluate the relative strength of an intervention, allowing an instructor to compare two or more interventions directly. According to Cohen (1988), the following rough guidelines help to evaluate the magnitude of effects: A small effect is 0.20 or less, a medium effect is between 0.30 and 0.70, and a large effect is 0.80 and above. An ES of 0.80 or more may demonstrate the power to help students catch up to their peers, while a small effect size demonstrates little growth at all. In education, an ES of 0.40 or larger is generally considered sufficiently large to merit attention (Lloyd, Forness, & Kavale, 1998), although the What Works Clearinghouse (2008) suggests 0.25 as the cutoff for an educationally meaningful effect. In order to close the achievement gap, it is my opinion that an ES of 0.50 or above is desired.

Intervention across Levels of Text

Whether to practice words in isolation or in context has garnered much attention and mixed results. Some studies have found strong improvements in students' passage reading rate and accuracy in unpracticed texts from repeated practice of isolated words (Levy, Abello, & Lysynchuk, 1997; Tan & Nicholson, 1997; Vadasy, Sanders, & Peyton, 2006), while others have not been as successful. Fleisher, Jenkins, and Pany (1979) found an improvement in text reading rate and accuracy in one experiment but not in another. They had fourth and fifth graders practice individual words from a passage until they could read them in a list quickly and accurately. The children then read aloud a passage containing these words and answered comprehension questions. Poor readers did better on reading the words in isolation, reading the passage accurately, and on rate than students in a no-practice condition. This improvement in passage reading fluency was not replicated in another study with similar procedures and practice reading the words in phrases. It is possible that this lack of effect is due to the short duration of practice. It is likely that struggling readers need more than three or four sessions to develop true automaticity. Other researchers have directly compared the two and found no difference between practice with words in isolation and words in context on transfer to unpracticed passages (LeVasseur, Macaruso, & Shankweiler, 2008; Levy, 2001) or a benefit to practice in context (Dahl, 1979; Daly & Martens, 1994; Morgan & Sideridis, 2006). The vast majority of interventions that focus on sublexical and lexical levels have been integrated with practice in connected text and are described in the section "Intervention at Multiple Levels."

Repeated Reading

In repeated reading, a common form of fluency intervention, a student reads the same connected text multiple times. There are many variations of repeated reading, ranging from reading connected text a specific number of times (Homan, Klesius, & Hite, 1993) to reading until a defined rate has been reached (Herman, 1985; Samuels, 1979). Researchers have studied repeated reading with students reading independently (Dahl, 1979), or with assistance from a peer (Mathes & Fuchs, 1993), an adult (Vadasy & Sanders, 2008a), or an audiotape (Shany & Biemiller, 1985). Repeated reading has been studied with average readers, struggling readers, and students with disabilities (Chard et al., 2002; Meyer & Felton, 1999; NRP, 2000). Positive effects have been found for practiced (Samuels, 1979) and unpracticed (O'Connor, White, & Swanson, 2007; Rashotte & Torgesen, 1985) passages.

The NRP (2000) examined 16 studies of guided oral repeated reading that used a wide range of instructional methods. Overall, the studies had an ES of 0.44 in reading rate and accuracy, and 0.35 in comprehension across all types of readers, suggesting that repeated reading has a moderate effect on reading achievement. Therrien (2004) found similar effects in his meta-analysis of repeated reading, and documented a mean rate and accuracy ES of 0.59 for students without disabilities and 0.79 for students with learning disabilities.

Among all of the varied methods to conduct repeated readings, some are more effective than others, especially for students with learning disabilities. The results reviewed below are for transfer effects to unpracticed passages, because generalized improvement in rate is the outcome most valued by instructors and students alike.

Types of Assistance

Repeated reading may be conducted independently, without assistance, and with modeling from a recording, or from an adult. The effect of assistance during reading practice is mixed. In some studies, modeling from either an adult or recording was better than no modeling in improving reading accuracy, rate, and comprehension (Chard et al., 2002; Kuhn & Stahl, 2003; Shany & Biemiller, 1985) while in studies that directly compared repeated reading, with and without assistance, no benefit for modeling was found for reading rate and accuracy in transfer text with fifth-grade struggling readers (Young, Bowers, & MacKinnon, 1996) or second-grade transitional readers (Dowhower, 1987), although Dowhower did find a small effect on prosody. Similarly, Rasinski (1990) did not find benefits for prosodic modeling in comparison to independent repeated reading in the reading rate or accuracy of third graders in the practiced text. In contrast, in a meta-analysis of repeated reading studies, Therrien (2004) found large differences depending on who conducted the reading intervention. Repeated readings led by an adult had a large mean ES of 1.37 on reading rate and accuracy, and 0.71 on comprehension, in comparison to those led by peers, which had small to moderate ESs of 0.36 on reading rate and accuracy, and 0.22 on comprehension. Because of these findings, my observation is that silent independent reading is of questionable value to improve the reading fluency of struggling readers (see also NRP, 2000), because these students may be too inaccurate for effective practice, or they may pretend to be reading when they are not (Greenleaf, Schoenbach, Cziko, & Mueller, 2001). It may be important for students to practice at least some of the time with an adult listener who can provide correction or modeling.

Reading a Set Number of Times or to a Criterion

There are two main ways to conduct repeated reading. In the first, students read a set number of times, while in the second, students read as many times as necessary to reach a criterion. Reading to a criterion is considerably more powerful in comparison to a control group (average ES = 1.70) than reading a set number of times (average ES = 0.38; Therrien, 2004), even among students with learning disabilities (Chard et al., 2002). If instructors decide to use a set number of readings, three to four readings appear to be optimal (O'Shea, Sindelar, & O'Shea, 1985).

Goal Setting and Feedback

Goal setting and corrective feedback are important elements to include in a repeated reading intervention. Students can set a goal for the amount of time they think it will take to read a passage or the number of errors they will make (Eckert, Ardoin, Daisey, & Scarola, 2000). After reading, the teacher provides feedback on whether students met the goal(s) and asks students to graph the scores. In their meta-analysis of single-subject research, Morgan and Sideridis (2006) found that across all reading fluency intervention methods they examined, goal setting and feedback were most effective in increasing reading rate and accuracy among struggling readers, many of whom were served in special education.

Corrective feedback can take several forms. In partner reading, peers are taught to monitor the reader's accuracy as they listen and to prompt the reader to decode any miscues or unknown words (McMaster, Fuchs, & Fuchs, 2006; Vaughn, Chard, Bryant, Coleman, & Kouzekanani, 2000). Alternatively, the teacher can provide the correct pronunciation of words while the student is reading (Mercer, Campbell, Miller, Mercer, & Lane, 2000), or conduct a scaffolded correction procedure on miscues after the student is done reading (Vadasy & Sanders, 2008a). This correction procedure includes increasing levels of support that begin with referring to a letter-sound card as a prompt; encouraging the student to say each sound, saying the whole word fast; assisting with segmentation and recoding of a multisyllabic word; and finally telling the nondecodable word and asking the student to reread it.

Reading Materials

The type and level of reading materials used in repeated reading is important to consider when implementing the method. The influence of reading level difficulty on the effectiveness of repeated readings has also been examined. Relatively easy text leads to higher gains than text that is very difficult for poor readers in grades 3–6 (O'Connor et al., 2002; Sindelar, Monda, & O'Shea, 1990). In addition, the effect of text difficulty depends on the reader's own fluency level. O'Connor et al. (2002) found that students who were least fluent (< 50 correct words per minute [CWPM]) made significantly greater gains on reading rate and accuracy with text at their instructional level than those who used text at their grade level; students using the grade-level text did no better than controls. For students with higher fluency (> 50 CWPM), the level of text difficulty did not appear to matter; practice in either text level improved reading rate over that of students in the control condition. When students read with an adult, somewhat more difficult text may be used, because assistance is provided. When reading with a peer or a recording, when little or no assistance is provided, text at an independent reading level is preferred.

In addition to difficulty, the amount of word overlap across texts is also important to consider. Overlap of words from one text to another appears to facilitate transfer to unpracticed text (Martin-Chang & Levy, 2005; Rashotte & Torgesen, 1985; Vadasy & Sanders, 2008a). When choosing text, it is important to attend to the number of unique words and to make sure there is some overlap (Hiebert, 2005). One way to accomplish this is to have students read in themes with overlapping vocabulary. Reading in themes should result in overlap between both content and individual words, which has been found to increase reading rate and accuracy among struggling readers in second (Dowhower, 1987), third, and sixth grades (Faulkner & Levy, 1994). An easy way for students to keep track of their repeated readings is with a book log, like that in Figure 8.1. As used in my former classroom with students with disabilities, students wrote the name of the passage, then checked off each time they read it. This log was effective in keeping students'

Name: _____

My Reading Log

Book	Type of Text	Adult	Friend	Self	Adult
Mac and Tab	*decodable*	✓	✓	✓	✓
Al	*decodable*	✓	✓	✓	

FIGURE 8.1. Repeated reading book log.

motivation to reread high; they enjoyed reading to multiple audiences and keeping track of the number of books they read over time.

Continuous Reading

Continuous (CR) or wide reading provides an alternative to repeated reading (RR) as a way to develop the reading fluency of struggling readers. While the NRP (2000) found a lack of evidence to support the use of independent wide reading to develop reading fluency, later experiments that addressed the weaknesses identified by the NRP have suggested that wide reading may be at least as effective as RR in developing reading rate, accuracy, and prosody. O'Connor et al. (2007) experimentally compared 15 minutes of RR (three times per page) and CR (no repetitions) with an adult listener who provided assistance as needed with struggling second and fourth graders, and found that both conditions resulted in better reading comprehension, accuracy, rate, and oral receptive vocabulary than did a control condition. The ESs were quite large in comparison to the control group: RR = 0.97 and CR = 1.04 on reading rate and accuracy; RR = 1.03 and CR = 1.00 on reading comprehension. The effects on vocabulary were moderate (RR = 0.63, CR = 0.46), an interesting finding, since O'Connor et al. had predicted that CR would have a larger effect on vocabulary by covering more material. In another study, Reutzel, Fawson, and Smith (2008) compared the effects of scaffolded silent reading and guided oral reading on the fluency of third-grade readers with a wide range of achievement levels. Each condition provided the same amount of reading practice time, used the same materials, included 5 minutes of modeled reading fluency, and was conducted by the same teachers. Scaffolded silent reading included at least six genre types, monitoring by teachers in short individual conferences, and completion of a reading log. Guided oral reading included repeated reading of texts aloud using choral reading, paired reading with a teacher or partner, and readers' theatre. There were no significant differences in gains in reading rate, accuracy, prosody, or comprehension between the two conditions. Kuhn (2004) also compared small-group instruction with struggling second-grade readers using teacher modeling, choral reading, and paired reading under three conditions: wide reading, RR, or listening only. The wide reading and RR groups were significantly better at word reading efficiency, passage reading rate and accuracy in connected text, and prosody than the control or listening-only groups. In addition, the wide reading group was significantly better than control or listening-only groups in reading comprehension. In another evaluation of wide reading with no or two RRs, Kuhn et al. (2006) found the wide reading group to be more effective than the control group on word reading efficiency, oral reading accuracy and rate, and comprehension.

Struggling readers tend to avoid the reading practice they need to increase their fluency, and motivation plays an even larger role in the reading of older struggling readers than it does with younger ones (Boardman et al., 2008). Because reading a variety of texts rather than a single one is likely to be more interesting and motivating, and because CR may expose readers to a variety of genres and topics, CR alone or in combination with RR may prove successful in motivating students to engage in the practice they need (Reutzel et al., 2008).

The following description is based on research by O'Connor et al. (2007), Reutzel et al. (2008), and Kuhn (2004). First, encourage students to choose reading materials at their instructional reading level across a variety of genres. Use of a genre list on which types of text, such as fantasy, newspapers, fables, humor, mystery, biography, short informational articles, historical fiction, and poetry, are listed may be useful, as is noting particular topics that interest each student. Because knowledge of text structure plays such a large role in reading comprehension (Catts & Kamhi, 2005; Duke & Pearson, 2002), ensuring that students read a variety of texts may have additional benefits beyond fluency improvement (see Williams & Pao, Chapter 11, this volume).

Second, have students read 10–20 minutes 3 days a week for several weeks, or until the appropriate level of reading fluency is reached. The appropriate level of fluency varies from grade to grade. A common way to determine a workable goal is to use the 50th percentile on a set of oral fluency norms (e.g., Hasbrouck & Tindal, 2006) or benchmarks established for a particular state or group of states (e.g., Roehrig, Petscher, Nettles, Hudson, & Torgesen, 2008). The CR method described by O'Connor et al. (2007) suggests that students work individually with an adult and read aloud. The adult listener provides assistance with difficult words and corrective feedback as students read. A reading log kept by both the students and adult listener keeps track of the text read and may help to monitor the types of text being read. In addition to reading individually, continuous or wide reading may also be used with choral reading in a small group or with pairs. Instead of reading chorally, then practicing individually, as in RR, the group continues to read chorally as long as is appropriate (Kuhn, 2004).

Intervention at Multiple Levels

For interventions to be successful for students with reading fluency problems, they likely need to focus simultaneously on multiple levels of reading fluency (Good et al., 2001; Torgesen & Hudson, 2006; Wolf & Katzir-Cohen, 2001). If a student's difficulty is with automaticity in letter sounds, it is possible that text-level practice will not be successful. For this reason, effective interventions often include practice at multiple levels of text.

RAVE-O

The RAVE-O (Retrieval, Automaticity, Vocabulary, Engagement with Language, and Orthography) program (Wolf et al., 2009; Wolf, Miller, & Donnelly, 2000) focuses on teaching phonological, orthographic, semantic, syntactic, and morphological aspects of a core set of words. This information is taught in a systematic fashion, making explicit connections among all of the sources of information. The premise of this program is that the more a reader knows about a word, the more quickly it will be retrieved while reading. RAVE-O is designed to be taught in connection with an explicit decoding program, such as Phonological and Strategy Training (PHAST; Lovett, Lacerenza, & Borden, 2000). In a series of studies of RAVE-O with second and third graders with reading difficulties (Wolf et al., 2009), the multidimensional program proved to be very effective. Children in the RAVE-O + decoding group outperformed children in the decoding only or control groups on word reading accuracy, word reading efficiency, passage reading fluency, and reading comprehension. The RAVE-O alone group was more effective than the decoding only or control groups in improving vocabulary knowledge (Wolf et al., 2009). While RAVE-O focuses primarily on sublexical and lexical elements, there is some practice in connected text, making it a multilevel intervention.

During RAVE-O, students are taught each week a core set of words representing common orthographic patterns and with multiple meanings. Students engage in a series of activities that focus on building knowledge of these words at multiple levels. Students spell words, sort them based on orthographic patterns, and read onsets and rimes in word families. Other forms of practice include semantic associations, sound sliders, semantic word games, and minute stories to develop automaticity at sublexical, lexical, and textual levels, as well as to build connections among a word's sound, spelling, and meaning.

Repeated Readings with Letter–Sound Instruction

This intervention for second- and third-grade struggling readers divided students into pairs for 30 minutes per day, 4 days per week, for 15 weeks (Vadasy & Sanders, 2008a; 2009) and combined within-word instruction with RRs of texts designed to foster fluency development. The texts comprised short, nonfiction passages organized into six topics, with specific text features designed to foster fluency and comprehension (Hiebert, 2005). The number of unique words was minimized, and high-frequency words and word patterns were included at high rates. Vadasy and Sanders (2008a) found that students in the intervention condition had moderate gains in word reading accuracy and passage reading. In their 2009 study, the students had moderate gains in knowledge of two- and three-letter spelling patterns (matching phonemes to graphemes), passage reading fluency, and reading comprehension. The 2009 study also revealed that pairs tutored by teachers were more successful than those tutored by paraeducators on word reading (ES = 0.43) and passage reading fluency (ES = 0.43). In contrast, when Vadasy and Sanders (2008b) used the same RR intervention combined with vocabulary instruction, which they expected to be more needed and appropriate than the letter sound instruction with fourth and fifth graders, they did not find significant improvements in text reading fluency. Instead, students in the intervention outperformed their control group peers in vocabulary, word comprehension, and reading comprehension. For older readers, RR did not differentially influence word reading accuracy or efficiency, or passage reading fluency. Without attention to the lower sublexical and lexical levels, the intervention was not successful in promoting reading fluency in these older readers.

In order to implement the intervention found to be effective with second- and third-grade struggling readers, follow these six steps (Vadasy & Sanders, 2008a, 2009):

- Review letter–sound correspondences with single letters (e.g., *l, a, m*) and digraphs (e.g., *ea, wh, ai*) for up to 5 minutes.
- Introduce the main idea for the first passage; point out one or two difficult words for students to practice before reading. Then have the students take turns reading sentences and following along. During each passage reading, provide scaffolded assistance when students struggle to decode unfamiliar

words by (1) prompting students to use the letter sounds they practiced; (2) reminding students to say each sound, then blend them to form the word; (3) assisting with segmenting and decoding multisyllabic words; and (4) supplying a nondecodable word and having the students reread the word. Review any mistakes after the reading.

- Read the passage twice in unison with the students to provide a model of smooth, accurate, and fluent reading.
- Have each student read the passage for 1 minute and record each student's rate and accuracy.
- Discuss two comprehension questions about the passage.
- Read a new passage following the same procedures, or reread a previous passage as time permits.

Word–Level Structural Analysis with Text Practice

Improvements in reading fluency and comprehension can also be found when the focus of the intervention shifts substantially from text to the lexical and sublexical levels, while still maintaining both in the intervention. Vadasy et al. (2006) experimentally studied an individualized 30-minute intervention delivered 4 days a week for an entire school year to a small number of second- and third-grade struggling readers (N = 35). They found large ESs on reading accuracy (ES = 1.06), word reading efficiency (ES = 0.70), and text reading fluency (ES = 1.09) for students in the experimental group in comparison to the students in the control group.

Second- and third-grade students who struggle reading longer words may benefit from this intervention. "In the first 12 lessons, the students reviewed reading and spelling words and nonwords that included two-letter combinations. The second group of 34 lessons provided practice reading and spelling multisyllable words. ... The third group of 20 lessons covered inflected words" (Vadasy et al., 2006, p. 372). In addition, during each 30-minute session, students practiced high-frequency words for 3–4 minutes, and read paragraphs and nonfiction passages that included the taught word types for 15 minutes. In summary, students engaged in sublexical word analysis for 11–12 minutes, practiced high-frequency words for 3–4 minutes, and practiced text-level reading for 15 minutes. Specific analytic skills that were taught included reading words with inflected endings, such as -s, -ed, -ing, and -y, and recognizing spelling changes that occur when these endings are added to words. Vadasy et al. also taught common affixes, such as dis-, mis-, -ly (read in isolation and in affixed words); how to chunk long words into syllables; and a strategy for how to put it all together. The opportunity for work with sublexical and lexical word reading and spelling, along with a chance to practice these patterns and strategies in connected text, is likely to be quite effective for struggling readers in mid-elementary grades.

Other Fluency Approaches

Readers' Theatre

Readers' theatre is another popular method used to increase the reading fluency of struggling readers. Despite its popularity, there is limited direct evidence of its effectiveness. To date, the evidence consists of anecdotal stories of increased motivation or reading achievement (Worthy & Prater, 2002), nonexperimental pre–post studies (Corcoran & Davis, 2005; Keehn, 2003), unpublished dissertations (Carrick, 2000; Maberry, 1975), and quasi-experimental studies (Keehn, Harmon, & Shoho, 2008; Martinez, Roser, & Strecker, 1998/1999; Millin & Rinehart, 1999) that all found improvement in oral reading rate, accuracy, prosody, and self-reported attitudes toward reading. No published experiments have produced data to suggest that readers' theatre is an evidence-based method, which leads one to wonder whether it should be used. The answer is a qualified "yes." Readers' theatre provides an authentic reason to reread a text, which may increase students' motivation to read a text multiple times. Struggling readers are provided with models of fluent reading via modeling from the teacher, a recording, or other readers. They read repeatedly and receive feedback on their reading. All of these aspects of fluency intervention have research support. If readers' theatre includes these elements, then it may be an effective method, because it may also provide the necessary motivation to help struggling readers engage in the practice they need. For these reasons, readers' theatre deserves experimental attention; without rigorous research, recommended instructional strategies cannot be provided here.

Fast Start Reading

Fast Start Reading (Rasinski & Stevenson, 2005) is a program that informs parents how to engage in reading practice with their first-grade children to improve reading fluency. Fast Start is a 10- to 15-minute daily lesson that involves parents reading a short, whole, predictable text, such as a poem, to the child several times, while pointing at the print, then discussing the content of the passage. Next, parent and child read the text together several times, until the child feels comfortable reading alone. At that point, the child reads the text alone, with the parent providing support as needed. Finally, parent and child engage in word study activities on words in the text or provided in a list. Rasinski and Stevenson studied this method with 30 first-grade students over 11 weeks and found that students in the Fast Start condition who began the study at a low level of reading achievement (composite of reading accuracy and a text fluency measure of words read correctly per minute) ended the study significantly higher than the students in the control group who also began at a low level of reading achievement. There were no differences between groups for students with higher reading achievement. Because of its potential to motivate students to practice reading through involvement with their families, this method deserves additional research.

Fluency-Oriented Reading Instruction

The Fluency-Oriented Reading Instruction (FORI) program (Stahl & Heubach, 2005) was designed for whole-class instruction for second graders using grade-level reading selections to scaffold text difficulty and maximize the amount of connected text children read. The teacher and students focus on one passage per week, with the teacher providing full support and modeling of the text with discussion afterward on the first day. On the second day, the class engages in echo reading, with the teacher reading two or three sentences aloud, followed by the whole class in unison. The students also bring the text home to practice with family or friends. On the third day, students read the text chorally, and they engage in partner reading on the fourth day. On the last day, children complete other extension activities related to the text. Like other fluency methods in this section, there is limited direct evidence of its effectiveness. In a nonexperimental pre–post study, Stahl and Heubach found evidence of reading improvement for students who participated in the program, but these gains are impossible to evaluate without a control group. In a later study comparing FORI to a control group and to a group that received wide reading of three texts with fewer repetitions, FORI and wide reading both led to improvements in word reading efficiency and comprehension in comparison to the control group, but there were no significant differences between FORI and the control group on reading accuracy and rate, or between FORI and wide reading (Kuhn et al., 2006).

Multilevel Timed Repeated Readings

In order to build students' automaticity at the sublexical, lexical, and passage levels of reading fluency, timed RRs may be used to practice letter sounds, high-frequency words, and connected text. Timed RRs are based on precision teaching, which has a long history of success in building fluency in many academic areas (e.g., Binder, 1993, 1996; Johnson & Layng, 1992, 1994). To date, the only published evaluation of timed RRs for building reading fluency was conducted by Mercer et al. (2000) with 49 middle school students with learning disabilities. This study is limited by design but provides tentative evidence for the effectiveness of timed RRs. Mercer et al. found that daily individualized sessions with a paraeducator focused on fluency-oriented practice in letter sounds, high-frequency words, and connected text led to large reading rate and accuracy gains among the students.

In order to use timed RRs, teachers follow a seven-step process that is the same regardless of the level practiced and does not vary from session to session. Once the instructor and students are familiar with the routine, the sessions proceed quickly. Each practice sheet is one page of letters, words, or connected text kept in a binder or hanging file folder. There are two versions of each page: one without numbers for the student, and the other with a word or letter count used by the instructor. The teacher previews the reading material with the student and provides modeling or error correction as needed. Next he or she reviews a graph and sets a rate and accuracy goal with the student for the reading session. Then the student reads for 1 minute, while the teacher records errors on the instructor's copy of the page. In addition, the instructor offers the correct pronunciations during the timed reading if the student hesitates for more than 3 seconds. After the timed reading, teacher and student review the student's performance on the page, correcting errors and practicing the correct pronunciations. Then the teacher records the score on the student's graph and together they decide whether the student has met the rate and accuracy goal for that page. If so, then the student goes to the next page; if not, then the student repeats the same page during the next session. Timed RR may be a promising practice to help students who lack automaticity at letter, word, and text levels, and it deserves additional research.

Conclusion: Determining the Appropriate Intervention

The challenge to provide intervention in reading fluency is to determine the intervention target. Because reading fluency is multidimensional and includes nearly every aspect of reading proficiency, there are many potential areas for instructional focus, not all of which have the effects that teachers desire.

In many instances, the first indication that a student has a reading fluency problem comes from an oral reading fluency (ORF) score during a progress-monitoring assessment. However, a low ORF score can be due to many things, and a low score alone does not indicate that the student needs a fluency intervention, nor does it indicate which method might be appropriate. Further diagnostic assessment is needed to discern the underlying cause and help the instructor determine the appropriate intervention. Students may have difficulty at letter, word, or text levels, and this difficulty may be due to inaccuracy, a slow rate, or both.

If the student is inaccurate, there are several potential areas for assessment and intervention. The first is at the sublexical level. Perhaps the reader lacks the phonemic awareness needed to blend letter sounds into words successfully, or may not know all the individual and digraph letter sounds. If this is the case, then work in phonics and phonemic blending is needed. Multilevel intervention may also prove effective (e.g., Vadasy & Sanders, 2009; Wolf et al., 2009). Second, it is possible that the reader is inaccurate because he or she does not have adequate background knowledge about the topic and lacks the oral vocabulary to match his or her decoding attempts. For example, if the word *splendid* or *cocoon* is not in a reader's receptive vocabulary, it is almost impossible for him or her to monitor pronunciation and determine whether the words are read correctly. If this is the case, then intervention might best target relevant word meanings to build the reader's oral vocabulary. Finally, the problem may be with metacognition; the reader may not be monitoring his or her accuracy and does not stop to correct errors when they are made. If the student is able to read accurately, but is not carefully monitoring his or her accuracy then instruction in self-regulation strategies might be effective.

If the student is reading slowly, there are several potential areas for assessment and intervention. First, readers may be slow because they are not efficient decoders. Readers who are inefficient often decode letter by letter or make several attempts to read a word, without successfully blending it together. If this is the case, then it is likely that practice at sublexical and lexical levels, designed to build automaticity with letter sounds, letter patterns, and isolated words, would be helpful (e.g., Vadasy & Sanders, 2009). Second, perhaps readers do not have a large enough number of words that they can read automatically. If this is the case, then practice with isolated words or connected text would be most appropriate (e.g., RR or CR) to build up sight word reading vocabulary. For students who read with poor prosody, oral reading practice with an adult model and listener may be especially important (e.g., O'Connor et al., 2007).

If the student is both inaccurate and slow, then a multilevel intervention that addresses accuracy and automaticity at letter, word, and text levels should be considered (e.g., Wolf et al., 2009). The teacher may need to adjust the intervention to find the most appropriate fluency component target. In some cases, metacognitive strategies may help the student to monitor accuracy and rate.

Spending time to diagnose why a student reads dysfluently usually leads to a set of interventions to try out, some linked to fluency interventions in this chapter, and others to decoding, vocabulary, or comprehension described elsewhere in this book. Using progress-monitoring data, the teacher can evaluate and change each intervention as needed. Reading fluency difficulties are most effectively addressed by matching the intervention to the underlying reading problem. Studies included in this chapter underscore the importance of intervening early and effectively. The goal is to help students develop the fluency skills needed for reading comprehension, which generates academic success in the intermediate and upper elementary grades.

References

Adams, M. J. (1990). *Beginning to read: Thinking and learning about print*. Cambridge, MA: MIT Press.

Allinder, R. M., Dunse, L., Brunken, C. D., & Obermiller-Krolikowski, H. J. (2001). Improving fluency in at-risk readers and students with learning disabilities. *Remedial and Special Education*, 22(1), 48–54.

Allington, R. L. (1983). Fluency: The neglected reading goal. *Reading Teacher*, 36(6), 556–561.

Armbruster, B. B., Lehr, F., & Osborn, J. (2001). *Put reading first: The research building blocks for teaching children to read*. Washington, DC: Partnership for Reading.

Berends, I. E., & Reitsma, P. (2007). Orthographic analysis of words during fluency training promotes reading of new similar words. *Journal of Research in Reading*, 30, 129–139.

Berninger, V. W., Abbott, R. D., Billingsley, F., & Nagy, W. (2001). Processes underlying timing and fluency of reading: Efficiency, automaticity, coordination, and morphological awareness. In M. Wolf (Ed.) *Dyslexia, fluency, and the brain* (pp. 383–414.) Timonium, MD: York Press.

Berninger, V. W., Abbott, R. D., Trivedi, P., Olson, E., Gould, L., Hiamatsu, S., et al. (2010). Applying the multiple dimensions of reading fluency to assessment and instruction. *Journal of Psychoeducational Assessment, 28*(1), 3–18.

Berninger, V. W., Abbott, R. D., Vermuelen, K., & Fulton, C. M. (2006). Paths to reading comprehension in at-risk second-grade students. *Journal of Learning Disabilities, 39,* 334–351.

Biancarosa, G., & Snow, C. E. (2006). *Reading next—a vision for action and research in middle and high school literacy: A report to Carnegie Corporation of New York* (2nd ed.). Washington, DC: Alliance for Excellent Education.

Biemiller, A. (1977–1978). Relationships between oral reading rates for letters, words, and simple text in the development of reading achievement. *Reading Research Quarterly, 13,* 223–253.

Binder, C. (1993). Behavioral fluency: A new paradigm. *Educational Technology, 33*(10), 8–14.

Binder, C. (1996). Behavioral fluency: Evolution of a new paradigm. *Behavior Analyst, 19*(2), 163–197.

Boardman, A. G., Roberts, G., Vaughn, S., Wexler, J., Murray, C. S., & Kosanovich, M. (2008). *Effective instruction for adolescent struggling readers: A practice brief.* Portsmouth, NH: RMC Research Corporation, Center on Instruction.

Breznitz, Z. (1987). Increasing first graders' reading accuracy and comprehension by accelerating their reading rates. *Journal of Educational Psychology, 79,* 236–242.

Breznitz, Z. (2006). *Fluency in reading: Synchronization of processes.* Mahwah, NJ: Erlbaum.

Carrick, L. U. (2000). *The effects of readers theatre on fluency and comprehension in fifth grade students in regular classrooms.* Unpublished doctoral dissertation, Lehigh University, Bethlehem, PA.

Catts, H. W., Gillispie, M., Leonard, L. B., Kail, R. V., & Miller, C. A. (2002). The role of speed of processing, rapid naming, and phonological awareness in reading achievement. *Journal of Learning Disabilities, 35,* 510–525.

Catts, H. W., & Kamhi, A. (2005). *Language and reading disabilities.* Needham Heights, MA: Allyn & Bacon.

Chard, D. J., Vaughn, S., & Tyler, B. J. (2002). A synthesis of research on effective interventions for building reading fluency with elementary students with learning disabilities. *Journal of Learning Disabilities, 35,* 386–406.

Cohen, H., Douaire, J., & Elsabbagh, M. (2001). The role of prosody in discourse processing. *Brain and Cognition, 46,* 73–82.

Cohen, J. (1988). *Statistical power analysis for the behavioral sciences* (2nd ed.). Hillsdale, NJ: Erlbaum.

Colón, E. P., & Kranzler, J. H. (2006). Effect of instructions on curriculum-based measurement of reading. *Journal of Psychoeducational Assessment, 24*(4), 318–328.

Corcoran, C. A., & Davis, A. D. (2005). A study of the effects of readers' theater on second and third grade special education students' fluency growth. *Reading Improvement, 42,* 105–111.

Daane, M. C., Campbell, J. R., Grigg, W. S., Goodman, M. J., & Oranje, A. (2005). *Fourth-grade students reading aloud: NAEP 2002 Special Study of Oral Reading* (NCES 2006-469, U.S. Department of Education, Institute of Education Sciences, National Center for Education Statistics). Washington, DC: Government Printing Office.

Dahl, P. R. (1979). An experimental program for teaching high speed word recognition and comprehension skills. In J. E. Button, T. Lovitt, & T. Rowland (Eds.), *Communications research in learning disabilities and mental retardation* (pp. 33–65). Baltimore: University Park Press.

Daly, E. J., & Martens, B. K. (1994). A comparison of three interventions for increasing oral reading performance: Application of the instructional hierarchy. *Journal of Applied Behavior Analysis, 27*, 459–469.

Denckla, M. B., & Rudel, R. G. (1976). Rapid "automatized" naming (R.A.N.): Dyslexia differentiated from other learning disabilities. *Neurosychologia, 14*, 471–479.

Dowhower, S. L. (1987). Effects of repeated reading on second-grade transitional readers' fluency and comprehension. *Reading Research Quarterly, 22*(4), 389–406.

Dowhower, S. L. (1991). Speaking of prosody: Fluency's unattended bedfellow. *Theory Into Practice, 30*(3), 165–175.

Duke, N. K., & Pearson, P. D. (2002). Effective practices for developing reading comprehension. In A. E. Farstrup & S. J. Samuels (Eds.), *What research has to say about reading instruction* (3rd ed., pp. 205–242). Newark, DE: International Reading Association.

Eckert, T. L., Ardoin, S. P., Daisey, D. M., & Scarola, M. D. (2000). Empirically evaluating the effectiveness of reading interventions: The use of brief experimental analysis and single case designs. *Psychology in the Schools, 37*, 463–473.

Ehri, L. C. (1987). Learning to read and spell words. *Journal of Reading Behavior, 19*, 5–31.

Ehri, L. C. (1992). Reconceptualizing the development of sight word reading and its relationship to recoding. In P. Gough, L. C. Ehri, & R. Treiman (Eds.), *Reading acquisition* (pp. 107–143). Hillsdale, NJ: Erlbaum.

Ehri, L. C. (1997). Sight word learning in normal readers and dyslexics. In B. Blachman (Ed.), *Foundations of reading acquisition and dyslexia* (pp. 163–186). Mahwah, NJ: Erlbaum.

Ehri, L. C. (1998). Grapheme–phoneme knowledge is essential for learning to read words in English. In J. L. Metsala & L. C. Ehri (Eds.), *Word recognition in beginning literacy* (pp. 3–40). Mahwah, NJ: Erlbaum.

Ehri, L. C. (2002). Phases of acquisition in learning to read words and implications for teaching. In R. Stainthorp & P. Tomlinson (Eds.), *Learning and teaching reading* (pp. 7–27). London: British Journal of Educational Psychology Monograph Series II.

Ehri, L. C. (2005). Learning to read words: Theory, findings, and issues. *Scientific Studies of Reading, 9*, 167–188.

Faulkner, H. J., & Levy, B. A. (1994). How text difficulty and reader skill interact to produce differential reliance on word and content overlap in reading transfer. *Journal of Experimental Child Psychology, 58*, 1–24.

Fien, H., Baker, S. K., Smolkowski, K., Smith, J. L. M., Kame'enui, E. J., & Beck, C. T. (2008). Using nonsense word fluency to predict reading proficiency in kindergarten through second grade for English learners and native English speakers. *School Psychology Review, 37*(3), 391–408.

Fleisher, L. S., Jenkins, J. R., & Pany, D. (1979). Effects on poor readers' comprehension of training in rapid decoding. *Reading Research Quarterly, 15*, 30–48.

Fuchs, L. S., Fuchs, D., Hosp, M. D., & Jenkins, J. (2001). Oral reading fluency as an indicator of reading competence: A theoretical, empirical, and historical analysis. *Scientific Studies of Reading, 5*, 239–259.

Fuchs, L. S., Fuchs, D., & Maxwell, L. (1988). The validity of informal reading comprehension measures. *Remedial and Special Education, 9*(2), 20–28.

Good, R. H., Baker, S. K., & Peyton, J. A., (2009). Making sense of nonsense word fluency: Determining adequate progress in early first grade reading. *Reading and Writing Quarterly, 25*, 33–56.

Good, R. H., Simmons, D. C., & Kame'enui, E. J. (2001). The importance and decision-making utility of a continuum of fluency-based indicators of foundational reading skills for third-grade high-stakes outcomes. *Scientific Studies of Reading, 5*(3), 257–288.

Greenleaf, C. L., Schoenbach, R., Cziko, C., & Mueller, F. (2001). Apprenticing adolescent readers to academic literacy. *Harvard Educational Review, 71,* 79–130.

Hasbrouck, J., & Tindal, G. A. (2006). Oral reading fluency norms: A valuable assessment tool for reading teachers. *Reading Teacher, 59*(7), 636–644.

Herman, P. (1985). The effect of repeated readings on reading rate, speech pauses, and word recognition accuracy. *Reading Research Quarterly, 20,* 553–565.

Hiebert, E. H. (2005). The effects of text difficulty on second graders' fluency development. *Reading Psychology, 26,* 183–209.

Homan, S., Klesius, P., & Hite, S. (1993). Effects of repeated readings and nonrepetitive strategies on students' fluency and comprehension. *Journal of Educational Research, 87,* 94–99.

Hudson, R. F., Lane, H. B., & Pullen, P. C. (2005). Reading fluency assessment and instruction: What, why, and how. *Reading Teacher, 58*(8), 702–714.

Jenkins, J. R., Fuchs, L. S., van den Broek, P., Espin, C., & Deno, S. L. (2003). Sources of individual differences in reading comprehension and reading fluency. *Journal of Educational Psychology, 95,* 719–729.

Johnson, K. R., & Layng, T. V. J. (1992). Breaking the structuralist barrier: Literacy and numeracy with fluency. *American Psychologist, 47*(11), 1475–1490.

Johnson, K. R., & Layng, T. V. J. (1994). The Morningside model of generative instruction. In R. Gardner, D. Sainato, J. Cooper, T. Heron, W. Heward, J. Eshleman, & T. Grossi (Eds.), *Behavioral analysis in education: Focus on measurably superior instruction* (pp. 173–197). Belmont, CA: Brooks/Cole.

Kail, R., & Hall, L. K. (1994). Speed of processing, naming speed, and reading. *Developmental Psychology, 30,* 949–954.

Kame'enui, E. J., & Simmons, D. C. (2001). Introduction to this special issue: The DNA of reading fluency. *Scientific Studies of Reading, 5*(3), 203–210.

Katzir, T., Kim, Y., Wolf, M., O'Brien, B., Kennedy, B., Lovett, M., et al. (2006). Reading fluency: The whole is more than the parts. *Annals of Dyslexia, 56,* 51–82.

Keehn, S. (2003). The effect of instruction and practice through readers' theatre on young readers' oral reading fluency. *Reading Research and Instruction, 42,* 40–61.

Keehn, S., Harmon, J., & Shoho, A. (2008). A study of readers theater in eighth grade: Issues of fluency, comprehension, and vocabulary. *Reading and Writing Quarterly, 24,* 335–362.

Kuhn, M. (2004). Helping students become accurate, expressive readers: Fluency instruction in small groups. *Reading Teacher, 58,* 338–344.

Kuhn, M. R., Schwanenflugel, P. J., Morris, R. D., Morrow, L. M., Woo, D. G., Meisinger, E. B., et al. (2006). Teaching children to become fluent and automatic readers. *Journal of Literacy Research, 38,* 357–387.

Kuhn, M. R., & Stahl, S. A. (2003). Fluency: A review of developmental and remedial practices. *Journal of Educational Psychology, 95,* 3–21.

LaBerge, D., & Samuels, S. J. (1974). Toward a theory of automatic information processing in reading. *Cognitive Psychology, 6,* 293–323.

LeVasseur, V. M., Macaruso, P., & Shankweiler, D. (2008). Promoting gains in reading fluency: A comparison of three approaches. *Reading and Writing: An Interdisciplinary Journal, 21,* 205–230.

Levy, B. A. (2001). Moving the bottom: Improving reading fluency. In M. Wolf (Ed.), *Dyslexia, fluency, and the brain* (pp. 367–379). Parkton, MD: York Press.

Levy, B. A., Abello, B., & Lysynchuk, L. (1997). Transfer from word training to reading in context: Gains in reading fluency and comprehension. *Learning Disabilities Quarterly, 20*, 173–188.

Lloyd, J. W., Forness, S. R., & Kavale, K. A. (1998). Some methods are more effective than others. *Intervention in School and Clinic, 33*, 195–200.

Logan, G. D. (1988). Toward an instance theory of automatization. *Psychological Review, 95*(4), 492–527.

Logan, G. D. (1997). Automaticity and reading: Perspectives from the instance theory of automatization. *Reading and Writing Quarterly, 13*, 123–146.

Lovett, M. W., Lacerenza, L., & Borden, S. (2000). Putting struggling readers on the PHAST track: A program to integrate phonological and strategy-based remedial reading instruction and maximize outcomes. *Journal of Learning Disabilities, 33*, 458–476.

Maberry, D. R. (1975). *A comparison of three techniques of teaching literature: Silent reading, solo performance, and readers' theatre.* Unpublished doctoral dissertation, North Texas State University, Denton, TX.

Manis, F. R., Doi, L. M., & Bhada, B. (2000). Naming speed, phonological awareness, and orthographic knowledge in second graders. *Journal of Learning Disabilities, 33*, 325–333.

Martin-Chang, S. L., & Levy, B. A. (2005). Fluency transfer: Differential gains in reading speed and accuracy following isolated word and context training. *Reading and Writing, 18*, 343–376.

Martinez, M., Roser, N. L., & Strecker, S. (1998/1999). "I never thought I could be a star": A readers' theatre ticket to fluency. *Reading Teacher, 52*, 326–334.

Mathes, P. G., & Fuchs, L. S. (1993). Peer mediated reading instruction in special education resource rooms. *Learning Disabilities Research and Practice, 8*, 233–243.

McMaster, K. L., Fuchs, D., & Fuchs, L. S. (2006). Research on peer-assisted learning strategies: The promise and limitations of peer-mediated instruction. *Reading and Writing Quarterly, 22*, 5–25.

Mercer, C. D., Campbell, K. U., Miller, M. D., Mercer, K. D., & Lane, H. B. (2000). Effects of a reading fluency intervention for middle schoolers with specific learning disabilities. *Learning Disabilities Research and Practice, 15*(4), 179–189.

Meyer, M. S., & Felton, R. H. (1999). Repeated reading to enhance fluency: Old approaches and new directions. *Annals of Dyslexia, 49*, 283–306.

Miller, J., & Schwanenflugel, P. J. (2006). Prosody of syntactically complex sentences in the real reading of young children. *Journal of Educational Psychology, 98*, 839–853.

Miller, J., & Schwanenflugel, P. J. (2008). A longitudinal study of the development of reading prosody as a dimension of oral reading fluency in early elementary school children. *Reading Research Quarterly, 43*, 336–354.

Millin, S. K., & Rinehart, S. D. (1999). Some of the benefits of readers' theater participation for second-grade Title 1 students. *Reading Research and Instruction, 39*(1), 71–88.

Morgan, P. L., & Sideridis, G. D. (2006). Contrasting the effectiveness of fluency interventions for students with or at risk for learning disabilities: A multilevel random coefficient modeling meta-analysis. *Learning Disabilities: Research and Practice, 21*, 191–210.

National Reading Panel (NRP). (2000). *A report of the National Reading Panel: Teaching children to read.* Washington, DC: National Institute of Child Health and Human Development.

O'Connor, R. E., Bell, K. M., Harty, K. R., Larkin, L. K., Sackor, S. M., & Zigmond, N. (2002). Teaching reading to poor readers in the intermediate grades: A comparison of text difficulty. *Journal of Educational Psychology, 94*, 474–485.

O'Connor, R. E., White, A., & Swanson, H. L. (2007). Repeated reading versus continuous reading: Influences on reading fluency and comprehension. *Exceptional Children, 74*, 31–46.

O'Shea, L. J., Sindelar, P. T., & O'Shea, D. J. (1985). The effects of repeated readings and attentional cues on reading fluency and comprehension. *Journal of Reading Behavior, 17,* 129–142.

Perfetti, C. A. (1985). *Reading ability.* New York: Oxford University Press.

Perfetti, C. A., & Hogaboam, T. (1975). Relationship between single word decoding and reading comprehension skill. *Journal of Educational Psychology, 67*(4), 461–469.

Posner, M. I., & Snyder, C. R. R. (1975). Facilitation and inhibition in the processing of signals. In P. M. Rabbitt & S. Dornic (Eds.), *Attention and performance* (Vol. 5, pp. 669–682). San Diego: Academic Press.

Rashotte, C. A., & Torgesen, J. K. (1985). Repeated reading and reading fluency in learning disabled children. *Reading Research Quarterly, 20*(2), 180–188.

Rasinski, T. V. (1990). Effects of repeated reading and listening-while-reading on reading fluency. *Journal of Educational Research, 83,* 147–150.

Rasinski, T. (2004). Creating fluent readers. *Educational Leadership, 61*(6), 46–51.

Rasinski, T., & Stevenson, B. (2005). The effects of Fast Start Reading, a fluency-based home involvement reading program, on the reading achievement of beginning readers. *Reading Psychology, 26,* 109–125.

Rayner, K., Foorman, B. R., Perfetti, C. A., Pesetsky, D., & Seidenberg, M. S. (2001). How psychological science informs the teaching of reading. *Psychological Science in the Public Interest, 2*(2), 31–74.

Reutzel, D. R., Fawson, P. C., & Smith, J. A. (2008). Reconsidering silent sustained reading: An exploratory study of scaffolded silent reading. *Journal of Educational Research, 102,* 37–50.

Roehrig, A. D., Petscher, Y., Nettles, S., Hudson, R. F., & Torgesen, J. K. (2008). Accuracy of the DIBELS Oral Reading Fluency measure for predicting third grade reading comprehension outcomes. *Journal of School Psychology, 46*(3), 343–366.

Samuels, S. J. (1979). The method of repeated readings. *Reading Teacher, 32*(4), 403–408.

Samuels, S. J. (2006). Toward a model of reading fluency. In S. J. Samuels & A. E. Farstrup (Eds.), *What research has to say about fluency instruction* (pp. 24–46). Newark, DE: International Reading Association.

Savage, R., & Frederickson, N. (2005). Evidence of a highly specific relationship between rapid automatic naming of digits and text-reading speed. *Brain and Language, 93,* 152–159.

Schatschneider, C., Fletcher, J. M., Francis, D. J., Carlson, C. D., & Foorman, B. R. (2004). Kindergarten prediction of reading skills: A longitudinal comparative analysis. *Journal of Educational Psychology, 96,* 265–282.

Schreiber, P. A. (1980). On the acquisition of reading fluency. *Journal of Reading Behavior, 7*(3), 177–186.

Schreiber, P. A. (1991). Understanding prosody's role in reading acquisition. *Theory Into Practice, 30*(3), 158–164.

Schwanenflugel, P. J., Hamilton, A. M., Kuhn, M. R., Wisenbaker, J. M., & Stahl, S. A. (2004). Becoming a fluent reader: Reading skill and prosodic features in the oral reading of young readers. *Journal of Educational Psychology, 96*(1), 119–129.

Schwanenflugel, P. J., Meisinger, E. B., Wisenbaker, J. M., Kuhn, M. R., Strauss, G. P., & Morris, R. D. (2006). Becoming a fluent and automatic reader in the early elementary school years. *Reading Research Quarterly, 41,* 496–522.

Shany, M. T., & Biemiller, A. (1985). Assisted reading practice: Effects on performance for poor readers in grades 3 and 4. *Reading Research Quarterly, 30,* 382–395.

Shinn, M. R., Good, R. H., Knutson, N., Tilly, W. D., & Collins, V. L. (1992). Curriculum-based measurement of oral reading fluency: A confirmatory analysis of its relation to reading. *School Psychology Review, 21*(3), 459–479.

Sindelar, P. T., Monda, L. E., & O'Shea, L. J. (1990). Effects of repeated readings on instructional- and mastery-level readers. *Journal of Educational Research, 83,* 220–226.

Speece, D. L., & Ritchey, K. D. (2005). A longitudinal study of the development of oral reading fluency in young children at risk for reading failure. *Journal of Learning Disabilities, 38,* 387–399.

Stahl, S. A., & Heubach, K. (2005). Fluency-Oriented Reading Instruction. In K. A. Stahl & M. C. McKenna (Eds.), *Reading research at work* (pp. 177–203). New York: Guilford Press.

Tan, A., & Nicholson, T. (1997). Flashcards revisited: Training poor readers to read words faster improves their comprehension of text. *Journal of Educational Psychology, 89,* 276–288.

Therrien, W. J. (2004). Fluency and comprehension gains as a result of repeated reading: A meta-analysis. *Remedial and Special Education, 25*(4), 252–261.

Thomson, J. B., Chenault, B., Abbott, R. D., Raskind, W., Richards, T., Aylward, E., et al. (2005). Converging evidence for attentional influences on the orthographic word form in child dyslexics. *Journal of Neurolinguistics, 18,* 93–126.

Torgesen, J. K., & Hudson, R. (2006). Reading fluency: Critical issues for struggling readers. In S. J. Samuels & A. Farstrup (Eds.), *Reading fluency: The forgotten dimension of reading success* (pp. 130–158). Newark, DE: International Reading Association.

Torgesen, J. K., Rashotte, C. A., & Alexander, A. (2001). Principles of fluency instruction in reading: Relationships with established empirical outcomes. In M. Wolf (Ed.), *Dyslexia, fluency, and the brain* (pp. 333–355). Parkton, MD: York Press.

Vadasy, P. F., & Sanders, E. A. (2008a). Repeated reading intervention: Outcomes and interactions with readers' skills and classroom instruction. *Journal of Educational Psychology, 100,* 272–290.

Vadasy, P. F., & Sanders, E. A. (2008b). Benefits of repeated reading intervention for low-achieving fourth- and fifth-grade students. *Remedial and Special Education, 29,* 235–249.

Vadasy, P. F., & Sanders, E. A. (2009). Supplemental fluency intervention and determinates of reading outcomes. *Scientific Studies of Reading, 13,* 383–425.

Vadasy, P. F., Sanders, E. A., & Peyton, J. A. (2006). Paraeducator-supplemented instruction in structural analysis with text reading practice for second and third graders at risk for reading problems. *Remedial and Special Education, 27,* 365–378.

Vaughn, S., Chard, D. J., Bryant, D. P., Coleman, M., & Kouzekanani, K. (2000). Fluency and comprehension interventions for third-grade students. *Remedial and Special Education, 21,* 325–335.

Vellutino, F. R., Scanlon, D. M., & Tanzman, M. S. (1994). Components of reading ability: Issues and problems in operationalizing word identification, phonological coding, and orthographic coding. In G. R. Lyon (Ed.), *Frames of reference for the assessment of learning disabilities: New views on measurement issues* (pp. 279–332). Baltimore: Brookes.

Wagner, R. K., & Torgesen, J. K. (1987). The nature of phonological processing and its causal role in the acquisition of reading skills. *Psychological Bulletin, 101,* 192–212.

Wagner, R. K., Torgesen, J. K., Laughon, P., Simmons, K., & Rashotte, C. (1993). Development of young readers' phonological processing abilities. *Journal of Educational Psychology, 85*(1), 83–103.

Wagner, R. K., Torgesen, J. K., & Rashotte, C. A. (1994). Development of reading-related phonological processing abilities: New evidence of bidirectional causality from a latent variable longitudinal study. *Developmental Psychology, 30*(1), 73–87.

Walczyk, J. J., Wei, M., Zha, P., Griffith-Ross, D. A., Goubert, S. E., & Cooper, A. L. (2007).

Development of the interplay between automatic processes and cognitive resources in reading. *Journal of Educational Psychology, 99,* 867–887.

What Works Clearinghouse. (2008). *Procedures and standards handbook, version 2.0.* Washington, DC: U.S. Department of Education.

Wolf, M. (1997). A provisional, integrative account of phonological and naming-speed deficits in dyslexia: Implications for diagnosis and intervention. In B. Blachman (Ed.), *Foundations of reading acquisition and dyslexia: Implications for early intervention* (pp. 67–92). Mahwah, NJ: Erlbaum.

Wolf, M., Barzillai, M., Gottwald, S., Miller, L., Spencer, K., Norton, E., et al. (2009). The RAVE-O intervention: Connecting neuroscience to the classroom. *Mind, Brain, and Education, 3,* 84–93.

Wolf, M., & Bowers, P. (1999). The double-deficit hypothesis for the developmental dyslexias. *Journal of Educational Psychology, 91,* 415–438.

Wolf, M., Bowers, P. G., & Biddle, K. (2000). Naming-speed processes, timing, and reading: A conceptual review. *Journal of Learning Disabilities, 33*(4), 387–407.

Wolf, M., & Katzir-Cohen, T. (2001). Reading fluency and its intervention. *Scientific Studies of Reading, 5*(3), 211–239.

Wolf, M., Miller, L., & Donnelly, K. (2000). Retrieval, automaticity, vocabulary elaboration, orthography (RAVE-O): A comprehensive, fluency-based reading intervention program. *Journal of Learning Disabilities, 33,* 375–386.

Worthy, J., & Prater, K. (2002). "I thought about it all night": Readers' theatre for reading fluency and motivation. *Reading Teacher, 56*(3), 294–297

Young, A. R., Bowers, P. G., & MacKinnon, G. E. (1996). Effects of prosodic modeling and repeated reading on poor readers' fluency and comprehension. *Applied Psycholinguistics, 17,* 59–84.

Zutell, J., & Rasinski, T. V. (1991). Training teachers to attend to their students' reading fluency. *Theory Into Practice, 30* (3), 211–217.

9

Main Idea and Summarization Instruction to Improve Reading Comprehension

Asha K. Jitendra
Meenakshi Gajria

It is well established that many students who struggle with reading have problems understanding text. Problems with comprehension, on the one hand, may be rooted in word recognition skills that are not automatic. The slow, inaccurate, and labored reading of poor readers often interferes with tasks that involve studying and learning from text. Unfortunately, these early skills deficits may result in an inordinate amount of time spent on decoding instruction that may in turn deprive the learner of the necessary experience with text for acquiring comprehension strategies (Rich & Shepherd, 1993). On the other hand, reading comprehension problems may stem from limited cognitive ability or problems with working memory, locating main ideas, inference making, flexibly selecting and applying strategies, and monitoring and evaluating strategy use (Gersten, Fuchs, Williams, & Baker, 2001; Palincsar, David, Winn, & Stevens, 1991; Rich & Shepherd, 1993; Williams, 2004). Learners with these types of problems may read fluently but have difficulty constructing meaning. Furthermore, there is empirical evidence that insufficient prior knowledge, discrepant language experiences, or lack of strategic skills may be associated with comprehension difficulties (Armbruster, Anderson, & Ostertag, 1987; Winograd, 1984).

Interest in higher-order comprehension problems that are not caused by decoding skill deficits or difficulties with lexical access (i.e., word finding abilities) has increased (Cain & Oakhill, 2007; van den Broek, Lynch, Naslund, Ievers-Landis, & Verduin, 2003; Winograd, 1984). When considering the advances made in designing effective interventions to remediate decoding deficits, there is considerably less research in comprehension strategy training to alleviate comprehension deficits of struggling readers (Gersten et al., 2001). Finding the main idea is integral to reading comprehension and often poses a challenge for struggling readers. Teaching readers to identify main ideas in texts is a promising approach that has a positive impact on comprehension skills. Although the research base on main idea intervention studies is limited, evidence supports instructional approaches focusing on identification and construction of main ideas, and skills essential for effective comprehension and studying from texts (Gersten et al., 2001). "Summarization," the ability to construct a concise account of the main ideas in a text, is also difficult for many students. Strategy training involving summarizing texts is known both to enhance written summaries and result in transfer effects on a variety of reading comprehension measures (Rinehart, Stahl, & Erikson, 1986). Winograd (1984) suggested that some of the strategies involved in summarization might also be used in comprehension globally, thereby highlighting the importance of teaching summarization strategies. Considerable evidence indicates that summarization training can transfer to comprehension when a direct instruction approach is used to teach the technique, when the learner has sufficient opportunities to apply the technique, and when specific instruction is provided on how to transfer the strategy to novel materials (see Rinehart et al., 1986).

Identifying and Generating Main Ideas

Getting the main idea from a text is central to summarization and reading comprehension (van den Broek et al., 2003). According to Williams (1988), the ability to find the main idea is fundamental to drawing inferences from texts, studying effectively, and thinking critically. Not only young children but also older students experience difficulty identifying main ideas (Williams, 1988). As such, identifying main ideas is of great importance and is an accepted goal of reading instruction in elementary school. The nature of the main idea differs between narrative and expository text types (see Baumann, 1986; Moore, Cunningham, & Rudisill, 1983; Pearson & Johnson, 1978). In narrative texts, the reader has to discern the theme of a story from the description of events and their temporal sequence. In contrast, expository text requires the reader to develop a generalization or a thesis based on the logical relationship of ideas about a topic. Because expository prose includes many different genres (e.g., description, compare–contrast, sequence, cause–effect, problem–solution), the main idea or what is important may be defined by a specific genre (Williams, 1988, 2004).

Teaching how to find the main idea is challenging and compounded by the difficulty many children, especially students with learning disabilities (LD), have in identifying and especially generating main ideas of simple texts (Baumann, 1984). Suggested instructional practices often involve teachers reading a passage and stating the main points as students follow along (Cunningham & Moore, 1986). However, such practices do not provide sufficient direction for finding a main idea, and they become more challenging in "inconsiderate" texts (Armbruster et al., 1987). As Afflerbach (1990) noted, "When the main idea of a text is not stated explicitly, the reader cannot simply *select* the main idea statement from surrounding statements, and must instead *construct* a statement to represent the main idea" (p. 33). The presence of extraneous information in text presents an additional challenge to identifying or constructing a main idea (Williams, 1986).

For students with LD, it is crucial to teach directly how to construct the main idea, and to emphasize metacognitive and strategic approaches to learning. Use of systematic, strategy training is known to improve the performance of students with LD in identifying important information in text (Englert & Lichter, 1982; Williams, 1986; Williams, Taylor, Jarin, & Milligan, 1983). Selection of a strategy for constructing main ideas may depend on the difficulty of the text (Bereiter, Burtis, & Scardamalia, 1988; Jitendra, Hoppes, & Xin, 2000). The early work of Baumann (1984) provides the foundation for the value of main idea comprehension instruction. Baumann used the principles of direct instruction to teach sixth-grade students to identify main ideas in paragraphs and stories that were explicitly or implicitly stated. The main idea strategy group outperformed students using the traditional textbook approach and the control group on several near- and far-transfer measures. Other researchers have reported positive effects of direct instruction in main idea comprehension, metacognitive skills, or a combination of strategies (i. e., previewing, clicking and clunking to self-monitor understanding, getting the gist, and wrapping up) with cooperative learning to enhance main idea comprehension of elementary-age students (e.g., Klingner, Vaughn, & Schumm, 1998; Stevens, Slavin, & Farnish, 1991).

Only in the past two decades or so have researchers investigated instructional strategies to help students with learning difficulties to identify or construct the main idea of texts. These investigations have typically included a direct instruction approach in isolation or in combination with metacomprehension skills, such as self-questioning or self-monitoring procedures. In an early investigation, Jenkins, Heliotis, Stein, and Haynes (1987) emphasized a comprehension-monitoring strategy to restate paragraph contents. Elementary-age students (grades 3–6) with LD learned a restatement procedure that involved asking themselves two questions related to the task of finding "who" the paragraph was about and "what was happening," and writing brief restatements that included three or four words to convey the gist of the story. The overall results supported the usefulness of writing brief statements of the important ideas of paragraphs to improve reading comprehension.

Other studies that focused on a paraphrasing or restatement strategy without metacomprehension training also produced similar results. For example, when Ellis and Graves (1990) taught upper-elementary and middle school (grades 5–7) students to state the main ideas in prose passages in their own words, students displayed improved comprehension and maintenance of strategy effects 2 weeks later. Bakken, Mastropieri, and Scruggs (1997) taught eighth-grade students to apply a text-structure-based or paragraph restatement strategy to science passages involving three types of text structures (main idea, list, or order), and students improved their performance on immediate and delayed recall of central and incidental information, as well as on transfer measures.

To understand better the effects of reading comprehension skills (e.g., finding main ideas), Graves (1986) conducted a study to separate the effects of instruction on finding the main idea from effects of instruction on metacomprehension skills (e.g., self-questioning, self-monitoring). Upper-elementary and middle school (grades 5–8) students with LD in both direct instruction only and direct instruction plus self-monitoring conditions were taught to identify main ideas of passages. Students were given explicit instruction in a rule to find main ideas of stories. For example, the teacher stated the rule: "A main idea tells what the whole story is about." The teacher then questioned students throughout the reading to help them determine whether each statement at the end of the story included the main idea. Students in the direct instruction plus self-monitoring condition were also taught to use a self-questioning procedure to check main idea comprehension. Both groups improved in comprehension performance, and self-monitoring added value in increasing comprehension of main ideas.

Similarly, work with middle and high school students supports these findings (Graves & Levin, 1989; Jitendra, Cole, Hoppes, & Wilson, 1998; Jitendra et al., 2000; Stevens, 1988). Graves and Levin (1989) documented that self-monitoring of main ideas is more effective than a mnemonic condition for identifying main ideas in texts for middle school students with LD. In an exploratory study, Jitendra et al. (1998) used a single-subject design with three sixth-grade students with LD to examine the effects of direct instruction in a main idea strategy followed by instruction in self-monitoring use of strategy. Results indicated an increase in students' ability to identify the main ideas of passages, with a greater increase following instruction in self-monitoring. Recognizing the importance of metacomprehension skills, Jitendra et al. (2000) extended their previous work and assessed the effectiveness of combining self-monitoring with a main idea strategy. Middle school students (grades 6–8) were taught to select or generate main idea sentences that summarized the passage, and use a procedure to self-monitor their comprehension. Results indicated that students not only improved but also maintained their performance 6 weeks after training. Furthermore, transfer effects to novel passages were found on selection items, but the effects were less robust on production responses, possibly due to a higher readability level and more implicit idea units in transfer passages compared to training passages.

In another study, Stevens (1988) successfully taught students in remedial reading classes (grades 6–11) to identify the main ideas of expository paragraphs, and provided training in related metacognitive strategies. This interesting study used computer tutorials to instruct students to identify the topic and the main idea of a paragraph from a list of both alternatives and modeled metacognitive strategies for self-checking main idea statements against information in the text. Results showed that students instructed in strategies outperformed their peers in a classification skills training group (categorizing words under topics) and control groups on both training content paragraphs (i.e., geology and weather) and transfer content paragraphs (i.e., biology, space, exploration, and Native Americans).

Using a different approach to main idea instruction, Wong and Jones (1982) employed self-questioning training to teach secondary (grades 8 and 9) students with LD to interact with the text by finding the main idea in the paragraph and underlining it, generating questions related to the main idea, and monitoring understanding of textual units. Results indicated that training led to increased awareness of important textual units, facilitated the ability to generate questions related to those units, and generally improved the comprehension performance of students with LD. Chan (1991) extended research on the use of a self-questioning strategy to upper-elementary students (grades 5 and 6) with reading disabilities with similar results that showed training facilitated identification of main ideas. The self-questioning procedure involved a series of questions that students were taught to ask themselves while reading to delete redundant or trivial information, locate topic sentences, and identify implicit main ideas.

Overall, these studies provide support for systematic instruction in main ideas to increase reading comprehension of poor readers and students with disabilities. The studies by Jenkins et al. (1987), Stevens (1988), and Jitendra et al. (2000) in particular supported the construction of meaning from text by teaching students to generate main idea statements rather than simply identify main ideas.

Summarization Skills

Although finding the main idea or gist of a text is a critical comprehension skill, summarization training that emphasizes the structure of ideas and their interrelationships within text is likely to lead to greater recall and retention of text than other strategies (Rinehart et al., 1986). The greater attention to text during this type of summarization training results in children not only spending more time engaged in reading but also focusing more closely on reading to monitor and evaluate their reading to comprehend text. As a consequence, summarization training has a reciprocal effect on improving students' self-regulation of cognitive processes essential for effective reading. The goal of summarization training is to make children aware of the highest level of information or main ideas in a text, as well as details that support the main ideas, because both are important to remember for school success. As a result, summarization is often a crucial component of strategy packages (e.g., reciprocal teaching: Brown & Palincsar, 1982; collaborative strategic reading: Klingner et al., 1998) that enhance comprehension.

One type of summarization training that has been thoroughly investigated and found to be effective is based on Kintsch and van Dijk's (1978) model of text processing, in which the essential components are the reader's schema (organized network of prior knowledge), the "microstructure" (the semantic content of sentences in text), and the rules for condensing information to develop the macrostructure or gist of the text (Winograd, 1984). In this model, the formulation of a "macrostructure" (i.e., global meaning of the text) is critical. When processing text, readers typically focus on the microstructure of text and engage in the process of converting sentences to propositions, as well as applying macrorules (i.e., deleting, generalizing, and constructing) to reduce the number of propositions to form a macrostructure, or gist. It is this macrostructure that a reader primarily remembers and uses as a cue to facilitate retrieval of detailed information from text. Thus, the macrostructure that one constructs during reading is like a summary: It represents the gist of the text. At the same time, the reader's schema plays an integral role in macroprocessing of text as he or she engages in the processes of deleting, generalizing, and constructing text based on not only the author's intent but also the reader's knowledge of the domain or text structure (stories or expository text).

Brown and Day (1983) studied the development of summarization skills from the standpoint of their usefulness as study techniques in learning from larger units of text (i.e., several passages). They proposed five basic rules of summarization derived from Kintsch and van Dijk's (1978) model. The first two summarization rules involve the deletion of unnecessary material (i.e., trivial and redundant). The third rule, superordination, which corresponds to Kintsch and van Dijk's generalization rule, entails the substitution of a superordinate term for a list of items or actions. The fourth and fifth rules approximate Kintsch and van Dijk's construction rule and require providing a topic sentence for each paragraph in the text. This involves selecting a topic sentence when it is explicitly stated in the paragraph, or inventing a topic sentence, if the author has not provided it. The five basic rules reflect the methods of condensation students typically use when summarizing text. In addition, these are the rules that more mature high-school students employ when note taking and outlining (Brown, 1981; Brown & Smiley, 1978). The Kintsch and van Dijk model posits that the macrorules of deleting, generalizing, and constructing are general rules underlying comprehension of texts, and not just specific rules for carrying out a summary writing task. Therefore, it can be assumed that the process of constructing a summary enhances comprehension and recall of texts.

Positive effects of summarization have been documented on students' sensitivity to text structure and on measures of reading comprehension. Research on summarization ability and text comprehension support the notion that good readers are more sensitive to important ideas in the text and use the structure of a passage to develop a summary of the passage ideas (Brown & Smiley, 1977; Meyer, Brandt, & Bluth, 1980; Smiley, Oakley, Worthen, Campione, & Brown, 1977). In addition, good readers have better comprehension and memory for what they have read compared to readers who do not develop a summary reflecting sensitivity to text structure.

Many struggling readers and students with LD lack sensitivity to important information in text, and experience difficulty in finding the main ideas and important supporting details (e.g., Wong, 1979). Also, they fail to relate main ideas and details to one another in a way that facilitates recall. More specifically, students with LD do not recall as much superordinate information as do normal peers, even though the two groups do not differ in the amount of subordinate information recalled from a set of short stories (Hansen, 1978). This pattern of results has been replicated by several researchers in different age groups of students with LD, and with both narrative and expository passages (Eamon, 1978; McGee, 1982; Worden & Nakamura, 1983). These studies have led to the conclusion that students with LD are less sensitive to differences in importance of propositions in stories and texts.

In summary, the body of research on summarization skills suggests several conclusions. First, text comprehension and production are functions of deliberate activities that readers employ to summarize information. Second, sensitivity to text structure is a substantial predictor of overall recall. Third, summarization strategies become increasingly efficient with age, such that simple strategies (e.g., copy or delete information) employed prior to the age of 12 years are replaced by more efficient strategies involving transformational and condensation rules to produce synopses in students' own words of the essential meaning of the text. Poor readers are more likely to make decisions about summary inclusions and deletions on a piecemeal, sentence-by-sentence basis, whereas good readers based their judgments on the meaning of the whole text (Brown, Day, & Jones, 1983; Kintsch & Kozminsky, 1977; Meyer et al., 1980; Winograd, 1984). As a result, summaries of poor readers are often list-like collections of descriptions about the passage topic that lack focus and connections between elements of the text. Fourth, comprehension differences between good and poor readers are a function of readers' sensitivity to text structure and, consequently, the use of summarization skills. As such, instruction focusing on summary formation or macrostructure for text may be beneficial for poor readers. Specifically, direct instruction in rule-based approaches has been shown to improve middle school students' written summaries (Armbruster et al., 1987; Bean & Steenwyk, 1984; Berkowitz, 1986; Hare & Borchardt 1984; Rinehart, Stahl, & Erickson, 1986; Taylor & Beach, 1984), and such training should be used to help poor readers become more aware of important information in text.

Summarization Research with LD Students

Early attempts to teach summary skills to students with learning difficulties focused on generating a single sentence to restate the main ideas in a paragraph. For example Malone and Mastropieri (1992) taught students in grades 6–9 to construct a summary sentence for each paragraph of the passage. Results indicated that students in summarization and summarization with self-monitoring conditions not only improved in their strategic knowledge but also outperformed students in the traditional reading comprehension training condition on several measures (immediate, near transfer, and far transfer tests). The results of this study are important given the short length of training (i.e., only 2 days of instruction) and the spontaneous transfer from narrative to expository material. Although the restatement approach to summarization was appealing given its simplicity of generating a single sentence that denotes the meaning of a paragraph (Pressley, Johnson, Symons, McGoldrick, & Kurita, 1989), later studies used more sophisticated summarization strategies based on the model of text comprehension postulated by van Dijk and Kintsch (1983; Kintsch, 1986). The studies by Nelson, Smith, and Dodd (1992), Gajria and Salvia (1992), and Rogevich and Perin (2008) in particular provide information that better explains the task of constructing the main idea when no main idea statement is presented in the text.

Nelson et al. (1992) examined the effects of a summarization strategy on comprehension of a science text by five students with LD (grades 4–8). Students were taught a nine-step summary skills strategy; the first seven steps focused on identifying and organizing main ideas and important information in writing a summary, followed by steps to reread and revise the summary. The instructional program was effective in improving both students' comprehension and quality of the written summaries, and the effects of instruction were maintained.

Gajria and Salvia (1992) used a direct instruction approach to teach middle school students with LD (grades 6–9) to develop a summary or gist of the main ideas of a passage by applying the five rules proposed by Brown and Day (1983): reduce lists, select topic sentences, construct topic sentences, delete redundancies, and delete unimportant information. After each rule was mastered in isolation, students received instruction and guided practice in the use of the combined rules. Instruction in inventing a main idea sentence and summarizing the information in expository passages not only led to improved summarization skill but students also maintained the skill and demonstrated generalization of the skill by spontaneously applying it to comprehend new reading passages that differed from the controlled materials used during the training.

Rogevich and Perin (2008) extended this research on summarization to secondary students with behavior disorders and comorbid attention-deficit/hyperactivity disorder (ADHD) using a self-regulated strategy development (SRSD) intervention: Think before Reading, Think while Reading, Think after Reading, with Written Summarization (TWA-WS). Students were taught to identify the author's purpose in the text, determine their prior knowledge about the topic, set a reading goal, focus on their reading speed, relate prior knowledge to new information in the text, reread parts of the text, identify the main idea, summarize the text, and reflect on what they learned. The intervention included Ogle's (1989) what I Know, what I Want to know, what I have Learned (K-W-L), strategy as well as Brown and Day's summarization steps. The overall results indicated the benefits of the intervention in improving reading comprehension, as measured by written summarization. Furthermore, the strategy effects generalized to reading a social studies text and to a more complex task that involved integrating information across two science passages.

In summary, progress has been made in improving reading comprehension skills by teaching students with learning difficulties to find the main idea and summarize to get the gist of the text. Explicit instruction using cognitive strategies, such as self-questioning, paragraph restatement, a text-structure-based procedure, SRSD, and rule-governed summarization approaches, is known to enhance ability to identify or construct main ideas and effectively summarize both narrative and expository text.

Teaching Main Idea and Summarization

Several instructional strategies noted in the literature teach main ideas and summarization skills to improve struggling readers' comprehension of text. One promising vehicle for facilitating such comprehension is the Direct Instruction approach. The following sample lessons from our work on main idea and summarization instruction reflect this approach.

The Main Idea Instructional Program described in Table 9.1 consists of a series of eight lessons adapted from the teaching procedures recommended by Carnine, Silbert, and Kame'enui, (1997), derived from successful studies of main idea strategies in the 1980s and 1990s. The program in Table 9.1 is based on our work with middle school students with learning difficulties (Jitendra et al., 1998, 2000). Although the order of lessons is not based on any definitive hierarchy of tasks in terms of difficulty level, we suggest that classroom teachers initiate instruction on the basis of instructional goals and students' prior knowledge. For example, students may have more difficulty in constructing rather than selecting main ideas, and it is appropriate to sequence the lessons accordingly, based on individual student needs. This may entail having students identify explicit main ideas in passages before requiring them to construct a main idea statement to convey the gist of the passage. For those students who have not mastered lower-level skills, such as finding the main ideas in lists of words or sentences, it may be necessary to teach classification activities using word lists or applying the main idea definition to smaller units of text (i.e., the sentence) than passages.

We incorporated several features into our instructional program for teaching main ideas. First, instruction was based on the following principles of instructional design: selection of appropriate examples of the prototypical task, optimal sequencing of skills (e.g., preskills taught before the strategy is presented), explicit explanation of the rules and consistent modeling of the strategies, and use of extensive practice and feedback (Carnine et al., 1997). Second, highly structured materials are included to provide consistency and allow for initial student success in finding main ideas. The average readability level of the training passages in our evaluation study was 3.3 (range: 1.2–4.9). Third, because there is evidence that requiring students to construct main ideas facilitates better com-

TABLE 9.1. Scope and Sequence of the Main Idea Instructional Program

Main idea lesson	Description
1. Construct main ideas in paragraphs by naming the subject (single) and categorizing the action.	Students are taught to generate the main idea by applying the rule "Name the person and tell the main thing the person did in all the sentences" (Carnine et al., 1997, p. 248). Students apply the rule by naming the subject and categorizing the action in which the subject engages. For example, in the paragraph, *The little bird gathered some sticks from the ground. She took them to the apple tree. She wove the sticks together. Then she added bits of string to make her nest soft.* the subject is *The little bird*, the action is *built a nest*, and the main idea of the paragraph is *The little bird built a nest*. *Prerequisite skills:* Students are able to analyze a list of related words to determine the superordinate category or class (e.g., *Ford*, *Chevy*, and *Dodge* are models of motor vehicles). Examples and nonexamples are used in words lists (e.g., *apples, oranges, carrots, bananas*) to discriminate those that belong or do not belong to the superordinate category (i.e., fruits).
2. Construct main ideas in paragraphs by naming the subjects (multiple) and classifying the action.	Students are taught to generate the main idea in paragraphs that involve multiple subjects by providing the group name for the different persons or things, and by classifying the group action. Instruction is the same as for Lesson 1, except that students construct the main idea sentence by naming the group and telling the main thing the group did. For example, in the paragraph *Carla scraped the leftover food off the dishes. Sue put the dishes into the dishwasher. Joanna put detergent into the dishwasher and turned it on.* the subject is *The women*, the action is *did the dishes*; and the main idea of the sentence is *The women did the dishes*.
3. Select main idea statements from multiple-choice options following a paragraph.	Students are taught to evaluate critically all the options prior to selecting the main idea sentence that best describes the paragraph. For example, in the paragraph *Paul stirred a huge pot of stew on the stove. Gina popped a pan of biscuits into the oven. Carl carried the dishes to the table. Dinner would be ready by the time their mother got home.* students select the main idea of the paragraph from the following options: 1. *Why kids should cook dinner.* 2. *How to cook dinner.* 3. *The kids like to cook dinner.* 4. *The kids were cooking dinner for their mother.* The main idea of the paragraph is *The kids were cooking dinner for their mother*. Instruction includes a discussion of why each statement is or is not a good main idea sentence for the paragraph.
4. Construct or select main ideas in paragraphs that include extraneous information by telling the main thing the person or group did in most of the sentences.	Students are taught to construct the main idea statement for a paragraph that includes one or more sentences not related to the main idea. Instruction for this task involves changing the rule for constructing a main idea from telling what a person or group did in all the sentences to specifying the main thing the person or group did in most of the sentences. The teacher emphasizes that except for the distractor sentence(s), all other sentences should support the main idea of the paragraph. For example, in the paragraph *(continued)*

TABLE 9.1. (*continued*)

Main idea lesson	Description

Linda got out flour and sugar. She took eggs from the refrigerator. The eggs were from her grandmother's chickens. Then, she got out the mixer and the cookie sheets.

the subject is *Linda*, the main thing the subject did in most of the sentences is *got ready to bake cookies*, and the main idea of the sentence is *Linda got ready to bake cookies.* So, the distractor sentence *The eggs were from her grandmother's chicken* does not provide information related to the main idea of the paragraph. Instruction also includes leading students to select a main idea statement that best tells about most of the information in the paragraph. For example, in the paragraph

It was a cold day in November. Tom took the football from the center. He ran down the field. He pushed a tackle out of the way and kept running. Finally, he crossed the goal line.

students select the main idea of the paragraph from the following options:
1. *It was a cold day in November.*
2. *Tom likes to play football.*
3. *When you can play football.*
4. *Tom ran for a touchdown.*

The main idea of the paragraph is *Tom ran for a touchdown.* So, the distracter sentence *It was a cold day in November* does not provide information related to the main idea of the paragraph

5–8. Select or construct main idea statements that tell *where*, *why*, *when* something occurs, *how* something is done, or *how* something looks.

Students are taught to select or construct the main idea sentence that best describes *where*, *why*, *when* something occurs, *how* something is done, or *how* something looks. For example, in the paragraph

Football is a lot of fun. You can play football in your own backyard, if there is plenty of room. You can play football in the park, if there aren't too many people or trees. You can also play football on a soccer field.

students select the main idea of the paragraph from the following options:
1. *What you can do in a street.*
2. *Where you can play football.*
3. *Why football is fun.*
4. *When you can play football*

The main idea of the paragraph is, *Where you can play football.* Instruction involves leading the students to examine each possible main idea option and to note how many sentences in the paragraph tell about that statement. If most of the sentences discuss the option (e.g., where you can play football), then that sentence is deemed to be the main idea of the paragraph.

Instruction also includes having students construct a main idea statement that conveys the gist of the paragraph. For example, in the paragraph

In my town, the best place to get pizza is a little restaurant called Mario's Pizza. It is right in the middle of town, next to the movie theater. The pizza at Mario's is always hot and very good. It is better than any other pizza in town.

the main idea of the paragraph is *The best pizza in my town is at Mario's Pizza.*

Prerequisite skills: Students are able to analyze sentences to determine if a sentence tells *where*, *why*, *when*, or *how*. For example, in the sentence *John ate in the kitchen*, the response to *Where John ate* is *In the kitchen*.

prehension than simply identifying main ideas (see Baumann, 1986), the majority of the tasks required students to generate main ideas. Fourth, we used distractor sentences in our main idea tasks to allow students to select or identify main ideas by discriminating between extraneous information and information related to the main idea.

We present two model lessons (Lesson 1 and Lesson 4) from our main idea instructional program to illustrate teacher-directed instruction in finding the main idea (see Figure 9.1). Lesson 1 involves instruction in constructing main ideas in passages by naming the subject (single) and categorizing the action (see Table 9.1). Lesson 4 teaches students to identify the distractor sentence(s), to cross it (them) out, and to generate a main idea for the passage. It is important to note that the teaching scripts help teachers to plan carefully and prepare instruction, and that teachers do not read verbatim from them. Rather, teachers familiarize themselves with the scripts to respond to students, and to modify examples and procedures as needed during the lesson.

Summarization Training Program

Similar to the Main Idea Instructional Program, the Summarization Training Program is based on principles of effective instruction (e.g., explicit explanation of the rules, modeling and applying the strategy, guided practice in controlled materials; see Gajria & Salvia, 1992). Expository passages are specially constructed or modified for a fourth-grade readability level to elicit the application of each summarization rule. During the application or final phase of training, we introduce students to real texts and provide several opportunities for practice, so that students assume responsibility for both applying and monitoring the strategy. This step allows students to transfer the learned strategy successfully to new reading tasks.

To maximize the effectiveness of summarization training with middle school students with LD, we applied a mastery learning paradigm (Bloom, 1976) and established a different performance criterion for each rule. For the rules related to reducing lists and selecting topic sentences, the criterion for mastery is set at 100% correct, because these tasks are relatively simple. For the remaining three rules (construct topic sentences, delete redundancies, delete unimportant information), the criterion is set at 80% accuracy. We developed short paragraphs to focus explicitly on different rules. For example, to ensure the application of the reduce lists rule, two to three lists of items/events are embedded in the paragraph. Once students demonstrate criterion performance on each rule in isolation, they receive instruction in the combined use of the five rules (i.e., the summarization strategy).

In our instructional program, we introduce students to one summary rule at a time. At the same time, prior to teaching a new rule, we review the rules learned in the previous lesson. Five lessons, each focusing on a specific summary rule,

FIGURE 9.1. Model lessons from the main idea instructional program.

LESSON 1

Lesson Objective: Students construct main ideas in paragraphs by naming the subject (single) and categorizing the action.

Preskills: To be able to categorize words in a list presented orally.

Materials: Prompt card and worksheets.

TEACHER: Listen to the following list of words and give me a name for the category: *Frankenstein, Dracula, Werewolf.* (*Possible student response: "Monsters."*) Yes, these are all terrifying monsters in the history of cinema. So we can say that *monsters* is the group name for this word list, because Frankenstein, Dracula, and Werewolf are all *monsters*. Here is another list of words that are verbs: *bite, chew, swallow.* A verb describes an action, so what would be the word that categorizes the action in this word list? (*Possible student response: "Eat."*) Can you think of another word that fits the category *eat*? (*Possible student response: "Gnaw".*) Yes, *gnaw* is another word that goes with the category *eat*. How about *sip*? Would *sip* refer to the action of eating? (*Possible student response: "Sip does not belong to the eat category; it is a word that would relate to the action, drink."*)

Now that you know how to categorize word lists to name the group or action, you are ready to identify the main idea of a paragraph by naming the subject and categorizing the action. Identifying main ideas can help you understand things you read, whether you are reading for school or reading about something that interests you. A main idea tells what the paragraph is mainly about. Now let's use the four steps on this card to help us identify the main idea.

The first step says to read the paragraph. (*Teacher reads aloud paragraph.*) "The little bird gathered some sticks from the ground. She took them to the apple tree. She wove the sticks together. Then she added bits of string to make her nest soft." I read the paragraph, so I will put a check by "read the paragraph." (*Teacher checks.*)

The second step tells me to use the prompt card to help me find the main idea of this paragraph. The prompt reminds me to name the subject (i.e., who the paragraph is mainly about) and categorize the action (i.e., the main thing the subject did in all the sentences). I used the prompt card to remind me of the rule or strategy, so I will put a check by "used the prompt card." (*Teacher checks.*)

The third step tells me to use the strategy to find the main idea. The rule tells me to name the subject and categorize the action. In this paragraph, the subject is the little bird. Because all the sentences tell that the little bird built a nest, the action category is *built*. Now I will put a check by "used the strategy." (*Teacher checks.*)

Next, I will write the main idea (i.e., "The little bird built a nest.") and put a check by the fourth step, "wrote the main idea." (*Teacher checks.*)

THE TEACHER PRESENTS TWO OR MORE EXAMPLES AND FACILITATES DISCUSSION OF THE MAIN IDEAS AND CHECKS STUDENTS' UNDERSTANDING AND MASTERY OF THE MAIN IDEAS IN PARAGRAPHS. THE STUDENTS THEN COMPLETE ADDITIONAL EXAMPLES ON THEIR OWN AS PART OF AN INDEPENDENT PRACTICE EXERCISE. THE TEACHER ENCOURAGES STUDENTS TO USE THE PROMPT CARD TO REMEMBER THE RULE FOR CONSTRUCTING A MAIN IDEA AND REMINDS THEM THAT A MAIN IDEA MUST TELL WHAT THE ENTIRE PARAGRAPH IS ABOUT.

LESSON 4

Lesson Objective: Students generate or select main ideas in paragraphs that include extraneous information by telling the main thing the person or group did in most of the sentences.

Materials: Prompt card and worksheets.

(*continued*)

FIGURE 9.1. (*continued*)

TEACHER: In the previous lesson, you learned to select the sentence that best describes the main idea of a paragraph. You read each sentence following the paragraph and asked yourself whether it is a good main idea sentence for the paragraph. You also learned in previous lessons to find the main idea in paragraphs by naming the person or group and the action. Today, we will look at paragraphs that include sentences not related to the main idea. We will identify these sentences as ones that do not tell what the person or group did, and we will figure out the main idea of the paragraph. The main idea rule for these types of paragraphs is to tell what the person or group did in most of the sentences rather than in all the sentences.

Let's look at the following paragraph: "Linda got out flour and sugar. She took eggs from the refrigerator. The eggs were from her grandmother's chickens. Then, she got out the mixer and the cookie sheets." First, let's figure out the main idea of the paragraph using the four steps on this card to help us identify the main idea. The first step says to read the paragraph. (*Teacher reads the paragraph aloud.*) I read the paragraph, so I will put a check by "read the paragraph." (*Teacher checks.*)

The second step tells me to use the prompt card to help me find the main idea of this paragraph. The prompt reminds me to name the subject (i.e., who the paragraph is mainly about) and categorize the action (i.e., the main thing the person or group did). I used the prompt card to remind me of the rule or strategy, so I will put a check by "used the prompt card." (*Teacher checks.*)

The third step tells me to use the strategy to generate the main idea. The rule tells me to describe the main thing the person or group did. This paragraph is about Linda, but notice that one sentence in the paragraph does not tell what Linda did. Now, who can tell me which sentence in this paragraph is not related to the main idea? How do you know? (*Possible student response:* "The sentence 'The eggs were from her grandmother's chickens' does not tell anything about what Linda did.") So, let's look at the sentences again and see if we can figure out what the main idea of this paragraph is. (*Teacher rereads the sentences in the paragraph.*) Now, what would be a main idea statement that tells us the main thing Linda did. (*Possible student response:* "Linda got ready to bake cookies.") Yes, "Linda got ready to bake cookies" tells us the main thing that Linda did in *most* of the sentences in the paragraph. Excellent! Now I will put a check by "used the strategy." (*Teacher checks.*)

Next, I will write the main idea (i.e., "Linda got ready to bake cookies") and put a check by the fourth step, "wrote the main idea." (*Teacher checks.*)

THE TEACHER PRESENTS TWO OR MORE EXAMPLES AND FACILITATES DISCUSSION OF THE MAIN IDEAS, AND CHECKS STUDENT UNDERSTANDING AND MASTERY OF THE MAIN IDEAS IN PARAGRAPHS WITH DISTRACTOR SENTENCES. NEXT, THE TEACHER PRESENTS MULTIPLE-CHOICE ITEMS (SEE BELOW) WITH THE POSSIBLE MAIN IDEA STATEMENTS (INCLUDING THE DISTRACTOR SENTENCE) (WRITTEN BELOW THE PARAGRAPH) FROM WHICH THE STUDENTS MUST SELECT.

It was a cold day in November. Tom took the football from the center. He ran down the field. He pushed a tackle out of the way and kept running. Finally, he crossed the goal line.

The main idea of the paragraph is:

A. It was a cold day in November.
B. Tom likes to play football.
C. When you can play football.
D. Tom ran for a touchdown.

TEACHER: Let's figure out the main idea of paragraphs by selecting the sentence that best describes the main idea of the paragraph. Remember, some paragraphs contain sentences that do not tell about or are not related to the main idea. Again, we will use the four steps on our card to find the main idea.

(*continued*)

FIGURE 9.1. (*continued*)

The first step says to read the paragraph. (Teacher reads aloud paragraph and the possible answers written under the paragraph.) I read the paragraph, so I will put a check by "read the paragraph." (Teacher checks.)

The second step tells me to use the prompt card to help me find the main idea of this paragraph. The prompt reminds me to name the subject (i.e., who the paragraph is mainly about) and categorize the action (i.e., the main thing the person or group did). I used the prompt card to remind me of the rule or strategy, so I will put a check by "used the prompt card." (*Teacher checks.*)

The third step tells me to use the strategy to find the main idea. The rule tells me to describe the main thing the person or group did. So, let's look at the possible answers and see which letter goes with the sentence you think best describes the main idea of this paragraph. (*Teacher rereads the answers.*) This paragraph is about Tom, but notice that answer choice A, "It was a cold day in November," does not tell what Tom did. So, we can cross out this sentence, because it is not related to the main idea of the paragraph. Now, who can tell us what the main idea is? (*Student response: "Answer choice 'D,' 'Tom ran for a touchdown,' is the main idea."*) Yes, "Tom ran for a touchdown" tells us the main thing that Tom did in *most* of the sentences in the paragraph. Why aren't answer choices "B" and "C" correct? (*Possible student responses: "Answer 'B' tells us that Tom likes to play football, but the paragraph only describes how he played football to get a touchdown. It does not tell anything about whether he likes to play football. Answer 'C' is also not correct, because there is nothing in the paragraph to tells us when you can play football. It only tells us that it was a cold day in November when Tom was playing."*) Now I will put a check by "used the strategy." (*Teacher checks.*)

Next, I will circle the answer choice for the main idea statement (i.e., "Tom ran for a touchdown") and put a check by the fourth step. (*Teacher checks.*)

THE TEACHER PRESENTS TWO OR MORE EXAMPLES AND FACILITATES DISCUSSION OF THE MAIN IDEA STATEMENT CHOICES TO IDENTIFY DISTRACTOR SENTENCES AND SELECT THE STATEMENT THAT BEST DESCRIBES THE MAIN IDEAS OF PARAGRAPHS. Students then complete additional examples on their own as part of independent practice exercise.

are planned and sequenced in increasing order of difficulty to ensure student success. After students master the application of each rule in isolation, they are given a prompt sheet that lists all the rules and components of the strategy (see Figure 9.2). We made this decision so that students do not become overwhelmed with the multiple components of the strategy and lose interest in the task. Figure 9.3 shows a model lesson (Lesson 6) from the instructional program to illustrate the summarization strategy. In this lesson, teachers specifically teach students to apply together the five rules previously learned in isolation, as a single strategy to form a summary of a reading passage (Figure 9.4). It is important to note that teachers are encouraged to modify the lessons in the summarization instructional program based on their students' learning needs and level of skills development.

Summary and Conclusion

On the basis of the success of students with learning difficulties in acquiring higher-order comprehension skills, generalizing to more complex text, and retaining main ideas in our evaluation studies, we draw some conclusions about how to improve comprehension of text.

FIGURE 9.2. Prompt sheet for summarization training

General Steps to Form a Summary

- *Understand the passage.* First, read the title to help you know what the passage is about. Then, read the passage slowly and ask yourself, "What is the general idea of this passage? What is the writer telling in this passage?" Try to say the general idea in your own words.
- *Check the passage.* Reread the passage to make sure you got the general theme. Then, apply the five summarization rules.

Rules for Writing a Summary

1. *Reduce lists.* If you come across a list of things in a passage, try to think of a word or a phrase that best describes the list of things. For example, if a list of items includes apples, peaches, grapes, plums, and strawberries, you could categorize the items in this list as *fruits*. Underline the list of items and write the category name for the list of items in the passage.
2. *Cross out repeated information.* Sometimes, information in a passage may be repeated; that is, the same thing may be said again in a different way in the same passage. So keep one sentence and get rid of the repeated statements by crossing them out with a red pen.
3. *Select a topic sentence.* Often authors write a sentence that gives the main idea of the passage. This is called a *topic sentence*. It is often the first sentence or last sentence in the paragraph. Read once again each paragraph of the passage. Try to say the main idea of each paragraph to yourself. Next, search for the topic sentence in the paragraph. If the author gives the topic sentence, underline it, and say it in your own words.
4. *Write your own topic sentence.* Sometimes the author does not write a topic sentence for a paragraph. Make up your own topic sentence for each paragraph that does not have one. Write your topic sentence in the margin. Use your topic sentences in your summary.
5. *Cross out unimportant details.* Sometimes passages contain unimportant or unnecessary details that do not deal directly with the general theme of a passage. Get rid of this information. Cross out unimportant sentences with a blue pen.

Check Your Work

- Have you underlined all lists in the passage and written a category name for each list?
- Do you have a topic sentence for each paragraph?
- Did you cross out information that is repeated?
- Did you cross out information that is not important?
- Have you applied the five rules to each paragraph in the passage?

Now use your marked passage to write a summary. Use connecting words (e.g., *and, so, or*) to join sentences. You can also join the paragraphs together. Try to say the information in your own words.

1. Provide explicit instruction in thoroughly learning the strategy (e.g., rule-based technique). Have students apply the strategy on a variety of materials and receive extensive practice and feedback. Instruction must also focus on when to use the strategy. It is only when students have acquired declarative knowledge of the strategy (what it is), procedural knowledge (how to apply it), and conditional knowledge (when to use it and why) that they are ready to consolidate their knowledge of strategy use and become more strategic learners who assume responsibility for their own learning. A salient feature of instruction is teacher modeling of the strategy; using think-alouds, teachers can share how they apply the strategy to comprehend the material, thereby making their thought processes transparent.

FIGURE 9.3. Model lesson from the summarization instructional program.

LESSON 6

Lesson Objective: Students write a summary of a passage.

Preskills: To be able to execute each summarization rule separately.

Materials: Reading passage (see Figure 9.4), prompt sheet (see Figure 9.2), blue and red pens.

TEACHER: Last week you learned and practiced applying each of the five rules to make a summary. Today, you will learn how to use those five different rules as one single strategy to form a summary of the reading passage. (*Teacher passes out prompt sheet.*) Let's use this prompt sheet that describes the general steps and the specific rules we learned to help us write a good summary. (*Teacher models by thinking aloud how to use the strategy to write a summary.*)

The first general step on the prompt sheet is "understand the passage." To understand the passage, I will read the title to figure out what this passage is about. (*Teacher reads aloud the title.*) The title of the passage is "Air Pollution." Based on the title, I think the author will talk about what air pollution is. Now, I will read the passage and ask myself, "What is the general idea of this passage?" (*Teacher reads aloud the passage.*) Can you tell me what this passage is about? (*Possible student responses: "Air pollution is harmful," "Polluted air is not good for the environment."*) Yes, I think the writer wants us to know that air pollution is harmful. (*Teacher writes the general idea or theme on the board.*) Is there anything more I can add to this statement that tells us more about air pollution? (*Possible student responses: "Pollution is caused by cars and pollen."*)

Good, now that we have the general idea that air pollution is harmful, we are ready for the second general step. This step tells me to reread the passage to make sure the general idea is correct. (*Teacher rereads the passage.*) Yes, I think the general idea that air pollution is harmful is correct.

Now that we are done with the general steps, we are ready to use the specific summary rules to write a summary. You can mark your passage as we go through it and use the summary rules. Let's begin with Rule 1: "Reduce lists." To reduce lists, I first need to read each paragraph to find lists of things. (*Teacher reads aloud the first paragraph.*) This paragraph has a list of things. What are the items in this list and the group name or category for this list? (*Student responses: "Cars, motorcycles, buses, and trucks are all vehicles."*) Excellent! Let's underline this list of items and write *vehicles* above the list. For each of the remaining paragraphs, let's use Rule 1 to reduce lists. (*Teacher guides students to find and underline the lists in their passage, and write the category name above each list.*)

Now that we have reduced the lists in the passage, let's use Rule 2: "Cross out repeated information." Let's read the passage to see if anything is repeated. In the third paragraph, the author says that trees are really hurt by air pollution. They also stop giving fruit. Well, I already read that trees do not grow well if the air is polluted. I think these sentences say the same thing but in different words. So I will keep one of these sentences and use my red pen to cross out the repeated sentences. Can anyone find something else that was repeated? (*Possible student response:* "Breathing problems and hard to breathe describe the same thing.") Good! let's cross out the repeated information and move to Rule 3: "Select a topic sentence."

The prompt sheet tells us that the topic sentence is the main idea and is generally the first or last sentence in a paragraph. Let's read each paragraph to see whether the author gives a topic sentence, and whether the main idea is in the first or last sentence. We know that the main idea is that air pollution is harmful. So the first sentence, "Air may contain matter that is harmful to people and other living things," is the topic sentence that I will underline. (*Teacher underlines the topic sentence.*) Now I will read the second paragraph and you tell me if the author gives the topic sentence. (*Possible student response: "The first and last sentences do not talk about the main idea of the paragraph, so there is no topic sentence."*) Good. Is there a topic sentence in the next

(continued)

FIGURE 9.3. (*continued*)

paragraph? (*Possible student response: "Trees do not grow well if the air is polluted is the topic sentence."*) *So, let's underline this sentence as the topic sentence and apply the rule to the next paragraph. Is there a topic sentence for this paragraph? (Student response: "No.") Because all paragraphs may not have topic sentences, we need to make up our own topic sentences.*

Rule 4, "Write your own topic sentence," can help us when a topic sentence is not given or not clearly written in the paragraph. We know that the second paragraph in this passage did not have a topic sentence. So we can create our own topic sentence for this paragraph. What is the main idea of this paragraph? (*Possible student response: "Pollen in the air also causes air pollution."*) That's right! This idea appears more than once in the paragraph, so it is the main idea. Now, let's put the main idea and any important details related to the main idea in our own words. We know that air pollution is also caused by wind blowing pollen and is called "natural pollution." So, this is the topic sentence I will write in the margin. (*Students copy the topic sentence in the margin. Teacher encourages students to come up with a topic sentence for the last paragraph.*) Yes, our topic sentence for the last paragraph is "Polluted air can cause many health issues."

Finally, we are ready for Rule 5: "Cross out unimportant details." To do this, we use the topic sentence of each paragraph and find sentences that do not tell anything important about the topic sentence. The first paragraph states that cars are important to many families, but this statement does not tell about air pollution. So I will cross this statement out. Is there anything else that is not important in this passage? Explain. (*Student response: "The sentence 'We need to eat fruit daily for good health' is not related to the topic sentence."*) Excellent! (*Teacher directs students to cross out unimportant information in the passage.*)

Now that we have used all five rules, let's check our work. (*Teacher points to the prompt sheet.*) Did we leave out any lists? Does each paragraph have a topic sentence? Did we cross out all the repeated sentences and unimportant details? OK, we are ready to make the summary by using the marked passage. Remember that a summary tells the main ideas in the passage, so we must use all the topic sentences. It also should include important details that support the main ideas. This means that we can use the information we did not cross out in the passage. Also, let's try to summarize in our own words, so that we can remember the passage. (*Teacher guides students to write the following summary.*)

Air may contain matter that is harmful to people and the environment. This is called *air pollution*. Air pollution is caused by a large number of vehicles that give off poisonous gases called *carbon monoxide*. Air pollution is also caused by wind blowing pollen, and this is called *natural pollution*. This causes trees not to grow well, and they stop bearing fruit. Polluted air can also cause many health issues, such as breathing problems and eye diseases.

This summary tells everything that is important in the passage and is much shorter than the original passage. Making a summary is a great way to understand what you have read.

IN THE NEXT SESSION, STUDENTS USE THE PROMPT SHEET AS A GUIDE TO WRITE THEIR OWN SUMMARY OF A DIFFERENT PASSAGE. THE TEACHER PROVIDES FEEDBACK AND ADDITIONAL INSTRUCTION AS NECESSARY. STUDENTS COMPLETE SEVERAL EXERCISES INDEPENDENTLY. THE TEACHER CHECKS STUDENTS' UNDERSTANDING AND MASTERY OF THE STRATEGY.

2. Emphasize the important elements and structural ideas in a text to help students with learning difficulties construct an accurate representation of the author's intent in the text. Given the attention and memory deficits that students with learning difficulties experience, having them focus on key elements and details connected to them is an effective way to remember information initially and retain it over time. Instruction during teacher-directed application should include informal checks for student sensitivity to important information. Com-

FIGURE 9.4. Sample reading passage.

Air Pollution

Air may contain matter that is harmful to people and other living things. Such air is said to be *polluted*. The large number of cars, motorcycles, buses, and trucks cause much air pollution. Many cities have a large number of cars and buses. Cars are important to many families. Cars, buses, and trucks produce waste gases from the fuel they burn. One of these gases called *carbon monoxide* is poisonous. Even a small amount of carbon monoxide can cause headaches and dizziness.

Windstorms blow large amounts of dust in the air. The wind also spreads pollen from daisies, dandelions, lilies, and tulips. Pollen adds to air pollution. Also, pollen in the air can make some people sneeze. Air pollution can also be caused by natural pollution. Natural pollution is not caused by people. It is different from pollution caused by automobiles.

Trees do not grow well if the air is polluted. The leaves turn yellow and fall off. Sometimes you may see brown spots on leaves. Trees are really hurt by air pollution. Orange, apple, peach, and plum trees are especially affected. These trees stop giving good fruit. We need to eat fruit daily for good health.

Polluted air can make your eyes red and watery. It can also make your eyes burn. It can give you a headache and make you feel dizzy. Air pollution can cause lung cancer, headaches, breathing problems, and eye diseases. It can also make it hard for you to breathe.

paring students' responses to those of their more capable peers can provide information on whether they need higher-order comprehension instruction in addition to or instead of instruction in decoding skills.

3. Use informal or formal assessment techniques to determine whether students need instruction in understanding larger units of text only, or would benefit from instruction in the basic concept of main idea using word lists and sentences prior to moving to paragraphs and longer passages. In addition, a teacher may decide to initiate instruction in identifying explicit main ideas in texts before inferring main ideas that are not stated directly in texts. Teachers may want to consider Baumann's (1986) hierarchy of main idea tasks and relations, and his tentative guideline that suggests the grade level at which main idea instruction in a particular task would be relevant.

4. Carefully consider the selection of text. When students are first learning the main idea or summarization strategy, the text should allow for application of the specific strategy. Also, the reading level of the text should not place heavy demands on students' decoding skills or vocabulary knowledge. Eventually, children should be provided systematic practice in applying the learned strategy on a range of content-area texts they will encounter in school, particularly social studies and science, to ensure transfer of the strategy.

In conclusion, the methods and materials we employ in our evaluation studies can be used to improve higher-order comprehension skills for students with learning difficulties. At the same time, the interventions described should be effective for all students and be used to differentiate instruction in general education classes on the basis of student difficulties in reading comprehension generally, and main idea construction and summarization specifically.

References

Afflerbach, P. P. (1990). The influence of prior knowledge on expert readers' main idea construction strategies. *Reading Research Quarterly, 25,* 3–46.

Armbruster, B. B., Anderson, T. H., & Ostertag, J. (1987). Does text structure/summarization instruction facilitate learning from an expository text? *Reading Research Quarterly, 22,* 331–336.

Bakken, J. P., Mastropieri, M. A., & Scruggs, T. E. (1997). Reading comprehension of expository science material and students with learning disabilities: A comparison of strategies. *Journal of Special Education, 31,* 300–324.

Baumann, J. F. (1984). The effectiveness of a direct instruction paradigm for teaching main idea comprehension. *Reading Research Quarterly, 20,* 93–115.

Baumann, J. F. (1986). *Teaching main idea comprehension.* Newark, DE: International Reading Association.

Bean, T. W., & Steenwyk, F. L. (1984). The effect of three forms of summarization instruction on sixth graders' summary writing and comprehension. *Journal of Reading Behavior, 15,* 297–307.

Bereiter, C., Burtis, P. J., & Scardamalia, M. (1988). Cognitive operations in constructing main points in written composition. *Journal of Memory and Language, 27,* 261–278.

Berkowitz, S. J. (1986). Effects of instruction in text organization on sixth-grade students' memory for expository reading. *Reading Research Quarterly, 21,* 161–178.

Bloom, S. S. (1976). *Human characteristics and school learning.* New York: McGraw-Hill.

Brown, A. L. (1981). Metacognitive development in reading. In R. Spiro, B. Bruce, & W. Brewer (Eds.), *Theoretical issues in reading comprehension* (pp. 453–482). Hillsdale, NJ: Erlbaum.

Brown, A. L., & Day, J. D. (1983). Macrorules for summarizing texts: The development of expertise. *Journal of Verbal Learning and Verbal Behavior, 22,* 1–14.

Brown, A. L., Day, J. D., & Jones, R. S. (1983). The development of plans for summarizing texts. *Child Development, 54,* 968–979.

Brown, A. L., & Palincsar, A. S. (1982). Inducing strategic learning from texts by means of informed, self-control training. *Topics in Learning and Learning Disabilities, 2,* 1–17.

Brown, A. L., & Smiley, S. S. (1977). The development of plans for summarizing texts. *Child Development, 54,* 968–979.

Brown, A. L., Smiley, S. S. (1978). Rating the importance of structural units of prose passages: A problem of metacognitive development. *Child Development, 48*(1), 1–8.

Cain, K., & Oakhill, J. (2007). Reading comprehension difficulties: Correlates, causes, and consequences. In K. Cain & J. Oakhill (Eds.), *Children's comprehension problems in oral and written language: A cognitive perspective* (pp. 41–75). New York: Guilford Press.

Carnine, D. W., Silbert, J., & Kame'enui, E. J. (1997). *Direct instruction reading* (3rd ed.). Upper Saddle River, NJ: Merrill.

Chan, L. K. S. (1991). Promoting strategy generalization through self-instructional training in students with reading disabilities. *Journal of Learning Disabilities, 24,* 427–433.

Cunningham, J. W., & Moore, D. W. (1986). The confused world of main idea. In J. F. Baumann (Ed.), *Teaching main idea comprehension* (pp. 1–17). Newark, DE: International Reading Association.

Eamon, D. B. (1978). Selection and recall of topical information in prose by better and poorer readers. *Reading Research Quarterly, 2,* 244–252.

Ellis, E. S., & Graves, A. W. (1990). Teaching students with learning disabilities: A paraphrasing strategy to increase comprehension of main ideas. *Rural Special Education Quarterly, 10*(2), 2–10.

Englert, C. S., & Lichter, A. (1982). Using statement-pie to teach reading and writing skills. *Teaching Exceptional Children, 14*(5), 164–170.

Gajria, M., & Salvia, J. (1992). The effects of summarization instruction on text comprehension of students with learning disabilities. *Exceptional Children, 58,* 508–516.

Gersten, R., Fuchs, L. S., Williams, J. P., & Baker, S. (2001). Teaching reading comprehension strategies to students with learning disabilities: A review of research. *Review of Educational Research, 71,* 279–320.

Graves, A. W. (1986). Effects of direct instruction and metacomprehension training on finding main ideas. *Learning Disabilities Research, 1*(2), 92–100.

Graves, A. W., & Levin, J. R. (1989). Comparison of monitoring and mnemonic text-processing strategies in learning disabled students. *Learning Disability Quarterly, 12,* 232–236.

Hansen, C. L. (1978). Story retelling used with average and LD readers as a measure of reading comprehension. *Learning Disability Quarterly, 1,* 62–69.

Hare, V. C., & Borchardt, K. M. (1984). Direct instruction of summarization skills. *Reading Research Quarterly, 20,* 62–78.

Jenkins, J. R., Heliotis, J. D., Stein, M. L., & Haynes, M. C. (1987). Improving reading comprehension by using paragraph restatements. *Exceptional Children, 54,* 54–59.

Jitendra, A. K., Cole, C., Hoppes, M. K., & Wilson, B. (1998). Effects of a direct instruction main idea summarization program and self-monitoring on reading comprehension of middle school students with learning disabilities. *Reading and Writing Quarterly, 14,* 379–396.

Jitendra, A. K., Hoppes, M. K., & Xin, Y. P. (2000). Enhancing main idea comprehension for students with learning problems: The role of a summarization strategy and self-monitoring instruction. *Journal of Special Education, 34,* 127–139.

Kintsch, W. (1986). Learning from text. *Cognition and Instruction, 3*(2), 87–108.

Kintsch, W., & Kozminsky, E. (1977). Summarizing stories after reading and listening. *Journal of Education Psychology, 69,* 497–499.

Kintsch, W., & van Dijk, T. A. (1978). Toward a model of text comprehension and production. *Psychological Review, 85,* 363–394.

Klingner, J. K., Vaughn, S., & Schumm, J. S. (1998). Collaborative strategic reading during social studies in heterogeneous fourth-grade classrooms. *Elementary School Journal, 99,* 3–22.

Malone, L. D., & Mastropieri, M. A. (1992). Reading comprehension instruction: summarization and self-monitoring training for students with learning disabilities. *Exceptional Children, 58,* 270–279.

McGee, L. M. (1982). Awareness of text structure: Effects on children's recall of expository text. *Reading Research Quarterly, 17,* 581–590.

Meyer, B. J. F., Brandt, D. M., & Bluth, G. J. (1980). Use of author's textual schema: Key for ninth graders' comprehension. *Reading Research Quarterly, 16,* 72–103.

Moore, D. W., Cunningham, J. W., & Rudisill, N. J. (1983). Readers' conceptions of the main idea. In J. A. Niles & L. A. Harris (Eds.), *Searches for meaning in reading/language processing and instruction: 32nd yearbook of the National Reading Conference* (pp. 202–206). Rochester, NY: National Reading Conference.

Nelson, J. R., Smith, D. J., & Dodd, J. M. (1992). The effects of teaching a summary skills strategy to students identified as learning disabled on their comprehension of science text. *Education and Treatment of Children, 15,* 228–243.

Ogle, D. M. (1989). The know, want to know, learn strategy. In K. D. Muth (Ed.), *Children's comprehension of text* (pp. 205–223). Newark, DE: International Reading Association.

Palincsar, A., David, Y., Winn, J., & Stevens, D. (1991). Enhancing the content of strategy instruction. *Remedial and Special Education, 12,* 43–53.

Pearson, P. D., & Johnson, D. D. (1978). *Teaching reading comprehension.* New York: Holt, Rinehart & Winston.

Pressley, M., Johnson, C. J., Symons, S., McGoldrick, J. A., & Kurita, J. A. (1989). Strategies that improve children's memory and comprehension of text. *Elementary School Journal, 90*, 3–32.

Rich, R., & Shepherd, M. J. (1993). Teaching text comprehension strategies to adult poor readers. *Reading and Writing: An Interdisciplinary Journal, 5*, 387–402.

Rinehart, S. D., Stahl, S. A., & Erickson, L. G. (1986). Some effects of summarization training on reading and studying. *Reading Research Quarterly, 21*, 422–438.

Rogevich, M. E., & Perin, D. (2008). Effects on science summarization of a reading comprehension intervention for adolescents with behavior and attention disorders. *Exceptional Children, 74*(2), 135–154.

Smiley, S. S., Oakley, D. D., Worthen, D., Campione, J. C., & Brown, A. L. (1977). Recall of thematically relevant material by adolescent good and poor readers as a function of written vs. oral presentation. *Journal of Educational Psychology, 69*, 381–387.

Stevens, R. J. (1988). Effects of strategy training on the identification of the main idea of expository passages. *Journal of Educational Psychology, 80*, 21–26.

Stevens, R. J., Slavin, R. E., & Farnish, A. M. (1991). The effects of cooperative learning and direct instruction in reading comprehension strategies on main idea identification. *Journal of Educational Psychology, 83*, 8–16.

Taylor, B. M., & Beach, R. W. (1984). The effects of text structure instruction on middle grade students' comprehension and production of expository text. *Reading Research Quarterly, 19*, 135–146.

van den Broek, P., Lynch, J. S., Naslund, J., Ievers-Landis, C. E., & Verduin, K. (2003). The development of comprehension of main ideas in narratives: Evidence from the selection of titles. *Journal of Educational Psychology, 95*, 707–718.

van Dijk, T. A., & Kintsch, W. (1983). *Strategies of discourse comprehension.* New York: Academic Press.

Williams, J. P. (1986). Teaching children to identify the main idea of expository texts. *Exceptional Children, 53*, 163–168.

Williams, J. P. (1988). Identifying main ideas: A basic aspect of reading comprehension. *Topics in Language Disorders, 8*(3), 1–13.

Williams, J. P. (2004). Teaching text structure to improve reading comprehension. In H. L. Swanson, K. R. Harris, & S. Graham (Eds.), *Handbook of learning disabilities* (pp. 293–305). New York: Guilford Press.

Williams, J. P., Taylor, M. B., Jarin, D. C., & Milligan, E.S. (1983). *Determining the main idea of expository paragraphs: An instructional program for the learning disabled and its evaluation* (Technical Report No. 25). New York: Columbia University, Teachers College, Research Institute for the Study of Learning Disabilities.

Winograd, P. N. (1984). Strategic difficulties in summarizing texts. *Reading Research Quarterly, 19*, 404–425.

Wong, B. Y. L. (1979). Increasing retention of main ideas through questioning strategies. *Learning Disability Quarterly, 2*, 42–47.

Wong, B. Y. L., & Jones, W. (1982). Increasing metacomprehension in learning disabled and normally achieving students through self-questioning training. *Learning Disability Quarterly, 5*, 228–240.

Worden, P. E., & Nakamura, G. V. (1983). Story comprehension and recall in learning disabled vs. normal college students. *Journal of Educational Psychology, 74*, 633–641.

10

Metacognition to Improve
Reading Comprehension

JANETTE K. KLINGNER
ANN MORRISON
AMY EPPOLITO

In this chapter, we discuss the very important role of metacognition in reading comprehension. We also convey different ways to help students summarize
text they read. We review relevant research, describe how to implement selected
approaches, and provide examples of teachers implementing certain practices.
The interventions we include are appropriate for differentiated instruction in
general education classrooms, specialized instruction in Title I classes, Tier 2
response-to-intervention (RTI) models, and/or special education classes. All of
the interventions are supported by research. Throughout the chapter, we provide
teaching tips based on our own experiences.

What Is Metacognition?

"Metacognition" involves planning for a cognitive task, self-instructions to control and complete the task, and self-monitoring or evaluation of whether the task
was completed appropriately (Bender, 2004). Metacognition is sometimes referred
to as "thinking about thinking," though that way of describing it may be over-
simplified. Definitions of metacognition emphasize the role of executive function
processes in overseeing and regulating cognitive processes. Gaskins and Pressley

(2007) explained, "Metacognition involves knowing about thinking and knowing about how to employ executive function processes to regulate thinking" (p. 262). They emphasized that metacognition also involves awareness of personal attributes (e.g., reflexivity and persistence), as well as beliefs (e.g., "I'm a poor reader, so I must be dumb").

Strategies are one aspect of metacognition. Metacognitive strategies can include planning, organizing, prioritizing, shifting mindsets, monitoring understanding, and self-checking. Metacognitive strategies for reading are often categorized into three types: planning strategies, monitoring strategies, and evaluation strategies. Pressley and Afflerbach (1995) studied the reading behaviors of good readers and ascertained that proficient readers use specific metacognitive strategies before, during, and after reading to assist their comprehension of text. Similarly, Jiménez, García, and Pearson (1996) compared the metacognitive strategies of (1) middle school bilingual Latina/o children who were considered successful English readers, (2) successful English readers, and (3) less successful bilingual Latina/o readers. They found that the successful Latina/o readers were more active readers and much more likely to use metacognitive strategies than the less proficient readers. Also, in comparison with proficient English-only readers, they were more likely to focus on the meanings of unknown words and to use their knowledge of "cognates" (i.e., words with similar spellings and meanings in two languages) to figure out word meanings.

Students who struggle with comprehension tend not to engage actively with text and often do not know how to use strategies effectively (Gersten, Fuchs, Williams, & Baker, 2001). Many students with learning disabilities (LD) have weak executive functioning and difficulty planning, organizing information and ideas, initiating and maintaining focus on activities, selecting relevant task goals, choosing and changing strategies, self-monitoring, and regulating behavior (Meltzer, 2007; Swanson, 1999). Yet students who learn to use even one metacognitive strategy can improve their comprehension of text. This idea—that teaching struggling readers how to use metacognitive strategies that good readers use to improve their comprehension—comes from cognitive psychology (e.g., Flavell, 1992). A significant amount of research supports instructional approaches that assist students in developing metacognitive strategies. Students who struggle with reading and students with LD can benefit from learning to utilize metacognitive strategies, and strategy instruction can begin in the very early grades.

Distinguishing between metacognitive and cognitive strategies can be confusing. Cognitive strategies help us achieve specific goals, and metacognitive strategies help us monitor whether we have met those goals. In other words, we use our metacognitive strategies to "oversee" our use of cognitive strategies. Think of the metacognitive strategies as the umbrella strategies that precede and follow the use of a cognitive strategy. For example, we use our metacognition to monitor whether we comprehend what we are reading. If we get to a word we do not understand, we then try a cognitive strategy to help us figure out what the word means, such as using our knowledge of prefixes and suffixes. Then we step back, figuratively speaking, to see whether the text now makes sense. Metacognitive and cognitive strategies do overlap somewhat, though, and trying to figure out whether our efforts are metacognitive or cognitive can be confusing.

How to Teach Metacognitive Strategies

Teachers should provide explicit instruction, model how to use strategies, and give students sufficient practice in utilizing the strategies (Baker, 2002). In a meta-analysis of instructional approaches for students with LD, Swanson and colleagues (Swanson, 2001; Swanson, Hoskyn, & Lee, 1999) found that direct instruction, strategy instruction, or a combination of both, were associated with the highest effect sizes in reading comprehension. When teachers provide explicit instruction, they should explain what the strategy is, why it is important, and how to use it. They should make sure to link the strategy with its applications to reading text in various contexts (Duffy, 2002). Not only explicit strategy instruction but also teachers' abilities to communicate the thinking processes behind the strategies improve comprehension (Block & Pressley, 2002). Teachers need to be able to make their thinking visible (or audible) as they demonstrate how to use strategies and build a framework for using a common language in the classroom. Having a common language for applying strategies allows students not only to discuss their strategies actively but also to learn from their peers (Pintrich, 2002). They can see how other students apply the strategies.

Regardless of which strategy students are learning, certain generic teaching steps can be applied. We adapted the following procedures from Swanson and De La Paz (1998):

1. Begin with reading material that is easy for the students to read. In the beginning, the point is to teach students how to use the strategy, so the text is a tool to that end.

2. Explain the target strategy step-by-step.

3. Activate background knowledge.

4. Provide information about students' current performance levels and emphasize the potential benefits of using the strategy.

5. Model the strategy for the students, repeating the steps you explained to them in step 2 and using a think-aloud procedure.

6. Provide several opportunities to practice the strategy as a whole class, in small groups, or in pairs. Help by prompting students to complete steps they might have missed or by assisting them to complete steps. Reexplain steps of the strategy as needed.

7. Provide opportunities for students to practice the strategy independently,

with feedback and support as needed. Gradually fade assistance, until students can apply the strategy on their own.

8. Help students generalize use of the strategy. Increase the difficulty level of the reading material students are using, and provide different types of reading materials. Remind students when it might be appropriate to use a strategy.

9. Provide students with a list or chart of the steps of the strategy, in case they need a reminder. Charts can be posted on the wall.

10. When students have used a strategy, they should self-evaluate how well it worked for them (Mason, 2004).

Many single-component cognitive strategies can be implemented in most classrooms in a short amount of time. These extensively researched strategies have been found to have effects on students' comprehension of text: main idea identification, summarization, imagery, story grammar, question generation, and question answering strategies (Gajria, Jitendra, Sood, & Sacks, 2007; Pressley, 2000). There are also effective multicomponent interventions (Gajria et al., 2007). These strategies include any combination of the single-component strategies and can be used with expository or narrative text, or both. Next we discuss single-strategy interventions and provide examples.

Before Reading: Activating Prior Knowledge and Making Connections

Each of the following strategies—setting a purpose, linking text to previous knowledge, previewing text, and predicting—may contribute to students' ability to approach text more deliberately, ready to monitor their reading and evaluate their learning. These strategies may be used individually or in combination based on students' needs and the nature of the text they are preparing to read.

Setting a Purpose

Good readers are knowledgeable about purposes for reading and able to develop a purpose even if one is not explicitly stated in the text (Pressley, 2000). Purpose setting allows students to develop a plan to guide their reading and to activate their background knowledge, and it helps them to sort out pertinent information (Blanton, Wood, & Moorman, 1990).

Conversely, not having a purpose, or having a poorly defined purpose, can lead to misunderstanding and poor comprehension (Pressley, 2000). If students are reading a passage on California farm workers, then a poorly defined purpose may lead them to look for information not provided in the text, such as the varieties of crops grown in California. Purposes for reading may also be too narrow or too broad. Students may read the passage on California farm workers for specific legislation enacted in response to violations against farm workers, or an entire history of farm worker culture.

Because purpose setting is both an important and challenging task, teachers should provide students with explicit instruction on how to set a purpose for reading. Teachers can model purpose setting, create purposes for reading with their students, and finally guide students in creating their own purpose for reading, with the hope that students will grow to be purposeful readers.

Setting a single purpose that is sustained throughout the reading tends to be more effective than having multiple purposes (Pressley, 2000). In other words, teachers should help students understand that they are reading not just because they are going to take a test or for a grade. Ask students for examples of all of the reasons we read in "real life." For example, we might read a recipe, a manual for how to assemble a new toy, want ads, a magazine article about our favorite actor, a newspaper article about last night's basketball game, a mystery, or a biography. We read for the following reasons:

- To enjoy ourselves
- To increase our knowledge about a topic
- To obtain information for a report
- To confirm or reject predictions
- To follow a set of instructions
- To answer specific questions

To teach students how to identify their purpose for reading, simply have them stop and ask themselves, "Why am I reading this?" (Neufeld, 2005/2006).

Linking Text to Prior Knowledge

Proficient readers also link the text to their prior knowledge and experiences, and make inferences based on that information (Paris & Oka, 1986). When students activate their background knowledge on a topic they are going to read, they are more likely to remember and understand new content (Pohlman, 2008). Prior knowledge affects reading comprehension in a few different ways (Pressley, Johnson, Symons, McGoldrick, & Kurita, 1989). It can help the student by creating expectations, then drawing attention to aspects of the text that are relevant to those expectations. It can also allow the reader to draw inferences and fill in gaps of information that are not explicit in the text. After reading, prior knowledge can help a student recall and reconstruct the text.

Whatever the topic of study, it is likely that some students have little prior knowledge about it. When students lack prior knowledge about a topic, their comprehension can be negatively affected. Thus, it is also important for teachers to help students build background knowledge. Because of differences in their background experiences, culturally and linguistically diverse students in particular may bring different prior knowledge to school tasks, and may lack the specific experiences required to understand the texts they read in school (August & Shanahan, 2006; Fitzgerald, 1995). When this is the case, teachers can make a concerted effort to provide students with the needed background knowledge to make sense of a story. They can provide shared experiences (e.g., by showing a video or arranging a field trip), or show and discuss pictures or objects.

Sachs (1983) demonstrated the effects of activating prior knowledge and providing prereading activities on reading comprehension for 36 elementary school students with LD. Teachers used two strategies that encouraged students to focus on illustrations and vocabulary words in context, the main idea, and predicting as prereading activities. Students were measured on different levels of reading comprehension: literal, inferential, evaluative, and appreciative. The students showed gains in evaluative reading comprehension, which is considered "higher level" reading comprehension. The students with LD were able to integrate their prior knowledge better to construct the meaning of the text when they were encouraged to engage actively in structured prereading activities. In another study, Hansen and Pearson (1983) taught 40 fourth-grade struggling readers to compare the text with their own lives and make predictions based on their experiences prior to reading. The teachers used talk-alouds and modeled questions, such as "What do I know about this? What can I predict here? And how can I combine it with what is in the text?" The training improved recall of the story and important details for the students involved.

One particular strategy that encourages students to activate their prior knowledge before reading is called FLASH (Ellis, 1993):

F: Focus on the topic.

L: Look for familiar information in the title, the pictures, or the text.

A: Activate knowledge and ask questions.

S: See what is connected. Think about what you already know and how it may be related to what you are about to read in the text.

H: Hypothesize about what will happen in the reading.

ᖇ *Tip:* Look for ways to connect students' prior knowledge to what they are learning. Sometimes this can be challenging, especially when a student's response seems a little off target. We provide two examples of teachers trying to do this. The first is a negative example, and the second, a positive one.

• *Negative*: We observed as one special education teacher asked her small group of students what they knew about alligators as part of a prereading activity. One student responded, "My father caught an alligator when we lived in Georgia!" The teacher chastised him: "Robert, we are in Florida, not Georgia, so we don't want to talk about Georgia." Robert did not respond again and started to fidget. Soon the teacher reprimanded him: "Robert, please sit up" (Klingner, Urbach, Golos, Brownell, & Menon, 2008). Clearly, the teacher missed an opportunity to tap into what the student knew and pull him into the story.

• *Positive*: Before reading a story called "The Class Photo" (in Spanish—this excerpt is translated into English), the teacher, Ms. Durcal, helps students activate their prior knowledge and connect the story to their lives. She uncovers a concept map with the word *fotos* ("photos") in the middle of a paper chart board.

> Ms. Durcal: Who in the class has taken photos before?
>
> Lupé. My cousin had her *quinceañera* [party to celebrate her 15th birthday, a coming-of-age party] on Saturday, and we took lots of photos.
>
> Ms. Durcal: (*Writes the word* quinceañera *and draws a line connecting it to the word* fotos.) Lupé, did you take photos with pretty dresses?
>
> Lupé. Yes, they were beautiful.
>
> Ms. Durcal: Who else?
>
> Jaime: When I had my birthday party, we took photos.
>
> Ms. Durcal: (*Writes the word* cumpleaños [birthday party] *and connects it to the word* fotos.) Did you take pictures of your cake?
>
> Jaime: (*smiling*) Yes.
>
> Rocky: This last year we took pictures of the end of the school year.
>
> Ms. Durcal: Good! Did you like how you looked in the photos? Who didn't? (*Calls on a few more students, and connects their ideas to the term* fotos.) Good, now we have enough ideas about photos. Photos are to help us remember important moments in our lives. (Orosco & Klingner, 2010, pp. 60–61)

Ms. Durcal's discussion served not only to engage her students' background knowledge on photos individually but also created a foundation for new information based on the combination of contributions from students. Students saw how their ideas were connected to one another as Ms. Durcal visually organized them.

Concept maps, or semantic maps, can be appropriate activities for students to link their knowledge with the text and make connections prior to reading. Some concept maps include story maps (Idol, 1987), story face (Staal, 2000), or K-W-L charts (what I Know, what I Want to know, what I have Learned) (Ogle, 1986).

Previewing Text

Previewing text involves looking through a passage or book before reading. Students who are reading a storybook can preview it by looking at the book's front and back covers and the illustrations. Previewing a storybook allows readers to orient themselves to the characters, setting, and major events. Students previewing expository text can scan section headings, photos, illustrations, graphs, and charts. These details can provide clues to the organization of a chapter, the "big picture" regarding the content, and important sections.

One way to prime students for new text content is to ask them to survey the title, headings, pictures or illustrations, graphs, charts, and any other text parts that create a connection. Next, ask students to turn to a partner and share what they already know about the topic they are studying and the connections they have made with the text. Students' sensitivity to important information increases as their familiarity with the content of the text increases (Winograd & Newell, 1985).

Previewing text can give students a guide that helps them tap into their prior knowledge and set a purpose for reading. One strategy that is particularly effective for previewing text is called TELLS Fact or Fiction (Idol-Maestas, 1985). Idol-Maestas showed the success of this strategy when working with elementary students with LD. Students who used the strategy improved their performance on comprehension questions and in oral reading and listening comprehension. TELLS Fact or Fiction helps to orient students before they read, with the help of an advance organizer. The goal of the organizer is to improve students' focus and activate their prior knowledge through the teacher's guidance. The acronym represents the following procedure:

T: Title—What is the title? Does it give any clues as to what the story is about?

E: Examine—Examine the text to see what the story is about.

L: Look—Look for important words and talk about what they mean.

L: Look—Look for difficult words, read them, and talk about what they mean.

S: Setting—What is the setting for the story? Where does it take place? When?

Fact or Fiction—Is the story true (fact) or pretend (fiction)?

The TELLS approach provides a format for previewing text with students, as well as a structure to preview text independently. Teachers can model the TELLS strategy, guide students in using the approach, prompt students to use the format independently, and, when learners are comfortable with the TELLS format, encourage students to preview text automatically as a regular part of their reading.

Predicting

Predicting helps students make connections between prior knowledge and new text, and it helps them set a purpose by anticipating what they will read. It is one of the strategies in reciprocal teaching (Palincsar & Brown, 1984), a multistrategy approach to enhancing reading comprehension, and collaborative strategic reading (CSR; Klingner, Vaughn, Argüelles, Hughes, & Ahwee, 2004; Klingner, Vaughn, & Schumm, 1998), another multistrategy model. When students are reading narrative text, as with reciprocal teaching, they predict what they think will happen next in a story. When they are reading expository text, as with CSR (described later), they predict what they think they are going to learn as a prereading activity.

When teaching how to predict expository text, the teacher first instructs students to preview the text by examining the title, subheadings, and any pictures to get a sense of what it is about. Students think about what they already know about the topic of the passage, then combine their prior knowledge with information they have been able to glean from the passage to come up with one or two predictions of what they will learn. When first teaching students about the strategy, the teacher explains what it is, why it is important, and how to do it. The teacher then models it for students, then guides them in practicing the strategy, perhaps putting up examples on an overhead transparency, and talks with the class about which predictions they think are the best and why.

Predictions do not have to be accurate to be "good." But they should be on topic. Mediocre predictions are those that are quite general or only peripherally related to the passage. For example, when predicting what they would learn about a passage titled "Earth-Friendly Fabrics," one seventh-grader wrote, "I predict I will learn about fabrics that help the earth." That prediction is acceptable but not excellent, because it only draws from information in the title. A better prediction is, "I predict I will learn about how earth-friendly fabrics help the earth, and about how they are made." Students should then read the passage to find out whether their predictions were correct.

   cg *Tip:* Make sure students check to see whether their predictions are
   accurate. Students can also discuss why their predictions are right or wrong,
   or how they diverge from the text. Often this step is omitted, but if students
   do not check their predictions, they soon learn that this strategy is not particularly important. They do it just to go through the motions.

During and after Reading Strategies: Monitoring Comprehension and Checking Understanding

Proficient readers are able to monitor their comprehension effectively and to implement procedures when difficulties arise. Some effective monitoring strategies include clarifying, self-questioning, question generating, and creating mental images. Students also apply many strategies after they have finished reading to make sure they understand what they have read and to help them remember it.

Clarifying

During reading, perhaps the most important metacognitive skill is being able to monitor understanding and to recognize when comprehension has broken down. It is only when we realize we do not understand that we can take steps to clarify our misunderstandings (Baker, 1985, 2002). How many times do we finish reading a paragraph or page and realize that we have not understood the text? We know at this point that we need to reread the passage and try to make some sense of it. It is essential that students learn to recognize and fix breakdowns in comprehension (Neufeld, 2005/2006).

When students are unclear about what a word or section of text means, teach them to use the techniques good readers typically try:

- Reread parts or all of the text.
- Think about what makes sense.
- Look ahead in the text for clues.
- Analyze word parts, looking for prefixes or suffixes or known words.
- Think about how the information in the text relates to what you already know about the topic.
- Consult other sources of information, such as a dictionary.
- Seek support from a peer or the teacher.

Being able to self-question is an important part of clarifying. Neufeld (2005/2006) suggests asking, "Is what I just read clear to me? "What parts are still unclear?" Another way to check for understanding is to try to identify the main idea of the passage, or to summarize it. If this task is difficult, it is a sign that a breakdown in comprehension might have occurred. At this point, it is a good idea to use "fix-up" strategies.

Self-Questioning and Question Generation

We ask questions for many reasons during and after reading: to check our understanding, to clarify meaning, to locate information in a text, or to focus on specific parts of a text. For question generation, students come up with their own questions to check how well they or their peers understand a passage. When Rosenshine, Meister, and Chapman (1996) reviewed the research on question generation, which is both a comprehension-fostering and a comprehension-monitoring strategy, they found it to be valuable. They concluded that using signal words to come up with questions and question stems may be the most effective way to generate questions. We describe this later in this chapter.

When students self-question, they are generating questions, but these questions may or may not be shared with others. When students are encouraged to self-question, they are more actively involved with the text and tend to process it at deeper levels. They may become more aware of the important text information and may be able to monitor their comprehension more efficiently (Wong, 1985). Self-questioning is an important metacognitive strategy. Mastriopieri, Scruggs, Bakken, and Whedon (1996) performed a meta-analysis of 68 studies of interventions to improve reading comprehension for students with LD. They found significant results for interventions that taught students some form of self-questioning strategies versus interventions that did not. The form and extent of student self-questioning varied, but the results were positive.

Kelley and Clausen-Grace (2008) described several reasons for students to come up with questions as part of their metacognitive teaching framework:

- To clarify something in the text.
- To figure out vocabulary.
- To find specific information in the text.
- To connect to the ideas and/or characters in the text.
- To use different senses (visualizing, tasting, smelling, feeling) to imagine the text.
- To understand why authors might have made the choices they did when writing the text.
- To identify the main idea.
- To summarize.
- To help extend learning beyond the text.

Thinking Aloud

Kelley and Clausen-Grace (2008) emphasize the importance of providing explicit strategy instruction that begins with "thinking aloud." Thinking aloud requires talking about the strategy you are using in a step-by-step fashion while reading a section of text. The purpose is to make the mental processes used by good readers accessible to students. Thinking aloud can be used when teaching any strategy; in this chapter, we describe how to think aloud with a self-questioning strategy as part of teaching students to monitor their comprehension. Kelley and Clausen-Grace suggest a four-step protocol for thinking aloud: (1) identify strategy components, (2) explain and define the components, (3) apply the strategy components using a variety of texts while "thinking aloud," and (4) clarify the strategy's purpose and when to use it.

When teachers have not engaged in a think-aloud before, they should practice the process before trying it with their students. Think-alouds should be well-planned and focused. One misconception is that when the teacher is thinking aloud, students should watch passively and not participate. Yet students can and should be involved in the process. Kelley and Clausen-Grace (2008) provide an example of a teacher explaining and defining the questioning strategy. The teacher has asked students to read the components of the strategy, and she is explaining what they mean (p. 26). Note how she connects the strategy with the students' prior knowledge and experiences to make it meaningful for them.

STUDENT: (*reading*) "I ask questions to put myself in the text by using my senses (visualizing, tasting, smelling, and feeling)."

TEACHER: For example, when you are reading, you might wonder what something tastes like. How many of you have thought about that in the Harry Potter series when the kids talk about the disgusting flavors of Bertie Botts Every Flavor Beans? Tell me the truth, how many of you have wondered what the vomit beans taste like? (*Students laugh, groan, and raise hands. Teacher calls on a student to read the next component.*)

After the teacher has explained the strategy, she moves on to the next step of the think-aloud in which she applies the strategy herself (p. 27).

TEACHER: The title of this book is *The Donner Party*, and in the right-hand corner, it says *Survivor*. I am wondering what kind of party would fit with survival. Does anyone know why I am asking that question?

STUDENT: To help you understand vocabulary?

TEACHER: Yes ... when I look inside the book at the title page, I notice a picture and caption. It reads, "Throughout the winter of 1846, the Donner Party huddled by the fire, struggling to survive." I am wondering why they are struggling to survive and also why they are called the Donner Party ...

STUDENT: I think you asked a question to clarify something in the text and to find specific information in the text.

TEACHER: Good. I looked at the text feature, and my question was based on that, because I am confused and need to clarify. I also think that this is the reason the text was written, so I expect to have my question answered [when I read].

&c *Tip:* One of the reasons thinking aloud can be so difficult is that teachers are not aware of the steps they follow when implementing a strategy. Therefore, to prepare for a think-aloud, it is a good idea to list the steps required to complete the strategy, asking oneself, "What do I do first?", "What do I do second?", and so on.

Signal Words

Students should be encouraged to ask themselves questions in a variety of ways. One interesting way is to use signal words and symbols. Assign signal words, "five W's and an *H*" (i.e., who, what, where, when, why, and how) with corresponding visual symbols. For example the question "When" could be paired with the symbol of a clock. Place the symbols on note cards as a point of reference. Have students ask themselves questions as they read. As they answer the questions, students can mark the section of the text with the appropriate symbol (Clark, Deshler, Schumaker, Alley, & Warner, 1984). This encourages students to read more actively in a fun way.

Using the five *W*'s and an *H* is also an effective way to help students summarize a text. Students question themselves and write their answers on a blank sheet of paper: Who is this story about? What is happening? When did it happen? Where did it happen? Why did it happen? How did it happen? Students might then give the piece of paper to a classmate who has not read the passage to see whether the partner can re-create the story using the answers provided.

Question Stems

Question stems can be used to foster critical thinking when interacting with text, improve comprehension, and increase knowledge (King & Rosenshine, 1993). Teachers can model this questioning strategy, provide students with opportunities for guided practice, then have students practice independently with partners or in small groups. Some examples of question stems include the following:

> "What are the strengths and weaknesses of . . . ?"
> "How does . . . affect . . . ?"
> "How are . . . and . . . similar?"
> "How do . . . and . . . differ?"
> "What is a new example of . . . ?"
> "What does . . . mean?"
> "Why is it important that . . . ?"
> "What do you think would happen if . . . ?"
> "Why is . . . better than . . . ?"

Self-Questioning Based on Story Grammar

Narrative texts share general organizational structures that provide clues to readers and support comprehension (Stein & Glenn, 1979). Stories often begin with information about the main characters, the setting in which the story takes place, and a time frame. The middle part of the story frequently describes events that lead up to a climax. The final part of the story includes some type of resolution to a problem or event described in the climax of the tale. Over the years, researchers have taught elementary and secondary school students to ask themselves questions based on story grammar to improve their understanding of narrative texts (e.g., Carnine & Kinder, 1985; Newby, Caldwell, & Recht, 1989; Singer & Donlan, 1982). Faggella-Luby, Schumaker, and Deshler (2007) taught ninth-grade students a self-questioning strategy based on story grammar as part of their embedded story structure intervention. The students with LD in general education literature classes who used the strategy outperformed students who used a different approach. The strategy incorporates self-questioning with story grammar elements. Students develop and answer questions related to each element of the story. They use general questions as models, then create their own questions and answers:

- Main character: Who is the main character?
- Central conflict or initiating event: What is the central conflict, and how does it begin?
- Time: When does the story take place?
- Place: Where does the story take place?
- Climax: Which decision or event is the turning point?
- Resolution: How is the central conflict resolved?
- Theme: Why did the author tell us the story in this way?

Question–Answer Relationship

Question–answer relationship (QAR; Raphael, 1982; Raphael & Au, 2005) is a strategy that can be used for both answering and generating questions. Simmonds (1992) conducted a study demonstrating significant effects of this strategy for students with LD across multiple measures. Twenty-four special education teachers implemented the strategies of distinguishing question types for 2 weeks. The students outperformed comparison groups on question–answer and maze tests constructed with actual classroom material.

The QAR strategy helps students to categorize questions by the type of information needed to answer them. Teachers point out that questions and answers come from two sources: text and our background knowledge and experiences. With this technique, students ask themselves: "Is the information located in the text or in my head?" If it is in the text, students determine whether the information is directly in the text (*Right There*) or in certain parts of the text (*Think and Search*). They then need to determine whether they need to integrate their own thinking with the author's words (*Author and Me*) or use their own thinking to answer the question (*On My Own*). This technique can be implemented with early primary-grade students with teacher-read text, or with more independent readers in older grades.

ᑡ *Tip:* Different types of student-generated questions can be used to play games such as Jeopardy. *Right There* questions are worth 1 point; *Think and Search* questions are worth two points, and *Author and You* questions are worth 3 points. We have used this game as a follow-up activity to CSR, a multicomponent approach we describe later for teaching comprehension strategies in which students work in cooperative learning groups. Students together decide on their best questions, write them on index cards, and indicate the level of each question. They also write down the correct answers. The teacher then sorts the cards into levels, shuffles each stack, and calls on groups to answer questions at the level of their choice (Klingner & Vaughn, 1999).

Summarization

Summarization of text is the process of writing the main thesis and supporting information in fewer words than the original text. Summarization is different from finding the main idea, in that finding the main idea involves identifying the single most important idea in a section of text (see Jitendra & Gajria, Chapter 9, this volume, for more information). The summary of a passage or text includes only the most relevant ideas and salient details. A summary is compact, includes only relevant details, and is uncluttered by extraneous or irrelevant information. This compact form is easier for students to remember, because the important ideas are clearer and easier to anchor in working or long-term memory (Pohlman, 2008).

Summaries written by the reader or someone else can be used in a variety of ways to increase understanding and memory of text. Summaries written by the reader can serve as good reference tools when answering questions or recalling information from a passage some time after it was read initially. Readers who are looking for a particular text can use a summary written by someone else to determine the appropriateness of the book, report, or article. It is helpful for students to compare essential information provided in a summary to other texts or to their own personal experiences. Reading a summary before reading the entire text can serve to activate background knowledge. Reading a summary after finishing a text can provide clarity about the main points of the passage, allowing the reader to have a stronger sense of the main points of the text. Summaries written by both the reader and others serve to facilitate recall and text selection, and to increase readers' understanding of the writer's primary message.

Several cognitive tasks are required to summarize well. Attention is required to read and think about text long enough to store meaning in working memory. Memory is required to retain meaning from one paragraph while reading the next (Siegel & Ryan, 1989; Swanson, Cochran, & Ewers, 1990). Students who are good summarizers relate new knowledge from text to previously learned knowledge, continuously revising their schemas. Sensitivity to the relative importance of one piece of information over another is required to understand the author's meaning and create a concise summary of the text. Sometimes problems in finding main ideas or summarizing are due to a lack of sensitivity to what is important (Hare & Borchardt, 1984). In addition, adults' and children's conceptions of importance are sometimes different.

Issues for Struggling Readers in Learning How to Summarize

Many students are unable to summarize well. The process of summarization requires the student to read text, identify significant ideas while reading, remember those ideas or pause to make notes about them, then compare the ideas to determine which was more significant than others. Immediately, some students experience barriers to doing this successfully. Less skilled readers who have trouble decoding the text may need to use a considerable portion of their cognitive energy for that task. Asking these students to determine whether an idea is important or not adds a cognitive task that further disrupts their already dysfluent reading. For these reasons, Swanson and De La Paz (1998) recommend teaching summarization using text that is easy for students to read.

Fortunately, numerous studies have demonstrated that students can be taught how to summarize effectively even if the skill does not come easily (Baumann, 1984; Brown & Day, 1983; Cordero-Ponce, 2000; Gajria & Salvia, 1992; Graves, 1986; Hare & Borchardt, 1984; Jenkins, Heliotis, Stein, & Haynes, 1987). Learning to summarize is a developmental process (Brown & Day, 1983) and some of our youngest or more struggling readers may need to begin with instruction that does not seem like summarization at all. Begin with instruction on how to determine whether a word or idea is important. These students especially benefit from direct instruction in the steps involved in summarizing.

Several researchers have had success by teaching "reduction," the act of eliminating unimportant or redundant information before looking for big ideas. Words that are frequently unimportant include conjunctions, prepositions, personal pronouns, and articles. The teacher should model how to reduce a text for students. Together teacher and students can practice crossing out unimportant and redundant information, and discuss why they selected these areas to eliminate. Students are left with text that makes it much easier to locate the important ideas for summarization.

How Metacognition Supports Readers in Summarization

The process of summarization is complex, and students are much more successful when their summarization efforts are paired with metacognition. Students who are taught how to summarize, without also being taught accompanying metacognitive processes, have more difficulty summarizing text. Adding components of metacognition supports students in learning how to summarize and to generalize summarization tasks from one type of text to others (Graves, 1986; Rogevich & Perin, 2008).

Utilizing metacognitive skills allows students to check their own thinking, determine whether their answers or ideas are correct, generate possible alternate answers, determine what "seems" right or wrong, evaluate their learning, and internalize learning (Joseph, 2005). Without using metacognitive strategies, a student can complete a summary without any understanding of whether is accurate. If it is not accurate, the student runs the risk of missing the author's intended meaning of the text. Self-monitoring allows students to determine whether the information from the text coincides with their previous knowledge of the topic, whether their summarization of the text "seems" right, and if not, how to go about fixing their summary.

How to Teach Summarization

The majority of research on summarization instruction uses one of two approaches. The first involves reading text and extracting out the most important information and main ideas (Baumann, 1984; Borkowski, Weyhing, & Carr, 1988; Graves, 1986; Jenkins et al., 1987; Jitendra, Hoppes, & Xin, 2000; Malone & Mastropieri, 1992; Nelson, Smith, & Dodd, 1992; Rinehart, Stahl, & Erickson, 1986; Taylor & Beach, 1984). These approaches vary in specifics, but all involve reading text, identifying primary characters or ideas and what is happening to or with these characters or ideas and why, then writing a summary statement from those answers. You will find examples of this approach in Jitendra and Gajria (Chapter 9, this volume).

The second approach takes the opposite perspective. Rather than teaching students to extract important information, students begin by deleting redundant and unimportant information. Then, the second step in this method is to look for similar things and ideas, and substitute a superordinate term to represent the group. The last step in this approach is to identify the most important characters, ideas, and events, then write a summary statement. Researchers who took this approach include Brown and Day (1983), Chan (1991), Cordero-Ponce (2000), and Gajria and Salvia (1992).

Both approaches require teaching students how to distinguish important ideas from supporting information or details. In order to be critical in determining how ideas relate to one another, students need to be able to determine the relative importance of ideas. Termed "sensitivity to importance," this skill has been shown to be critical for the successful production of summaries and comprehension of text (Winograd, 1983). The following activity helps students develop sensitivity to the importance of ideas.

Developing Sensitivity to Importance

Having students prioritize the importance of the ideas in a passage is good practice for summarizing. This exercise also helps them see the relationships between ideas or characters. To teach students this skill, begin by selecting a text with a similar structure to the one that students will use independently. Select the main idea and several secondary ideas, and write them on small pieces of paper or index cards. Have students read the practice text. Then, give each student or pair of students a set of the pieces of paper. Ask students to arrange the pieces of paper in a hierarchy that identifies the ideas in order of importance. Have them explain why they organized the ideas as they did and how secondary ideas relate to one another. Students put the most important idea at the top, then place the secondary ideas below it. Students who are confident with this process can also identify details that support the secondary ideas as an extension.

How to Teach Summarization Using Main Idea Instruction

Many researchers have demonstrated that students who are taught explicitly how to identify main ideas in text and write summary statements improve their ability to do so and achieve enhanced comprehension when tested on those tasks (Baumann, 1984; Jitendra, Cole, Hoppes, & Wilson, 1998; Jitendra et al., 2000; Malone & Mastropieri, 1992). Malone and Mastropieri taught 45 students with LD in grades 6, 7, and 8 how to summarize. Students in one group were given narrative text and instructed to ask themselves, "Who or what is this paragraph about?", "What is happening to them?", then to write a summary sentence based on the answers to their questions. A second group was provided the same instructions but given an index card with prompts for the two questions and the summary statement. The second group placed a check mark on the index card next to the appropriate prompt after completing each task for each paragraph. Although the authors did not find a significant difference between the two groups in the posttest results, they did find that the students who had used the note card for prompting performed significantly better than those who did not when tested on far transfer measures. They concluded that either condition was suitable for conventional reading and summarizing, but as the reading content became more difficult, the self-monitoring component became increasingly important for comprehension of the text.

Baumann (1984) took main idea instruction one step further in his study instructing sixth-grade students to identify explicit and implicit main ideas and supporting details in text. Students learned how to identify both clearly stated and implied main ideas in paragraphs and passages. They also received instruction on how to create an outline of the main and supporting ideas. Students began by learning that text with an explicit main idea has a clear topic sentence. Students also learned that text with an implicit main idea includes subordinate ideas that point to a single dominant idea. Students used explicit and implicit dominant and supporting ideas to create main idea outlines of text. A second experimental group received basal instruction on how to identify main and supporting ideas. The group that was taught to identify and outline explicit and implicit ideas in text significantly outperformed students who received basal instruction and a control group on all measures of finding main ideas and supporting details, and outlining main ideas. High student achievement in identifying implicit main ideas is particularly significant, because it has proven to be difficult for students to learn (Hare & Borchardt, 1984) and is an essential step in summarizing text.

How to Teach Summarization by Deleting Unimportant Information

Numerous researchers have taught students to summarize text by first deleting redundant and unimportant information. Chan (1991) developed a list of questions for students with LD to ask themselves while summarizing text.

1. Delete redundant information.
   a. Does this sentence repeat something that has already been said?
   b. Should I leave it out?
2. Delete trivial information.
   a. Does this sentence tell me anything new or more important?
   b. Should I leave it out?
3. Locate topic sentences.
   a. What does the paragraph seem to be about?
   b. Does this sentence tell us anything new or more important about the main idea?
   c. Which sentence gives the main idea?
4. Identify implicit main ideas.
   a. What does the paragraph seem to be about?
   b. Does this sentence tell me more about the main idea?
   c. What is the main idea?

Macrorules for Summarizing

Many successful summarization interventions require students to do three things: (1) Delete unimportant and redundant information; (2) substitute groups of words or ideas with a superordinate term; and (3) either select a topic sentence or generate one, if none is apparent. The most prominent approach using this structure, developed by Brown and Day (1983), is called macrorules for summarizing.

Garjia and Salvia (1992) taught 15 middle school students with LD how to use macrorules to summarize text. They included a second group of 15 students with LD who served as a control group, and a third group of 15 students not identified with a disability. At pretest, students who were not identified with a disability significantly outperformed both the experimental and the control group on measures of reading comprehension and summarization. Both on the posttest and a delayed posttest (between 25 and 36 days), students with LD who had received macrorules instruction outperformed the nondisabled comparison students in comprehension and summarization skills.

To teach macrorules for summarizing, show students the delete–substitute–keep process for summarizing. The first and second macrorules, requiring students to delete unnecessary and redundant material, is generally easy to do, even for students as young as fifth graders (Brown & Day, 1983). Substituting terms and finding or writing topic sentences are more difficult, however. Writing topic sentences can be a difficult task even for students in high school and college. Explicit instruction in how to use these macrorules has been shown to improve student performance (Brown & Day, 1983; Cordero-Ponce, 2000; Gajria & Salvia, 1992). Brown and Day's macrorules are as follows:

1. Delete unnecessary words or sentences. Unnecessary words may include conjunctions, prepositions, personal pronouns, and articles.

2. Delete redundant words or sentences. Text that is redundant covers content that has previously been mentioned.

3. Substitute for categories (e.g., *trees* for pines, oaks, and maples).

4. Substitute superordinate terms (e.g., *housework* for vacuuming, dusting, and laundry).

5. Select a topic sentence from the text.

6. Create a topic sentence if none exists.

Give students a pen to cross out deletions, one color highlighter for terms that need to be grouped, and another color highlighter to mark the topic sentence. After reading, students can go back to their words for substitution to find appropriate category or superordinate terms. They can also find possible topic sentences, without having to remember where they were in the text.

Multicomponent Strategies

Next we describe multicomponent interventions that can be implemented with small groups or in heterogeneous classrooms with cooperative grouping. These multicomponent approaches include metacognitive strategies, as well as procedures for summarizing text. They include similar strategies, but with different ways of presenting or using them. They provide instructional frameworks designed to facilitate their use in the classroom (see Liang & Dole, 2006). Some are more appropriate for expository text, others work well with narrative text, and still others are effective with different kinds of text. By no means is this an exhaustive list of multicomponent interventions. We do not describe Peer-Assisted Learning Strategies (PALS; Fuchs, Fuchs, Mathes, & Simmons, 1997) because it is described by Abbott, Greenwood, Buzhardt, Wills, and Terry (Chapter 12, this volume). Other effective approaches we do not explain include reciprocal teaching (Palincsar & Brown, 1984), concept-oriented reading instruction (CORI; Guthrie et al., 1996, 1998), and transactional strategies instruction (Pressley et al., 1992), among others.

Reciprocal Questioning

The reciprocal questioning (ReQuest) procedure was originally developed as a remedial reading strategy in one-on-one situations, but it can also be used in large, heterogeneous classrooms (Manzo & Manzo, 1990). It has been used successfully with students with LD and with English language learners. The purpose of ReQuest is for teachers to model relevant and appropriate questions for engaging with text (Manzo & Manzo, 1990). ReQuest shares similar features with reciprocal teaching. There are a few rules to follow with this strategy:

- The answer "I don't know" is not allowed.
- Unclear questions are to be restated.
- Uncertain answers are to be justified by using the text and other sources.

Students and teachers read the same shared text and follow a set of procedures. Consider the following example taken from *Tuck Everlasting*, read in a fifth-grade literature circle.

1. The teacher declares the purpose or goal for reading the text.

   "The goal for reading today is to discuss one of the main themes in the story: eternal life. Remember that the Tuck family drank from a spring that allows them to live forever."

2. *Silent reading*: The student and teacher silently read the title and first sentence of the text (or the first paragraph).

   "Winnie—Isn't it peculiar? And kind of wonderful? Just think of all the things we've seen in the world! All the things we're going to see!"

   "That kind of talk'll make her want to rush back and drink a gallon of the stuff," warned Miles. "There's a whole lot more to it than Jesse Tuck's good times, you know."

3. *Student questioning*: The student questions the teacher about what he or she has read, and the teacher encourages the student to ask questions the teacher might ask.

   TEACHER: Now think of a question that you would ask if you were the teacher.

   STUDENT: Does Jesse want Winnie to drink the water?

   TEACHER: Hmmm. I think he does, because he says it is wonderful. What do you think?

   STUDENT: I think so too, because he might want a friend to live forever with him.

4. *Teacher questioning*: After the teacher answers the student's questions, the teacher then asks the questions, modeling how to ask questions and focusing the discussion.

   TEACHER: I am going to use the following sentence frame from our question chart: How does _____ affect _____? OK? My question is: How does living forever affect Jesse?

STUDENT: Well, he seems happy.

TEACHER: Why do you say that? Which words make you think that?

STUDENT: When he says, "Just think of all the things we've seen in the world!" He gets to do lots of things, because he lives so long.

5. When students come across a teacher-generated question they can't answer, they are prompted to explain why they can't answer it.

TEACHER: How does living forever affect Miles?

STUDENT: I'm not sure.

TEACHER: Go back and reread the text. Are there words you don't understand?

STUDENT: I don't know what the last sentence means.

TEACHER: Well, I am looking at the word *warned*. If Miles is warning Jesse and Winnie, to me a *warning* means some kind of danger or something bad might happen. How do you think Miles feels?

STUDENT: That maybe it could be bad.

TEACHER: Yes. That it might not all be good times like Jesse says.

6. *Integration of the text*: If the passage contains multiple paragraphs, the teacher then models how to integrate information among the paragraphs. For example:

"Judging from the first paragraph in this chapter I think people in the Tuck family feel differently about living forever."

Creating Mental Images

Students who use imagery to picture what they are reading are more likely to understand complex relationships in text (Sadoski, 1983; 1985). Struggling readers can be taught to create mental images using explicit guided practice, thereby improving their comprehension (Clark, Deshler, Schumaker, Alley, & Warner, 1984; Gambrell & Bales, 1986; Gambrell & Jawitch, 1993; Oakhill & Patel, 1991). One way is to help students create representational images using single sentences that became increasingly more complex. For example, using a sentence such as "The boy sat on the bench and ate an ice cream cone," have the students imagine the sentence or draw a picture of the sentence, then show them a picture representing the major elements of the sentence. The teacher can begin with a sentence that has one or two major elements, then increase the number of elements (Joffe, Cain, & Maric, 2007). A more complex sentence would be "The large pink pig was eating hot brown potatoes." Instruct the students to break the sentence into individual parts (e.g., first picture a "pig," then a "large pink pig"; first visualize "potatoes," then "hot brown potatoes"). Point out to the students that the image does not have to match the teacher's image exactly, but it has to contain the important elements of the sentence. One of the key features of this training is that students should be instructed not to attempt to read and to create the image at the same time. They should be taught to read a sentence, then stop and create an image. Incorporating this process into oral reading time encourages students to build it into their independent reading.

Clark et al. (1984) described a method they successfully taught to secondary students with LD. Students followed these procedures:

1. *Read*: Read the first sentence.

2. *Image*: Try to make an image in your mind.

3. *Describe*: Describe the image.
   a. If you cannot make an image, explain why and go on to the next sentence.
   b. If you can make an image, decide whether it is the same as an old image (one that is held in your memory from a recent image), the old image changed somewhat, or an entirely new image. Make a changed image by adding or erasing from the picture items you had in your mind.
   c. If you have an image, describe it.

4. *Evaluate*:
   a. Reread the sentence.
   b. Evaluate the image for its completeness. Make sure the image includes as much of the sentence content as possible.
   c. If anything is missing, then adjust the image and continue.

5. *Repeat*: Repeat Steps 1–4.

Scaffolded Reading Experience

Scaffolded reading experience (SRE) incorporates specific activities to implement before, during, and after reading (Graves & Graves, 2003). SRE can be used with a variety of texts. It has been used effectively with students from third through ninth grades. Rothenberg and Watts (1997) successfully used SRE to help eighth and ninth graders with LD understand Shakespeare. Fournier and Graves (2002) implemented the model with seventh-grade students and demonstrated that their comprehension improved, as measured by multiple-choice tests. Students read two short stories ("Last Cover" by Paul Annixter [1994] and "The Medicine Bag" by Virgini Driving Hawk Sneve [1994]) from a seventh-grade literature anthology called *Literature and Language*. Students reported a more positive attitude toward reading and the reading instruction after using the strategy. Liang, Peterson, and Graves (2005) effectively applied SRE with culturally and linguistically diverse third graders in an urban elementary school. The students read two folktales: *The Legend of the Indian Paintbrush* by Tomie dePaola and *Two of Everything* by Lily Toy Hong. The teachers found preteaching vocabulary before reading and the use of a story map during a rereading to be the most useful strategies for their students.

The major focus of SRE is on understanding the meaning of text. SRE has two major phases: planning phase and implementation. The planning phase takes a great deal of preparation, during which the teacher considers the students, the text, and the purpose for reading. The teacher plans very specific before-, during-, and after-reading activities. The *pre-reading* activities include motivating, activating, and building background knowledge; providing text-specific knowledge; relating the reading to students' lives; teaching vocabulary and concepts; and questioning, predicting, direction setting, and suggesting strategies. *During-reading* activities include silent reading, reading to students, guided reading, oral reading by students, and modifying the text. The *after-reading* activities include questioning, discussion, writing, and drama; artistic, graphic, and nonverbal activities; application and outreach activities; building connections; and reteaching. Daily lessons may vary in length, content, and activities.

  &ca; *Tip:* The SRE framework is designed to flexibly meet different students' needs. Not all strategies are intended to be used in a given unit, but the framework provides different combinations of the strategies for specific situations. For example: English language learners may need more time building background knowledge for new concepts and vocabulary. The teacher might focus on previewing the text, explaining main concepts and vocabulary, and letting them get a head start on the reading. The teacher might encourage the students to listen to an audio recording of the text or read with a native English-speaking peer while some students work silently to complete a story map.

Questioning the Author

Questioning the author (QtA; Beck, McKeown, Sandora, Kucan, & Worthy, 1996) is an instructional framework designed to help students construct meaning from text. The focus is on helping students to question what they read and to think critically. Beck et al. taught QtA to at-risk fourth graders in an inner-city, low socioeconomic status (SES), predominantly African American school over a year-long period. The quality of classroom discussions improved, with students grappling with text in much more complex ways than previously. Similarly, Sandora, Beck, and McKeown (1999) taught QtA to sixth and seventh graders considered "at risk" for reading difficulties in another urban, low SES, predominantly African American school. Students who learned QtA outperformed students who participated in Great Books discussions.

  QtA has four essential features:

1. Students view the text as a fallible product written by fallible authors.
2. Students question the text, with the purpose of making sense of it.
3. They question the text while reading.
4. Teachers encourage student collaboration in the construction of meaning.

QtA uses queries about an author's ideas or about students' ideas and can be used with text of any length. The student and teacher co-construct meaning by asking questions such as "What is the author trying to tell us here? Where is the author going with this? Is that clearly stated?" QtA is not a scripted approach, nor it is intended to be implemented in a particular sequence; rather, it is meant to be used flexibly.

    ☙ *Tip:* Some students may be used to answering questions as if there are only right or wrong answers. The goal of QtA is for students to build meaning through the text, not to check for understanding of text. Sometimes the author's message or writing is not clear to the reader, and this strategy can help students make sense of the text. Teachers need to be explicit about the kinds of responses they expect of students. They can demonstrate what they expect by paraphrasing a student's response, changing the wording but leaving the meaning intact. Or teachers can refine and refocus a response to clarify main concepts.

Collaborative Strategic Reading

CSR (Klingner et al., 1998; Klingner, Vaughn, Dimino, Schumm, & Bryant, 2001) uses four specific reading comprehension strategies to help students understand all kinds of informational and expository texts. Students work in cooperative groups while reading content-area text and applying the strategies. One goal of CSR is to maximize student involvement. Another goal is to increase students' metacognitive awareness and help them become more strategic readers, even when they are reading on their own. CSR started out as an adaptation of reciprocal teaching (Palincsar & Brown, 1984).

    Research on CSR has yielded positive results in a variety of settings with struggling readers and students with LD, and with English language learners. In two separate studies, fourth-grade students who used CSR outperformed comparison students on the Gates–MacGinitie Reading Test and improved in social studies content knowledge (Klingner et al., 1998, 2004). In another study, fifth grade students, many of whom were English language learners, demonstrated high levels of academic engagement and cooperative learning (Klingner & Vaughn, 2000). Most recently, middle school students who learned CSR in language arts or reading classes improved in reading comprehension significantly more than their peers who learned other comprehension strategies but did not learn CSR (Vaughn et al., in press).

    To teach CSR, the teacher models the strategies for the whole class and uses a think-aloud procedure to demonstrate how to use them. The teacher explains why they are important and helps students apply the strategies. Once students are familiar with the strategies, they then work in cooperative, mixed-ability groups. Each student performs a specific role that helps the group function: as leader, as an expert in one of the strategies, or as the group's timekeeper. Student learning is scaffolded using cue sheets and cue cards for the strategies. Students record what they are learning in learning logs.

Like other approaches, CSR includes before-, during-, and after-reading strategies:

- *Preview:* Before reading, students use the visual cues in the text, such as the title and pictures, as well as the headings and subheadings. They brainstorm what they already know about the topic and predict what they think they will learn in the day's passage.

- *Click and Clunk:* During reading, students use this strategy to monitor comprehension. When they do not understand a word (or words), they use fix-up strategies to help them figure out word meanings (described earlier in this chapter).

- *Get the Gist:* Also during reading, students synthesize the information in a section of the passage and restate the main idea (gist) in their own words. As in PALS, they first identify the "who" and "what" the section is about, then they state what they read about the who or what. It is important that they state the gist in their own words. Sometimes teachers put a word limit on the gist (10 words or less).

- *Wrap-up:* After reading, students review main ideas and generate questions about what they have read. The students learn to use question starters and pretend they are teachers asking key questions to check whether they and their classmates understood the passage. They are encouraged to ask different types of questions.

The following brief excerpt is from an actual CSR group in a heterogeneous, inclusive fifth-grade class. Students are generating and asking each other questions as part of wrap-up (Hoover, Klingner, Baca, & Patton, 2007, p. 251). Note that Carolina did not accept an incorrect response. We found that students are very good at helping one another and following up on each other's responses if they believe a response can be improved (Klingner & Vaughn, 2000).

CAROLINA: What does the spinal cord do?

JUAN: The spinal cord? The spinal cord is a thick cord on a nerve in the middle of the back bone.

CAROLINA: I'm sorry, but you didn't answer the question.

JUAN: The spinal cord carries messages to and from the brain.

CAROLINA: OK, now that's more like it.

ଛ *Tip:* Use CSR to take the place of whole-class reading activities in which students read silently or take turns reading aloud then answer questions. Many students, especially students with disabilities, tend to tune out with such approaches. One of the benefits of CSR is that everyone is involved. Tracy, a seventh-grade teacher using CSR, explained:

> "Having a role in the group and having a purpose for being in the group, and having something that you're in charge of, I think, has been really beneficial. Knowing that you can't necessarily kind of hide in your group; there are only four of them. The leader has to call on people, so pretty soon it's coming around to you, so I think that part of it, just that kind of accountability and purpose that you have for being there, and something that you're in charge of, has been good. I've really, really liked it. . . . I think it's been really good. I like the cards that kind of lead them through the group and keep them focused on things."

Like other multicomponent interventions, CSR takes time to get up and running in the classroom, but it is well worth the effort. It is important for teachers to emphasize that the reasons for using CSR are to learn the content covered in the text, to help others learn the content, and to improve reading comprehension. These mastery-oriented goals also improve motivation and persistence. We have noticed real differences between classrooms in which students just go through the motions, treating the CSR strategies as something to check off a list as completed, and classrooms in which teachers emphasize the importance of using CSR to learn (Klingner et al., 2004). Carolina, Juan's teacher, and Tracy were experts at setting up classrooms focused on learning and collaboration.

TWA-WS

Developed by Rogevich and Perin (2008), TWA-WS includes macrorules for summarizing, plus additional components. Rogevich and Perin tested it with 63 boys with behavioral concerns and/or ADHD between the ages of 13 and 16, teaching them to activate background knowledge, to link prior knowledge actively to new knowledge gained from text, and to use Brown and Day's (1983) macrorules for summarizing. The combination of these tasks, first designed by Mason (2004), were termed TWA—"think before reading," "think while reading," "think after reading." Rogevich and Perin (2008) added a written summarization component, and added WS at the end of the strategy name to indicate this. TWA-WS emphasizes the metacognitive component of summarization. Both groups that participated in the TWA-WS intervention performed well on the posttest, with no significant difference between group scores. However, students without ADHD performed better than those with ADHD.

Think Before Reading

1. Lead students in thinking about the author's purpose, including the type of text structure and the information discussed in the passage.

2. Have students think about what they already know.

3. Encourage students to identify what they want to learn.

Think While Reading

1. Prompt students to think about their reading speed in order to be aware of how quickly they are reading and to focus on increasing their speed.

2. Encourage students to link the new knowledge they are learning to what they already know.

3. Have students think about which parts of the text they are unclear about and reread portions to increase clarity.

Think After Reading

1. Have students think about the main idea of the text.

2. Guide students in the use of the five steps of writing summaries, based on Brown and Day's macrorules (1983):
    a. Delete unimportant information.
    b. Delete redundant information.
    c. Substitute common terms or actions with one word or phrase.
    d. Identify a topic sentence and rewrite it in your own words.
    e. In case there is no explicit topic sentence, make one up.

3. Spend time with students talking about their summary and why they chose some ideas over others.

    ℭ *Tip:* The TWA-WS process includes many important elements of reading comprehension. As students learn how to use this approach, ensure that they are completing each step with fidelity. Begin with simple text and the goal of learning the process rather than learning the text. As students are able to use the approach with manageable texts, increase the reading level of the text.

Conclusion

In this chapter, we have explained metacognition and described different ways to help students become more strategic readers. By acquiring the techniques good readers have learned to do automatically, students with LD and other struggling readers *can* improve their comprehension. Yet comprehension strategies are challenging to teach. Although we know a great deal about the features of effective comprehension instruction and which strategies are helpful for students, we know less about how to help teachers become proficient in teaching strategies to their students (Deshler & Schumaker, 1993; Hilden & Pressley, 2007; Klingner et al.,

2004; Pressley & El Dinary, 1997). It is our hope that this chapter, and this book, will help teachers learn to implement interventions that improve their students' comprehension.

References

Annixter, P. (1994). Last cover. In *Literature and language* (pp. 523–530). Evanston, IL: McDougal Littell.

August, D., & Shanahan, T. (2006). *Developing literacy in second-language learners: Report of the national literacy panel on language-minority children and youth*. Mahwah, NJ: Erlbaum.

Baker, L. (1985). How do we know when we don't understand?: Standards for evaluating text comprehension. In D. L. Forrest-Pressley, G. E. MacKinnon, & T. G. Waller (Eds.), *Metacognition, cognition, and human performance* (pp. 155–206). New York: Academic Press.

Baker, L. (2002). Metacognition in comprehension instruction. In C. C. Block & M. Pressley (Eds.), *Comprehension instruction: Research-based best practices* (pp. 77–95). New York: Guilford Press.

Baumann, J. F. (1984). The effectiveness of a direct instruction paradigm for teaching main idea comprehension. *Reading Research Quarterly, 20*(1), 93–115.

Beck, I. L., McKeown, M. G., Sandora, C., Kucan, L., & Worthy, J. (1996). Questioning the author: A yearlong classroom implementation to engage students with text. *Elementary School Journal, 96,* 385–414.

Bender, W. N. (2004). *Learning disabilities: Characteristics, identification, and teaching strategies* (5th ed.). Boston: Allyn & Bacon.

Blanton, W., Wood, K., & Moorman, G. (1990). The role of purpose in reading instruction. *Reading Teacher, 43,* 486–495.

Block, C. C., & Pressley, M. (2002). *Comprehension instruction: Research-based best practices*. New York: Guilford Press.

Borkowski, J., Weyhing, R. S., & Carr, M. (1988). Effects of attributional retraining on strategy-based reading comprehension in learning-disabled students. *Journal of Educational Psychology, 80,* 46–53.

Brown, A. L., & Day, J. D. (1983). Macrorules for summarizing texts: The development of expertise. *Journal of Learning and Verbal Behavior, 22*(1), 1–14.

Carnine, D., & Kinder, B. D. (1985). Teaching low performing students to apply generative and schema strategies to narrative and expository material. *Remedial and Special Education, 6*(1), 20–30.

Chan, L. K. S. (1991). Promoting strategy generalization through self-instructional training in students with reading disabilities. *Journal of Learning Disabilities, 24,* 427–433.

Clark, F. L., Deshler, D. D., Schumaker, J. B., Alley, G. R., & Warner, M. M. (1984). Visual imagery and self-questioning: Strategies to improve comprehension of written material. *Journal of Learning Disabilities, 17,* 145–149.

Cordero-Ponce, W. L. (2000). Summarization instruction: Effects on foreign language comprehension and summarization of expository texts. *Reading Research and Instruction, 39*(4), 329–350.

dePaola, T. (1988). *The legend of the Indian paintbrush*. New York: Scholastic.

Deshler, D. D., & Schumaker, J. B. (1993). Strategy mastery by at-risk students: Not a simple matter. *Elementary School Journal, 94,* 153–167.

Driving Hawk Sneve, V. (1994). The medicine bag. In *Literature and language* (pp. 558–565). Evanston, IL: McDougal Littell.

Duffy, G. G. (2002). The case for direct explanation of strategies. In C. C. Block & M. Pressley (Eds.), *Comprehension instruction: Research-based best practices* (pp. 28–41). New York: Guilford Press.

Ellis, E. S. (1993). Integrative strategy instruction: A potential model for teaching content area subjects to adolescents with learning disabilities. *Journal of Learning Disabilities, 26*(6), 358–383.

Faggella-Luby, M., Schumaker, J. S., & Deshler, D. D. (2007). Embedded learning strategy instruction: Story-structure pedagogy in heterogeneous secondary literature classes. *Learning Disability Quarterly, 30*, 131–147.

Fitzgerald, J. (1995). English-as-a-second-language learners' cognitive reading processes: A review of research in the United States. *Review of Educational Research, 65*, 145–190.

Flavell, J. H. (1992). *Cognitive development* (3rd ed.). Saddle River, NJ: Prentice-Hall.

Fournier, D. N. E., & Graves, M. F. (2002). Scaffolding adolescents' comprehension of short stories. *Journal of Adolescent and Adult Literacy, 45*, 30–39.

Fuchs, D., Fuchs, L. S., Mathes, P. G., & Simmons, D. C. (1997). Peer-assisted learning strategies: Making classrooms more responsive to diversity. *American Educational Research Journal, 34*(1), 174–206

Gajria, M., Jitendra, A. K., Sood, S., & Sacks, G. (2007). Improving comprehension of expository text in students with learning disabilities: A research synthesis. *Journal of Learning Disabilities, 40*(3), 210–225.

Gajria, M., & Salvia, J. (1992). The effects of summarization instruction on text comprehension of students with learning disabilities. *Exceptional Children, 58*(6), 508–516.

Gambrell, L. B., & Bales, R. J. (1986). Mental imagery and the comprehension-monitoring performance of fourth- and fifth-grade poor readers. *Reading Research Quarterly, 21*(4), 454–464.

Gambrell, L. B., & Jawitch, P. B. (1993). Mental Imagery, text illustrations, and children's story comprehension and recall. *Reading Research Quarterly, 28*(3), 265–276.

Gaskins, I. W., & Pressley, M. (2007). Teaching metacognitive strategies that address executive function processes within a schoolwide curriculum. In L. Meltzer (Ed.), *Executive function in education: From theory to practice* (pp. 261–286). New York: Guilford Press.

Gersten, R., Fuchs, L. S., Williams, J. P., & Baker, S. (2001). Teaching reading comprehension strategies to students with learning disabilities: A review of research. *Review of Educational Research, 71*, 279–320.

Graves, A. W. (1986). Effects of direct instruction and metacomprehension training on finding main ideas. *Learning Disabilities Research, 1*(2), 90–100.

Graves, M. F., & Graves, B. B. (2003). *Scaffolding reading experience: Designs for student success* (2nd ed.) Norwood, MA: Christopher Gordon.

Guthrie, J. T., Van Meter, P., Hancock, G. R., Alao, S., Anderson, E., & McCann, A. (1998). Does concept-oriented reading instruction increase strategy use and conceptual learning from text? *Journal of Educational Psychology, 90*, 261–278.

Guthrie, J. T., Van Meter, P., McCann, A. D., Wigfield, A., Bennett, L., Poundstone, C. C., et al. (1996). Growth of literacy engagement: Changes in motivations and strategies during concept-oriented reading instruction. *Reading Research Quarterly, 31*, 306–332.

Hansen, J., & Pearson, P. D. (1983). An instructional study: Improving the inferential comprehension of good and poor fourth-grade readers. *Journal of Educational Psychology, 75*(6), 821–829.

Hare, V. C., & Borchardt, K. M. (1984). Direct instruction of summarization skills. *Reading Research Quarterly, 20*(1), 62–78.

Hilden, K. R., & Pressley, M. (2007). Self-regulation through transactional strategies instruction. *Reading and Writing Quarterly, 23,* 51–75.

Hong, L. T. (1993). *Two of everything.* Morton Grove, IL: Albert Whitman.

Hoover, J., Klingner, J. K., Baca, L., & Patton, J. (2007). *Methods for teaching culturally and linguistically diverse exceptional learners.* Upper Saddle River, NJ: Merrill/Prentice-Hall.

Idol, L. (1987). Group story mapping: A comprehension strategy for both skilled and unskilled readers. *Journal of Learning Disabilities, 20,* 196–205.

Idol-Maestas, L. (1985). Getting ready to read: Guided probing for poor comprehenders. *Learning Disability Quarterly, 8,* 243–254.

Jenkins, J. R., Heliotis, J. D., Stein, M. L., & Haynes, M. C. (1987). Improving reading comprehension by using paragraph restatements. *Exceptional Children, 54*(1), 54–59.

Jiménez, R. T., García, G. E., & Pearson, P. D. (1996). The reading strategies of bilingual Latino students who are successful English readers: Opportunities and obstacles. *Reading Research Quarterly, 31*(1), 90–112.

Jitendra, A. K., Cole, C. L., Hoppes, M. K., & Wilson, B. (1998). Effects of a direct instruction main idea summarization program and self-monitoring on reading comprehension of middle school students with learning disabilities. *Reading and Writing Quarterly, 14*(4), 379–396.

Jitendra, A. K., Hoppes, M. K., & Xin, Y. P. (2000). Enhancing main idea comprehension for students with learning problems: The role of summarization strategy and self-monitoring instruction. *Journal of Special Education, 34*(3), 127–139.

Joffe, V., Cain, K., & Maric, N. (2007) Comprehension problems in children with specific language impairment: does mental imagery training help? *International Journal of Language and Communication Disorders, 42*(6), 648–664.

Joseph, L., (2005). The role of self-monitoring in literacy learning. In S. E. Israel, C. C. Block, K. L. Bauserman, & K. Kinnucan-Welsch (Eds.), *Metacognition in literacy learning: Theory, assessment, instruction, and professional development* (pp. 199–214). Mahwah, NJ: Erlbaum.

Kelley, M., & Clausen-Grace, N. (2008). Ensuring transfer of strategies by using a metacognitive teaching framework. *Voices from the Middle, 15,* 23–31.

King, A., & Rosenshine, B. (1993). Effects of guided cooperative questioning on children's knowledge construction. *Journal of Experimental Education, 61*(2), 127–148.

Klingner, J. K., Urbach, J., Golos, D., Brownell, M., & Menon, S. (2008, April). *How do special education teachers promote reading comprehension for their students with learning disabilities?* Paper presented at the annual meeting of the American Educational Research Association, New York, NY.

Klingner, J. K., & Vaughn, S. (1999). Promoting reading comprehension, content learning, and English acquisition through collaborative strategic reading (CSR). *Reading Teacher, 52,* 738–747.

Klingner, J. K., & Vaughn, S. (2000). The helping behaviors of fifth graders while using collaborative strategic reading during ESL content classes. *TESOL Quarterly, 34*(1), 69–98.

Klingner, J. K., Vaughn, S., Argüelles, M. E., Hughes, M. T., & Ahwee, S. (2004). Collaborative strategic reading: "Real world" lessons from classroom teachers. *Remedial and Special Education, 25,* 291–302.

Klingner, J. K., Vaughn, S., Dimino, J., Schumm, J. S., & Bryant, D. (2001). *Collaborative Strategic Reading: Strategies for improving comprehension.* Longmont, CO: Sopris West.

Klingner, J. K., Vaughn, S., & Schumm, J. S. (1998). Collaborative strategic reading during social studies in heterogeneous fourth-grade classrooms. *Elementary School Journal, 99,* 3–21.

Liang, L. A., & Dole, J. A. (2006). Help with teaching reading comprehension: Comprehension instructional frameworks. *Reading Teacher*, 59(8), 742–753.

Liang, L. A., Peterson, C. A., & Graves, M. F. (2005). Investigating two approaches to fostering children's comprehension of literature. *Reading Psychology*, 26, 387–400.

Malone, L. D., & Mastropieri, M. A. (1992). Reading comprehension instruction: Summarization and self-monitoring training for students with learning disabilities. *Exceptional Children*, 58(3), 270–279.

Manzo, A., & Manzo, U. (1990). *Content area reading: A heuristic approach*. Columbus, OH: Merrill.

Mason, L. H. (2004). Explicit self-regulated strategy development versus reciprocal questioning effects on expository reading comprehension among struggling readers. *Journal of Educational Psychology*, 96, 283–296.

Mastropieri, M. A., Scruggs, T. E., Bakken, J. P., & Whedon, C. (1996). Reading comprehension: A synthesis of research in learning disabilities. In T. E. Scruggs & M. A. Mastropieri (Eds.), *Advances in learning and behavioral disabilities* (Vol. 10, Part B, pp. 201–227). Greenwich, CT: JAI Press.

Meltzer, L. (Ed.). (2007). *Executive function in education: From theory to practice*. New York: Guilford Press.

Nelson, J. R., Smith, D. J., & Dodd, J. M. (1992). The effects of teaching a summary skills strategy to students identified as learning disabled on their comprehension of science text. *Education and Treatment of Children*, 15(3), 228–243.

Neufeld, P. (2005/2006). Comprehension instruction in content area classes. *Reading Teacher*, 59(4), 302–312.

Newby, R. F., Caldwell, J., & Recht, D. R. (1989). Improving the reading comprehension of children with dysphonetic and dyseidetic dyslexia using story grammar. *Journal of Learning Disabilities*, 22, 373–380.

Oakhill, J., & Patel, S. (1991). Can imagery training help children who have comprehension difficulties? *Journal of Research in Reading*, 14, 106–115.

Ogle, D. (1986). K-W-L: A teaching model that develops active reading of expository text. *The Reading Teacher*, 39, 564–571.

Orosco, M., & Klingner, J. K. (2010). Bilingual first-grade instruction. In D. Haager, J. K. Klingner, & T. C. Jimenez, *How to teach English language learners: Effective strategies from outstanding educators* (pp. 53–77). San Francisco: Jossey Bass.

Palincsar, A. S., & Brown, A. L. (1984). Reciprocal teaching of comprehension-fostering and comprehension-monitoring activities. *Cognition and Instruction*, 1, 117–175.

Paris, S., & Oka, E. (1986). Children's reading strategies, metacognition, and motivation. *Developmental Review*, 6(1), 25–56.

Pintrich, P. (2002). The role of metacognitive knowledge in learning, teaching, and assessing. *Theory Into Practice*, 41(4), 219–225.

Pohlman, C. (2008). *Revealing minds: Assessing to understand and support struggling learners*. San Francisco: Wiley.

Pressley, M. (2000). What should comprehension instruction be the instruction of? In M. L. Kamil, P. B. Mosenthal, P. D. Pearson, & R. Barr (Eds.), *Handbook of reading research* (Vol. 3, pp. 545–561). Mahwah, NJ: Erlbaum.

Pressley, M., & Afflerbach, P. (1995). *Verbal protocols of reading: The nature of constructively responsive reading*. Hillsdale, NJ: Erlbaum.

Pressley, M., & El Dinary, P. B. (1997). What we know about translating comprehension-strategies instruction research into practice. *Journal of Learning Disabilities*, 30, 486–488.

Pressley, M., El Dinary, P., Gaskins, I., Schuder, T., Bergman, J. L., Almasi, J., et al. (1992).

Beyond direct explanation: Transactional instruction of reading comprehension strategies. *Elementary School Journal, 92*(5), 513–555.

Pressley, M., Johnson, C., Symons, S., McGoldrick, J., & Kurita, J. (1989). Strategies that improve children's memory and comprehension of text. *Elementary School Journal, 90*(1), 3–32.

Raphael, T. E. (1982). Question-answering strategies for children. *The Reading Teacher, 36,* 186–190.

Raphael, T. E., & Au, K. H. (2005). QAR: Enhancing comprehension and test taking across grade and content levels. *Reading Teacher, 59*(3), 206–221.

Rinehart, S. D., Stahl, S. A., & Erickson, L. G. (1986). Some effects of summarization training on reading and studying. *Reading Research Quarterly, 21*(4), 422–438.

Rogevich, M. E., & Perin, D. (2008). Effects on science summarization of a reading comprehension intervention for adolescents with behavior and attention disorders. *Exceptional Children, 74*(2), 135–154.

Rosenshine, B., Meister, C., & Chapman, S. (1996). Teaching students to generate questions: A review of the intervention studies. *Review of Educational Research, 66,* 181–221.

Rothenberg, S. S., & Watts, S. M. (1997). Students with learning difficulties meet Shakespeare: Using a scaffolded reading experience. *Journal of Adolescent and Adult Literacy, 40*(7), 532–540.

Sachs, A. (1983). The effects of three prereading activities on learning disabled students' reading comprehension. *Learning Disability Quarterly, 6*(3), 248–251.

Sadoski, M. (1983). An exploratory study of the relationship between reported imagery and the comprehension and recall of a story. *Reading Research Quarterly, 19*(1), 110–123.

Sadoski, M. (1985). The natural use of imagery in story comprehension and recall: Replication and extension. *Reading Research Quarterly, 20*(5), 658–667.

Sandora, C., Beck, I., & McKeown, M. (1999). A comparison of two discussion strategies on students' comprehension and interpretation of complex literature. *Reading Psychology, 20,* 177–212.

Siegel, L. S., & Ryan, E. B. (1989). The development of working memory in normally achieving and subtypes of learning disabled children. *Child Development, 60*(4), 973–990.

Simmonds, E. P. M. (1992). The effects of teacher training and implementation of two methods for improving the comprehension skills of students with learning disabilities. *Learning Disabilities Research and Practice, 7,* 194–198.

Singer, H., & Donlan, D. (1982). Active comprehension: Problem-solving schema with question generation for comprehension of complex short stories. *Reading Research Quarterly, 17,* 166–186.

Staal, L. (2000). The story face: An adaptation of story mapping that incorporates visualization and discovery learning to enhance reading and writing. *Reading Teacher, 54,* 26–31.

Stein, N. L., & Glenn, C. G. (1979). An analysis of story comprehension in elementary school children. In R. O. Freedle (Ed.), *New directions in discourse processing* (pp. 53–120). Norwood, NJ: Ablex.

Swanson, H. L. (1999). Reading comprehension and working memory in learning-disabled readers: Is the phonological loop more important than the executive system? *Journal of Experimental Child Psychology, 72,* 1–31.

Swanson, H. L. (2001). Reading intervention research outcomes and students with learning disabilities: What are the major instructional ingredients for successful outcomes? *Perspectives, 27*(2), 18–20.

Swanson, H. L., Cochran, K. F., & Ewers, C. A. (1990). Can learning disabilities be determined from working memory performance? *Journal of Learning Disabilities, 23,* 59–67.

Swanson, H. L., Hoskyn, M., & Lee, C. (1999). *Interventions for students with learning disabilities: A meta-analysis of treatment outcome.* New York: Guilford Press.

Swanson, P. N., & De La Paz, S. (1998). Teaching effective comprehension strategies to students with learning and reading disabilities. *Intervention in School and Clinic, 33*(4), 209–218.

Taylor, B. M., & Beach, R. W. (1984). The effects of text structure instruction on middle-grade students' comprehension and production of expository text. *Reading Research Quarterly, 19*(2), 134–146.

Vaughn, S., Klingner, J. K., Swanson, E. A., Boardman, A. G., Roberts, G., Mohammed, S. S., et al. (in press). The efficacy of collaborative strategic reading with middle school students. *American Educational Research Journal.*

Winograd, P. N. (1983). *Strategic difficulties in summarizing texts* (Technical Report No. 274). Washington, DC: National Institute of Education.

Winograd, P., & Newell, G. (1985). *The effects of topic familiarity on good and poor readers' sensitivity to what is important in text* (Technical Report No. 337). Washington, DC: National Institute of Education.

Wong, B. Y. L. (1985). Self-questioning instructional research: A review. *Review of Educational Research, 55*(2), 227–268.

11

Teaching Narrative and Expository Text Structure to Improve Comprehension

Joanna P. Williams
Lisa S. Pao

Children often struggle with reading comprehension, and there are many reasons for their difficulties. One common problem is a lack of reading fluency. Substantial correlations have been found between oral reading fluency measures and standardized measures of reading comprehension (Lyon, Fletcher, Fuchs, & Chhabra, 2006), suggesting that nonfluent readers must allocate some of their cognitive resources to basic word recognition instead of comprehension. However, many children can read fluently but do not comprehend what they read because of cognitive processing problems, such as working memory limitations, lexical processing difficulties, poor inference making, and ineffective comprehension monitoring (Gersten, Fuchs, Williams, & Baker, 2001).

Another common problem arises from the frustration that children may experience when reading is difficult. This lowers their motivation to read; they begin to avoid reading, and so lose opportunities for further practice and achievement (Guthrie & Ozgungor, 2002; Stanovich, 1986). Additional problems then arise, because successful reading involves persistence. Torgesen (1977) noted that some students are chronically inactive as learners. Even when taught specific ways to get more out of their reading by using comprehension strategies, these students remain passive and do not greatly improve their reading performance.

In other cases, comprehension is hindered by minimal knowledge of word meanings or of a particular domain (Perfetti, Marron, & Foltz, 1996). A lack of vocabulary knowledge and general background knowledge, both of which are acquired through reading and general interaction with the world, can contribute seriously to comprehension difficulties (Bos & Anders, 1990). One specific aspect of general knowledge, knowledge about text, is the focus of this chapter.

The Importance of Text Structure

An extensive literature demonstrates that readers who are knowledgeable about text structure can use that knowledge to enhance their understanding (Pearson & Dole, 1987). Moreover, instruction designed to teach students to recognize the underlying structure of text improves comprehension (Gersten et al., 2001). Not all text follows the same structure, of course. The difference between narrative and expository text is probably the most basic distinction. "Narrative text" typically follows a single general structural pattern that has been described in several ways, notably in terms of *story grammar* (Mandler & Johnson, 1977). Children develop knowledge of narrative structure early in life. Parents read stories to them, they watch television, and they hear others talking about real-life events. These experiences usually can be parsed into the basic narrative categories of setting, initiating event, reaction (emotional or cognitive), goal, action, outcome, and ending (Pearson & Fielding, 1991). Even before they enter school, children note the most salient categories (initiating event and outcome). By the end of the primary grades, most children are familiar with all of the categories and usually are proficient at understanding simple stories. However, this story grammar represents narrative only at the plot level, and many narratives have meaning beyond the plot level. Mature comprehension involves generalization beyond the story characters and events to "real-life" people and events. This requires comprehension at the level of the *story theme*, and this level is sometimes not easy for children to attain and is usually neglected in school (Wilder & Williams, 2001; Williams, Brown, Silverstein, & deCani, 1994; Williams et al., 2002).

Unlike narrative text, which typically follows one structural pattern, "expository text" is structured in several different ways, such as description, sequence, compare–contrast, cause–effect, and problem–solution (Meyer, 1985). Because of the variety of structures found in expository text, and because this type of text often deals with unfamiliar content, it is generally more difficult to comprehend (Kucan & Beck, 1997). Moreover, many children come to school with practically no experience with expository text, so there is not much of a foundation that the school can build on.

Of course, these narrative and expository structures are not limited to text; they are rhetorical structures that embody universal cognitive processes (Dickson, Simmons, & Kame'enui, 1998). The thinking of young children reflects all of these structures, albeit in simplified form. By the time children enter school, they tell stories, compare and contrast objects, order events in a temporal sequence, and attribute causality (Carey, 1990). But children have not had sufficient experience to be able to use these structures with ease when they read, and sometimes they do not even recognize opportunities to use them to enhance their comprehension. We believe that teaching students to recognize the structure inherent in a text—and to match it to their own cognitive structures—helps them to understand the text. They come to expect structure. When they encounter text whose structure is complex, or text that is poorly organized, they are able to simplify or reorganize it mentally to comprehend it better (Graesser, Millis, & Zwaan, 1997).

The Nature of Strategy Instruction

Today's approach to comprehension instruction centers around teaching children the strategies used by proficient readers. Studies have consistently shown that comprehension strategies can be taught, and when they are applied, better comprehension follows (Pressley & McCormick, 1995). A hallmark of the strategy approach (which really encompasses a wide variety of approaches) is that children are taught to take an active stance in their reading. They learn that it takes mental effort to understand what they read. Sometimes, in fact, reading is described as problem solving (Duffy, 2005). Children learn to visualize a scene or to take notes, or to pose a question; the list of strategies that have been incorporated into instructional programs is a long one (National Reading Panel [NRP], 2000). These strategies can be thought of as ways of putting oneself in a position to comprehend. Good readers seem to use strategies without specific instruction and, indeed, without ever being aware of using them. However, most struggling readers need instruction.

Much strategy instruction involves a strong emphasis on metacognition, that is, instruction geared toward an awareness of one's own cognitive processes and how to deploy them (Swanson & Hoskyn, 1998). Students are directed to stop occasionally during their reading to monitor their comprehension by asking themselves questions or by summarizing. They are taught to take steps to ensure their understanding by rereading, trying to connect the material to be learned with what they already know, and using other general study skills (Swanson & Hoskyn, 1998). In fact, some researchers and educators go beyond this; they claim that emphasizing a conscious awareness of one's mental processes is essential to strategy instruction. Activities that foster this awareness include practice in thinking aloud about one's cognitive processing (Duffy, 2005; Pressley & McCormick, 1995) and discussion of the ways in which individuals vary in how they think and learn (Schreiber, 2005).

Others, however, consider this emphasis on awareness and understanding of mental processing inappropriate. Clay (1998) argues that having children focus on such matters interferes more than it helps with their reading, and that the awareness children need will develop naturally as they gain experience in reading. Beck and McKeown (1998) and Chall and Squire (1991) agree with Clay; for them, anything that distracts readers from giving their full attention to the text and its message is detrimental to comprehension.

Our approach to comprehension instruction involves teaching strategies, but there is no emphasis on awareness of students' mental processing. We focus on the characteristics of various types of text and teach students to use text structure to organize the content and construct a mental representation of a text (Williams et al., 1994; Williams, Hall, & Lauer, 2004). They are taught to identify the important structural elements of a particular type of text and to use them strategically.

Many elements of text can serve as cues to what a text is about—titles, headings, italics, paragraph indenting, and so forth. A good reader learns to pay particular attention to these typographical features. Also, more subtle cues, inherent in a text's organizational pattern, reflect the logical connections among the ideas in the text that indicate meaning (Meyer, Brandt, & Bluth, 1980; Meyer & Poon, 2001). Proficient readers have a sense of the structure that exists in a text, so that even when there are no easy cues to a text's structure, or when a text is not organized effectively, they can organize the information into a well-structured mental representation.

The strategies involved in teaching text structure are not necessarily metacognitive in nature (Williams & Atkins, 2009), although some of them are. To make certain elements of text structure salient, the teacher has students learn to take steps that help them identify the structure of a given text and use it to select important information to remember. The instruction reduces the burden of executive functioning by helping the child internalize and automatize the necessary cognitive and metacognitive processes. At the end of our instruction, students have available to them a greater number of comprehension strategies and have practiced them enough that they can use them on their own.

Our Instructional Model

Our Theme Identification and Close Analysis of Texts with Structure (CATS) programs teach students to comprehend what they read by using the respective narrative and expository structures inherent in the text. Both programs take a structured and explicit approach that has been found to be effective in teaching academic content to at-risk children. They follow classic principles of good instructional design, introducing content in small increments, moving from the simple to the complex, and providing the following: modeling by the teacher; scaffolding that fades as instruction progresses; and, at each step, substantial practice, first guided and then independent, with feedback. In the same spirit, instructional texts and materials are simple; in fact, they are sometimes developed specifically for the instruction, so that they exemplify with clarity the particular textual patterns that are the focus of instruction.

Most second-grade instruction involves a great deal of speaking and listening, since many students are not yet fluent readers. We include a typical second-grade mix of listening–speaking and reading–writing tasks in our programs. The same cognitive processes are basic to both listening and reading comprehension (Perfetti et al., 1996), and our goal is to improve comprehension as demonstrated in either oral or written language. Language production is important, too. We want students to learn to frame their own reports of what they have read, both orally and in writing. The programs are aligned with New York State learning standards in English language arts and in the appropriate content area (literature, social studies, or science). They are designed to serve as first-tier interventions, that is, research-principled, validated classroom instruction in a multitiered response-to-intervention (RTI) system (Fuchs et al., 2008).

Teaching Students to Understand Theme in Narrative Text

One important challenge for any instructional program that focuses on narrative text (usually in the literature curriculum) is to move children from simple plot-level comprehension to higher-order abstract understanding. Many stories have meaning beyond the plot level in the form of a theme or lesson that relates not only to the story characters and events but also to real-life people and events; that is, the theme can be applied more generally beyond the story itself. However, most instruction at the elementary level and even beyond has focused almost entirely on the concrete plot level (Idol & Croll, 1987).

Research has suggested that young children do have a sense of theme, and that it is possible and appropriate to incorporate theme into elementary school instruction. Lehr (1988) demonstrated that kindergarten children can match stories that exemplify the same theme, though they cannot generate themes. Au (1992) found that more than one-third of young children participating in classroom discussion made theme-related statements. Morrow (1992) found that second graders' sensitivity to theme increased as a result of exposure to a literature-based program, corroborating Au's observation of students' use of theme in class discussion. These important observations suggest that instruction targeted specifically at an understanding of theme is appropriate for elementary school children.

Although sometimes these studies (e.g., Morrow, 1992) have included children from low-income families, there has not been specific emphasis on how higher-order comprehension might best be fostered in elementary school-age children at risk for academic failure. Moreover, the few studies to date that have focused on teaching theme to older children have not been highly successful (e.g., Dimino, Gersten, Carnine, & Blake, 1990; Gurney, Gersten, Dimino, & Carnine, 1990; Singer & Donlan, 1982). Although their instruction was well structured, these investigators used complex stories that incorporated multiple perspectives, and they did not include an explicit focus on theme identification in the instruction.

In our instructional approach, we start with a model of how a theme is identified. Dorfman and Brewer (1994) posit that in order to identify the theme of a fable, one must attend to two of the basic plot components, the central event and the outcome. Given the event, one evaluates the outcome in terms of one's moral understanding; this evaluation is essentially a moral judgment. The combination of plot components and evaluation results in the theme. For example, if the event is an evil action, such as stealing, and the outcome is negative for the thief, the story communicates a lesson or theme, such as "One should not steal."

Our definition of "theme" follows and expands on that of Dorfman and Brewer (1994). A *theme* expresses a relationship among story components in a form that is abstracted from the specific story context, and it comments on that relationship in some way. The commentary can take the form of a lesson with a value judgment, as in a fable (e.g., "When he is hungry, a person may do bad things"), or it can consist simply of an observation, with no value judgment attached (e.g., "Some people steal"). This commentary operates at the concept level, not at the plot level; that is, the lesson or the observation is generalized beyond the specifics of the particular story plot.

This conceptualization underlies the design of our instructional program (Wilder & Williams, 2001; Williams, 1998; Williams et al., 1994, 2002). The purpose of the program is to help students learn about the concept of theme, identify themes in stories, and apply themes to real life. The instruction follows the instructional model described earlier. It focuses on teaching plot-level components, using four organizing (schema) questions, as previous studies have done (Mandler & Johnson, 1977; Pearson & Fielding, 1991). Then, it teaches theme identification, using four additional questions. These eight questions (which appear in the next section) are called the Theme Scheme. An additional pair of questions helps students generalize the theme to relevant life situations. Lessons also contain substantial discussion about the story and similar real-life situations. Students take the lead to the extent they are able, but the overall direction of the discussion is shaped and steered by the teacher.

In one of our studies (Williams et al., 2002), we administered our Theme Identification program to students in second- and third-grade classrooms, including students with learning disabilities and those referred for special education evaluation. We randomly assigned classrooms to the Theme Identification program or to a comparison program that represented a more typical type of instruction. Both the Theme Identification and the comparison conditions relied on carefully selected stories and well-organized lessons that were delivered by competent teachers over the same number of lessons and incorporated substantial discussion, a prime instructional technique in comprehension instruction. Students in the comparison condition received the same reading matter and participated in the same learning activities, except that they did not receive instruction in the eight-question Theme Scheme.

The Theme Identification program, which focused on the concept of theme and provided a strategy specifically geared toward theme identification, proved the superior treatment, as indicated by students' posttest scores. As expected, the program helped students learn the fundamental aspects of theme comprehension: to understand the concept of theme and to recognize themes when they are encountered in stories.

The largest difference between the effects of the two programs was on identifying the instructed themes presented in stories the students had not previously encountered. Students in the Theme Identification program were able to generalize what they learned; that is, when confronted with a novel story, they could identify themes on which they had been instructed. The comparison program was successful to some extent in terms of promoting acquisition of what was explicitly taught, but students did not generalize (i.e., they could not identify a theme in novel stories). Thus, to promote generalization, the more direct and structured instruction about theme provided in our Theme Identification program was necessary. (It should be noted that the program did not help students generalize what they had learned to a story that contained a theme they had *not* encountered in instruction, although in a previous study we had found that older students (fifth and sixth grade) improved on such a measure. This may indicate the difficulty that abstract thinking poses for younger children.)

Overall, these results indicate that as early as the second and third grade, students at risk for academic failure can be taught higher-order comprehension skills, and an effective approach is one that features direct instruction of structured, explicit lessons, along with teacher-led discussion.

Overview of the Theme Identification Program (the Theme Scheme)

The program consisted of a series of 14 lessons: two introductory lessons and 12 theme lessons (Williams et al., 2002). The introductory lessons focused on particular plot components rather than on theme. The first lesson emphasized the central event of the story, and the second, story outcome. The purpose of the introductory lessons was to ensure that students were able to comprehend key plot components before moving on to the more difficult task of identifying theme. Each of the 12 theme lessons was organized around a single story and consisted of the following six parts:

1. Introduction and prereading discussion

2. Reading the story ("read aloud")

3. Discussion of the story using organizing questions as a guide, leading to theme identification

4. Transfer and application of the generalized theme to other story examples and real-life experiences, using discussion and additional organizing questions

5. Review

6. Activity

The stories were taken from current trade books and included both fables and realistic fiction. We revised four of the stories for clarity. Each of the stories used in the theme lessons contained a single clear theme, as judged by a consensus of four adult readers. Four stories exemplified each of the following three themes: "We should be honest," "We should keep trying," and "We should not be greedy."

1. *Introduction and prereading discussion.* In the first part of each lesson, the teacher defined theme, discussed the value of understanding themes, and introduced the background for the specific story for that lesson. We incorporated these components, because both explaining the purpose of instruction and activating prior knowledge improve comprehension (Anderson & Pearson, 1984; Baumann, 1984). The instruction was scaffolded, with teachers initially modeling each step and moving toward letting students take on more responsibility (Brown & Palincsar, 1989). In the first three lessons, teachers explicitly defined theme and directly stated the lesson's theme for students. Starting in Lesson 7, students offered definitions of theme, led the discussions themselves, and identified the theme independently. In this manner, the instruction combined direct instruction and interaction scaffolding (Pressley et al., 1992).

2. *Reading the story.* Next, the teacher read the story aloud while students followed along with their texts. At various points during the reading, the teacher interposed questions designed to encourage students to process the text actively (i.e., to make associations between their own knowledge and the text information). The teacher asked the students to make predictions about what would happen next in the story and to explain major story events. The class discussed student responses, and the teacher encouraged students to ask their own questions.

3. *Discussion using organizing questions (the Theme Scheme).* The teacher and students discussed eight questions designed to help organize the important story components and derive the thematic material. The teacher encouraged students to internalize these generic questions over the course of the lesson series.

The first four organizing questions focused on the important plot components from which a theme concept would be derived—main character, problem, solution, and outcome. The questions directed students to focus on the important information and enabled them to develop and internalize questions to help extract and organize important plot components independently (Carnine & Kinder, 1985; Idol & Croll, 1987):

Who is the main character?
What is the main character's problem?
What did the main character do about the problem?
And then what happened?

The answers reflected the content of the story summary. Again, instruction was scaffolded, so that teachers initially modeled each step, both asking and answering the questions. This responsibility was then transferred to students, with additional modeling as needed.

The next four organizing questions included two questions and two theme statements:

Was what happened good or bad?
Why was it good or bad?
The main character learned that he or she should _____.
We should _____.

Through Lesson 6, teachers modeled the way in which their own answers to the eight questions led to a theme, then stated the theme. After Lesson 7, responsibility for identifying and stating the theme was gradually transferred to the students.

4. *Transfer and application of the generalized theme.* Teachers introduced students to a one-paragraph vignette that provided another example of the theme. Teachers and students discussed the example by referring to the eight organizing questions. Teachers then taught students to ask two additional questions to help generalize the theme to other relevant life situations:

When is it important to _____?
In what situation is it easy/difficult to _____?

5. *Review.* Teachers reviewed the eight organizing questions and encouraged students to think about other examples of how the theme could be demonstrated.

6. *Activity.* An enrichment activity, such as writing, drawing, discussion, or role playing, was included at the end of each lesson to heighten student interest and focus on the theme of the story.

Appendix 11.1 presents an example of a Theme Identification lesson.

Teaching Students to Understand Cause–Effect Text

Many researchers have noted the lack of expository text in the primary-grade classroom. In observational studies of first-grade classrooms, Hoffman et al. (1994) and Duke (2000) found very little use of expository text. Moss and Newton (2002) found that less than one-fifth of the selections in school reading textbooks were informational texts. A national survey of elementary classrooms by Campbell, Kapinus, and Beatty (1995) indicated that few, if any, of the books read aloud to students include expository text. Yet by the time students reach fourth grade, much of the content they encounter in the classroom is presented in the form of expository text (Moss, 2005). Without an adequate understanding of the structures inherent in expository text and the strategies needed to comprehend the text that is organized within these structures, many students struggle with this rather sudden shift to informational texts (Duke, 2000). Evidence of this struggle is highlighted by the well-documented slump in fourth-grade reading achievement (Chall, Jacobs, & Baldwin, 1990).

The social studies classroom is one of the major places where proficiency in comprehending expository text is needed, and where students' difficulties become apparent. As much as 90% of social studies content is derived from and structured around informational text presented in textbooks (Myers & Savage, 2005). In fact, many educators view textbooks as the primary source of the social studies curriculum (Brophy, 1992). Unfortunately, these texts are often dense, poorly structured, and riddled with irrelevant information that can distract readers from the important concepts (Beck, McKeown, & Gromoll, 1989). Students are not given the tools with which to read such text, and without adequate skills, students—particularly students with learning disabilities and others at risk for academic failure—may be unable to access and comprehend the information presented to them (De La Paz & MacArthur, 2003).

There is evidence, however, that through explicit instruction in text structure, low-achieving students can develop and refine their ability to comprehend expository text. Bakken, Mastropieri, and Scruggs (1997) found that eighth-grade students with learning disabilities who were taught explicitly to apply specific strategies toward the reading of expository text were better able to recall important information from the text. Dickson (1999) found that instruction in compare–contrast structure was effective for middle school students with a range of learning needs.

Our work (Williams et al., 2004, 2005, 2007, 2009) has demonstrated the effectiveness of explicit instruction in text structure (sequence, compare–contrast, and cause–effect) in helping second graders at risk for academic failure to improve their reading comprehension. It corroborates the finding of the review by Gersten et al. (2001) that low-achieving students benefit from systematic and intensive instruction. In this chapter we describe our cause–effect program (Williams et al., 2007).

The basic concept of causality is seen early in life; two-year-olds can make rudimentary causal predictions and provide causal explanations (Gopnik et al., 2004). As with other text structures, the task for beginning readers is to tap into their underlying knowledge structures and map textual information onto their existing representation of causal structure. Nubla-Kung (2008) investigated the difficulty of several text structures for second graders and found that the order of difficulty depended on the particular measure of comprehension that was used.

The overall goal of our program was the same as the goal of our narrative work, and we used the same instructional model as in our previous work on narrative. We wanted to ensure that children's knowledge of structure (in this case, of causality) could be utilized in reading as well as it is in listening. Since causal structure is a real challenge for primary-grade children and they probably have not reached a mature understanding of causality (Ciardiello, 2002), we had another goal as well. We wanted to lay the foundation for further development of the knowledge structure of causality, which comes in part as the result of the more advanced texts that children read as they move through the grades.

The core of the instruction consisted of teaching children three well-researched strategies to help them identify text structure: clue words, generic cause–effect questions, and graphic organizers. In addition, we incorporated an instructional strategy that is rarely used at the elementary and middle school levels, the close analysis of well-structured paragraphs that embody the characteristics of the cause–effect text structure. Students used these paragraphs, which were written specifically for the instructional program, to identify clue words, to answer generic questions, and to analyze paragraph structures with the help of a graphic organizer.

The comprehension instruction was embedded in social studies content, because the nature of social studies lends itself to opportunities for cause–effect analysis. Students learned about three historical communities of the United States: Cherokee, Colonist, and Pioneer. They learned about homes, schools, jobs, and other features of these communities. Our expectation was that students would learn the social studies content, as well as improve their ability to comprehend cause–effect text.

We administered our text structure program to second graders at risk for academic failure. We randomly assigned classrooms to the text structure program; to a comparison program that taught the same content using the same materials and activities, and that consisted of the same number of lessons but did not include instruction on text structure; and to a no-instruction control group.

At the end of instruction, students were asked to reread instructional paragraphs and also to read novel paragraphs with social studies content. Students who had received the instruction in text structure were better able to answer both cause questions and effect questions than were students in the other two groups. The differences were larger for the effect questions than for the cause questions. Students who received text structure instruction did not show superiority on questions that asked for paragraph details (noncausal questions). This finding speaks to the precision of the instructional effects. Because the instruction focused specifically on the cause–effect nature of the paragraph, there was no reason to expect differences in the number of details recalled.

These effects did not appear only when the test paragraphs had been seen in instruction; there was transfer to novel content. In addition, the effects were seen in both an individual interview, in which an adult read the paragraph to the student and the student responded orally, and in a group-testing situation, in which students read independently and responded in writing.

We also looked at how much social studies content the students had acquired. We asked questions about community features that were the focus of the content instruction, about other information presented and discussed in the lessons, and about vocabulary definitions. On all three measures, students who had received the text structure training did as well as students given the comparison content-only training, indicating that the embedded text structure instruction had not lessened the amount of social studies content learned.

We concluded from this study that explicit instruction of text structure has the potential to improve comprehension on both oral and written tasks, while giving students the opportunity to acquire basic content knowledge.

Overview of the Cause–Effect Program (CATS: Close Analysis of Texts with Structure)

The program consisted of a series of 22 lessons (Williams et al., 2009). First, an introductory lesson introduced the concept of cause–effect; it also introduced the program content (living in a community) through two narrative books. Then, there were three units, one devoted to each community (Cherokee, Colonists, Pioneers). The first of the seven lessons in each unit introduced the community via a biography of a young person living in that community. This lesson included a read-aloud and discussion, as well as an introduction to the clue words and relevant vocabulary. Following this first lesson were two lessons each on homes, schools, and jobs. Each pair of lessons (e.g., the two lessons on Cherokee schools) was organized around a target paragraph and included further read-alouds from a second trade book.

Each pair of lessons consisted of the following parts:

1. *Introduction.* Teachers introduced the definition of cause and effect. "Effect" was defined as a thing or event that happens, and "cause," as the person, thing, or event that makes the effect happen. Students developed their understanding of these concepts through matching, picture cards, and cloze activities.

2. *Vocabulary.* The vocabulary concepts were related to the social studies content of the program. Vocabulary words were incorporated in two ways: They were embedded in the target paragraphs and were also presented as a list of words explained and illustrated through examples.

3. *Trade book read-aloud and discussion.* Teachers read specific passages from a trade book out loud. Students were encouraged to ask questions and share comments.

4. *Cause–effect clue words.* Throughout the unit, students were introduced to four cause–effect clue words: *because, so, since,* and *therefore.* As the program continued, they memorized clue words and used them to identify paragraphs as cause–effect paragraphs.

5. *Text analysis.* Students read the target paragraph, first silently and then aloud. Teachers reviewed vocabulary words in the paragraph, then asked students to go on a "clue word hunt." Students used blue crayon to circle cause clue words

and to underline causes, and green crayon to circle effect clue words and to underline effects.

6. *Graphic organizer.* The teacher used the cause–effect graphic organizer to help students visually organize the three elements (*cause, effect,* and *clue word*) in a cause–effect sentence. The graphic organizer consisted of a blue oval for the cause linked by an arrow to a green oval for the effect.

7. *Comprehension questions.* Students answered comprehension questions about the paragraph independently on their worksheets. We showed the students that they could find the answers to the comprehension questions in the completed graphic organizer as well as in the target paragraph. The students were encouraged to answer in complete cause-effect sentences.

8. *Cause–effect activity.* Students completed activities, such as matching, cloze, picture cards, and sentence generation, first with familiar content and then with social studies content.

9. *Community chart.* There was a community chart for each unit, which was used for further review of the content vocabulary. During the second and third units, words from previous charts were reviewed.

10. *Review.* At the end of the lesson, the teacher reviewed the definition of *cause* and *effect,* the cause-effect clue words, the vocabulary word list, and the strategies (clue-words, cause-effect questions, and graphic organizers), as well as the content covered.

Appendix 11.2 presents a lesson plan from the CATS Cause–Effect Program. Each lesson in the program took two class sessions.

Concluding Thoughts

We have not yet addressed two important topics in this chapter. First is the powerful role that writing can play in improving reading comprehension. We discuss what we have done to incorporate writing into our instruction. Second is the major influence of the teacher in any type of instruction. The teachers who have worked with us throughout the development and evaluation of our programs have made important contributions to our work.

Writing

Writing can play a major role in improving reading. There are many ways in which writing can enhance comprehension and learning beyond the obvious point that writing promotes the skill of writing itself, making students more fluent in expressing themselves on paper. Reading and writing are largely overlapping language processes that support each other. Writing, like reading, can be used to acquire both new content and new skills (Bangert-Drowns, Hurley, & Wilkinson,

2004; Graham & Hebert, 2010). Perhaps the most important distinction between oral expression and writing is that writing leaves a permanent record. Writers can review what they have written, and this helps them reexamine and critique their thoughts (Applebee, 1984).

The Theme Identification program includes three writing activities, each of which involves a step in the process of improving students' writing proficiency. These activities also help students focus on evaluating their own work, an important part of developing self-regulation (Harris, Graham, & Mason, 2006). Students needed a basic familiarity with the Theme Scheme before they began these activities. For this reason, we did not start them until several lessons had been completed. Each activity was completed first orally by the class, then as independent written work, and finally as homework. First, students read very brief stories and wrote, independently, answers to each of the Theme Scheme questions. Then, they went over their answers as a class. In the second activity, they read a story stem and, as a class, brainstormed possible endings. They wrote three possible endings on an activity sheet, and after the group decided which ending best fit the theme, each student rewrote it as the ending of the story. This activity contained goal setting, brainstorming, and organizing, all important features of self-regulation training (Harris et al., 2006). The third activity involved self-monitoring. Students discussed as a group the answers to the Theme Scheme questions for the story whose ending they had previously written. Then they reviewed their answers, marking those they thought were good answers and making changes to the others. Finally, they evaluated whether their story was a "good" story (i.e., that all the Theme Scheme questions could be answered about it).

In the version of the CATS Cause–Effect program described in this chapter, the main writing activities were based on the short cause–effect paragraphs used in the text analysis, although familiar content was used in the beginning lessons. Students worked on sentence completion and sentence generation. They started this by completing a cause–effect sentence, filling in the missing clue word. Next, they read a sentence fragment that contained a cause and completed it by adding an effect (with an appropriate clue word), or, given an effect, they completed the sentence by adding a cause plus a clue word. They then generated their own sentences based on picture sequences and text. Students also answered questions, some of which called for noncausal details and others, for causes or effects. All of these activities they first conducted orally, as a class, then independently in writing.

These writing activities are helpful in many ways. First, they help students learn about text structure. While students may learn to recognize a cause–effect sentence simply from reading, it is likely that by dint of having to formulate such a sentence themselves, then examine it for accuracy and work to improve it, they will attend more to details and thereby learn to recognize a cause–effect sentence in text more quickly.

The iteration of the expository text structure program on which we are currently working contains three structures—sequence, compare–contrast, and cause–effect—and introduces an additional writing activity. In the later lessons on each structure, students write summaries of texts they have read, first with picture cards and graphic organizers, then without. This writing task is designed to help students produce full and accurate summaries; by providing a written record, students may be better able to note omissions in their recall of important content and retrieve more of the content to add to their summary. The task also aids them in organizing their recall and summary according to the structure of the text, because of the opportunities for review and reflection that writing offers.

The Teacher's Role

Our intent is for our programs to be presented as completely as possible. We describe activities thoroughly, include many procedural details, and provide samples of the student materials for teachers to copy. But no matter how much effort is put into the development of a program or how carefully the program is described, successful instruction in reading comprehension cannot be achieved without a competent teacher. The success of programs like ours will always depend on the teacher who delivers it. Moreover, teachers have their own individual styles, which is an important element of delivery and cannot be captured in a written lesson plan. Program developers understand this and want teachers to be engaged enough in the instruction to be willing to put out their best efforts.

Teachers must use their own professional knowledge and expertise to teach comprehension effectively. We suggest that one way for teachers to prepare to teach these programs, or any program dealing with comprehension, is to pay attention to what their own comprehension entails. Teachers benefit from taking the time to become aware and conscious of their own cognitive processing. In fact, this type of metacognition is more important for teachers than for students. Being reflective about how they themselves read, as well as about their own teaching, helps teachers assess how their instruction is affecting their students.

Throughout the development and evaluation of our programs we regularly call on the teachers who have worked with us for guidance. We ask them for suggestions for content and specific activities. We consult with them about our observations to get their views on what has gone on in the classroom during a lesson. During the postinstruction debriefings we have received some excellent suggestions for improving our work. We have asked teachers to help edit lessons. In these and other ways, teachers are collaborators and invaluable contributors to our work. On the basis of questionnaires and postprogram interviews, we have found that most of our teachers like our approach. They like the explicitness, repetition, and organization of our programs (Williams, 2003). While student outcomes are, of course, the final arbiter of success or failure, we know that a teacher's enthusiasm is an important element in ensuring successful student outcomes.

References

Anderson, R. C., & Pearson, P. D. (1984). A schema-theoretic view of basic processes in reading comprehension. In P. D. Pearson, R. Barr, M. L. Kamil, & P. Mosenthal (Eds.), *Handbook of reading research* (Vol. 1, pp. 255–291). White Plains, NY: Longman.

Applebee, A. (1984). Writing and reasoning. *Review of Educational Psychology, 54,* 577–596.

Au, K. H. (1992). Ownership, literacy achievement, and students of diverse cultural backgrounds. In J. T. Guthrie & A. Wigfield (Eds.), *Reading engagement: Motivating readers through integrated instruction* (pp. 168–182). Newark, DE: International Reading Association.

Bakken, J. P., Mastropieri, M. A., & Scruggs, T. E. (1997). Reading comprehension of expository science material and students with learning disabilities: A comparison of strategies. *Journal of Special Education, 31,* 300–324.

Bangert-Drowns, R. L., Hurley, M. M., & Wilkinson, B. (2004). The effects of school-based Writing-to-Learn interventions on academic achievement: A meta-analysis. *Review of Educational Research, 74,* 29–58.

Baumann, J. (1984). The effectiveness of a direct instruction paradigm for teaching main idea comprehension. *Reading Research Quarterly, 20,* 93–115.

Beck, I. L., & McKeown, M. G. (1998). Comprehension: The sine qua non of reading. In *The keys to literacy* (pp. 40–52). Washington, DC: Council for Basic Education. [Reprinted in *Teaching and Change, 6*(2), 197–211]

Beck, I. L., McKeown, M. G., & Gromoll, E. W. (1989). Learning from social studies texts. *Cognition and Instruction, 6,* 99–158.

Bos, C. S., & Anders, P. L. (1990). Effects of interactive vocabulary instruction on the vocabulary learning and reading comprehension of junior-high learning disabled students. *Learning Disability Quarterly, 12,* 31–42.

Brophy, J. (1992). The de facto national curriculum in U.S. elementary social studies: Critique of a representative example. *Journal of Curriculum Studies, 24,* 401–447.

Brown, A. L., & Palincsar, A. S. (1989). Guided, co-operative learning and individual knowledge acquisition. In L. B. Resnick (Ed.), *Knowing and learning: Essays in honor of Robert Glaser* (pp. 393–451). Hillsdale, NJ: Erlbaum.

Campbell, J. R., Kapinus, B., & Beatty, A. S. (1995). *Interviewing children about their literacy experiences: Data from NAEP's integrated reading performance at grade 4.* Washington, DC: U.S. Department of Education.

Carey, S. (1990). On the relations between the description and the explanation of developmental change. In G. Butterworth & P. Bryant (Eds.), *Causes of development* (pp. 135–160). New York: Harvester Wheatsheaf.

Carnine, D., & Kinder, B. D. (1985). Teaching low-performing students to apply generative and scheme strategies to narrative and expository material. *Remedial and Special Education, 6*(1), 20–27.

Chall, J. S., Jacobs, V. A., & Baldwin, L. E. (1990). *The reading crisis: Why poor children fall behind.* Cambridge, MA: Harvard University Press.

Chall, J. S., & Squire, J. R. (1991). The publishing industry and textbooks. In R. Barr, M. L. Kamil, P. B. Mosenthal, & P. D. Pearson (Eds.), *Handbook of reading research* (Vol. 2, pp. 120–146). White Plains, NY: Longman.

Ciardiello, A. V. (2002). Helping adolescents understand cause/effect text structure in social studies. *Social Studies, 93,* 31–36.

Clay, M. M. (1998). Literacy awareness: From acts to awareness. In M. M. Clay (Ed.), *By different paths to common outcomes* (pp. 41–84). York, ME: Stenhouse.

De La Paz, S., & MacArthur, C. (2003). Knowing the how and why of history: Expectations for secondary students with and without learning disabilities. *Learning Disability Quarterly, 26*(2), 142–154.

Dickson, S. (1999). Integrating reading and writing to teach compare–contrast text structure: A research-based methodology. *Reading and Writing Quarterly, 14,* 49–79.

Dickson, S. V., Simmons, D. C., & Kame'enui, E. J. (1998). Text organization: Research bases. In D. C. Simmons & E. J. Kame'enui (Eds.), *What reading research tells us about children with diverse learning needs* (pp. 239–278). Mahwah, NJ: Erlbaum.

Dimino, J., Gersten, R., Carnine, D., & Blake, G. (1990). Story grammar: An approach for promoting at-risk secondary students' comprehension of literature. *Elementary School Journal, 91,* 19–32.

Dorfman, M. H., & Brewer, W. F. (1994). Understanding the points of fables. *Discourse Processes, 17,* 105–129.

Duffy, G. G. (2005). Developing metacognitive teachers: Visioning and the expert's changing role in teacher education and professional development. In S. E. Israel (Ed.), *Metacognition in literacy learning: Theory, assessment, instruction, and professional development* (pp. 299–314). Mahwah, NJ: Erlbaum.

Duke, N. K. (2000). 3.6 minutes per day: The scarcity of informational texts in first grade. *Reading Research Quarterly, 35,* 202–224.

Fuchs, L. S., Fuchs, D., Craddock, C., Hollenbeck, K. N., Hamlett, C. L., & Schatschneider, C. (2008). Effects of small-group tutoring with and without validated classroom instruction on at-risk students' math problem solving: Are two tiers of prevention better than one? *Journal of Educational Psychology, 100,* 491–509.

Gersten, R., Fuchs, L. S., Williams, J. P., & Baker, S. (2001). Teaching reading comprehension strategies to students with learning disabilities: A review of research. *Review of Educational Research, 71,* 279–320.

Gopnik, A., Glymour, C., Sobel, D. M., Schulz, L. E., Kushnir, T., & Danks, D. (2004). A theory of causal learning in children: Causal maps and Bayes nets. *Psychological Review, 111,* 3–32.

Graham, S., & Hebert, M. (2010). *Writing to read: Evidence for how writing can improve reading. Carnegie Corporation Time to Act Report.* Washington, DC: Alliance for Excellent Education.

Graesser, A., Millis, K., & Zwaan, R. (1997). Discourse comprehension. *Annual Review of Psychology, 48,* 163–189.

Gurney, D., Gersten, R., Dimino, J., & Carnine, D. (1990). Story grammar: Effective literature instruction for high school students with learning disabilities. *Journal of Learning Disabilities, 23,* 335–348.

Guthrie, J., & Ozgungor, S. (2002). Instructional contexts for reading engagement. In C. C. Block & M. Pressley (Eds.), *Comprehension instruction: Research-based best practices* (pp. 275–288). New York: Guilford Press.

Harris, K. R., Graham, S., & Mason, L. (2006). Improving the writing, knowledge, and motivation of struggling young writers: Effects of self-regulated strategy development with and without peer support. *American Educational Research Journal, 43,* 295–340.

Hoffman, J. V., McCarthy, S. J., Abbott, J., Christian, C., Corman, L., Curry, C., et al. (1994). So what's new in the new basals?: A focus on first grade. *Journal of Reading Behavior, 26,* 47–73.

Idol, L., & Croll, V. (1987). Story mapping training as a means of improving reading comprehension. *Learning Disability Quarterly, 10,* 214–230.

Kucan, L., & Beck, I. L. (1997). Thinking aloud and reading comprehension research: Inquiry, instruction, and social interaction. *Review of Educational Research, 67*, 271–299.

Lehr, S. (1988). The child's developing sense of theme as a response to literature. *Reading Research Quarterly, 23*, 337–357.

Lyon, G. R., Fletcher, J., Fuchs, L., & Chhabra, V. (2006). Learning disabilities. In E. Mash & R. Barkley (Eds.), *Treatment of childhood disorders* (3rd ed., pp. 512–591). New York: Guilford Press.

Mandler, J. M., & Johnson, N. S. (1977). Remembrance of things parsed: Story structure and recall. *Cognitive Psychology, 9*, 111–151.

Meyer, B. J. F. (1985). Prose analysis: Purposes, procedures, and problems. In B. K. Britton & J. B. Back (Eds.), *Understanding expository text* (pp. 11–65). Hillsdale, NJ: Erlbaum.

Meyer, B. J. F., Brandt, D. M., & Bluth, G. J. (1980). Use of top-level structure in text: Key for reading comprehension of ninth-grade students. *Reading Research Quarterly, 16*, 72–103.

Meyer, B. J. F., & Poon, L. W. (2001). Effects of the structure strategy and signaling on recall of the text. *Journal of Educational Psychology, 93*, 141–159.

Morrow, L. M. (1992). The impact of a literature-based program on literacy achievement, use of literature, and attitudes of children from minority backgrounds. *Reading Research Quarterly, 27*, 251–275.

Moss, B. (2005). Making a case and a place for effective content area literacy instruction in the elementary grades. *Reading Teacher, 59*(1), 46–55.

Moss, B., & Newton, E. (2002). An examination of the informational text genre in basal readers. *Reading Psychology, 23*, 1–13.

Myers, M. P., & Savage, T. (2005). Enhancing student comprehension of social studies material. *Social Studies, 96*, 18–24.

National Reading Panel (NRP). (2000). *Teaching children to read: An evidence-based assessment of the scientific research literature on reading and its implications for reading instruction.* Washington, DC: National Institute of Child and Human Development.

Nubla-Kung, A. M. (2007). *The effects of text structure and signals on second graders' recall and comprehension of expository text.* Unpublished doctoral dissertation, Teachers College, Columbia University, New York, NY.

Pearson, P. D., & Dole, J. A. (1987). Explicit comprehension instruction: A review of research and a new conceptualization of instruction. *Elementary School Journal, 88*, 151–165.

Pearson, P. D., & Fielding, L. (1991). Comprehension instruction. In R. Barr, M. L. Kamil, P. Mosenthal, & P. D. Pearson (Eds.), *Handbook of reading research* (Vol. 2, pp. 815–860). White Plains, NY: Longman.

Perfetti, C. A., Marron, M. A., & Foltz, P. W. (1996). Sources of comprehension failure: Theoretical perspectives and case studies. In C. Cornoldi & J. Oakhill (Eds.), *Reading comprehension difficulties: Processes and interventions* (pp. 137–165). Mahwah, NJ: Erlbaum.

Pressley, M., El-Dinary, P. B., Gaskins, I., Schuder, T., Bergman, J. L., Almasi, J., et al. (1992). Beyond direct explanation: Transactional instruction of reading comprehension strategies. *Elementary School Journal, 92*, 511–554.

Pressley, M., & McCormick, C. (1995). *Advanced educational psychology.* New York: Harcourt Brace.

Schreiber, F. J. (2005). Metacognition and self-regulation in literacy. In S. E. Israel, C. C. Block, K. L. Bauserman, & K. Kinnucan-Welsch (Eds.), *Metacognition in literacy learning: Theory, assessment, instruction, and professional development* (pp. 215–239). Mahwah, NJ: Erlbaum.

Singer, H., & Donlan, D. (1982). Active comprehension: Problem-solving schema with question generation for comprehension of complex short stories. *Reading Research Quarterly*, *17*, 166–186.

Stanovich, K. E. (1986). Cognitive processes and the reading problems of learning-disabled children: Evaluating the assumption of specificity. In J. K. Torgesen & B. Y. L. Wong (Eds.), *Psychological and educational perspectives on LD* (pp. 87–131). Orlando, FL: Academic Press.

Swanson, H. L., & Hoskyn, M. (1998). Experimental intervention research on students with learning disabilities: A meta-analysis of treatment outcomes. *Review of Educational Research*, *68*(3), 277–321.

Torgesen, J. (1977). The role of nonspecific factors in the test performance of learning disabled children: A theoretical assessment. *Journal of Learning Disabilities*, *10*(1), 33–39.

Wilder, A. A., & Williams, J. P. (2001). Students with severe learning disabilities can learn higher order comprehension skills. *Journal of Educational Psychology*, *93*, 268–278.

Williams, J. P. (1998). Improving the comprehension of disabled readers. *Annals of Dyslexia*, *48*, 213–238.

Williams, J. P. (2003). Teaching text structure to improve reading comprehension. In H. L. Swanson, K. Harris, & S. Graham (Eds.), *Handbook of learning disabilities* (pp. 295–305). New York: Guilford Press.

Williams, J. P., & Atkins, J. G. (2009). The role of metacognition in teaching reading comprehension to primary students. In D. J. Hacker, J. Dunlosky, & A. C. Graesser (Eds.), *Handbook of metacognition in education* (pp. 26–43). Mahwah, NJ: Erlbaum.

Williams, J. P., Brown, L. G., Silverstein, A. K., & deCani, J. S. (1994). An instructional program for adolescents with learning disabilities in the comprehension of narrative themes. *Learning Disabilities Quarterly*, *17*, 205–221.

Williams, J. P., Hall, K. M., & Lauer, K. D. (2004). Building the basics of comprehension instruction: Teaching expository text to young at-risk learners. *Exceptionality*, *12*, 129–144.

Williams, J. P., Hall, K. M., Lauer, K. D., Stafford, K. B., De Sisto, L. A., & deCani, J. S. (2005). Expository text comprehension in the primary grade classroom. *Journal of Educational Psychology*, *97*, 538–550.

Williams, J. P., Lauer, K. D., Hall, K. M., Lord, K. M., Gugga, S. S., Bak, S. J., et al. (2002). Teaching elementary school students to identify story themes. *Journal of Educational Psychology*, *94*, 235–248.

Williams, J. P., Nubla-Kung, A. M., Pollini, S., Stafford, K. B., García, A., & Snyder, A. E. (2007). Teaching cause–effect structure through social studies content to at-risk second graders. *Journal of Learning Disabilities*, *40*, 111–120.

Williams, J. P., Stafford, K. B., Lauer, K. D., Hall, K. M., & Pollini, S. (2009). Embedding reading comprehension training in content-area instruction. *Journal of Educational Psychology*, *101*, 1–20.

APPENDIX 11.1. The Theme Scheme

Lesson 14: "The Woodcutter and His Ax"

I. Lesson Purpose and Prereading Discussion
- Remind students that we are discussing themes without telling them the theme of today's story.
  ○ "Do you remember what a theme is?"
  ○ "The theme for today's story is *different* from the themes of the stories we read in the last few lessons."

II. Reading of the Story: "The Woodcutter and His Ax"
- Introduce the story and remind students to ask themselves questions as they listen.
  ○ "Today we are going to read a story about the honest woodcutter. As I read, ask yourself, 'What happened to the honest woodcutter that teaches us a lesson?' or 'What is the lesson of this story?' "
- Interpose and discuss the following questions at the appropriate points in the story:
  ○ "Why does the woodcutter work in the oldest part of the forest?" (He is a very good woodcutter and can easily chop down the biggest trees.)
  ○ "What did the fairy do when the woodcutter told the truth?" (She gave the woodcutter all three axes.)
  ○ "Why did the woodcutter buy fine china for his wife and toys for his children?" (They had told him that they would buy themselves those things if they had money.)
- After reading, summarize the story with students. Please be sure that your summary includes the four points that are <u>underlined</u> in the example summary:
  ○ <u>There once was a poor woodcutter</u>, who lived in a small cabin with his family. One day he went to the woods to work, to chop wood. He wasn't paying attention to where he was going and he tripped. <u>His ax fell into the river.</u> A fairy rose out of the river. She pulled a silver ax out of the river. The woodcutter said that it did not belong to him. Then she pulled out a gold ax. The woodcutter said it did not belong to him. <u>Then the fairy pulled the woodcutter's old steel ax out of the river, and the woodcutter said that one was his.</u> <u>The fairy gave him all three axes as a reward</u> and the woodcutter sold the gold and silver axes to buy gifts for his family.

III. Organizing Questions and Theme Statements
- Read all eight questions aloud and have students repeat each question aloud before answering. For questions 7 and 8, students should respond with the *entire* sentence.

1. Who is the main character? (The woodcutter.)
2. What is the main character's problem? (He lost his ax.)
3. What did the woodcutter do about the problem? (He told the fairy the truth when she brought him the three axes.)
4. And then what happened? (The fairy gave the honest woodcutter all three of the axes.)
5. Was what happened good or bad? (Good.)
6. Why was it good? (Because he could sell the gold and silver axes to buy gifts for his family.)
7. The woodcutter learned that he should ... (The woodcutter learned that he should be honest.)
8. We should ... (We should be honest.)
- Discuss theme (honesty) with respect to the story "The Woodcutter and His Ax."

IV. Generalization to Real-Life Experiences
- Start discussion by reading the example below.
    o One day, Ann was feeling silly. Ann made a paper airplane. She threw it across the room at her friend. The teacher saw it. She turned around to face the class. She asked who threw it. No one said anything. Then the teacher said that there would be no recess for the whole class until whoever threw the paper airplane spoke up. No one said a word. Then Ann raised her hand. She said that she had thrown it. The teacher let the rest of the class go to recess, but Ann had to stay behind. After the class had left, she told Ann that she was disappointed by her behavior but glad that she was honest.
- Help students to provide "real-life" examples from their own experience by asking the following questions:
    o "When is it important to be honest?"
    o "In what situation is it easy/difficult to be honest?"
- After each example, ask students to identify the theme or lesson illustrated by the example and to talk about how they were able to identify it.
- Have students complete Activity Sheet 1 by using the Theme Scheme questions to identify the theme of the story.

V. Activity (Writing)
- Ask students to use Activity Sheets 2 and 3 to write an ending to the given story about honesty and to evaluate their completed story by answering the Theme Scheme questions about it.

VI. Review
- Review the eight questions that students should learn to ask themselves in order to identify the theme.
- Encourage students to think further about this theme ("We should be honest"). Ask them to think about other examples of how this theme could be demonstrated or other experiences they have had with learning about this theme.

APPENDIX 11.2. CATS: Close Analysis with Text Structure

Lesson 19: Pioneers and Their Schools (Part 1)

I. Vocabulary
- Display vocabulary poster and review the words.
  - *community, home, school, job, pioneer, prairie, sod, sod house, schoolhouse, farmer*

II. Cause–Effect Clue Words
- Display clue word poster and review with students.
  - Remind students that we have two cause clue words and two effect clue words.
  - "*Cause* and *effect* clue words help us to connect a sentence together. They also help us to figure out which part in a sentence is the cause and which part is the effect. They can even help by giving us clues that a paragraph includes cause and effect sentences!"

Cause clue words	Effect clue words
Since	*Therefore*
Because	*So*

III. Text Analysis
- Pass out copies of the "Pioneers and Their Schools" paragraph, and have students put their names on them.

Pioneers and Their Schools

Pioneer children went to school in a schoolhouse. Children of all ages were taught in the same classroom, because most schools had only one teacher. Pioneer children went to school only for 4 months a year, since they had to work the rest of the year. Even before leaving for school in the morning, children had to do their chores. Pioneer schools did not have books; therefore, children brought books from home. Pioneer schools had spelling teams that would compete in spelling contests with other schools.

- Have students read the paragraph silently to themselves.
- Review the vocabulary words in the paragraph (*pioneer, schoolhouse*).
- Read the paragraph aloud as a class.
- Pass out crayons, and have students go on a clue word hunt.

- Working sentence by sentence, have students use blue to circle cause clue words and underline causes, and green to circle effect clue words and underline effects as you model circling and underlining on chart paper.
- Remind students that if a sentence has a cause–effect clue word, then one part is the cause and the other is the effect.
    o "Since we underlined the *cause*, we know that the part we didn't underline is the *effect*."

IV. Graphic Organizer
- Post your Velcro graphic organizer.

- Remind students that blue cause oval comes before the green effect oval, because the cause happens before the effect in real life, even though sometimes the effect is written first when we read.
- Model placing Velcro sentence strips of causes and effects from the "Pioneers and Their Schools" paragraph into the cause and effect ovals on your Velcro graphic organizer.

V. Comprehension Questions
- Pass out copies of the "Pioneers and Their Schools" comprehension questions worksheet.
- Have students use the graphic organizer and their copy of the paragraph to answer the following questions in complete sentences with clue words (if applicable):
    1. Where did pioneer children go to school?
        - Pioneer children went to school in a schoolhouse.
    2. Why were all students taught in the same classroom?
        - Children were all taught in the same classroom because most schools only had one teacher.
            - If students give "Because most schools only had one teacher" as an answer, encourage them to answer as a complete cause–effect sentence with a cause, an effect, and a clue word.
    3. What happened because there were no books in school?
        - Pioneer schools did not have books; therefore, children brought books from home.
            - If students give "Children brought books from home" as an answer, encourage them to answer as a complete cause–effect sentence with a cause, an effect, and a clue word.

VI. Lesson Review
- Review the definitions of cause and effect.
- Review the cause–effect clue words.
- Review the vocabulary word list.
- Review the content of the graphic organizer.
- Review the comprehension questions.

Lesson 20: Pioneers and Their Schools (Part 2)

I. Cause–Effect Activity: Sentence Generation
- Write the following cause sentence on your chart paper, and write a line for the clue word and an empty box for the effect. Work with students to complete the sentences using the cause–effect questions.

Maria's backpack ripped	_____	
CAUSE	CLUE WORD	EFFECT

	_____	the water on the pond froze
CAUSE	CLUE WORD	EFFECT

- Completed sentences:
  - ○ Maria's backpack ripped so her books fell out.
  - ○ It was a very cold winter so the water on the pond froze.
- Please hand out Lesson 20 Student Page 1 so that students can practice generating their own causes, effects, and cause–effect sentences. Make sure to move around the room to help students who need assistance.

II. Pioneer Community Chart
- Display the pioneer community chart, and make sure that students can see the vocabulary poster and community charts from previous units as well.
  - ○ "We're going to organize some of the words we learned on this community poster. The three parts of this poster—homes, schools, and jobs—are the three features of the pioneers that we're going to learn about. Can anyone tell me where we can write the word *schoolhouse*?"

Pioneer community chart		
Homes	Schools	Jobs
Sod House	*Schoolhouse*	

- Ask a student to read the definition of *schoolhouse* from the vocabulary poster to double check.
- Review the vocabulary words under the "schools" section of the Cherokee and Colonial community charts to help students understand the differences among the three historical communities for each feature.

III. Read-Aloud
- Please read pages 54–55 from the trade book *If You Were a Pioneer on the Prairie* aloud.
- Make sure you go over all the vocabulary words in the read-aloud as you read through the pages.
- Show students the pictures and invite them to ask questions.
- Involve students in a discussion about pioneer homes.

IV. Lesson Review
- Review the cause–effect clue words.
- Review the Pioneer, Colonist, and Cherokee community charts.

12

Peer–Mediated Approaches

Mary Abbott
Charles R. Greenwood
Jay Buzhardt
Howard P. Wills
Barbara Terry

One may ask, "What unique contributions to reading instruction do peer-mediated approaches make?" In peer-mediated approaches, students practice and learn academic content from their peers. Peer-mediated approaches provide classroom teachers with an evidence-based Tier 1 educational strategy that can meet the academic and social skills needs of diverse learners simultaneously regardless of ability level. Peer-mediated approaches can help teachers effectively manage the challenges of limited instructional time, multiple curricular requirement, and appropriate social engagement among students. Peer-mediated approaches engage students in active learning, hold students accountable for their achievement, and motivate them with social or tangible rewards. Work on peer-mediated strategies (e.g., Fuchs et al., 2001; Greenwood, Maheady, & Delquadri, 2002) has supported the goal of general education teachers to help enable all students be more "responsive to learning tasks" in terms of what they actually do, how often they do it, and how they interact with each other, using a range of functional skills and roles (Greenwood, 1991). Essentially, peer-mediated approaches have proven to be a powerful Tier 1 strategy for engaging students in a classroom in active academic responding and in complex behaviors focused on academic tasks.

One may also ask, "Why do general education teachers need strong evidence-based classroom interventions?" Evidence-based Tier 1 classroom general education practices produce better student outcomes. Within the context of schoolwide academic improvement, the goal of Tier 1 general education is to provide a sufficient quality and quantity of core general education instruction to enable 80% of students to meet academic benchmarks (Kame'enui & Simmons, 2008). When fewer than 80% of a school's students meet academic benchmarks, the school may become overtaxed in terms of the number of personnel needed to provide small-group (Tier 2) and individual academic intervention (Tier 3).

Peer-mediated strategies provide a method for strengthening Tier 1 instructional effectiveness using classroom peers as tutors. Peer-mediated instruction may be used to differentiate instruction throughout the tutoring process. In creating differentiated instruction, the teacher actively uses varied materials or amount of content completed during tutoring (Bender, 2002). For example, during peer-tutoring, the lower-performing student of the peer pair may be asked to read half a page of text orally, while the higher-performing peer reads two pages of text. The lower-performing student still participates in learning the content of the two pages of text, because the higher-performing peer reads the additional page and a half orally during peer tutoring. This allows the lower-performing peer to read the same smaller amount of text repeatedly and work on reading accuracy. The teacher monitors the implementation of differentiated instruction by facilitating and overseeing peer tutoring across all tutoring pairs. This increased flexibility of material usage and content coverage at the Tier 1 level strengthens instruction and potentially reduces the percentage of students requiring more costly intervention.

As an educational interventionist, ask yourself the following questions:

1. Does our school have fewer than 80% of students who reach reading benchmarks?
2. Would students who fail to meet reading benchmarks benefit from increased skills instruction and text reading?
3. Do students who fail to reach benchmark lack motivation to participate?

If you answered "yes" to any of these questions and are interested in strategies that strengthen Tier 1 classroom-level instruction to improve general reading ability and the specific skills associated with reading, then you will want to learn more about peer-mediated strategies.

How Do Peer-Mediated Strategies Work?

The two most widely used, evidence-based peer-mediated approaches are Class-wide Peer Tutoring (CWPT) and Peer-Assisted Learning Strategies (PALS). Both approaches have been successful in improving literacy outcomes across varied student populations, academic environments, and student age levels. Our chapter includes general information about both approaches and why they strengthen student outcomes at the Tier 1 classroom level of instruction. The specific steps of CWPT classroom implementation, training, and suggestions that promote full and sustained implementation are also provided. The chapter ends with a discussion that includes suggestions for further study and work to improve the implementation process.

Classwide Peer Tutoring

CWPT was originally developed by researchers at Juniper Gardens Children's Project and an urban core classroom teacher in the 1970s. The intent was to integrate six students with learning disabilities into a general education classroom in a manner that did not isolate them into the lowest reading group or require a separate, parallel curriculum. CWPT provided the students with similar opportunities for active participation, respect, and interaction with peers not struggling to learn to read and spell (Delquadri, Greenwood, Stretton, & Hall, 1983).

CWPT was also developed to remove inequities often observed in general education classroom instruction. As research investigators of reading instruction, we reported that struggling readers in low-achieving reading groups, who needed more intensive instruction, often received less reading instruction per day than did higher achieving groups. These groups were frequently scheduled to read last in order, bounded by transitions to recess or lunch, so that if other groups ran long, and they often did, the lowest-achieving group met less per day and per week (Greenwood, Carta, Whorton, & Hall, 1988).

CWPT overcame these general education challenges by creating a regular 35 to 45 minutes per day in which all students in the classroom were engaged for the same amount of time in reading with a peer tutor or peer coach using a game-based activity system. Compared to teacher-led instruction or independent study, in which attention and self-managed passive responding is the norm, one hears a buzz of responding and reading aloud in the CWPT activity system, along with discussion and responding among peers. Student errors are corrected, and positive feedback is provided. There is continual assessment of student performance through daily measurement of student engagement. Weekly student academic achievement determines future instruction (see Greenwood, 1991). Effectiveness can be boosted when the CWPT activity system is combined with (1) teaching of evidence-based skills in the curriculum, (2) tutors using evidence-based teaching strategies taught to them by the classroom teacher, and (3) skills-based pairing strategies.

Peer–Assisted Learning Strategies

The PALS program in reading, developed at Vanderbilt University and modeled after CWPT (e.g., Fuchs, Fuchs, & Kazdan, 1999), is similar to CWPT in that all students in a class (1) are paired; (2) trained to use specific prompts, corrections and feedback; (3) tutor each other; and (4) award points to their peers. Additionally, PALS Reading for elementary school (Mathes, Torgesen, & Allor, 2001) consists of three structured activities, which students are taught to implement independently. The first activity is Partner Reading with Retell, during which each student in the peer pair reads aloud, with the higher-performing student reading first. After both students have read, the lower-performing student retells the sequence of events just read. During the second PALS activity, Paragraph Shrinking, designed to develop comprehension through summarization and main idea identification, after each paragraph the reader must condense or "shrink" information within the paragraph into 10 or fewer words. The last activity, Prediction Relay, requires students to make predictions, then to confirm or disconfirm them. During Prediction Relay the reader (1) makes a prediction about what will happen on the next half-page to be read, (2) reads the half-page aloud, (3) confirms or disconfirms the prediction, and (4) summarizes the main idea. PALS instruction occurs three times a week for 35 minutes each session.

Although PALS research began at the elementary school level, with a few modifications to the point reward system PALS was successfully implemented at the middle and high school levels (Fuchs et al., 1999). A more recent focus of PALS has included beginning reading programs that explicitly teach critical skills for early literacy acquisition. Kindergarten PALS (K-PALS) and First Grade PALS activities address phonological awareness, beginning decoding, and word recognition skills (Mathes, Clancy-Menchetti, & Torgesen, 2001). K-PALS has 60 lessons or sessions. During K-PALS sessions, the teacher first models activities to the whole class. Then students tutor each other and award points by marking the smiley-face point card. Each lesson includes a specific series of early literacy activities in a consumable worksheet format. In early lessons, students practice quickly recognizing letters–letter sounds, and by the end of K-PALS, sight words and decodable words. First Grade PALS follows the same format of teacher introduction, with student peer tutoring on preestablished worksheets. The lesson begins with segmenting and blending and letter and sound activities, and ends with peer practice on sight and decodable word text reading.

Both CWPT and PALS keep motivation and interest high, because all students are actively engaged in reading both as learners (tutees) and teachers (tutors). These features of peer mediation are combined to increase active engagement in learning tasks, acquisition of practiced skills, and the number and breadth of peer social relations. Students routinely indicate that they prefer learning with peer-mediated compared to teacher-mediated instruction (Ginsburg-Block, Rohrbeck, & Fantuzzo, 2006; Rohrbeck, Ginsburg-Block, Fantuzzo, & Miller, 2003).

The Research Base for Peer–Mediated Strategies

Peer-mediated strategies are supported by more than two decades of experimental research (e.g., Greenwood, Maheady, & Delquadri, 2002; Rohrbeck, Ginsburg-

Block, Fantuzzo, & Miller, 2003). Randomized trials of peer-mediated strategies consistently report medium to large effect sizes that indicate the strength or effect of treatment (i.e., 0.3 to 0.8, Cohen, 1988; see Table 12.1). CWPT and PALS are, to date, the most researched peer-mediated strategies and both CWPT and PALS have been recognized as effective by the United States government's What Works Clearinghouse website (*ies.ed.gov/ncee/wwc*).

There is an extensive body of research on peer-mediated strategies within the general areas of achievement and student engagement, literacy achievement, social behavior, and scaling up widespread use of peer-mediated strategies. In a seminal 12-year CWPT longitudinal study (Greenwood, Hou, Delquadri, Terry, & Arreaga-Mayer, 2001), students in first through fourth grades who received CWPT instruction (1) showed significantly higher growth in a variety of achievement areas; (2) had significantly higher rates of academic engagement; (3) achieved significantly greater academic growth into middle school, with fewer special education services; and (4) had significantly fewer incidents of leaving school prior to high school graduation (Greenwood, & Delquadri, 1995; Greenwood, Delquadri, & Hall, 1989: Greenwood, Terry, Utley, Montagna, & Walker, 1993). Long-term results from PALS studies also indicate improvement in student outcomes. In a synthesis of 90 PALS elementary school research studies Rohrbeck et al. (2003) reported (1) moderate effect sizes in favor of PALS, (2) larger academic gains for students from urban rather than suburban areas, (3) larger gains for younger students than for older students, (4) larger gains when fidelity or quality of classroom implementation is monitored and controlled, and (5) greater achievement when peer rewards of points and praise are implemented.

Extensive research has investigated peer-mediated strategies associated

TABLE 12.1. Results of Randomized Trials Supporting the Efficacy of Peer–Mediated Strategies

Citation	Description	Indicator	Effect size
Greenwood, Delquadri, & Hall (1989)	Longitudinal randomized CWPT trial; grades 1–4 (N = 416)	Reading achievement total Language achievement Arithmetic achievement Academic engagement	0.57 0.60 0.37 1.41
Greenwood (1991)	Multiyear behavioral trajectories; grades 1–3 (N = 115)	Academic engagement Task management Inappropriate behavior	0.63 0.61 0.83
Greenwood, Kamps, Terry, & Linebarger (2007)	Middle school follow-up of elementary school use of CWPT (N = 303)	Reading achievement Language achievement	0.39 0.35
Fuchs, Fuchs, Mathes, & Simmons (1997)	Randomized PALS trial; grades 2–4 (N = 120)	Reading achievement Reading	0.22 0.56
Fuchs, Fuchs, Thompson, et al. (2001)	Randomized PALS trial; grade K	Segmentation Blending Alphabetics	0.34 0.02 1.96

Note. Effect sizes are in Cohen's *d*.

directly with literacy achievement in a wide variety of learning environments. Much of this research has occurred with children in low socioeconomic status (SES) elementary schools. Early studies of CWPT focused primarily on reading, spelling, vocabulary, and math for students in urban core schools (see Greenwood et al., 2002). A large-scale, experimental field trial of elementary school students found that those in PALS classrooms significantly outperformed their comparison peers in reading fluency and comprehension (Fuchs, Fuchs, Mathes, & Simmons, 1997). These results for CWPT and PALS were consistent for average and low-literacy achievers.

Peer-mediated strategy studies have also investigated outcomes with different student populations. Harper, Mallette, and Moore (1991) reported significant improvement in spelling scores for elementary school children with mild learning disabilities. Greenwood, Arreaga-Mayer, Utley, Gavin, and Terry (2001) reported that English language learners (ELLs) made considerable progress in mastering the curriculum when teachers implemented CWPT to high standards of fidelity or quality. Herring-Harrison, Gardner, and Lovelace (2007) reported success in adapting CWPT for students who are deaf or hard of hearing.

Additionally, literacy-related studies have occurred with early childhood and older student populations. In a K-PALS experimental study of 33 randomly assigned urban and suburban kindergarten classrooms, Fuchs et al. (2001) reported that after approximately 20 weeks of intervention, significant differences were found in phonological awareness and beginning reading skills favoring the K-PALS group. McMaster, Kung, Han, and Cao (2008) reported that kindergarten ELLs who participated in K-PALS instruction performed better than comparison ELLs on measures of phonemic awareness and letter-sound recognition. Their non-ELL K-PALS counterparts also performed better than non-ELL who did not received K-PALS instruction. PALS has also proved successful in improving reading comprehension of high school students with serious reading delays (Fuchs et al., 1999).

Some evidence suggests that peer-mediated strategies improve social skills and on-task behavior. A study with students who exhibited autism and their non-autistic peers found that CWPT not only improved reading fluency and comprehension but also increased the free-time social interactions between students with autism and their typically developing peers (Kamps, Barbetta, Leonard, & Delquadri, 1994). Pressley and Hughes (2000) reported that when CWPT was used to teach social skills, fewer intensive anger behavior episodes occurred during other parts of the school day. Van Norman (2007) reported improved social conversation skills in students with disabilities through the use of a sports trivia CWPT game. Fuchs et al. (2002) indicated that PALS students with learning disabilities gained greater social acceptance than those with learning disabilities in non-PALS classes. In social studies classes in a middle school for students with emotional or behavioral disorders, Spencer, Scruggs, and Mastropieri (2003) reported that students participating in CWPT scored higher on content tests and on-task behavior. Similarly, in an alternative middle school study of students with emotional and behavioral disorders, Bowman-Perrott, Greenwood, and Tapia (2007) reported an increased amount of time spent on-task with CWPT compared to conventional instruction.

In summary, for Tier 1 instruction, research-validated peer-mediated approaches accelerated the academic and behavioral outcomes of students with a wide range of abilities and instructional settings. Large-scale studies indicate medium to large effect sizes that describe treatment impact. Additionally, embedded within peer-mediated instruction are evidence-based individual instructional features known to improve student outcomes significantly. These features include increased student engagement, consistent assessment that determines the future direction of instruction, and teacher adherence to procedures creating strong fidelity of implementation.

Instructional Procedures

Peer-mediated strategies allow students to engage in the curriculum and learn new skills in a systematic and fun way. Both CWPT and PALS include the following components: (1) peer-mediated instruction, with active responding and repeated practice; (2) immediate corrective feedback and positive reinforcement from peers, as well as from the teacher; (3) student evaluation, with daily in-class performance and weekly curriculum-based assessment; and (4) teacher monitoring that manages tutoring sessions and provides feedback and positive reinforcement. Both CWPT and PALS include a well-structured process that engages all of the learning modalities of hearing, seeing, saying, and writing the content for more sustained learning, while having fun, enjoying competition, and improving student academic outcomes. In the remainder of this chapter, we focus on CWPT instructional procedures.

One of its strengths is that CWPT can be adapted for various curricula, standards, and instructional activities covering all areas of literacy, as well as other subject matter, such as math, social studies, and science. When using CWPT with simple rote tasks, such as learning spelling words, letter names, or math facts, lists or cards may be used. For example, for learning multiplication facts the teacher creates various lists or sets of math fact cards. Depending on student proficiency, the teacher assigns a list or set of math fact cards to each peer-tutoring pair, and the peer-tutoring session focuses on learning the list of math facts. The peer tutor has the answers and provides corrective feedback. Study guides are recommended for more advanced subjects, such as social studies and science. For example, for learning the content for a history unit about the Civil War, the teacher creates a unit study guide that covers vocabulary, conceptual information, and important dates. Students peer-tutor together to read several pages of the chapter or content, then work together in peer pairs to complete a portion of the study guide. The basic procedures for implementing CWPT are described below.

CWPT Overview

Briefly, CWPT involves daily 35- to 45-minute sessions, three to five times a week, within a game format of team competition. Prior to tutoring, the teacher establishes the tutor and tutee pairings, and distributes the pairs across two teams. Tutor and tutee pairings change weekly or with every new unit/content. During tutoring, half the students in the classroom are the "tutors" and supervise the academic activities of the other half, known as the "tutees" (see Table 12.2). Midway through the session, the partners switch roles; the tutor becoming the tutee, and vice versa. As students tutor each other on the assigned content, the tutor frequently awards points to the tutee for successfully completing small increments of lesson content. During the tutoring period, the teacher's role is to facilitate, supervise, coordinate, award bonus points, and provide additional feedback to students. At the end of the full tutoring session, students report individual points earned and the class recognizes the winning team with the highest point total for the day. On the final day of the tutoring week, the teacher administers the posttest that assesses mastery over material the students have been learning all week. Immediately following the posttest, the teacher administers the pretest for the content that the students will learn for the upcoming week.

Prior to Implementation

Essential to the success of CWPT is student training prior to implementation. Student training covers (1) establishing rules for appropriate social and tutoring behavior during tutoring, (2) peer teaching interactions for task presentation and error correction procedures, (3) awarding points, and (4) giving praise for correct responses. For example, the following sequence illustrates error correction, awarding points, praise, and the tutor–tutee interaction during an oral reading session:

TUTOR: Go ahead and start on page 12.

TUTEE: It was a warm and sunny day.

TUTOR: Good, two points.

TUTEE: Will and Paul went to the park to play.

TABLE 12.2. Tutor, Tutee, and Classroom Teacher Roles during CWPT

Tutor	Tutee	Classroom teacher
• Present new items to the tutee.	• Work quickly reading, writing, or saying the item presented.	• Facilitate by moving among tutor pairs.
• Make corrections when necessary.	• Correct errors when made.	• Verbally reinforce good tutoring behavior.
• Award points based on tutee's performance.	• Work until timer signals the end of session.	• Award bonus points.

TUTOR: Two points!

TUTEE: Paul sug ... " (*hesitation and pause*).

TUTOR: (*pointing to the word*) "Suggested."

TUTEE: Suggested.

TUTOR: Right! Reread the sentence.

TUTEE: Paul suggested that they first play on the swings.

TUTOR: Good, one point.

These procedural skills needed to make implementation successful must be explicitly taught prior to CWPT implementation.

Before tutoring begins, the teacher pretests students on the material from the unit to be tutored and then prepares the required tutoring materials. Figure 12.1 shows tutoring materials, which include point sheets and instructional materials, such as spelling lists, reading materials, or study guides. The teacher makes team assignments by pairing students at similar academic levels and randomly assigning each pair to one of two teams.

CWPT Spelling Implementation Procedures

To describe further the process of implementing CWPT tutoring procedures and point reporting, we depict one day of CWPT spelling instruction. We chose spelling instruction, because it is the least complex type of literacy instruction to implement. Prior to tutoring, the teacher compiles a weekly or unit list of spelling words from the spelling text or theme-related words from the literacy curriculum.

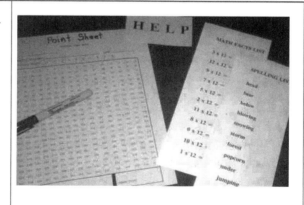

- Move/stay assignments (self-determined or computer-generated)

- Point total charts (commercial or computer)

- Tutoring point sheets

- Help cards

- Student tutoring materials

- Pencils/markers/crayons

- Timer

FIGURE 12.1. Materials required for CWPT.

After establishing peer pairs, one member of the student pair is designated as the "mover." The mover's responsibilities include checking the partner pairing chart to identify his or her partner, picking up the tutoring packet with all the tutoring materials inside, and quietly sitting next to his or her "stayer" partner. The responsibility of the "stayer" is to assume the role of first tutor. When all students are seated and have removed the tutoring materials, the teacher reminds students to begin at the top of the spelling list, asks if everyone is ready, sets the timer for 10 minutes, and says "Begin."

The tutor in each pair says the first spelling word on the list aloud. The tutee repeats the word, and writes and spells the word aloud. The tutee writes it in the first trial box on the tutee practice page (see Figure 12.2 for an example). If the word is written and spelled correctly the first time, the tutor awards 2 points on the tutee point sheet and says "good job." The tutor then dictates the second word on the list. Again the tutee writes the word and spells it aloud. As soon as the tutee makes an error in the spelling, the tutor says "Stop," immediately shows the word to the tutee, and spells the word correctly for the tutee. The tutee then moves to the second practice trial box on the practice page, and writes and spells the word correctly as the tutor has modeled. The tutee repeats writing and spelling the corrected word in each of the remaining practice trial boxes on the practice page, and if all three practice trials are correct, the tutee is awarded 1 point. If at any point during the error-correction process, the tutee makes a second error on a previously corrected word, the tutor stops the tutee and no points are awarded. The tutor moves to the next word on the list. This practice and error-correction procedure continues until the timer rings, ending the first tutoring session. The list of words should be short enough that the tutee can complete spelling the entire list at least two times within the 10-minute tutoring segment. Then the partners immediately switch roles and materials, the teacher sets the timer for 10 minutes, and the roles are reversed. The pairs go through the tutoring process as many times as they can in the 10 minutes and repeat the words on the list as many times as the session permits. When the timer sounds, the tutoring pairs immediately stop tutoring.

Throughout the tutoring process, the teacher's role is one of facilitation. The teacher circulates while peers are tutoring one another. While the students are actively peer tutoring, the teacher equally awards and distributes bonus points by marking on the student point sheet. Additionally, the teacher provides specific verbal praise for appropriate tutoring behavior. The teacher also responds to student pairs that require assistance. This may be student-initiated assistance if a member of the student pair holds up a "help" card, or by the teacher-initiated if the teacher notices that a pair is having difficulty with an aspect of the tutoring process.

At the completion of the peer-tutoring sessions, the teacher shows the team point chart and asks students to call out the total number of points each pair earned for the day. Daily point totals help the teacher monitor level of implementation. Generally, daily point totals should increase during the course of a unit of

Practice each missed spelling word three times.			
Word	**1**	**2**	**3**
heard			
bear			
beloe	*below*	*below*	*below*
snowing			
storm			
forr	*forest*	*forest*	*forest*
popcorn			
under			
jump	*jumping*	*jumping*	*jumping*
heard			
bear			
below			

FIGURE 12.2. Tutee practice sheet for CWPT spelling.

material. Increased points indicate an improved fluency of unit content (i.e., more repetitions of the spelling list in a tutoring session). The sum of each tutor–tutee pair's points constitutes the two class team totals and determines the winning team for the day. The teacher praises the winning team and encourages the other team. Finally, the teacher awards some type of tangible "prize" (e.g., a special activity reward or privilege) to the winning team, such as being the first group of students to line up for recess or lunch.

The preceding description outlines what takes place during one day of CWPT spelling instruction. Over the course of an academic year, consistent implementation of these same CWPT procedures can translate into strong academic gains for children (see Figure 12.3). This graph illustrates 17 weeks of CWPT classroom spelling instruction in which the teacher closely followed implementation procedures. Note that average pretest scores for students were in the 30% range, and average posttest scores were in the 80–90% range. Through strong, consistent implementation, these students dramatically improved their spelling scores throughout the 17 weeks of instruction. However, like many evidence-based classroom strategies, consistent, long-lasting implementation can be challenging to achieve. Over the decade of our research into scaling up peer-mediated strategies, we have found that many factors unrelated to the actual instructional strategy procedures can have dramatic impacts on implementation fidelity, sustainability and, therefore, student outcomes.

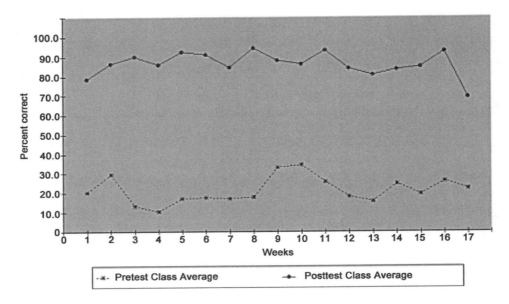

FIGURE 12.3. CWPT graph of mean class spelling accuracy over weeks for one teacher with high implementation fidelity.

Recommendations for Implementation

The struggle to translate educational research findings from the lab to the classroom has been well documented (Abbott, Walton, Tapia, & Greenwood, 1999; Cuban, 1990; Greenwood, & Abbott, 2001; Vaughn, Klingner, & Hughes, 2000). Because new evidence-based instructional strategies can take years to implement fully and integrate into school practices, evidenced-based strategies are often abandoned for other strategies that lack empirical support, or new strategies are modified to the point that they no longer resemble the original procedures that made them effective (Fixsen & Blase, 2009; Gersten, Vaughn, & Kim, 2004). Therefore, one aspect of CWPT research has been to identify implementation and sustainability barriers that exist at the classroom, system, or administrative levels. This work guides our current efforts to deliver CWPT professional development that offers built-in implementation and administrative support tools that streamline and encourage high-fidelity CWPT implementation.

Evidence–Based Recommendations to Improve Implementation and Sustainability

The recommendations that follow are the result of studies that investigated the usability and effectiveness of specific components of CWPT, including instructional strategies, and administration procedures and barriers that impede or prevent the implementation of these components. Careful implementation is important, because Greenwood and Finney (1993) reported that when research-validated CWPT procedures were not followed, there was a reduction in student achievement. Some of the procedural changes that decreased the effects of CWPT were variations in scripted interactions between tutors and tutees (Greenwood, Delquadri, & Hall, 1984), error-correction procedures (Harper, Mallette, Maheady, & Clifton, 1990), fewer than three CWPT sessions per week across academic weeks (Dinwiddie, Terry, Wade, & Thibadeau, 1982), use of content that did not challenge students, and conducting CWPT with only a portion of the class rather than classwide (Greenwood, Terry, Arreaga-Mayer, & Finney, 1992). Additionally, once teachers deviate from specified procedures, it is often difficult to improve fidelity of implementation. Such improvement usually requires extensive professional development and fidelity monitoring that are often costly and laborious, limiting CWPT's ability to become more widely implemented and to sustain long-term implementation. Widespread, sustainable implementation of peer-mediated strategies requires a built-in system of teacher and administrator accountability to fidelity of implementation in procedures, as well as in data collection and use.

Training

A strong recommendation that increases sustainability of peer-mediated strategies is training. In our experience, training requires a minimum of 1–3 days of professional development for teachers who have never implemented CWPT. During the first day of teacher training for general implementation, teachers trainees are introduced to the research base of CWPT; learn about the different materials, procedures and roles; watch video clips of students implementing CWPT; and practice the procedures of CWPT with a peer teacher during training.

During the practice phase of the training, teachers use the materials needed for CWPT implementation and participate in an actual learning experience with spelling words. In order to simulate a week's worth of CWPT, three back-to-back sessions of peer-tutoring practice occur. Prior to peer-tutoring practice, teachers take a spelling pretest on a list of challenging spelling words (e.g., *gallimaufry, diarrhea, ptomaine, chauffer, acquiescence*). The teacher trainees are divided into peer pairs, assigned to one of two teams, and review materials to be used during tutoring. During tutoring practice, pairs follow the tutoring procedures, and the CWPT trainers circulate around the room, award bonus points, and remind teachers of procedures as needed. Between each tutoring segment, questions about procedures are discussed. After peer-tutoring practice, the teacher trainees report points and take the posttest. Pre- and posttests are graded and trainees have the opportunity to see the improvement in their spelling scores as a result of peer tutoring.

CWPT Reading

For school personnel who want to implement CWPT for reading instruction, a second day of training is recommended. During CWPT Reading training, teachers learn the difference between CWPT Reading and other subject matter, decide on a student pre- and postassessment plan that will work within their classroom and school environment, and learn how to create pre- and postreading assessments. CWPT Reading is different from other content areas, in that it requires both oral reading and comprehension segments of instruction. These activities increase the daily time spent on CWPT and require more teacher preparation, because the teacher prepares daily (as opposed to weekly) passages that will be read by students and also creates appropriate comprehension questions that pertain to the passages and fit the level of student development.

During CWPT Reading, peer-tutoring pairs first read the passage assigned by the teacher. The passage should be long enough that students make progress toward unit completion and also short enough that the average student is able to read the complete passage two times during the peer-tutoring day. For a student who is unable to read the entire passage twice, a portion of the passage is read repeatedly. This student is paired with a more advanced reader, which enables the slower reader to gain oral reading mastery on a short passage, then hear the more advanced reader read the remainder of the passage, so that comprehension of the entire passage is possible. The second segment of CWPT reading is comprehension. During the comprehension segments, students quiz each other on predetermined questions created by the teacher. These questions are prepared by the teacher prior to the peer tutoring session.

For CWPT reading, teachers need to select a method for pre- and posttesting of reading passages. Assessment data drive the selection of content used for instruction and are significantly linked to suitable student reading progress; however, it is unrealistic to think that teachers will find time weekly to collect individual students' pre- and postreading assessments. Therefore, an acceptable, manageable system of pre- and postreading assessment must be determined. The CWPT teacher's manual explains in detail the assessment options (Greenwood, Delquadri, et al., 2001; for more information about the full CWPT Learning Management System teacher manual, visit *www.jgcp.ku.edu/~jgcp/products/CWPT-LMS/ projectinfo/cwpt-lms_info.htm*). Usually, teachers choose a staggered approach in which students are pre- and postassessed every 2 to 3 weeks. Such assessments are usually created using the school district's reading curriculum.

Fidelity

In order to ensure that procedures are being implemented with high fidelity, CWPT implementation needs to be observed, with teachers receiving feedback about their quality of implementation. Data collection on fidelity of implementation is a critical aspect of CWPT that is ongoing. Because this requires administrative staff time and specific knowledge about the instructional strategy, collection of fidelity data can often be a challenging aspect of the implementation process.

Research into streamlining evaluation of implementation fidelity led to the creation of the CWPT Learning Management System (CWPT-LMS) software tool

(Abbott, Greenwood, Buzhardt, & Tapia, 2006; Greenwood, Hou, et al., 2001), which monitors and provides a record of different aspects of fidelity during CWPT implementation, including number of weekly sessions of implementation, time spent on CWPT during each session, and aspects of how instruction affects student outcomes. Through use of classwide and individual student data, the CWPT-LMS's Advisor tool evaluates implementation and provides teachers with specific recommendations regarding their use of CWPT and how to optimize student outcomes. Recommendations from the Advisor include identification of students who fail to make expected gains or are not being challenged by the instructional content. The Advisor also conducts more complex analyses that consider point allocations and pretest scores to identify students who may be awarding too many or too few points, which is indicative of improper tutoring procedures (e.g., point cheating, improper error-correction procedures, and unresponsiveness to the material).

In addition to providing teachers with data-based advice, the CWPT-LMS offers tools that make it easier to adhere to best practices. For example, the CWPT-LMS provides teachers with a way to group students automatically on the class roster into tutoring pairs according to skill level (recommended), randomly, or manually. The CWPT-LMS also allows teachers to calculate and graph pretest–posttest gains, tutoring points, and average performance by student and week. Studies (Greenwood, Delquadri, & Bulgren, 1993; Greenwood & Finney, 1993; Greenwood, Hou, et al., 2001) indicate that this technology improves the fidelity of CWPT implementation procedures, thus helping to maintain consistent improvements in student outcomes across a wide range of students and teachers.

Sustained Schoolwide, High-Quality Implementation

In addition to increased fidelity of implementation within the classroom, a final recommendation is to establish a schoolwide effort to improve and encourage sustainability. Recent research on CWPT has focused on identifying the barriers and facilitators to schoolwide implementation, including those that inhibit or slow down full implementation (Abbott et al., 2006; Buzhardt, Abbott, Greenwood, & Tapia, 2005). It has been well established that any school- or districtwide reform effort requires strong support from all levels of personnel, from the principal and teachers to the students and parents (Carnine, 1997; Elmore, 1996; Greenwood & Abbott, 2001). Figure 12.4 shows the CWPT Administrative Adoption Model, which describes the top-down personnel support structure recommended for CWPT. The key to this model is a strong advocate for CWPT at the top, who plans CWPT professional development activities, coordinates schoolwide preparation of CWPT materials before each academic year, and ensures that CWPT is being implemented with high fidelity. We have found that when the CWPT Site Coordinator is an upper-level administrator and a strong advocate, CWPT implementation occurs much faster and survives longer (Abbott et al., 2006; Buzhardt, Greenwood, Abbott, & Tapia, 2006).

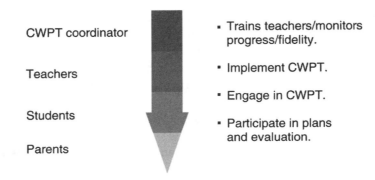

CWPT coordinator · Trains teachers/monitors
progress/fidelity.

Teachers · Implement CWPT.

· Engage in CWPT.

Students · Participate in plans
and evaluation.

Parents

FIGURE 12.4. Administrative/adoption model for implementing CWPT within a school.

Additionally, Table 12.3 describes the primary components, activities, and personnel our research has identified as critical for successful implementation in *most* school settings under almost *any* conditions (Buzhardt et al., 2006). It is important to keep in mind that each school has a unique set of challenges and sometimes situations that may preclude the need for one or more of these recommendations. In summary, systematic training, collection of fidelity of implementation information, and a focus on the factors of school- and districtwide implementation improves the likelihood of full, sustainable implementation of peer-mediated strategies.

Discussion

Our purpose in this chapter has been to provide an overview of PALS and CWPT peer-mediated strategies, and the research behind those approaches, and to outline the components of instructional implementation and provide recommendations to improve implementation efforts. As schools struggle to meet increased accountability for student academic achievement, peer-mediated strategies provide an evidenced-based Tier 1 method for responding to a wide variety of academic needs. The flexibility of peer-mediated strategies across varying student groups and content areas provides a unique way to differentiate instruction by using peers as teachers. The role of monitoring implementation of instruction allows classroom teachers to facilitate and orchestrate increased student opportunities to respond and practice essential skills and subject content. On a broader scale, a peer-mediated strategy focused at the Tier 1 level equips schools and districts with a model that potentially reduces the number of students who require Title and Special Education services. As with any intervention, the good news is that it works when implemented well, and the bad news is that strong implementation can be a time-consuming, effortful process. Our research indicates that

TABLE 12.3. Recommended Practices for Sustained CWPT Implementation

Recommendation	Ideal parameters	Minimum parameters
CWPT site coordinator	Experienced administrator (e.g., vice principal, Special Education coordinator, etc.)	Experienced CWPT teacher
Use of CWPT-LMS	Use by each teacher, and administrative CWPT-LMS for CWPT coordinator	Use by each CWPT teacher
Site coordinator training	Onsite training and consultation by experienced CWPT Coordinator	Thorough review of CWPT training materials and distance consultation
Teacher CWPT training and preparation	One- to 2-day professional development by an experienced CWPT coordinator	N/A
Begin classroom implementation early	Begin implementation at the beginning of the academic year	Begin implementation upon return from winter break
Early and continuous communication between teacher and coordinators	Weekly or biweekly coordinator consultations with teachers	Monthly coordinator consultations with teachers
Technology/computer support	Onsite technology support	Outsourced technology support or teacher with advanced computer experience

peer-mediated strategies work best when a schoolwide or districtwide system is established in which buy-in is from students all the way through the highest levels of school district administration, and that full implementation may take multiple years of concentrated effort (Fixsen & Blase, 2009).

The Future of Peer–Mediated Strategies

Peer-mediated strategies can be expanded to meet the academic needs of more diverse groups of students across different subject matters. This can be especially true in content areas for which proficient reading is essential. For example, a recent middle school study of social studies classrooms reports results that favor CWPT on weekly quizzes (Kamps et al., 2008). In the CWPT classrooms, students tutored each other during text reading and while working on study guides. Because reading is integral to nearly all academic content, peer-mediated strategies have the potential to provide a strong Tier 1 treatment intervention across grade levels and content areas.

The future of peer-mediated strategies at the Tier 2 and Tier 3 levels is not as clear. One advantage of implementing peer-mediated strategies at the Tier 1 level is that mixing of student peer pairs at different academic levels provides the opportunity for high-achieving peers to model instructional content for low-achieving peers. At Tier 2 and Tier 3 levels of instruction, high-achieving peers are not available. This challenge became evident in an experimental study that examined the efficacy of alternative PALS Tier 2 interventions. McMaster, Fuchs, Fuchs, and Compton (2005) reported that students identified for Tier 2 intervention who received the unmodified PALS intervention performed less well than Tier 2 students who received modified PALS instruction that was adult-directed. More study is required to evaluate alternative modifications to peer-mediated strategies at Tiers 2 and 3. It may be that cross-age or adult-directed tutoring is needed at Tiers 2 and 3.

Finally, for Tier 1 classroom instruction, we envision technology as a potential remedy for some challenges in attaining full implementation. By moving assessment databases and decision-making tools to Web-based formats, information about the process and speed of implementation can be streamlined. With online data systems, teachers have more immediate access to their students' outcome data and tools that support their analysis and interpretation of those data (e.g., graphs and reports) for data-based decision making. Administrators can have this information for all classrooms. Online databases also address issues of accountability, in that they provide a written, real-time record of implementation and the resulting outcomes.

It can be difficult in educational settings to find instructional strategies that students enjoy, that allow classroom teachers to differentiate instruction to meet the needs of all students, and that improve student outcomes. Peer-mediated strategies provide an evidenced-based Tier 1 strategy for classroom teachers to make a big difference in the academic lives of their students.

References

Abbott, M., Greenwood, C., Buzhardt, J., & Tapia, Y. (2006). Using technology-based teacher support tools to scale up the classwide Peer Tutoring program. *Reading and Writing Quarterly, 22,* 47–64.

Abbott, M., Walton, C., Tapia, Y., & Greenwood, C. R. (1999). Research to practice: A blueprint for closing the gap in local schools. *Exceptional Children, 65,* 339–352.

Bender, W. N. (2002). *Differentiating instruction for students with learning disabilities: Best teaching practices for general and special educators.* Thousand Oaks, CA: Corwin Press.

Bowman-Perrott, L. J., Greenwood, C. R., & Tapia, Y. (2007). The efficacy of CWPT used in secondary alternative school classrooms with small teacher/pupil ratios and students with emotional and behavioral disorders. *Education and Treatment of Children, 30,* 65–87.

Buzhardt, J., Abbott, M., Greenwood, C., & Tapia, Y. (2005). Usability testing of the Classwide Peer Tutoring Learning Management System. *Journal of Special Education Technology, 20,* 19–29.

Buzhardt, J., Greenwood, C., Abbott, M., & Tapia, Y. (2006). Rate of implementation progress: A formative measure of scaling up evidence-based instruction. *Educational Technology Research and Development, 54,* 467–492.

Carnine, D. (1997). Bridging the research-to-practice gap. *Exceptional Children, 63,* 513–521.

Cohen, J. (1988). *Statistical power analysis for the behavioral sciences* (2nd ed.). Hillsdale, NJ: Erlbaum.

Cuban, L. (1990). Reforming again, again and again. *Educational Researcher, 19*, 3–13.

Delquadri, J., Greenwood, C. R., Stretton, K., & Hall, R. V. (1983). The peer tutoring spelling game: A classroom procedure for increasing opportunity to respond and spelling performance. *Education and Treatment of Children, 6*, 225–239.

Dinwiddie, G., Terry, B., Wade, L., & Thibadeau, S. (1982). *The effects of peer tutoring and teacher instructional allocation on academic achievement outcomes.* Poster presented at the 8th annual meeting of the Association for Behavior Analysis, Milwaukee, WI.

Elmore, R. (1996). Getting to scale with good educational practice. *Harvard Educational Review, 66*, 1–26.

Fixsen, D. L., & Blase, K. A. (2009). *Implementation: The missing link between research and practice* (NIRN Implementation Brief No. 1). Chapel Hill: University of North Carolina.

Fuchs, D., Fuchs, L. S., Mathes, P. G., & Simmons, D. C. (1997). Peer-assisted learning strategies: Making classrooms more responsive to diversity. *American Educational Research Journal, 34*, 174–206.

Fuchs, D., Fuchs, L. S., Thompson, A., Al Otaiba, S., Yen, L., Yang, N., et al. (2001). Is reading important in reading-readiness programs?: A randomized field trial with teachers as program implementers. *Journal of Educational Psychology, 93*, 251–267.

Fuchs, D., Fuchs, L. S., Thompson, A., Svenson, E., Yen, L., Al Otaiba, S., et al. (2002). Peer-assisted learning strategies in reading: Extensions for kindergarten, first grade and high school. *Remedial and Special Education, 22*, 15–21.

Fuchs, L. S., Fuchs, D., & Kazdan, S. (1999). Effects of Peer-Assisted Learning Strategies on high school students with serious reading problems. *Remedial and Special Education, 20*, 309–318.

Gersten, R., Vaughn, S., & Kim, A.-H. (2004). Introduction: Special issue on sustainability. *Remedial and Special Education, 25*, 3–4.

Ginsburg-Block, M. D., Rohrbeck, C. A., & Fantuzzo, J. W. (2006). A meta-analytic review of the social, self-concept and behavioral conduct outcomes of peer assisted learning. *Journal of Educational Psychology, 98*, 732–749.

Greenwood, C. R. (1991). Longitudinal analysis of time engagement and academic achievement in at-risk and non-risk students. *Exceptional Children, 57*, 521–535.

Greenwood, C. R., & Abbott, M. (2001). The research to practice gap in special education. *Teacher Education and Special Education, 24*, 276–289.

Greenwood, C. R., Arreaga-Mayer, C., Utley, C. A., Gavin, K., & Terry, B. J. (2001). ClassWide Peer Tutoring Learning Management System: Applications with elementary-level English language learners. *Remedial and Special Education, 22*, 34–47.

Greenwood, C. R., Carta, J. J., Whorton, D., & Hall, R. V. (1988). The use of Classwide Peer Tutoring strategies in classroom management and instruction. *School Psychology Review, 17*, 258–275.

Greenwood, C. R., & Delquadri, J. (1995). Classwide Peer Tutoring and the prevention of school failure. *Preventing School Failure, 39*, 21–25.

Greenwood, C. R., Delquadri, J., & Bulgren, J. (1993). Current challenges to behavioral technology in the reform of schooling: Large-scale high-quality implementation and sustained use of effective educational practices. *Education and Treatment of Children, 16*, 401–440.

Greenwood, C. R., Delquadri, J., & Hall, R. V. (1984). Opportunity to respond and student academic performance. In W. L. Heward, T. E. Heron, J. Trap-Porter, & D. S. Hill (Eds.), *Focus on behavior analysis in education* (pp. 58–88). Columbus, OH: Merrill.

Greenwood, C. R., Delquadri, J., & Hall, R. V. (1989). Longitudinal effects of Classwide Peer Tutoring. *Journal of Educational Psychology, 81*, 371–383.

Greenwood, C. R., Delquadri, J., Hou, L. S., Terry, B. J., Arreaga-Mayer, C., & Abbott, M. (2001). *Together we can: Classwide Peer Tutoring—Learning Management System (CWPT-LMS) teacher's manual.* Kansas City: University of Kansas, Juniper Gardens Children's Project.

Greenwood, C. R., & Finney, R. (1993). Monitoring, improving and maintaining quality implementation of the Classwide Peer Tutoring using behavioral and computer technology. *Education and Treatment of Children, 16,* 19–29.

Greenwood, C. R., Hou, L.-S., Delquadri, J., Terry, B., & Arreaga-Mayer, C. (2001). Classwide Peer Tutoring programs: A learning management system, *Technology, Curriculum, and Professional Development, 4,* 61–86.

Greenwood, C. R., Kamps, D., Terry, B., & Linebarger, D. (2007). Primary intervention: A means of preventing special education. In C. Haager, J. Klingner, & S. Vaughn (Eds.), *Validated reading practices for three tiers of intervention* (pp. 73–106). New York: Brookes.

Greenwood, C. R., Maheady, L., & Delquadri, J. (2002). Classwide Peer Tutoring. In M. R. Shinn, H. M. Walker, & G. Stoner (Eds.), *Interventions for achievement and behavior problems* (2nd ed., pp. 611–649). Washington, DC: National Association for School Psychologists.

Greenwood, C. R., Terry, B., Arreaga-Mayer, C., & Finney, R. (1992). The Classwide Peer Tutoring program: Implementation factors moderating students' achievement. *Journal of Applied Behavior Analysis, 25,* 101–116.

Greenwood, C. R., Terry, B. J., Utley, C. A., Montagna, D., & Walker, D. (1993). Achievement, placement and services: Middle school benefits of Classwide Peer Tutoring used at the elementary school. *School Psychology Review, 22,* 497–516.

Harper, G., Mallette, B., Maheady, L., & Clifton, R. (1990). Applications of peer tutoring to arithmetic and spelling. *Direct Instruction News, 9,* 34–38.

Harper, G. F., Mallette, B., & Moore, J. (1991). Peer-mediated instruction: Teaching spelling to primary school children with mild disabilities. *Journal of Reading, Writing, and Learning Disabilities International, 7,* 137–151.

Herring-Harrison, T. J., Gardner, R., & Lovelace, T. S. (2007). Adapting peer tutoring for learners who are deaf or hard of hearing, *Intervention in School and Clinic, 43,* 82–87.

Kame'enui, E., & Simmons, D. (2008). *The schoolwide model* (DIBELS resources 2008). University of Oregon, Retrieved September 13, 2010, from *dibels.uoregon.edu/swm/index.php.*

Kamps, D., Barbetta, P. M., Leonard, B. R., & Delquadri, J. (1994). Classwide Peer Tutoring: An integration strategy to improve reading skills and promote peer interactions among students with autism and general education peers. *Journal of Applied Behavior Analysis, 27,* 49–61.

Kamps, D., Greenwood, C. R., Arreaga-Mayer, C., Veerkamp, M. B., Utley, C., Tapia, Y., et al. (2008). The efficacy of Classwide Peer Tutoring in middle schools. *Education and Treatment of Children, 31,* 119–152.

Mathes, P. G., Clancy-Menchetti, J., & Torgesen, J. K. (2001). *Kindergarten Peer-Assisted Literacy Strategies (K-PALS).* Longmont, CO: Sopris West.

Mathes, P. G., Torgesen, J. K., & Allor, J. H. (2001). The effects of Peer Assisted Learning Strategies for first grade readers with and without additional computer assisted instruction in phonological awareness. *American Educational Research Journal, 38,* 371–410.

McMaster, K. L., Fuchs, D., Fuchs, L. S., & Compton, D. L. (2005). Responding to nonresponders: An experimental field trial of identification and intervention methods. *Exceptional Children, 71,* 445–463.

McMaster, K. L., Kung, H., Han, I., & Cao, M. (2008). Peer-Assisted Learning Strategies: A

"Tier 1" approach to promoting responsiveness to beginning reading instruction for English learners. *Exceptional Children, 74,* 194–214.

Pressley, A. J., & Hughes, C. (2000). Peers as teachers of anger management to high school students with behavioral disorders. *Behavioral Disorders, 25,* 114–130.

Rohrbeck, C. A., Ginsburg-Block, M. D., Fantuzzo, J. W., & Miller, T. R. (2003). Peer-assisted learning interventions with elementary school students: A meta-analytic review. *Journal of Educational Psychology, 95,* 240–257.

Spencer, V. G., Scruggs, T. E., & Mastropieri, M. A. (2003). Content area learning in middle school social studies classrooms and students with emotional or behavioral disorders: A comparison of strategies, *Behavioral Disorders, 28,* 77–93.

Van Norman, R. K. (2007). "Who's on first?": Designing a sports trivia peer tutoring program to teach and support conversations between peers. *Intervention in School and Clinic, 43,* 88–100.

Vaughn, S., Klingner, J., & Hughes, M. (2000). Sustainability of research-based practices. *Exceptional Children, 66,* 163–171.

What Works Clearinghouse. (2006). *What Works Clearinghouse intervention reports.* Retrieved September 13, 2010, from *ies.ed.gov/ncee/wwc.*

13

Supplemental Reading Instruction by Paraeducators and Tutors

Recent Research and Applications

PATRICIA F. VADASY

In schools that serve large numbers of students with diverse instructional needs, teachers face the difficult challenge to increase reading achievement for all of their students. Teachers often find themselves concerned about a handful of students for whom they would like to offer more assistance. These may be students whose families are unable to provide important language and literacy experiences that lay foundations for learning to read. These may be students who are struggling to keep up with grade-level expectations for early literacy foundation skills. Or these may be students who receive special education or bilingual education services, yet continue to make very slow progress in word identification or fluency. Even when classroom and specialist resources have been fully tapped, teachers look for ways to provide more intensive attention to students who experience problems learning to read.

Often schools find ways to offer supplemental reading instruction or tutoring to their neediest students. In high needs or Title I schools, tutoring may be provided in coordination with community agencies, the federal America Reads program, the school Parent–Teacher–Student Association (PTSA), or building-level parent volunteers. Because resources to coordinate and evaluate carefully the effectiveness of this type of tutoring are usually limited, this added instruction may often be less effective than it otherwise might be.

Earlier chapters in this book clearly outline empirical findings that support effective classroom instructional approaches in reading foundation skills such as word reading or fluency. Research findings on supplemental reading instruction also provide a guide to practitioners who want to increase instructional intensity for struggling readers.

This chapter reviews research from the last decade on tutoring and supplemental instruction in reading. These research findings may, first, provide guideposts for how to add more effective and necessary instruction and practice for struggling students. Second, the findings may help schools consider ways to supplement limited specialist time. Third, the findings support ways in which paraeducators in particular can be effectively utilized in high needs schools. The studies describe effects of particular interventions on students' reading skills. Finally, as Gelzheiser (2005b) points out, research on supplemental tutoring, because it has the flexibility to address questions of intensity, tutor experience, and reading skill targets, may also help to inform remedial and special education instruction for children with reading difficulties. Many of these studies add to our knowledge of instructional content and design features that address the needs of struggling readers.

One of the underlying questions that research on supplemental tutoring addresses is the potential instructional efficacy of nonteacher tutors. In most of the studies that follow, these tutors are "paraeducators," school staff members that are most widely utilized to deliver supplemental reading instruction. Schools increasingly employ paraeducators (also called "instructional aides," or "teacher assistants"). In fall of 2004, 707,028 instructional aides were employed in U.S. public schools (National Center for Education Statistics, 2007a). Most of these staff members (75%) work in elementary schools (Northwest Regional Educational Laboratory, 1999). Between 1980 and 2005 the numbers of instructional assistants employed in public schools increased by 114% (National Center for Education Statistics, 2007b). This review on supplemental instruction focuses on instructional assistants, because they often work with bilingual and Title I students, and furthermore, are often personally involved in and committed to their school community (Darling-Hammond, 1998). This review does not include studies of supplemental instruction provided by volunteer and typically unpaid tutors (see meta-analysis by Ritter, Barnett, Denny, & Albin, 2009). Nor does this review include studies on supplemental instruction delivered by certificated teachers, researchers, or graduate students—individuals who would not be available to tutor in most school settings.

Most of the intervention studies in this review target alphabetic, phonological, phonics, and fluency skills—early literacy skills in which students often need more explicit intensive instruction or practice opportunities. In contrast to these early reading skills, supplemental reading instruction in comprehension skills for older students necessarily increases in complexity and skilled diagnosis of underlying problems. When a tutor is enlisted to work with a student on comprehension skills, lower-level skills deficits must often be addressed. Without more extensive training, many tutors are not prepared to detect and adapt their instruction to address these deficits. For example, comprehension problems may be due to poor word identification skills for one student and to limited oral language skills for another. Not surprisingly, research on effective supplemental comprehension interventions is more limited. It should be noted that many supplemental interventions in this review include some comprehension activities, although comprehension is not the primary skill target.

These research findings are presented with one caveat: Most of the studies that follow have *not* measured the direct effects of tutoring on student motivation. Over two decades of working with paraeducator tutors we have found that these interventions are often a source of motivation for discouraged and struggling students. The power of the relationship that develops between students and tutors in one-to-one and small-group instruction is difficult for researchers to measure, yet is frequently part of the student (and tutor) experience. Although we have not measured motivation outcomes in our research, we and the tutors in our studies have noted changes in students' self-efficacy and confidence in their ability to read well. This is an area that calls for more careful measurement.

In the summaries that follow, key features of interventions are listed, as well as fidelity of implementation when available. To maintain a focus in this chapter on intervention features and variables, treatment effectiveness is summarized broadly in terms of effect sizes for specific reading outcomes. Readers should refer to the original studies for more fine-grained information about research designs and statistical analyses.

Many supplemental reading interventions for struggling and at-risk students are delivered to individual students. Elbaum, Vaughn, Hughes, and Moody (2000) conducted a meta-analysis of research on supplemental one-to-one reading interventions delivered by adults to at-risk students. They considered the immediate reading gains and intervention features associated with intervention effectiveness. Although most of the interventions in this review were delivered by teachers or volunteers (only one of the interventions was delivered by paraeducators), the review provides general support for individual tutoring in reading and identifies features of interventions associated with positive reading outcomes. The researchers found the overall mean weighted effect size for a total of 42 effect sizes from 29 treatment–control studies was $d = 0.41$. The effect size for college student tutors was $d = 1.65$; that for teacher tutors was $d = 0.36$, and that for community volunteer tutors $d = 0.26$. Tutoring was found to be most effective for students in grades 1 ($d = 0.46$) and 2–3 ($d = 0.37$) (no kindergarten interventions were included in this review). Elbaum et al. (2000) found that average effect sizes were largest for reading comprehension interventions ($d = 2.41$), and moderate for phonemic awareness–phonics interventions ($d = 0.44$).

The more recent studies reported here have added considerably to our understanding of reading outcomes for students who receive supplemental tutoring in specific reading skills. Two features in particular characterize these recent tutoring studies. First, many of these studies utilize paraeducator tutors, making the findings of practical importance to many schools. Second, a growing awareness of alphabetic and phonological prerequisites for learning to read and the effectiveness of kindergarten instruction in these skills has resulted in a large research base on kindergarten supplemental interventions. Many interventions used in these studies include instruction in more than one skill, however; they are organized into four areas that reflect their primary instructional focus: alphabetics, phonological awareness, phonics, and fluency. In several cases when the intervention cuts across several reading skills, this is noted. Each study is briefly described to highlight reading skills targets, intervention intensity, treatment fidelity, and effect sizes for primary student outcomes. Table 13.1 summarizes key features of these studies.

Alphabetics

Alphabetic and phonological skills were targets in a kindergarten prereading intervention evaluated for its effectiveness with two cohorts of children at risk for both behavior disorders and reading difficulties (Nelson, Benner, & Gonzalez, 2005; Nelson, Stage, Epstein, & Pierce, 2005). In both studies, paraeducator tutors were trained to implement a supplemental literacy intervention, Stepping Stones to Literacy (Nelson, Cooper, & Gonzalez, 2004), designed for use by nonteachers. The tutors were provided a background on the importance of the intervention's target literacy skills: matching sounds to symbols, letter identification, phonological awareness, and serial processing of visual stimuli. Trainers modeled the instructional activities. Tutors practiced using the lessons with trainer feedback, then demonstrated teaching several lessons. Tutors were required to demonstrate 90% implementation fidelity before they were assigned to students.

Stepping Stones to Literacy (Nelson et al., 2004) consists of 25 scripted lessons, with additional serial processing activities. Instruction may be provided to small groups or individual students. Lessons are designed for 10–20 minutes of daily guided activities and practice in the following skills:

- *Identification, manipulation, and memory of environmental sounds.* Children practice listening for animal names, matching animal names and animal sounds, identifying sequences of sounds, and identifying sounds missing from a sequence.

- *Letter naming and sentence meaning.* Children practice identifying the content of a sentence in a nursery rhyme, generating descriptions of pictures, pointing to and naming letters presented in a left-to-right format, practicing letter naming for 1 minute, and reviewing letter names.

- *Phonological awareness.* Children practice identifying words that rhyme, generating rhyming words, clapping the words in a nursery rhyme, blend-

TABLE 13.1.

Primary target reading skills	Grade level	Study	Intervention	Tutor: student ratio	Tutor type	Intensity	Effect sizes (*d*) for study outcomes	What Works Clearinghouse rating of effectiveness
Alphabetics	K	Nelson, Benner, et al. (2005)	*Stepping Stones to Literacy*	1:1	Paraeducators	42 sessions	Phonological awareness: 1.13 Word reading: 1.32 Rapid naming: 1.0	+30 across both studies
		Nelson, Stage, et al. (2005)	*Stepping Stones to Literacy*	1:1	Paraeducators	62 sessions	Phonological awareness: 0.58 Word ID: 0.94 Word attack: 0.92 Letter naming fluency: 0.79	See above
Mixed: Phonological awareness, alphabetics, decoding, comprehension	1	Ehri et al. (2007)	*Reading Rescue*	1:1	Paraeducators, reading specialists, teachers	26 weeks	Phoneme segmenting: 0.81 Pseudoword reading: 1.09 Sight word reading: 0.61 Comprehension: 0.96	NA
	K–3	Gunn et al. (2005)	*Reading Mastery, Corrective Reading*	1:2–3	Instructional assistants	2 years	Word attack: 0.38 Oral reading fluency: 0.24 Reading comprehension: 0.29 Vocabulary: 0.28	NA
	1	Lane et al. (2007)	*Phonological Awareness Training in Reading*	1:4	Paraeducators	15 hours	Phonological awareness: 0.71 Nonword fluency: 0.40	NA
	2	O'Shaughnessy & Swanson (2000)	*Phonological Awareness Training in Reading vs. Word Analogy*	1:5	Paraeducators	9 hours	PATR effects—Phonological awareness: 2.15 Word list reading: 1.73 WAT effects—Phonological awareness: 1.37 Word list reading: 1.64	NA

Alphabetics, phonics

	Study	Program	Ratio	Tutor	Hours	Findings	Notes
1 (at risk)	Hatcher et al. (2006)	*Reading Recovery* adaptations	1:6	Teaching assistants	20 hours	Tutored students made significant gains in letter-sound knowledge, phoneme awareness, word reading, and spelling.	NA
1 (at risk)	Savage & Carless (2005)	Alphabetics, phonemic awareness, onset–rime	1:4	Teaching assistants	12 hours	Significantly greater gains for treatment students in phonological awareness, letter-sound knowledge, and decoding.	NA
1 (at risk)	Vadasy et al. (1997).	*Sound Partners*, beta version	1:1	Community tutors, parents	53 hours	Decoding: 0.47 Word reading: 0.31 Spelling and segmenting: 0.47	Average across studies: Alphabetics +21 Fluency +19 Comprehension +21
1 (at risk)	Vadasy et al. (2000)	*Sound Partners*, beta version	1:1	Community tutors	36 hours	Decoding: 1.16 Word reading: 0.69 Spelling: 0.84	
K (at risk)	Vadasy et al. (2006a)	*Sound Partners*, kindergarten adaptation	1:1	Paraeducators	28 hours	Word reading accuracy: 1.02 Oral reading fluency rate: 0.81 Word reading efficiency: 0.61 Developmental spelling: 0.57	
K (at risk)	Vadasy & Sanders (2008)	*Sound Partners*, kindergarten adaptation	1:2	Paraeducators	28 hours	Phonological awareness: 0.59 Word reading accuracy: 0.63 Oral reading fluency: 0.46 Spelling: 0.49 Comprehension: 0.41	
K (at risk)	Vadasy & Sanders (2009a)	*Sound Partners*, kindergarten adaptation	1:1	Paraeducators	26 hours	Alphabetics: 0.83 Phonological awareness: 0.93 Decoding: 1.09 Word reading: 0.89	

(continued)

TABLE 13.1. (continued)

Primary target reading skills	Study	Grade level	Intervention	Tutor: student ratio	Tutor type	Intensity	Effect sizes (d) for study outcomes	What Works Clearinghouse rating of effectiveness
	Jenkins et al. (2004)	1 (at risk)	*Sound Partners* (2005) (using either decodable or nondecodable storybooks)	1:1	Paraeducators	50 hours	Decoding: 0.76 Word reading: 0.68 Fluency: 0.48 Comprehension: 0.81 Spelling: 0.62	
Fluency	Vadasy & Sanders (2008c)	2–3	*Quick Reads*	1:2	Paraeducators	25 hours	Word reading accuracy: 0.29 Fluency rate: 0.31 Passage reading fluency: 0.37	NA
	Vadasy & Sanders (2009b)	2–3	*Quick Reads*	1:2	Paraeducators and teachers	25 hours	Letter-sound knowledge: 0.41 Fluency: 0.37 Comprehension: 0.30	NA
	Vadasy & Sanders (2008a)	4–5	*Quick Reads*	1:2	Paraeducators	28 hours	Curriculum-based vocabulary: 0.42 Word comprehension: 0.27 Passage comprehension: 0.50	NA
Interventions for older readers	Gelzheiser (2005a)	4 (at risk)	Reading aloud from texts related to classroom social sciences	1:1	Community volunteers	46 hours	Major finding: Pretest decoding skills were correlated with reading gains.	NA

306

ing into a word two or more syllables spoken by the tutor, and blending into a word an onset and rime spoken by the tutor.

- *Phonemic awareness.* Children practice deleting a phoneme, identifying each phoneme, and segmenting the phonemes in words spoken by the tutor.
- *Serial processing.* Children practice naming arrays of objects, colors, letters, and numbers presented by the tutor.

Figure 13.1 shows a sample lesson format for teaching phonemic awareness, including the tutor script for teaching phoneme deletion (initial sounds) and phoneme identification for three-phoneme words. Stepping Stones lessons are designed for model–lead–test presentation, and error correction and progress tracking procedures are outlined in the instructor's manual. In both studies, the at-risk kindergarten students were randomly assigned to Stepping Stones or to a nonspecific core kindergarten literacy instruction.

In the first study (Nelson, Stage, et al., 2005), the Stepping Stones students received sixty-two 10- to 20-minute, one-to-one tutoring sessions. Children who received Stepping Stones made significantly greater gains in phonological awareness, word reading, and letter-naming skills compared to the children who received only core kindergarten literacy instruction. Effect sizes computed on mean posttest scores were large for word identification ($d = 0.94$), word attack ($d = 0.92$), and letter-naming fluency ($d = 0.79$), and were small to moderate for rapid naming ($d = 0.07$) and phonological awareness ($d = 0.58$). Tutor fidelity based on random independent observations averaged 98%. Important features of the instruction included clear instructional prompts to guide the teacher and effective error correction activities. In the second study (Nelson, Benner, et al., 2005), students in the Stepping Stones group received a total of forty-two 10- to 20-minute, one-to-one tutoring sessions. Nelson, Benner, et al. reported that the Stepping Stones students made significantly greater gains in phonological awareness (average $d = 1.13$), word reading ($d = 1.32$), and rapid naming ($d = 1.00$). Tutor fidelity using the lessons averaged 97%. In its review of Stepping Stones to Literacy, the What Works Clearinghouse (2007) determined the program to have positive effects in the area of alphabetics, with an average improvement index of +30 percentile points across these two studies.

Phonological Awareness

Several studies have evaluated the effectiveness of supplemental instruction with a focus on phonological skills. Lane, Fletcher, Carter, Dejud, and DeLorenzo (2007) trained a paraeducator to provide instruction to first graders at risk for behavior and emotional disorders, and with below-average reading skills. Students were randomly assigned to treatment and control groups. The paraeducator provided instruction to small groups of four students in 30-minute sessions, 3

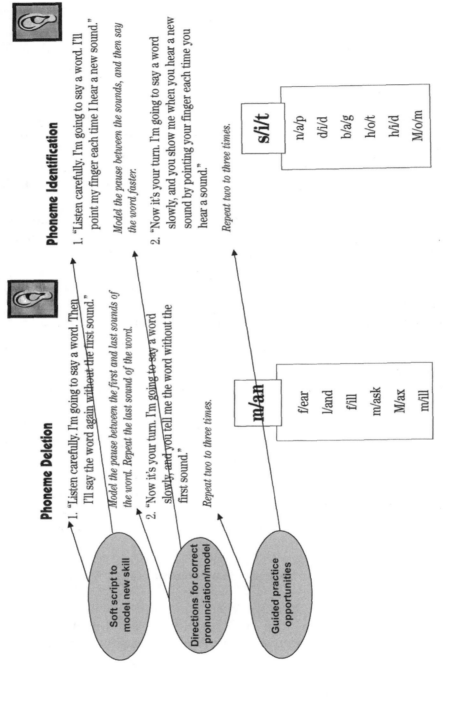

FIGURE 13.1. Sample lesson on teaching phonemic awareness. From *Stepping Stones to Literacy* by J. Ron Nelson, Penny Cooper, and Jorge Gonzalez (2004–2005). Reprinted with permission from Sopris West Educational Services.

days a week, for a total of 15 hours. The intervention, Phonological Awareness Training for Reading (PATR; Torgesen & Bryant, 1994), included instruction in rhyming, sound blending, sound segmenting, reading, and spelling. Treatment integrity averaged 95%. At posttest, the treatment students scored significantly higher than controls in phonological skills ($d = 0.71$), and reading effects maintained at a 4-week follow-up. As found in other reading interventions for students with both poor reading and behavior skills (Nelson, Benner, et al., 2005), the intervention did not have collateral effects on behavior.

The PATR intervention was also used in a treatment comparison study of supplemental instruction for second-grade students with reading disabilities (O'Shaughnessy & Swanson, 2000). At pretest, student reading scores were in the lower 10th percentile. Students were randomly assigned within schools to one of three treatment conditions: PATR, which featured instruction in rhyming, phoneme blending and segmenting, a small set of letters, reading, and spelling; Word Analogy Training (WAT) in rhyming, onset–rime blending, whole-word identification, word identification by analogy, and a compare-and-contrast strategy using key words, based in part on the Benchmark School Decoding Program; or, training in math skills. Paraeducator tutors received 10 hours of training in the programs and ongoing weekly supervision. Tutors worked with groups of five students for 30 minutes a day, 3 days a week, for 6 weeks. Treatment fidelity averaged 95%. Both the PATR and WAT programs resulted in significant reading gains. Effect sizes for the PATR instruction were 2.15 in phonological awareness and 1.73 in word list reading. Effect sizes for the WAT instruction were 1.37 in phonological awareness and 1.64 in word list reading. Students in both groups also demonstrated skills transfer in word attack, passage comprehension, and spelling. Effect sizes for students in the PATR treatment were 0.45 for word attack, 0.36 for passage comprehension, and 0.42 for spelling. Effect sizes for students in the WAT treatment were 0.47 for word attack, 0.65 for passage comprehension, and 0.65 for spelling. Average effect sizes for each intervention (compared to the math control group) across reading outcomes were greater than 1.0.

Finally, in a British study, Savage and Carless (2005) evaluated the efficacy of teaching assistants in one of four 9-week reading interventions. The lowest skilled 6-year-olds, identified based on a decoding, alphabetic, and phonological screening test, were assigned to one of four interventions: (1) instruction in phoneme segmenting, blending, and spelling of consonant–vowel–consonant (CVC) words; (2) instruction in generating words from rime families and applying an onset–rime strategy to read and spell the words; (3) a mixed program teaching both phonemic analysis and onset–rime word building; or (4) a control condition of classroom word-level instruction outlined by the National Literacy Strategy, including sight word and phonemic awareness instruction. All three intervention groups received instruction in letter–sound correspondence and phonological awareness activities that matched their respective phoneme or rhyme program. All three groups taught by the teaching assistants made significant progress in decoding, alphabetic, and phonological skills, and the phoneme-based group made significantly greater gains in letter-sound knowledge than the other groups. The authors noted that these effects were obtained by teaching assistants trained to use highly structured programs, and who received ongoing teacher supervision.

Phonics

A larger number of phonics-based interventions have been evaluated for use by paraeducators. Because schools serve a diversity of students at risk for poor reading outcomes, Gunn, Smolkowski, Biglan, Black, and Blair (2005) tested the efficacy of two published reading curricula for students in grades K–2 with behavior problems and early literacy deficits. The study sample included both Hispanic and non-Hispanic students. In this study, most of the tutors were instructional assistants trained to use either Reading Mastery (Engelmann & Bruner, 1988) or Corrective Reading (Engelmann, Carnine, & Johnson, 1988) to supplement classroom instruction in word recognition skills and reading practice. Both Reading Mastery and Corrective Reading are sequenced and scripted programs that use a Direct Instruction approach. The programs have carefully described placement and progress-monitoring procedures, and emphasize brisk instructional pacing. Eligible students were randomly assigned to treatment or control groups, with the treatment group receiving a three-part intervention: 30 minutes daily of supplemental reading instruction in groups of two or three students, parent training, and social skills instruction. Students received 2 years of intervention. The intervention group scored significantly higher at immediate posttest in word attack ($d = 0.38$), oral reading fluency ($d = 0.24$), reading comprehension ($d = 0.29$), and vocabulary ($d = 0.28$). At the 2-year follow-up, intervention students scored significantly higher than controls in letter–word identification ($d = 0.25$), oral reading fluency ($d = 0.29$), and reading comprehension ($d = 0.29$). The Hispanic students who received the supplemental instruction made similar or greater gains in skills than the non-Hispanic students, regardless of their initial English oral language proficiency skills. Fidelity of instruction was 90–100% across bimonthly observations. Although the interventions used in this study, Reading Mastery, and Corrective Reading were not specifically designed for use by nonteachers, the study demonstrated that instructional assistants—when provided with training—were able to implement these scripted reading programs effectively, with benefits for students across reading skills subsets. Both of these programs, which had been previously evaluated for small-group and whole-class use (Stahl & Miller, 1989), include critical alphabetic, decoding, and fluency components identified for inclusion in effective early reading programs, and incorporate features of effective instructional design (e.g., explicit skills instruction, teacher modeling, review cycles).

In our own work over the past decade, our research team has specifically addressed the question: What early reading skills are nonteacher or paraeducator tutors able to effectively supplement for young students at risk for reading disability? In 1994 we began to field-test a supplemental phonics intervention with at-risk first graders. We evaluated several iterations of this intervention in a series of small quasi-experimental studies. During that time we collected and incorporated informative tutor feedback and staff observations. We used this feedback to refine the tutor scripts to be as clear and concise as possible; adjust the scope, sequence, and cycles of review; and identify necessary training procedures and coaching strategies to prepare tutors to deliver instruction with a small repertoire of skills in effective scaffolding, pacing, and corrective feedback. The phonics intervention was later published as Sound Partners (Vadasy et al., 2005). More recently we have evaluated a kindergarten version of the instruction, as well as instruction in more advanced word reading skills for second and third graders with poor reading skills (Vadasy, Sanders, & Peyton, 2006b; Vadasy, Sanders, & Tudor, 2007). Figure 13.2 includes a sample Sound Partners lesson page, showing the tutor script on the right. The figure highlights design features that support effective tutor use, such as the scripted correction procedure for student errors in reading silent-*e* words.

In one of our early studies (Vadasy, Jenkins, Antil, Wayne, & O'Connor, 1997), we trained tutors drawn from the school community to provide individual phonologically based reading instruction to first graders who scored lowest on phonological and alphabetic screening measures. Most of these tutors were mothers of students in the research sites or high school students. The tutors were paid a nominal hourly wage. Students were randomly assigned within schools to tutoring or to a control group. Students received an average 53 hours of instruction in alphabetic, rhyming, blending, segmenting, spelling, and story reading practice in decodable texts. At posttest, the tutored students scored higher than the controls in decoding ($d = 0.47$), reading ($d = 0.31$), and spelling/segmenting ($d = 0.47$), with significant differences between groups on a nonword reading measure ($d = 0.70$) and a curriculum-based spelling measure ($d = 0.75$) favoring tutored students. When we examined the influence of tutor fidelity and compared the students with high-implementing tutors to a combined group of students with low-implementing tutors and controls, the effect sizes for the high-implementing tutors averaged 1.09 for word reading, 0.90 for decoding, and 0.68 for spelling/segmenting. We found no differences in the mean performance at posttest between the control and low-implementing tutor groups. These findings made clear the importance of tutor selection, training, and supervision.

In our next study (Vadasy, Jenkins, & Pool, 2000) we tested refinements in the instructional materials, including added tutor training and supervision, as well as maintenance of effects of tutoring. During this time we observed first-hand the challenges schools face in funding and coordinating community tutors. We understood the value of information on sustained effects that would help schools better weigh the costs and benefits of adding a supplemental tutoring program. In this intervention study, tutoring was again delivered by paid hourly tutors recruited from the school community. We used a quasi-random assignment procedure to assign students to treatment or control groups. Students received an average 36 hours of instruction. Treatment fidelity averaged 89%. At posttest,

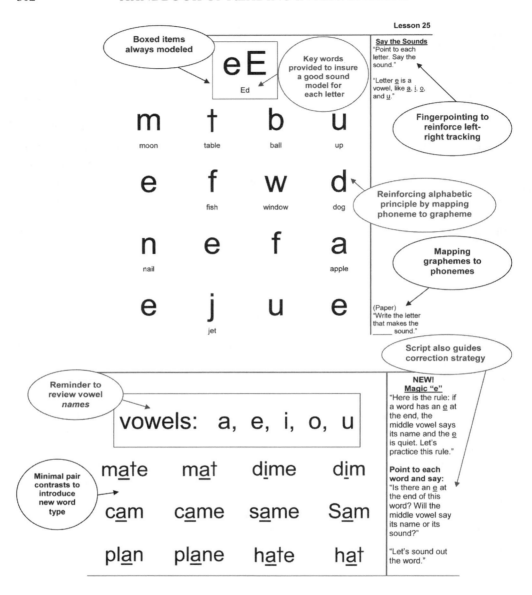

FIGURE 13.2. Sample phonics lesson. From *Sound Partners* by Patricia Vadasy, Susan Wayne, Rollanda O'Connor, Joseph Jenkins, Kathleen Pool, Mary Firebaugh, and Julia Peyton (2005). Reprinted with permission from Sopris West Educational Services.

tutored students scored significantly higher than the controls on most outcome measures, and effect sizes averaged $d = 0.69$ for reading, $d = 1.16$ for decoding, and $d = 0.84$ for spelling. We found that when students were tested at the end of second grade, the tutored students continued to score significantly higher than controls in decoding ($d = 0.87$) and spelling ($d = 0.82$). In a later follow-up study

(Vadasy, Sanders, & Abbott, 2008) of a second cohort of first graders who received Sound Partners tutoring, students maintained gains in word reading and fluency rate through the end of third grade.

Like many of the interventions in this review, Sound Partners includes multiple components that individually and collectively contribute to student outcomes. In a later first-grade study (Jenkins, Peyton, Sanders, & Vadasy, 2004) we examined the value of a particular component of the intervention. We compared the effects of using the Sound Partners phonics instruction with more decodable (based upon the letter–sound relations taught in the phonics lessons) versus less decodable texts in the storybook reading portion of the tutoring sessions. Although research suggests that decodable texts contribute to the effects of multicomponent reading interventions, the separate effects of text type had not previously been tested. At this point in time, Sound Partners (Vadasy et al., 2005) was in its final published form, and included the following phonics components.

- *Practicing letter–sound relations.* Instruction targeted the most common sounds associated with single letters and digraphs. Approximately one new letter–phoneme relation was introduced per lesson, along with a review of previously taught relations. Students also practiced writing letters and letter pairs.

- *Reading decodable words.* In each lesson, students practiced sounding out and reading eight to 20 words that comprised previously introduced letter sounds. Blending letter sounds was taught as a strategy until it was mastered, and students later read words independently and were encouraged to develop fluent word reading.

- *Spelling.* In each lesson students practiced spelling three words selected from the lesson's decodable words. Students were taught to stretch words into their constituent sounds and represent the sounds with written letters, then blend the written product into a spoken word.

- *Reading nondecodable words.* Students practiced reading high-frequency and sight words (that were not decodable in relation to the phonics taught up to that point) scheduled to appear in their text reading.

- *Oral text reading practice.* Students read aloud for 10–15 minutes per session from texts matched to the lessons. The more decodable books (primarily *Bob Books*; Maslen, 2003) were very carefully matched to the phonics skills sequence, and about 85% of unique words were decodable. The less decodable books (about 11% of unique words decodable) were drawn from several books in the Wright Group storybook series, and featured fewer words that were decodable based on previous phonics skills instruction.

Students were screened to score in the lower 25th percentile in reading, and assignment of students to treatment and control conditions was either by convenience or based on a random selection procedure. All tutored students were then randomly assigned within school to one of two treatment conditions (more vs. less decodable texts). Students received an average 25 weeks of individual tutoring. Treatment fidelity averaged 96%. At posttest, the combined treatment groups significantly outperformed controls on all reading and spelling outcomes. Effect sizes averaged $d = 0.76$ for decoding, and $d = 0.68$ for word reading. There were no differences between the two treatment groups (more-decodable or less-decodable texts), suggesting that many instructional variables overshadowed differences in the type of texts used in these tutoring sessions.

Having established a strong and consistent record for improving student reading outcomes in these first-grade studies, we undertook the evaluation of a kindergarten version of the intervention. During the course of our research on first-grade supplemental phonics instruction, we began to pilot-test a version of this instruction for kindergarten students. We intended this instruction for use beginning in midkindergarten, after children had been screened and had an opportunity to respond to initial classroom alphabetic and reading instruction. In a later randomized controlled trial (Vadasy, Sanders, & Peyton, 2006a), we evaluated the effects of this instruction. Kindergarten students averaging in November in the 10th to 25th percentile in receptive vocabulary, phonological awareness, and reading accuracy were randomly assigned to either individual tutoring or classroom literacy instruction. Tutoring was initiated in January, and students received an average 28 hours of instruction. Implementation fidelity ratings averaged 3.64 on a 4-point scale. At spring posttest, tutored students significantly outperformed controls in reading accuracy ($d = 1.02$), and oral reading fluency rate ($d = 0.81$), with moderate treatment effects for developmental spelling ($d = 0.57$). The kindergarten students maintained reading gains at follow-up at the end of first grade. In a replication study (Vadasy & Sanders, 2009a) with a new cohort of kindergarten students, treatment effects were also positive, with significant differences between treatment and control groups in: alphabetics ($d = 0.83$), phonological awareness ($d = 0.93$), decoding ($d = 1.09$), and word reading ($d = 0.89$). Finally, we compared the efficacy of this code-oriented instruction (based on Sound Partners) for kindergarten students tutored individually or in dyads (Vadasy & Sanders, 2008b). We found overall treatment effects in phonological awareness ($d = 0.59$), word reading accuracy ($d = 0.63$), oral reading fluency ($d = 0.46$), spelling ($d = 0.49$), and comprehension ($d = 0.41$). When we compared students tutored individually versus students tutored in dyads, we found they had similar outcomes. Together, this series of studies on supplemental kindergarten tutoring in phonics-based skills supports the benefits of this instruction across key early reading skills sets. Findings (Vadasy & Sanders, 2008b) also suggest that schools might arrange this tutoring for pairs of students in order to serve greater numbers of students.

In another kindergarten study that considered the effect of tutoring intensity, Al Otaiba, Schatschneider, and Silverman (2005) randomly assigned students at risk for reading difficulties into one of three intervention conditions: 30-minute tutoring sessions for 2 or 4 days per week that featured a focus on several reading skills, or a control condition of small group storybook reading 2 days per week. The tutoring intervention, Tutor-Assisted Intensive Learning Strategies (TAILS), based upon the Peer-Assisted Learning Strategies for Kindergarten (K-PALS; Fuchs et al., 2000) program, was specifically developed for use by nonteacher tutors. In addition to the basic phonological awareness and phonics skills taught in K-PALS, tutors also provided instruction in fluency, vocabulary, and comprehension. Tutors worked with students for 30 minutes a day for the school year. Tutors were recruited from the community; most had no previous tutoring experience, were paid, and were provided 13 hours of training. Fidelity of treatment averaged 97%. Students who were tutored 4 days a week made significantly greater gains in word identification ($d = 0.79$) and comprehension ($d = 0.90$) than students tutored 2 days a week. Students tutored 2 days a week made significantly greater improvement in sound-blending skills ($d = 0.68$) than students in the control group. The findings from this study suggest that a minimal level of tutoring intensity is required to detect treatment effects. The authors discussed the logistical challenges of recruiting tutors, and scheduling tutoring time and space in the research sites.

Finally, British researchers (Hatcher et al., 2006) compared the effectiveness of a more scripted versus a more individualized early literacy intervention for 6-year-olds performing at about the 25th percentile in reading. Students were matched on pretest measures and demographics, and assigned to tutoring from a teaching assistant in one of the two programs. Assignment was based on the program, or programs, offered in the participating schools. Teaching assistants in each group received 3 days of training, and teaching assistants in the Reading Intervention group received an additional five tutorials from the researchers during the intervention. Both programs were offered in 20-minute sessions that included elements adopted from the Reading Recovery program. The highly scripted Early Literacy Support program that included phonics, text reading, and writing was used by teaching assistants in 20 hours of small-group instruction with groups of six children. The Reading Intervention program content was determined by the teaching assistant and individualized to the child's reading development, including alphabetics, phonological awareness, phonics, reading and rereading, and writing. Children in the Reading Intervention program received 10 hours of small-group (groups of six students) and 10 hours of individual instruction (i.e., half of the intervention time was allocated for one-on-one instruction). Both groups made comparable gains in alphabetics, reading, and spelling, although the Reading Intervention group scored significantly higher at posttest in alphabetics. Overall, gains were maintained for 3 months after the intervention. Hatcher et al. noted that both programs were effectively implemented by teaching assistants, who were able to individualize the instruction successfully in the Reading Intervention approach for students with below average reading skills needing added support.

In summary, these studies identify the following features of supplemental

tutoring in early reading skills (alphabetics, phonological awareness, and phonics):

- Instruction is explicit and intensive, with learning goals that are clear to both tutor and student.
- Supplemental instruction in these early reading skills has been effectively implemented by paraeducator tutors.
- Features of effective interventions include scripted lessons and tutor training in high-fidelity instructional delivery.
- Large effect sizes in more recent studies support the benefits of supplementing instruction in phonics skills for at-risk kindergarten students.
- Effects of scripted phonics-based tutoring for at-risk kindergarten students appear comparable when implemented one-on-one or with dyads.
- Treatment effects for kindergarten and first-grade phonics-based tutoring appear to maintain at 1-year follow-up.

Fluency

Fluent reading reflects accurate and consolidated word reading skills and develops with practice. Fluency develops when word reading subskills are automatic and allow the student to retrieve words easily and allocate attention to the meaning of the text. Fluency is highly correlated with comprehension, and fluency deficits are often persistent and difficult to remediate (Kamps & Greenwood, 2005; O'Connor et al., 2002; Vadasy & Sanders, 2009b). Students who have difficulty learning to read often lose motivation to read because they struggle with the mechanics. They may have poor word reading skills, limited background knowledge, and less well-developed language skills. Schools often seek ways to increase students' reading practice through volunteer "buddy reading" and more structured oral reading practice. A second group of studies examined the benefits of supplemental instruction that targets fluency: reading aloud and repeated reading instruction. The intervention research conducted by Torgesen, Rashotte, and Alexander (2001) underscores that although remedial interventions often close the gap for at-risk students in word reading skills, fluency deficits are more intractable (Torgesen, 2004).

Generally, tutoring interventions that target early elementary students have a phonics and decoding focus, whereas interventions for older students may offer book reading activities to develop fluency or comprehension skills. However, enduring decoding deficits may compromise older students' ability to benefit from partner reading activities. In Gelzheiser's (2005a) study, low-skilled fourth graders in the lowest 30th percentile in reading skills were assigned to volunteer tutors. The students read aloud with tutors from a mix of texts related to students' social studies curriculum. Texts were balanced in terms of genre and difficulty.

Tutors worked with students after school in 50-minute sessions for a total of 46 hours. Students who entered the intervention with higher decoding skills made greater reading gains. The authors cautioned that older students who continue to have decoding deficits are best served either by special education teachers or in programs specifically designed to teach decoding skills.

One means to build fluency for students who need extra reading practice is through repeated reading, a technique with a long history and strong empirical support (Dahl, 1979; Kuhn & Stahl, 2003; LaBerge & Samuels, 1974; National Reading Panel, 2000; see Hudson, Chapter 8, this volume). Repeated reading is the most successful intervention used to help children with poor reading fluency. In its varied forms, it provides the added practice in reading text that is needed to increase children's sight word vocabularies. Repeated reading procedures often utilize short motivating passages that can be read at about 95% accuracy, an adult who provides a fluent reading model, identification and review of miscues, and a timing procedure that often motivates readers.

We examined the benefits of repeated reading instruction in a series of three experimental studies. We wanted to evaluate the effectiveness of paraeducator tutors in supplementing classroom reading instruction for students with poor reading fluency. We chose a particular fluency intervention, Quick Reads (Hiebert, 2003) for these studies because of its careful consideration of text characteristics and engaging nonfiction reading passages aligned with grade-level science and social science topics. In a series of three studies, we randomly assigned low-skilled students to either supplemental instruction with Quick Reads delivered by a paraeducator tutor to a pair of students or to a classroom control group. Students in the control group received regular reading instruction. Treated students in each of these three studies were tutored for 30 minutes a day, 4 days a week, for 15–20 weeks.

In two of these studies, the tutoring was provided to second and third graders. Students at pretest averaged below grade level in fluency, rapid automatized naming (RAN), word reading accuracy and efficiency, and comprehension. Students randomly assigned to supplemental tutoring received 15 weeks of instruction. The paraeducator tutors used the Quick Reads program procedures, having students reread passages with and without a model. Tutors also added word-level instruction that they adjusted to meet students' needs. In the first study (Vadasy & Sanders, 2008c), students were tutored in dyads for 30 minutes a day, 4 days a week. Treatment fidelity averaged 4.76 on a 5-point scale. At posttest the tutored students had significantly greater gains in word reading accuracy ($d = 0.29$) and fluency ($d = 0.35$).

In the second study with second- and third-grade students (Vadasy & Sanders, 2009b), we included a treatment comparison of paraeducator and teacher tutors. Treatment fidelity on the instructional protocols for paraeducators averaged 4.4, and for teachers 4.7, on a 5-point scale. Although students in both tutor groups outscored control students in letter-sound knowledge ($d = 0.41$), fluency ($d = 0.37$), and comprehension ($d = 0.30$), we found that students who had certificated teacher tutors made greater gains in word reading ($d = 0.43$) and in one fluency measure ($d = 0.43$). These findings of an advantage for teachers in word-level instruction are similar to those reported in two other comparisons of teacher and paraeducator or tutor instruction. Ehri, Dreyer, Flugman, and Gross (2007) conducted a quasi-experimental study of a comprehensive tutoring intervention model that included the five areas of reading outlined by the National Reading Panel (2000). Language-minority first-grade students were assigned to individual tutoring by reading specialists, certificated teachers, or trained paraprofessionals. Ehri et al. (2007) reported that paraprofessionals delivered the instruction less effectively than teachers and specialists in two areas: They were less effective in teaching pseudoword decoding, and they provided more tutoring sessions, and were therefore less efficient, than the teachers. Gelzheizer (2005a) reported a similar finding that suggests decoding deficits in older students are better served by skilled teachers rather than by volunteer tutors. We hypothesized that in our second Quick Reads study (Vadasy & Sanders, 2009b), perhaps teachers were better able than nonteachers to scaffold added and incidental word reading instruction that becomes more complex once students have acquired basic decoding skills. We also found that students whose tutors had higher fidelity ratings and implemented the instruction more closely made greater gains in word reading and in fluency. In both of these interventions for second and third graders, tutored students continued to read below grade level in fluency at the end of the instruction. The added word-level instruction in the second study had only a small effect on students' word reading skills. Both of these studies raised the question of whether students require a certain level of word reading skill in order to make optimal gains from fluency practice. In both studies, however, added tutoring in fluency provided by paraeducators resulted in significant gains in important reading skills: word reading and fluency in one study (Vadasy & Sanders, 2008c), and alphabetic skills, fluency, and comprehension in the other (Vadasy & Sanders, 2009b). The findings support that paraeducator tutors can effectively provide this fluency practice when they receive adequate training and supervision, and are equipped with well-designed materials.

We also evaluated the use of Quick Reads fluency instruction for fourth- and fifth-grade students (Vadasy & Sanders, 2008a). Students averaged in the 20th to 25th percentile at pretest in reading skills, and student dyads paired for reading levels were provided 20 weeks of instruction (30 minutes a day, 4 days a week) by paraeducator tutors. The tutors followed the basic Quick Reads procedures and also provided brief direct instruction in vocabulary words that were challenging and important for understanding the passages. Treatment fidelity averaged 3.7 on a 5-point scale. At posttest the tutored students significantly outperformed controls on measures of curriculum-based vocabulary ($d = 0.42$), word comprehension ($d = 0.27$), and passage comprehension ($d = 0.50$). Similar to the earlier intervention studies with younger students, although tutored students made gains, they continued to average at the 30th percentile in reading fluency at the end of the intervention.

One question that arises is why these intensive repeated reading interventions failed to raise students to grade-level fluency. One answer is that fluency is a complex skill that reflects consolidation of lower-level word reading skills, and the coordination of syntactic and comprehension skills. It may require more skilled and extended instruction by teachers to target specific component skills prerequisite for an individual student to develop fluency. Furthermore, many students in these treatment groups who entered with poor word reading skills had not yet attained grade-level word reading accuracy and efficiency skills by the end of the intervention. Students may require a basic level of word reading accuracy in order to build their text reading rate. Finally, other students in these interventions demonstrated deficits in rapid naming (e.g., rapid naming of letter or numbers) that may have prevented them from benefiting from the oral reading practice.

One implication from this series of studies on supplemental tutoring in fluency skills is that students should be selected carefully for fluency practice. Findings from Vadasy and Sanders (2008a) suggest that selection of texts for fluency practice take into account students' word identification skills. Word reading deficits may prevent students from benefiting from repeated reading in practice materials that are too difficult. Tutors may not have the skills to match students to texts, or to recognize and provide individualized incidental instruction to address deficits in lower-level word reading skills.

Findings from Vadasy and Sanders (2008a) suggest that tutors can effectively add direct instruction in word meanings for fourth and fifth graders in the context of fluency instruction. What may have allowed tutors to be effective is that this vocabulary instruction was carefully scripted and straightforward, requiring minimal adaptation. In Vadasy and Sanders (2008c), we found that tutors were able to supplement word reading instruction in the context of repeated reading practice for second- and third-grade students with word reading skills averaging in the lowest 40th percentile. This instruction appeared to allow students with lower word reading skills to make the greatest gains across reading skills areas. In Vadasy and Sanders (2009b), on the other hand, we found that teachers, compared to paraeducator tutors, were better able to promote gains in word reading accuracy in the context of repeated reading. The effect size in word reading was highest for teacher tutors in this latter study. This suggests that as word reading complexity increases, instruction for students with these word reading deficits may be best provided by teachers who can target specific aspects of word reading (e.g., multisyllabic words or words with vowel digraphs or consonant blends).

Implications for Supplementing Reading Instruction with Tutoring

In a now classic paper, the cognitive psychologist Benjamin Bloom (1984) described what is termed the "2 sigma dilemma" regarding individual tutoring: that although tutoring offers students the potential to attain significantly higher levels of learning than does group instruction (an average effect size of 2.0), one-to-one tutoring is far too costly for widespread use. Bloom summarized research on instruction to identify *alterable* intervention variables that might enhance learning in more typical educational conditions. Two variables were found to have quite large effect sizes:

- Student time on task (effect size 1.0)
- Corrective feedback (i.e., providing students with cognitive and affective prerequisites for each new learning task, using a mastery learning approach that includes formative testing with feedback and corrective procedures; effect size 1.00)

Interestingly, the research studies summarized in this chapter help to inform more fully Bloom's findings. All of the supplemental interventions summarized here in effect increased student time on task for the particular reading skills focus of the program, and were provided most often in addition to regular classroom reading instruction. Many of the interventions included corrective feedback procedures that Bloom estimated to help students learn more effectively. For example, the Reading Mastery intervention used in the Gunn et al. (2005) study, the Stepping Stones to Literacy alphabetic intervention used in the Nelson, Stage, et al. (2005) study, and the Sound Partners intervention (Vadasy et al., 2005) included these cognitive and affective features that Bloom (1984) identified.

- Sequenced hierarchy of skills
- Integrated alphabetic and phonological instruction
- Explicit connections between skills sets
- Scripted format to ensure consistency of instruction
- Explicit modeling and instruction
- Multiple response and practice opportunities
- Generalization of isolated skills instruction to text practice
- Ongoing mastery assessment

Instruction for use *with* struggling students *by* nonteacher tutors must be designed to take into account both student prerequisites for learning and instructor prerequisites for teaching. It is important that future studies add to this growing body of evidence on specific intervention features associated with student learning.

Summary

Effective tutoring interventions reviewed in this chapter have included the following design and implementation features:

- Materials are specifically designed for nonteacher tutors, or with their use in mind. In some cases, these "soft-scripted" programs are considerate of the tutors' backgrounds and the typical conditions of tutoring.

- Tutors receive initial and ongoing training in use of materials. Training often includes an overview of the theory and research supporting the intervention, trainer modeling of practices, and supervised practice opportunities.

- Research-based materials reflect intervention strategies previously found effective. Materials reflect practices with strong research support, and many intervention features have been demonstrated to be effective in previous intervention studies (often initially implemented by teachers or researchers).

- Tutoring fidelity is monitored. Procedures are designed to measure implementation fidelity and to provide structured feedback to improve instruction.

- Tutors provide scaffolding, modeling, and response to student errors. Instruction incorporates these generic and established principles of instructional design.

- A tutoring coordinator provides ongoing support and coaching. Tutors do not work unsupervised or unsupported, and they receive ongoing coaching to refine their teaching skills.

- Tutors are paid (or hired as paraeducators); they are not volunteers. The research suggests that it is not realistic to expect volunteer tutors to commit the time needed to become skilled implementers or to offer the intensive instruction needed by struggling readers.

Over the past decade a small but strong body of research has grown on the effectiveness of supplemental instruction, often provided by paraeducator tutors, for students at risk and with reading difficulties. Many of these studies have used careful experimental designs that add confidence in these findings. The growing evidence summarized in this chapter suggests that paraeducator tutors can effectively supplement instruction in early alphabetic, phonological awareness, and phonics skills. The findings from this first group of studies highlight the intervention features that across many studies are associated with reading growth:

- Explicit instruction in letter sounds
- Integrated instruction in phonological awareness and alphabetic skills
- Explicit instruction in a phonemic decoding strategy
- Integrated skills instruction in phonological, alphabetic, phonics, and text reading, with explicit connections across these skills sets
- Scripted instructional formats to support consistency

- Massed practice opportunities and cumulative cycles of review
- Mastery assessment to track learning progress

A smaller group of studies offers more limited support for supplemental tutoring in fluency skills. Poor reading fluency may mask underlying deficits in word reading accuracy and efficiency, as well as other deficits in vocabulary and language associated with limited reading practice. The cumulative deficits that often characterize fluency delays present more complex instructional challenges for teachers and may reduce the effectiveness of interventions implemented by nonteachers. Despite these challenges in closing the fluency gap for students, we can draw the following tentative conclusions about supplemental instruction by paraeducators in fluency skills:

- Repeated reading procedures with carefully selected texts matched to student reading levels, and with incidental alphabetic or vocabulary instruction, produce gains in alphabetic skills, word reading accuracy, fluency, vocabulary, and comprehension.
- Repeated reading interventions appear to have stronger fluency benefits for younger (second- and third-grade) compared to older (fourth- and fifth-grade) students. It may be more difficult for supplemental interventions to benefit students with cumulative fluency deficits.

In order to close the reading achievement gap, schools must often look beyond group instruction. In our efforts to close this gap, we often overlook the potential of two universal features in many U.S. schools: teaching assistants and reading curricula. As noted earlier, increasing numbers of paraeducators work in U.S. schools. Many students with reading difficulties receive some assistance from these school staff members. These paraeducators use a variety of materials and curricula in tutoring students. The most recent wave of research on supplemental reading interventions identifies conditions under which paraeducator tutors have the potential to improve discrete, foundation reading skills significantly for children who are underachieving and at risk for falling behind in reading. Findings on effective phonics and fluency interventions describe favorable conditions for learning in these supplemental interventions. These conditions include tutor training; consistency of instruction; and research-based, carefully designed curricula. These alterable variables merit more careful consideration to help students learn more effectively within the current infrastructure of our public schools.

References

Al Otaiba, S., Schatschneider, C., & Silverman, E. (2005). Tutor-assisted intensive learning strategies in kindergarten: How much is enough? *Exceptionality, 13,* 195–208.

Bloom, B. S. (1984). The 2 sigma problem: The search for methods of group instruction as effective as one-to-one tutoring. *Educational Researcher, 13,* 4–16.

Dahl, P. R. (1979). An experimental program for teaching high speed word recognition and comprehension skills. In J. E. Button, T. Lovitt, & T. Rowland (Eds.), *Communications research in learning disabilities and mental retardation* (pp. 33–65). Baltimore, MD: University Park Press.

Darling-Hammond, L. (1998). *How can we ensure a caring, competent, qualified teacher for every child?: Strategies for solving the dilemmas of teacher supply, demand, and standards.* Washington, DC: Education Commission of the States.

Ehri, L. C., Dreyer, L. G., Flugman, B., & Gross, A. (2007). Reading Rescue: An effective tutoring intervention model for language-minority students who are struggling readers in first grade. *American Educational Research Journal, 44,* 414–448.

Elbaum, B., Vaughn, S., Hughes, M. T., & Moody, S. W. (2000). How effective are one-to-one tutoring programs in reading for elementary students at risk for reading failure?: A meta-analysis of the intervention research. *Journal of Educational Psychology, 92,* 605–619.

Engelmann, S., & Bruner, E. C. (1988). *Reading Mastery.* Chicago: Scientific Research Associates.

Engelmann, S., Carnine, L., & Johnson, G. (1988). *Word attack basics (Corrective reading series).* Chicago: Scientific Research Associates.

Fuchs, D., Fuchs, L. S., Thompson, A., Al Otaiba, S., Yen, L., & Braun, M. (2000). *Peer-assisted learning strategies: Kindergarten: A teacher's manual.* Unpublished training manual, Vanderbilt University, Nashville, TN.

Gelzheiser, L. M. (2005a). Maximizing student progress in one-to-one programs: Contributions of texts, volunteer experience, and student characteristics. *Exceptionality, 13,* 229–243.

Gelzheiser, L. M. (2005b). Tutoring and literacy: Insights from one-to-one tutoring programs. *Exceptionality, 13,* 193–194.

Gunn, B., Smolkowski, K., Biglan, A., Black, C., & Blair, J. (2005). Fostering the development of reading skill through supplemental instruction: Results for Hispanic and non-Hispanic students. *Journal of Special Education, 39,* 66–85.

Hatcher, P. J., Goetz, K., Snowling, M. J., Hulme, C., Gibbs, S., & Smith, G. (2006). Evidence for the effectiveness of the Early Literacy Support programme. *British Journal of Educational Psychology, 76,* 351–367.

Hiebert, E. H. (2003). *Quick Reads: A research-based fluency program.* Parsippany, NJ: Modern Curriculum Press, Pearson Learning Group.

Jenkins, J. R., Peyton, J. A., Sanders, E. A., & Vadasy, P. F. (2004). Effects of reading decodable texts in supplemental first-grade tutoring. *Scientific Studies of Reading, 8,* 53–85.

Kamps, D., & Greenwood, C. (2005). Formulating secondary-level reading interventions. *Journal of Learning Disabilities, 38,* 500–509.

Kuhn, M. R., & Stahl, S. A. (2003). Fluency: A review of developmental and remedial practices. *Journal of Educational Psychology, 95,* 3–21.

LaBerge, D., & Samuels, S. J. (1974). Toward a theory of automatic information processing in reading. *Cognitive Psychology, 6,* 293–323.

Lane, K. L., Fletcher, T., Carter, E. W., Dejud, C., & DeLorenzo, J. (2007). Paraprofessional-led phonological awareness training with youngsters at risk for reading and behavioral concerns. *Remedial and Special Education, 28,* 266–276.

Maslen, B. L. (2003). *Bob Books.* New York: Scholastic.

National Center for Education Statistics. (2007a). *Digest of Education Statistics: 2007.* Retrieved January 24, 2009, from *nces.ed.gov/programs/digest/d07/ch_2.asp.*

National Center for Education Statistics. (2007b). *Digest of Education Statistics: 2007 (Table 77: Staff employed in public elementary and secondary school systems, by functional area*). Retrieved January 24, 2009, from *nces.ed.gov/programs/digest/d07/tables/dt07_077. asp?referrer=report.*

National Reading Panel. (2000). *Report of the subgroups: National Reading Panel.* Washington, DC: National Institute of Child Health and Development.

Nelson, J. R., Benner, G. J., & Gonzalez, J. (2005). An investigation of the effects of a prereading intervention on the early literacy skills of children at risk of emotional disturbance and reading problems. *Journal of Emotional and Behavioral Disorders, 13,* 3–12.

Nelson, J. R., Cooper, P., & Gonzalez, J. (2004). *Stepping Stones to Literacy.* Longmont, CO: Sopris West.

Nelson, J. R., Stage, S. A., Epstein, M. H., & Pierce, C. D. (2005). Effects of a prereading intervention on the literacy and social skills of children. *Exceptional Children, 72,* 29–45.

Northwest Regional Educational Laboratory. (1999). *Designing state and local policies for the professional development of instructional paraeducators.* Portland, OR: Author.

O'Connor, R. E., Bell, K. M., Harty, K. R., Larkin, L. K., Sackor, S. M., & Zigmond, N. (2002). Teaching reading to poor readers in intermediate grades: A comparison of text difficulty. *Journal of Educational Psychology, 94,* 474–485.

O'Shaughnessy, T. E., & Swanson, H. L. (2000). A comparison of two reading interventions for children with reading disabilities. *Journal of Learning Disabilities, 33,* 257–277.

Ritter, G. W., Barnett, J. H., Denny, G. S., & Albin, G. R. (2009). The effectiveness of volunteer tutoring programs for elementary and middle school students: A meta-analysis. *Review of Educational Research, 79,* 3–38.

Savage, R., & Carless, S. (2005). Learning support assistants can deliver effective reading interventions for "at-risk" children. *Educational Research, 47,* 45–61.

Stahl, S., & Miller, P. (1989). Whole language and language experience approaches for beginning reading: A quantitative research synthesis. *Review of Educational Research, 59,* 87–116.

Torgesen, J. K. (2004). Lessons learned from research on interventions for students who have difficulty learning to read. In P. McCardle & V. Chhabra (Eds.), *The voice of evidence in reading research* (pp. 355–382). Baltimore: Brookes.

Torgesen, J. K., & Bryant, B. (1994). Phonological Awareness Training in Reading (PATR). Austin, TX: Pro-Ed.

Torgesen, J. K., Rashotte, C. A., & Alexander, A. W. (2001). Principles of fluency instruction in reading: Relationships with established empirical outcomes. In M. Wolf (Ed.), *Dyslexia, fluency, and the brain* (pp. 333–356). Timonium, MD: York Press.

Vadasy, P. F., Jenkins, J. R., Antil, L. R., Wayne, S. K., & O'Connor, R. E. (1997). The effectiveness of one-to-one tutoring by community tutors for at-risk beginning readers. *Learning Disability Quarterly, 20,* 126–139.

Vadasy, P. F., Jenkins, J. R., & Pool, K. (2000). Effects of tutoring in phonological and early reading skills on students at risk for reading disabilities. *Journal of Learning Disabilities, 33*(6), 579–590.

Vadasy, P. F., & Sanders, E. A. (2008a). Benefits of repeated reading intervention for low-achieving fourth- and fifth-grade students. *Remedial and Special Education, 29,* 235–249.

Vadasy, P. F., & Sanders, E. A. (2008b). Code-oriented instruction for kindergarten students at risk for reading difficulties: A replication and comparison of instructional groupings. *Reading and Writing, 21,* 929–963.

Vadasy, P. F., & Sanders, E. A. (2008c). Repeated reading intervention: Outcomes and interactions with readers' skills and classroom instruction. *Journal of Educational Psychology, 100,* 272–290.

Vadasy, P. F., & Sanders, E. A. (2009a). Individual tutoring for struggling readers: Moving research to scale with interventions implemented by paraeducators. In G. Reid, A. Fawcett, F. Manis, & L. Siegel (Eds.), *The Sage handbook of dyslexia* (pp. 337–355). London: Sage.

Vadasy, P. F., & Sanders, E. A. (2009b). Supplemental fluency intervention and determinants of reading outcomes. *Scientific Studies of Reading, 13*, 383–425.

Vadasy, P. F., Sanders, E. A., & Abbott, R. D. (2008). Effects of supplemental early reading intervention at 2-year follow up: Reading skill growth patterns and predictors. *Scientific Studies of Reading, 12*(1), 51–89.

Vadasy, P. F., Sanders, E. A., & Peyton, J. A. (2006a). Code-oriented instruction for kindergarten students at risk for reading difficulties: A randomized field trial with paraeducator implementers. *Journal of Educational Psychology, 98*(3), 508–528.

Vadasy, P. F., Sanders, E. A., & Peyton, J. A. (2006b). Paraeducator-supplemented instruction in structural analysis with text reading practice for second and third graders at risk for reading problems. *Remedial and Special Education, 27*(6), 365–378.

Vadasy, P. F., Sanders, E. A., & Tudor, S. (2007). Effectiveness of paraeducator-supplemented individual instruction: Beyond basic decoding skills. *Journal of Learning Disabilities, 40*(6), 508–525.

Vadasy, P. F., Wayne, S. K., O'Connor, R. E., Jenkins, J. R., Pool, K., Firebaugh, M., et al. (2005). *Sound Partners: A tutoring program in phonics-based early reading.* Longmont, CO: Sopris West.

What Works Clearinghouse. (2007). *Stepping Stones to Literacy* (June 25, 2007). Retrieved February 10,2009, from *ies.ed.gov/ncee/wwc/reports/beginning_reading/ssl.*

14

On the Comprehension and Production of Written Texts

Instructional Activities
That Support Content-Area Literacy

Ralph P. Ferretti
Susan De La Paz

Literacy is critical to our children's development and their participation in our nation's economic future. The growing reliance on sophisticated information technology and the increasing importance of specialized knowledge, coupled with diminishing opportunities for blue-collar jobs, make salient the value of sophisticated reading and writing skills in the workplace (Biancarosa & Snow, 2006; Graham & Perin, 2007). Unfortunately, the evidence shows that students neither read nor write proficiently (National Center for Education Statistics [NCES], 2007, 2008). For example, the 2007 National Assessment of Educational Progress (NAEP) Writing Report Card (NCES, 2008) showed that only 33% of eighth graders and 24% of 12th graders scored at or above the "proficient" level, which represents "solid academic performance" and "competency over challenging subject matter" (NCES, 2008, p. 6). Perhaps more disturbing is that 12% of eighth graders and 18% of 12th graders fail to achieve even "partial mastery of prerequisite knowledge and skills that are fundamental for proficient work at a given grade level" (NCES, 2008, p. 6). These data are problematic, because writing proficiency affects prospective employers' hiring and promotion decisions (National Commission on Writing, 2004, 2005).

In a similar vein, the Nation's Reading Report Card (NCES, 2007) reported that no more than 33% of fourth and eight graders were "proficient" readers. Proficient readers are able not only to recognize facts and support for interpretation of text ("basic" level) but also to retrieve relevant information and use it to provide an opinion about the text. While the reading and writing performance of elementary students has shown some modest improvement over time (Graham & Perin, 2007; NCES, 2007; Olson, 2006), too few students are skilled enough to meet the escalating literacy demands of the workplace (Biancarosa & Snow, 2006). Data about adolescents' literacy skills are especially disconcerting, because these students will soon transition from school to work. The Nation's Reading Report card showed that only about 35% of 12th graders were "proficient" readers (NCES, 2007), and the percentage of proficient readers has declined since 1992. These challenges are especially pronounced for students with learning disabilities (LD), who often experience chronic problems in reading (Fletcher et al., 1994; Kavale & Forness, 2000) and writing (Troia, 2006).

The aforementioned observations raise serious questions about adolescents' vocational prospects, but there is another, related reason for concern. Basic reading and writing skills are not sufficient to ensure adolescents' academic success as they progress through the curriculum (Shanahan & Shanahan, 2008). Literacy and content-area learning become inextricably interlinked, so academic progress increasingly depends upon the acquisition of highly specialized knowledge and skills that are often discipline dependent. Vocabulary becomes increasingly specific and complex, and the comprehension and production of text become more dependent on domain-specific knowledge and strategies. Students need to read and write to communicate and to understand, but they must understand and communicate about increasingly specific, domain-dependent, and intellectually challenging issues. In short, basic literacy skills are not sufficient to ensure students' academic success. They are expected to think, read, and write like disciplinary experts (De La Paz, 2005; Ferretti & Okolo, 1996; Shanahan & Shanahan, 2008).

In this chapter, we offer evidence for our views about a range of issues related to the acquisition of content-area literacy. First, we discuss factors that affect students' comprehension and their production of comprehensible texts in the content areas. Second, we describe some of the specific challenges in reading and writing experienced by students with LD. Third, we summarize representative interventions that target domain-specific knowledge and skills, and impact students' performance in the areas of the language arts and historical interpretation. We conclude with some illustrations about how instructional activities can be designed to promote the understanding and production of texts in these areas.

Factors Affecting the Comprehension and Production of Content–Area Text

Reading and writing are complementary and purposeful communicative activities that are meant to accomplish human intentions (Olson, 1994; Searle, 1998). Texts are structured to clarify their communicative purposes, and both readers and writers rely on knowledge of text structure to infer the author's intended purposes and meanings (RAND Reading Study Group, 2002; Williams, Safford, Lauer, Hall, & Pollini, 2009). Reading and writing are interpretive processes (Lewis & Ferretti, 2009) that draw upon a common pool of background knowledge and skills (Graham & Perin, 2007). However, the skills that undergird reading and writing are not simply interchangeable. Many adolescents are able to meet expectations for reading but have severe writing difficulties (Graham & Perin, 2007). Furthermore, improvements in reading and writing require their own dedicated instruction (Graham & Perin, 2007). For these reasons, care must be given to the design of content-area instruction that involves reading and writing.

A number of factors complicate the comprehension of text and production of comprehensible text. Understanding and producing text involves interpretive transactions between the author and text, the reader and the text, and the myriad purposes that motivate communicative acts (Lewis & Ferretti, 2009; Rosenblatt, 1995). Text is sometimes confusing and ambiguous; nevertheless, comprehension demands its representation in memory. At least three levels of representation are involved (Kintsch, 1988, 1994; Kintsch & Kintsch, 2005; van Dijk & Kintsch, 1978, 1983): (1) as a surface code that links graphemic and phonemic elements with linguistic structures; (2) as a propositional text base that strips away the surface features and preserves the text's gist; and (3) as a "situation model" in which the textbase is elaborated upon and integrated with a reader's prior knowledge. Clearly, comprehending text is highly dependent on the student's background knowledge, which includes not only general world knowledge and knowledge of text structure (Englert & Thomas, 1987; RAND Reading Study Group, 2002; Williams et al., 2009) but also specific disciplinary knowledge (De La Paz, 2005; Ferretti, MacArthur, & Okolo, 2001; Shanahan & Shanahan, 2008).

Furthermore, comprehension is a nonunitary construct that involves different subskills across types of texts and content (Duke, 2005). Texts also have different purposes (i.e., genres), and there is tremendous variability within genres with respect to the type of texts they subsume. For example, expository text, which is critical to content-area learning (Williams et al., 2009), subsumes many different text subtypes, including description, sequence, compare–contrast, causation, and problem–solution (Meyer & Freedle, 1984; Meyer et al., 2002). Students have differential exposure to and experience with various genres, and the emergence of genre knowledge involves developing understandings of the linguistic features of different text types (Donovan & Smolkin, 2006).

Writing high-quality text is no less challenging for students. Writing, which is a problem-solving process (Bereiter & Scardamalia, 1987; Hayes, 1996; Hayes & Flower, 1980), involves the use of goal-directed self-regulatory procedures to plan, write, and revise essays (Graham, 1997; Graham & Harris, 1997). In contrast to expert writers, novices often retrieve and write down topically relevant information, then use this information as a stimulus for retrieving and reporting related information (Page-Voth & Graham, 1999). Not surprisingly, the failure to use genre-specific goals results in the production of essays that lack critical components and are of poor quality (De La Paz & Graham, 1997a; Graham, 1990; Graham & Harris, 1989; Graham, MacArthur, Schwartz, & Page-Voth, 1992). Furthermore, expert writers draw on their background knowledge to plan, write, and revise their essays. These sources include general world knowledge, knowledge of text structure (Englert & Thomas, 1987; RAND Reading Study Group, 2002), and disciplinary knowledge (De La Paz, 2005; Lewis & Ferretti, 2009; Shanahan & Shanahan, 2008). The retrieval and use of relevant background knowledge is guided by an expert writer's purposes and rhetorical goals (Bereiter & Scardamalia, 1987; Hayes, 1996; Hayes & Flower, 1980).

Academic progress depends on the development of literacy skills that become increasingly specific and dependent on disciplinary knowledge and skills (De La Paz, 2005; Lewis & Ferretti, 2009; MacArthur, 2009; Shanahan & Shanahan, 2008). Research now indicates how disciplinary experts think and reason in literary studies (Fahnestock & Secor, 1991; Lewis & Ferretti, 2009, in press; Wilder, 2005), history (De La Paz, 2005; Stearns, Seixas, & Wineburg, 2000; Wineburg, 1991a, 1991b, 2001), and other disciplines. We review representative studies later in this chapter, but suffice it to say that experts engage in interpretive processes that are highly dependent on their disciplinary knowledge and skills. To promote acquisition of disciplinary expertise, we must design instructional activities that encourage students to read and write like domain experts.

Challenges to Reading and Writing
in the Content Areas for Students with LD

Students with LD experience myriad challenges to comprehending written texts and producing comprehensible texts (Faggella-Luby & Deschler, 2008; Troia, 2006). A well-established literature shows that students with LD are most frequently referred for special education services because of reading problems (Fletcher et al., 1994; Kavale & Forness, 2000). During the elementary school years, these problems often result from difficulties with phonological awareness and the inability to retrieve rapidly the names of visually presented information (Lovett, Steinbach, & Frijters, 2000; Torgesen & Wagner, 1998). Not surprisingly, problems with these basic reading processes adversely affect the reading comprehension of students with LD (Jenkins & O'Connor, 2002). However, the comprehension problems of these students may also result from the lack of relevant background knowledge, impoverished vocabularies, limited knowledge of text structure, and limits in the self-regulatory skills needed to monitor their comprehension and repair misunderstandings (Faggella-Luby & Deschler, 2008; Gersten, Fuchs, Williams, & Baker, 2001; Mastropieri, Scruggs, & Graetz, 2003; Vaughn, Gersten, & Chard, 2000). The latter issues are especially taxing for adolescents with LD (Faggella-Luby & Deschler, 2008).

Not surprisingly, students with LD also experience a plethora of writing problems. Compared to their normally achieving peers, the essays of students with LD contain more spelling, punctuation, and grammatical errors (Graham, 1990, 1999). These production problems may not only affect adversely teachers' perceptions of the writing quality (Graham, Harris, & Chorzempa, 2002) but also tax the writer's working memory capacity, thereby limiting the processing resources available for planning, revising, and regulating the writing process (Graham, 1990, 1999). In addition, students with LD often write shorter, incomplete, and poorly organized essays of lower quality (MacArthur & Graham, 1987; Troia, 2006). The poor quality of their essays may be due to their inability to generate relevant content (Graham, 1990; Graham & Harris, 1997); to set genre-specific writing goals (Ferretti, Lewis, & Andrews-Weckerly, 2009; Ferretti, MacArthur, & Dowdy, 2000); and more generally, to engage in the self-regulatory processes needed to plan, write, and revise their essays. These conclusions are drawn largely from evidence about the narrative and expository writing of students with LD (Graham, Harris, MacArthur, & Schwartz, 1991; MacArthur, Harris, & Graham, 1994). Although limited, the available evidence suggests that the argumentative essays of students with LD frequently lack critical discursive elements and fail to consider alternative perspectives (Ferretti et al., 2000, 2009; Graham, 1990; Graham et al., 1992).

The research evidence shows that common principles undergird effective writing and reading instruction for students with LD (Faggella-Luby & Deschler, 2008; Graham, 2006; Graham & Perin, 2007; Mastropieri et al., 2003; Troia, 2006). Vaughn et al. (2000) summarized the major findings about effective interventions from a number of meta-analyses that focused on a range of outcomes, including higher-order processing, writing and reading comprehension, and grouping practices in reading instruction. In general, effective instruction is explicit and visible, and makes clear to students the knowledge and skills needed to be self-regulating learners. Effective writing instruction teaches students with LD the mechanical skills (e.g., spelling, handwriting) needed to produce accessible text (Graham, 1990, 1999). In addition, students learn to set clear writing goals to guide the retrieval of task-relevant information (De La Paz, Swanson, & Graham, 1998; Ferretti et al., 2000, 2009; Graham, 1997), and explicit procedures and strategies that the writer can use to regulate the writing process (Graham, 2006; Graham & Perin, 2007; Troia, 2006). Effective reading comprehension instruction for adolescents with LD (Mastropieri et al., 2003) promotes word recognition skills, teaches students about text structure and vocabulary, and makes instruction explicit and students' thinking visible (Bransford, Brown, & Cocking, 2000).

Vaughn et al. (2000) also found that interactive small-group instruction and peer tutoring is usually more effective for students with LD than whole-class recitations and lectures, because they afford teachers and peers the chance to check on students' understandings, provide feedback, and diagnose and correct potential misconceptions. This finding is echoed in the instructional literatures about reading comprehension (Mastropieri et al., 2003) and writing (Graham & Perin, 2007; MacArthur, Schwartz, & Graham, 1991). For example, peer tutoring of students with LD can help ensure that essential content is acquired and accessible, that relationships among big ideas are represented and made salient, and that comprehension-relevant knowledge is activated and critically evaluated (Mastropieri et al., 2003).

Finally, effective instruction also controls task difficulty (Vaughn et al., 2000). Tasks that are challenging and meaningful to students sustain engagement (Troia, 2006). To control task difficulty, it is important to teach strategies that can be used by children to guide their thinking and problem solving. This is especially important for children with LD, because they may not generate strategies or use them flexibly without these supports. Strategies have the potential to reduce task difficulty for many students with LD. In brief, these students benefit from explicit instruction that teaches them basic skills, directly targets the strategic processes and background knowledge needed to understand and produce text, and makes thinking visible, so that their peers and teachers can provide critical feedback about their communicative intentions (Faggella-Luby & Deshler, 2008; Graham, 2006; Mastropieri et al., 2003; Vaughn et al., 2000).

A Perspective on Designing
Literacy Instruction in the Content Areas

Our discussion of reading and writing in the content areas highlights the many complicated instructional decisions that await teachers, most especially when they design instruction for students with LD. First, they must collaborate with colleagues to establish instructional objectives that are valued by members of the community and promote the long-term development of their students. These objectives often focus on reading, writing, and content knowledge and skills; they may also include expectations related to comportment, social behavior, and the like. Second, they must choose texts and other materials that support the attainment of these objectives because they are accessible, coherent, and motivating. Third, they must design writing tasks that are not only sufficiently challenging to promote the development of writing skills but also considerate of students' current levels of skill, knowledge, and capacities. Fourth, they must fashion and implement instructional procedures that (1) make explicit the knowledge and strategies used by skilled readers, writers, and disciplinary experts; (2) model the use of the knowledge and strategies; (3) structure tasks so that students take independent control of the knowledge and strategies; (4) monitor students' use of the knowledge and strategies, and provide corrective feedback; (5) make adaptations in the materials and instruction that accommodate individual differences in students' capacities, knowledge, and skills; and (6) if the instruction involves peers, teach students how to support and evaluate each other's performance. These issues only hint at the instructional challenges that await teachers!

Interventions That Promote Content-Area Literacy

Most of the aforementioned ideas about content-area literacy have been implemented in some form in the instructional literature. However, no studies report a
design of instructional activities that addresses the full range of challenges related
to content-area reading and writing, especially for students with LD. For this
reason, we present studies that illustrate how instructional activities have been
designed to achieve particular purposes in three areas: literary analysis, writing
to learn in social studies and science, and historical interpretation.

Literary Analysis

Proficiency in the analysis and interpretation of literary text is an important goal of
the English curriculum for high school students (Lewis & Ferretti, 2009). Despite
the significance of these analytic and interpretive skills (Zbikowski & Collins,
1994), students are rarely able to construct arguments about literary interpretation
(Marshall, 2000) or go beyond basic plot summary to engage in substantive thematic issues of a text (Persky, Daane, & Jin, 2003). This difficulty in part is because
little instructional time is devoted to interpretive or analytic writing (Applebee &
Langer, 2006; Gamoran & Carbonaro, 2002; Kiuhara, Graham, & Hawken, 2009),
especially for low-achieving students (Applebee & Langer, 2006).

Before students are able to write analytic arguments about literature, they must
be able to analyze and interpret the literature about which they write. The analysis
and interpretation of literature depends on two interdependent processes (Lewis
& Ferretti, 2009, in press). First, students must be able to recognize patterns of
language created by the author that enable them to comprehend the text and interpret the writer's intentions. Second, students must translate these interpretations
into a written argument that supports their interpretations. According to Fahnestock and Secor (1991), disciplinary experts use "literary topoi" to interpret literature and write literary arguments. For example, the "ubiquity topos" is used to
show how a pattern (e.g., image, symbol, syntactic element) is repeated throughout
a work, and the "paradox topos" is used to reconcile contradictory patterns in the
work. These topoi are used not only to represent and interpret the text but also
to warrant arguments in support of the interpretation (Lewis & Ferretti, 2009,
in press). Evidence shows that topoi are used by literary scholars (Wilder, 2005)
and appear in the discourse of college instructors and students in college English
classes (Wilder, 2002). In addition to invoking topoi, literary critics bolster their
arguments with quotations, textual references, and explanations that warrant the
use of these sources as evidence (Lewis & Ferretti, 2009, in press).

A short vignette from Hemingway's *In Our Time* (1958) illustrates how the
ubiquity and paradox topoi can be used to construct meaningful interpretations
of literary texts (see Lewis & Ferretti, 2009).

> It was a frightfully hot day. We'd jammed an absolutely perfect barricade across
> the bridge. It was simply priceless. A big old wrought-iron grating from the front

of the house. Too heavy to lift and you could shoot through it and they would have to climb over it. It was absolutely topping. They tried to get over it, and we potted them from forty yards. They rushed it, and officers came out alone and worked on it. It was an absolutely perfect obstacle. Their officers were very fine. We were frightfully put out when we heard the flank had gone, and we had to fall back. (p. 37)

Both the paradox and ubiquity topoi can be used to help interpret this passage. Hemingway's use of genteel British speech stands in paradoxical contrast to the description of violence. Perhaps the affected manner represents a verbal barrier that the narrator has erected to deal with the violence and death of which he is part (Lewis, 1997). In addition, the ubiquitous descriptions of the excellence of the barrier reinforce the interpretation that the most important barrier is the psychological one that the narrator has erected to shield himself from the horrors of war.

To demonstrate the instructional importance of these ideas, Lewis and Ferretti (2009, in press) taught high school students, who were judged by their teachers to be poor writers, about figurative language and literary topoi, as well as an argumentative writing strategy that could be used to tie interpretive claims to these literary elements. The argumentative writing strategy, called THE READER, was based on De La Paz and Graham's (1997a) STOP and DARE strategy, which provided procedural support for students with LD to stop, reflect, and plan their opinion essays using elements of argumentative discourse. THE READER strategy was designed to help students plan and write arguments about their interpretation of literature using figurative language and literary topoi. In brief, students were taught to develop a THEsis, back up the thesis with REAsons, include Details as illustrations of those reasons (direct quotes or references to the text), Explain how those quotes and references are related to their reasons or thesis (warrant), and Review their main points in a conclusion. In addition, a graphic organizer was used to help plan the elements of the essay.

Six lessons, based on the self-regulated strategy development (SRSD) model of Graham and Harris (2005), were used to teach THE READER strategy and the disciplinary knowledge needed to use it effectively. In the first lesson, students learned about figurative language, such as simile and metaphor, that authors sometimes use to highlight themes in literature. In the second and third lessons, students were taught to use THE READER strategy to develop a point of view about a piece of literature, then write an interpretive argument based on their knowledge of figurative language, with the help of a graphic organizer. In the fourth lesson, students were taught to recognize and use examples of patterns of imagery, symbolism, or language use, and to use these patterns to support an analytical argument about literature. Half of the students were taught to recognize and use the ubiquity topos, in which a pattern is repeated throughout the text to highlight a theme. In the fifth lesson, the instructor and students engaged in collaborative practice in using THE READER strategy, the graphic organizer, and knowledge of topoi to plan and write essays about literary passages. In the sixth lesson, the graphic organizer was systematically withdrawn after students demonstrated that they could recreate its format on plain notebook paper. In the final lesson, students were required to use THE READER strategy to write an essay without using either the graphic organizer or the instructor's assistance.

The intervention was assessed using a multiple-probe, multiple-baseline design with six high school students. Baseline and posttest essays about literary passages were scored for inclusion of text structure elements (standpoint, topoi, textual citations, warrants), use of the ubiquity and paradox topoi, and overall quality. At the completion of instruction, students were able to invoke the topoi (Fahnestock & Secor, 1991), use textual citations to support their standpoints, and warrant the relationship between the textual evidence and their standpoints. In general, the quality of students' literary arguments improved as a result of instruction; furthermore, they showed a rudimentary understanding of discourse about literary analysis and argument (Fahnestock & Secor, 1991; Lewis & Ferretti, 2009; in press; Wilder, 2002, 2005). The participants showed some evidence of writing arguments and understanding literature like disciplinary experts.

The researchers found that experienced English teachers favorably evaluated Lewis and Ferretti's (in press) instructional protocol, which supported the social validity of the intervention. However, the study was not conducted in the conditions of everyday classroom instruction. Individual students were provided intensive and explicit instruction about the background knowledge and skills used by experts in literary analysis, which allowed for relatively strong inferences about the internal validity of the intervention. Evidence about the intervention's external validity, and especially about how it might be adapted to the complexities of the everyday classroom, was not provided. Nevertheless, Lewis and Ferretti's research shows that strategy instruction grounded in the disciplinary knowledge used in literary analysis produced marked improvements in students' written arguments about literature.

Writing to Learn in Social Studies and Science

ACCelerating Expository Literacy (ACCEL; Englert, Okolo, & Mariage, 2009) is a specific instructional program designed to integrate a series of interrelated reading and writing strategies in learning about science and social studies from expository texts. The ACCEL instruction includes strategies that are called upon flexibly, depending on the nature of the reading and writing science or social studies task; collectively, they include PLAN It, Highlight It, Read It, Mark It, Note It, Map It, Respond to It, and Write It. Each strategy becomes a tool to be used in conjunction with knowledge about common text structures in expository text: cause–effect, problem–solution, compare–contrast, time (sequential order), classification, and explanation. Together, strategies and text structure form the basis of the overall curriculum.

Theoretical principles inherent in ACCEL feature a gradual release of responsibility model, as with most cognitive apprenticeships: (1) modeling the new literacy strategy through teacher think-alouds as the teacher makes public his or her inner thoughts and demonstrates overt actions; (2) providing cue cards to prompt strategy steps, self-instructions, and self-questions; (3) providing guided practice using sample texts as the teacher prompts students to perform the think-alouds and strategy steps, while continuing to monitor, reteach, and support performance; (4) placing students in collaborative arrangements with partners to encourage strategy use and talk; (5) making knowledge public by summarizing and discussing the strategy and the content knowledge of students; and (6) providing further modeling, prompting, and coaching on an as-needed basis through responsive dialogues.

In addition, Englert, Okolo, et al. (2009) provided notes, diagrams, and concept maps to help students coordinate use of the individual strategies and apply the strategies as part of an inquiry process. The planning (PLAN It), reading (Highlight It, Mark It), organizing (Note It, Map It), and writing (Respond to It, Report It) strategies were situated within a learning-to-learn inquiry process, in which students applied their knowledge about text comprehension and composition to support the development of disciplinary knowledge in social studies and science.

The inquiry process began as teachers engaged students in activities geared for planning to learn, such as considering the purpose for reading (P: Why am I reading this?) and overview of the topics (L: List Topics—What is it about?), activating prior knowledge (A: Activate prior knowledge and connect to self, text, world—What do I know?), asking questions (N: Note your questions—What do I want to know?), and surveying the structure of the passage (S: Structure and organization—How is it organized?). Moreover, the defining goal of these activities was to link common reviewing and paraphrasing strategies, whether students were highlighting, taking notes, summarizing, or writing (Englert, Okolo, 2009, et al., 2009).

Students learned strategic reading behaviors as they gathered information from text, then interpreted and organized that information. Thus, Reads It broadly included highlighting, marking, note taking, and creating concept maps:

1. During the Highlight It strategy, students highlighted the main ideas and details of an expository passage.

2. The Mark It strategy encouraged students to underline main ideas, to make connections between the text information and their knowledge of the world or self, and to summarize the information about the main ideas and details in the margins.

3. During Note It, students took notes on an expository passage that they had highlighted, using a hierarchical structure or outline to represent the superordinate–subordinate relationship among the main ideas and details.

4. During Map It, students were taught to construct a semantic map of the important ideas and details from the passage, or to use a discipline-specific

graphic organizer (e.g., problem–solution) to take notes of the important ideas.

During Respond to It students learned additional disciplinary tools, such as identifying author credibility and bias, and multiple perspectives, and attempted to query texts, as well as interpret evidence. In this phase, students transitioned from processing content to interacting with content in preparation for writing. Thus, some of the actions in the Respond to It phase included using evidence to support claims, and connecting to self, texts, and world, and giving and receiving feedback to and from peers. Finally, during Report It, students shared their findings by generating a written report, selecting a relevant expository text structure, then discussing their findings with peers. Information gathered by students in earlier phases was assembled in this culminating phase of the inquiry curriculum, and they employed all of the learning-to-learn tools (notably, text structure), in writing.

Englert and her colleagues evaluated the ACCEL program in a series of studies over a 3-year period (Englert et al., 2007, 2008; Englert, Mariage, et al., 2009) by comparing learning outcomes for students in general education classrooms without learning problems to learning outcomes for students with LD. In their most recent program evaluation, students completed tasks in social studies and science domains. For social studies, students wrote an informational news article, in which they retold main ideas and facts from text they learned to highlight and take notes on. For science, students synthesized information from text into a semantic map and used it to write an informational essay. Both activities required students mentally to construct, represent, and orchestrate the informational relationships among main ideas and details, developing a macrostructure for the expository texts (Englert, Mariage, et al., 2009).

Not surprisingly, general education students outperformed students in special education on measures related to note taking, highlighting, comprehension, and writing. Moreover, organizing information was difficult for students in both groups. In an evaluation that focused on learning differences between students who learned the ACCEL curriculum and students who did not, students without learning problems demonstrated gains in note taking and highlighting, whereas students with special needs only showed gains in highlighting. Reliable gains were not evident in overall writing ability for either group.

However, use of the ACCEL program has been credited for other improved literacy outcomes. In the earliest study (Englert et al., 2007), seventh-grade students became skilled readers by using the highlighting and note taking strategies proficiently, leading to improved literacy performance in content-area classrooms. In later studies (Englert et al., 2008; Englert, Mariage, et al., 2009) students with special educational needs made relatively larger gains than students in general education, based on their improved ability to identify main ideas selectively and details in printed texts, take well-organized notes, and generate written retellings that contained related details and ideas. Finally, observers noted that, at the end of the study, students were making spontaneous use of the strategies, which may suggest generalization.

Historical Understanding

Despite differing perspectives about its purposes (see Ferretti et al., 2001; Wineburg, 1996), there is general agreement that history instruction should promote the acquisition of disciplinary knowledge and critical habits of mind needed to participate in democratic decision making (Ferretti & Okolo, 1996; Ferretti et al., 2001; MacArthur, Ferretti, & Okolo, 2002). Historical thinking requires that students "sift through *traces* of the past (e.g., artifacts, documents, and the physical environment) as well as *accounts* of the past (e.g., stories, films, television news, and historical fiction) to construct an interpretation of an event" (Ferretti et al., 2001, p. 60, emphasis in original). Because these sources reflect a *representation* of the past (Seixas, 1996), historians and students alike must analyze evidence to determine how the sources came into existence, who constructed them and for what purposes, what other accounts exist, and which of these accounts merit trust (Seixas, 1996).

Historical analysis is informed by evidence that can be brought to bear on potentially contestable interpretive claims. In judging and evaluating these claims, historians, like other disciplinary experts, use strategies and standards shared by members of their discourse community. Wineburg's (1991a, 1991b) research shows that historians use the strategies of corroboration, contextualization, and sourcing to judge the trustworthiness of the evidence. They compare the details of one source against those of another ("corroboration"), situate the event in its temporal and spatial context ("contextualization"), and check the document's source to determine the purposes for which it was created ("sourcing"). Unfortunately, the evidence shows that students' understanding of historical perspective and their ability to conduct historical analysis are limited. For example, the results of the 2006 NAEP history test (Lee & Weiss, 2007) showed that about one-third of fourth and eighth graders, and over 50% of 12th graders, performed below the "basic" level.

De La Paz (2005) conducted a study designed in part to demonstrate how writing may be infused into content classrooms. The social studies teacher helped validate a historical reasoning strategy by applying Wineburg's strategies with students and using primary source documents. The English teacher taught a previously validated planning strategy for persuasive writing (De La Paz & Graham, 1997a, 1997b) using the same sources. Participants came from one middle school in northern California. A total of 70 students (19 gifted, 39 average, and 12 students with mild disabilities, primarily LD) learned the historical reasoning and persuasive writing strategies. In addition, although the primary purpose of the study was to conduct a descriptive comparison of the essays written by students with varying learning profiles in the experimental group, the data also included papers written at the same school by students who comprised a posttest-only control group. The control participants (N = 62; 17 gifted and 46 average students) included 28 students randomly assigned to read and respond to the pretest topic, and 34 students randomly assigned to read and respond to the posttest topic.

The materials in this study included six westward expansion topics, from 1830 to 1850, prepared for both assessment and instruction purposes. Before the study began, primary source excerpts (e.g., published remarks by missionaries) and secondary sources (historians' interpretations of the events summarized as "textbook" versions of an event) were simplified, until teachers were confident that students would understand the vocabulary and be able to read each text. Passage length was held constant for each set of materials. Each set contained three accounts (with conflicting viewpoints and/or contrasting information) on the following topics.

The first topic (which was used as a pretest measure) was President Andrew Jackson's Indian Removal Act and its impact on the Cherokee Nation. The second topic was an event known as the Whitman Massacre, which occurred because of a series of cultural misunderstandings between U.S. missionaries and Native Americans in the state of Oregon. The third topic was about a Mormon leader named John D. Lee and his role in the Mormon massacre of then U.S. emigrants at Mountain Meadows, Utah. The fourth topic was the Texas War for Independence from Mexico. The fifth topic included differing views by women during the Suffrage Movement. The last topic (which was used as a posttest measure) retold a series of events that led to the war between the United States and Mexico; this territorial dispute ended with a huge increase in the size of the United States.

The three-step historical reasoning strategy was based on Wineburg's seminal work (1991a, 1991b) and contained two self-questioning routines and a prompt for students to generate notes about the topic. During the first step, students considered the author, or source, of a text and, based on that information, analyzed the text for potential inaccuracies in reporting an event. Students answered three questions: 1. What was the author's purpose?; 2. Do the reasons make sense?; 3. Do you find evidence of bias? To detect bias, students were guided to examine the author's *word choice* and whether there was *only one point of view* in the document.

The second step of the strategy was to compare details across sources and look for conflicting points of view or information by answering five questions: 1. Is the author inconsistent?; 2. Is a person described differently?; 3. Is an event described differently?; 4. What is missing from the author's argument?; 5. What can you infer from reading *across* sources? Thus, students learned to identify then ignore misleading and untrustworthy information, and to focus on facts that appeared consistent across multiple sources (i.e., corroboration). The final step prompted students to make notes on what seemed believable from each source.

Students learned to read and take notes on primary source documents and to use their notes to prepare for a second task, writing opinion essays. Planning instruction was similar to that used by De La Paz and Graham (1997a); however, it was changed to meet the needs of older, more capable writers by increasing expectations for length, elaborations, and number of supporting reasons to multiparagraph essays. The strategy was also modified to address historical elements of the argumentative writing task, using suggestions by Karras (1994), specifically adding historical evidence as the basis for one's argument and refutation of a potential rebuttal. Thus, the strategy prompted students to use historical content from their reading and to organize these ideas for use in their papers before composing.

The mnemonic STOP reminded students to consider and list content on both sides of the topic before deciding which side to support in their essays. The steps of the mnemonic prompted them to Suspend judgment, Take a side, Organize ideas (choose from among the ideas listed and number), and Plan more as they wrote. A second mnemonic and subroutine, DARE, was incorporated in the strategy to reinforce the need to consider text structure (i.e., to include important elements of argumentative essays and to consider the reader's perspective when writing). Students were prompted to Develop a topic sentence, Add supporting ideas, Reject an argument for the other side, and End with a conclusion. Students learned to use each element within each paragraph, with one exception: The idea to "reject an argument for the other side" was to be accomplished once in the essay.

The historical reasoning instruction lasted 12 days, and the writing instruction lasted 10 days (taught simultaneously over the course of 1 month). During instruction, teachers and students worked collaboratively to apply both strategies, then teacher assistance and other instructional scaffolds were gradually faded.

Evidence that students internalized instructional content came from results of formal comparisons of their pre- to posttest performance (in reading and writing from primary sources) in which they worked without teacher assistance (De La Paz, 2005). In general, the results indicated that after instruction, students wrote longer and more persuasive papers containing more arguments and more accurate historical content. In addition, both the length and persuasive quality of papers written by students with disabilities at posttest were comparable to the pretest papers written by talented writers. Students' work at posttest also included the use of mnemonics in their work, and they generated written notes (on regular lined paper) before composing essays without prompting. A few caveats are worth noting regarding this study: First, students in the control group did not receive comparable instruction; rather, they read one set of historical documents and produced a written argument. Second, some students who received instruction did not master the reading and writing strategies. Five students with disabilities (29%) and seven average students (15%) were not proficient in using the historical reading and writing strategies, as evidenced by their work completion during independent practice (given time constraints to plan and write an essay in one class period) before the posttest.

Making Historical Reasoning Visible

The coordination of historical reasoning and writing strategy instruction has been described with an emphasis on how teachers made use of the reasoning and writing heuristics (De La Paz, Morales, & Winston, 2007). A more recent study (De La Paz & Felton, 2010) used documents about the 20th century with academically diverse high school students. These documents were part of a semester-long social studies unit for 11th-grade students who were poor and average writers; moreover, the study took place at two schools; at each site, one general education teacher provided the experimental instruction and another provided a comparison form of instruction. One special education teacher who was certified in history cotaught at one school, because some students in the setting had high incidence disabilities.

The social studies teachers in the experimental condition collaborated with researchers on the instructional objectives and gave considerable input on the final source selection (see Figures 14.1–14.4). They chose *Prohibition* as a topic for instruction because it not only is a required 20th-century American history element but it also seemed to be an accessible topic for high school students not yet eligible to drink legally. Second, this topic appeared to be appropriate for students' attempts at sourcing and corroborating collaboratively, because their teacher had described and modeled his thinking using a document set about the Philippine War a few weeks earlier.

Instruction began with the same document set that students had grappled with as their pretest content. The teacher used the materials, knowing they were familiar, to describe both historical reasoning (reading) and writing strategies that students were going to learn in the upcoming unit. He also showed two finished argumentative essays, written from opposing stances, and explained how they had been composed from a plan that followed text structure that students would learn to follow. Finally, the teacher modeled how to engage in a close reading of one of the documents that students read, and demonstrated how to annotate the sources as he talked, using Figure 14.1 as a means for making the sourcing, corroboration, and contextualization strategies explicit. At the end of the first 3-day sequence, the teacher told students that they would engage in similar actions the next time they encountered primary source documents.

What now follows is a presentation of how this teacher engaged his students in a joint reading of three primary sources—two texts and one political cartoon. The teacher and students read and discussed each source, then applied the historical reasoning strategy. In the dialogue that follows, *bold italic font* highlights statements that provide examples of sourcing, corroboration, and contextualization (see Figure 14.1). The meaning of each excerpt is noted in brackets using language that was presented to students (e.g., Consider the author) and language that indicates more abstract terminology (e.g., contextualization).

Finally, while none of the following students was recognized as a high achiever according to typical academic standards, such as grades or test scores, Melissa, Maria, and Amanda consistently participated in class with high levels of engagement. Stephen qualified for special education services as a student with emotional and behavioral disorders. This particular teacher, Mr. H., should be credited for the high levels of student involvement in his classroom, because he was a very motivating person. Moreover, not all of his classes responded as well as this particular group of youngsters.

TEACHER: We are going to talk about Prohibition today. Amanda, please start reading. (*Hands out Prohibition sources*)

AMANDA: (*Reads the first source attribution.*) "Excerpt from the 1926 testimony before the U.S. Senate Committee on the Judiciary by Fiorello H. LaGuardia, New York City politician who served several terms in the House of Representatives."

TEACHER: **LaGuardia was probably a credible source** but it is hard to tell if there are factual errors. . . . [Consider the author; *sourcing*] **1926 was in the middle of prohibition when it was not enforced**. [Understand the source; *contextualization*]

CLASS: (*Reads the rest of the document aloud, commenting and clarifying meanings of vocabulary items together.*)

MELISSA: (*Reads the title of the cartoon,* "The Devil Fish.") This is a political cartoon . . .

TEACHER: The Prohibition Party stabs an octopus with *saloon* written on it. **This suggests that if saloons are done away with, then** all the problems associated with the saloons, political corruption, and partnership with thieves, gambling, defiance of the law, and trafficking in girls, will be effectively done away with. That is **an assumption underlying the argument**, that drinking alcohol and spending time in saloons is a bad thing to do. [Understand the source; *sourcing*]

JUAN: (*Reads the third source attribution.*) "Excerpt from the 1926 testimony by two officers of the Federal Council of Churches before the U.S. Senate Committee on the Judiciary." OK, **so this is from the same time**, and is also testimony to the U.S. Senate." [Understand the source; *contextualization*]

TEACHER: What do you think is going to be the position of officers of the Federal Council of Churches?

Thinking with historical documents

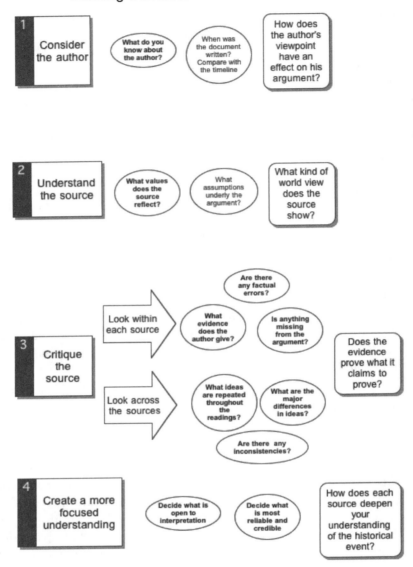

FIGURE 14.1. Historical reasoning strategy.

MELISSA: They are *ministers, so they are going to be against ending Prohibition.* [Consider the author; *sourcing*]

CLASS: (*Reads third document.*)

THANH: (*commenting on first fundamental assertion, lines 3–5.*) *Looking across sources*, a couple of ideas are repeated, the evils are the problems caused

1 It is impossible to tell whether Prohibition is a good thing or a bad thing. It has never been
2 enforced in this country.
3 There may not be as much liquor in quantity consumed today as there was before Prohibition,
4 but there is just as much alcohol.
5 At least 1,000,000 quarts of liquor is [*sic*] consumed each day in the United States. In my opinion
6 such an enormous traffic in liquor could not be carried on without the knowledge, if not the
7 connivance [support] of the officials entrusted with the enforcement of the law....
8 I believe that the percentage of whisky drinkers in the United States now is greater than in
9 any other country of the world. Prohibition is responsible for that....
10 At least $1,000,000,000 a year is lost to the National Government and the several States and
11 counties in excise taxes. The liquor traffic is going on just the same. This amount goes into the
12 pockets of bootleggers and in the pockets of the public officials in the shape of graft....
13 I will concede that the saloon was odious but now we have delicatessen stores, poolrooms,
14 drug stores, millinery shops, private parlors, and 57 other varieties of speak-easies selling liquor and
15 flourishing....
16 It is my calculation that at least a million dollars a day is paid in graft and corruption to
17 Federal, State, and local officers. Such a condition is not only intolerable, but it is demoralizing and
18 dangerous to organized government....
19 The Government even goes to the trouble to facilitate the financing end of the bootlegging
20 industry. In 1925, $286,950,000 more of $10,000 bills were issued than in 1920 and $25,000,000
21 more of $5,000 bills were issued. What honest business man deals in $10,000 bills? Surely these
22 bills were not used to pay the salaries of ministers. The bootlegging industry has created a demand for
23 bills of large denominations, and the Treasury Department accommodates them....

FIGURE 14.2. Excerpt from the 1926 testimony before the U.S. Senate Committee on the Judiciary by Fiorello H. LaGuardia, New York City politician who served several terms in the House of Representatives.

by saloons ... [Critique the source—Look across the sources; *corroboration*]

AMANDA: (*Commenting on LaGuardia's testimony, lines 8–9.*) See, LaGuardia said that Prohibition caused more people to drink whiskey ...

TEACHER: Yes, good point, and when LaGuardia concedes that the saloon was "odious" [line 13], *that point is in agreement with that made by the council of churches* ... [Critique the source—Look across the sources; *corroboration*] *but what do you make of other ideas in LaGuardia's testimony?* [Critique the source—Look within each source; *corroboration*]

LARA: (*reading lines 10–12.*) This shows that *LaGuardia thinks Prohibition is ineffective*, that it is wasting money, and people are still drinking alcohol, and that you can still get it to drink. [Critique the source—Look within each source; *corroboration*]

TEACHER: Uh-huh. **What is the premise of the Federal Council of Churches?** … [Critique the source—Look across the sources; *corroboration*]

MELISSA: (*Reads lines 28–32.*) "Least of all should our prohibition law be changed in response to the cry of those who by their own disrespect for the law are preventing it from receiving a fair trial or who, because of their special interest in the return of the liquor traffic, are artificially stimulating an agitation for changing our present law."

TEACHER: OK, fine. Let's take a break and partner off. (*Assigns the following task to each group of students.*) These groups will look for corroborating evidence in agreement, and the other groups will look for contrasting examples, different points of view…. Did you find *any similarities in positions across sources*? … [Critique the source—Look across the sources…*corroboration; repeats throughout remaining excerpt*]

SHARON AND MARIA: (*Reads.*) "The liquor traffic with the accompanying saloon was allied with political corruption, crime, gambling, and prostitution"

FIGURE 14.3. Political cartoon: The devil fish.

[lines 22–23, Federal Council of Churches]. *This is consistent with the cartoon* ...

EDUARDO AND LAWRENCE: LaGuardia and the Federal Council of Churches *really don't agree* ...

ROCHELLE AND UYEN: Yeah. Like when the Federal Council says, "If serious evils have sprung up since Prohibition, they are far less than the evils, which

1 The support of national Prohibition by the Federal Council of the Churches rests
2 upon four fundamental considerations.
3 First. The belief that in dealing with gigantic social evils like disease or crime,
4 individual liberty must be controlled in the interest of the public welfare. Second. The
5 belief that the liquor traffic is beyond question such an evil. Third. The conviction that no
6 plan less thoroughgoing than Prohibition is sufficient to eradicate the evils of the liquor
7 traffic. Fourth. The evidence of history that other methods of attempting to control the
8 traffic have failed and that Prohibition, despite inadequacies of enforcement, is
9 succeeding better than any other program.
10 ... The policy of prohibition was not adopted hastily nor was it foisted upon the
11 country by a puritanical minority. It was first voted in most of the States separately and
12 then nationally, because the people had become convinced that the liquor traffic was a
13 social evil of such magnitude that it had to be destroyed. The Eighteenth Amendment was
14 made a part of the Constitution by the regular methods which the founders of the Republic
15 devised with a view to making the amendment to the Constitution difficult rather than
16 easy. Yet this amendment was adopted more promptly than any other change in the
17 Constitution ever proposed.
18 The reasons which led to Prohibition not only remain to-day but have been
19 reinforced by the experience of other nations. The social peril of alcoholism is becoming a
20 growing concern to statesmen throughout the world. If serious evils have sprung up since
21 Prohibition, they are far less than the evils which arose from the liquor traffic prior to the
22 amendment. The liquor traffic with the accompanying saloon was allied with political
23 corruption, crime, gambling, and prostitution. It meant the wreckage of men and the
24 degradation of families, which social workers and ministers saw constantly in their daily
25 work. It produced needless inefficiency in industry....
26 The one path of advance is for all good citizens personally to observe the law and
27 to support the great enterprise ... of completely ridding the Nation of as demoralizing a
28 business as the liquor traffic has always proved itself to be. Least of all should our
29 Prohibition law be changed in response to the cry of those who by their own disrespect
30 for the law are preventing it from receiving a fair trial or who, because of their special
31 interest in the return of the liquor traffic, are artificially stimulating an agitation for
32 changing our present law. The call of the hour is for such a thoroughgoing work of moral
33 persuasion and legal enforcement as will give the policy of Prohibition an adequate
34 opportunity to demonstrate its full value to the Nation and to the world.

Rev. S. Parkes Cadman, President
Rev. Charles S. Macfarland, General Secretary

FIGURE 14.4. Excerpt from the 1926 testimony by two officers from the Federal Council of Churches before the Senate Committee on the Judiciary.

arose from the liquor traffic prior to the amendment," [lines 20–22] *that goes against what LaGuardia says* . . .

TRINH AND STEPHEN: Right, and the Council said, "The evidence of history that other methods of attempting to control the traffic have failed and that Prohibition, despite inadequacies of enforcement, is succeeding better than any other program," [lines 7–9]. *This is something else in conflict with LaGuardia* . . .

TEACHER: OK. So now we are going to end with a 5-minute debate on the two positions. Write down the reasons for each side. Then tomorrow you are going to plan using the STOP process and a T-chart, and start drafting an essay. . . .

In the preceding situation, the teacher divided the room in half and reminded students that they were focused on the time period in which the end of Prohibition was being debated. Their task was to present reasons for and against each position, and to provide evidence from the documents that supported their reasons, in a quick whole-class debate. The reader may believe that this type of thinking is not realistic for struggling students, and in some ways that is true. The number of students who engaged actively was relatively few, and a handful of students did not even pay attention. However, most students did work in groups to prepare for the upcoming debate, because they had followed along as the previous discussion had taken place, and several teacher actions had prepared students for the activity.

First, the teacher had modeled this type of thinking in response to another document set, before students examined this set of documents. When he had done so before, Mr. H. had made explicit reference to sourcing, corroboration, and contextualization strategies routinely used by disciplinary experts. As in other forms of self-regulatory strategy instruction (De La Paz, 2005; Graham, 2006), the teacher used metacognitive statements as he explained his thinking while reading the primary source documents. Second, the teacher connected the task of reading with that of writing. He informed his class that the debate was a way to solidify their thinking about the topic of Prohibition, and that after the debate, students would be developing a plan and subsequent essay on that topic.

To prepare students for the planning and writing process, the teacher kept track of the main ideas that students presented for continuing or ending Prohibition during the class debate. As each new idea was mentioned, he recorded it on one side or the other (using a T-chart) on the blackboard. Students copied these ideas as the debate ensued. Then, after the debate was over, Mr. H. transformed the ideas into a plan, using the STOP process. He acknowledged that the first step in the planning process had now been accomplished, because ideas on both sides of the topic were noted. Students were told that they could decide which side they wished to take when they composed their own essays (to be done for homework), but because most students were likely to believe that Prohibition should end, he chose to "take the other side" and argue that this law should be continued.

To accomplish the next step, "organize ideas," the teacher chose one argument from the side that he planned to refute, then an idea that could be used for its rebuttal, and labeled them as the third and fourth ideas. He explained why it was important to decide on this argument rebuttal dimension first, based on De La Paz's prior experience that secondary students with and without LD were most successful in planning multiparagraph essays when they considered the overall scheme for the essay, rather than organize ideas in a sequential manner. He ended this step by identifying the first and second ideas for his essay, and numbering them. The final step, "plan more as you write" was adapted to follow Karras's (1994) text structure rather than DARE, as De La Paz and Graham (1997a) had originally developed the writing structure for younger students. As mentioned earlier, this decision was based partly on the need to adapt the writing process for *disciplinary* purposes, and because writing expectations in a high school general education (social studies) setting were quite different from original expectations held for middle school resource (English/language arts) settings.

Outcomes in De La Paz and Felton's 2010 study were compared to those of different groups of students at the same schools who had access to the same topics and received a traditional form of instruction with feedback about writing. Results demonstrated that the historical reasoning and writing strategies helped students write evidence-based arguments that were superior to peers who practiced reading and writing from the same sources. More specifically, students who received the experimental form of instruction learned how to consider several aspects of the sources they were given to read, and to corroborate and contextualize aspects across sources with events of the time period in which they were situated. They also learned how to use evidence from these sources as a means for substantiating claims in their written arguments.

In addition, the instruction had a positive effect on the writing performance of the participating high school students. They were much more likely to be able to cite documents or quotes, or use quotes to further an argument after instruction. This was not a subtle change in growth among students in the experimental group, because students in the comparison group had outperformed them at pretest on the number of documents cited and the level of document use. Students in the experimental group also wrote argumentative essays with more advanced development of claims and rebuttals after instruction, after controlling for the length of their essays.

Disciplinary Learning with Young Students

Modifications may be needed to promote disciplinary learning with younger students; however, these changes require changes in scaffolds and materials rather than changes in the decision to engage younger students in historical analysis. VanSledright and colleagues (Afflerbach & VanSledright, 2001; VanSledright &

Frankes, 2000; VanSledright & Kelly, 1998) have demonstrated that students in general education classrooms as young as fourth and fifth grade are capable of achieving these outcomes. Books have also been written by and for practitioners. For example, Monica Edinger's *Seeking History: Teaching with Primary Sources in Grades 4–6* (2000) offers ample suggestions for making primary sources come alive for young students. Findings from Ferretti et al. (2001) also provide support for these approaches in elementary school with poor readers and writers. Students with disabilities made significant gains in historical knowledge and historical reasoning, although students without disabilities made larger gains. Both groups of students made gains in self-efficacy for learning social studies.

We describe specific adaptations to historical reasoning and persuasive writing strategies for younger students based on De La Paz's (2004) work with fourth- and fifth-grade teachers on a Teaching American History grant and her current work with collaborators Monte-Sano and Felton (De La Paz, Monte-Sano, & Felton, 2009). Rather than reproduce actual documents on topic of the Gold Rush here, it may be more helpful to suggest that essential features of appropriate sources should (1) all be on the same topic; (2) present similar voices (e.g., two letters from miners rather than one newspaper advertisement calling prospective miners to the West and one letter); (3) show contrasting views, opinions, or evidence; and (4) be corroborated with a secondary source, such as a textbook excerpt. Sources framed in this way encourage a more disciplinary approach to looking for evidence when students read and compare points of view about particular topics (Monte-Sano, 2010). Finally, recall that students should situate their work with sources in the context of a broader unit in which they have an understanding of the overall topic, such as a unit on the growth of our nation or the Gold Rush, which are required topics in California history classes. The final section of this chapter provides a description of how teachers might choose to engage upper elementary school students in planning to write an argumentative essay on this topic. Just as the vignette on Prohibition portrayed the historical reading process in action with older students, the following information is intended to show how teachers might engage younger students with the writing process, in activities that support content-area literacy. To accomplish this, we share a familiar writing strategy originally developed by Steve Graham and Karen Harris.

The Graham and Harris planning strategy and accompanying mnemonic TREE (Topic sentence, Reasons, Explain reasons, Ending; 1989; Harris, Graham, & Mason, 2002) was modified for planning evidence-based argumentative essays. The original purpose was for persuasive writing rather than disciplinary writing. While there is an adequate match between the mnemonic and its original purpose, in the current context students need to invoke disciplinary content that aligns with argumentative text structure.

De La Paz (2004) and De La Paz et al. (2009) provided new meanings for the mnemonic TREE. First, students wrote a Topic sentence *that explains the situation, controversy, or dilemma.* Depending on how the learning activity is structured, the topic sentence acknowledges the historical dilemma at hand. For example, if given two primary source excerpts from miners' letters sent to family members living "back East" during the Gold Rush, a student might write, "During the Gold Rush, miners sent letters home telling different stories about what happened when they went looking for gold."

The second element, Reasons, was the same as the one proposed by Graham and Harris, with one important caveat. Rather than brainstorming reasons from what they know about the world in general, students identify claims, or reasons from the available sources, to support the topic sentence. In this example, they look for evidence in the miners' letters showing different accounts of events, attitudes, or experiences. To illustrate further (but without actually providing specific documents), reasons might include evidence that some miners had financial success in mining for gold, whereas the vast majority found that daily expenses far outweighed the limited sums of money they made from minute discoveries of gold. Moreover, eventually, many miners gave up mining for agricultural pursuits in California.

The original intent of the third element in TREE prompted students to elaborate on content. For historical reasoning, this element was changed to *Evaluate the Evidence*. To better promote disciplinary thinking in history, this step prompts students to evaluate the reasons just written as they compared the primary and secondary sources in the reading and writing activity. Structured discussion may facilitate this process (see Felton, Garcia-Mila, & Gilabert, 2009) as students select reasons that they judge to be strong and ones that can be supported with facts, quotes, or details from the documents. This step involves some sophistication, because noting which content from the reading to use in the writing activity may be difficult for elementary school students.

The last element was to ask students to *End with your position or interpretation*. This element was similar to the topic sentence or premise; however, in a truly disciplinary sense in the social studies, an important goal is for students to form an argument or position based on the available evidence (Monte-Sano, 2010). Thus, a given student may decide to end his or her paragraph with a statement indicating that "some miners ended their search for gold without reaching their dreams," while another student may finish with a more nuanced appreciation that "searching for gold led some miners to true wealth in ways they had not imagined." The important point here is that the writing assignment has supported students' thinking about the primary and secondary documents, and that the mnemonic and accompanying strategy has been recrafted from its original purpose to support a disciplinary use.

Summary

Our purpose in this chapter was to identify the factors and illustrate instructional activities that influence the development of literacy in the content area. We began by reviewing evidence about the factors that contribute to the comprehension and production of texts, and concluded that the academic progress of students depends on the development of literacy skills that become increasingly specific and dependent on disciplinary knowledge and skills. We then discussed some of the specific challenges experienced by students with LD in the comprehension and production of text, and concluded that a lack of relevant background knowledge, which includes disciplinary knowledge, as well as impoverished vocabularies; limited knowledge of text structure; and problems with self-regulation negatively impact their comprehension and production of text. Representative interventions in the language arts and history were summarized to illustrate how instructional activities can and have been designed to promote content-area literacy. While imperfect, these interventions illustrate how the purpose-driven design of instructional activities might promote the development of disciplinary literacy. In short, instructional activities that promote content-area literacy support students in thinking, communicating, writing, and interacting like disciplinary experts. We ended the chapter with two illustrations of how reading and writing activities might look in secondary and elementary settings in the context of social studies instruction. We hope our examples help readers envision why it is important to change the nature of reading and writing instruction in content-area learning situations, as well as suggest ways to do so within one discipline.

References

Afflerbach, P., & VanSledright, B. (2001). Hath! Doth! What?: Middle graders reading innovative history text. *Journal of Adolescent and Adult Literacy, 44*, 696–707.

Applebee, A. N. (1993). *Literature in the secondary schools: Studies of curriculum and instruction in the United States.* Urbana, IL: National Council of Teachers of English.

Applebee, A., & Langer, J. (2006). *The state of writing instruction: What existing data tell us.* Albany, NY: Center on English Learning and Achievement.

Bereiter, C., & Scardamalia, M. (1987). *The psychology of written composition.* Hillsdale, NJ: Erlbaum.

Biancarosa, G., & Snow, C. E. (2006). *Reading next: A vision for action and research in middle and high school literacy: A report from the Carnegie Corporation of New York* (2nd ed.). Washington, DC: Alliance for Excellent Education.

Bransford, J. D., Brown, A. L., & Cocking, R. R. (2000). *How people learn: Brain, mind, experience, and school.* Washington, DC: National Academy Press.

De La Paz, S. (2004, August). *Thinking and writing with primary and secondary documents.* Presented at the Teaching American History Summer Workshop, Santa Clara, CA.

De La Paz, S. (2005). Effects of historical reasoning instruction and writing strategy mastery in culturally and academically diverse middle school classrooms. *Journal of Educational Psychology, 97*(2), 137–156.

De La Paz, S., & Felton, M. (2010). Reading and writing from multiple sources in history: Effects of strategy instruction. *Contemporary Educational Psychology, 35*(3), 174–192.

De La Paz, S., & Graham, S. (1997a). Strategy instruction in planning: Effects on the writing performance and behavior of students with learning difficulties. *Exceptional Children, 63*, 167–181.

De La Paz, S., & Graham, S. (1997b). The effects of dictation and advanced planning instruction on the composing of students with writing and learning problems. *Journal of Educational Psychology, 89*(2), 203–222.

De La Paz, S., Monte-Sano, C., & Felton, M. (2009). Disciplinary writing instruction for the social studies classroom: A path to adolescent literacy. Institute for Education Sciences, U.S. Department of Education through Grant R305A090153 to the University of Maryland.

De La Paz, S., Morales, P., & Winston, P. (2007). Source interpretation: Teaching students with and without learning disabilities to read and write historically. *Journal of Learning Disabilities, 40*(2), 134–144.

De La Paz, S., Swanson, P., & Graham, S. (1998). The contribution of executive control to the revising of students with writing and learning difficulties. *Journal of Educational Psychology, 90*, 448–460.

Donovan, C. A., & Smolkin, L. B. (2006). Children's understanding of genre and writing development. In C. A. MacArthur, S. Graham, & J. Fitzgerald (Eds.), *Handbook of writing research* (pp. 131–143). New York: Guilford Press.

Duke, N. K. (2005). Comprehension of what for what: Comprehension as a nonlinear construct. In S. G. Paris & S. A. Stahl (Eds.), *Children's reading comprehension and assessment* (pp. 93–104). Mahwah, NJ: Erlbaum.

Edinger, M. (2000). *Seeking history: Teaching with primary sources in grades 4–6*. Portsmouth, NH: Heinemann.

Englert, C. S., Mariage, T., Okolo, C., Billman, A., Courtad, C. A., Moxley, K. D., et al., (2007, April). *Project ACCEL: A study of content area literacy in middle grade classrooms*. Paper presentation at the Annual Meeting of the American Educational Research Association, Chicago.

Englert, C. S., Mariage, T. V., Okolo, C. M., Chen, H.-Y., Courtad, C. A., Moxley, K. D., et al. (2008, March). *Content area literacy in inclusive middle grade classrooms: A two-year study of Project ACCEL*. Paper presentation at the Annual Meeting of the American Educational Research Association, New York.

Englert, C. S., Mariage, T. V., Okolo, C. M., Martin, N., Courtad, C. A., Sevensma, K., et al. (2009). *ACCELerating the Expository Literacy of middle-school students through strategy instruction in the content areas*. Unpublished paper, Literacy Achievement Research Center of Michigan State University, East Lansing.

Englert, C. S., Okolo, C. M., & Mariage, T. V. (2009). Informational writing across the curriculum. In G. Troia (Ed.), *Instruction and assessment for struggling writers: Evidence-based practices* (pp. 132–161). New York: Guilford Press.

Englert, C. S., & Thomas, C. C. (1987). Sensitivity to text structure in reading and learning: A comparison between learning disabled and non-learning disabled students. *Learning Disability Quarterly, 10*, 93–105.

Faggella-Luby, M. N., & Deshler, D. D. (2008). Reading comprehension in adolescents with LD: What we know; what we need to learn. *Learning Disabilities Research and Practice, 23*, 70–78.

Fahnestock, J., & Secor, M. (1991). *The rhetoric of literary criticism*. In C. Bazerman & J. Paradis (Eds.), *Textual dynamics of the professions: Historical and contemporary studies of writing in professional communities* (pp. 77–96). Madison: University of Wisconsin Press.

Felton, M., Garcia-Mila, M., & Gilabert, S. (2009). Deliberation versus dispute: The impact of argumentative discourse goals on learning and reasoning in the science classroom. *Informal Logic, 29*(4), 417–446.

Ferretti, R. P., Lewis, W. E., & Andrews-Weckerly, S. (2009). Do goals affect the structure of students' argumentative writing strategies? *Journal of Educational Psychology, 101,* 577–589.

Ferretti, R. P., MacArthur, C. A., & Dowdy, N. S. (2000). The effects of an elaborated goal on the persuasive writing of students with learning disabilities and their normally achieving peers. *Journal of Educational Psychology, 92,* 694–702.

Ferretti, R. P., MacArthur, C. A., & Okolo, C. M. (2001). Teaching for historical understanding in inclusive classrooms. *Learning Disability Quarterly, 24,* 59–71.

Ferretti, R. P., & Okolo, C. M. (1996). Authenticity in learning: Multimedia design projects in the social studies for students with disabilities. *Journal of Learning Disabilities, 29,* 450–460.

Fletcher, J. M., Shaywitz, S. E., Shankweiler, D. P., Katz, L., Liberman, I. Y., Fowler, A., et al. (1994). Cognitive profiles of reading disabilities: Comparisons of discrepancy and low achieving definitions. *Journal of Educational Psychology, 86,* 1–18.

Gamoran, A., & Carbonaro, W. J. (2002). High school English: A national portrait. *High School Journal, 86,* 2–15.

Gersten, R., Fuchs, L., Williams, J., & Baker, S. (2001). Teaching reading comprehension strategies to students with learning disabilities: A review of research. *Review of Educational Research, 71,* 279–320.

Graham, S. (1990). The role of production factors in learning disabled students' compositions. *Journal of Educational Psychology, 82,* 781–791.

Graham, S. (1997). Executive control in the revising of students with learning and writing difficulties. *Journal of Educational Psychology, 82,* 223–234.

Graham, S. (1999). Handwriting and spelling instruction for students with learning disabilities: A review. *Learning Disabilities Quarterly, 22,* 78–98.

Graham, S. (2006). Strategy instruction and the teaching of writing. In C. A. MacArthur, S. Graham, & J. Fitzgerald (Eds.), *Handbook of writing research* (pp. 187–207). New York: Guilford Press.

Graham, S., & Harris, K. (1989). Improving learning disabled students' skill at composing essays: Self-instructional strategy training. *Exceptional Children, 56,* 201–214.

Graham, S., & Harris, K. R. (1997). It can be taught, but it doesn't develop naturally: Myths and realities in writing instruction. *School Psychology Review, 26,* 414–424.

Graham, S., & Harris, K. R. (2005). *Writing better: Effective strategies for teaching students with learning difficulties.* Baltimore: Brookes.

Graham, S., Harris, K. R., & Chorzempa, B. F. (2002). Contribution of spelling instruction to the spelling, writing, and reading of poor readers. *Journal of Educational Psychology, 94,* 669–686.

Graham, S., Harris, K., MacArthur, C. A., & Schwartz, S. S. (1991). Writing and writing instruction with students with learning disabilities: A review of a program of research. *Learning Disability Quarterly, 14,* 89–114.

Graham, S., MacArthur, C. A., Schwartz, S., & Page-Voth, V. (1992). Improving learning disabled students' compositions using a strategy involving product and process goal setting. *Exceptional Children, 58,* 322–334.

Graham, S., & Perin, D. (2007). *Writing Next: Effective strategies to improve writing of adolescents in middle and high schools.* New York: Carnegie Corporation.

Harris, K., Graham, S., & Mason, L. (2002). POW plus TREE equals powerful opinion essays. *Teaching Exceptional Children, 34,* 70–73.

Hayes, J. R. (1996). A new framework for understanding cognition and affect in writing. In C. M. Levy & S. Ransdell (Eds.), *The science of writing: Theories, methods, individual differences, and applications* (pp. 1–28). Mahwah, NJ: Erlbaum.

Hayes, J. R., & Flower, L. S. (1980). Identifying the organization of writing processes. In L. Gregg & E. Steinberg (Eds.), *Cognitive processes in writing: An interdisciplinary approach* (pp. 3–30). Hillsdale, NJ: Erlbaum.

Hemingway, E. (1958). *In our time.* New York: Scribner's.

Jenkins, J., & O'Connor, R. (2002). *Early identification and intervention for young children with reading/learning disabilities.* In R. Bradley, L. Danielson, & D. Hallahan (Eds.), *Identification of learning disabilities: Research to practice* (pp. 99–149). Mahwah, NJ: Erlbaum.

Karras, R. W. (1994). Writing essays that make historical arguments. *OAH Magazine of History, 8,* 54–57.

Kavale, K. A., & Forness, S. R. (2000). History, rhetoric, and reality: Analysis of the inclusion debate. *Remedial and Special Education, 21,* 279–296.

Kintsch, W. (1988). The role of knowledge in discourse comprehension: A construction–integration model. *Psychological Review, 95,* 163–182.

Kintsch, W. (1994). Text comprehension, memory, and learning. *American Psychologist, 49,* 294–303.

Kintsch, W., & Kintsch, E. (2005). Comprehension. In S. G. Paris & S. A. Stahl (Eds.), *Children's reading comprehension and assessment* (pp. 71–92). Mahwah, NJ: Erlbaum.

Kiuhara, S. A., Graham, S., & Hawken, L. S. (2009). Teaching writing to high school students: A national survey. *Journal of Educational Psychology, 101,* 136–160.

Lee, J., & Weiss, A. (2007). *The Nation's Report Card: U.S. History 2006* (No. NCES 2007-474). Washington, DC: U.S. Department of Education, National Center for Education Statistics.

Lewis, W. E. (1997). *Gender, identity and the power of the narrative structure: Hemingway's postwar consciousness.* Unpublished manuscript, Millersville University, Millersville, Pennsylvania.

Lewis, W. E., & Ferretti, R. P. (2009). Defending interpretations of literary texts: The effects of topoi instruction on the literary arguments of high school students. *Reading and Writing Quarterly, 25,* 250–270.

Lewis, W. E., & Ferretti, R. P. (in press). Topoi and literary interpretation: The effects of a critical reading and writing intervention on high school students' analytic literary essays. *Contemporary Educational Psychology.*

Lovett, M. W., Steinbach, K. A., & Frijters, J. C. (2000). Remediating the core deficits of developmental reading disability: A double-deficit perspective. *Journal of Learning Disabilities, 33,* 334–358.

MacArthur, C. A., Ferretti, R. P., & Okolo, C. M. (2002). On defending controversial viewpoints: Debates of sixth-graders about the desirability of early 20th century American immigration. *Learning Disabilities Research and Practice, 17,* 160–172.

MacArthur, C. A., & Graham, S. (1987). Learning disabled students' composing with three methods: Handwriting, dictation, and word processing. *Journal of Special Education, 21,* 22–42.

MacArthur, C. A., Harris, K. R., & Graham, S. (1994). Improving students' planning processes through cognitive strategy instruction. In E. C. Butterfield & J. S. Carlson (Eds.), *Advances in cognition and educational practice: Vol. 2. Children's writing: Toward a process theory of the development of skilled writing* (pp. 173–198). Greenwich, CT: JAI Press.

MacArthur, C. A., Schwartz, S. S., & Graham, S. (1991). Effects of a reciprocal peer revision strategy in special education classrooms. *Learning Disabilities Research and Practice, 6,* 201–210.

Marshall, J. (2000). Research on response to literature. In R. Barr, M. L. Kamil, P. Mosenthal,

& P. D. Pearson (Eds.), *Handbook of reading research* (Vol. III, pp. 381–402). Mahwah, NJ: Erlbaum.

Mastropieri, M., Scruggs, T., & Graetz, J. (2003). Reading comprehension instruction for secondary students: Challenges for struggling students and teachers. *Learning Disability Quarterly, 26*, 103–116.

Meyer, B. J. F., & Freedle, R. O. (1984). Effects of discourse type on recall. *American Educational Research Journal, 21*, 121–143.

Meyer, B. J. F., Theodorou, E., Brezinski, K. L., Middlemiss, W., McDougall, J., & Barlett, B. J. (2002). Effects of structure strategy instruction delivered to fifth-grade children using the Internet with and without the aid of older adult tutors. *Journal of Educational Psychology, 94*, 486–519.

Monte-Sano, C. (2010). Disciplinary literacy in history: An exploration of the historical nature of adolescents' writing. *Journal of Learning Sciences, 19*, 539–568.

National Center for Educational Statistics. (2007). *The Nation's Report Card: Reading 2007.* Washington, DC: U.S. Government Printing Office. Retrieved July 31, 2009, from *nces. ed.gov/pubsearch/pubsinfo.asp?pubid=2007496.*

National Center for Educational Statistics. (2008). *The Nation's Report Card: Writing 2007.* Washington, DC: U.S. Government Printing Office. Retrieved July 31, 2009, from *nationsreportcard.gov/writing_2007.*

National Commission on Writing. (2004, September). *Writing: A ticket to work ... or a ticket out: A survey of business leaders.* Retrieved August 1, 2009, from *www.writingcommission. org/pr/writing_for_employ.html.*

National Commission on Writing. (2005, July). *Writing: A powerful message from state government.* Retrieved July 31, 2006, from *www.nwp.org/cs/public/print/resource/2541.*

Olson, D. R. (1994). *The world on paper.* Cambridge, UK: Cambridge University Press.

Olson, L. (2006). A decade of effort. *Quality Counts, 25*, 8–10, 12, 14, 16, 18–21.

Page-Voth, V., & Graham, S. (1999). Effects of goal-setting and strategy use on the writing performance and self-efficacy of students with writing and learning problems. *Journal of Educational Psychology, 91*, 230–240.

Persky, H. R., Daane, M. C., & Jin, Y. (2003). *The Nation's Report Card: Writing 2002, NCES 2003.* Washington, DC: National Center for Educational Statistics.

RAND Reading Study Group. (2002). *Reading for understanding.* Santa Monica, CA: RAND Corporation.

Rosenblatt, L. M. (1995). *Literature as exploration.* New York: Modern Language Association.

Searle, J. R. (1998). *Mind, language, and society.* New York: Basic Books.

Seixas, P. (1996). Conceptualizing the growth of historical thinking. In D. R. Olson & N. Torrance (Eds.), *The handbook of education and human development* (pp. 765–783). Oxford, UK: Blackwell.

Shanahan, T., & Shanahan, C. (2008). Teaching disciplinary literacy to adolescents: Rethinking content-area literacy. *Harvard Educational Review, 78*, 40–59.

Stearns, P. N., Seixas, P., & Wineburg, S. (Eds.). (2000). *Knowing, teaching, and learning history.* New York: New York University Press.

Torgesen, J. K., & Wagner, R. K. (1998). Alternative diagnostic approaches for specific developmental reading problems. *Learning Disabilities Research and Practice, 13*, 220–232.

Troia, G. A. (2006). Writing instruction for students with learning disabilities. In C. A. MacArthur, S. Graham, & J. Fitzgerald (Eds.), *Handbook of writing research* (pp. 324–336). New York: Guilford Press.

van Dijk, T. A., & Kintsch, W. (1978). Cognitive psychology and discourse: Recalling and summarizing stories. In W. U. Dressler (Ed.), *Current trends in linguistics* (pp. 61–80). New York: de Gruyter.

van Dijk, T. A., & Kintsch, W. (1983). *Strategies of discourse comprehension*. New York: Academic Press.

VanSledright, B., & Frankes, L. (2000). Concept- and strategic-knowledge development in historical study: A comparative exploration in two fourth-grade classrooms. *Cognition and Instruction, 8*, 239–283.

VanSledright, B., & Kelly, C. (1998). Reading American history: The influence of multiple sources on six fifth graders. *Elementary School Journal, 98*, 239–265.

Vaughn, S., Gersten, R., & Chard, D. J. (2000). The underlying message in LD intervention research: Findings from research synthesis. *Exceptional Children, 67*, 99–114.

Wilder, L. (2002). "Get uncomfortable with uncertainty": A study of the conventional values of literary analysis in an undergraduate literature course. *Written Communication, 19*, 175–221.

Wilder, L. (2005). "The rhetoric of literary criticism" revisited: Mistaken critics, complex contexts, and social justice. *Written Communication, 22*, 76–119.

Williams, J. P., Stafford, K. B., Lauer, K. D., Hall, K. M., & Pollini, S. (2009). Embedding reading comprehension training in content-area instruction. *Journal of Educational Psychology, 101*, 1–20.

Wineburg, S. (1991a). Historical problem solving: A study of the cognitive processes used in the evaluation of documentary and pictorial evidence. *Journal of Educational Psychology, 83*, 73–87.

Wineburg, S. (1991b). On the reading of historical texts: Notes on the breach between school and the academy. *American Educational Research Journal, 28*, 495–519.

Wineburg, S. (1996). The psychology of learning and teaching history. In D. C. Berliner & R. Calfee (Eds.), *The handbook of educational psychology* (pp. 423–437). New York: Macmillan.

Wineburg, S. (2001). *Historical thinking and other unnatural acts: Charting the future of teaching the past*. Philadelphia: Temple University Press.

Zbikowski, J., & Collins, J. (1994, November). *Literature as the laboratory of the moral life: building moral communities through literature study*. Paper presented at the Annual Conference of the Association for Moral Education, Banff, Alberta, Canada.

15

Cultural Aspects of Teaching Reading with Latino English Language Learners

MICHAEL J. OROSCO
ROLLANDA E. O'CONNOR

Research over the past several decades has improved instruction in basic reading skills. This research is the base for interventions that teach critical foundation reading skills, including phonemic awareness, fluency, and comprehension. Yet despite the research that enables many children to become proficient readers, culturally and linguistically diverse students continue to underachieve in our schools. As evidence, education reports document academic failures for these students in comparison to white students. According to the Nation's Report Card 2007 only 17% of Hispanic students, 14% of black students, 20% of Native American/Alaska Native students, and 45% of Asian/Pacific Islander students in the fourth grade are reading at the proficient or advanced levels (Lee, Grigg, & Donahue, 2007). In addition, Orfield, Losen, Wald, and Swanson (2004) reported that although the high school completion rate for the general population (18–24 years of age) was approximately 68%, Hispanics lagged behind in high school completion in comparison to most other racial groups at 53.2%, black students graduated at 50.2%, whites at 74.9% and Asians/Pacific Islander at 76.8%. This gross underachievement of culturally and linguistically diverse students has added an impetus for teachers to seek viable support options to close this achievement gap.

A large and increasing proportion of students in U.S. schools are from varied cultural backgrounds and come from homes in which a language other than English is spoken. This change has led some researchers to examine carefully research on the development of literacy for these culturally and linguistically diverse students, not only in schools but also in the communities in which these students live. For the purpose of building a knowledge base on the educational development of language-minority students, three major reviews were conducted by the National Research Council's Institute of Medicine on Improving School for Language-Minority Children (August & Hakuta, 1997), the National Literacy Panel on Language-Minority Children and Youth (August & Shanahan, 2006), and the National Center for Education Evaluation and Regional Assistance (Gersten et al., 2007). Because these reviews are the most comprehensive syntheses of this type of student research conducted prior to 2006, they serve as the first sources for research studies cited in this chapter, along with more recent sources.

In this chapter, we describe some of these viable support options and cultural aspects of teaching reading studied through a coherent body of interrelated descriptive and experimental methods. Interventions that address literacy learning with Latino English language learners (ELLs) are the major focus of this chapter, because these ELLs are the fastest growing student population in the United States. Topics comprise language of instruction; cultural factors, including attitudes, beliefs, knowledge, and motivation; and culturally meaningful material and instructional approaches that may impact learning to read. We have guided this review with the following three questions, for which tentative conclusions can be drawn from the research literature:

1. What does current research tell us about the influence of the child's home language on learning to read?

2. What does research tell us about the influence of culture (e.g., home and family interactions and communication norms) on children's literacy learning and outcomes?

3. What is the influence of providing culturally meaningful reading materials and instructional approaches on children's literacy outcomes?

The Influence of the Child's Home Language on Learning to Read

Research is slowly emerging to identify effective teaching practices for students from culturally and linguistically diverse backgrounds. The majority of this research currently being conducted is with Spanish-speaking ELLs (in some studies these students are identified as Latino ELLs) (García & Cuéllar, 2006). It is important to note that one of the reasons this research has been slow in developing is due to the political nature of education (Cummins, 2007). For instance, in the 1990s the political tide in favor of bilingual education turned, with many states such as California, Arizona, Massachusetts, and others, enacting policies that diminished bilingual education programming (Slavin & Cheung, 2005). As a result, today many ELLs receive minimal or no specialized instruction in reading in their native language, even though research has found that language comprehension in Spanish contributes to comprehension development in English (Proctor, August, Carlo, & Snow, 2006). Research with ELLs repeatedly indicates that learning to read in the native language is the strongest predictor of improving English reading performance (Slavin & Cheung, 2005).

One major theme that has emerged from this research is the critical importance of intensive, interactive reading instruction with ELLs that promotes not only English as a second language (ESL) but also native language development. This effective instruction focuses on explicit instruction and intervention in teaching seven core reading elements (phonological awareness, phonics, reading fluency, vocabulary, comprehension, oral language, and motivation), or oral language development that fosters native and English language academic development (August & Hakuta, 1997; August & Shanahan, 2006; Gersten et al., 2007).

As an example of explicit focus on phonological awareness, Leafstedt, Richards, and Gerber (2004) examined the effects of 300 minutes of intervention with low socioeconomic status (SES) Latino ELLs in one kindergarten class over a 10-week period. The students were instructed in ability-level groups of three to five students based on pretest word-reading scores and teacher recommendation. Students were taught phonological awareness skills, such as rime, onset, segmenting and blending for 15 minutes twice a week. Pacing was driven by student growth in these skills, so lower-skilled children received less advanced content than children who learned at a faster pace. Posttest scores were compared with kindergartners who had received the district-mandated curriculum. Overall, results indicated that intensive phonological awareness instruction in English produced higher levels of phonemic awareness and word reading following the treatment. Although even the least skilled children in the treatment improved their phonemic awareness, only the middle and more skilled groups improved in word reading over students in control classes. Because the slower-learners also had less developed vocabulary in English, the authors speculated that intervention in Spanish might be more successful for these students.

To test this possibility, Gerber et al. (2004) conducted a small-group, intensive Spanish phonological awareness intervention study with Latino K–1 ELLs. The lowest 20% of readers in five schools (15 classes) were selected, and almost all of these students were ELLs. Kindergarten instruction was similar to that used in Leafstedt et al. (2004), except that lessons were delivered in Spanish. For first graders, language of the small-group intervention was matched to classroom reading instruction, which was English in all but two classes. First-grade supplemental intervention was provided in 10 half-hour sessions and focused on teaching phonological awareness and decoding through a scaffolded Direct Instruction approach. The comparison following treatment was with students who had not been selected because their reading scores were in the average range. Postassessment findings indicated positive gains in favor of intensive native language phonological awareness support, and the gap between those who began in the bottom 20% narrowed with their average-achieving peers. Although the kindergarten instruction and some of the first-grade instruction was in Spanish, these gains were apparent on English measures, as well as those in Spanish.

In a series of large-scale studies, Vaughn, Linan-Thompson, and colleagues investigated the effectiveness of Spanish and English reading interventions for ELLs at the primary (K–2) level (Linan-Thompson, Vaughn, Hickman-Davis, & Kouzekanani, 2003; Linan-Thompson, Vaughn, Prater, & Cirino, 2006; Vaughn, Cirino, et al., 2006; Vaughn, Linan-Thompson, et al., 2006; Vaughn, Mathes, et al., 2006). First, Linan-Thompson et al. (2003) conducted a study on the effectiveness of an intensive supplemental reading intervention in English with 26 second-grade ELLs identified as being at risk, using oral reading fluency, phoneme segmentation fluency, nonsense word reading, and reading comprehension assessments prior to, immediately after, and twice following interventions (4 weeks and 4 months). Students received 13 weeks (58 sessions) of daily supplemental reading instruction in small groups (two or three) for 30 minutes per day. During the intervention phase, students worked on developing (1) reading rate in English with familiar text, using paired reading formats, tape-assisted reading, and echo reading; (2) phonemic awareness skills, with blending, segmenting, and manipulating sounds in words; (3) word analysis strategies, using word sorts, word building, and chunking; and (4) instructional-level reading skills, with texts in which students made no more than 10 errors per 100 words. Scores at 4-week follow-up increased significantly for word attack, passage comprehension, and phoneme segmentation. Long-term follow-up after 4 months indicated that students maintained these gains and also improved their oral reading fluency significantly.

Next, Vaughn, Cirino, et al. (2006) conducted two first-grade studies of reading interventions for Latino ELLs at risk for reading problems. Students were given pre- and postassessments in letter knowledge, phonological awareness, rapid naming, language proficiency, decoding, comprehension, reading fluency, and spelling. Students who scored below the 25th percentile were selected for the intervention. Two samples of students were randomly assigned to a treated or untreated comparison group on the basis of their language of instruction for core reading (i.e., Spanish or English). In all, 91 students completed the English study (43 treatment and 48 comparison) and 80 students completed the Spanish study (35 treatment and 45 comparison). Students in the treatments received 115 sessions of supplemental reading daily in phonemic awareness, phonics, word study, and text reading for 50 minutes per session in groups of three to five. Findings from the English study revealed statistically significant differences in favor of treated students on English measures of phonological awareness, word attack, and word reading. Findings from the Spanish study revealed significant differences favoring treated students on Spanish measures of phonological awareness, letter-sound and letter–word identification, verbal analogies, word-reading fluency, and spelling.

Subsequently Vaughn, Linan-Thompson, et al. (2006) continued their study of first-grade reading and language intervention in the same language as the students' core reading instruction. In this study, small-group intervention provided by trained bilingual reading intervention teachers for 50 minutes per session focused on systematic and explicit core reading development in both languages. After 7 months, the intervention students significantly outperformed contrast students on multiple measures of reading in English and Spanish, including letter naming, phonological awareness, reading comprehension, and other related language skills.

Expanding on this work, Vaughn, Linan-Thompson, Mathes, et al. (2006) examined the effectiveness of an explicit, systematic reading intervention that matched core reading program components for first-grade Latino bilingual students at risk for reading difficulties in 20 classrooms in seven schools from three districts. Again, students scoring below the 25th percentile were selected for intervention, and 69 participants were randomly assigned within schools to a treatment or a comparison group. Intervention groups (three to five students) met daily for 7 months and were provided instruction for 50 minutes in oral language and reading by trained bilingual intervention teachers. Comparison students received the school's recommended intervention program for at-risk readers. Posttest results indicated significant gains in favor of the treatment group in letter-sound identification, phonological awareness, fluency, oral language development, word attack, and reading comprehension.

To determine whether these early gains made a long-term difference in reading development, Cirino et al. (2009) conducted a follow-up study of students from the first-grade interventions conducted by Vaughn and her colleagues (described earlier). These students had received supplemental instruction in the language (English–Spanish) of their core reading instruction. Findings indicated that at the end of second grade, modest effect sizes favored students who received their instruction in English, and moderate effects were maintained for students whose intervention was in Spanish. Neither intervention had a strong, continued effect on oral language. Moreover, the design of the studies did not determine the effect of bilingual instructors on student outcomes.

These studies of early intervention with ELLs have direct implications for schools and districts implementing responsiveness-to-instruction (RTI) models, in which students are screened for potential reading difficulties, small-group interventions are implemented for low-skilled students, student progress is monitored, and instruction is adjusted based on this progress. The first tests of these models were conducted with English-only students (e.g., O'Connor, 2000; Torgesen, 2000); however, these interventions appear to be effective for ELLs also. Specifically employing a three-tier model, Kamps et al. (2007) compared the impact of a Direct Instruction Tier 2, small-group (three to six students) intervention for ELLs with a small-group (six to 15 students) ESL intervention, both supplemental to whole-group reading instruction in general education first- and second-grade classes. Students in the Direct Instruction Tier 2 intervention, which shared similar components with the interventions of Vaughn, Linan-Thompson, and colleagues (2006) described earlier, made higher reading gains. While these studies support including students who are ELLs in RTI models, several caveats should be mentioned. In many studies, the comparison instruction was delivered in larger groups than the experimental treatments, and students in some cases could only be placed in interventions that focused on reading, or that focused on language. School systems may not always have the staff support or flexibility to provide both types of intervention, even though they may be needed.

Although the studies described earlier indicate that interventions can have an impact on Spanish-speaking ELLs' reading basics and that many phonemic features in same-typology languages transfer (e.g., Spanish–English; Herrera, Perez, & Escamilla, 2010), it is important to note that these interventions failed to improve the vocabulary development of ELLs in English or Spanish. Researchers may fail to realize that certain target phonological features of a native language do not transfer to English, and vice versa. As an illustration, a native Spanish speaker who knows the Spanish phoneme *b* may have an easy time transferring this sound into English but a difficult time pronouncing vowels controlled by *r*, such as in the blending example *B ... art the b ... ard*, because the *art* and *ard* sound sequences do not exist in Spanish.

Well-developed vocabulary exerts some influence on phonemic awareness and word recognition (Ehri & McCormick, 1998); however, studies of children who are native English speakers have found these relationships to be weak (O'Connor, Jenkins, & Slocum, 1995; Steubing, Barth, Molfese, Weiss, & Fletcher, 2009). Roberts' (2005) study of Spanish- and Hmong-speaking children also found no strong effect of vocabulary on phonemic awareness or word reading. Findings from the studies of Vaughn, Linan-Thompson, and their colleagues (2006) described earlier endorse early intervention in reading development regardless of the students' first language, and O'Connor, Bocian, Beebe-Frankenberger, and Linklater (2010) found no difference in responsiveness to early intervention in kindergarten between ELLs and native English speakers. Nevertheless, vocabulary exerts a strong influence on reading comprehension (Hoover & Gough, 1990; Perfetti, 1985; Rupley, Willson, & Nichols, 1998) in third grade and beyond. As might be expected, ELLs consistently perform lower than non-ELLs on measures of vocabulary in English, so interventions directed specifically toward building oral and academic vocabulary of ELLs should be considered.

As a place to start, Tran (2006) summarized resources for finding and teaching the 2,000 to 3,000 basic words that ELLs need for colloquial listening, speaking, and reading, including the Dolch list of 220 sight words (Jesness, 2004) and the General Service List (GSL) of English words, with just over 2,000 high-frequency words (West, 1953; updated by Bauman & Culligan, 1995). Another useful word corpus is Coxhead's (2006) Academic Word List of 570 word families that appear frequently in school texts. Although these sources can help to jump-start vocabulary development for ELLs, Cummins (2007) points out that they fall short of the academic vocabulary needed for successful reading comprehension, especially after third grade.

To explore the feasibility of teaching new vocabulary in general education settings that included ELLs and native English speakers, August, Carlo, Dressler, and Snow (2005) introduced an instructional procedure for fifth graders that included Direct Instruction in the meanings of words and word-learning strategies. Students learned morphological analysis that encouraged them to reflect on cross-linguistic aspects of word meaning, including "cognates" (i.e., words that look and sound similar across languages) and affixes. These procedures were effective for ELLs, along with their classmates, with moderate effects for mastery of the words taught and a small but significant effect on reading comprehension. In addition to positive effects for the students, teachers reported heightened sensitivity to Spanish–English cognates and word relationships that could help them perpetuate these practices during daily instruction. Earlier and later studies (e.g., Kieffer & Lesaux, 2009; Nagy, García, Durgunoğlu, & Hancin-Bhatt, 1993) demonstrated that ELL students who understand derivational morphology and use cognates across languages are better comprehenders. Carlo et al. (2004) showed how these understandings can be taught.

Several researchers have studied the effect of storybook reading on young children's learning of new vocabulary. Biemiller and Boote (2006) tested effects of reading storybooks multiple times, and found that more rereading generates better vocabulary learning. Although their study included ELLs, they did not analyze their data for effects on these students specifically. With a focus on oral language, Silverman (2007) compared three methods of improving vocabulary of kindergarten students through storybook read-alouds in classes where one-third of students were ELLs. Using the same set of six storybooks and 30 focus words, Silverman varied level of discussion, linkage to children's personal lives, and focus on sounds and letters in the focus words. In addition to a standardized measure of English language, she constructed receptive and expressive measures for the focus words she taught in the lessons. Overall, the instructional approaches that encouraged children to think about words analytically outside the context of the stories produced the strongest results. Discussing the words in multiple contexts (rather than their meaning in a particular sentence in a book) developed more depth of vocabulary knowledge and usage for the students. She also found an advantage for including demonstration of sounds and letters in words, with discussion of their meanings. Although only small differences were found overall on a custom measure of receptive language (e.g., "Point to the picture that shows *disgusted.*"), larger differences were found on a custom expressive measure (e.g., "Tell me about *quarrelsome*"). These differences were especially apparent for the students learning English and those from high-poverty families. With the time constraints teachers face amid multiple instructional goals, Silverman recommended that teachers use storybook time to integrate discussion of unusual words and meanings, with decoding instruction.

Using words in multiple contexts can be difficult for teachers to manage. Silverman and Hines (2009) designed another study to investigate the contribution of multimedia to teaching vocabulary to students in PreK–2 classes where 32% of students were ELLs. In one condition, teachers taught the science curriculum about habitats (rainforests, savannahs, coral reefs, and deserts) for 45 minutes, 3 days per week, using books representing these concepts. One hundred content words were selected for the 12 weeks of instruction. In the multimedia instruction, the amount of time, books, and content words were the same; however, one-third of instructional time was spent watching video clips that illustrated each of these habitats and reinforced some of the content words. The native English speakers improved their vocabulary knowledge in both of these treatments (i.e., no significant differences); however, students learning English in the multimedia classes not only improved their knowledge of the content words but also made substantial improvements on normed vocabulary measures. Although the gap between ELLs and non-ELLS persisted on posttests of science vocabulary in the book-only condition, ELL and non-ELL students who received the multimedia condition did not differ at the close of the treatment.

Another important concern investigated by Silverman and Hines (2009) was the impact on native English speakers in classes where teachers planned vocabulary instruction to benefit the ELLs in particular. Their results demonstrated that the non-ELL and ELL students both improved on the normed measure of vocabulary. Moreover, ELLs gained 11 standarized score points (over three times the growth of non-ELL students), suggesting that the use of multimedia may help to close the vocabulary gap between ELL and non-ELL students, without slowing the progress of the non-ELL students in the same classes.

Not all studies of vocabulary instruction with ELLs are as successful as those reported earlier. Townsend and Collins (2009) developed an afterschool Language Workshop to teach 11- to 15-year-old ELLs science vocabulary. They ran the workshop for 5 weeks, 4 days per week, with 75-minute sessions. They focused instruction on words drawn from two of the California standards for middle school: history of inventions, and space and the solar system. Disappointingly, the greatest overall predictor of how well students' vocabulary would grow during treatment was the rate of growth during the control weeks prior to treatment. Nevertheless, for students with the lowest levels of vocabulary in English, the intervention improved their rate of vocabulary growth. Several possibilities may account for the low overall gains, including the afterschool delivery and the older age of participants. Studies of non-ELL poor readers in middle school also show typically less growth than similar interventions achieve in elementary school settings. Another glaring difference was that students in the more successful interventions (e.g., Silverman & Hines, 2009) were in classes that mixed ELL and non-ELL students in the same instruction, suggesting benefits of peer models and interactions. More studies that compare instructional contexts and optimal ages for vocabulary interventions are clearly needed.

Overall, these studies demonstrate that carefully planned instruction incorporating some of the effective procedures developed in studies with English-only students can be beneficial for ELLs. These strategies include (1) introducing new vocabulary in a powerful context, (2) discussing word meanings across a range of appropriate uses, and (3) reviewing words in ways that encourage students to use them in their own speech. Moreover, strategies that help students to notice morphological similarities across words and word families, and cognates across languages may be particularly beneficial for ELLs, because these strategies may transfer to increased word awareness and inferring word meanings that were not taught specifically. Although the findings are not yet conclusive, there may also be benefits to delivering vocabulary instruction to ELL and non-ELL students in the same settings, such as in many general education environments.

Recently, reading intervention researchers (e.g., Cirino et al., 2009) have begun to acknowledge that factors such as language dominance and proficiency across first and second languages, teacher knowledge about effective ELL reading instruction and intervention, and variations in reading program implementation across classrooms and schools can impact reading intervention application and effectiveness. Moreover, few intervention programs have integrated vocabulary and comprehension instruction with early reading foundation skills, such as phonemic awareness, decoding, and word reading. Much more work remains to identify language aspects of teaching reading that are supported by rigorous scientific research and remain faithful to social and cultural factors that support reading development.

The Influence of Culture on Children's Literacy Learning and Outcomes

Culture is a complex concept that integrates psychological and socially inherited knowledge driven by various cultural, institutional, and political contexts (Irvine & Armento, 2001) that people use to interpret and create behaviors. Culture is reflected in a group's common values, beliefs, language, and life experience that contribute to a community's cultural norms (Cole, 2005; Geertz, 1973; Spindler & Spindler, 1990; Villegas & Lucas, 2002). Culture is continuously shaped through enculturation and socialization. "Enculturation" is the process of a person becoming knowledgeable and competent in his or her culture throughout life, while "socialization" is the process of assuming or taking on inherited cultural norms, customs, and ideologies based on social experiences (Pinker, 2002; Tomasello, 1999). Many students encounter formal schooling as separate cultural experiences from their own, which may conflict with mainstream educational standards and instructional principles (Cole, 2005; Gutiérrez & Rogoff, 2003). Learning to read may be difficult if instructional practices mirror a dominant society's socialization practices and disregard minority students' enculturation processes (Au, 2005; Gipe, 2006; Herrera et al., 2010).

In this vein, many culturally and linguistically diverse students come from homes and communities that emphasize collectivist approaches to learning, such as interdependence, sharing, and collaboration (Au, 2005; Gonzales, Moll, & Amanti, 2005; Greenfield, 1999; Williams, 2003). Genesse and Riches (2006), in a review of research, found that teachers who use interactive approaches (e.g., small-group collaboration) that reinforce students' home structures improve these students' literacy engagement and motivation. In contrast, American public schooling practices promote individualistic instructional approaches (e.g., declarative, direct approaches), such as independent reading and writing (Au, 2005; Cazden, 2001; Heath, 1983; Valdez, 1996). Understanding the differences between these two value systems becomes a critical first step in recognizing the cultural aspects of reading instruction and intervention.

Next, it is important to understand that many of these students use their native language as a cognitive medium through which they communicate, learn, and transmit knowledge in their homes and communities. English-speaking students are encouraged to draw upon their own cultural experiences as they relate to discussions in English content and vocabulary; however, culturally and linguistically diverse students are discouraged from using their native language to relate their cultural experiences to discussion topics (Au, 1998, 2005). Furthermore, these students may place more emphasis on collaborative forms of reading discourse, based on social practices, to contextualize what they learn by sharing their knowledge and by understanding new knowledge using their home languages (Au, 2005; Cazden, 2001; Rogoff, 2003; Wells, 1999). One attempt to combine these aspects of cultural responsiveness through student-based discussions using home languages and interdependent group learning has to led to the development of a promising strategy called Collaborative Strategic Reading (CSR; see Klingner, Morrison, & Eppolito, Chapter 10, this volume).

Although the majority of public education teachers understand that culture is important to their students and is practiced at home, community, and school levels, they may not see its relevance to themselves and to their instruction (Irvine & Armento, 2001). One reason may be that teachers who have been raised in white, mainstream, middle-class communities may not have had experiences that cause them to reflect on their own cultural identities (Au, 2005; Florio-Ruane, 2001). Research has indicated that before teachers can address their students' learning needs, they must first become aware and understand the influence (e.g., beliefs, experiences, and stereotypes) of their own culture on their instruction (Abt-Perkins & Rosen, 2000; Howard, 2006; Nieto, 2002).

Consequently, teachers may not recognize their stereotypes for students whose cultures differ from their own. A "stereotype" is a perception based on the belief that members of a group share similar attitudes, appearances, or behaviors, a belief that often forms the basis for prejudices (Howard, 2006). Intercultural awareness allows teachers to discover assumptions prevalent in their own culture about those who are different (Schmidt, 1999). As an illustration, McCarty, Lynch, Wallace, and Benally (1991) conducted an ethnographic study with Navajo students, who were often stereotyped by their teachers as being "nonanalytical and nonverbal learners." The teachers therefore believed that these students would not benefit from inquiry-based instructional approaches (i.e., questioning, speaking up, and inductive reasoning). Over a 3-year period, the researchers expanded a K–2 inquiry-based culturally responsive curriculum that drew from Navajo cultural and linguistic values through grade 8. Students were encouraged to discuss social studies concepts in English and Navajo languages, and relate concepts to their agrarian community. Classroom observations suggested that students' oral discourse improved, which researchers credited to teachers making use of their students' culture to learn. Unfortunately, when the grant funding ended, the researchers terminated their plan to expand these practices into other curricular areas. Effects on students' reading were not evaluated.

In another example, Jiménez (1997) used culturally relevant materials and instruction with five low-achieving seventh-grade middle school Latina students. This formative experiment consisted of eight 1-hour lessons that emphasized resolving the meanings of unknown vocabulary, asking questions, and making inferences. Students were encouraged to use their bilingualism by searching for cognates and reflecting on text in Spanish. Findings indicated that as students extended their discourse while reading culturally familiar text that related to this groups' ethnic background (e.g., Mexican cuisine), they were able to draw from their background knowledge, which improved engagement, motivation, and reading comprehension. Given the small sample, limited study duration, and lack of direct measures of reading, these results are only suggestive. Clearly, more rigorous studies of alternative approaches to improve the cultural relevance of instruction and intervention are warranted.

Nevertheless, these studies suggest that the conditions within which reading instruction takes place may be important for students from minority cultures. Perhaps learning may be improved for culturally and linguistically diverse students by changing their learning contexts, such as giving students the opportunity to discuss, read, and write about experiences in their native language or second language, or by using a culturally relevant curriculum (Goldenberg, Rueda, & August, 2006).

For all students, teachers can create exemplary contexts for instruction when they provide students with opportunities to use what they already know as a basis for learning new material. Culturally and linguistically diverse students enter school with various experiences that foster their reading development, so assumptions about what students already know can be misleading (Gay, 2000; Villegas & Lucas, 2002). Many students face reading comprehension obstacles due to limited vocabulary development in the English language, and linking new English vocabulary and concepts to concepts that students may understand in their own language is an additional instructional challenge. To create this linkage, cognate instruction may be useful. Cognates are similar words related across languages with shared roots (e.g., *hospital* [English], *el hospital* [Spanish]; see August, Calderón, & Carlo, 2002; Jiménez, García, & Pearson, 1996). Nagy et al. (1993) found improved reading comprehension in English expository text when 74 upper elementary school Hispanic students were briefly instructed in the concept of cognates. Studies of vocabulary interventions that included a cognate instruction component have had positive effects in improving reading comprehension (e.g., Carlo et al., 2004; Carlo, August, & Snow, 2005). Use of cognates may be one way to validate students' home cultures, while introducing a strategy students can use throughout their schooling to improve vocabulary and learning.

The Influence of Culturally Meaningful Reading Materials and Instructional Approaches on Children's Literacy Outcomes

Many public school teachers are not well prepared (e.g., with relevant content knowledge, experience, and training) to address culturally and linguistically diverse students' learning needs (e.g., Au, Raphael, & Mooney, 2008; Cummins, 2007; Jerald & Ingersoll, 2002). This lack of training can create a cultural gap between teacher and students (Gay, 2000; Ladson-Billings, 1994; Nieto, 2002; Walker, Shafer, & Liams, 2004), and limit teachers' ability to choose effective instructional approaches or materials (Gollick & Chinn, 2002; Ladson-Billings, 1994). Teachers should be aware that some classroom materials, passages, and texts used in reading interventions with Spanish-speaking children may be culturally irrelevant and incomprehensible to ELLs if they have never encountered them in everyday life.

Macleod (1995) proposed that structuring school to support mainstream cultural practices may lead to differential academic aspirations for culturally and linguistically diverse students. Teachers' instructional beliefs, practices, and values reinforce middle-class norms that emphasize individualistic learning styles, such as self-reliance, independence, and competition, with a lesser focus on the cooperative and noncompetitive learning that may be valued by some minority groups. When such cultural differences exist, teachers may utilize reading interventions that are at odds with students' cultural backgrounds.

The National Clearinghouse for English Language Acquisition and Language Instructional Educational Programs (Ballantyne, Sanderman, & Levy, 2008) reports that nearly 30% of K–12 teachers have training in working with ELLs. Inadequate preparation could contribute to the "reading gap" if primarily white, middle-class, English-speaking public school teachers enter classrooms with subjective personal and instructional dispositions toward cultural differences (e.g., Au, 2005; Gutiérrez & Rogoff, 2003; Irvine, 1990; Ladson-Billings, 1994). Yoon (2008) found a strong link between teachers' past personal and professional experiences and how their cultural experiences contributed to ELLs positioning themselves to learn. This positioning was dependent on how well teachers understood ELLs' cultural and linguistic identity, and how they proactively promoted ELLs' learning engagement through interactive teaching experiences. In this study, teachers who had culturally responsive practice and preparation in schools tended to provide instructional methods that improved ELL engagement and motivation.

Over the years, researchers (August & Hakuta, 1997; August & Shanahan, 2006) have indicated that professional learning can have a powerful effect on teachers' skills and knowledge if teachers are assisted in (1) learning instructional approaches that are effective with culturally and linguistically diverse learners; (2) understanding the language acquisition process and how it affects learning to read in ESL; (3) building on ELLs' background knowledge and making connections with prior learning; and (4) differentiating instruction to meet students' various learning needs. As an example, Gere, Buehler, Dallavis, and Haviland (2009) found that when given culturally responsive preparation that incorporated multicultural texts, discussions of attitudes toward race and racism, and explicit engagement with how race consciousness shapes learning, teachers created more culturally encompassing classrooms.

In addition, Haager and Windmueller (2001) evaluated a professional development program's capacity to improve reading instruction for 17 first- and second-grade urban teachers with Hispanic students. Teachers were provided intensive training on teaching phonemic awareness, the alphabetic principle, oral reading fluency, and English language development. The authors concluded that, due to professional development, outcomes for their students showed gains in all areas assessed. Because professional development in effective instructional practices stands out as a key predictor of student achievement (Nye, Konstantopoulos, & Hedges, 2004; Wenglinsky, 2002), its potential for improving the reading achievement of ELLs deserves more research attention.

Theoretically, cultural aspects of teaching reading are embedded within the social constructivist perspective. Through this perspective, reading instruction is viewed as a social practice that relies on social context. In the social constructivist approach, instruction is a socially mediated individual, interpersonal, and community process based on the cultural activities of everyday life that integrate historical sources of individual predispositions, semiotics (signs, symbols, tools, and language), and biological development (e.g., Moll, 1990; Vygotsky, 1962, 1978; Wertsch, 1991). Instruction is embedded in these dynamic planes due to mutual influences between the student and teacher; one is constantly shaping the other (Scribner & Reyes, 1999); that is, reading instruction is an actively reciprocated process between a student and teacher, bound by students' socially inherited knowledge that contains rich cultural and cognitive capital that a teacher can use to help students construct meaning (Gonzalez et al., 2005). This type of instructional mediation is also known as *Funds of Knowledge* (Gonzales et al., 2005).

Gonzales et al. (2005) collaborated with teachers to conduct field-based research that involved observations, interviews, and case studies of several of these teachers' Spanish-dominant student households. The goal of this research was to understand the information, methods, and ways of thinking and learning related to a community's everyday life. This socially and culturally developed knowledge contributes to the everyday accumulation of intellectual capital that provides a powerful nexus in associating new information with prior knowledge. Gonzales et al. indicated that a community's funds of knowledge can become a valuable resource for classroom teaching. Teachers found that their students' international travel experience, along with their parents' skills and knowledge, could be used to reinforce classroom practices. For example, teachers formed Spanish literacy circles with many of the parents to explain and foster critical analysis skills. In return, these parents were able to use these critical analysis skills in conversations with their children to reinforce classroom-based practices. By applying the funds of knowledge concept, teachers encompassed student households as useful sociocultural, cognitive resources that allowed them to enrich their classroom instruction through culturally responsive and meaningful lessons that tapped students' background knowledge.

Tharp and Gallimore (1988, 1991) and Monzó and Rueda (2001) have suggested that instruction should weave aspects of reading, such as vocabulary and comprehension into aspects of everyday life; instruction cannot be meaningful without incorporating students' system of meaning and understandings. In what is now considered a classic study, Heath's (1983) *Ways with Words* examines the everyday linguistic functions of white and black Southern, rural, working-class communities and compares them to the linguistic patterns of the middle-class community, including teachers. Her classroom observations indicate that when instruction is aligned with the explicit and declarative discourse zones of white working- and middle-class parents, her black working-class students were disengaged and unmotivated. Another classic, Cazden's (2001) *Classroom Discourse*, also affirms the impact of classroom language patterns. When teachers connected student sociolinguistic patterns with those required in academic dialogue through various student–peer collaborative activities, such as sharing time, debate groups, and conversation, students became more engaged and motivated, and showed a deeper understanding of classroom content. Throughout this process, students gain extended opportunities for discussion in the context of these shared instructional activities, in which comprehension is collaboratively constructed, negotiated, and improved. By implication from these studies, when teachers learn how to activate and incorporate students' discourse patterns, they also improve oral language development, which has been found to be a key component in reading comprehension. These studies also suggest that motivation improves when teachers incorporate student discourse patterns in learning activities.

Researchers have explored whether collaborative approaches to reading instruction are more effective than individual approaches for Latinos. An evidence-based example of this approach has been CSR (see Klingner et al., Chapter 10, this volume, for an extensive discussion), which includes aspects of reciprocal teaching, such as collaborative group work and interactive dialogue (Palincsar & Brown, 1984), combined with explicit instruction in procedural strategies (Klingner & Vaughn, 1996, 1999). In the CSR approach students engage collaboratively in small groups in academically related strategic discussion and assist one another in understanding word meanings, deriving the main idea, asking and answering questions, and relating what they learn to their own cultural backgrounds. When students do not have cultural background knowledge (e.g., vocabulary) to understand a text passage, they are encouraged to generate questions for clarification that are further discussed in a small group with the teacher to facilitate comprehension. By encouraging discussion in students' home languages, CSR provides culturally responsive teaching that integrates learning strategies with student cultural and linguistic knowledge.

In an early exploration of CSR, Klingner and Vaughn (1996) conducted a two-phase study at the middle school level (10 classrooms) with Hispanic ELLs with learning disabilities. Five teachers and their classrooms were assigned to the CSR condition, while five others were assigned to the control group. All participants were given pre- and postassessment in reading comprehension in English. Phase 1 of the study consisted of fifteen 25- to 30-minute sessions in groups of eight to nine students. Teachers first modeled the comprehension strategies, then supported students' learning through these strategies, decreasing support as students became more strategy proficient. In Phase 2 of the study (12 sessions), students were divided into two groups. One group engaged in cross-age tutoring with younger students, using reciprocal teaching, and the other group worked in small, cooperative groups, using reciprocal teaching. Results indicated that both types of CSR were effective, with no differences between these variations. Students in the CSR condition made significantly greater reading comprehension gains than those in the control group.

Another promising collaborative based reading strategy, called Peer-Assisted Learning Strategies (PALS), combines peer tutoring with instructional principles and practices found to be effective in improving reading development, while allowing student native language discourse (Calhoon, Al Otaiba, Cihak, King, & Avalos, 2007; Calhoon, Al Otaiba, Greenberg, King, & Avalos, 2006; McMaster, Kung, Han, & Cao, 2008; Sáenz, Fuchs, & Fuchs, 2005). PALS sessions implement reading activities two to four times a week for 25 to 35 minutes to complement, not replace, the existing reading curriculum. In PALS, teachers evaluate and identify and pair students (players) who need help with specific reading skills with more skilled classroom members (coaches) to practice what the teacher has taught them. The PALS peer-tutoring strategy enables teachers to circulate around the classroom, observe students, and provide feedback and remedial lessons when necessary.

Most importantly from the sociocultural framework, through observation of peer interactions and small-group instruction, teachers become familiar with not only their students' cultural and linguistic differences but also their cultural and linguistic experiences. This deep understanding may allow teachers to develop more culturally responsive instruction and to combine the best of high-quality instructional practices with students' cultural and linguistic knowledge. The incorporation of effective, well-researched instructional procedures with students' cultural frames of reference may facilitate learning and development for novice readers (Herrera et al., 2010; Villegas & Lucas, 2002). Experimenting with these and other forms of peer-mediated instruction with ELLs deserves more research attention.

The recommendation to implement culturally responsive literacy instruction stems from observations that to do so may activate engagement and motivation, and incorporate literacy practices from the home and community. Incorporating these characteristics may also promote cross-cultural communication within diverse student populations. Teachers tap into and connect with students' prior knowledge, interests, motivation, and home language (August & Hakuta, 1997). Ladson-Billings (1994) conducted a literacy study of five black and three white teachers with black students, and found that the white teachers were just as effective as the black teachers when they followed the same culturally relevant principles to black discourse. The primary principle was making students' culture a point of assertion by embedding reading instruction within students' real-life experiences, community-based knowledge, and oral language development. Although teachers need not be "insiders" in a particular culture to offer culturally responsive instruction (Osborne, 1996), they should make an effort to learn about the cultures represented in their classrooms, respect students' values, and view differences as strengths, not deficits (Howard, 2006; Ladson-Billings, 2001).

Research studies have shown a positive relationship between the use of instructional standards and student improvement. Tharp, Estrada, Dalton, and Yamauchi (2000) suggested five standards for effective pedagogy to improve learning outcomes for culturally and linguistically diverse students. These five standards were extracted from three decades of research across cultural and linguistic contexts: (1) teacher and student joint collaboration; (2) development of language/literacy across the curriculum; (3) contextualization of instruction in students' home and community experiences; (4) engagement of students in challenging activities; and (5) and emphasizes on dialogic inquiry during teacher instruction. In a series of studies, Doherty, Hilberg, Pinal, and Tharp (2003) investigated the influence of Tharp et al.'s standards for effective pedagogy (2000) through teacher professional development in a public elementary school serving low-SES Latino ELLs. Fifteen elementary school teachers were given professional development training to use these fives standards in everyday classroom instruction. Study 1 found that teachers who implemented these standards at a higher rate during reading instruction improved their students' achievement on the Stanford Achievement Test (SAT-9) of comprehension, reading, spelling, and vocabulary. Study 2 found that the achievement gains on the SAT-9 were higher in this population when teachers used culturally responsive pedagogy across multiple subject areas.

Legitimizing the cultural heritage of diverse learners may improve not only students' attitudes but also their engagement and motivation, which is critical in learning to read (Guthrie, Alvermann, & Au, 1998). Bell and Clark (1998) compared 109 first- through fourth-grade black students' recall and comprehension in books with culturally consistent black themes and characters in comparison to white characters. They found that the participants in the culturally relevant treatment recalled events better than those in the control group. Similarly, when Diamond and Moore (1995) observed students' oral language participation in classrooms, they found that use of culturally relevant grade-level-appropriate books increased students' engagement and motivation.

The similarities between descriptions of culturally responsive teaching and generally effective teaching are striking. Culturally responsive teachers are aware that when children start school, they may not have experienced all the same interactions with print as their mainstream peers. Various studies have examined the impact of economic disparities on early childhood development with print (e.g., Dickinson & Neuman, 2006). One major implication from these studies is the role of student knowledge in learning to read. For example, in the Kamehameha Education Project in Hawaii (Au, 1980), teachers adjusted their reading instruction with culturally and linguistically disadvantaged students to provide more culturally congruent language, based on differing language practices found in the home and schools, along with direct and explicit instruction in phonological awareness, the alphabetic code, and vocabulary development. As a result, the children's time on task, and their engagement and motivation with classroom activities increased, as did their scores on standardized reading tests.

Similarly, in a family biliteracy project with fourth-grade Latino students, Dworin (2006) encouraged students to write about topics from their homes and communities using their own understanding and experiences of their families' stories. Children interviewed parents and relatives, drafted the stories in Spanish, discussed them with Spanish-speaking peers, and revised them based on peers' and teachers' feedback. Last, students and teachers worked together to translate the stories into English. Dworin speculated that using two languages in a writing workshop approach strengthened students' metalinguistic and vocabulary connections, while valuing the knowledge and experiences in students' home communities.

Other valuable programs have focused on developing partnerships with parents and teachers to enhance home literacy experiences that promote literacy achievement (Arnold, Lonigan, Whitehurst, & Epstein, 1994; Dickinson & Smith, 1994; Valdez-Menchaca & Whitehurst, 1992). Rueda and García (2002) found that when teachers instructed parents and family members of ELLs to read to their children at home and discuss story content in their native language, this home practice fostered improved biliteracy skills that also improved classroom English reading comprehension. In essence, culturally responsive teachers see learning as an active process in which learners give meaning to new information and ideas. They design literacy interventions that build on what students already know and guide them beyond the known to impact reading achievement.

Conclusion

Research that disentangles culturally responsive teaching from good teaching is difficult to design. No one would advocate assigning ELLs purposefully to less-skilled and more-skilled teachers to test the value added by a culturally relevant teacher orientation. Nevertheless, consideration of the cultural aspects of reading may provide a promising approach in which teachers incorporate their students' cultural experiences to combine culturally responsive pedagogy with evidence-based practices. Researchers have developed procedures for implementing culturally responsive teaching; however, few studies have tested the outcomes of implementation, and even fewer have found significant achievement effects. It makes sense to provide reading instruction that is both considerate of students' cultural values and effective. Just how teachers should make use of this balance is less clear, but research that is currently underway might help to define the key elements of culturally responsive instruction that influence students' motivation and long-term reading achievement (Orosco & Klingner, 2010). Once these elements are understood, professional development in culturally responsive teaching may help teachers not only learn the most effective practices but also apply these practices with expertise.

References

Abt-Perkins, D., & Rosen, L. (2000). Preparing English teachers to teach diverse student populations: Beliefs, challenges, and proposals for change. *English Education, 32*(4), 251–266.

Arnold, D. H., Lonigan, C. J., Whitehurst, G. J., & Epstein, J. N. (1994). Accelerating language development through picture book reading: Replication and extension to a videotape-training format. *Journal of Educational Psychology, 86,* 235–243.

Au, K. H. (1980). Participation structures in a reading lesson with Hawaiian children: Analysis of a culturally appropriate instructional event. *Anthropology and Education Quarterly, 77,* 91–115.

Au, K. H. (1998). Social constructivism and the school literacy learning of students of diverse cultural backgrounds. *Journal of Literacy Research, 30*(2), 297–319.

Au, K. (2005). *Multicultural issues and literacy achievement.* New York: Routledge/Taylor & Francis.

Au, K., Raphael, T. E., & Mooney, K. C. (2008). What we have learned about teacher education to improve literacy achievement in urban schools. In L. C. Wilkinson, L. M. Morrow, & V. Chou (Eds.), *Improving literacy achievement in urban schools: Critical elements in teacher preparation* (pp. 159–184). Newark, DE: International Reading Association.

August, D., Calderón, M., & Carlo, M. (2002). *Transfer of skills from Spanish to English: A study of young learners.* Washington, DC: Center for Applied Linguistics.

August, D., Carlo, M., Dressler, C., & Snow, C. E. (2005). The critical role of vocabulary development for English language learners. *Learning Disabilities Research and Practice, 20*(1), 50–57.

August, D., & Hakuta, K. (1997). *Improving schooling for language-minority children.* Washington, DC: National Academy Press.

August, D., & Shanahan, T. (2006). *Developing literacy in second-language learners.* Mahwah, NJ: Erlbaum.

Ballantyne, K. G., Sanderman, A. R., & Levy, J. (2008). *Educating English language learners: Building teacher capacity.* Washington, DC: National Clearinghouse for English Language Acquisition.

Bauman, J., & Culligan, B. (1995). About the General Service List. Retrieved March 1, 2010, from *jbauman.com/aboutgsl.html*.

Bell, Y. R., & Clark, T. R. (1998). Culturally relevant reading material as related to comprehension and recall in African American children. *Journal of Black Psychology, 24*(4), 455–475.

Biemiller, A., & Boote, C. (2006). An effective method for building vocabulary in primary grades. *Journal of Educational Psychology, 98,* 44–62.

Calhoon, M. B., Al Otaiba, S., Cihak, D., King, A., & Avalos, A. (2007). Effects of a peer-mediated program on reading skill acquisition for two-way bilingual first-grade classrooms. *Learning Disability Quarterly, 30,* 169–184.

Calhoon, M. B., Al Otaiba, S., Greenberg, D., King, A., & Avalos, A. (2006). Improving reading skills in predominantly Hispanic Title 1 first-grade classrooms: The promise of peer-assisted learning strategies. *Learning Disabilities Research and Practice, 21,* 261–272.

Carlo, M. S., August, D., McLaughlin, B., Snow, C. E., Dressler, C., Lippman, D. N., et al. (2004). Closing the gap: Addressing the vocabulary needs of English-language learners in bilingual and mainstream classrooms. *Reading Research Quarterly, 39*(3), 188–215.

Carlo, M. S., August, D., & Snow, C. E. (2005). Sustained vocabulary-learning strategies for English language learners. In E. H. Hiebert & M. Kamil (Eds.), *Teaching and learning vocabulary: Bringing research to practice* (pp. 137–153). Mahwah, NJ: Erlbaum.

Cazden, C. B. (2001). *Classroom discourse: The language of teaching and learning* (2nd ed.). Portsmouth, NH: Heinemann.

Cirino, P. T., Vaughn, S., Linan-Thompson, S., Cardenas-Hagan, E., Fletcher, J. M., & Francis, D. J. (2009). One-year follow-up outcomes of Spanish and English interventions for English language learners at risk for reading problems. *American Educational Research Journal, 46*(3), 744–781.

Cole, M. (2005). Cross-cultural and historical perspectives on the developmental consequences of education. *Human Development, 48,* 195–216.

Coxhead, A. (2006). *Essentials of teaching academic vocabulary: English for academic success.* Boston: Thomson Heinle.

Cummins, J. (2007). Pedagogies for the poor?: Realigning reading instruction for low income students with scientifically based reading research. *Educational Researcher, 36,* 564–572.

Diamond, B. J., & Moore, M. A. (1995). *Multicultural literacy: Mirroring the reality of the classroom.* White Plains, NY: Longman.

Dickinson, D. K., & Neuman, S. B. (2006). *Handbook of early literacy research* (Vol. 2). New York: Guilford Press.

Dickinson, D. K., & Smith, M. W. (1994). Long-term effects of preschool teachers' book readings on low-income children's vocabulary and story comprehension. *Reading Research Quarterly, 29,* 104–122.

Doherty, R. W., Hilberg, R. S., Pinal, A., & Tharp, R. G. (2003). Five standards and student achievement. *NABE Journal of Research and Practice, 1*(1), 1–24.

Dworin, J. (2006). The family stories project: Using funds of knowledge for writing. *Reading Teacher, 59,* 510–520.

Ehri, L., & McCormick, S. (1998). Phases of word learning: Implications for instruction with delayed and disabled readers. *Reading and Writing Quarterly, 14,* 135–164.

Florio-Ruane, S. (with De Tar, J.). (2001). *Teacher education and cultural and cultural imagination: Autobiography, exchange and narrative.* Mahwah, NJ: Erlbaum.

García, E., & Cuéllar, D. (2006). Who are the linguistically and culturally diverse students? *Teachers College Record, 108*(11), 2220–2246.

Gay, G. (2000). *Culturally responsive teaching*. New York: Teachers College Press.

Geertz, C. (1973). *The interpretation of cultures*. New York: Basic Books.

Genesse, F., & Riches, C. (2006). Literacy: Instructional issues. In F. Genesse, K. Lindholm-leary, W. Saunders, & D. Christian (Eds.), *Educating English language learners: A synthesis of research evidence* (pp. 109–175). New York: Cambridge University Press.

Gerber, M. M., Jiménez, T., Leafstedt, J. M., Villacruz, J., Richards, C., & English, J. (2004). English reading effects of small-group intensive intervention in Spanish for K–1 English learners. *Learning Disabilities Research and Practice, 19*(4), 239–251.

Gere, A. R., Buehler, J., Dallavis, C., & Haviland, V. S. (2009). A visibility project: Learning to see how preservice teachers take up culturally responsive pedagogy. *American Educational Research Journal, 46*(3), 816–852.

Gersten, R., Baker, S. K., Shanahan, T., Linan-Thompson, S., Collins, P., & Scarcella, R. (2007). *Effective literacy and English language instruction for English learners in elementary grades: A practice guide* (NCEE 2007–4011). Washington, DC: National Center for Education Evaluation and Regional Assistance, Institute of Education Sciences, U.S. Department of Education. Retrieved March 31, 2010, from *ies.ed.gov/ncee*.

Gipe, J. P. (2006). *Multiple paths to literacy: Assessment and differentiated instruction for diverse learners*. Boston: Allyn & Bacon.

Goldenberg, C., Rueda, R. S., & August, D. (2006). Synthesis: Sociocultural contexts and literacy development. In D. August & T. Shanahan (Eds.), *Developing literacy in second-language learners* (pp. 249–267). Mahwah, NJ: Erlbaum.

Gollick, D. M., & Chinn, P. C. (2002). *Multicultural education in a pluralistic society*. Upper Saddle River, NJ: Merrill.

Gonzalez, N., Moll, L., & Amanti, C. (Eds.). (2005). *Funds of knowledge: Theorizing practices in households and classrooms*. Mahwah, NJ: Erlbaum.

Greenfield, P. M. (1999). Cultural change and human development. *New Directions for Child and Adolescent Development, 83*, 37–59.

Guthrie, J. T., Alvermann, D. E., & Au, K. H. (1998). *Engaged reading: Process and policy implications*. New York: Teachers College Press.

Gutiérrez, K., & Rogoff, B. (2003). Cultural ways of learning: Individual traits or repertoires of practice. *Educational Researcher, 32*(5), 19–25.

Haager, D., & Windmueller, M. (2001). Early literacy intervention for English language learners at-risk for learning disabilities: Student and teacher outcomes in an urban school. *Learning Disability Quarterly, 24*(4), 235–250.

Heath, S. B. (1983). *Ways with words: Language, life, and work in communities and classrooms*. New York: Cambridge University Press.

Herrera, S. G., Perez, D. R., & Escamilla, K. (2010). *Teaching reading to English language learners: Differentiated literacies*. Boston: Allyn & Bacon.

Hoover, W. A., & Gough, P. B. (1990). The simple view of reading. *Reading and Writing: An Interdisciplinary Journal, 2*, 127–160.

Howard, G. (2006). *We can't teach what we don't know: White teachers, multiracial schools*. New York: Teachers College Press.

Irvine, J. J. (1990). *Black students and school failure: Policies, practices, and prescriptions*. Westport, CT: Greenwood.

Irvine, J. J., & Armento, B. J. (2001). *Culturally responsive teaching: Lesson planning for elementary and middle grades*. Boston: McGraw-Hill Higher Education.

Jerald, C. D., & Ingersoll, R. M. (2002). *All talk, no action: Putting an end to out-of-field teaching*. Washington, DC: Education Trust.

Jesness, J. (2004). *Teaching English language learners K–12: A quick start guide for the new teacher.* Thousand Oaks, CA: Corwin Press.

Jiménez, R. T. (1997). The strategic reading abilities and potential of low-literacy Latina/o readers in middle school. *Reading Research Quarterly, 32*(3), 224–243.

Jiménez, R. T., García, G. E., & Pearson, P. D. (1995). Three children, two languages, and strategic reading: Case studies in bilingual/monolingual reading. *American Educational Research Journal, 32*(1), 67–97.

Kamps, D., Abbott, M., Greenwood, C., Arreaga-Mayer, C., Wills, H., Longstaff, J., et al. (2007). Use of evidence based, small-group reading instruction for English language learners in elementary grades: Secondary-tier interventions. *Learning Disability Quarterly, 30*(3), 153–168.

Kieffer, M. J., & Lesaux, N. (2009). The role of derivational morphology in the reading comprehension of Spanish-speaking English language learners. *Reading and Writing: An Interdisciplinary Journal, 21*, 783–804.

Klingner, J. K., & Vaughn, S. (1996). Reciprocal teaching of reading comprehension strategies for students with learning disabilities who use English as a second language. *Elementary School Journal, 96*, 275–293.

Klingner, J. K., & Vaughn, S. (1999). Promoting reading comprehension, content learning, and English acquisition through collaborative strategic reading (CSR). *Reading Teacher, 52*, 738–747.

Ladson-Billings, G. (1994). *The dreamkeepers: Successful teaching for African American Students.* San Francisco: Jossey-Bass.

Ladson-Billings, G. (2001). *Crossing over to Canaan: The journey of new teachers in diverse classrooms.* San Francisco: Jossey-Bass.

Leafstedt, J. M., Richards, C. R., & Gerber, M. M. (2004). Effectiveness of explicit phonological-awareness instruction for at-risk English learners. *Learning Disabilities Research and Practice, 19*(4), 252–261.

Lee, J., Grigg, W., & Donahue, P. (2007). *The nation's report card: Reading 2007* (NCES 2007-496). Washington, DC: National Center for Education Statistics, Institute of Education Sciences, U.S. Department of Education.

Linan-Thompson, S., Vaughn, S., Hickman-Davis, P., & Kouzekanani, K. (2003). Effectiveness of supplemental reading instruction for second-grade English language learners with reading difficulties. *Elementary School Journal, 103*, 221–238.

Linan-Thompson, S., Vaughn, S., Prater, K., & Cirino, P. T. (2006). The response to intervention of English language learners at risk for reading problems. *Journal of Learning Disabilities, 39*, 390–398.

Macleod, J. (1995). *Ain't no makin' it: Leveled aspirations in a low-income neighborhood.* Boulder, CO: Westview Press.

McCarty, T. L., Lynch, R. H., Wallace, S., & Benally, A. (1991). Classroom inquiry and Navajo learning styles: A call for reassessment. *Anthropology and Education Quarterly, 22*(1), 42–59.

McMaster, K. L., Kung, H., Han, I., & Cao, M. (2008). Peer-assisted learning strategies: A "tier 1" approach to promoting English learners' response to intervention. *Exceptional Children, 74*, 194–214.

Moll, L. C. (Ed.). (1990). *Vygotsky and education.* Cambridge, UK: Cambridge University Press.

Monzó, L., & Rueda, R. (2001). Constructing achievement orientations toward literacy: An analysis of sociocultural activity in Latino home and community contexts. *National Reading Conference Yearbook, 49*, 405–420.

Nagy, W., García, G. E., Durgunoğlu, A., & Hancin-Bhatt, B. (1993). Spanish–English bilingual students' use of cognates in English reading. *Journal of Reading Behavior, 25*, 241–259.

Nieto, S. (2002). *Language, culture, and teaching: Critical perspectives for a new century.* Mahwah, NJ: Erlbaum.

Nye, B., Konstantopoulos, S., & Hedges, L. V. (2004). How large are teacher effects? *Education Policy Analysis Archives, 26*(3). Retrieved September 7, 2009, from *epaa.asu.edu/epaa/v26n3.*

O'Connor, R. E. (2000). Increasing the intensity of intervention in kindergarten and first grade. *Learning Disabilities Research and Practice, 15*, 43–54.

O'Connor, R. E., Bocian, K., Beebe-Frankenberger, M., & Linklater, D. (2010). Responsiveness of students with language difficulties to early intervention in reading. *Journal of Special Education, 43*, 220–235.

O'Connor, R. E., Jenkins, J. R., & Slocum, T. A. (1995). Transfer among phonological tasks in kindergarten: Essential instructional content. *Journal of Educational Psychology, 2*, 202–217.

Orfield, G., Losen, D., Wald, J., & Swanson, C. B. (2004). *Losing our future: How minority youth are being left behind by the graduation rate crisis.* Cambridge, MA: Civil Rights Project at Harvard University.

Orosco, M. J., & Klingner, J. K. (2010). One school's implementation of RTI with English language learners: "Referring into RTI." *Journal of Learning Disabilities, 43*, 269–288.

Osborne, A. B. (1996). Practice into theory into practice: Culturally relevant pedagogy for students we have marginalized and normalized. *Anthropology and Education Quarterly, 27*(3), 285–314.

Palincsar, A. S., & Brown, A. L. (1984). Reciprocal teaching of comprehension monitoring activities. *Cognition and Instruction, 1*, 117–175.

Perfetti, C. A. (1985). *Reading ability.* New York: Oxford University Press.

Pinker, S. (2002). *The blank slate: The modern denial of human nature.* New York: Penguin Group.

Proctor, C. P., August, D., Carlo, M. S., & Snow, C. (2006). The intriguing role of Spanish language vocabulary knowledge in predicting English reading comprehension. *Journal of Educational Psychology, 98*, 159–169.

Roberts, T. (2005). Articulation accuracy and vocabulary size contributions to phonemic awareness and word reading in English language learners. *Journal of Educational Psychology, 97*, 601–616.

Rogoff, B. (2003). *The cultural nature of human development.* New York: Oxford University Press.

Rueda, R., & García, G. E. (2002). *How do I teach reading to English language learners?* Ann Arbor, MI: Center for the Improvement of Early Reading Achievement.

Rupley, W. H., Willson, V. L., & Nichols, W. D. (1998). Exploration of the developmental components contributing to elementary school children's reading comprehension. *Scientific Studies of Reading, 2*, 143–158.

Sáenz, L. M., Fuchs, L. S., & Fuchs, D. (2005). Peer-assisted learning strategies for English language learners with learning disabilities. *Exceptional Children, 71*, 231–247.

Schmidt, P. R. (1999). Focus on research: Know thyself and understand others. *Language Arts, 76*(4), 332–340.

Scribner, J. D., & Reyes, P. (1999). Creating learning communities for high performing Hispanic students: A conceptual framework. In P. Reyes, J. D. Scribner, & A. P. Scribner (Eds.), *Lessons from high-performing hispanic schools: Creating learning communities* (pp. 188–210). New York: Teachers College Press.

Silverman, R. (2007). A comparison of three methods of vocabulary instruction during read-alouds in kindergarten. *Elementary School Journal, 108*, 97–113.

Silverman, R., & Hines, S. (2009). The effects of multimedia-enhanced instruction on the vocabulary of English-language learners and non-English-language learners in pre-kindergarten through second grade. *Journal of Educational Psychology, 101*, 305–314.

Slavin, R. E., & Cheung, A. (2005). A synthesis of research on language of reading instruction for English language learners. *Review of Educational Research, 75*(2), 247–248.

Spindler, G., & Spindler, L. (1990). *The American cultural dialogue and its transmission*. London: Falmer.

Steubing, K. K., Barth, A. E., Molfese, P. J., Weiss, B., & Feltcher, J. M. (2009). IQ is not strongly related to response to reading instruction: A meta-analytic interpretation. *Exceptional Children, 76*, 31–51.

Tharp, R. G., Estrada, P., Dalton, S. S., & Yamauchi, L. (2000). *Teaching transformed: Achieving excellence, fairness, inclusion, and harmony*. Boulder, CO: Westview Press.

Tharp, R. G., & Gallimore, R. (1988). *Rousing minds to life: Teaching, learning and schooling in social context*. Cambridge, UK: Cambridge University Press.

Tharp, R. G., & Gallimore, R. (1991). A theory of teaching as assisted performance. In P. Light, S. Sheldon, & M. Woodhead (Eds.), *Learning to think* (pp. 42–62). London: Routledge, in association with The Open University.

Tomasello, M. (1999). *The cultural origins of cognition*. Cambridge, MA: Harvard University Press.

Torgesen, J. K. (2000). Individual differences in response to early interventions in reading: The lingering problem of treatment resisters. *Learning Disabilities Research and Practice, 15*, 55–64.

Townsend, D., & Collins, P. (2009). Academic vocabulary and middle school English learners: An intervention study. *Reading and Writing: An Interdisciplinary Journal, 22*, 993–1019.

Tran, A. (2006). An approach to basic-vocabulary development for English-language learners. *Reading Improvement, 43*, 157–162.

Valdez, G. (1996). Con respeto: *Bridging the distances between culturally diverse families and schools: An ethnographic portrait*. New York: Teachers College Press.

Valdez-Menchaca, M. C., & Whitehurst, G. J. (1992). Accelerating language development through picture book reading: A systematic extension to Mexican day care. *Developmental Psychology, 28*, 1106–1114.

Vaughn, S., Cirino, P. T., Linan-Thompson, S., Mathes, P. G., Carlson, C. D., Hagan, E. C., et al. (2006). Effectiveness of a Spanish intervention and an English intervention for English language learners at risk for reading problems. *American Educational Research Journal, 43*, 449–487.

Vaughn, S., Linan-Thompson, S., Mathes, P., Cirino, P., Carlson, C., Pollard-Durodola, S., et al. (2006). Effectiveness of Spanish intervention for first-grade English language learners at risk for reading difficulties. *Journal of Learning Disabilities, 39*(1), 56–73.

Vaughn, S., Mathes, P., Linan-Thompson, S., Cirino, P., Carlson, C., & Pollard-Durodola, S. (2006). Effectiveness of an English intervention for first grade English language learners at risk for reading problems. *Elementary School Journal, 107*(2), 153–181.

Villegas, A. M., & Lucas, T. (2002). Preparing culturally responsive teachers: Rethinking the curriculum. *Journal of Teacher Education, 53*(1), 20–32.

Vygotsky, L. S. (1962). *Thought and language*. Cambridge, MA: MIT Press.

Vygotsky, L. S. (1978). *Mind and society*. Cambridge, MA: Harvard University Press.

Walker, A., Shafer, J., & Liams, M. (2004). "Not in my classroom": Teacher attitudes towards

English language learners in the mainstream classroom. *National Association of Bilingual Education Journal of Research and Practice*, 2(1), 130–160).

Wells, G. (1999). *Dialogic inquiry: Towards a socio-cultural practice and theory of education.* Cambridge University Press.

Wenglinsky, H. (2002). How schools matter: The link between teacher classroom practices and student academic performance. *Education Policy Analysis Archives*, 10(12), 58–63. Retrieved September 7, 2009, from *epaa.asu.edu/epaa/v10n12.*

Wertsch, J. (1991). *Voices of the mind: A sociocultural approach to mediated action.* Cambridge, MA: Harvard University Press.

West, M. (1953). *A General Service List of English Words.* London: Longman, Green, & Co.

Williams, B. (2003). *Closing the achievement gap: A vision for changing beliefs and practices.* Alexandria, VA: Association for Supervision & Curriculum Development.

Yoon, B. (2008). Uninvited guests: The influence of teachers' roles and pedagogies on the positioning of English language learners in the regular classroom. *American Educational Research Journal*, 45, 495–522.

16

Teaching Older Students to Read

ROLLANDA E. O'CONNOR
VANESSA GOODWIN

Teachers often wonder whether instructional methods designed for young poor readers are appropriate for older students who read far below grade level. On the one hand, processes such as identifying words on the page and understanding what they mean must be crucial for readers of all ages; on the other hand, materials designed for young children that start with simple word forms and build skills gradually may be demeaning or boring for older students. Materials at appropriate levels with content interesting to older students may be difficult to find. Moreover, older poor readers are well aware of their reading problems and have faced years of frustration over their laborious reading progress.

Authors of other chapters in this book describe reading interventions that have been evaluated for younger and in some cases older readers, such as main idea identification and summarization (Jitendra, Hoppes, & Xin, 2000; Rogevich & Perin, 2009) in Jitendra and Gajria Chapter 9; metacognitive strategies (Klingner, Vaughn, & Boardman, 2007) in Klingner, Morrison, and Eppolito, Chapter 10; and the Theme Identification program (Wilder & Williams, 2001) in Williams and Pao, Chapter 11. In this section we discuss interventions that focus specifically on students in fifth through 12th grade.

Differences between instructional focus in grades K–4 and in grades 5–12 are many. While reading instruction in the early years emphasizes word-level skills, these skills are assumed to be fully developed as students enter middle school. Text is largely narrative in the early grades, but the balance shifts to expository text predominantly in secondary schools. Story grammar-based comprehension strategies for reading and writing in the early grades are less effective when discussion and writing require cross-text integration. Along with the major shift in the task demands of secondary classrooms, poor readers are hampered by serious delays in word-level, fluency, and summarization skills compared to their peers, who mastered the reading basics years before.

Providing intensive instruction is more difficult in secondary than in elementary schools, because coursework required for graduation limits opportunities for teaching reading and spelling to poor readers. Even in middle school, reading instruction can be difficult to manage if special education focuses on tutoring or support for passing courses, instead of improving reading skills (Deshler, Ellis, & Lenz, 1996; O'Connor et al., 2002). Educators are faced with the dilemma of weighing the importance of content acquisition over reading skills.

While research has spotlighted intervention for elementary school students for many years, intervention for older students is a burgeoning field. Many of these students carry the label of "learning disability" or other categories of special services; however, our review also includes unlabeled poor readers who may (or may not) receive remedial services in middle or high school. Often, these students lack one or more of the complex skills needed to read effectively at the word level or for understanding. In this chapter we explore interventions designed to be effective for older students, utilizing not only established methods for elementary students but also adaptations and, at times, novel approaches to the instruction of reading.

Word Study

Older poor readers may fail in secondary school due to their difficulty understanding and using text materials written many grade levels above their reading ability, but the first hurdle for comprehending text may be deciphering the words on the page. Word-level difficulties of students with reading disabilities (RD) have been well documented (see Rack, Snowling, & Olson, 1992, for a review); however, effective interventions to address this problem may differ from those designed for younger students.

For example, young poor readers are likely to have difficulties with phonemic awareness, so improving phonemic awareness often improves their ability to read words. In a study of sixth-, seventh-, and eighth-grade poor readers (average reading grade level of 2.2), Bhat, Griffin, and Sindelar (2003) found phonological deficits similar to those of younger poor readers (i.e., standardized score of 79, on average). They provided 18 lessons of focused phonemic awareness instruction delivered one-to-one across a 4-week period, an amount likely to influence the phonemic awareness of young children. Their repeated measures analysis found that students improved in phonemic awareness; nevertheless, word reading scores did not improve.

The boost that phonemic awareness provides young children beginning to decode one-syllable words with regular spellings may be irrelevant to older poor readers, who can read simple word forms but balk at the multisyllabic words they see in textbooks. For older students, instruction in preparatory skills such as letter–sound correspondences, affixes, and morphemes may need to be integrated from the beginning with opportunities to apply these skills to words that are more age- and grade-appropriate.

Older poor readers often have a larger available sight word vocabulary than younger students, with similar overall word identification ability (Rack et al., 1992). Some years ago, Glass developed an approach (Glass Analysis; Glass & Glass, 1976) to help older students make use of their sight word knowledge by identifying and rehearsing letter sequences, such as rime and syllable units, to decode long words. Few studies have evaluated its effects; however, Penney's (2002) use of this approach experimentally with high school students in remedial reading classes showed promise. Students received 15–18 one-hour lessons, spaced once per week, that began with the student reading aloud from a text, while the teacher noted words missed. During this part of the one-to-one instruction, the teacher provided the missed word without decoding assistance. Patterns in the missed words were used for Glass Analysis, in which students read a simple word with the missed pattern (e.g., *sad*), identified the pattern (e.g., "Which letters say /ad/? What do the letters *a-d* spell?"), and used the pattern to read at least three longer words (e.g., *glad, gladly, saddle*). Following Glass Analysis, students reread the passage in which the focus pattern was formerly missed. Students who received these lessons made significantly greater progress than untreated students in the same remedial reading classes, with gains of over 2 years on word-level skills in 4 months. In addition to improvement in reading words and nonwords, students also gained significantly more than controls in comprehension. Penney suggested that the comprehension improvement may have been a result of extracting the taught patterns from text and rereading the same text passages after instruction, which may have made word study interesting and relevant to students.

This approach shares some similarity with the Benchmark Reading Program (Gaskins et al., 1988), in which students study high-frequency words and extract relevant patterns to apply to decoding new words. Few controlled experiments have been conducted with the Benchmark approach, and while studies have included students in the upper elementary school grades, results were rarely analyzed separately for the older students.

The research of Lovett and Steinbach (1997) provided an exception. In a study that contrasted phonological decoding with Word Identification Strategy Training (WIST) based on the work of Gaskins et al. (1988), students receiving phonological decoding instruction improved, as shown through their generalization to nonsense words. Students in WIST training also generalized to real, untaught words that shared the taught spelling patterns, including rime patterns that did not follow decoding rules. The study included students in grades 2–3, 4, and 5–6. In a comparison of effects across ages, fifth and sixth graders improvement was similar to that of younger students in both reading approaches. Lovett and colleagues have continued to refine the approach and now recommend PHAST (Phonological and Strategy Training; Lovett, Steinbach, & Frijters, 2000) as their preferred reading approach for older students, because it improves phonological skills, while teaching students to take advantage of their relatively advanced sight word knowledge to read longer words.

"Morphology," or the study of meaningful word parts (called "morphemes") such as prefixes, roots, and suffixes (Ebbers & Denton, 2008), has been influential in improving phonological awareness, vocabulary expansion, and reading comprehension for older readers (Nagy, Berninger, & Abbott, 2006). Nagy and Anderson (1984) estimated that about half of the words in English are morphologically complex; in other words, for about half of the new words that students encounter when reading, morphological strategies might help both decoding and comprehension. Moreover, the proportion of morphologically complex words increases as students get older. Consider science expository texts. Morphologically, *microbiology* comprises *micro-* (small), *bio-* (life), and *ology* (study or science). As exposure to expository texts increases, so does exposure to complex words, often with Greek or Latin roots; thus, morphology would seem to be increasingly useful. Results from the Nagy and colleagues (2006) study with typical readers found that understanding of morphology was moderately correlated with vocabulary and comprehension for students grouped in grades 4–5, 6–7, and 8–9, but these relations have received less research attention for poor readers.

Lenz and Hughes (1990) developed an effective model of word recognition strategy instruction for older students with RD in middle school. The DISSECT strategy (Discover the context, Isolate the word's prefix, Separate the word's suffix, Say the word's stem, Examine the word's stem, Check with another person to see if you are correct, Try to find the word in the dictionary) is designed to provide a collection of flexible strategies for students who lack a strong decoding base. The fourth step in the strategy—Say the word's stem (or base word), which is central to this method, introduced the Rules of Twos and Threes to decode the base word, which often has more than one syllable, in addition to attached affixes. The researchers taught students that when a stem begins with a vowel, separate the first two letters; when a stem begins with a consonant, separate the first three letters, then say the syllable. After that, repeat the process until the whole stem has been recognized. Once the stem is recognized, the other affixes are added back on, and the student pronounces the whole word. The instructional routine includes teacher modeling of the entire strategy, student paraphrasing of each step, memorizing the steps, then several weeks of controlled practice and feedback on the individual steps. Learning the strategy and applying it accurately required 20–25 minutes at least three times per week over a 6-week period. Generalization probes 1 week, 3 weeks, and 5 weeks after training demonstrate that students maintain use of the strategy after it is learned thoroughly. Although not labeled as a morphological approach, DISSECT teaches students to recognize word parts and to use morphemes to improve their word reading.

Bhattacharya and Ehri (2004) also considered adolescent poor readers' problem identifying multisyllabic words. Studies designed to teach syllabication rules to students with reading difficulties have shown little success. Instead of rules, Bhattacharya and Ehri developed a program based on multiple exemplars of syllables within words. Their hypothesis was that teaching students first to pronounce syllables in isolation, then to pronounce them nested in many appropriate examples of those syllables within words would improve both reading and spelling of multisyllabic words. To test the hypothesis, they randomly assigned poor readers (i.e., students reading 2–5 years below grade assignment) in grades 6–10 to one of three conditions: syllable analysis and practice (graphosyllabic treatment), whole-word practice with the same core of words, or a no-treatment control. Four 30-minute sessions were conducted with each treatment, and pre- and posttesting took two additional meetings. In the graphosyllabic treatment, students learned to identify the vowel(s) in each syllable, identify and pronounce affixes, separate off each syllable in the word with their thumbs, then blend syllables to say the word. Students were allowed to choose alternative breaking points between syllables if these did not alter the word's pronunciation.

Students in both treatments learned the 25-word sets they practiced; however, students in the graphosyllabic treatment reliably outperformed students in the whole-word treatment on transfer of syllable types to unpracticed words. They demonstrated their ability to segment words into spoken syllables, match them to spellings, and read long words correctly. Moreover, learning to analyze words fully benefited their detection of spelling errors and correct spelling of multisyllabic words. The most exciting finding in the study was the strong transfer to reading untaught words after just four treatment sessions totaling 2 hours of instruction.

In all, studies that replicated the methods found effective with younger students showed smaller effects for older students; however, interventions that applied decoding skills to words that were more age appropriate (multisyllabic words) improved the word-reading skills of older students, even when instruction was relatively short term (e.g., as little as 4–5 hours). Key to the most effective interventions were analyses of long words that contained known patterns, and teaching patterns with immediate utility for reading long words.

Vocabulary

Of course, recognizing words is only the first step to improving overall reading ability. Interventions for older, struggling readers tend to have a spiraling effect: Vocabulary improvement increases text comprehension, and one of the most effective ways of increasing vocabulary is by increasing proficient reading skills so that students read more (Jitendra, Edwards, Sacks, & Jacobson, 2004). As Stanovich suggested in his theory of Matthew effects, "The very children who are reading well and who have good vocabularies will read more, learn more word meanings, and hence read even better. Children with inadequate vocabularies—

who read slowly and without enjoyment—read less, and as a result have slower development of vocabulary knowledge, which inhibits further growth in reading ability" (Stanovich, 1986, p. 381). Interventions for older students require multifaceted strategies. Word analysis, content driven vocabulary, and making words meaningful through discussion and contextual reading all interplay in effective vocabulary intervention (see Chapter 7); however, educators also should be aware of the additional difficulties older poor readers may have with memory.

Students with learning disabilities (LD) frequently show concomitant difficulty with memory (Swanson & Alexander, 2000; Torgeson, 1988), and both short- and long-term memory play a role in acquiring new vocabulary. Mnemonic devices help students compensate for memory difficulties by forging auditory and visual connections. One specific intervention using mnemonics is the keyword strategy. To use this method, students "recode" a new word they are trying to learn with a concrete keyword they can picture. For example, in a study with LD students in sixth and eighth grades, Veit, Scruggs, and Mastropieri (1986) used the keyword method to teach students dinosaur names. Students in the experimental treatment were provided cards with the dinosaur name, a word clue, attributes of the dinosaur, and an interactive picture. The authors described the word cards to teach students about the attributes of the tyrannosaurus. The word clue was *tie*, which was colored red to indicate a red meat eater. An owl and a night scene indicated that this dinosaur was from the "late" period. The interactive picture showed owls with red ties (red meat eater), dancing through the night (late period) with bows and arrows (to indicate hunting). The keyword strategy was compared with direct questioning, in which students were told the word definition and asked to repeat it. Students who used the keyword method scored significantly higher on a test of the vocabulary words that required students to link the specific dinosaurs with their attributes.

Although the keyword method was successful for vocabulary tasks that required learning a new word and its attributes, often science vocabulary requires memorizing sequences and orders. Mastropieri, Scruggs, and Levin (1985) used a combined keyword–pegword strategy in a study with ninth graders with LD who needed to learn the hardness of various minerals in science. First, students were instructed using keyword strategies to learn the mineral names. Next, rhyming pegwords were taught for hardness levels (1–10). The mineral *corundum* was represented by the keyword *car*, then shown in a picture entangled by a vine (rhyming word for hardness *Level 9*). Students were given one of three treatments: the mnemonic condition with the keyword–pegword method, a questioning condition (5-minute lesson and 30 seconds of questioning for each target mineral), and a free-study condition (5-minute lesson and student self-study). The keyword–pegword condition was found to be more effective for both recall and "response latency" (defined by the authors as the time between the researcher's question and the beginning of the student's relevant response) than questioning and self-study conditions.

In another study, Mastropieri, Scruggs, and Fulk (1990) examined how effectively keyword strategies support comprehension. Students with LD in grades 6–8 were taught either a keyword mnemonic strategy or a rehearsal strategy (drill and practice). Students using the keyword strategy outperformed rehearsal students on both outcome measures, with large effect sizes—a production test for recall of the word (overall effect size 3.25) and a comprehension test for matching the word with the meaning (overall effect size 1.83). The authors concluded that although the keyword strategy was designed primarily to address vocabulary, positive effects were found for comprehension (Mastropieri et al., 1990).

The tests in these studies of mnemonics require recall of words and meanings; however, students also need to use words in appropriate conversational settings and discussions (Beck, McKeown, & Kucan, 2002). Ebbers and Denton (2008) underscore the importance of developing meaning of new words through practical and conversational connections, in addition to reading instruction. Teachers can help to facilitate deeper word knowledge by incorporating new vocabulary into classroom conversations, in both academic (in lecture and instruction) and nonacademic exchanges, such as classroom procedures and personal exchanges. Bos and Anders (1990) found better results for middle school students with LD using interactive vocabulary instruction rather than definition instruction. Students worked with context clues and were encouraged to think about what they already knew about new words through activation, sharing, and elaboration of prior knowledge. Students in the interactive treatment condition performed better than students in the definition instruction group, and maintained their new vocabulary knowledge on delayed posttests 1 month later.

Using context to learn new vocabulary may require considerable instruction and adult assistance. Making use of peers as motivators, Harmon (2002) worked with pairs of students in high school remedial reading classes to develop their ability to infer the meanings of words in narrative and expository texts. In facilitated peer dialogues, a teacher and two struggling readers discussed words and identified clues to possible meanings, along with their metacognitive strategies for identifying and testing clues. Through discussion the teacher not only offered strategies and demonstrated how to use them but also assessed students' current strategies and logic. Key components in the intervention included teaching students how independent word-learning strategies work, encouraging students to select the words in texts that were most troublesome, facilitating peer interaction, and discussing with students the focus word and related concepts to build rich definitions. Through transcriptions of these discussions, Harmon identified the strategies that required the most teacher support: "(a) awareness of the function of a word in relation to the context . . . , (b) ability to discern the helpfulness of the immediate context, (c) reference to text events or the broader story line beyond the immediate sentence level, and (d) ability to make connections with personal background knowledge or explicitly state text information" (p. 609). Segments of discussion with students demonstrated the importance of shaping students' dialogue and rationale as they puzzled with word meanings. It is unclear, however, whether students were able to use the strategies and processes independently.

In all, vocabulary interventions for older poor readers have had encouraging results in research. Some studies have shown generalization of improved vocabulary to increased reading comprehension. Findings suggest important implications for practitioners. First, both strategic and direct vocabulary instruction can be effective for older students. Several successful interventions have addressed the memory concerns of poor readers by providing visual and auditory links, and extensive opportunity to practice new words and appropriate associations with those words. Although these interventions required considerable effort and support by teachers, they suggest that deficits in overall reading skills can, to some extent, be ameliorated by vocabulary intervention.

Computer-Assisted Instruction

Finding the time to implement interventions, such as those described earlier, has led some researchers to consider computer-assisted instruction (CAI) for vocabulary acquisition, as well as other components of reading. The unique niche that CAI fills for older students is to reconcile intense student academic need and the demands of secondary classrooms. Several studies have demonstrated significant improvements in vocabulary and comprehension on both researcher-made and standardized tests with use of CAI.

Johnson, Gersten, and Carnine (1987) compared differences in the size of learning sets using CAI. Working with high school students with LD, two computer-directed interventions were compared: one targeting only words a student did not know on a pretest (the small teaching set group), and the other presenting vocabulary in sets of 25 words (the large teaching set group). In the small set of words condition, students had individualized lessons targeting only words they did not already know, with no more than seven words in a set, which addressed two instructional principles: optimal set size and cumulative review. Students were required to demonstrate mastery of the seven words in two consecutive lessons, and cumulative review of learned words was used to ensure retention. The large teaching set was based on a commercial program and presented words to students in sets of 25, regardless of student prior knowledge. For the large set condition, students had the option of selecting displays of the word with definition and example sentence, multiple-choice quiz, complete the blank, or an arcade game–like visual. Both conditions included immediate feedback to the students; however, the small teaching set provided periodic cumulative review, whereas the large teaching set kept no cumulative record of student progress. Students in the targeted group achieved mastery in an average of 7.6 sessions compared to students in the large teaching set group, averaging 9.1 sessions. Sessions were ceased at the discretion of the researcher for students who reached Session 11 without mastery (two in the small set, four in the large set). Students in both groups improved significantly on posttests and maintained new vocabulary.

Among the promising programs for secondary students, READ 180 (Scholastic, 1999) combined software with teacher instruction to improve word iden-tification, fluency, and content-area learning for middle and high school students who read poorly. Based on principles of anchored instruction, students viewed a brief video on CD-ROM that contained background information relevant to the passages they would read. The CAI portion of the lesson (Hasselbring & Goin, 2004) was designed to improve motivation for reading by providing background knowledge and word-level assistance to enable adolescents to engage with mean-ingful text. Instruction centered on a video anchor that depicted a contemporary situation likely to be of interest to adolescents. Viewing each section of the video was followed by reading text related to the video, word-level assistance with rel-evant vocabulary, and comprehension tasks in which students sought discrepan-cies between text segments and video portrayal of events. An animated figure with a human voice guided students, tracked student responses, and adjusted instruction accordingly. Spelling (linked to the anchor video) was also included to improve orthographic knowledge.

Students listened to a taped model of fluent reading as they followed along in the text, then read the passage independently. Teachers directed word study, vocabulary, and comprehension lessons in small groups. Other materials for inde-pendent reading were selected from lists matched to the student's current reading ability based on the Lexile Framework for Reading, and students took quizzes on the computer to assess comprehension of these materials. Although only a few studies have been conducted on this system to date (Goin, Hasselbring, & McAfee, 2004; Hasselbring & Goin, 2004; Papalewis, 2004), the results have been positive, and the content-area reading materials may help to provide age-appropriate world knowledge for students who have difficulty reading grade-level text materials.

The 5- or 6-period day and the stringent course requirements for graduation combine to make intensive reading instruction in secondary schools difficult to provide. Several structural modifications in the school day were made in a large urban district to evaluate the effects of READ 180 with students who were failing eighth-grade English, failing the district writing test, and in most cases repeating the eighth grade (Papalewis, 2004). Class size was reduced to 15–20 students, and the period was lengthened to 90 minutes. Teachers in the experimental classes were trained to implement 20 minutes of whole-group instruction that included shared reading, reading aloud, and word-level skills. Next, the group was bro-ken into thirds, with one-third working directly with the teacher, one-third read-ing independently, and one-third reading with CAI using READ 180 and text matched to student reading ability. The groups rotated through all three sessions, then ended with a 10-minute whole-group wrap-up.

Over the course of the school year, students whose teachers used READ 180 improved significantly on standardized and state-mandated tests of reading and language arts, while matched control students lost ground. The advantages for students using READ 180 over control students may be due to matching extended time for instruction to students' reading ability; nevertheless, abundant research suggests that maintaining the status quo for poor readers in secondary schools is ineffective. The results were especially strong for students who were English learners, perhaps due to the video context for the reading and spelling activities in the CAI portion of instruction.

CAI interventions offer the distinct advantage of individualizing instruction and providing additional practice without expending teacher time. In a review of program features, Hall, Hughes, and Filbert (2000) reported that CAI programs frequently provided systematic instruction and immediate feedback—instructional attributes that are particularly helpful for struggling readers. Although studies of CAI to improve reading for older students are sparse, strategic use of CAI to supplement teacher-led instruction (not to replace it) may be able to extend appropriate practice at useful levels of difficulty, and all with infinite patience.

Improving Fluency

Reading rate is difficult to shift for poor readers in secondary schools. Interventions designed to improve reading rate along with word reading and passage comprehension tend to have stronger effects on comprehension than on rate.

Peer-Assisted Learning Strategies (PALS; Fuchs, Fuchs, Mathes, & Simmons, 1997), a variation of classwide peer tutoring, has been widely researched for elementary-age students. The PALS approach includes peers reading aloud to each other and summarizing what they have read. Fuchs, Fuchs, and Kazdan (1999) adapted PALS for high school students in remedial and special education classes. Although PALS often improves the fluency of elementary students, the high school students showed no more improvement in reading rate than control students, although students in PALS improved their reading comprehension. In another study of this intervention, Calhoun (2005) combined PALS with phonological skills instruction for middle school students in special education classes, most of whom were in grade 6. Following 31 weeks of treatment, students participating in PALS improved significantly more than controls on passage comprehension but not fluency.

In a 10-week study with seventh graders, Allinder, Dunse, Brunken, and Obermiller-Krolikowski (2001) compared two practice conditions on the read-aloud portion of a program that included phonics, comprehension, and reading text. In the strategy practice condition, students were given a particular focus as they read aloud, based on teacher and researcher observation of the type of student fluency problem. As examples, students were instructed to pause at periods, follow with their finger, read with expression, or watch for word endings, among other strategies. Students in the alternative treatment were told generically to do their best. Bookmarks with the key focus typed across them were tailored for each student. Comprehension improvement was found for students in both conditions. The only significant difference favored the specific focus treatment on slope of improvement on a reading maze task, in which students read an unfamiliar passage with every seventh word deleted and selected an appropriate word from three choices. Because oral reading rate was not measured directly, it is difficult to interpret the maze difference between treatments. Students read silently on the maze task, and supposedly used their comprehension of the passage to choose the appropriate word. Perhaps the most notable component of this multifeature reading intervention for poor readers in seventh grade was time spent reading orally, because by middle school, reading aloud is often omitted from instruction.

Therrien, Wickstrom, and Jones (2006) focused on reading aloud in a study that included fourth- through eighth-grade poor readers and required 50 sessions of repeated reading. Students read each passage two to four times, until they met a specific rate criterion or completed four readings. Comprehension was addressed by asking students to identify main characters and events following the last reading, with assistance provided as needed. Students in the intervention generalized their improved rate to untaught passages and gained 12 words per minute, on average, across the 4 months of intervention, which was significantly greater than those in the control condition, though less than gains of typical readers in earlier grades. Generalized gains in comprehension were not found. In contrast to other studies, when Therrien (personal communication, June 20, 2009) later compared the data from the students in grades 5–8 with the fourth graders, he found that the older students who practiced with repeated reading made stronger gains than the younger students in reading rate. Nevertheless, gains were still less than 1 word per week during the 16-week treatment.

In all, studies designed to improve reading rate have had only minimal success beyond the elementary years. Some might argue that rate is the least of concerns for older poor readers, whose deficits in word reading, vocabulary, comprehension, and motivation to work hard are the immediate problems. If, however, improving rate influences reading comprehension, as it seems to for younger students (O'Connor, Swanson, & Geraghty, 2010), researchers might want to find more successful methods for doing so beyond fifth grade.

Approaches to Reading Comprehension

Reading comprehension becomes increasingly critical for older students. Not only is K–12 education centered on reading to learn (Denton, Wexler, Vaughn, & Bryan, 2008; Roberts, Torgesen, Boardman, & Scammacca, 2008; Swanson, 1999), but reading comprehension is also an essential life skill for postsecondary outcomes, such as employment and going to college or vocational school. Several important components construct the processes of comprehension, including accessing texts (text structure), identifying the main idea, organizing key information, and employing strategies at each step to access and maintain new information. In this section we discuss research strategies that have been shown to be effective in improving reading comprehension for older struggling students.

Prior Knowledge

The role of prior knowledge as a conceptual framework for reading comprehension (Anderson & Pearson, 1984) is widely accepted, but how to develop and ensure sufficient conceptual knowledge for reading comprehension is less clear. Several methods have shown some success, such as previewing (Graves, Cooke, & Laberge, 1983), discussion of vocabulary and content (Beck, Omanson, & McKeown, 1982), and semantic mapping (Anders, Bos, & Filip, 1984). Morris, Stein, and Bransford (1979) found a strong association between prior knowledge and comprehension for college students. Building upon this work, Dole, Brown, and Trathen (1996) expanded the model to fifth- and sixth-grade students at risk for reading difficulties. They assigned students randomly to 5 weeks of instruction in story content, strategies for deriving text structure, or a basal approach that followed the teacher's guide recommendations. The text material was consistent across groups and drawn from basal readers.

Instruction in *story content* was similar to the previewing technique developed by Graves et al. (1983) and designed to develop the knowledge necessary for understanding the day's story. It included key vocabulary, concepts, and related ideas, such as the central problem to be faced by protagonists. *Strategy instruction* led students to identify main characters, the central problem, and the problem's resolution. Students were taught to jot down key ideas on story maps, first modeled by the teacher, and gradually taken over by the students. Over time, students led discussions on features necessary to capture the central story ideas and adapt the map to fit each story's features. In the traditional *basal approach*, researchers followed the instructional manual, which identified vocabulary and word recognition activities, as well as discussion points to elicit student knowledge about the topic. Time spent on reading and writing was similar across the three groups.

Although students in all three groups demonstrated good comprehension of the stories taught, students who received the strategy instruction outscored the other groups on comprehension posttests of new material, which indicates generalization. Moreover, they maintained the ability to derive meaning independently from new text 7 weeks later. The authors interpret these results in terms of scaffolding. In particular, the teacher modeled procedures, coached students to use them, and faded assistance over time, which led students toward independent use of the strategy without teacher support.

Organizing Key Information

The use of graphic or cognitive mapping and visual representation serve to impose structure through organizing and sequencing information (Kavale, Forness, & Bender, 1987). Cognitive maps and visual displays encompass a broad set of tools to help students organize chunks of reading visually (component ideas and details) and to help connect the implicit relationships between ideas and details (Boyle, 1996). Cognitive maps can be made by students, by teachers, or by both (e.g., through reciprocal teaching, discussed below). Use of cognitive maps has had mixed results in research literature. They generally help students score better on activities during treatment, when strategies are reinforced and maintained externally, and on researcher-made outcome measures that parallel the instruction closely. On standardized outcomes, however, results are rarely significant (Kim, Vaughn, Wanzek, & Wei, 2009). In other words, evidence is inconclusive about whether students generalize the skills of using concept maps from one task to another.

Questions of how organizers are constructed remain as well. In a series of studies by Horton, Lovitt, and Bergerud (1990), middle school students (typical, remedial, and LD) either constructed their own graphic organizers or used a teacher-constructed organizer for content-area classes in science, social studies, and health. In the first study, they compared teacher-directed graphic organizers with self-study. All three types of students demonstrated significantly increased outcomes with use of the graphic organizer. In the second and third studies, researchers examined student-generated graphic organizers compared to self-study, and again results were significant for remedial students and those with LDs. Variation in these two studies involved how the graphic organizers were constructed: In Experiment 2, the teacher provided referential cues to help students locate information in the text, and in Experiment 3, study teachers provided clues about information to be included. Results were more favorable when students with LD were provided information location cues (Experiment 2) rather than content clues alone. Teachers' strategic choice of how and when to use graphic organizers (teacher- or student-directed, and which information to provide for students when constructing their own) appears to be a factor in effectiveness. Table 16.1 describes ways for teachers to choose the kind of visual representation for students based on task type.

Strategy Instruction

High school interventions must contend with dual challenges of preparing struggling students for postsecondary instruction and bridging instruction to the skills needed in real life. In a study that connected adolescent comprehension teaching strategies with adult outcomes, Hock and Mellard (2005) identified organization strategies such as looking for clues, summarizing, generating questions, and drawing inferences as preparatory for adult outcomes. Using a survey of literature, exams, and outcomes (National Assessment of Educational Progress for eighth-grade skills, the General Educational Development (GED) exam, and employability ratings for 12th-grade skills), investigators worked backward through review of items occurring most frequently and made specific recommendations for how to design high school instruction strategically to support reading comprehension on particular kinds of tasks. Summarizing and drawing inferences were the most effective strategies for adult-focused tests; paraphrasing and self-questioning were also beneficial. The authors point out that knowing the type of test (school- or

TABLE 16.1. Use of Visual Representation/Concept Mapping in the Classroom

Student directed: *Provide student with procedures or teacher-made map.*	**Teacher supported:** *Teacher and group create and complete visual representation together.*
Explicit information	Implicit information
For gathering specific information about a reading, such as the W (who, what, when, where, why) questions, or plot, scene, characterization	*For information that requires students to use inferential skills, draw on prior knowledge, or prior text structure instruction (i.e., theme, characterization, compare–contrast, descriptive)*
• Outlining a narrative chapter • Completing a biology lab assignment in science • Organizing information about the Vietnam War	• Comparing two texts (e.g., *One Flew over the Cuckoo's Nest* and *Hamlet*) • Brainstorming what the student knows about the Civil War before instruction begins
Single task	To generalize
When the purpose is to complete a single text or project	*When the purpose is to teach a strategy that students might be expected to use for other texts, in other content areas, or independently in the future*
• Organizing for prewriting (parts of an essay, brainstorming maps) • Chunking a larger project into parts (e.g., a history paper that must cover five or more events)	• Generic map for Know, Want, Learned (K-W-L) chart as a strategy to generalize for independent use on future readings • Venn diagram organizer for shared and distinct attributes

employment-based) to prepare for suggests different instructional strategies. For example, the employability measure relies heavily on looking for clues, whereas the GED requires more summarizing and main idea skills. Teachers also must evaluate tasks when determining which test-based strategies will be most beneficial to students. Gersten, Fuchs, Williams, and Baker (2001), in a review of literature, differentiated between two major kinds of texts that older students regularly encounter: narrative and expository. Hock and Mellard (2005) add documents. Narrative texts include stories and fiction, whereas expository texts consist of information and explanations. Documents, a subset of expository writings, include items such as job applications and want ads associated with postsecondary life. Expository text is particularly problematic for struggling readers, because it comprises a variety of text structures, such as description, cause–effect, and sequences (Gajria, Jitendra, Sood, & Sacks, 2007). In a study by Meyer, Brandt, and Bluth (1980), struggling readers with limited text structure knowledge retrieved text randomly without a plan. For maximum success, struggling readers need both explicit instruction in text structures and guided practice to generalize the strategy to new texts.

Cognitive strategy instruction for text structures, or teaching *processes* on how to learn (Gajria et al., 2007), involves providing direct instruction to students on how to recognize key text structures and approach problem solving with that process (generalizing to novel situations). One chief decision that teachers must make is determining which text structures are most critical. Complexity and variety of text structures increase as students get older, so strategic choices must be prioritized. For example, in an experimental high school treatment with students with LD, Smith and Friend (1986) identified *time–order, problem–solution, comparison, description,* and *cause–effect* as important structures. Students in their treatment group received training to recognize and use these text structures, whereas the control group received training on generic problem solving. The treatment group significantly outscored the control group on posttest measures of structure recognition (identifying text structures) and recall of the main idea, and maintained their advantage on a delayed posttest.

Bakken, Mastropieri, and Scruggs (1997) taught eighth-grade students to identify three text structures—*main idea, list,* and *order*—in science passages. This text-based group was compared to a treatment group receiving instruction on paragraph restatement, and to a control group that received traditional classroom instruction. Students instructed in text-based strategies outperformed traditional and paragraph-restatement treatment groups. Effects remained for transfer to a new, grade-level social studies task and to a delayed posttest.

Choice of text structures to teach depends on specific content area and required assignments. For example, studies with college-level students with LD have included a story grammar framework, with *setting* (social, physical, or temporal context) and *episode,* broken down into *initiating event* (a change in the story environment), *internal response* (of the protagonist and goals), *attempt* (protagonist's action), *consequence* (outcome and attainment or nonattainment of goal) and *reaction* (Bacon & Carpenter, 1989). Meyer (1975) sorted readings into *collective/descriptive* (a list of elements that are attributes of a topic or sequenced events), *causation* (if–then or antecedent–consequence), *problem–solution* (causation with at least one aspect of a solution that impacts the problem) and *comparison* (similarities and difference). The frameworks, while designed for college-age students, might be adapted for high school texts.

Using a more generic process to encourage students to explore text, Schumaker, Deshler, Alley, Warner, and Denton (1982) taught teachers of students with LD, ages 14–18 the Multipass strategy, which required students to review text three times, each time with a different purpose. Building upon the Survey, Question, Read, Recite, and Review (SQ3R) technique (Robinson, 1946), the Survey Pass helps students identify the main idea and organization of the chapter. Students read the title and introductory paragraph, review the chapter's relationship to adjacent chapters (how it fits in with what they have already read), survey subtitles, inspect illustrations and captions, read the summary paragraph, and paraphrase information. In the Size-Up Pass, students read the questions at the end of the chapter. If they already know the answer, they place a check next to the question. If they do not, they look through the chapter again to identify text cues (e.g., bold or italicized words), turn cues into questions, skim through text surrounding text cues, and paraphrase answers in their own words. In the final pass, students Sort Out information. Going back to the questions at the back, students placed a check next to questions to which they now have answers. If they do not know the answer, they considered the section in which the answer is most likely to be found, skim through those sections, and repeat the process as needed.

Students were given explicit instruction on the Multipass strategy. Important findings included not only increases in reading comprehension using the strategy (baseline to posttest), but also ability to generalize use of Multipass to other grade-level material without further training (Schumaker et al., 1982). Initially, materials at students' current independent reading level were used, so that students could concentrate on the strategies without struggling to read the words. As students progress toward independence, the Multipass strategy is used with more difficult text. The amount of time for students to master the strategy varies from 4.5 to 11.5 hours of instruction. Like other procedures that have demonstrated positive effects, teachers explain the purpose for the strategy, model how to do it, coach students through it, have students verbally rehearse what they would do, then gradually released assistance as students gain independence through multiple opportunities to apply Multipass. Following this training, students are able to apply Multipass to their social studies texts, with the important outcome of improvement on grades in their classes and on experimenter tests.

Discussion can also help students to structure information from materials they read. Reciprocal teaching is a four-step teaching method to increase comprehension through strategies based on scaffolded instruction, influenced by Vygotsky (1978), in which teacher and student take turns leading discussions about sections of a text (Brown & Palincsar, 1989; Palincsar & Brown, 1984). Instruction occurs in guided cooperative learning groups, in which teachers encourage students to think actively while they read. The four strategies in reciprocal teaching include questioning, summarizing, attempting to clarify word meanings and other confusions, and predicting what will come next. Although studies often show positive effects on experimenter measures, in controlled experiments they rarely find measurable improvement on standardized tests. Alfassi (1998) used reciprocal teaching in remedial classes of high school freshmen who were poor comprehenders but good decoders. Her comparison students were in traditional remedial classes. Following 4 days of teacher-led training (1 day on each of the four methods: questioning, summarizing, clarifying, and predicting), students used the approach for 15 days. The teacher was available for guidance but students assumed increasing responsibility for leading the discussions. Students were explicitly told the utility of each strategy (e.g., saying something in one's own words or predicting the test questions demonstrates comprehension of what was read).

On researcher-developed tests (i.e., 350- to 500-word passages followed by text-explicit and text-implicit questions), students in the reciprocal teaching groups significantly outperformed those in traditional classes and maintained superior comprehension 8 weeks later. Positive results for reciprocal teaching were also demonstrated by Lysynchuk, Pressley, and Vye (1990), who worked with 11- and 12-year-old students with reading difficulties. As in earlier studies, no difference was found on the standardized measures.

Clearly the researcher-developed tests were more closely aligned to reciprocal teaching instruction, but these measures are also arguably more aligned to what students need to do in the real world, where they rarely face multiple-choice decision making. One limitation is that reciprocal teaching is based on a small-group design (groups of two students in Palincsar & Brown, 1984; groups of two to five students in Lysynchuck et al., 1990). As an intervention, reciprocal teaching is designed and best situated for intense, small-group instruction for at least 30 minutes, three times a week or more.

Discussion techniques attempt to engage students in literature (story texts) through active questioning and collaborative problem solving. In an investigation of 64 middle and high school classrooms, Applebee, Langer, Nystrand, and Gramoran (2003) demonstrated that discussion strategies (exploratory questioning, more time allocated for open discussion, and teacher questions designed to build on students' comments) were influential, regardless of student academic ability. Comprehension improved for students in remedial English classes, as well as for students in more challenging academic classes. Some studies have adopted procedures designed for typical readers for older students with RD (Peverly & Woods, 2001; Sandora, Beck, & McKeown, 1999). Results have been positive, and below we describe discussion techniques that have been most beneficial.

In a study of high school students with LD, Peverly and Wood (2001) investigated the effect of inserting questions, with and without feedback, either during or following student reading. Postquestions, in which students are asked about passages they have already read either concurrent with or after reading, have been demonstrated to be more advantageous than prequestions, such as predictions (Hamaker, 1986). Groups were designated to conditions in which questions were inserted during or after reading, with and without feedback. Students who were asked questions as they read and received feedback on their responses had the greatest gains. Additionally, questioning while reading as a discussion technique was found to be beneficial for main idea and inferential comprehension.

In a similar vein, Sandora et al. (1999) investigated other discussion strategies with older, at-risk students (75% scoring below the 50th percentile on the Iowa Test of Basic Skills) in grades 6 and 7 in an inner-city school. The study used two discussion techniques. The first was the Great Books series discussion program, in which a group leader asked three types of questions after students completed reading (Dennis & Moldof, 1983). The second discussion technique was Questioning the Author (Beck, McKeown, Sandora, & Worthy, 1996), in which teachers encourage students to assume that the author is human and fallible, and that the text is incomplete. The group constructs meaning through discussion that occurs during the reading of the text. Results were significantly higher for comprehension (measured using story recall) and interpretation (measured using open-ended questions) using the Questioning the Author method. Authors suggest that discussion generates "a cycle of encountering information, interpreting, discussing, and reevaluating, . . . providing students with numerous opportunities to discuss key concepts or points of confusion" (Sandora et al., 1999, p. 208).

In summary, the purpose of teaching comprehension strategies transcends a single text, single assignment, or single class. We note that many of the most effective strategies for older poor readers scaffold students through a process by demonstrating how and why to use an approach; close monitoring and "just in time" assistance as students learn the steps or process; and extensive practice, in which students gain autonomy over the procedures and explain to peers when and how to use a particular strategy.

Although narrative text continues to be available through high school and beyond, the requirements for extracting information in the workplace, in the daily news, and in other adult endeavors are based inevitably on reading expository text with comprehension. Findings from these studies are particularly important to teachers as they structure discussions in their own classrooms. Questions addressing main idea and inference, during and after reading, and with feedback to shape discussion, are most effective (Peverly & Wood, 2001). Discussions that occur during the reading of a text and are open-ended and collaborative yield higher comprehension and interpretation of novel texts (Sandora et al., 1999).

Improving Motivation

Motivation may be particularly important for older students, first because motivation may be poor due to years of struggling, and second because evidence suggests that individual differences in motivation play a key role in the efficacy of interventions (Guthrie & Humenick, 2004).

In a synthesis of 22 studies designed to increase students' motivation for reading (Guthrie & Humenick, 2004), two types of interventions were especially effective for adolescents: establishing knowledge goals and providing interesting texts. Teachers can pursue themes that increase students' background knowledge and interest, arouse students' curiosity on a topic, and enable students to become eager readers. Schiefele (1999) found that students rate a text as interesting if they already know something about it. Therefore, establishing some familiarity with a topic, whether through discussion, activity, or prior reading, is likely to influence motivation to read. Students who form goals for reading that relate to mastering content and improving their knowledge of a topic become intrinsically motivated to improve their expertise and to read carefully for their own purposes. Providing supportive feedback on how well students achieve these goals allows them to assume mastery-oriented goals that increase persistence. In studies of students in grades 8–11 (Ames & Archer, 1988), and middle school students (Anderman, Maehr, & Midgley, 1999), those who perceived their class as mastery oriented, rather than competitive or grade oriented, expressed more interest in class content, were more willing to tackle difficult material, and recalled more of what they read. In their analysis of overall effects on motivation and reading, Guthrie and Humenick (2004) found that improving students' motivation for reading had a large positive effect on reading achievement and comprehension. Although teachers still need to address specific reading skills for these older poor readers, addressing motivation to read more and more carefully may encourage students to engage in the practice required to improve proficiency.

In a study that combined motivation for reading and instruction, Ivey and Broaddus (2007) developed an instructional intervention for middle school language English learners (ELLs) beginning to read and write in English. Based on theories of motivation and engagement, their instruction included self-selected and teacher-directed reading and writing. Students in the participating language arts class had emigrated to the United States 1–24 months earlier, and were all considered to be at Level 1, with little conversational or reading skill in English, although some students were good readers in Spanish. In this formative experiment, the researchers participated in class instruction several times a week, and used student interviews and observations to consider influences on learning and to adjust instruction throughout the year. They increased accessibility of reading materials by using books augmented with photographs to stimulate acquisition of reading and speaking vocabulary around interesting content (e.g., the natural world, family life).

When students lack a functional core of sight words, matching books with appropriate reading levels to student interests is difficult. In one promising compromise, researchers used a Language Experience Approach (LEA; Stauffer, 1970; Stokes, 1989), which is often used with much younger poor readers. Working one-on-one, the teacher shows the student a picture or suggested a topic, and the student dictates his or her story. In another study with middle school students, Stratton, Grindler, and Postell (1992) used photographs to encourage middle school students to write stories on a computer and read them back. Through repeated reading of this self-generated text, students gained reading practice with exposure to their own high-frequency speaking vocabulary, which may improve motivation and persistence, as well as memory for useful words. Bos and Vaughn (2002) have suggested that this approach be used only until poor readers can identify 30–100 words, which may be a sufficient initial core of words to begin reading other kinds of text. Although LEA may encourage engagement with text, the approach does little to establish the specific word study strategies so needed by older poor readers.

Marginalization is both a cause and an effect of poor motivation for reading. Students may feel unconnected to instruction because their poor reading makes it difficult to access materials or engage in assignments, whether their poor reading is due to lack of opportunity to learn, disabilities, or learning English. Marginalization is also a key issue for poor readers in the adolescent years (Franzak, 2006). For these students, establishing viable reading opportunities through interesting reading materials at lower levels of difficulty, and providing choices among materials and assignments, may increase persistence and engagement; however, studies have not tested these possibilities.

The Landscape of Secondary Schooling

The ability to read well with comprehension may be the single most important educational skill for passing the high school exit exams many states require for graduation. The Center for Education Policy (2008) has identified three types of exit exam currently being used in the USA. Minimum Competency Exams evaluate basic skills, often below the high school level; however, these exams are being phased out. The number of states with a minimum competency testing system decreased from 10 states in 2002 to two in 2008, with only one state projected to continue by 2012. Instead, states are adopting comprehensive exams that target skills at the high school level and are aligned to state standards, or end-of-course exams based on content of high school courses (also aligned to state standards) and given at the conclusion of each specific course. While in 2002 only two states had comprehensive exams, by 2008 the number had increased to 17. The nature of comprehensive exams, which are given all at once and cover large amounts of information, is particularly problematic for poor readers and students with disabilities.

For example, since the California Comprehensive Exam System was instituted in 2006, a student cannot receive a high school diploma without passing both the English Language Arts and Math portions of the California High School Exit Exam (CAHSEE). Although a class action lawsuit postponed the accountability of CAHSEE for students with disabilities until 2008 (*Kidd v. CDE*), they too now must pass in English Language Arts and Math to receive a diploma. The subgroup of students with disabilities is especially vulnerable, with a passing rate in 2008 of only 54.5% compared with 93.7% for students without disabilities (Becker, Wise, & Watters, 2008).

The outlook beyond graduation for students who do not acquire strong reading skills is bleak. The National Joint Committee on Learning Disabilities (2008) reports that only 11% of students with LDs go to college within 2 years of graduation, compared with 53% of the general education population. Faggella-Luby and Deshler (2008) point out that the changing job market places more and more demand on literacy skills. Reading in the workplace requires acquisition of novel information through expository sources (e.g., job applications, manuals, taxes, bills, memos, and employee handbooks).

These changes for high school graduation are relevant for teaching poor readers in secondary schools to read effectively. They suggest that the current trend to tutor students to pass courses without improving their reading skill may be detrimental to their life choices as they exit the K–12 system. Studies have shown how we can improve reading skills of older, poor readers; however, changes in secondary schooling that allow the required instructional intensity are likely to be needed.

In Appendix 16.1, we show how teachers of older poor readers might incorporate the effective research findings described in this chapter to improve reading development.

References

Abbott, S. P., & Berninger, V. W. (1999). It's never too late to remediate: Teaching word recognition to students with reading disabilities in grades 4–7. *Annals of Dyslexia, 49,* 223–250.

Alfassi, M. (1998). Reading for meaning: The efficacy of reciprocal teaching in fostering reading comprehension in high school students in remedial reading classes. *American Educational Research Journal, 35,* 309–332.

Allinder, R., Dunse, L., Brunken, C., & Obermiller-Krolikowski, H. (2001). Improving fluency in at-risk readers and students with learning disabilities. *Remedial and Special Education, 22,* 48–54.

Ames, C., & Archer, J. (1988). Achievement goals in the classroom: Students' learning strategies and motivation processes. *Journal of Educational Psychology, 94,* 545–561.

Anderman, E. M., Maehr, M. L., & Midgley, C. (1999). Declining motivation after the transition to middle school: Schools can make a difference. *Journal of Research and Development in Education, 32,* 131–147.

Anders, P. L., Bos, C. S., & Filip, D. (1984). The effect of semantic feature analysis on the reading comprehension of learning disabled students. In J. Niles & L. Harris (Eds.), *Changing perspectives in research on reading/language processing and instruction* (33rd yearbook of the National Reading Conference, pp. 162–166). Rochester, NY: National Reading Conference.

Anderson, R. C., & Pearson, P. D. (1984). A schema-theoretic view of the basic processes in reading. In P. D. Pearson (Ed.), *Handbook of reading research* (pp. 255–292). New York: Longman.

Applebee, A. N., Langer, J. A., Nystrand, M., & Gramoran, A. (2003). Discussion-based approaches to developing understanding: classroom instruction and student performance in middle and high school. *American Education Research Journal, 40*(3), 685–703.

Bacon, E. H., & Carpenter, D. (1989). Learning disabled and nondisabled college students' use of structure in recall of stories and text. *Learning Disability Quarterly, 12*(2), 108–118

Bakken, J. P., Mastropieri, M. A., & Scruggs, T. E. (1997). Reading comprehension of expository science material and students with learning disabilities: A comparison of strategies. *Journal of Special Education, 31*(3), 300–324.

Beck, I., McKeown, M., & Kucan, L. (2002). *Bringing words to life: Robust vocabulary instruction.* New York: Guilford Press.

Beck, I. L., McKeown, M. G., Sandora, C., & Worthy, J. (1996). Questioning the Author: A year-long classroom implementation to engage students with text. *Elementary School Journal, 96*(4), 385–414.

Beck, I. L., Omanson, R. C., & McKeown, M. G. (1982). An instructional redesign of reading lessons: Effects on comprehension. *Reading Research Quarterly, 17,* 462–481.

Becker, D. E., Wise, L., & Watters, C. (Eds.). (2008). *Independent evaluation of the California High School Exit Examination (CAHSEE): 2008 evaluation report.* Retrieved June 10 2009, from *www.cde.ca.gov/ta/tg/hs/documents/cahsee08evalrpt.pdf.*

Bhat, P., Griffin, C. C., & Sindelar, P. T. (2003). Phonological awareness instruction for middle school students with learning disabilities. *Learning Disability Quarterly, 26,* 73–87.

Bhattacharya, A., & Ehri, L. (2004). Graphosyllabic analysis helps adolescent struggling readers read and spell words. *Journal of Learning Disabilities, 37,* 331–348.

Bos, C. S., & Anders, P. L. (1990). Effects of interactive vocabulary instruction on the vocabulary learning and reading comprehension of junior-high learning disabled students. *Learning Disability Quarterly, 13,* 31–42.

Bos, C. S., & Vaughn, S. (2002). *Strategies for teaching students with learning and behavior problems*. Boston: Allyn & Bacon.

Boyle, J. R. (1996). The effects of a cognitive mapping strategy on the literal and inferential comprehension of students with mild disabilities. *Learning Disability Quarterly, 19*, 86–98.

Brown, A., & Palincsar, A. (1989). Guided, cooperative learning and individual knowledge acquisition. In L. Resnick (Ed.), *Knowing, learning, and instruction: Essays in honor of Robert Glaser* (pp. 393–451). Hillsdale, NJ: Erlbaum.

Calhoun, M. B. (2005). Effects of a peer mediated phonological skill and reading comprehension program on reading skill acquisition for middle school students with reading disabilities. *Journal of Reading Disabilities, 38*, 424–433.

Center on Education Policy. (2008). *State high school exit exams: A move toward end-of-course exams*. Washington, DC: Author.

Dennis, R., & Moldof, E. (1983). *A handbook on interpretative reading and discussion*. Chicago: Great Books Foundation.

Denton, C. A., Wexler, J., Vaughn, S., & Bryan, D. (2008). Intervention provided to linguistically diverse middle school students with severe reading difficulties. *Learning Disabilities Research and Practice, 23*(2), 79–89.

Deshler, D. D., Ellis, E. S., & Lenz, B. K. (1996). *Teaching adolescents with learning disabilities: Strategies and methods* (2nd ed.). Denver: Love.

Dole, J. A., Brown, K. J., & Trathen, W. (1996). The effects of strategy instruction on the comprehension performance of at-risk students. *Reading Research Quarterly, 31*, 62–88.

Ebbers, S. M., & Denton, C. A. (2008). A root awakening: Vocabulary instruction for older students with reading difficulties. *Learning Disabilities Research and Practice, 23*(2), 90–102.

Faggella-Luby, M. N., & Deshler, D. D. (2008). Reading comprehension in adolescents with LD: What we know; what we need to learn. *Learning Disabilities Research and Practice, 23*, 70–78.

Franzak, J. K. (2006). Zoom: A review of the literature on marginalized adolescent readers, literacy theory, and policy implications. *Review of Educational Research, 76*, 209–248.

Fuchs, D., Fuchs, L. S., Mathes, P. G., & Simmons, D. C. (1997). Peer-assisted learning strategies: Making classrooms more responsive to diversity. *American Educational Research Journal, 34*, 174–206.

Fuchs, L. S., Fuchs, D., & Kazdan, S. (1999). Effects of peer-assisted learning strategies on high school students with serious reading problems. *Remedial and Special Education, 20*, 309–318.

Gajria, M., Jitendra, A. K., Sood, S., & Sacks, G. (2007). Improving comprehension of expository text in students with LD: A research synthesis. *Journal of Learning Disabilities, 40*(3), 210–225.

Gaskins, I. W., Downer, M. A., Anderson, R. C., Cunningham, P. M., Gaskins, R. W., Schommer, M., et al. (1988). A metacognitive approach to phonics: Using what you know to decode what you don't know. *Remedial and Special Education, 9*, 36–41, 66.

Gersten, R., Fuchs, L. S., Williams, J. P., & Baker, S. (2001). Teaching reading comprehension strategies to students with learning disabilities: A review of research. *Review of Educational Research, 71*(2), 279–320.

Glass, G. G., & Glass, E. W. (1976). *Glass-analysis for decoding only: Teacher guide*. Garden City, NJ: Easier to Learn.

Goin, L., Hasselbring, T., & McAfee, I. (2004). *Executive summary, DoDEA/Scholastic READ 180 project: An evaluation of the READ 180 intervention program for struggling readers*. New York: Scholastic Research and Evaluation Department.

Graves, M., Cooke, C. L., & Laberge, M. J. (1983). Effects of previewing short stories. *Reading Research Quarterly, 18,* 262–276.

Guthrie, J. T., & Humenick, N. M. (2004). Motivating students to read: Evidence for classroom practices that increase reading motivation and achievement. In P. McCardle & V. Chhabra (Eds.), *The voice of evidence in reading research* (pp. 329–354). Baltimore: Brookes.

Hall, T. E., Hughes, C. A., & Filbert, M. (2000). Computer assisted instruction in reading for students with learning disabilities: A research synthesis. *Education and Treatment of Children, 23*(2), 173–193.

Hamaker, C. (1986). The effects of adjunct questions on prose learning. *Review of Educational Research, 56,* 212–242.

Harmon, J. M. (2002). Teaching independent word learning strategies to struggling readers. *Journal of Adolescent and Adult Literacy, 45,* 606–615.

Hasselbring, T., & Goin, L. (2004). Literacy instruction for older struggling readers: What is the role of technology? *Reading and Writing Quarterly, 20,* 123–144.

Hock, M., & Mellard, D. (2005). Reading comprehension strategies for adult literacy outcomes. *Journal of Adolescent and Adult Literacy, 49*(3), 192–200.

Horton, S. V., Lovitt, T. C., & Bergerud, D. (1990). The effectiveness of graphic organizers for three classification of secondary students in content area classes. *Journal of Learning Disabilities, 23*(1), 12–22.

Horton, S. V., Lovitt, T. C., & Givens, A. (1988). A computer-based vocabulary program for three categories of student. *British Journal of Educational Technology, 20*(4), 206–213.

Ivey, G., & Broaddus, K. (2007). A formative experiment investigating literacy engagement among adolescent Latina/o students just beginning to read, write, and speak English. *Reading Research Quarterly, 42,* 512–545.

Jitendra, A. K., Edwards, L. L., Sacks, G., & Jacobson, L. A. (2004). What research says about vocabulary instruction for students with learning disabilities. *Exceptional Children, 70*(3), 299–322.

Jitendra, A. K., Hoppes, M. K., & Xin, Y. P. (2000). Enhancing main idea comprehension for students with learning problems: The role of a summarization strategy and self-monitoring instruction. *Journal of Special Education, 34,* 127–139.

Johnson, G., Gersten, R., & Carnine, D. (1987). Effects of instructional design variables on vocabulary acquisition of LD students: A study of computer assisted instruction. *Journal of Learning Disabilities, 20,* 206–213.

Kavale, K. A., Forness, S. R., & Bender, M. (1987). *Handbook of learning disabilities: Vol. I. Dimensions and diagnosis.* Boston: College-Hill Press.

Kim, A., Vaughn, S., Wanzek, J., & Wei, S. (2009). Graphic organizers and their effects on the reading comprehension of students with LD: A synthesis of research. *Journal of Learning Disabilities, 37*(2), 105–118.

Klingner, J. K., Vaughn, S., & Boardman, A. (2007). *Teaching reading comprehension to students with learning difficulties.* New York: Guilford Press.

Lenz, B. K., & Hughes, C. A. (1990). A word identification strategy for adolescents with learning disabilities. *Journal of Learning Disabilities, 23,* 149–163.

Lovett, M. W., & Steinbach, K. A. (1997). The effectiveness of remedial programs for reading disabled children of different ages: Is there decreased benefit for older children? *Learning Disability Quarterly, 20,* 189–210.

Lovett, M. W., Steinbach, K. A., & Frijters, J. C. (2000). Remediating the core deficits of developmental reading disability: A double-deficit perspective. *Journal of Learning Disabilities, 33,* 334–358.

Lysynchuk, L. M., Pressley, M., & Vye, N. J. (1990). Reciprocal teaching improves standardized reading-comprehension performance in poor comprehenders. *Elementary School Journal, 90*(5), 469–484.

Mastropieri, M. A., Scruggs, T. E., & Fulk, J. M. (1990). Teaching abstract vocabulary with the keyword method: Effects on recall and comprehension. *Journal of Learning Disabilities, 23*(2), 92–96.

Mastropieri, M. A., Scruggs, T. E., & Levin, J. R. (1985). Mnemonic strategy with learning disabled adolescents. *Journal of Learning Disabilities, 18,* 94–100.

Meyer, B. J. F. (1975). Identification of the structure of prose and its implications for the study of reading and memory. *Journal of Reading Behavior, 7,* 7–47.

Meyer, B. J. F., Brandt, D. M., & Bluth, G. J. (1980). Use of top-level structure in text: Key for reading comprehension of ninth-grade students. *Reading Research Quarterly, 16*(1), 72–103.

Morris, C. D., Stein, B. S., & Bransford, J. D. (1979). Prerequisites for the utilization of knowledge in the recall of prose passages. *Journal of Experimental Psychology: Human Learning and Memory, 5*(3), 253–261.

Nagy, W., & Anderson, R. C. (1984). The number of printed words in printed school English. *Reading Research Quarterly, 19*(3), 304–330.

Nagy, W., Berninger, V. W., & Abbott, R. D. (2006). Contributions of morphology beyond phonology to literacy outcomes of upper elementary and middle-school students. *Journal of Educational Psychology, 98*(1), 134–147.

National Joint Committee on Learning Disabilities. (2008). Adolescent literacy and older students with learning disabilities: A report from the National Joint Committee on Learning Disabilities. *Learning Disability Quarterly, 31,* 211–218.

O'Connor, R. E., Bell, K. M., Harty, K. R., Larkin, L. K., Sackor, S. M., & Zigmond, N. (2002). Teaching reading to poor readers in the intermediate grades: A comparison of text difficulty. *Journal of Educational Psychology, 94*(3), 474–485.

O'Connor, R. E., Swanson, H. L., & Geraghty, C. (2010). Improvement in reading rate under independent and difficult text levels: Influences on word and comprehension skills. *Journal of Educational Psychology, 102,* 1–19.

Palincsar, A. S., & Brown, A. L. (1984). Reciprocal teaching of comprehension-fostering and monitoring activities. *Cognition and Instruction, 1,* 117–175.

Papalewis, R. (2004). Struggling middle school readers: Successful, accelerating intervention. *Reading Improvement, 41,* 24–37.

Penney, C. G. (2002). Teaching decoding skills to poor readers in high school. *Journal of Literacy Research, 34,* 99–118.

Peverly, S. T., & Wood, R. (2001). The effects of adjunct questions and feedback on improving reading comprehension skills of learning-disabled adolescents. *Contemporary Educational Psychology, 26,* 25–43.

Rack, J. P., Snowling, M. J., & Olson, R. K. (1992). The nonword reading deficit in developmental dyslexia: A review. *Reading Research Quarterly, 27,* 29–53.

Roberts, G., Torgesen, J. K., Boardman, A., & Scammacca, N. (2008). Evidence-based strategies for reading instruction of older students with learning disabilities. *Learning Disabilities Research and Practice, 23*(2), 63–69.

Robinson, F. P. (1946). *Effective study.* New York: Harper & Brothers.

Rogevich, M. E., & Perin, D. (2009). Effects on science summarization of a reading comprehension intervention for adolescents with behavior and attention disorders. *Exceptional Children, 74,* 135–154.

Sandora, C., Beck, I., & McKeown, M. (1999). A comparison of two discussion strategies on students' comprehension and interpretation of complex literature. *Journal of Reading Psychology, 20,* 177–212.

Schiefele, U. (1999). Interest and learning from text. *Scientific Studies of Reading, 3,* 257–279.

Scholastic. (1999). *Read 180.* New York: Scholastic.

Schumaker, J., Deshler, D., Alley, G., Warner, M., & Denton, P. (1982). Multipass: A learning strategy for improving reading comprehension. *Learning Disability Quarterly, 5,* 295–304.

Schumaker, J., Deshler, D., Nolan, S., & Alley, G. (1994). *The self-questioning strategy: Instructor's manual.* Lawrence: University of Kansas Institute for Research on Learning Disabilities.

Smith, P. L., & Friend, M. (1986). Training learning disabled adolescents in a strategy for using text structure to aid recall of instructional prose. *Learning Disability Research, 2,* 38–44.

Stanovich, K. E. (1986). Matthew effects in reading: Some consequences of individual differences in the acquisition of literacy. *Reading Research Quarterly, 21*(4), 360–407.

Stauffer, R. G. (1970). *The language experience approach to the teaching of reading.* New York: Harper & Row.

Stokes, S. M. (1989). LD students and language experience. *Journal of Language Experience, 10,* 19–23.

Stratton, B. D., Grindler, M. C., & Postell, C. M. (1992). Discovering oneself. *Middle School Journal, 24,* 42–43.

Swanson, H. L. (1999). Reading research for students with LD: A meta-analysis of intervention outcomes. *Journal of Learning Disabilities, 32*(6), 504–532.

Swanson, H. L., & Alexander, J. E. (2000). Cognitive processes as predictors of word recognition and reading comprehension in learning disabled and skilled readers. *Journal of Educational Psychology, 89,* 128–158.

Therrien, W. J., Wickstrom, K., & Jones, K. (2006). Effect of a combined repeated reading and question generation intervention on reading achievement. *Learning Disabilities Research and Practice, 21,* 89–97.

Torgesen, J. K. (1988). Studies of children with learning disabilities who perform poorly on memory span tasks. *Journal of Learning Disabilities, 21,* 605–612.

Veit, D. T., Scruggs, T. E., & Mastropieri, M. A. (1986). Extended mnemonic instruction with learning disabled students. *Journal of Educational Psychology, 78*(4), 300–308.

Vygotsky, L. S. (1978). *Mind in society: The development of higher psychological processes.* Cambridge, MA: Harvard University Press.

Wilder, A. A., & Williams, J. P. (2001). Students with severe learning disabilities can learn higher order comprehension skills. *Journal of Educational Psychology, 93,* 268–278.

APPENDIX 16.1. Shackleton Lesson Plan, Chapter 7

Ernest Shackleton Gripped by the Antarctic
By Rebecca L. Johnson
Carolrhoda Books, 2003
ISBN: 0-87614-920-4

Word Study

Guidelines:
- Students work in pairs or small groups to increase motivation (Harmon, 2002).
- Each student fills out his or her own organizer.
- Can be done with pencil and paper or on a computer.
- Provide page numbers for word usage.
- Use a DISSECT model for reading (see a modified DISSECT model below in the graphic organizer), including use of morphology (Lenz & Hughes, 1990).
- Use personal/prior experiences to assist with word meaning and memory (see example below for "emotion" vocabulary; Bos & Anders, 1990; Ebbers & Denton, 2008).

Scaffolding:
- Provide a list of common prefixes and suffixes.
- Use an age-appropriate dictionary, or a dictionary with translations for ELLs.
  - *The American Heritage Student Dictionary*, Houghton Mifflin Harcourt; updated edition (May 3, 2006)
  - *The American Heritage High School Dictionary*, Houghton Mifflin Harcourt; fourth edition (February 7, 2007)
  - *Merriam-Webster's School Dictionary*, Merriam-Webster; revised edition (July 2004)
  - *Merriam-Webster's Intermediate Dictionary*
  - *Merriam-Webster*; revised edition (July 2004)
  - *Merriam-Webster's Elementary Dictionary*, Merriam-Webster; first edition (January 2009)
  - *Scholastic Children's Dictionary*, Scholastic Reference; revised edition (June 1, 2007)
  - *Webster's New World Children's Dictionary*, Webster's New World; second edition (May 1, 2006)
  - *Hippocrene Children's Illustrated Spanish Dictionary*: English–Spanish/Spanish–English (Hippocrene Children's Illustrated Foreign Language Dictionaries), Hippocrene Books; bilingual edition (September 2003)
  - *Webster's Spanish–English Dictionary for Students*, Federal Street Press (July 1, 2003)

- Students can use online dictionaries.
  - *www.merriam-webster.com*
  - *www.onelook.com*
  - *www.dictionary.com*
  - *www.yourdictionary.com*
  - *dictionary.cambridge.org*
  - *dictionary.msn.com*

Read the Text

Guidelines:
- Use focused read-alouds. One student reads, then another student reads the same paragraph. If either student struggles, switch and read again (total reading two to four times). Students alternate reading first. Students follow along and help with difficult words. Students are instructed to delay help 3 seconds.

Scaffolding during reading:
- Teacher works with struggling students by modeling.
  - Teacher models sentence by sentence and has student read second.
  - Teacher models reading paragraph, with student repeating.

Example teacher corrections for fluency from Chapter 7

(p. 78)

Student reading: For hours they rowed, fighting waves and ~~dodging~~ [dogging] ~~floes~~ [floss].

Teacher correction: This word (pointing) is *dodging*. It means to try to miss something, like dodge ball. This word (pointing) is *floes*. It means large ice chunks. Listen to me read this sentence: *For hours they rowed, fighting waves and dodging floes.* Read that sentence and keep going.

Student reading: For hours they rowed, fighting waves and dodging floes. At sunset, Shakleton could see the men were exhausted. Before the light faded completely from the sky, he spotted a floe that looked large enough to hold them all. They rowed to it, drew up the boats, and set up camp on its slushy ~~surface~~ [surfak].

Teacher correction: This word (pointing) is *surface*. The *c* is soft and makes the *s* sound. Listen to me read this sentence: *They rowed to it, drew up their boats, and set camp on its slushy surface.* Read just this sentence again (points to last sentence only).

Student reading: They rowed to it, drew up their boats, and set camp on its slushy surface.

Teacher: Great job! Let's read the paragraph one more time.

Graphic organizer for word study

Vocabulary word	Provided word meaning	What does the dictionary say? Any new information?	Break word into parts (morphology); read parts aloud	What parts do you already know?	What do you think the word means? (context clues)	Give a situation that made you feel this way (to help remember what it means)
Dismay				p. 78		
Inspired				p. 80		
Encouragement Encouraging Encouragingly				p. 77, p. 78, p. 80		
Dehydrated				p. 80		
Exhausted				p. 80		

Sample filled-out graphic organizer

Vocabulary word	Provided word meaning	What does the dictionary say? Any new information?	Break the word into parts (morphology) and read parts aloud	What parts do you already know?	What do you think the word means? (context clues)	Give a situation that made you feel this way (to help remember what it means)
Dismay	To feel very disappointed. To feel hopeless.	To lose courage	Dis-may	dis = not, negative	p. 78 The men's feelings "turn to" dismay, so they had a change of feeling. They feel it when something bad happens.	When there was a pop-quiz and I hadn't read, I was dismayed.

(continued)

Sample filled-out graphic organizer (continued)

Inspired	A sudden good idea.	To be given spirit to do something	In-spire-ed	in = into -ed = something already happened	p. 80 The men feel this way when Shackleton gives them good news. They feel hope.	I didn't know what to write my paper about, but then I was inspired when I saw a picture that gave me a good idea.
Encouragement Encouraging Encouragingly	To feel like things are going to turn out OK.	To help somebody do something through helpful words	En-courage-ment En-courage-ing En-courage-ing-ly	en = in courage = to be brave -ment = noun -ing = something is happening right now -ly = adverb (the way something is being done)	p. 77 Shackleton shouted encouragement. It might mean he said things to help them feel better. p. 79 Shakleton is trying to make them feel better in a bad situation. p. 80 Shackleton is trying to help the men try again. He wants them to do something.	My best friend encouraged me to talk to a boy, even though I was afraid.
Dehydrated	When your body does not have enough water. It can be very dangerous.	To be deprived or water	De-hydrate-ed	de = opposite Hydrate = water -ed = something already happened	p. 80 The men's lips are cracked and tongues are swollen. They are ill. They have not had enough water.	One time when it was very hot, I forgot my water bottle, and the drinking fountain was broken. By the end of the day I was dehydrated.
Exhausted	To be very tired.	Drained of strength or energy; very tired	Ex-haust-ed	ex= out of -ed = something already happened	p. 80 The men were worn down.	When I was done with my unit test, I was exhausted!

*Using online dictionary, Dictionary.com (dictionary.reference.com).

Read for Comprehension with Motivation

Guidelines:
- Review prior reading. (What has happened so far?)
- Have student read summaries of previous chapters to each other. Students should expand/correct their own summaries if needed to include critical information.
- Establish goals (What do we want to learn today?) and use prediction.
- Use Multipass (Schumaker et al., 1982). Students skim text for structure (survey pass). Pre-determine critical stop-points and stop. Ask for main idea. Have students look back to find important information. Organize information visually during reading (consider graphic support i.e., sequence of events) (Anders et al., 1984; Kavale et al., 1987). Graphic organizers can be teacher-guided or teacher-created.
- Use inserted questions to increase comprehension (Peverly & Wood, 2001).
- Use strategy instruction (a framework for structuring the meaning of the chapter) (Gajria et al., 2007).

Scaffolding:
- For student summary shares, group students heterogeneously (better reader with at-risk reader). Ask students to edit each other's work for the following:
  - Are sentences complete sentences?
  - Are all of the main ideas included?
  - Use of proper nouns for characters in favor of pronouns (i.e., *Shackleton* rather than *he*).
- Increase number of critical stop points (stop more frequently) to reduce information included in main idea statements.
- Use a teacher-created graphic organizer. Complete organizer as a whole-class activity, or in cooperative groups rather than individually.
- Students state sentences aloud before writing.
- Increase frequency of inserted questions (Peverly & Wood, 2001).

Example from Chapter 7

(pp. 77—78: Passage chosen as a critical "stop place" for sequence of events)

Review prior reading:
- Who is the captain of *Endurance?* What do we know about him?
- What has happened so far to *Endurance?* Where is the ship? Where are the men? Why are they there? Where have the men been staying?
- How do the men feel about getting into the lifeboats? Think about the vocabulary we've learned. Do they feel dismayed? Inspired? Encouraged? Why do you think they feel that way?

Set learning goals:
- What do you want to find out today?
- What do you think this chapter will be about? (prediction)
- What does the title tell you? (story structure)
- Read the quotation on the top of page 77. What does that tell you about this chapter? What can you expect?

    Crashing waves gave way to huge swells that came at them one after another. First the boat would be swept up one side of a swell, and then hurled at great speed down the other side. (p. 77)

- What could make the men feel dehydrated? Exhausted? Inspired? Encouraged?

Multipass Strategy with inserted questions (read pp. 77–78):

Paragraph 1 (p. 77)
- *Provide word:* floes
- *Inserted question:* What was it like in the boats? What challenges did the men face?
- Scaffolding:
  - **Say:** The ice hit their boats over and over again. What did they do?
  - **Point to:** *The men leaned into the oars with all their might and slipped out of harm's way just in time.*
  - **Say:** What does it mean to slip out of harm's way? Tell me in your own words.

Paragraph 2 (p. 77)
- *Inserted question:* What were the three boats named?
- *Inserted question:* What was Shackleton doing?

Paragraph 3 (p. 78)
- *Inserted question:* The sun was setting. What did Shackleton decide?

Paragraph 4 (p. 78)
- *Inserted question:* What was Shackleton worried about?
- *Inserted question:* What actually happened?
- *Inserted question:* Describe Shackleton's actions. What words could you use to tell me about what he did?

Paragraph 5 (p. 78)
- *Inserted question:* What were the men working for? Did it happen?
- *Inserted question:* How did the men feel? Use a vocabulary word [*encouraged, inspired, exhausted*].

Paragraph 6 (p. 78)
- *Inserted question:* What obstacles stood in the way?
- *Inserted question:* What finally happened?
- *Scaffolding*
  - **Point to:** *dismay*
  - **Say:** The men felt dismay. Tell me in your own words what that means.
  - **Say:** The men were feeling relieved. They were feeling good, then something happened that made them feel dismayed. What happened?

Main idea and structure (end of section, bottom of p. 78):
- What is the main idea of this passage? Tell me in about 10 words.
- Let's write that as a complete sentence in the graphic organizer.

Graphic organizer made with Inspiration Software

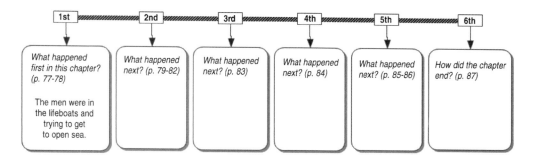

At the conclusion of the chapter, use strategy instruction to structure the chapter meaningfully:

In this chapter, Shackleton and his men face many challenges! Let's look at what those challenges were, and how the crew resolved those challenges. Use your sequence of events organizer. Think about what happened again, but this time, think about what the challenge (problem) was, and how Shackleton and his crew solved those problems.

Table made with Microsoft Word Software		
Section (pages)	Problem	Solution
pp. 77–78	Shackleton and the men are tying to get free of the ice flows, but the conditions are dangerous. The temperature is freezing cold, waves are large, and there are large ice floes in the water.	The men row very hard and try to navigate the floes. They camp out on one of the floes to get some rest. They finally decide to retreat rather than risk getting smashed by the big waves and ice floes.
pp. 79–82		
p. 83		
p. 84		
pp. 85–86		
p. 87		

Author Index

413

Kaderavek, J., 146
Kail, R., 172, 173
Kame'enui, E. J., 17, 67, 97, 144, 146, 170, 172,
    174, 206, 255, 280
Kamhi, A., 183
Kamil, M. L., 145
Kamp, N., 41
Kamps, D., 18, 283, 284, 295, 316, 360
Kapinus, B., 262
Kapp, S., 146, 147
Karras, R. W., 339
Katzir, T., 172, 174
Katzir-Cohen, T., 170, 172, 177, 184
Kauffman, J. M., 129
Kavale, K. A., 178, 327, 329, 391, 409
Kazdan, S., 281, 389
Keehn, S., 187
Kelley, M., 230
Kelly, C., 348
Kemp, N., 100
Kessler, B., 35, 41, 42, 117
Kieffer, M. J., 362
Kim, A.-H., 290, 392
Kinder, B. D., 232, 261
King, A., 232, 370
Kintsch, E., 328
Kintsch, W., 202, 203, 204, 205, 328
Kirby, J., 97
Kiuhara, S. A., 332
Klesius, P., 179
Klingner, J. K., 5, 200, 202, 220, 226, 228, 234,
    244, 245, 246, 247, 290, 365, 369, 370, 373,
    380
Knutson, N., 169
Konstantopoulos, S., 368
Kouzekanani, K., 181, 359
Kozminsky, E., 204
Kranzler, J. H., 177
Kucan, L., 148, 243, 255, 386
Kuhn, M. R., 176, 180, 183, 184, 188, 317
Kung, H., 284, 370
Kurita, J. A., 205, 224
Kurland, B. F., 138
Kwong, T., 121, 129

Laakkonen, E., 31
LaBerge, D., 170, 171, 317
Laberge, M. J., 391
Lacerenza, L., 72, 184
Ladson-Billings, G., 367, 371
LaGuardia, F. H., 343, 346
Landauer, T. K., 143, 145
Landen, E., 143
Landry, S. L., 49
Lane, H. B., 169, 181
Lane, K. L., 304, 307
Lanford, C., 28
Langer, J., 332
Langer, J. A., 396
Lauer, K. D., 257, 328

Laughon, P., 12, 173
Lawrence, F. R., 27
Layng, T. V. J., 188
Leach, J. M., 64
Leafstedt, J. M., 358
Lee, C., 222
Lee, J., 337, 356
Lee, J. S., 31
Lehr, F., 169
Lehr, S., 258
Lemos-Britton, Z., 18
Lenz, B. K., 381, 383, 405
Leonard, B. R., 284
Leonard, L. B., 173
Leong, C. K., 90, 91
Leong, D. J., 45, 50
Lepola, J., 31
Lepper, M. R., 102
Lesaux, N. K., 18, 362
Leung, C., 146
LeVasseur, V. M., 179
Levin, I., 35
Levin, J. R., 201, 385
Levine, S., 46
Levy, B. A., 178, 179, 181
Levy, J., 367
Lewis, W. E., 328, 329, 330, 332, 333, 334
Liams, M., 367
Liang, L. A., 239, 242
Liberman, A. M., 48
Liberman, I., 12
Lichter, A., 200
Linan-Thompson, S., 18, 359, 360, 361
Lindamood, C., 12
Lindamood, P., 12, 41
Lindo, E. J., 145
Linebarger, D., 283
Linklater, D., 18, 361
Lively, T. J., 97
Lloyd, J. W., 178
LoCasale-Crouch, J., 28
Loftus, S., 146, 147
Logan, G. D., 170, 171
Longcamp, M., 35
Lonigan, C. J., 27, 32, 53, 372
López, L. M., 38, 40
Losen, D., 356
Lovelace, T. S., 284
Lovett, M. W., 16, 69, 72, 73, 184, 329, 382, 383
Lovitt, T. C., 392
Loynanch, C., 130
Lucas, T., 364, 366, 370
Lull, H. G., 113
Lundberg, I., 10, 17, 38
Lynch, J. S., 199
Lynch, R. H., 365
Lynch-Brown, C., 146
Lyon, G. R., 64, 254
Lyster, S. H., 98, 100, 106
Lysynchuk, L. M., 178, 395, 396

Subject Index

Handbook of reading
  interventions